DATE DUE

DE 16 94			
JY 6 '95			
AP 19 '96			

DEMCO 38-296

BUSINESS OPPORTUNITIES IN THE UNITED STATES

THE COMPLETE REFERENCE GUIDE TO PRACTICES AND PROCEDURES

BUSINESS OPPORTUNITIES IN THE UNITED STATES

THE COMPLETE REFERENCE GUIDE TO PRACTICES AND PROCEDURES

Edited by
Robert F. Cushman
Pepper, Hamilton & Scheetz

R. Lawrence Soares
Price Waterhouse

Price Waterhouse

BUSINESS ONE IRWIN
Homewood, Illinois 60430

Project editor: Gladys True
Production manager: Diane Palmer
Jacket designer: Sam Concialdi
Artist: TCSystems, Inc.
Compositor: TCSystems, Inc.
Typeface: 11/13 Times Roman
Printer: Arcata Graphics/Martinsburg

Library of Congress Cataloging–in–Publication Data

Business opportunities in the United States : the complete reference
  guide to practices and procedures / edited by Robert F. Cushman and
  R. Lawrence Soares.
    p.   cm.
  Includes index.
  ISBN 1-55623-493-7
   1. Investments, Foreign—United States—Handbooks, manuals, etc.
  2. Investments, Foreign—Law and legislation—United States-
  -Handbooks, manuals, etc.   I. Cushman, Robert Frank, 1931-
  II. Soares, R. Lawrence.
  HG4921.B87   1992
  332.6′73′0973—dc20   91–38717

Printed in the United States of America

1 2 3 4 5 6 7 8 9 0   AGM   9 8 7 6 5 4 3 2

PREFACE

Foreign investment in the United States continues to be a dynamic force in the international investment scene—an arena offering a complex, changing array of requirements, opportunities, challenges and pitfalls.

For the foreign investor attracted to the profit potential, tax advantages, and security of the U.S. market, help is on the way. In fact, it has already arrived: *Business Opportunities in the United States: The Complete Reference Guide to Practices and Procedures* presents a unique compilation of comprehensive, in-depth writings by leaders in international business, law, accounting, finance, and related disciplines. The authors' specialized knowledge will inform and guide foreign investors regarding the major considerations involved in entering and growing in the American economy.

Business Opportunities in the United States: The Complete Reference Guide to Practices and Procedures identifies the key business issues the foreign investor needs to consider and provides general technical guidance concerning the methods of addressing them. The experts whose contributions are provided in this volume examine a broad range of topics, including strategic planning, communications and marketing, banking, finance, insurance, legal matters, taxation, accounting, employee relations, and real estate and construction. The book includes chapters on special considerations for the German investor and tax planning for Japanese investment in the United States. Especially timely are writings updating such key areas as transfer pricing, U.S. environmental law, and American product liability law.

Here, in a single volume, is the collective knowledge of well-qualified professionals, providing readily accessible answers to the foreign investor's questions about the U.S. market. The accountants, attorneys, bankers, and business executives who were invited to write these chapters—from international organizations such as Price Waterhouse, Union Carbide, Cushman & Wakefield, Hill and Knowlton, and major U.S. law firms—are all prominent authorities in their particular fields; and, they have the ability to write in clear, nontechnical, understandable language.

We believe this book, thanks to the skilled efforts of the distinguished authors, will prove to be a valuable reference work, encouraging and assisting foreign investors in taking advantage of the abundant opportunities in the Unites States.

Robert F. Cushman, Esquire
R. Lawrence Soares

ABOUT THE EDITORS

Robert F. Cushman is a partner in the national law firm of Pepper, Hamilton & Scheetz and is a recognized specialist and lecturer on all phases of real estate and construction law. He serves as legal counsel to major construction, development, and bonding companies.

Mr. Cushman is the co-editor of *A Guide for the Foreign Investor, Handbook for Raising Capital, The Handbook of Joint Venturing, High Tech Real Estate,* and *The Professionals' Guide to Commercial Property Development,* all published by Dow Jones-Irwin, the predecessor to Business One Irwin, as well as many other handbooks and guides in the insurance, real estate, and construction fields.

Mr. Cushman, who is a member of the Bar of the Commonwealth of Pennsylvania and who is admitted to practice before the Supreme Court of the United States and the United States Claims Court, has served as executive vice president and general counsel to the Construction Industry Foundation. He is a founding member of the American College of Construction Lawyers.

R. Lawrence Soares is a partner in Price Waterhouse, an international accounting and consulting firm. He is partner-in-charge of inbound
investment for his firm's Southeast Region. In
this capacity, he is actively involved in assisting and advising overseas investors on the
business, financial and tax aspects of investments in the United States.

ABOUT THE AUTHORS

Robert L. Anderson is the partner responsible
for the Southeast Region Real Estate Practice
for the Atlanta office of Price Waterhouse and
has extensive experience working with multinational corporations and international organizations, particularly those that deal with the
unique tax aspects of inbound investment opportunities. Prior to joining Price Waterhouse,
Mr. Anderson was Executive Vice-President
of Finance for Lehndorff Management, USA,
a foreign owner, manager and syndicator of U.S. real estate property.
He was also a partner with Arthur Andersen & Company where he
had firmwide responsibility for the international real estate tax specialty group. He was one of the co-authors of "Federal Taxes Affecting Real Estate" and has authored numerous booklets on investment
in U.S. real estate. He is a member of the American Institute of
Certified Public Accountants as well as the Georgia Society of Certified Public Accountants. Mr. Anderson graduated from the University of Florida with a B.S./B.A. degree.

Michael Budnick is the national director and
practice leader of Price Waterhouse's International Assignment Tax Services (IATS) Specialized Practice Unit. He has over 20 years of
experience in coordinating expatriate programs for international corporations.

Mr. Budnick received a B.S. from Boston
University in 1972 and a J.D. from New York
Law School in 1977. His professional affili-
ations include: the American Institute of
CPAs, the New York State Society of CPAs, and the American and
New York State Bar Associations. He is a member of Organization
Resources Counselors Advisory Board.

Mr. Budnick has spoken and written articles for many professional and personal organizations such as Employee Relocation
Council, Runzheimer International, and Organization Resources
Counselors, on the subject of compensation and tax planning for
international assignments.

Marylouise Dionne is a tax manager (International Tax Services) with the New York Practice Office of Price Waterhouse. Previously,
she was an attorney-advisor with the Internal
Revenue Service, Associate Chief Counsel (international).

Hisashi Doi is a tax director in the Tokyo office
of Price Waterhouse. He previously worked in
the Southern California offices of Price Waterhouse and served various Japanese owned
companies operating in the United States. He
is now a member of the International Tax Service Group in the Tokyo office and has been
assisting Japanese companies investing overseas, particularly in the United States. Mr. Doi
is a Certified Public Accountant in the state of
California.

Carol Dudnick heads Union Carbide Chemicals and Plastics Company Inc.'s group of environmental attorneys. She has been with Union Carbide for 10 years, and has responsibility for environmental aspects of acquisitions, divestitures and joint ventures, and day-to-day environmental regulatory and compliance matters. Previously, she worked at the U.S. Environmental Protection Agency in New York City for about 8 years. Ms. Dudnick received her J.D. from New York University in 1972. She is admitted to practice in New York and Connecticut.

Charles H. Eggleston is a partner in the Financial Services Industry Practice of Price Waterhouse and is the editor of the Price Waterhouse banking newsletter, "Banking Trends and Events." He previously served as an ex officio member of the AICPA Banking Committee and played an active role in the development of the *AICPA Auditing Procedure Study: Auditing the Allowance for Credit Losses of Banks.* Previously, Mr. Eggleston served as Vice President and Manager of Financial Planning and Analysis at Centerre Bank, St. Louis, Missouri.

A Certified Public Accountant, he is the author of articles on banking and finance which have appeared in *The Magazine of Bank Administration, The Bankers Magazine, Burroughs Clearing House, Mid-Continent Banker, Illinois Banker,* and the *Journal of Bank Accounting and Auditing.* Mr. Eggleston is a member of the faculty of the Graduate School of Banking at the University of Wisconsin and the Illinois Bankers School at the University of Illinois and is listed in *Who's Who in Finance and Industry.* He holds an M.B.A. in Finance from the University of Massachusetts and a B.A. in Mathematics and Accounting from Kent State University.

Donald I. Feiner is a senior director at Cushman & Wakefield, Inc. He has and A.B. and an M.B.A. in finance from Columbia College. His tenant representation includes: Prudential Insurance Company of America, Societe Generale, Pfizer Inc., and Parsons Brinckerhoff.

Howard M. Fischer is founder and president of Howard Fischer Associates, Inc., the leading Philadelphia-based Executive Search firm.

Mr. Fischer entered the recruitment business in 1972, and by 1976, he had become one of the leading executive recruiters in the country for a national recruitment firm headquartered in New York City. In 1976, Mr. Fischer opened his own Executive Search firm in Philadelphia to provide Delaware Valley-based companies with "the highest quality" executive search and selection capabilities.

During his eighteen-year career as an Executive Search consultant, Mr. Fischer has filled more than 500 management positions, ranging from middle managers to CEO's, and has a special interest in recruiting Outside Directors for Public and Private companies. The firm's clients run the gamut from Fortune 500 companies to venture capital state-ups, both profit and non-profit.

Marc R. Garber is a partner of Pepper, Hamilton & Scheetz, resident in the Philadelphia office, where he is a member of the firm's Employee Benefits Group. Mr. Garber concentrates his practice on employee benefit matters with a particular emphasis on business transactions, plan design, counselling plan sponsors and plan fiduciaries with respect to compliance with applicable laws and regulation, and executive compensation matters. He  graduated from Duquesne University School of Law in 1981 and received his Bachelor of Arts degree from Temple University. Mr. Garber is a member of the Pennsylvania and Massachusetts bars, and is active in the Employee Benefits Committee of the Tax Section of the American Bar Association. He is an instructor at the Institute for Employee Benefits Training and has lectured on a variety of subjects regarding employee benefits.

Jack P. Gibson is president of International Risk Management Institute, Inc. a Dallas-based publisher of risk management and insurance reference books. He holds BBA and MBA degrees from the University of Georgia where he majored in risk management. He has also earned the Chartered Property Casualty Underwriter (CPCU), Associate in Risk Management (ARM), and Chartered Life Underwriter (CLU) designations. Mr. Gibson has au-  thored many articles, is the co-author of 10 books, and is a frequent speaker on insurance and risk management topics.

Scott L. Gorland is a partner in the Detroit office of Pepper, Hamilton & Scheetz. His practice is focused on the litigation of products liability matters, including pharmaceutical products liability and toxic tort litigation, as well as environmental litigation. Prior to joining the firm in 1983, he was a Trial Attorney in the Torts Branch, Civil Division, U.S. Department of Justice in Washington, D.C., involved in defending the federal government in negligence and toxic tort litigation. He received a Bachelor of Arts degree in 1971 from the University of Michigan, and is a *cum laude* graduate of the University of Detroit School of Law where he served as Associate Editor of the law review.

David K. Grevengoed is a senior manager in Price Waterhouse's International Assignment Tax Services (IATS) Specialized Practice Unit. He previously spent five years in Price Waterhouse's Atlanta office, followed by a two-year tour of duty in the firm's National office tax department in New York City. He has a Bachelor's Degree in Economics from Wheaton College (Illinois) and a Master's Degree in Accounting from the University of Georgia. Mr. Grevengoed has been a speaker at the World Trade Institute and has written articles for "The Tax Adviser" and New York University's "Forty-Eighth Annual Institute on Federal Taxation." He is a member of the American Institute of Certified Public Accountants and the Georgia Society of CPAs.

Anthony B. Haller is a partner resident in the
Philadelphia office of the law firm of Pepper,
Hamilton & Scheetz and his practice covers all
aspects of labor and employment law and litigation. Mr. Haller received a Bachelor's and
Master's degree in law from the University of
Cambridge in England. After graduation from
the University of Cambridge, Mr. Haller was
awarded a Thouron Fellowship to study at
the University of Pennsylvania Law School,
where he received an L.L.M. He is admitted to practice in Pennsylva-
nia, before the U.S. District Court for the Eastern District of Pennsylvania and in the U.S. Court of Appeals for the Third Circuit. Mr.
Haller is also admitted as a barrister in England. Mr. Haller is a
member of the Labor and Employment Law and Litigation Section of
the American Bar Association and the Labor and Employment Law
Section's Committee on International Labor Law. He is a member of
the American Trial Lawyer's Association and is currently serving on
the Labor Subcommittee of the International Young Lawyers Association. Mr. Haller has written and lectured on labor, employment and
comparative labor law.

Richard M. Hammer joined Price Waterhouse
in New York in 1956, and now he serves as
National Director, International Tax Policy.
He earned a B.A. degree from Princeton Uni-
versity and M.B.A. degree from Harvard
Graduate School of Business Administration.
Currently, he serves as Chairman of the Tax
Committee of the U.S. Council for Interna-
tional Business, as Chairman of the Taxation
Committee of the Business and Industry Ad-
visory Committee to be OECD and as a member of the Taxation
Commission of the International Chamber of Commerce. He is a past
president of the International Fiscal Association.

Howard B. Hill is a partner in the Detroit office of the national law firm of Pepper, Hamilton & Scheetz, specializing in international, corporate and commercial matters for U.S. and foreign investors for over 20 years. Prior to joining Pepper, he was Assistant General Counsel for Chrysler Corporation dealing with international, mergers and acquisitions and its components subsidiary. Mr. Hill has also worked in Hong Kong as Asian Counsel for Union Carbide Corporation and in New York and London, England with the Coudert Brothers law firm. He is a graduate of Northwestern University and Columbia University Law School and a member of the New York and Michigan Bars. He currently serves as an officer and/or director of several organizations including the American Branch of the International Law Association, the International Law Section of the State Bar of Michigan, and the French American Chamber of Commerce.

Klaus H. Jander is the partner in charge of the German Practice Group at Rogers & Wells in New York and Frankfurt. He was born in Germany and educated both in Germany and in the United States. He earned his J.D. from Cornell University Law School and has been admitted to the Bar in the United States since 1964. Mr. Jander has specialized in transnational commercial law, antitrust law, and product liability litigation. He also has expertise in transnational mergers and acquisitions and other corporate matters and counts amoung his clients many German companies with U.S. subsidiaries and U.S. companies with interests in Europe.

Louis L. Joseph is a senior manager with the Price Waterhouse Employee Benefits Services Group specializing in U.S. and international benefits and remuneration planning. He is currently completing a two year assignment as a managing consultant with the Price Waterhouse Benefits Group's London office, where his responsibilities include advising U.K. and European companies on U.S. benefits issues. Mr. Joseph joined Price Waterhouse in 1988  following service with the U.S. Department of Labor, where he was in charge of the Solicitor's Office ERISA division. He is a graduate of Indiana University and the University of Michigan Law School.

Hiroo Kato is a tax partner in the Tokyo office of Price Waterhouse, specializing in international taxation for both Japanese owned and foreign owned multinational companies. He is responsible for the International Tax Service Group in the Tokyo office serving Japanese corporations' outbound investments. He is a member of the Price Waterhouse World Firm's International Tax Service Development Group and its Transfer Pricing Network.  Mr. Kato is a Certified Public Accountant and a Certified Tax Accountant in Japan.

David F. Kleeman is a tax partner at the Price Waterhouse, Philadelphia office. He has a Bachelor of Science degree from the Wharton School, University of Pennsylvania, and a J.D. from Harvard Law School.

Mr. Kleeman specializes in the international tax area and serves as the tax partner on a number of large multinational clients.

He has been an Adjunct Professor of Taxation in the graduate tax program at Widener University and authored the international tax chapter in the recent Dow Jones book, *The Handbook of Joint Venturing*.

Mr. Kleeman is a member of the American Institute of Certified Public Accountants, American Bar Association and the International Fiscal Association.

Larry L. Klein is senior manager with Price Waterhouse. He is in the Financial Services Consulting Group based in Philadelphia, PA. He provides property and liability risk management and insurance consulting services to national and international clients. He holds a B.A. degree from Rutgers University and also earned the Chartered Property Casualty Underwriter (CPCU) and Accredited Advisor in Insurance (AAI) designations. He has nearly two decades of insurance industry experience as a risk manager, broker and underwriter. Mr. Klein is a frequent speaker on risk management topics for industry and business groups and has authored several articles for accountants on insurance issues.

Frank A. Klepetko is a senior managing director in the Corporate Finance Group of Price Waterhouse in New York. Mr. Klepetko has been engaged in investment banking services throughout his career, primarily assisting corporations in raising capital and in merger and acquisition advisory activities. He is a graduate of Princeton University and the Graduate School of Business, The University of Chicago.

Christopher P. A. Komisarjevsky is executive vice president of Hill and Knowlton, Inc., the international public relations and public affairs counseling firm.

He is responsible for client counseling covering a broad range of industries and companies, both in the United States and internationally.

In 1988, Mr. Komisarjevsky was named president and chief executive officer of Carl Byoir & Associates. Prior to that, Mr. Komisarjevsky was president and chief executive officer of Hill and Knowlton International S.A., the headquarters for Hill and Knowlton operations in Europe, the Middle East and Africa.

Mr. Komisarjevsky holds a Master's degree in business administration, has done graduate work in German literature and international affairs in the United States and Europe, has attended the Wharton School and has a Bachelor of Arts degree in political science.

He served in the U.S. Army from 1967 to 1972 as a captain, helicopter pilot, instructor pilot, flight commander and plans officer, seeing combat service in Vietnam with the First Cavalry Division in 1969 and 1970.

John J. Korbel is a partner in Price Waterhouse's Management Science and Economics Specialty Practice Unit based in Washington, D.C. Mr. Korbel is an economist who specializes in the areas of international trade, financial and economic analysis, and international business and strategic planning. Mr. Korbel has a M.A. and Ph.D. in Economics from the University of Colorado and a B.A. in History from Williams College.

Robert D. Lane, Jr. is the chairman of the Real Estate Group at Pepper, Hamilton & Scheetz where his practices encompass all aspects of commercial real estate transactions as well as real estate litigation. Mr. Lane is also currently the chairman of the Real Property Section of the Philadelphia Bar Association and is a frequent lecturer and author on zoning and land use, real estate taxation, real estate finance and commercial leasing. He has also served on the Board of Directors of the Central Philadelphia Development Corporation, the Mayor's Advisory Committee on Center City Zoning (Philadelphia), the Board of Governors of the Philadelphia Bar Association, the House of Delegates of the Pennsylvania Bar Association and on the Boards of various other community and civic organizations.

Ruurd G. Leegstra is the national director of Multistate Tax Consulting Services for Price Waterhouse. In this capacity, he is responsible for developing the Firm's expertise in state and local taxation and for managing this rapidly growing area of the Price Waterhouse tax practice. Mr. Leegstra is experienced in all aspects of state and local taxation in a wide variety of industries. He is a frequent conference speaker as well as a prolific contributor to technical literature devoted to state and local tax topics. Mr. Leegstra is a C.P.A. who received a B.A. degree from Duke University and a J.D. degree from St. John's University, School of Law.

Thomas R. Lucke is a senior manager in the Strategic Consulting Group at Price Waterhouse. Mr. Lucke focuses on providing consulting in corporate and business unit strategy to large multinational corporations in technology-based industries, including consumer and industrial electronics, pharmaceuticals, aerospace, telecommunications and microelectronics. He has frequently been called upon by clients in North America, the Far East  and Europe to assess the strategic and economic aspects of business opportunities in the United States, including direct market entry, joint ventures, strategic partnerships, acquisitions and technology licensing. In addition, Mr. Lucke has directed engagements in the areas of worldwide competitive strategy, product planning, new business development, market entry and manufacturing strategy. He holds an M.S.I.A. from the Graduate School of Industrial Administration at Carnegie Mellon University and a B.S. from Rensselaer Polytechnic Institute.

Joellen Mazor is a search consultant with Howard Fischer Associates, Inc., and has recruited senior level executives in diverse functional roles throughout a broad spectrum of industries.

Prior to entering the field of recruitment, Ms. Mazor spent over five years with SAF Products, Inc., the American subsidiary of Societe Industrielle Lasaffre, of Marcq en Baroeul, France. There, she held a variety of  sales positions, the last of which was Northeast Regional Manager.

Ms. Mazor is a graduate, with honors, of The University of Pennsylvania.

John Mucha III is an associate in the Detroit office of Pepper, Hamilton & Scheetz, practicing in the area of products liability, employment and commercial litigation. He received a Bachelor of Arts degree in 1977 from the University of Michigan, and a Master of Public Policy Studies degree in 1979, also from the University of Michigan. He is a graduate of the University of Michigan Law School where he served as a Contributing Editor for the *Journal of Law Reform*.

Richard B. Nash, Jr., a senior associate in the Washington, D.C. office of Pepper, Hamilton & Scheetz, practices in the fields of antitrust and international business. His antitrust work has involved counseling and defending a variety of mergers, joint ventures and other transactions for U.S. and European-based clients. Mr. Nash's international work has involved U.S. regulation of foreign investment (Exon-Florio), export controls, and privatization of state-owned enterprises in former socialist economies.

   Mr. Nash's articles on antitrust and foreign investment topics have appeared in the *Financial Times* and *International Merger Law*. Mr. Nash received his J.D. from Columbia Law School in 1984 and his A.B. from Princeton in 1981, where he studied at the Woodrow Wilson School of Public & International Affairs. He is a member of the New York and District of Columbia bars.

Dennis L. Neider is a partner and the National Director of Price Waterhouse's United States German Business Services Group. He is a graduate of Drexel University and received an M.B.A. from the University of Florida. His twenty year career with Price Waterhouse has been focused on services to multinational companies and in the last eight years primarily on services to foreign investors in the United States. Mr. Neider is a member of the AICPA,  PICPA, NJSCPA and NYSCPA and is currently serving as a National Vice President of the Institute of Management Accountants.

S. Sandile Ngcobo is a graduate of the University of Natal, South Africa, and is a member of the Bar of South Africa, where he has practiced as a barrister in the field of Commercial and Employment Law. In 1986, he was awarded a Fulbright Scholarship to the University of Harvard Law School, where he received a Master's degree in Labor Law and International Law. Since 1987, he has been associated with the Labor Law Department of  Pepper, Hamilton & Scheetz, which represents corporations in all aspects of their labor and employment relations. After working as a Law Clerk and Research Associate to Honorable A. Leon Higgenbotham, Jr., of the U.S. Court of Appeals for the Third Circuit, Philadelphia, he joined the firm of Pepper, Hamilton & Scheetz permanently in November 1989.

Daniel A. Noakes is a senior tax manager with Price Waterhouse in Charlotte, North Carolina. He recently completed a two-year tour of duty with the Tax Consulting group in the Price Waterhouse national office in New York. He coordinated the 1990 version of *Doing Business in the United States,* which is part of the prestigious series of Price Waterhouse information guides. He has also been involved in writing the Price Waterhouse *Personal Tax*  *Advisor,* the Price Waterhouse *Investors' Tax Advisor,* and *The Price Waterhouse Book of Personal Financial Planning.* He has authored many articles and lectured on a variety of tax topics. Mr. Noakes is a member of the North Carolina Association of Certified Public Accountants and the American Institute of Certified Public Accountants.

Gail T. Rold is a certified public accountant with Price Waterhouse in Philadelphia, PA. She specializes in German business and has been involved with several multinational companies requiring specialized foreign financial reporting. She is a graduate of Lehigh University and is an active member of the American and Pennsylvania Institutes of CPAs.

H. David Rosenbloom is an attorney specializing in international tax matters and a member of the law firm of Caplin & Drysdale, Chartered, in Washington, D.C. Born in New York, New York in 1941, he attended Princeton University, the University of Florence in Florence, Italy, and Harvard Law School. Mr. Rosenbloom has been with Caplin & Drysdale intermittently since 1968. He served as International Tax counsel in the United States  Treasury Department from January 1978 through January 1981. A frequent speaker and author on tax subjects, Mr. Rosenbloom has lectured on international taxation at Harvard and Stanford Law Schools, and is presently a lecturer at Harvard.

Bernard M. Shapiro is the national director of
Tax Policy and Legislative Affairs for Price
Waterhouse. Prior to joining the firm in 1981,
Mr. Shapiro was Chief of Staff of the Joint
Committee on Taxation of the U.S. Congress,
and had been a member of that staff since 1967.

As National Director of Tax Policy, Mr.
Shapiro is responsible for development and
coordination of the firm's opinions concerning
matters of tax policy and for articulating the
firm's views on various tax proposals. Because of his experience in
advising the Congressional tax-writing committees on technical
aspects and potential economic effects of proposed legislation, Mr.
Shapiro is able to provide a unique perspective and guidance on
current tax issues and legislation.

R. Desmond Shaw is a senior manager in Price
Waterhouse where he directs the firm's International Trade Consulting Services practice.
He has consulted to companies on direct investment in the United States, Eastern and
Western Europe and Southeast Asia. He has
also consulted to U.S. and foreign government
agencies at the national and local levels on
ways to attract foreign investment.

Kenneth A. Shearer, is executive director at
Cushman & Wakefield, Inc. He holds a Bachelor of Science in Mechanical Engineering from
New York University. He is a consultant to all
of Cushman & Wakefield's 100 million square
foot Management Portfolio, Project Development Services, and the Brokerage and Appraisal Divisions. He has 45 years experience
in the design, development and management of
major high rise commercial buildings and optimizing their operation.

Joanne M. Sisk is a manager of International Tax Services at Price Waterhouse. She holds a B.S. in Accounting from Case Western Reserve University (CWRU), an M.B.A. with Emphasis in Management Information Systems, from Weatherhead School of Management, CWRU, and an M.S. in Accounting with Emphasis in Taxation from Weatherhead School of Management, CWRU. She is a Member of the American Institute of Certified  Public Accountants and District of Columbia Institute of Certified Public Accountants. She is a co-author of an article in *Warren, Gorham & Lamont's Journal of Taxation of Investments,* "Foreign Investments in U.S. Partnerships Can Produce Varying Tax Consequences", Winter, 1992.

Robert A. Skitol is a partner in the Washington, D.C. office of Pepper, Hamilton & Scheetz. His principal areas of expertise are antitrust and trade regulation, practice before the Federal Trade Commission and the Antitrust Division of the Department of Justice, franchising, and contract and trademark licensing. He has extensive experience in merger counseling and litigation, advertising and other consumer protection issues, and liti-  gation involving a broad range of antitrust and related commercial law issues in the federal courts. He has written and lectured extensively in the antitrust and trade regulation field, is a co-author of *Mergers in the New Antitrust Era* published in 1985, and is also co-founder and co-editor of a monthly journal entitled *International Merger Law.* He is a 1970 graduate of New York University Law School, was Order of the Coif and Research Editor of the NYU Law Review.

Richard B. Stanger is national director of Employee Benefits Services for Price Waterhouse.

He has extensive experience in all aspects of employee benefits.

Mr. Stanger is a member of the Pension Research Council of the Wharton School of the University of Pennsylvania and an adjunct professor of law at Georgetown University Law Center. He was a member of the FASB, Task Force on Statement of Financial Accounting Standards No. 87. Mr. Stanger has numerous published writings and is a frequent speaker on employee benefits-related issues.

John J. Sullivan is a partner of Walter, Conston, Alexander & Green, P.C. Mr. Sullivan is a graduate of Yale University (B.A. 1974) and Georgetown University Law Center (J.D. 1977). He is a member of the American Bar Association and is the author of numerous articles on international banking and securities issues.

Donald E. Wilson is an international tax partner in the Detroit office of Deloitte & Touche and is Director of the Michigan Region International Tax Practice. His clientele includes over 90 foreign owned companies and 500 foreign nationals as well as major U.S. based multinational companies. He received his B.A. in economics from the University of Michigan and his J.D., cum laude, from Wayne State University Law School in Detroit. Mr. Wilson

teaches international tax at the Walsh College Master of Tax Program and is a frequent speaker at seminars in the United States and abroad. He is the editor of his firm's quarterly international tax newsletter and

Chairman of the International Tax Committee of the State Bar of Michigan, International Law Section. Mr. Wilson is a member of the AICPA, MACPA, ABA, State Bar of Michigan, International Business Forum, World Trade Club, International Fiscal Association, Michigan District Export Council and the Council on Foreign Relations.

Alan S. Woodberry is an international tax partner with Price Waterhouse in San Francisco. He has over 23 years of international tax and accounting experience with emphasis on tax planning for Japanese and other Pacific Rim Investment in the United States. Mr. Woodberry has assisted many Japanese companies in tax planning for acquisitions of U.S. businesses and U.S. real estate as well as tax planning for their ongoing U.S. operations.

David A. Wormser is a partner in the national law firm of Pepper, Hamilton & Scheetz. Mr. Wormser's practice focuses on services required by high technology and industrial companies, including the perfection, protection, licensing and sale of intellectual property, commercial contracts and agreements, state and federal telecommunications regulation and limitations on foreign investment in the United States. He is a frequent lecturer and writer on export administration issues, and has helped numerous companies identify and comply with their export licensing obligations. Mr. Wormser received his B.S. degree from Miami University and his J.D. degree from the Ohio State University. He joined Pepper, Hamilton & Scheetz after serving as Assistant General Counsel to ADAPSO (now called the "Information Technology Association of America"), the computer software and services industry association.

Lloyd R. Ziff is a partner in the litigation department of Pepper, Hamilton & Scheetz and is primarily engaged in complex litigation matters and advising and negotiating in connection with complex business structuring and transactions both internationally and domestically. His experience includes dealing with issues arising from contemplated and completed acquisitions, mergers, joint ventures, contracts, licensing and related transactions, international and domestic market entry, antitrust, intellectual property, sales and distribution including the resolution of disputes both before and after the commencement of litigation with government and among private parties. He is co-author of "Transatlantic M&A: Springing the U.S. Anti-trust Trap" in the *International Financial Law Review* (May 1989). Mr. Ziff received his undergraduate and law degrees from the University of Pennsylvania, the latter *magna cum laude* in 1971. In 1970 he served on a task force of a Presidential Commission investigating campus and civil unrest; in 1978 he was a Fellow at the Salzburg Seminar in American Studies; he has taught legal advocacy; served as chairman of the federal courts committee at the Philadelphia Bar Association; has served as counsel to the Philadelphia Vietnam Veterans Memorial Fund; and is presently Chairman of the Local Rules Advisory Committee of the U.S. District Court for the Eastern District of Pennsylvania.

Neal W. Zimmerman is an international tax partner with Price Waterhouse. For over 25 years, he has been advising U.S. and foreign companies on international tax and accounting matters. During the past 14 years, he has consulted extensively with Japanese companies investing in the United States. Since 1986, he has been located in the Tokyo office of Price Waterhouse. Mr. Zimmerman is a U.S. Certified Public Accountant and a frequent contributor to professional journals.

Philip M. Zinn is a Senior Tax Manager and the practice leader of Multistate Tax Consulting Services in the Southeast Region for Price Waterhouse. His responsibilities with the firm include handling state and local tax issues for clients of the Philadelphia office and the Southeast Region. Mr. Zinn has an extensive knowledge of state and local taxation with particular emphasis on corporate reorganizations and the use of holding companies. He has significant experience in the cable, telecommunications and manufacturing industries. Mr. Zinn received his B.B.A. degree from Temple University, a J.D. degree from Dickinson School of Law and an L.L.M. degree from Villanova University Graduate Tax Program.

CONTENTS

PART 1

GENERAL AND PLANNING

CHAPTER 1

STRATEGIC PLANNING—THE KEY TO OPTIMIZING OPPORTUNITIES IN THE UNITED STATES

Thomas R. Lucke, Senior Manager
Price Waterhouse

In 1986, Sir Gordon White, then chairman of Hanson Industries, vividly and metaphorically expressed the frustrations of many foreign investors with their U.S. investments: "I don't believe you can run a major U.S. company from abroad. George III tried to run the United States from Britain, and look what happened to him!" Frustrations come directly from the bottom line: According to the Department of Commerce, the return on assets earned by the U.S. affiliates of foreign companies hovered at 1 percent in 1988, less than half what it was in 1978—2.6 percent (see Exhibit 1-1 for a breakdown by sector).

Consider what happened to four foreign investors with long track records outside of the United States when they entered this market:

- Global Bank entered the U.S. market from the European continent amid great fanfare, buying a majority interest in a regional bank for $900 million in 1981. In the beginning of 1985, it pumped another $300 million into the subsidiary to buy the rest of it, bringing its total investment to $1.2 billion.

EXHIBIT 1–1
ROA Earned by U.S. Affiliates of Foreign Companies (%)

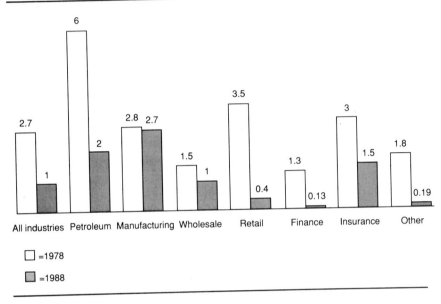

Source: U.S. Department of Commerce, PW analysis.

At the end of 1985, Global sold the regional bank to a U.S. money center for $1.23 billion, citing years of declining earnings, and lack of a "good fit."

• Electric International suffered dramatic losses over a 10-year period in its North American subsidiary (in its best year, the company only made a 4 percent return on sales). In 1990, it finally spun off what it considered the weakest unit, which lost almost $8 million in 1987 marketing a hodge podge of consumer products.

• Asia Computers, a powerhouse in the Korean computer market, had a disastrous entrance into the U.S. computer market by trying to sell the same computer in the United States that it did in Asia and then proliferating activities into every conceivable product line, including television. After several years of fruitless effort, Asia Computers began to retrench by exiting the conventional consumer sector to concentrate on its main businesses.

• The Hefty Finance Bank (Australia), one of the largest in the world, wanted to make the United States the cornerstone of a push into global investment banking. It bought a small boutique bank which was a U.S. subsidiary of a European Global Bank, and began to get into many investment-related businesses, including mergers and acquisitions, leveraged buyouts, and investment management. The subsidiary proceeded to make two related acquisitions—a U.S. Treasury securities primary dealer and a small brokerage house that specialized in executing and clearing securities trades for financial institutions. Then, in a dramatic reversal, the subsidiary began to retrench, drastically cutting staff and announcing it was going to concentrate on the small- to medium-sized corporate market. When it also announced, in the same year, that it was setting up a subsidiary to specialize in mergers and acquisitions, observers began to believe that Hefty would soon sell and would not exist for much longer.

Similar frustrations have been experienced by foreign investors in a variety of industries and from a myriad of countries. Despite them, the United States continues to attract a sizeable amount of foreign investment—the total value of assets owned by U.S. affiliates of foreign companies, for example, rose from $181 billion in 1978 to $1,147 billion in 1988 (an increase of more than 600 percent). For these investors, the attractions of the market have not dimmed. Even in the midst of a recession, the United States has significant personal disposable income, high aggregate industrial capital investment, a diverse economy, almost no ownership limits on foreign investors, and increasingly good labor relations. Moreover, with a weakened dollar, U.S. assets remain significantly less expensive than comparable assets in Europe and Japan. Government attempts to limit foreign investment (most notably felt following the 1973 oil price shock) have been replaced by a welcome mat for investors in a variety of industries, from publishing to banking. In fact, in some individual states, the marketing of the state economy abroad has become the governor's main job and preoccupation, not to mention the centerpiece of any reelection campaign.

The gap between inherent attractiveness and investor success demonstrates how difficult a U.S. investment can be—for any company. In the case of the four firms mentioned above, for example, the parent organizations were all known for being well-managed, excellent international companies. Hefty Finance Bank is one of the most cost-conscious and successful banks in its domestic market, with strong ties, both financially and through the employment of its alumni, to many major manufacturing companies. Asia Computers is a successful Korean computer company, and Electric International, a multinational of long standing. Certainly, they might have been expected to do better in the United States.

The Strategic Consulting Group of Price Waterhouse has worked with the senior management of a variety of foreign companies in analyzing the attractiveness of the U.S. market, as well as proposed U.S. investments and entry strategies. It is our belief that experience and success in other markets, even those judged most sophisticated, are not enough. Instead, we have found that the probability of success increases when investments are consistent with the long-term strategic objectives of the parent, when tactics take into account the sources of competitive advantage, and when a precise game plan has been developed detailing how to operate successfully in the United States. In short, investments that have been subjected to the scrutiny and structure of the strategic planning process (see Exhibit 1-2) are most likely to succeed. More specifically, this entails:

- *Proper consideration and analysis of a parent's overall corporate strategy to sharpen the focus on precise objectives and rationale for doing business in the United States.* It is best to start in the context of the overall strategic goals of the parent company. Taking this step avoids the problem of making an investment either without a clearly articulated goal or with a goal not central to the parent company's strategy. In either case, the result is too often a well-publicized, unceremonious exit after it becomes clear that the investment is not

EXHIBIT 1–2
Strategic Planning for U.S. Investment

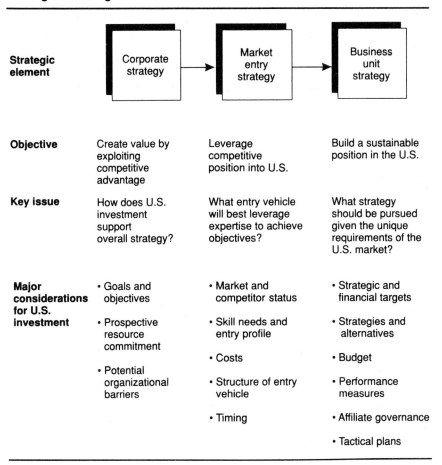

Strategic element	Corporate strategy	Market entry strategy	Business unit strategy
Objective	Create value by exploiting competitive advantage	Leverage competitive position into U.S.	Build a sustainable position in the U.S.
Key issue	How does U.S. investment support overall strategy?	What entry vehicle will best leverage expertise to achieve objectives?	What strategy should be pursued given the unique requirements of the U.S. market?
Major considerations for U.S. investment	• Goals and objectives • Prospective resource commitment • Potential organizational barriers	• Market and competitor status • Skill needs and entry profile • Costs • Structure of entry vehicle • Timing	• Strategic and financial targets • Strategies and alternatives • Budget • Performance measures • Affiliate governance • Tactical plans

a key part of the parent company's strategy. Our experience is that defining what a U.S. investment *should* be doing to further a company's ends improves the ability to judge specifically whether a particular opportunity is the best way for those ends to be met.

• *A well-thought-out entry strategy, linked directly to the parent's corporate strategy, to define a vehicle that is built on the parent's expertise, and therefore likely to achieve its objectives.* One of the main criticisms made of many failed foreign investments is that they involved an excessive acquisition premium—one that would not necessarily have been paid by a U.S. investor. Such criticisms are typically made, however, after it has become clear that an investment is in trouble and reflect the view that the required strategic synergies were never likely to have emerged. In other words, while the strategic objective of the investment may have been correct, the particular vehicle chosen could not have enabled the company to achieve that objective. By providing a thorough understanding of the U.S. market as well as the strengths and weaknesses of each potential investment vehicle, a clear entry strategy puts the emphasis on achieving long-term goals rather than short-term opportunities related to particular deals.

• *Carefully developed, yet flexible, business unit strategy to build on the entry strategy and provide a blueprint for success of U.S. operations.* The final issue is concerned with guiding the U.S. affiliate in the most effective manner, consistent with the requirements of the U.S. competitive arena and the parent company's strategy and organization. One reason for failure in the United States is that foreign investors, when acquiring a U.S. company, often believe that management should be allowed to function as it has always done; this attitude expresses, in part, a reaction to the experience of U.S. multinationals in the 50s and 60s, when foreign governments and common sense ultimately pushed them into relying more on local managers than on American expatriates. In the case of the United States, however, each of the foreign investors we have mentioned ultimately had to exert more and more control over its U.S. operations in an attempt to turn around increasingly disastrous situations. Too many problems can be traced to a lack of clear understanding between affiliate managers and the parent company as to what the real strategic issues are and how (and when) they will be addressed. Drawing up a precise plan for the unit helps set realistic expectations for the parent and affiliate, and also provides a framework and set of benchmarks to help manage decisions as the investment goes along.

Of course, there can be no guarantees with any investment, and strategic planning and analysis are not the only factors that lead to investment success. Environmental factors, which are often unavoidable, come into play and change the rules. Cultural and organizational variables can sometimes get out of control. Even so, we have found that strategic planning can improve the odds—if not the inevitability—of success.

BUILDING A FRAMEWORK FOR SUCCESS

Before foreign investors can understand whether their proposed investment has a good chance of succeeding they must put the theory of the investment in the context of their own strategic design. After more than a decade of strategic thinking, most companies have become quite adept at articulating strategies. Whether each tactical move they make, or plan to make will actually support the strategy is another question. As applied to a decision to invest in the United States, the problem is that the intrinsic attractiveness of the U.S. market can become an end unto itself, so that investments are launched without proper consideration of the market's requirements versus the resources that a parent company has on hand to commit. In that case, the foreign investment may be analyzed without a level of rigor that questions fundamental assumptions or without connecting the investment properly to the parent company's strategy.

In the case of one superior European machine tool manufacturer, for example, its U.S. involvement developed in fits and starts as a marketing and sales operation with little or no support from the parent company. Although this company was a European market leader in several product segments and had a long-lived reputation for production innovation and quality, it could not sell its products in the United States. After two initially fair introductory years, profits began to decline substantially over the three succeeding years, per-unit sales plummeted, and, to add insult to injury, the market perceived the company's products as substandard. The parent company began to reevaluate its options, realizing that it had to structure a planning framework, and that succeeding in the U.S. market was not possible simply "by falling into it."

To put the investment in the context of the objectives of the parent and the ultimate rationale for U.S. entry, the investor needs to answer three basic questions, which help avoid very real pitfalls:

1. *What does the company want to achieve through a U.S. investment?* Considering this issue helps avoid pursuing the wrong objective for the wrong reasons and places the burden on the company to clearly enumerate the strategic as well as financial justifications.

2. *What resources is the company willing to apply to achieving that goal?* Answering this question explicitly gets around the potential difficulty faced by many foreign investors that have a good strategic objective but risk the investment by virtue of insufficient resources committed to carrying it out.

3. *Are there organizational factors that will interfere with the management of the investment?* This question addresses the problems that can result when differences in management style, culture, or approach arise and threaten the value of an otherwise successful venture.

The end result of the process should be a charter for the U.S. investment specifying precisely the objectives as well as the organizational resources that will be used to achieve the objectives. This will lead directly to the development of a market entry strategy.

Consider the first question—*What does the company want from the United States?* At first glance, the answer may be easy for any foreign investor if it rests on the market's intrinsic attractiveness as one of the world's largest and most sophisticated. But it is the strategic goal that must be investigated and fully developed. This might be to meet competitive challenges (such as fighting on the home front of your major competitors, or beating them in the world's toughest market) or to drive product innovation by learning about where the market is going. Or it might be that, to be a global player, the company must have a presence in industries that are undergoing globalization.

Problems arise when entry into the United States is seen as an end in itself and is not directly connected with the parent's overall strategic goals. One global transportation company, for example, was attempting to expand its reach in travel services in a number of different directions in the global market, while the larger parent's goal was always the same—to increase the number of travelers using its diverse modes of transportation. When an enthusiastic planning group came up with the idea of a U.S. investment, however, it was not a direct way to achieve the goal of expanding transportation services. Rather, the group suggested an indirect and very expensive method of expansion—credit cards. They believed that offering a credit card would tie the customer more closely to the means of transportation offered by the company. But this particular tactic would not directly further the larger strategic goal. The gap between the chosen tactic and the larger strategic goal would prove to be one of the reasons for subsequent problems when the parent finally approved the initial U.S. investment.

Another foreign investor's basic strategic goal—to be the preeminent provider of financial information worldwide—was more directly facilitated by its investment in a U.S. manufacturer of video equipment. The parent reasoned that it could provide not only the information but also the equipment on which the information was viewed. The technology that came along as part of the investment would allow the parent to dominate the U.S. market more effectively, and, down the road, leverage that technological base on the worldwide market.

Once the precise strategic attraction is identified, however, the investigation into this issue cannot stop—it must be backed up with realistic analysis. For example, before a company can decide whether the United States will help with the push to globalization, it must ask whether it can be a global player. Could the company survive the competitive wars that it will face?

The second question is more important than the first, because it brings the strategic idea down to earth—*What resources are the company willing to apply to achieving the strategic goal?* Answering this question has two distinct components. The first concerns the company's ability to commit the capital necessary for the investment. (This requires understanding the size of the capital investment necessary and the reality of the company's ability to make the necessary commitment). As important, however, is the second component, concerning the ability to commit other resources that are just as necessary to the success of the investment—senior management time and functional expertise. In order to realistically appraise the feasibility of parental resource commitment, it is necessary to take an honest look at where the U.S. investment falls in relation to the parent's other businesses. The following specific questions should be considered in analyzing resource constraints:

- How well does the company's existing portfolio of businesses generate cash?
- What are the foreseeable cash requirements, and how will they be funded across businesses?
- What level of investment could be supported? How would this vary under different competitive scenarios?
- When does the parent expect (or require) a positive cash flow from the U.S. investment?
- What is the nature and extent of management time that can be devoted to the investment (both initially and on an ongoing basis)?

The main reason for the initial failure of the European machine tool manufacturer in the United States, for example, was the lack of resources targeted at the market. Like many others, the company wanted simply to "wet its feet" but wound up "losing its shirt." Not only was the sales and marketing effort inordinately low key but the service personnel were also poorly trained, without the same understanding or career development afforded their counterparts in the company's domestic European market. The resources committed were below par—as were the first five-year results.

In another foreign investment, the first visible signs of success for its market entry into the shipping business (and also in attracting some other investors) can be traced, in part, to the involvement of senior management throughout the process. That involvement included direct participation and access to functional experts for help in drawing up the plans and in tailoring them for the targeted market niche in the U.S.

The third question that should be answered in the initial investigation is this: *Are there organizational factors that will interfere with the management of the investment?* To answer this question, management must put its new understanding of the investment into the context of the organizational and cultural realities of the parent company. Even if top management is willing to commit resources to the investment, and actually has the resources to commit, organizational factors or management style can prove impediments to the success of the venture.

In acquiring a diverse business publishing house in the United States, for example, a prestigious British publisher believed it could allow the organization to run on its own, as it always had, with some managerial input from the parent. The publisher, however, did not realize how strongly its own British organization would require that it institute the same personnel policies in the U.S. organization that it had in the United Kingdom. After a time, the British team protested that U.S. employees were too highly favored; the parent subsequently gave in to British demands, ending time-honored methods of incentive compensation in the United States and bringing them strictly in line with U.K. policies. In addition, the parent did not consider that none of the more promising members of the British organization wanted to be involved with the United States, which they considered a publishing backwater. The managers who finally oversaw the U.S. investment were the least efficient in the British group and they proceeded to run the U.S. investment into the ground.

In the case of the foreign investment into shipping, on the other hand, substantive analysis was undertaken, the company had experience with foreign investments in Europe, and the senior management committed more than enough staff and capital resources. The result was an initially happy investment experience. If, however, none of these pieces had been in place, the result might have been entirely different.

The question of potential organizational or cultural limitations to success is particularly important for companies with little overseas investment experience. From that perspective, management should ask the following questions:

- How is middle management likely to view the U.S. investment—as a threat or opportunity?

- Will functional management raise concerns about the potential to drain funds away from domestic priorities?
- How willing are top managers to spend substantial amounts of time to launch and sustain the investment?
- Is the organization able to accept a possibly different culture at the U.S. affiliate?

Negative responses to these questions should not dissuade the potential investor from the United States. Rather, they should serve to point up critical issues that must be addressed in formulating an entry strategy.

PUTTING THE PLAN INTO THE RIGHT SYSTEM

Once the organization has put the goal of a U.S. investment into the context of the parent's overall strategy, it must develop a specific strategy for entry into the U.S. market—tied to the capabilities of the parent and new subsidiary rather than the market opportunity. Simply put, this is a gradual process of narrowing options. There are five basic steps to be taken in analyzing the various options for entry:

1. *Developing a perspective on the status of the market and competitors.* Before an investor can decide its point and mode of entry into the U.S. market, it must develop a high-level viewpoint about what is going on in the market, and who the chief competitors are. Unless it has a clear understanding of such competitive realities, it will not understand how to choose among the wealth of entry opportunities that will certainly be presented.
2. *Determining the fit.* What capabilities and activities must the investment encompass within the company's internal business system? Management should identify the critical factors for success in the U.S. market and then identify the functions and activities that the company must control in the United States in order to meet these requirements.

3. *Analyzing the costs and comparing them with available resources.* Given the range of activities that the investment should include (from a strategic perspective), what are the economic implications? The cost analysis should go beyond superficial cost comparisons to identifying the structural drivers of costs, and differences in factor input rates and usage levels. The cost structures of the whole and of potential activities should then be contrasted with the best available evaluation of the parent's resource constraints.

4. *Specifying the best entry vehicle—and quantifying the impact of a specific choice in risk and return.* Given the cost realities of the investment and the resources available from the parent, the investor will be able to determine precisely which potential entry vehicle will not only fill the strategic and operational requirements but will also fit within the resource constraints of the parent.

5. *Understanding the importance of timing.* The impact of timing shows in every aspect of the investment decision, and is not really a step but rather a critical factor that is ignored at the investor's peril.

While a general rule of thumb is that this analysis should be as detailed as possible, it is also true that, at some point, successive layers of complexity can be more debilitating than helpful in making a decision. Analytical focus depends on what is of strategic importance in the business under consideration and the level of detail required to consider properly what needs to be done locally versus what needs to be done by the parent.

Understand the Market and the Competition

To start with, the investor needs to develop a picture, both qualitatively and quantitatively, of the U.S. market. The point of this is to understand better where the market is today and where and how it is going to change over time. These two bits of analysis lay the foundation for the market entry strategy. They help determine the choice of the entry vehicle and where the strategic opportunities lie.

In evaluating whether to enter the U.S. market for mortgage servicing, for example, a foreign investor was alerted to a wealth of opportunities. The decline in the fortunes of the financial services industry meant that not only were both healthy and unhealthy institutions attempting to sell their mortgage servicing portfolios but also whole institutions were themselves for sale. Management agreed that evaluating the industry had to begin with the general overview of financial services and then go into the specific outlook in mortgage servicing. But, given the complexity and sophistication of the market, management decided it needed to deepen its investigation. It analyzed first restructuring in mortgage originations, and then the imbalance that existed between supply and demand for servicing rights. Finally, it thought about likely changes to the situation, including a growing trend toward consolidation in the industry as well as new players, powerful in other industries, who had begun to infiltrate the servicing market. Despite the complexity of the analysis, the investor came away with an understanding of not only the market and the competition, but, as important, how the situation would likely change over time as the competitive environment shifted.

Systemic Fit

The next step in understanding the breadth and depth of the type of market-entry vehicle required to establish a solid competitive position is to lay out precisely the structure of the parent company's business system, including the important activities and how they are accomplished. Exhibit 1-3 illustrates the six most generic sections of any system—Technology, Product Development, Manufacturing, Marketing, Distribution, and Service.

The map of the parent's own system should be as detailed as necessary. Manufacturing, for example, can be broken down into subcomponents such as sourcing, component building and assembly, which can be further divided. Under each category, the precise list of activities should include which facilities are responsible for what, and to what extent.

Next, management details the critical success factors for its U.S. goal. Then, it begins to envision the broad outline of the

EXHIBIT 1–3
Systemic Fit and U.S. Entry Profile

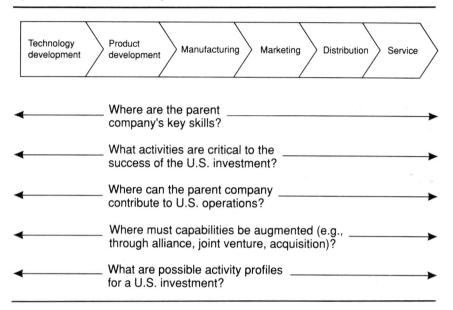

| Technology development | Product development | Manufacturing | Marketing | Distribution | Service |

Where are the parent company's key skills?

What activities are critical to the success of the U.S. investment?

Where can the parent company contribute to U.S. operations?

Where must capabilities be augmented (e.g., through alliance, joint venture, acquisition)?

What are possible activity profiles for a U.S. investment?

required U.S. business system. The analysis must explicitly consider the strategic impact of alternative ways of handling each key activity in the United States. For example, should the parent perform the activity itself or transplant it to the United States? Should it purchase the product or service from a third party? Or should the production of this particular product or service be part of the actual investment? At this point, the analysis should go into as much detail as possible. In the case of sales, for example, management would have to consider whether to go direct or through dealers or distributors. Moreover, it must evaluate the competitive impact of the options. Can the parent really provide the activity from overseas? Does the parent have the requisite skills and/or knowledge, or must these skills be part of the ideal investment vehicle?

If the strategic goal, as was the case with one foreign cheese manufacturer, was to become the leader in the processed cheese market (both private label and branded), identifying the required investment started with a consideration of the extreme competitiveness of the market. To come out on top would require economies of scale in sourcing, manufacturing, and distribution to generate sufficient volume to defray the high promotional costs of supporting a branded product; flexibility in supply relationships to facilitate shifting product between plants to accommodate market shifts; superior product quality (based on consistent quality of raw materials and the most modern manufacturing operations); cost effectiveness, in part through the use of the latest technology in processing equipment to cut down on labor costs; proximity of manufacturing operations to major markets; and excellent distribution channels through high-volume retail segments (for branded products) and fast-food chains and restaurants (for private labels).

Cross-checking these success factors against the parent company's existing system in its own country, which included raw materials procurement, processing, packaging, and distribution, made it apparent that this investment would have to cut across the whole business system. The foreign cheese company could not hope to achieve its goal unless it held a strong foothold throughout the entire market. Only a large-scale, fully integrated investment could succeed.

Setting up the system is a critical piece of the evaluation. It helps define the scope of the investment by matching the parent's capabilities and the requirements for U.S. success—at the same time identifying skills and activities that must be part of the investment. Will it be necessary to mirror the parent company's entire business system within the United States? Or, more likely, will the company be entering initially through one piece of the system? Will that new offshoot feed back into the parent's own system, or will it be self-contained? Which of its functions or activities must occur in the United States, and what can be centralized back home?

**Analyzing Costs and Cross-checking Against
Resource Constraints**

An investment may be of strategic importance, but if the costs involved will have a large negative impact on the parent company, then it must be reevaluated. A cost analysis is used to decide among various options or alternatives within the business system. The first step is to identify the drivers of cost for critical business system activities (at least those for which there are alternatives). These cost drivers include such obvious examples as cost per unit for factor inputs and level of usage for each of these inputs, related to operational decisions, for example, on location. But to be effective, the analysis must also include other structural drivers—such as scale economies, learning curve and cumulative volume, and product-line complexity—that relate to some of the large strategic decisions, about, for instance, how broad a product line the affiliate will handle. After identifying the cost drivers, the company should assess the overall relative cost impact for various alternatives and then compare costs with the most likely entry point within the business system structure.

This cost analysis will add a different dimension to the various business system options. It will illuminate exactly what the company can and cannot change to affect its cost position among and within business options.

The European machine tool manufacturer, for example, planned to correct its initial failure in the United States by setting up a small assembly operation in the South, which, management reasoned, would cost little to operate and would enjoy the same input cost as the U.S. competition. This plan, however, failed to address the cost realities of U.S. machine tool manufacturing, which were heavily affected by economies of scale. Competitors enjoyed an enormous cost advantage (calculated to be 15 percent in some market segments) because of economies of scale enjoyed through shared facilities, equipment, and factory support services in administration, quality control, and maintenance among their various operations. The European company, on the other hand, was not thinking in terms of economies of scale in the U.S. market. Management wanted to hold the line on initial spending through the acquisition of a small assembly operation. While it could control initial costs, however, the assembly plant suffered from the same underlying difficulties as the sales operation. Neither of the two identified investment options would allow the company to benefit from the advantages of scale, and either eventually would result in a long-term drain on resources.

This type of cost analysis will help force the parent to reconsider the realities of its resource constraints and make decisions among alternative profiles (business system layouts) for the investment. It may be that the costs could overrun the parent's resources—or the opposite may prove true. But without the most sophisticated cost understanding possible, an investment should not be made. In the cases of the foreign credit card company and the cheese manufacturer, for example, the attractions of the market paled alongside the costs of the investments needed to take advantage of these attractions—costs that were completely beyond the parent companies' available resources under any reasonable scenario.

Which Way to Enter?

At this point, the foreign investor analyzes the specific mode of entry. Exhibit 1-4 compares four major types of investment: minority position, joint venture, complete acquisition, and de novo investment. Each has basic attractions in terms of risk, return, control, strategic direction, and organizational impact, but these basic attractions have to be viewed in light of the strategic, market, and organizational realities that have already been analyzed.

Consider, for example, that any investment in the U.S. service industry will have a hefty systems component for information processing. For a foreign investor, it often may seem sensible to consider a joint venture or strategic alliance with a third-party processor in the United States, which would ostensibly be familiar with the most efficient types of systems in use. Depending on the importance of information systems to the parent corporation, however, it may also be possible to centralize operations and benefit from economies of scale. One global French bank acquired 100 percent of a mortgage servicing operation that had historically outsourced its processing. After analyzing the situation, however, and seeing that it could obtain a long-term competitive advantage in servicing by doing its own processing, the bank purchased the processing operation as well and integrated it into the mortgage servicing subsidiary. The result was initially successful as the mortgage servicing unit had a distinct cost advantage in data processing, which translated into a 5 to 6 percent cost advantage in total cost per loan.

EXHIBIT 1–4
Entry Mode Comparison

Mode	Issues		
	Financial	Strategic	Organizational
Minority position	• Modest investment • Limited/no premium • Returns dependent on payout decisions by board majority holders	• Limited control • Low-profile entry to U.S. • Potential to shift to J.V./acquisition	• Few resources required • Limited ability to learn
Joint venture	• Investment dependent on specific structure and company needs • Must consider price at which parent would sell/buy partner's stake	• Moderate control • Likely to become competitive with parent • Unlikely to continue indefinitely	• Potentially good learning vehicle • Different cultures may make management difficult
Complete acquisition	• Premium for control may raise financial hurdle • Greatest financial flexibility • Known cost of entry	• Aquisition may adversely affect competitive performance • Post-acquisition integration difficult • High-profile entry	• Learning highly dependent on management team • Cultural clashes possible • Potential loss of key people
De Novo investment	• Significant cost risk if experience limited • Long lead time to profitability • Full ownership of results	• Complete control • Potentially easiest integration with parent strategy • Time to build organization may adversely affect competitive position	• Greatest resource requirement • Need to build an affiliate culture • Human resource infrastructure must be built from scratch

The specification of the entry vehicle involves complex trade-offs. If labor costs are found to be the main structural cost driver, for example, then a de novo investment in facilities located in non-union areas in the U.S. South might prove initially attractive.

This potential advantage, however, would need to be evaluated against the resources, capabilities, and goals of the company related to the U.S. investment. With limited time for management oversight, for example, or little experience constructing facilities outside the domestic market, a de novo plant could be a very risky (and ultimately costly) alternative.

Thus, the key to the analysis resides in assessing proposed returns from the investment. Will expected results allow the investment to meet the company's target hurdle rate? Most important, how long is the parent willing to wait for a positive payback from the investment?

In analyzing the financial impact of the investment in the U.S. processed cheese industry, for example, the foreign cheese manufacturer had to analyze not only the cost of acquiring a manufacturer in the United States, but also the costs of solving the problems inherent in the company. The foreign company realized that it could achieve its market goals only with a strong presence across the board in the market. The U.S. company offered a start on fulfilling some of the foreign firm's strategic requirements especially in the private label market, including manufacturing facilities located near key markets, good supplier relationships, and excellent distribution outlets with fast-food chains and restaurants.

In order to play a part in the parent company's achievement of its larger strategic goals, however—to become a global player in the cheese processing business—the parent would have to correct the remaining faults of the U.S. target, first by instituting a system of cost control, and then by introducing a regional branded label, acquiring continuous processing equipment, making higher promotional expenditures, and increasing market penetration in the food processor/manufacturer market segment and in independent and small restaurant chains. Outside the initial cost of the acquisition, then, and even taking into account the positive impact of expected cost reductions in labor and supply costs, the parent estimated that achieving the strategic goal would still cost millions more in product and production enhancements over a five-year period of heavy investment. After that time, it was estimated that the profitability of the proposed subsidiary would more than double. Upon reaching this understanding of the true costs, and recognizing the scope of management talent necessary to oversee the operation, the foreign investor did not enter the market.

Given that this particular foreign investor wanted to enter a highly competitive market in a big way, only an aggressive push could ensure profitability. This resource constraint precluded the investment. In the case of other investments, however, the costs are outweighed either by strategic or economic returns. In the shipping example, top management anchored the investment squarely on the company's existing strategies and resources. The company went ahead with good results because the costs did not weight it down.

Timing

An added dimension in assessing the plan for an investment is time. As with life, timing in a U.S. investment "is everything," and can often mean the difference between success and failure. If the credit card investor mentioned earlier had begun to make an aggressive push in the late 1970s, for example, its investment outlook might have been entirely different.

Some market-entry vehicles will look better in the short term and worse in the long run; for others, the situation will be reversed. Often, however, the mere existence of the opportunity will drive the company's decisions, no matter what type of vehicle looks good on paper. In such cases, the parent organization may push a deal along because, from its point of view, the timing is right to "seize a U.S. opportunity." The investor must look beyond what is a "great deal" to whether the timing is right according to the market and the competitive situation. It may often turn out that the market has changed and is no longer as attractive—no matter how ready the parent company is to plunge in.

In the case of the one bank's disastrous investment in Colorado, for example, the Colorado real estate and retail markets started into a downturn precisely when the parent made its investment. This was not the only reason for the difficulties the British parent had with the subsidiary, but it was a contributing factor. In the same way, and despite its size, the Honda investment in U.S. auto manufacturing was extremely well timed in terms of the target market and the investment vehicle. Ohio was beginning to pull itself out of a recession and could offer a lucrative package of incentives to Honda in return for the promise of significant job creation. More important in the long run, the company has managed to sell the output from the plant because of the right combination of opportunities in the medium to upper end of the auto market and the Japanese reputation for quality.

Remember that timing will never be as crucial in the long run as the strategic importance of the investment. While the United States continues to suffer recessionary symptoms, particularly with regard to property values, the price of U.S. assets looks comparatively good to foreign investors. Once again, however, the parent company management must step back from existing opportunities and put them in the context of its overall strategic aims. In fact, the recent slowdown in financial markets means that there is time for more thinking and analysis before a deal must be consummated. It is unlikely that bargains will be snatched up before they can be properly evaluated—and there can be no excuse for forgetting strategic elements in the rush to make a deal.

A FLEXIBLE STRATEGY FOR THE BUSINESS UNIT

Once the appropriate entry vehicle has been decided upon, the parent should develop a specific strategy for the unit emphasizing the key targets that the investment is to achieve, whether strategic or financial. Depending on the affiliate's position within the parent's overall business system, it will be necessary to have a precise plan to best integrate operations. At the same time, specific measures should be decided upon for judging the unit's performance.

Through our work with foreign investors, Price Waterhouse has identified the six most important operational components of a business unit strategy. It is important to include all six in the strategy in order to set realistic expectations and align them between the parent and the new subsidiary:

1. *Setting key strategic and financial targets.* These targets will flow naturally from the objectives that have been articu-

lated. They help bring the idea of the investment down to earth.

2. *Selecting among strategies and major alternatives.* This requires careful consideration and analysis following on the preliminary market and competitive analysis done earlier. Contingencies should be developed to show the impact of various alternatives and changes within them.

3. *Analyzing the financial impact under a range of likely scenarios.* Even with one set of budget figures, the plan should explicitly address the range of likely outcomes, enumerate the competitive risk factors, and identify possible actions to mitigate their impact on the investment.

4. *Setting up a system of performance measures.* Even if the subsidiary already has an existing set of measures, the plan should come up with a new set of measures, including those relating to outcomes, those that come out of leading indicators and those that monitor intermediate processes. The measures linked to outcomes will bring key targets to life for both strategies and markets. Those tied to leading indicators will help the parent monitor the investment's progress toward certain objectives. Those that monitor processes provide keys to identifying solutions for different business problems.

5. *Developing a design for management decision making at the affiliate.* This should clearly lay out the scope of the authority for affiliate management as well as the scope of oversight responsibility for the parent. It should also include trigger points for reevaluation of the target's strategy or decision-making ability.

6. *Setting up an action plan.* Supporting these higher-level components should be a set of detailed action plans outlining functional strategies in areas such as marketing, sales, manufacturing, and product development. The action plans should also describe the means that will be used to ensure appropriate levels of coordination and integration with the parent company.

If the new unit is being built from the ground up, an action plan may be set in place relatively easily and a new system of performance measures drawn up without much difficulty. If, as is generally the case, the unit is an acquisition or joint venture, setting new targets may prove a time-consuming and wrenching process because it will necessitate revamping and reorienting existing systems.

Once the targets are set, however, detailed strategies should be drawn up that relate specifically to each target. In that way, parent company management will be able to guide actions in a direction consistent with its own strategies. The process will involve parent company negotiation and agreement with affiliate management, first on strategic direction and then on individual strategies to arrive at strategic goals.

These strategic goals should then form the basis of the management action plans for the U.S. subsidiary, which should be as detailed as possible. Many of the foreign investment mistakes made in the United States are the result of allowing the new subsidiary to continue in its own direction without much interference from the new parent. The fact that so many foreign investors must subsequently increase their stake, both managerially and financially, within a subsidiary testifies to the wisdom of beginning the process in a more hands-on fashion.

BEATING THE RECORD OF GEORGE III

It is true that many of the reasons for the poor showing of the American investment made by the Hanoverian dynasty still obtain:

- The natives are fiercely independent and devoted to their own way of doing things.
- The continent is so large that it is difficult to connect widely dispersed parts of the organization, although success depends on it.
- Unless expectations of the investor and the subsidiary align and reinforce one another in a positive fashion, the investment is doomed to progress in fits and starts, at best, or by open revolt, at worst.

The lessons from the ensuing two hundred years demonstrate, however, that investment success is possible if it is planned for sufficiently. Careful strategic planning holds the key to any investment in the United States. It must be strategic planning that sets up a system and rationale for the investment, from the conception until it is up and running, and even after. Only if the planning exercise becomes integrated with the operations of the investment and is not ignored and/or bypassed in favor of immediate action will it ensure success.

CHAPTER 2

COMMUNICATIONS: THE KEY TO SUCCESSFUL MARKETING

Christopher P. A. Komisarjevsky
Executive Vice President
Hill and Knowlton, Inc.

OVERVIEW

In the United States, perhaps more than anywhere else in the world today, effective communications is the key to marketing success.

For the foreign company entering the U.S. market, there are several considerations:

- *Corporate image* is a critical element in the marketing process and it can be shaped through communications.
- Companies must communicate with and market products to a *host* of different audiences.
- Foreign companies must communicate their *participation* in the U.S. economy through the practice of good public affairs.
- Companies need effective *corporate positioning* through the use of proactive, coordinated communications about themselves and their product; they must be aware of individual issues to be confronted and must know how to shape the image of the company and the product to turn these issues to their advantage.

The U.S. Market Environment

Entering any new market presents an array of challenges. For the overseas company attempting to market its products or services in the United States, the challenges are unique. Far from presenting a homogeneous target, the U.S. market is fragmented and specialized along complex demographic lines. In fact, it would be more accurate to refer to a variety of U.S. *markets*.

In the United States, millions of consumers are split along such lines as age, residence location (urban/suburban/rural), region (Northeast, Midwest, West Coast, etc.), employment, income, buying habits, size of family, sex, racial/ethnic divisions, and many other factors.

Companies need to communicate to many other audiences in addition to consumer segments, including shareholders; employees or other stakeholders; local, state, and federal government representatives; opinion leaders; and the media.

THE IMPORTANCE OF IMAGE

Right or wrong, and like it or not, each company has a public image. Corporate image is the sum total of perceptions held by all the company's various audiences. Each corporate action affects that image, whether in a positive or negative manner. The question is: Do you want to shape that image or let others do it for you?

Corporate image can be shaped and influenced through **corporate positioning**—that is, the process of managing communications and perceptions. The goal is understanding, not just awareness.

In a rapidly changing international/global marketplace, the key issue is whether companies want to be proactive, exerting a voice to shape corporate image and help create marketing opportunities. Here, corporate communications play a critical role.

The core corporate question is one of corporate policy and strategy: It's important to remember that **policy** is established first, **strategy** to carry out that policy is second, and **tactics** to implement strategy run third.

There is no magic to the corporate positioning process. It is a matter of disciplined, planned, coordinated communications involving these eight key steps:

- Research—defining the current corporate image.
- Issues analysis.
- Developing core strategic messages, themes, and illustrations.
- Planning, discipline, and coordination.
- Use of the communications matrix.
- Monitoring.
- Midcourse corrections.
- Evaluation.

In the corporate positioning process, a research base must first be gathered. Perceptions involving the following areas should be measured:

- Quality of management.
- Quality of products and services.
- Innovativeness.
- Ability to attract, develop, and keep talented people.
- Financial stability.
- Sense of community and environmental responsibility.
- Commitment to research and development.
- Technological expertise.
- Diversity of products and markets.
- International scope.
- Growth potential.
- Integrity.

THE NEED FOR A MARKETING COMMUNICATIONS STRATEGY

In today's marketing environment, it is no longer sufficient to rely on ad hoc communications about the issues, opportunities, or problems affecting companies. There should be careful public relations planning that has its roots in corporate goals, objectives, and strategy. Furthermore, out of that planning should arise an overall communications strategy that effectively organizes and coordinates what, when, how, and whether a company speaks. That strategy forms the base of effective public relations efforts and constitutes the foundation of a clear, purposeful, and credible way of communicating.

To help you deal with marketing your product in the United States, an overall communications strategy should work in a number of specific ways:

- Create a climate of understanding within which the company's goals and strategies will be viewed.
- Increase the ability of the company to anticipate and respond to issues that affect its business, assisting in strategic planning and identifying new audiences that may be important to the company.
- Increase understanding of the company among its various audiences so that actions and policies can be understood and fairly evaluated.
- Enable the various departments or divisions to develop a cohesive position and speak with one voice on issues that can and should be dealt with publicly.
- Help establish a unified tone to communications that encourages consumers and others to respect the information, products, and opinions of the company.
- Provide an opportunity for the company to participate in issues important to the industry.
- Support and make more effective existing marketing efforts.

Experience has shown that coordinated and effective communications require the strong support of top management. Recognition that you are under public scrutiny as you enter a new national market often begins the process, followed by a mandate to the public relations or communications function.

Top management support includes involving public relations in the strategic planning process. Developing communications strategy requires an examination of the internal and external environments within which the corporation does business; an understanding of the goals of the corporation and the objectives of business units, departments, or divisions; and a translation of those business goals and objectives into communications goals and objectives.

The public relations process requires an analysis of those issues critical to the continued productivity and profitability of the business. Management then makes fundamental policy decisions on those important issues, and then a public relations strategy and company policy statements support the corporate strategy and provide the framework for organized communications.

Reviewing Strategy: Some Case Studies

No strategy is permanent, and that certainly includes communications, which should be reviewed on a regular basis. The most critical factor is change as needed: as the company's needs change, as the issues change, and as the external and internal environments change.

To anticipate change, there should be a means of monitoring issues. As issues important to the company emerge and then intensify, an evaluation is required of their impact on the company, its products, and the industry, followed by a reexamination of the communications efforts. Perhaps the strategy might remain the same but the projects and techniques might change, or nothing might need to be revised, or everything might.

The experiences of several companies entering the U.S. market serve as appropriate illustrations. The giant Japanese company Shiseido is the third-largest cosmetics company in the world, behind only Avon and L'Oreal. Their experience in the U.S. market can be considered somewhat typical in that they did not realize the vast differences between the American market for cosmetics and the Japanese market, which they dominated. In Japan, the company established intense personal relationships with its customers, complete with calls from salespeople to wish them a happy birthday. The U.S. market is far different, with most sales made through relatively impersonal department stores that depend on give-away promotions to capture customer attention.

In addition, Shiseido had not changed its cosmetics line to be more appropriate to the needs of American women and makeup needs that differ with the culture. The company lost $2 million in the

United States in 1974 before it pulled its product line and designed an all new line to meet the needs of the American market. The American subsidiary's sales reached $60 million in 1988. In 1989, Shiseido launched a new line of makeup after a careful, six-month study of American consumers.

After several false starts in the American market, Shiseido did not just fold up its tent and leave. Instead, it learned from its mistakes, performed extensive market research, and got back in the game. And Shiseido's persistence is paying off: The company is shifting production of its U.S. product line to a manufacturing facility in New Jersey, where it will produce most of the products it sells in the United States. In addition, the company puts local people in charge of its non-Japanese operations whenever possible. These are both important steps to stay in touch with the changing local market.

To take another example: the popular Danish plastic toy blocks made by Lego were introduced in the United States in 1961 through a licensing agreement with Samsonite, the luggage maker. Samsonite banked on its experience in plastics and retailing to succeed in the new venture, but instead found the toy business a jungle of special deals that it did not really understand. "Kids are kids and alike around the world" is Lego's company motto. However, Samsonite thought that U.S. children were different from European children, and that Lego would not catch on here. In 1973, Samsonite gave up its U.S. license and Lego started its own subsidiary. Since then, brilliant marketing has caused U.S. sales to soar to around $140 million—about a quarter of Lego's worldwide sales. In addition, about 65 percent of American households with children under age 12 have at least one Lego product.

Furthermore, the company shows its highly savvy marketing through joint promotions with other companies, including McDonald's, Jell-O dessert, and Crest toothpaste, that help it reach its young audience. Lego is also active in the educational market, developing products for elementary schools.

But even Lego has encountered a few bumps along the way. The company faced major competition and numerous imitators beginning in the 1980s. One competitor in particular, Tyco, introduced a bucket in which to store the plastic toys. Lego had always used an elegant see-through carton, which was standard for the company's operations worldwide. On this point the Danish head office would not budge, despite the U.S. subsidiary's insistence that market research showed that parents, who controlled the purse strings, preferred the buckets. Finally, facing a massive loss of market share in the United States, the company reversed its position, and buckets are now outselling cartons. This example shows the need to adapt to change as well as the importance of tailoring global marketing strategy to meet local needs.

Durand International, the U.S. subsidiary established in 1970 by a French glassware manufacturer, encountered initial marketing problems stemming from poor communications. The company was charged with not being responsive to the American market—of trying to force European-style products on the market. As a result, Durand has worked to create closer ties with retailers and take into account the differing nature of the U.S. retail market.

Setting Up a Communications Matrix

Effective and coordinated corporate communications goes far beyond the best techniques for telling your story to the customers, the media, or the financial community. It brings together a variety of elements in a skillful and creative way. It fosters a close working relationship among communications experts, staff, and line managers. And it becomes interwoven in many business decisions—whether they deal with business goals and the financial community, issues analysis, product marketing, management strengths and corporate identity, internal relations and productivity, strategic planning, or the role of executives in the business community.

Today's business decisions are increasingly complex. Issues surface, the winds of politics change, and new forces must be reckoned with. The need to communicate ideas and positions to corporate stakeholders is balanced by the need to be aware of and sensitive to changes in public moods and perceptions.

The public relations process is integral to marketing strategy. If it is coordinated, purposeful, and well managed, public relations assists staff and line officers in implementing strategy and in reaching goals and business objectives. Moreover, it helps management broaden its perspective when it has to deal with the many dimensions of today's business environments.

A communications matrix helps to visualize communications as a management function. It creates a broad vantage point from which management looks at business decisions, adopting a communications perspective.

The communications matrix in Exhibit 2-1 shows how and why communications is part of marketing strategy. It outlines how and why top management should look to members of a communications department for advice on corporate decisions that have strong communications components. It stresses communications planning, input, output, feedback, listening, and talking so that corporate decisions are well grounded.

The Legacy of the 1960s, 1970s, and 1980s

Consumer activism has a profound effect on product marketing. This kind of activism had its roots in the Civil Rights movement and Vietnam War protests of the 1960s. At the same time, some larger companies were abruptly tossed into the limelight through editorial attacks in such books as Vance Packard's *The Waste Makers,* Rachel Carson's *Silent Spring,* Ralph Nader's *Unsafe at Any Speed,* and John Kenneth Galbraith's *The New Industrial State.*

The 1970s added to the list when questions about the environment, governance, and profits touched companies of all sizes. Unprepared to deal head-on with those issues or having dealt with them badly, industry was faced with pressure from the legislature, the marketplace, and shareholders.

In the 1980s, the trend toward activism continued. While there were fewer public demonstrations such as sit-ins and mass protest marches, a segment of the U.S. population continued to feel that business was driven by greedy men and women who were to blame for an extensive laundry list of the world's ills, including poverty, racism, drug abuse, the plight of the homeless, pollution, depletion of the ozone layer, nuclear waste dumping, and the destruction of the world's rain forests.

The litmus test is one's reaction to the mention of a single name: Reagan. For many in the business community, the Reagan years represented a period of prosperity and growth unparalleled in recent American history. For many others, the Reagan years will be

EXHIBIT 2–1
Corporate Positioning Matrix: Information Sharing Before, During, and After Decision Making

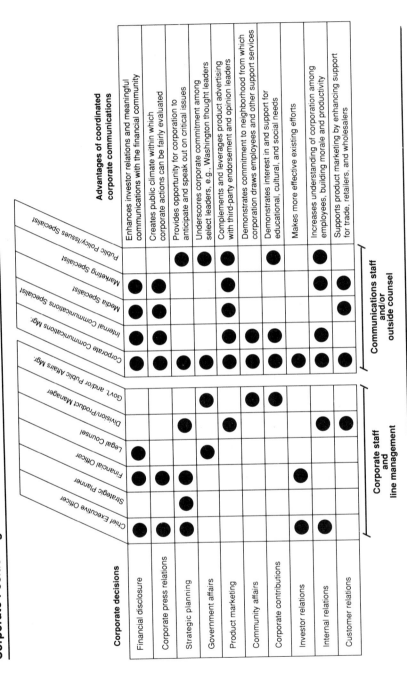

Corporate decisions (rows):
- Financial disclosure
- Corporate press relations
- Strategic planning
- Government affairs
- Product marketing
- Community affairs
- Corporate contributions
- Investor relations
- Internal relations
- Customer relations

Corporate staff and line management (columns):
- Chief Executive Officer
- Strategic Planner
- Financial Officer
- Legal Counsel
- Division/Product Manager
- Gov't and/or Public Affairs Mgr.

Communications staff and/or outside counsel (columns):
- Corporate Communications Mgr.
- Internal Communications Specialist
- Media Specialist
- Marketing Specialist
- Public Policy/Issues Specialist

Advantages of coordinated corporate communications:
- Enhances investor relations and meaningful communications with the financial community
- Creates public climate within which corporate actions can be fairly evaluated
- Provides opportunity for corporation to anticipate and speak out on critical issues
- Underscores corporate commitment among select leaders, e.g., Washington thought leaders
- Complements and leverages product advertising with third-party endorsement and opinion leaders
- Demonstrates commitment to neighborhood from which corporation draws employees and other support services
- Demonstrates interest in and support for educational, cultural, and social needs
- Makes more effective existing efforts
- Increases understanding of corporation among employees, building morale and productivity
- Supports product marketing by enhancing support for trade, retailers, and wholesalers

remembered as the greedy "me" decade personified by the case of Michael Milken and the collapse of the high-yield "junk" bond market, and Charles Keating's role in the huge savings and loan scandal, which led to the collapse of many S&Ls across the country.

The Outlook for the 1990s

The 1990s have started off as a time of retrenchment, recession, and a reversal of many of the excesses of the 1980s. Milken's firm, Drexel Burnham Lambert, went out of business. The high-yield bond market still exists, but at a much lower profile. The high-flying proxy fights, mergers, and acquisitions of the 1980s have all but vanished; most big-money deals in the early '90s have been corporate spin-offs, restructurings, and bankruptcies.

Insurance companies, banks, and other financial institutions are much more careful about the amount of assets they hold in risky high-yield bonds. Furthermore, a collapsing real estate market has led these institutions to reexamine their holdings in real estate as well. The American taxpayer will be cleaning up after the S&L mess for a long time to come. The mood has clearly shifted.

Despite the Bush Administration's obvious sensitivity to business concerns, corporations and industry associations still face a serious challenge. Public interest groups will have no less an influence on public attitudes and on government actions. Business has made considerable progress in consumer and environmental areas, but corporate executives themselves readily acknowledge that business still has a long way to go in educating the public and opinion leaders about its attitudes and accomplishments.

Public interest groups that are sophisticated in using media, grass-roots lobbying, and public relations techniques are also putting pressures on business. Even the conservative Reagan and Bush administrations have had to deal with those who have not found them conservative enough.

In the last few years, many issues with potentially far-reaching effects on companies have suddenly arisen. The drama and tragedy of hazardous waste disposal set corporations against the public. Product litigation and the issue of industry liability have put asbestos companies out of business and pose long-term questions for the pharmaceutical industry. Oil spills, ozone depletion, rain forest destruction, and the problem of solid and liquid waste disposal are environmental issues that have come to the fore recently.

Every day brings new findings concerning the role of consumer products in the public health. Studies have linked numerous products, from coffee to artificial sweeteners, to cancer and heart disease. And the S&L scandal, mergers and acquisitions, and changes in the regulatory climate have created new breeds of financial institutions, sending shock waves through the investment, insurance, and banking industries.

Some Examples: Financial Services Firms

A basic change in strategic direction may provide one of the most far-reaching needs for meaningful communications. The acquisitions of Bache by Prudential, Shearson by American Express, and Salomon Brothers by Phibro Corporation signal substantial changes for the insurance, investment, and banking industries. Such strategic decisions require timely communications—not so early that they divulge plans, but timely enough that the new directions are adequately explained to employees, public policymakers, shareholders, and the financial community.

The Work Force's Changing Values

To take another situation: The 1990s show strong signs of new values continuing to emerge among the work force. Higher levels of expectation and midcareer changes are only two of the elements at work. For example, as a response to both the demands for corporate social responsibility and the demands among employees for greater personal fulfillment, a corporation might experiment with a social leave policy, giving employees an opportunity to spend time working with social service organizations. To be successful, such a program requires communications input about the needs of communities, about career issues, and about social trends. It also offers communications output opportunities that can go far beyond the obvious and can reach audiences in local plant communities and the financial community, the consumer, the legislator, the regulator, and other Washington thought leaders.

The changing work force provides another example. A new source of employees is helping corporate productivity, and corporations are seeking new ways to enhance productivity and morale. Recognizing that retirees have valuable experience and well-hewn skills, corporations are finding innovative ways to entice them back into the work force.

In yet another case, issues analysis should provide topics that can be shared with a host of audiences. They in turn may provide some feedback that helps the company further refine its product or marketing direction. The concern over additives and "natural foods" has affected the food industry considerably. Sugars, fats, cholesterol, artificial sweeteners, caffeine, other ingredients, and safety and labeling are topics that will be around for quite some time. They cannot be ignored and actually force changes in new product development. Communications has a role in identifying those individuals or groups who are opinion leaders. Hearing what the opinion leaders say, researching why they say it, and learning what underlies their opinions are the first steps to a successful communications program. This is the listening stage. The talking stage follows, when sophisticated opinion and attitude research provide insights into what themes will change or reinforce attitudes.

The Looming Issues in Health Care

For a final example in another industry: In developing a marketing strategy, a company in the health care business needs to go through a systematic process of issues and communications analysis. As a starting point and as a minimum it might look at the following:

Issues affecting the company:
- Product testing and efficacy.
- Ingredient safety.
- Medical instrument testing and safety.
- Production control—clean room standard.
- Acquisitions and divestitures.
- Long-term goals as seen by management.

- Long-term goals as seen by shareholders.
- Future of the company as seen by financial community.
- Company description.
- Relations in plant communities.
- Domestic versus international earnings.
- Problems and opportunities in foreign countries.
- New product development.

Issues affecting business in general:
- Capital markets in an inflationary economy.
- Corporate social responsibility.
- Product liability.
- Corporate governance.
- Productivity.
- Government regulation (e.g., OSHA, EEOC).
- Energy.
- Mandatory retirement.
- Corporate ethics.
- Changing values of employees and customers.
- Changing face of the work force.

Issues affecting the health care and personal health care products industry:
- Efficacy.
- Independent testing.
- Ingredient monograph.
- Self-medication in a drug culture.
- Ingredient safety.
- Risk and benefit analysis—risk assessment.
- The government as health administrator.
- Role of FDA—FDA reform.
- Potential for an "international FDA-type regulatory body.
- Hospital care.
- Clinic care.

Marketing communications strengths.
Marketing communications weaknesses.

These steps represent only the beginning. Out of this analysis comes a marketing communications effort that builds on the strengths and takes steps to shore up the weaknesses. This effort ensures that the company speaks with one voice to its many audiences. If the issues are to be discussed publicly, position papers need to be developed and systems established so that all spokespeople have the correct information and know what they can say and when they can say it. One of the important ways to accomplish this, especially for an international company, is through a public relations procedures manual. It outlines which topics are left to the discretion of the local area or country management, and it identifies those topics that must be referred to headquarters. This may be particularly critical for a pharmaceutical company when it comes to product liability lawsuits. Under such circumstances, the company faces a host of marketing communications problems since the outcome of these lawsuits affects other products, customer confidence, shareholder relations, and financial community perception of the company's future. Noting what can be said and by whom is critical to underscoring confidence in the company.

PARTICIPATING IN THE U.S. ECONOMY

It is important for foreign companies to be seen as *participants* in the U.S. economy. Companies encounter difficulty from the beginning when they are perceived as "outsiders" coming in to take jobs and dollars out of the United States. It is the practice of good public affairs to enhance the company's image as a participant in the economy, positively changing and being changed by the local business environment.

There are many ways to achieve this objective. A foreign company entering the U.S. market should find ways to communicate a sense of corporate social responsibility, respond to environmental issues that concern the community, and establish a solid reputation as a good corporate citizen.

Corporate Social Responsibility

The trend toward strategic social responsibility probably originated and developed first in the United States, due in large part to tax policies. The concept of corporate social responsibility is a crucial one, particularly for the foreign investor, because evidence of this demonstrates that your company is participating in the economy and the community of which it is a part.

In recent years, the impact of foreign companies on the U.S. economy has been great and has raised some degree of frustration and resentment among the public at large. American auto workers, for example, blamed Japanese auto companies for the loss of jobs in U.S. factories. In response, many foreign companies have built plants in the United States where they make products on American soil, creating jobs for U.S. workers.

While building plants that employ U.S. workers and recycle American dollars locally is certainly one way—perhaps the best way—to turn around the perception of being an outsider, many other methods can be used to enhance a company's status as a responsible participant in the economy.

For some businessmen, social responsibility means "delivering the goods and making a profit." To others, the term simply implies sticking rigidly to the letter of the law. Still others equate social responsibility with good labor relations. And finally there is social or cause-related marketing.

In reality, a company's social responsibility is all of these things and more, and unless your company is about to go bankrupt, you already represent social responsibility, simply because you exist as a viable, profitable enterprise.

For example:

- You provide jobs to your employees.
- You produce products or services that directly benefit your customers.
- Simply by generating cash flow, you're able to reinvest in the community; you support other community businesses; and, of course, you support your stakeholders, whether they are employees, shareholders, or customers.

The highly publicized social consciousness of the 1960s and 1970s left a legacy that is even more vocal in the 1990s: Corporations, and not just governments, are being asked to demonstrate a real sensitivity and a true commitment to social issues. On a local, national, and global scale, the social community is looking to you to make life better.

This legacy continues even in these days of relative corporate austerity. In the late 1980s and early '90s, many companies have tightened their belts, streamlining departments and operations to cut costs and boost their bottom lines. There is a new emphasis on being "lean."

Nonetheless, the patterns and expectations for corporate action and performance have been set and we cannot retreat. This is especially true for foreign investors seeking to open new markets in the United States.

A Link Between Responsibility and Profitability

The fact is that companies have actually discovered a link between responsibility and profitability.

Consider the experience of Johnson & Johnson, which has been in the forefront of this issue for many years. This company's commitment to social responsibility is very real and extends throughout its worldwide network of companies.

In fact, it was its experience in the United States with the over-the-counter drug Tylenol that (1) established for many companies the direct correlation between a company's image and its sales, and (2) has come to represent the definitive case study in crisis communications preparedness.

When cyanide-laced Tylenol capsules resulted in seven deaths in Chicago in 1982, Johnson & Johnson immediately opted for an expensive nationwide recall of the pain reliever—even though the poisonings were in no way the company's fault and there was no evidence of tampering outside of those few cases in Chicago.

The company very quickly reintroduced the product in tamper-resistant packages, but kept the product name—a calculated gamble that proved successful. In fact, the company's introduction of tamper-resistant packaging was a first, and quickly became an industry standard. Without any sort of government intervention, hundreds of companies voluntarily rushed to introduce their products in tamper-resistant packaging, and now when you visit a grocery or drugstore in the United States, virtually every product on the shelf is clearly wrapped in tamper-resistant packaging.

In 1986, in the face of a second poisoning incident, the company took the potentially costly step of ceasing to market Tylenol in capsule form. It began marketing the product in tablet form only, as the measure most clearly in the interest of public safety.

These actions enabled Johnson & Johnson to weather both crises, even in the face of intense advertising efforts by their competition. Their success was due, at least in part, to the company's excellent reputation for serving the public good, which had been nurtured over many years. As their former chairman, James E. Burke, said, "The Tylenol situation dramatically proved that serving the public good is what business is all about."

A similar example happened with Perrier, the French imported sparkling water. The product was introduced in the United States in 1976 with a brilliant campaign that targeted a young, affluent market whom research had shown to be casting about for an alternative to both alcohol and soft drinks. Despite a host of competitors who flocked to the market niche that Perrier first exploited, Perrier became the top-selling water brand in the United States—so much so that the product name itself became synonymous with bottled water. Instead of asking for generic bottled water, customers in restaurants and stores asked for Perrier by name.

In early 1990, the benzene contamination scare threatened to sink Perrier. A few samples of the water were found to contain benzene, a known carcinogen. Although the amounts found were relatively harmless, and the substance was discovered in only a few bottles, Perrier recalled all bottles worldwide to determine the source of the problem. It was found that the benzene originated in the carbon dioxide gas that gives the beverage its bubbles. The problem was traced to a charcoal filter that workers at Perrier's bottling plant in Vergeze, France, had failed to change.

Four months later, having taken steps to ensure that its filters were changed more frequently, Perrier was ready to go back into stores and restaurants. In a short time, the company recovered a substantial portion of its market share, but it has had to face two problems stemming from the benzene incident. First, while Perrier was absent from the scene, competitors rushed to fill the void and consumers got used to trying other bottled waters, many of them cheaper. Second, there is an issue of public trust: Perrier has been forced by the FDA to eliminate the words *naturally sparkling* from its label. As a result of the benzene recall, it has been discovered that Perrier is not naturally carbonated spring water; its sparkling bubbles are in fact created by carbon dioxide gas forced through filters.

Despite these problems, Perrier's forthright action has earned it marks and has helped preserve a portion of its earlier market share.

In contrast, there are the problems encountered by Exxon over several recent oil spills, most notably the Exxon *Valdez* tanker disaster in Prince William Sound, Alaska. Rightly or wrongly, the public perception following the *Valdez* oil spill was that the company did not respond forthrightly by acknowledging responsibility for the action and acting quickly to clean it up. In fact, Exxon did clean up the damage caused by the oil spill; nonetheless, in the public mind, there is a lingering perception that the company acted irresponsibly and was defensive in its response to the public outcry. In protest, many consumers returned their Exxon credit cards, and the incident certainly has done no good for the company's image.

Health, Safety, and Environmental Issues

In recent years, a triumvirate of related issues has risen to the forefront of American consumer consciousness and had an enormous impact on products in the marketplace: health, safety, and the environment. Far from being passing trends, all show signs of continuing and even increasing in importance throughout the 1990s and into the next century.

The American consumer has become increasingly aware of health issues, including the importance of proper exercise, nutrition, and diet. Smoking and second-hand smoke have been recognized as health dangers, and federal, state, and local governments and private companies have curtailed or outlawed smoking in most offices, airports, train terminals, and public areas nationwide.

In the 1970s and '80s, an exercise boom caused millions to take up jogging, dancing at aerobic studios that proliferated nationwide, and working out at home with exercise videotapes.

In the marketplace, every conceivable edible consumer product has rushed to label itself *no-fat, low-fat, low-sodium, low in cholesterol, rich in fiber,* and so on.

Safety represents another pressing concern in the U.S. market, especially in toys or products that are in the home or may be found or used by young children.

Recently, environmental concerns have become an issue and a hot selling point for all sorts of products, from soap and detergents to fast-food restaurants such as McDonald's. To counter the problems of global warming, ozone depletion, air and water pollution, and the need to recycle natural resources, everyone is rushing to claim that their product or product packaging is environmentally "safe" and recyclable, or at least that the company is concerned.

This market deluge was prompted by increased consumer awareness and concern. It is a worldwide trend, but consumer awareness and sophistication in the United States are probably the greatest. It is also a nearly predictable function of changing demographics: As the post–World War II Baby Boomers age, they have turned their attention to health and working out to stay in shape. Since they are now having children of their own, children's safety is an issue for them. Similarly, the aging of the Baby Boomers will cause increased growth among health care and pharmaceutical companies and ultimately nursing home facilities in the coming years.

However, consumer sophistication in the United States is causing some problems for companies who are seen as trying to cash in on the trend by making overinflated claims for the health or environmental purity of their products. Faced with a bewildering and over-hyped array of such claims, consumers are showing some evidence of backlash, and the government in the U.S. is also striking back. Most recently FDA Commissioner Kessler raided food manufacturers to force off the shelf products that the FDA believed were deceptionally labeled.

Not only is the American consumer sophisticated and knowledgeable, but also the media, government, and independent consumers' organizations are skeptical about product claims and will not hesitate to unmask any assertion found to be spurious or exaggerated. By all means, communicate the healthful advantages of your product, but don't insult the consumer's intelligence and risk negative exposure by making wildly unfounded assertions that will only backfire in the end.

Environmental social responsibility is particularly critical in the energy, oil, and chemical industries—the industries most easily attacked because the potential problems are so devastating. Oil and chemical companies face environmental issues, field hazardous waste questions, and deal with worker safety issues virtually every day. Problems are a fact of life for these companies. But responsible leaders in the industry anticipate the problem and follow nine steps of planning and communications:

1. Create policies for decision making.
2. Publish white papers and policy statements.
3. Create board-level committees to evaluate pricing, pollution control, worker safety, and government contract policies.
4. Develop crisis management plans.
5. Rehearse emergency procedures.
6. Evaluate managerial performance on factors such as social awareness and responsibility.
7. Take the lead in researching alternative energy sources, working for a clean environment and safe chemical usage.
8. Participate in public policy and legislation formation.
9. Communicate positions, policies, research, and corporate action.

Anticipate and Be Innovative

In short, companies should not wait, but rather must lead the industry by being innovative and tackling problems before they arise. The basic principle is to anticipate and to participate in forming public policy.

As already mentioned, all profitable companies are socially responsible to a certain extent. A successful business is good for the community and society. But while you may be good citizens, you may not be telling people about it—you may not be communicating. If you are going to set aside 2, 3, or 4 percent of your profits each year to put back into community works, you should talk about it and gain the good reputation you deserve.

In the end, a strategic approach to social responsibility should benefit both the company and the community. It is probably true that enlightened self-interest has always played a role in corporate efforts toward social responsibility. Especially today, however, the companies that get the most out of it are those that are most visible about it, so we urge our clients to target their contributions by determining what makes the most sense from a business standpoint, how accountable the results will be, and how visible the project will make them. Increasingly, contributions and community sponsorship programs are tied directly to corporate marketing strategies, with many donation dollars coming from marketing budgets.

Market and Goal Driven

One example is a program developed in 1984 by American Express to support the fund-raising campaign to renovate the Statue of Liberty in the United States. Many private and corporate contributions were raised in this effort. American Express advertised that it would donate a penny to the fund each time a cardholder charged a purchase, and would donate a dollar for each new card application.

The response was overwhelming, raising $1.7 million for the statue renovation fund and causing AMEX credit card use and applications to soar. Initially, AMEX had expected an 18 percent increase in credit card transactions as a result of the promotion. Actually, credit card usage jumped 28 percent and applications shot up 45 percent.

In order to double-check their strategy, American Express even conducted a follow-up telephone survey of cardholders. The survey revealed a high awareness of the promotion, and a large number of the respondents said they had actually used the card more frequently to "help this good cause."

The same strategy was used by American Express rival VISA to support the 1988 Winter Olympics. In both cases, advertising campaigns effectively wed the promotions to the company's social responsiveness.

This type of creative, market-driven philanthropy can occasionally appear too self-serving, and it's possible that the public will get a negative impression. In some cases, a program's image can cross the line from being innovative to being tasteless.

Communicate Your Efforts

By and large, though, the strategic mistakes made in communicating social responsibility are related to a lack of effort, rather than from trying too hard. There are two common problems.

First, follow these six steps of communications:

- Communicate with the local and regional media.
- Tell your employees through internal publications.
- Tell your shareholders through your regular financial publications.
- Initiate a corporate advertising campaign.
- If appropriate, even put it in your product advertising.
- Always be sure to tell opinion leaders, such as politicians and influential community leaders.

The second-most common problem occurs when companies follow outdated, uninventive patterns. There are five kinds of "uninventive giving":

- **Reactive giving** responds in an unplanned way to requests from outside the company. The contributions are usually nonstrategic, unrelated to the corporation's business or its image, and scattered among many recipients without any coherence.
- **Location giving** goes to causes in communities where headquarters or plants are located, and for no other reason than that. If you simply donate to local charity without any relation to strategic priorities, you may be just giving, period.

- **Safe giving** implies grants to traditional, prestigious, and non-controversial causes. Again, if such support is unavoidable, the company should at least attempt to target the gift for a specific purpose.
- **Me-too giving** shows that a company feels it must be seen on a major cultural institution's roster of donors as being "present and accounted for." It is usually a waste from a marketing standpoint because you are just part of a long list of participating sponsors.
- Finally, there are always a number of **causes with low visibility** that are seen as unimportant by community opinion leaders. By giving to them, you may actually do more damage than good to your corporate image.

The Role of the CEO

One point that should not be underestimated is the role of the CEO. The greatest single influence on the size and nature of a company's social commitment is its chief executive officer. Because a corporate image is going to be developed and nurtured over time, a forceful commitment from top management is essential to any program you may begin.

For companies in the energy, chemical, pharmaceutical, or any manufacturing business, social commitment is particularly critical and communicating on environmental issues is of paramount importance.

Environmental policies are at the core of sound, responsible corporate action. They form the basis for policy, action, and regular corporate performance. They are not mere words on pieces of paper, but rather codes by which to make decisions and against which to be measured.

What You Stand For

What you stand for must be communicated, both inside your company and outside. All your publics need to know the principles that underlie your business. These principles should be part of your newsletters, releases, annual reports, and speeches—and part of your everyday actions in communities where you operate.

While there is no guarantee that social responsibility assures profits, or that all profitable companies are socially responsible, recent findings are encouraging. One study of American companies found that the stock of the companies mentioned in the book, *100 Best Companies to Work for in America,* dramatically outperformed the Standard and Poor's 500 stock price average over a 10-year period. The stocks rose from a value of just over 100 in 1975 to 700 in 1985, compared with a rise of just over 200 for the S&P 500.

In the end, a carefully planned, strategic approach to social responsibility will provide a measurable difference to the bottom line. In addition, the better blue-chip companies make what they're doing exceedingly clear to their constituencies through effective communications. Moreover, it helps you attract quality employees, and those people are perhaps your most critical asset for long-term performance and success.

Key Questions and Opportunities

In examining the issue of your company's social responsibility, ask yourself the following six key questions:

- Have you established a corporate strategy for social responsibility?
- How do you allocate budgets in this area?
- Does your program relate to corporate and marketing objectives?
- Are you achieving credibility with consistent giving programs?
- Are you prepared to give even when earnings are down?
- Is it possible to extend your strategy internationally?

Once you have decided on your strategy, do not neglect the importance of communications. To start with, put aside a percentage of corporate social responsibility budget for public relations support. Also, explore program ideas that will benefit most from communications.

For example, specifically look at the following opportunities:

- Look for charitable donation and sponsorship programs that are inherently newsworthy because they interest others.

- Consider tying your social responsibility strategy into marketing programs for your products.
- Once you are ready to announce and implement the program, prepare local and regional news or feature releases to send to the press and opinion leaders.
- Publicize your involvement through internal communications, to inform your employees and to encourage subsidiary locations to be socially responsible as well.
- Mention your good works in the annual report and other financial communications during the year.
- Be candid about issues—environmental, social, and ethical—that are important to your company.
- Consider scheduling external speaking opportunities for your top management at seminars or annual meetings related to the programs you support. These provide an appropriate forum for management to talk publicly about what you've accomplished.
- Get involved in public and legislative issues that affect your business—speak out, be heard.

Public Affairs and Communications

Without clear corporate policy positions convincingly presented, companies entering the U.S. market will encounter problems and miss out on some marvelous opportunities.

In most situations, especially complex ones, the real challenge for corporations is not the act of communicating, but rather the process of figuring out just what you want to say.

There are countless corporate communications opportunities, including the annual meeting and other shareholder and financial communications, takeovers, mergers, expansion of operating facilities, new product introductions, annual reports, public speeches, public affairs issues, and internal discussions with senior management and other employees.

Whatever the circumstance, shortchanging the often painful and time-consuming process of figuring out what you really want to say leads inevitably to muddied, confusing, and often conflicting communications.

Preparation for those opportunities constitutes a potent tool for strategy, goal definition, and change. We call such preparation **corporate positioning**, and it is critical to marketing in any environment.

To Talk or Not to Talk

Deciding whether to speak out publicly—and then deciding how to deal with that decision—is a crucial matter. It is not a simple question. It is based on strategy. The answer for one company may be entirely different from that for another, even though the companies may be in the same industry. Also, no one company can or should speak out on too many issues: Its expertise and resources couldn't possibly be sufficient for this.

Public relations planning and strategy are basic to deciding whether to take a public stand on a given issue. That decision is built on a number of important considerations—for example:

- What are the issues that affect the industry and the company?
- What is the public profile of the company on those issues?
- What are the pros and cons of speaking out on a given issue?
- Is your public stand built on strength and experience, and is the issue important to your business?
- Do you have enough facts?
- Are you confident about your position? Is it responsible and honest?
- Are your words supported by actions?
- What are the long-term implications of speaking out publicly?
- How do you prepare to deal with the media?
- How do you respond if you decide not to take a public position?

Planning, issues analysis, and strategy are at the core of answering those questions.

Selecting a Corporate Spokesperson

Once you've decided whether to speak out or not, you will need to select a corporate spokesperson. Even if you are not planning to speak out on any particular issue, a corporate spokesperson should be chosen ahead of time because, literally overnight, events can cause the press to contact you for comments or answers. Having a spokesperson designated in advance will prevent confusion and last-minute infighting that can lead to problems within your company and cast your company in a bad light externally.

Being the spokesperson for a company is a demanding task—and one that is only sometimes rewarding. Beyond having the authority to speak out on the issues when appropriate, what kind of person is needed?

- Is authoritative and confident.
- Conveys understanding and compassion.
- Knows when to talk and when not to talk.
- Thinks well in a crisis.
- Remains objective when the going gets hot.
- Understands the media and their need to capture complete thoughts in 30-second "sound bites".
- Is trained in front of the camera.
- Understands an interview as beneficial to both parties.

Speaking Out

In many cases, companies respond to public pressure by speaking out on the important issues that affect their businesses. For example, in the United States, the Coalition for Better Television and a number of special-interest groups have threatened boycotts against advertisers supporting television programs that the groups felt contained too much sex, violence, and profanity.

In a 1981 speech before the Academy of Arts and Sciences in Los Angeles, Owen B. Butler, chairman of the board of the Procter & Gamble Company—which, as the largest single advertiser on network television, had the most to lose from a boycott—said: "We will not have our programming dictated by threats of boycott, but we will surely listen to those who have strong views about our programming whether they threaten boycott or not."

In addition to Procter & Gamble, other companies pointed to long-standing corporate policies that required a case-by-case examination of episodes. Even though the threat of a boycott was withdrawn at the time, the issue has returned repeatedly throughout the past decade.

In addition, many companies have been vocal about their support of the arts. Philip Morris, Exxon, Mobil, Xerox, Consolidated Edison, Mead, Texaco and countless other companies both large and small have been forthright in their conviction that the arts do more than foster goodwill. The arts, they believe, play a vital role in society and can help in tangible ways to improve marketing and recruitment. Companies have gone further than just being vocal and have provided considerable financial support to the arts—another means of speaking out.

As a foreign company entering the U.S. market, the Japanese cosmetics giant Shiseido sponsored a retrospective of 113 years of its advertising art in New York. Titled "The Art of Beauty," the exhibition was a blend of Japanese history, avant-garde beauty, and the Western influence of art nouveau that captured attention by subtly playing on the company's Japanese heritage.

Moreover, some pharmaceutical companies facing product liability claims have become increasingly courageous in supporting the safety and testing of their products by briefing the media and responding to press inquiries.

Finally, Mobil Oil has shown no lack of courage in its aggressively thought-provoking Op-Ed page advertisements that have appeared regularly in the national print media for the better part of two decades.

When to Keep Silent

In other cases, though, companies shun the limelight for any of hundreds of reasons, some good, some bad. Indeed, there are times when a corporation should not get involved in a controversy: Perhaps it is not germane to the business or perhaps the company's position has not been formulated, or the issue may be too volatile and may pose a "no-win" situation. For companies with large constituencies of employees, shareholders, and consumers above the age of 50, the Mandatory Retirement Bill some years ago was such an issue. While there may have been valid operating reasons to oppose extending the age at which employees must be retired, taking a visible position that offended their important constituencies risked lower morale, hostile proxy resolutions, and losing customers. Here, silence was probably the best policy.

Carcinogens, waste management, industry downturns, foreign trade restrictions, the profit motive—these are just some of the many other issues that have served notice that they won't fade away.

They are hot topics. They give focus to pressure groups that may be hostile to business motives. They are the current wave of a trend that started back in the 1960s.

CORPORATE POSITIONING AND A GLOBAL MARKETING STRATEGY

In planning a global marketing strategy for your company—one that can cross borders anywhere in the world—it's important to maintain a global-international perspective, coupled with an awareness of and respect for national-local differences.

Just as communications are global, so is corporate positioning. In a world of satellites, computer modems, faxes, and high-tech telecommunications, global communications are instantaneous today. Messages and strategies must be understood internationally as well as locally. Developing a network is critical, and companies should feed the network with ideas and suggestions, rather than abusing it with orders and tasks.

The following are some key **policy** questions cross-border companies need to ask:

- Who takes responsibility for global positioning and communications?
- How can communications be pushed through the firm? Does it have firmwide senior executive support and involvement?
- What kind of global presence exists?
- How can culture of intense pride be encouraged?
- What level of resources are needed?

These are some key **organizational** questions for your company:

- What skills are needed?
- What is the best reporting relationship?
- Does the function deliver? Is it cost-effective?
- Is it global?
- Does it reflect strategic directions?

Finally, here are some important points to keep in mind regarding your company's **communications policy and structure**:

- Reports to CEO.
- Total support and commitment.
- Interface with strategic planning committee.
- Worldwide function.
- Centrality of drive.
- Global image and positioning.
- Direct reports to senior communications professional.
- One voice—one style—one positioning.
- Economies of scale.

Policy, Strategy, and Tactics

Establishing sound corporate positions with respect to the United States is complex. Companies can't afford to view the landscape from just one vantage point—you must be really international. It is no longer enough merely to transport an idea across borders: Those ideas must be international in scope, but with a national emphasis on the U.S. market being entered.

The process of developing corporate policy, strategy, and communications is at least three-dimensional: It involves culture, geography and time. For most companies, traditional corporate communications in the home countries has been only one-dimensional, guided by local needs.

Corporate planning and communications reflect very careful listening. No need is greater than that of listening attentively to a wide range of economic voices, both positive and negative, and capturing the nuances beneath the surface.

The person who must control the process of corporate positioning is the chief executive. The implications are simply too vast. Marketing, planning, government relations, public relations, legal, and finance professionals all are essential. These are the key executives, reporting to the chief executive, who must be part of the senior team—and communications is an integral part.

Five Marketing Communications Concepts

While this process is at work, we cannot lose sight of five marketing communications concepts:

- Corporate positioning and effective communications objectives must flow from and support corporate policy positions, core strategies, and business plans. This is essential so that the corporation and its words and deeds reflect and enhance one another. Otherwise, marketing initiatives are useless or even counterproductive.
- Both business and marketing strategies must be flexible and adaptable to unforeseen change. What seems right today may be very wrong tomorrow. There should always be a Plan B readily at hand in case Plan A is not on target.
- Marketing must be tailored to the local culture. Strategic messages must be international, but they must be phrased in the context of each national culture.
- Credible communications must always be candid and consistent. When changes in direction are dictated by circumstances, these changes should be communicated swiftly and candidly as well. Whatever you say goes down the drain if your credibility is in doubt.
- The best—or worst—spokesperson is the chief executive officer. This person is the chief policymaker and strategist, and only he or she has the vision and weight to communicate fully. The chief executive is best if properly prepared—and worst if not.

Marketing Communications Techniques

Marketing communications is necessary to sell products and services of any kind. The time is past when a few press releases or simply blitzing the airwaves with advertising can perform marketing communications. Today's rapidly changing U.S. markets and the explosive growth of specialized trade and consumer media demand innovative, increasingly sophisticated approaches.

Here is a list of marketing communications functions that should be developed by your company, with the help of an outside consultant, if necessary:

- Marketing public relations programs and marketing communications consulting.
- New product introductions.
- Product defense.
- Dealer-distributor relations programs.
- Publicity and media relations.
- Materials development: press kits, releases, photos, brochures, direct mail pieces, and other materials for media and other audiences, including sales forces, retail and wholesale outlets, and legislative or regulatory bodies.
- Bylined articles by the company CEO or spokesperson for placement in important trade or consumer media.
- Products and/or company name placement in motion pictures or TV shows.
- Investor relations programs for public companies, including security analyst surveys.
- Media tours.
- Nonmedia communications, including mall demonstrations, dealer meetings, sales meetings, and other special events.
- Consumer education programs.
- Trade show support.
- Specialized marketing tools, such as videotapes, satellite video feeds, and computer programs.
- Technical counseling and trade media relations.
- Sampling programs.
- Point-of-sale-premium support.
- Contest-sweepstakes management.
- Presentation training.

CONCLUSION

Marketing your product in the United States requires a knowledge of U.S. culture and demographics, your various audiences, and your potential competition. It requires you to be an active *participant* in the local economy. And it requires companies to be proactive in their communications through the process of corporate positioning. This entails being aware of the issues to be confronted, and knowing how to shape the image of the company and the product to turn these issues to your advantage.

The public relations process plays a role that goes beyond the best in strategy and implementation. It keeps a watchful eye on public attitudes, changing perceptions, and emerging issues. Its role requires it to be in touch with opinion leaders, the media, shareholders and other corporate stakeholders, employees, customers, and other important groups. As a result, it is in a unique position to provide management with valuable insights into those forces within and outside the corporation that affect actions, decisions, strategy, and future directions.

Communications can never make the problems go away or make the most of the opportunities. But coupled with strong management support and some good thinking, it can make your marketing efforts much more effective.

CHAPTER 3

IDENTIFYING AND EVALUATING ACQUISITION CANDIDATES

Frank A. Klepetko
Senior Managing Director
Price Waterhouse

INTRODUCTION

America has long been regarded as a land of economic opportunity, and for many years, this concept has been reflected in the flow of foreign capital into the United States. The United States should remain attractive to foreign investors, and opportunities to purchase American businesses with the expectation of good returns on capital should remain available for the foreseeable future.

The extent of foreign purchases of businesses in the United States is evidenced by the recent example of the entertainment industry, certainly one of the most visible businesses in the world and historically representing a strong American presence. During the past several years, several major motion picture studios have been acquired by foreign concerns, including Sony's purchase of Columbia Pictures, Matsushita's $7 billion acquisition of MCA, and Pathe's purchase of MGM. In addition, when the Walt Disney Company built overseas versions of Disneyland, one of America's most cherished institutions, Disney utilized foreign capital through public offerings in Europe and Japan rather than domestic sources.

In short, the United States has long been a popular arena for foreign investment, which is demonstrated by the large foreign ownership interests in several prominent American industries. The flow of capital into the United States is due in large part to the strong political environment for capitalism, the safety of investment, and other factors, and any change in these factors may affect the opportunity (both positively and negatively) for investing in America. The following factors influence the flow of capital into the United States:

- *Currency differentials.* The relationship of foreign currencies to the dollar obviously has a significant effect. The strengthening of most European currencies and the yen against the dollar has permitted foreigners to purchase assets in the United States at prices considerably lower than if denominated in their local currencies. This opportunity also applies to financial assets, which would include operating businesses. Thus, by merely purchasing a business located in North America rather than a comparable enterprise domiciled elsewhere, a foreign investor often can obtain a higher return on capital.
- *America as a market for goods and services.* North America is a large, attractive marketplace, and ownership of businesses that tap that market seems obviously desirable for an investor, foreign or otherwise. This could be particularly true if a foreign investor could enhance an acquisition in North America through, as examples, importation of additional products, more efficient production processes, or technology transfers. A foreign investor need not address only the manufacturing sector; numerous other opportunities to participate in the North American consumer and industrial markets are available, such as distribution, merchandising, and marketing enterprises.
- *Availability of financing.* The financial markets of the United States and Canada provide funds for business acquisitions relatively efficiently from a wide variety of domestic debt and equity sources. The large financial services industry in the United States is highly accommodative in working with foreigners to assist with acquisitions.

- *Sophistication of financial markets.* The financial markets in the United States and Canada offer a variety of services in addition to financing capability that can enable a foreign investor to minimize certain risks through interest rate, currency, and commodity hedging. This helps to protect an overseas investor's capital applied to a dollar-denominated acquisition.
- *Receptiveness to foreign investment.* The United States was industrialized by foreign capital, and America remains a stronghold of free flow of capital. The United States capital market regulations do not differentiate with respect to sources of funds, with only minor exceptions (e.g., certain defense-oriented and communications companies).
- *Flow of information.* Investment decision making is a function of information, and in-depth information concerning corporations (particularly publicly-held companies) in the United States is widely available. The process of deriving information for investigation and analysis of investment opportunities in North America is efficient and usually relatively inexpensive. The Securities and Exchange Commission (SEC) has standard reporting requirements that are uniform across companies, which greatly facilitate the flow of information and availability of financial data for publicly-held companies. In addition, the Financial Accounting Standards Board (FASB) has created standard accounting practices that are uniform for both publicly and privately-held companies. These factors help assure accuracy of information, a consideration that should not be overlooked when contemplating investment in the United States.
- *Deleveraging of the industrial base.* During the 1980s the United States capital markets went on a leveraging spree. This movement had many successes, but in general left many corporations inadequately funded. The opportunity for investment in companies that are overleveraged but nonetheless well regarded may be unusually attractive.
- *Decline of regulatory controls.* One of the hallmarks of the conservative Republican administrations in the 1980s and early 1990s is the deemphasis on governmental activism at the federal level. This deregulation movement, which empha-

sizes free enterprise and competitive markets as means of regulation, should be viewed favorably by foreign investors.

In short, the climate for foreign investment in North America should remain attractive for the foreseeable future, which should offer foreign investors good opportunities to achieve attractive returns on capital. Also, the likelihood that the United States government will continue operating on a deficit budget suggests an extended need to attract external financial resources which American business will require for capital replacement and expansion.

AMERICA TO THE FOREIGN INVESTOR: WHERE TO BEGIN?

It is relatively easy to establish the concept that owning some type of interest in a business in the United States or Canada appears desirable. The forms of investment are extensive (the financial markets of the United States are particularly good at inventing new ways to invest) and are generally available equally to foreign and domestic investors.

It is simple to purchase debt or equity of publicly-held U.S. companies. Some foreign investors, including institutions or wealthy overseas individuals, may have a passive approach and therefore would prefer to invest in public securities. However, it is assumed that many foreign investors wish to participate actively in managing a company and accordingly would prefer, as a part of an investment, to achieve either control or at least a position of significant influence in an acquisition candidate.

Criteria for an Investment

In deciding to acquire a company in the United States, the investor should establish the criteria for investment by addressing both the type of opportunity sought and the constraints surrounding the investors' objectives.

A foreign investor should carefully specify and prioritize the objectives of an investment to help establish the criteria for selection and evaluation of opportunities. The investor's objective will generally be either to (1) invest in similar businesses that can be enhanced by active participation in the management; or (2) diversify into new lines of business. If the objectives relate to expanding the foreign investor's existing overseas business (which has generally been the case), the foreign investors likely will have somewhat stringent criteria already established because they specifically seek to invest in businesses in which they have a thorough knowledge and can use their managerial skills and other resources.

What Is the Foreign Investor's Objective, Stated in the Broadest Terms?

Since the principal criterion is usually the opportunity to obtain greater sales in the North American markets for the investor's products or services, often this objective is translated into acquisition of an American company that manufactures a complementary or competitive product. Accordingly, the search for a target opportunity may be narrowed quickly to corporations related to the investor's industry. However, in many instances, an investor's objective of achieving a strong (or stronger) sales base in North America can be achieved by means other than simply investing in the manufacturer of a look-alike or competitive product. Alternative opportunities might include acquiring a distribution concern with access to specific targeted markets or users. Starting with a broad definition, more specific criteria can be established, such as the following:

Product or Industry Interests.   Keeping the criteria somewhat broad at the early stage of the search is helpful since it permits the later stages to be pursued more effectively. Narrowly defining objectives and criteria too early generally rules out numerous valid investment opportunities. However, to the extent that an investor has very specific interests, limiting the search to businesses engaged either directly or indirectly in a specific industry is the most appropriate initial step.

Strategic Interests.   Strategic concerns often motivate an investment in America. The concept of a "strategic interest" covers many considerations, such as trade issues, cost structure differentials, competitors' undertakings, long-term and short-term product development, and the like. Achieving strategic objectives is not necessarily effected merely by a purchase of a company. For example, a joint venture (or series of ventures) with a corporation that has marketing, product development, or other complementary resources might accomplish the strategic objective.

Diversification. Fortunes were established in the Middle East as a result of cartelization of the oil industry, and among Japanese groups and individuals as a result of the dramatic success of the post–World War II economic revitalization of Japan. These investors often have relatively broad appetites for U.S. investments, primarily related to diversification of their interests or utilization of excess cash flow from their foreign business interests.

In short, the first step is to determine the investor's objectives. Presumably the investor wishes to maximize return on capital; however, more specific criteria are required. Maintaining flexibility in establishing criteria and avoiding an overly narrow search are important to avoid losing an opportunity that might meet the investor's objectives.

Operating Requirements and Financing Constraints
The second stage of establishing investment criteria is to determine the investor's operating requirements as well as financial constraints. For a strategic investor the operating characteristics primarily focus on the foreign investor's ability to affect the target company's operations. The opportunities for improvements between a foreign investor's existing business and the target usually address possible interchanges in product characteristics, manufacturing techniques, product development, research, or other areas. The potential for improvement in an acquisition also significantly affects the expectations for return on investment.

Profitable Enterprises and Traditional Criteria
Assuming that the foreign investor prefers to consider successful businesses (rather than troubled situations), the investors' criteria might have more traditional elements, including the following:

Size. A foreign investor could target an acquisition according to its level of sales, profitability, or asset size. Although the investor's criteria could be altered if an attractive target that was not in the original criteria was identified, it is desirable to start by defining some basic limits related to the overall scale of the target in terms of sales volume, market share, or the like.

Amount of Investment.   Investors usually consider the monetary size of the investment to be a high priority. However, numerous financing techniques and practices can be utilized to permit considering a much larger target than was originally intended. The obvious first issue is the leverageability of the transaction. Based on the historic earning capacity, as well as a plan for changes (presumably improvements) in the business, debt funds could be obtained from banks, institutional lenders, and/or equity-related investors. The United States capital markets are adept at providing funds for acquisitions, particularly if the acquiring party can contribute operationally to the acquiree.

Financing.   Further, a foreign investor could consider raising additional funds from joint venture partners or from institutional investors. Numerous large, highly regarded financial institutions in the United States are quite interested in providing funds to investors with expertise in an industry in an amount significantly disproportionate to the level of commitment of the foreign investor. Often such an institutional investor who participates in an acquisition will provide essentially all of the funds, primarily in the form of debt, and will co-invest in the equity of the acquired company. Because of the availability of acquisition funding from passive institutional investors, a foreign investor can consider an acquisition much larger than that originally targeted.

The use of third-party U.S. funding can work quite well for a foreign investor because mechanisms are available to permit the repurchase over time of an institutional co-investor's equity position. A repurchase option initially may appear expensive to the foreign investor; however, this cost usually is offset overwhelmingly by the incremental returns achievable by the leveraging. In short, if a foreign investor decides to pursue an acquisition somewhat larger than originally intended, the investor could consider co-investing with a passive financial institution and, over time, repurchase the institution's ownership of the target company.

Turn-Around Situations

An initial question concerns the investor's willingness to consider underperforming or even troubled situations. If an investment in a troubled (or even merely overleveraged) business is acceptable, numerous ancillary issues arise, including the following:

In-depth Analysis of the Situation. A thorough understanding of the issues affecting a troubled company's future and the ability to correct the problems are clearly required. The success of an investment in a turnaround company would be based largely upon the investor's ability to develop a plan for correcting the investee's problems.

Form of Investment. An investor (particularly a foreign investor) needs as much control as possible over the form of investment. A purchase of assets, rather than stock, may be appropriate as a means of addressing problem issues because the purchaser often can wipe the slate clean by starting fresh with a new company to continue the business. A corporate reorganization may be advisable, possibly including the use of a prearranged bankruptcy.

Change of Management. Investment in an underperforming company often requires changes in management. A foreign investor should be prepared to address the need for changes in top management at a very early point of analysis of the investment opportunity. Although investing in problem companies represents additional risks, it also offers opportunities for incremental rewards. Acquiring an underperforming business usually permits the investor to have a particularly large voice in structuring the transaction, which offers additional elements of protection as well as greater upside potential.

Other Criteria

In addition to these criteria, which are typical for any type of investor, foreign investors must examine and understand other criteria affecting a potential investment in the United States. Specifically, foreign investors must examine the tax treaties existing between their country and the United States, trade treaties that may affect their ability to import and export certain products or components, and any foreign currency restrictions. Foreign investors should also address and have a thorough understanding of certain U.S. laws including, among others, the antitrust laws, environmental pollution and control laws, and product liability laws. Knowledge of these factors will be important in choosing financial and legal advisors to assist in an acquisition.

To summarize, investors should establish broad criteria for an acquisition, including general industry characteristics and some basic elements concerning size of the investment, in terms of both the scope of the business and the level of investment. Perhaps the most important reason for foreign investors to consider defining their investment criteria carefully is that the ensuing search process will likely be more productive, which in turn will increase the probability of high-quality results. To the extent that investors have defined their criteria somewhat narrowly, the search process may focus too quickly on several specific companies. In addition, the possibility exists that an attractive industry or businesses tangential to the target might be overlooked. With a carefully constructed set of criteria, the search process should permit an orderly review of alternatives, leading to a thorough analysis of specifically targeted investments.

THE SEARCH PROCESS

In general, the efficiency and effectiveness of the search will be enhanced significantly by obtaining outside assistance. Most investors retain the services of a financial advisor, primarily because the cost of the advisory services will likely be recovered by the advisor's success in enhancing the search process or avoiding mistakes, primarily by helping analyze the business to identify potential problems and to avoid overpaying for an investment. The process of identifying and evaluating investment opportunities invariably involves a variety of outside parties, such as industry consultants, financial advisors, accountants, and attorneys. The process of successful investment includes utilizing professionals as efficiently as possible, so that the investor maximizes the benefits and minimizes the costs of these services.

Selecting an Advisor

A wide variety of firms are able to assist an investor, including experts in specific industries, management consulting firms, and financial services firms (banks, investment banks, accounting firms, and boutique-type investment firms). Among the major financial services firms, almost all have groups dedicated to assisting with the processes of searching, analyzing, and negotiating investments in North America. There are several criteria the investor should consider in selecting an advisor:

Industry Expertise. An investor should always seek a firm (or group within a larger firm) with expertise in the industry or type of investment sought by the foreign party. A foreign investor should contact the target industry's appropriate trade association, which can be located easily in a directory of U.S. associations. In addition, many U.S. law firms, banks, and consulting firms have expertise in the industries identified by the search process, and in general these firms can assist in identifying financial advisory groups that specialize in the investor's area of interest.

Financial Services Capability. Most large financial services firms are organized according to specializations, and often a large firm will have a group that concentrates on the foreign investor's area of interest. These groups can be identified in the same manner as the specialist firms. Although a large financial services firm may not have the depth of specific industry expertise of a specialist firm, a larger firm generally will offer a greater array of services. For example, large financial services firms can generally assist an investor in raising debt or equity funds for an acquisition.

Compatibility. The key here is to select a firm and a team of individuals with which the investor group could work effectively. All firms can provide résumés of prior experience, and the direct contributions, personalities, and other considerations related to prior engagements could be reviewed with officers of those companies.

Financial Modeling Capability. The effectiveness of the investor's search and analysis process can be significantly enhanced through financial modeling. Computer modeling and database management, although largely staff functions, are important in evaluating a firm's overall capacity to serve an investor.

Compensation of an Advisor. The compensation of a financial advisor has become almost a form of art. Most advisors seek to be compensated based upon a retainer-type relationship, with incremental income reflecting the success of the effort. Financial advisory firms often accept the concept that much of their compensation can depend on completion of a transaction and can be somewhat at risk for the success of the effort side-by-side with the investor. The art form in negotiating the advisor's fee is to encourage as much as possible of the total compensation to have interests parallel with the investor's (i.e., subject to a successful investment) while maintaining the lowest possible overall cost. Although the retainer represents an out-of-pocket expenditure at risk by the investor, having a financial services firm work on an all-contingency basis does not necessarily result in the best service to the client. It is easier to maintain a work discipline if the servicer is being paid, however modestly, to respond to the client's (the investor's) needs.

An argument can be made that if an advisor is paid based largely on completion of a transaction, the advisor has too great an incentive to complete a deal as opposed to rendering impartial advice regardless of the outcome. While this issue exists, in general a retainer relationship in which the advisor is paid based upon the success of the search helps to maximize the benefits to the investor.

IDENTIFYING AND ANALYZING TARGETS

The work plan for identifying targets should entail a process of developing a broad list of targets and then winnowing that list with the advisor(s) working in tandem with the investor. The first step, assembling basic information, can be completed relatively easily, since a wealth of information is readily available from a variety of sources.

Large statistical databases encompassing essentially all industries have been compiled by numerous services, and access to those databases through computers is easy. Screening for SIC (Standard Industrial Classification) size according to revenues, asset base, profitability, location, and other factors (including combinations of the above) is a simple task. The principal requirement is to screen a vast amount of data to arrive at a more specific array of targets.

After an initial culling of targets from a database, the process of analysis of the information commences. There are two primary areas of further evaluation: qualitative review and quantitative analysis.

Qualitative Review

The qualitative review may be done reasonably easily in the United States because of the vast financial reporting requirements of FASB and the SEC. These reporting requirements result in quarterly and annual financial reports to securities holders that generally include reports from top management allowing the investor to obtain a feel for style, outlook, operating policies, and other elements of a target company's managerial group. This insight will enable the investor to look for management synergies that will help select and eliminate potential target companies.

Industry Characteristics. The analysis should identify the forces and factors common to the entrants of a target company's industry. The desired result is to identify the factors affecting a business, starting with the issues common to all the companies in a target's industry. These generally include sensitivity to overall economic cycles, interest rates, consumable trends, and the like. These common factors usually can be identified and analyzed through publications of (or about) the industry as well as through consulting firms with expertise in the target industry. If the target industry includes publicly-held companies, brokerage reports concerning companies in the industry will be particularly helpful.

Characteristics of the Target.   The second stage is deriving an understanding of the individual characteristics of a specific target concern. Assessing a company's unique traits constitutes the most important task of the investor. The process of determining what causes one corporation to perform better than its competitor represents the essence of evaluating an investment opportunity.

Quantitative Analysis

The second aspect of evaluation, the quantitative analysis, will allow systematic historical reviews of the company's target financial performance. The objective of quantitative analysis is to create a financial model that will permit testing various sensitivities of the target business, and the model should be based upon a comprehensive understanding of the factors that might affect an industry and or a specific corporation.

Financial Statements

Comparing the financial statements of two (or more) concerns in the same industry will reveal information helpful in developing an understanding of the earnings potential of both the industry and the specific target. Again, because of the SEC reporting requirements, these data are readily available for public companies. It is important to evaluate the trends over time in order to help determine the growth stage of the company.

Income Statements.   The statements of income are particularly useful, and investors should focus on several particular items.

Sales. Ideally, a target business would have regular sales increases, but such is not always the case. A summary of sales, both in dollar amounts and units of sales, provides valuable information concerning the corporation's prospects. However, because of the large number of acquisitions and divestitures that occurred in the 1980s, it is important to use comparable numbers in analyzing revenue growth to determine internal versus external growth. These data are usually disclosed in footnotes or in pro forma information.

Operating expenses. In the case of most manufacturing businesses, the cost of goods sold will be a substantial factor in determining the profitability of a business. The operating margin, which is the income after cost of goods sold divided by revenues, usually indicates the operating efficiencies of the underlying assets. This ratio may indirectly reflect certain other aspects of the operations, such as the condition of manufacturing facilities or intrinsic labor practices (i.e., the influence of the target company's labor unions).

Selling, general, and administrative expenses. The costs of the corporate overhead can provide an understanding of some of the basic costs of operating the business. Several important costs, such as research and development expenditures, are usually included in selling, general, and administrative expenses. Obtaining a breakout of research and development, owner manager perquisites (in the case of private businesses), extraordinary and nonrecurring expenses, and other costs is sometimes more difficult, but represents an important element of evaluating the business's ongoing profitability.

Depreciation and amortization. Depreciation and amortization levels should be reviewed to determine the prior levels of capital spending as an aid in evaluating the condition of physical assets. An analysis of book and tax differences in depreciation and amortization will help in understanding the potential target's tax position.

Earnings before interest and taxes. Earnings before interest and taxes, commonly referred to as EBIT, is a measure that has become popular in recent years as a result of the impact of the financial capital structure on the income statement. A review of EBIT will isolate the true income-producing capability of a company, independent of interest expense, which may fluctuate from changes in interest rates and debt levels.

Income taxes. A thorough understanding of the income tax liability of the company is critical in order to evaluate potential tax savings or exposure that will result from an acquisition. Understanding the tax treaties between the United States and the foreign investor's country is also critical in this evaluation.

Net income. The simplest measure of a business's success is its ability to command an attractive price for its goods or services as indicated by return on sales or net income margin. A business with at least a 10 percent net income margin can be deemed an attractive concern, whereas a low return on sales margin sometimes implies a lesser control of the company's basic profitability.

Balance Sheet Analysis. An analysis of the balance sheet's components is useful in analyzing the value of an enterprise, particularly with respect to undervaluations of assets or unrecorded (i.e., "hidden") liabilities. Balance sheet analysis can most easily be done by a series of ratios.

Current ratio. The ratio of current assets to current liabilities measures the short-term operating position of a company. A ratio of less than one to one may indicate difficulties in paying current payables; however, there are certain businesses in the United States that normally operate on a low or negative current ratio, such as cable television, restaurants, and other service businesses. Hence, it is important to look for company-specific as well as industry-standard ratio levels and trends.

Working capital productivity. A review of the histories of inventory turns and collection of receivables will provide insight into both potential issues and opportunities. A history of low inventory movement and/or slow conversion of receivables to cash implies some difficulties with the operations or a lack of attention on the part of management. Conversely, these deficiencies may represent an opportunity for improvement, with a high return obtainable to an investor in a short-term horizon. Some of the most successful LBO investments have been achieved by implementing changes in work-product flow to achieve greater inventory turns or sacrificing sales made to slow-paying customers, both of which increased returns on capital significantly. In addition, implementation of just-in-time inventory practices can free up working capital tied up in excess inventories.

Return on equity. A business that achieves a good return on equity indicates, in simple terms, that capital is employed productively and that acquiring the ownership of the business should result in a sound investment, unless the superior return on equity has been accomplished with a significant amount of leverage.

Capitalization ratios. The ratio of long-term debt to equity measures the extent to which a company has been leveraged. If the target company has recently been leveraged, it is important to look at these trends over time to determine whether the company is successful in generating cash to repay debt, or whether additional equity infusions have been (or should be) made. If debt exceeds equity, then additional review should be made of the capital structure to ascertain how much risk to the equity is represented by the amount and terms of the debt being employed.

In order to help further understand the impact of the capital structure, an investor may want to evaluate the relationship of EBIT to equity, as well as net income to equity. It should be noted that while the capital structure will probably change on acquisition, the historical ratios will still provide data on the ability of company's operations to support debt in the past.

Statement of Cash Flows.   The statement of cash flows (formerly sources and uses of funds) is useful in analyzing the cash-generating potential of the company.

Noncash charges. Noncash charges to the income statement, primarily depreciation and amortization and deferred taxes, represent a significant source of funds for debt repayment, reinvestment in the business, or other uses. Companies in the United States often report losses for financial statement purposes but generate substantial cash flow as a result of the tax treatment of capital spending.

Capital spending. The statement of cash flows identifies the levels of capital spending. A review of the requirements for replacement or refurbishment of existing facilities and equipment, as well as expenditures to accommodate growth or to protect the existing sales base, is also part of an initial analysis.

Free cash flow. A measure that has become popular in various industries is to evaluate "free cash flow," which is cash flow from operations less capital expenditures. This analyzes the amount of cash that may be available on an ongoing basis to service the capital structure or for other purposes.

Footnotes to Financial Statements and Other Information.   It is imperative to review thoroughly and understand the footnotes to the financial statements as part of any investment review. Additionally, it is important to review all SEC filings, which will provide further information on changes in the company's business and operations.

These items establish criteria for the initial analysis of an investment in a target business and can help to determine the investment's attractiveness as well as identifying key ongoing managerial issues.

Asset Review

In addition to evaluating the earnings potential of a company, an investor should undertake a thorough review of an acquisition candidate's assets. Evaluating the physical facilities by an industry expert always is desirable. A target company's fixed asset base should be analyzed for productivity, and an acquiror should evaluate the fixed assets with respect to opportunities for improvements, including the following:

Excess and Underutilized Assets.
The classic analysis of an acquisition includes assessing opportunities to identify and dispose of excess or underutilized assets. The most typical example is the opportunity to consolidate facilities of a purchaser and a target, thereby freeing up plant and equipment that might be sold.

The investor's managerial skill can contribute to identifying opportunities to free up fixed assets. Changes in manufacturing processes, sometimes assisted by capital investment improvements (such as investments to increase production by "de-bottlenecking" a manufacturing facility), can create additional capacity or saleable assets.

Hidden Assets.
A thorough review of the overall asset base for undervaluation of assets should be undertaken. Older assets, such as real estate, often have appreciated significantly, particularly if an alternative, higher-quality use of the asset is possible. Such appreciation in value will not generally be reflected on the financial statements, and a financial advisor's expertise will be particularly useful in evaluating potential hidden assets.

A second source of value in hidden assets includes undervalued operating assets, which may encompass entire operating divisions. Equity values of subsidiaries may exceed the value of an entire enterprise, and this value could be captured either through the sale of the entire subsidiary or the public offering of a partial interest in the subsidiary.

Search for Hidden Liabilities

While the potential for discovery of hidden asset values always exists, the converse also is true: The risk exists of unrecognized future liabilities. Although this list is by no means complete, the following are potential hidden liabilities to watch for: (1) unforeseen environmental liabilities that represent particularly significant elements of exposure over an extended period of time; (2) product liability, which is fairly stringent in the United States relative to many other countries; (3) requirements for capital spending to modernize assets to compete effectively, particularly in industries undergoing significant transformation; and (4) liabilities to former employees.

For example, in the case of liabilities to former employees, a company's health benefits often extend to the retiree base, which can create a large, ongoing cost to an acquiror. Similarly, a retirement program represents a long-term obligation that usually is offset by separate assets administrated by outside parties. In some instances the retirement plan's assets may exceed the obligations; however, altogether too often the obligations significantly exceed the assets. Underfunded pensions represent a major ongoing liability, and servicing of that liability should be analyzed thoroughly by an acquiror.

Financial Modeling

The historical financial statements will provide investors with an understanding of the business to permit forecasting of the operations under their control. Creating a financial model, with which investors can vary assumptions and changes in the business, represents the key tool for analyzing the investment.

Financial modeling has become quite sophisticated through utilization of various software programs, including programs that enable the development of short and long-term financial projections. Investors are able to develop their own view of the future business, including any synergies that may occur from business combinations or any contemplated asset sales. From there, investors can measure discounted cash flows and determine valuations of the business. Additionally, they will be able to test various financing strategies in order to determine the optimal capital structure for the acquisition. This quantitative analysis will give investors a base of information from which to determine pricing and negotiating strategies.

CONCLUSION

The United States continues to be fertile ground for investment by both foreign and domestic investors alike. America has certain inherent country characteristics that make it a good base for expansion by foreign investors, and that are enhanced from time to time by market changes such as currency and interest rate differentials. The capital markets are highly sophisticated, with substantial availability of information to aid an investor in the investment process.

Selecting a competent financial advisor will help a foreign investor through the maze of information and assist in a thorough digestation of financial and industry data. Developing a specialized financial model will enable a foreign investor to optimize financing and negotiation strategies in making an acquisition in the United States. Finally, the level of sophistication of the United States capital markets will enable a foreign investor to minimize risk through use of the wide variety of interest rate, currency, and other hedges.

CHAPTER 4

SPECIAL CONSIDERATIONS FOR THE GERMAN INVESTOR

Dennis L. Neider
Partner
National Director, German Business
Price Waterhouse
Klaus H. Jander, Esq.
Rogers & Wells

While the desire always is to keep transactions as simple as possible, our experience has taught us that in order to protect our clients' interests, it is very important to be meticulous and diligent in addressing all potential problems, particularly in such a litigious environment as that of the United States.

The cross-border element of such transactions brings to the surface a number of problems that might not be present in a purely domestic transaction. Parties experienced in doing purely domestic transactions have learned to accept that certain issues will arise as a matter of course. Parties to cross-border transactions, however, often will find that what is routine for one party is unanticipated for the other. This is especially true for German investors coming to the United States, mainly because of differing legal and cultural backgrounds. We find it therefore essential to a prospective German investor to obtain legal and financial advice from professionals based in the United States who understand and have experience in the legal and financial system of Germany and who know how to reconcile these cultural differences.

An important role for the lawyers and accountants involved in such transactions is therefore to help bridge gaps in understanding so that the parties reach an agreement that both understand and can live with.

It might help in approaching the problem to summarize some of the issues that arise in such circumstances, taking as example a general cross-border transaction.

PARTIES TO THE TRANSACTION

Deals are normally negotiated between representatives of the major corporate entities involved—often the parent corporation of a group or a significant operating subsidiary within that group. One significant difference is that the U.S. representatives often bring with them attorneys who also play an active role in the negotiations. For tax, third-party liability, and other reasons, the corporate vehicle that often will make the acquisition in the United States is a newly formed subsidiary with no assets or liabilities. This is not a device by the purchaser to avoid responsibility to the seller. Persons selling businesses to such new companies are concerned that, having negotiated with a major corporation, the obligation to complete the deal will be that of a company with little or no net worth. The seller normally is satisfied by receiving a guarantee from a financially responsible member of the purchaser's group of companies that the new company making the acquisition will perform its obligations.

SCHEDULE

In the United States, very often there is a significant period of time, sometimes more than one or two months, between the signing of an acquisition agreement and the actual closing or completion of the transaction. In addition to the delay normally required in the United States to pre-notify the U.S. antitrust authorities, this period of time is usually used by the purchaser to conduct a diligence review of the business being acquired. This review will include meeting with management, operating personnel, outside accountants and lawyers for the seller, commercial lenders to the seller, and perhaps its major customers; it also usually includes inspections of the important operating and production facilities of the business being acquired. Where organized labor plays an important role in the seller's business, often a purchaser will meet with the leaders of the union. Obviously, these inquiries are all made with the consent, cooperation, and participation of the seller, and are necessary partly because of the lack of public records in the United States for privately owned companies. It is not uncommon to include in a purchase agreement a provision allowing the purchaser to abandon the transaction if in the course of its due diligence review it discovers a condition materially adverse to those represented to it at the time the agreement was signed. In addition, sellers usually require that the purchaser enter into a separate agreement to keep the information obtained confidential.

If financing is involved, this period of time is also used for putting the financing in place and allowing the lenders an opportunity to participate in the same due diligence process. In addition, this period is used to process any registration statements or proxy material required by U.S. or state securities law and to hold any required shareholder meeting to approve the transaction.

REPRESENTATIONS AND WARRANTIES

It is customary in United States acquisition agreements for the seller of a business, as a corporation, to make extensive representations and warranties to the purchaser regarding the results of operations and the financial condition of the business being acquired, the absence of materially adverse changes, the value of accounts receivable and inventories, the absence of undisclosed contingencies, the propriety of the accounting practices and principles, the condition of and title to property, the status of litigation, employee relations, the condition of property and equipment, the enforceability of and the absence of default under material contracts, compliance with laws, and the like. The reason to ask for representations is to be found in the regulatory environment. There are very few public records for privately owned companies and there is, for example, no statutory law requiring disclosure or filing with an authority if a corporation becomes insolvent. Also, insolvency is not a criminal offense of the managers of the company (Zahlungsunfähigkeit, Antrag auf Konkurseröffnung, Konkursverschleppung). These representations serve not only as conditions to the closing (if they are not correct and this fact is discovered prior to the closing, the purchaser may abandon the transaction and depending on the terms of the acquisition agreement, may also have a claim for damages) but also as a basis for a claim for damages if it is discovered after the closing that a representation is not correct. Thus, it is very important in negotiating a contract that the clients are clear on the representations that they require of the other party and on the representations that they can give.

Normally only the corporate parties are liable for the accuracy of these representations, rather than the individual officers and directors of the corporation. Exceptions to these general rules can be and are negotiated. When the business being sold has been held by a very few shareholders who also are the officers and directors of the seller, those individuals sometimes are asked to be personally responsible for the accuracy of representations and warranties. As a general rule, however, individual as compared to corporate responsibility for the accuracy of representations and warranties is unusual.

If all of the business is being sold, it is not uncommon for the purchaser to insist that a portion of the purchase price be held in escrow for a fixed period of time (which is also negotiated) to permit time for assuring that in fact the representations were correct. This process can lead to intensive negotiations, and there is no set pattern. Sometimes representations and warranties do not continue beyond the closing, and sometimes they continue for as many as three or four years (or even longer for claims based on taxes); sometimes there is no escrow and other times the escrow can be as much as 15 to 20 percent of the total purchase price.

Representations and warranties also are given by the purchaser. The extent of the representations and warranties that a purchaser gives usually depends upon the nature of the consideration being paid to the seller. If the transaction involves only cash, the purchaser's representations and warranties normally are quite limited. If the consideration involves equity issued by the purchaser or a corporate entity of the purchaser, or if it involves a delayed payment, the representations and warranties can be as extensive as those required of the seller.

CLOSING CONDITIONS

The closing is the event at which the transfer of title of the business being acquired takes place. A number of conditions must normally be satisfied before closing may proceed. These include not only the continued accuracy of material representations and warranties, but also the following six components:

1. Obtaining consents of third parties, such as lenders, whose consent is required by reason of preexisting contractual obligations of one of the parties (leases, for example, are often deemed "assigned" by reason of business acquisitions, and the leases customarily prohibit assignments without the consent of the lessor).

2. The absence of governmental objection to the transaction (most transactions in the United States require pre-notification under the Hart-Scott-Rodino Antitrust-Improvements Act and the passage of an appropriate waiting period following that filing; also the Exon-Florio Act has to be considered, providing formal authority to the President to restrict foreign acquisitions if deemed harmful to national security).

3. The satisfaction of any financing requirements of the purchaser that are made conditions to the transaction.

4. Advice from independent accountants of the seller (and of the purchaser if consideration other than cash is involved) regarding the audited and, in some instances, the unaudited financial statements of the seller and adverse changes in the results of operations and financial condition of the seller since the date of last full financial statements (the "comfort" letter).

5. Opinions of legal counsel to the sellers and to the purchaser covering a variety of subjects including due authorization, execution and approval of the basic agreements, the binding nature of those agreements, compliance of the parties with their obligations under the agreements and other instruments affecting the transaction, the absence of governmental objection to the transaction, and other subjects, often the result of extended negotiations. If the transaction requires approval by the shareholders of either party (usually approval by the shareholders of the seller is required), the opinions also address Securities and Exchange clearances (if required) and the accuracy and completeness of proxy material used to solicit the shareholders' votes; opinions of legal counsel are uncommon in Germany because of the legal background. In the United States they are essential because of the lack of statutory law and public records. Legal opinions serve to safeguard the clients' interest, evidencing that a professional who is familiar with the deal as well as the federal and state laws and regulations has examined the transaction.

6. Special conditions tailored to the transaction, such as a requirement that the earnings of the business being purchased must be at not less than a certain level or that its net worth be not less than a certain amount.

These closing conditions are negotiated at the time the acquisition agreement is signed and are specified therein. When the seller or purchaser is a U.S. company whose equity securities are publicly traded, the investment community within the United States is especially interested in knowing the nature of the closing conditions in order to determine the likelihood of the transactions being completed. Thus, if a public announcement of the transaction is required in the United States, it is important, if possible, to satisfy this in the public announcement by outlining, in at least general terms, the closing conditions.

POSTCLOSING COVENANTS

If the seller is disposing less than all its business, often it will be required to agree to do or not to do certain things following the closing. Most commonly these agreements pertain to not competing with the business being sold and obviously must be carefully crafted to assure that they do not result in antitrust and similar violations. In addition, in the case of a claim for breach of representations and warranties, the agreement will specify the postclosing procedures to be followed. These procedures sometimes include arbitration by third parties.

The foregoing are the highlights of typical acquisition agreements. Depending upon the complexity of the transaction, these agreements with schedules and appendices attached can run over one hundred pages. In general, the American legal system allows the parties to "write the law" of the agreement because statutory law in the United States has relatively limited impact on the rights and obligations of the parties to a negotiated transaction. This is also one of the basic cross-border differences: The legal system in the United States is based on common law, while the legal system in Germany is basically statutory law. This difference influences not only the size of the agreements and the amounts of skill, negotiations, and costs related thereto, but also the general attitude of approaching and negotiating transactions. It is because of those differences that negotiating in the United States is very often time-consuming, and also why American attorneys have a direct approach to the various topics, which sometimes seems impolite to a German businessman. As a generalization one could say that every side is asking for the maximum and then compromising while negotiating, and that actions not prohibited by the written contract are per se permissible; the German general principle of "Treu und Glauben" is unknown to the American business world. We understand that those reasons explain why German investors are most times taken by surprise to be facing lengthy and detailed negotiations, and complicated procedures and formalities to be dealt with in what they thought was the model state of free enterprise and trade.

In what follows we will describe in brief the different types of business entities available to a foreign investor, making reference where possible to the German equivalent. The United States is a common law jurisdiction that recognizes various business forms controlled by the laws of the individual states. The most usual forms are corporation, general partnership, limited partnership, joint venture, branch of a foreign corporation, or sole proprietorship. The basic decision to be made is whether to incorporate the business in the United States and operate it as a subsidiary, or to operate the business as a U.S. branch or division. In general, the trend is toward declining use of U.S. branches mainly because of the Tax Reform Act of 1986, wherein a branch profits tax was imposed on earnings and profits of U.S. branches of foreign corporations, regardless of any actual distribution of such profits. An exemption exists for reinvestment of profits in the United States. It is, therefore, favorable for German investors to form a separate legal entity in the United States.

CORPORATION

A corporation may be equated with the German "Aktiengesell-schaft." Ownership of the corporation is evidenced by shares of stock and the liability of the shareholders in general is limited to their investment in the company. The incorporation procedures and capital requirements vary from state to state, but in general the incorporation is inexpensive and can be accomplished in a short time. Because of its very liberal corporation law and the ease of getting documents from the state, as well as the long history of judicial decisions making that law predictable to all concerned, the state of Delaware is often chosen for incorporation. The initial and annual filing requirements are not very difficult, and there are no restrictions for corporations to be fully owned by foreign investors. The standard documents necessary consist of a certificate of incorporation to be filed with the applicable Secretary of State, wherein the basic business purposes of the corporation are enumerated. By filing, the corporation becomes a legal entity. In addition, by-laws are necessary, stipulating topics not covered by the certificate of incorporation, such as time and place of required annual shareholders meeting, election and removal of officers and directors, voting requirements, and the like. Any amendment of the certificate of incorporation has to be approved by the shareholders. The same can be stipulated with regard to the by-laws. The shareholders have to elect a board of directors, which is a body combining the powers of a German "Aufsichtsrat" and "Vorstand." The board of directors elects and supervises the officers who run the day-to-day business of the corporation.

Since this management structure has no equation in Germany we will explain it in more detail. The board of directors supervises the officers but has an executive function as well. Except for the day-to-day business, most actions to be taken by the officers on behalf of the corporation need the consent of the board of directors. Because the statutory law is very limited, the by-laws of the corporation stipulate what corporate actions need the consent of the board of directors. Ordinarily the directors will sign a unanimous written consent specifying the corporate action to be taken and carried out by the officers. This consent is prepared by the secretary, who is an officer of the corporation. Commonly the secretary is also the general counsel of the corporation. This is advisable because as an attorney, he or she has the legal expertise to review the documentation for the proposed corporate action with regard to liability and legal pitfalls, and to act in a way as an independent register by keeping the minute books, records, and seal of the corporation. There exists no official register in the United States, comparable to the German Handelsregister. The only public records that can be obtained with regard to a corporation are a certified copy of the Certificate of Incorporation and a Certificate of Good Standing, both available from the Office of the Secretary of State of the state where the corporation was incorporated. As mentioned, the Certificate of Incorporation basically states that the named corporation is an existing legal entity, but does not contain any information regarding capitalization, ownership of the shares, and other legal or financial issues of interest. The Certificate of Good Standing may be obtained as of a current date but only evidences the corporation's legal existence and that it has complied with the filing requirements and payments of fees under the applicable state law. Any other information—such as the number of issued shares, the current stockholders, and names of the directors and officers—can be evidenced only by an officer's certificate, which is commonly issued by the Secretary of the corporation. Such a certificate may be issued under penalty of perjury and can be notarized (Unterschriftsbeglaubigung).

GENERAL PARTNERSHIP

A general partnership can be compared with "Offene Handelsgesellschaft," consisting of two or more persons whose liability is not limited. The partnership agreement should include the name and purpose of the business, the capital contributions, management powers, allocation for profits and losses, dissolution procedures, and the like. It is not necessary to file the agreement with the state, but ordinarily one has to file with a record office a certificate stating the names and residences of the partners. There is no minimum capital requirement. The partners are jointly and severally liable, and each can bind the partnership legally by acting in the ordinary course of business.

LIMITED PARTNERSHIP

The limited partnership may be compared with a "Kommand-itgesellschaft," having one or more general partners with unlimited liability and one or more limited partners. Limited partners have no right to participate in the management or control of the partnership and are liable for obligations only to the extent of their contributions. The partnership is formed by executing the agreement between the partners and filing a certificate with the state indicating the partners and the profit share of each limited partner.

JOINT VENTURE

In most instances the joint venture is a special type of partnership created for a single purpose and terminated when the project is completed. A joint venture can be established as a partnership or a corporation. In our experience, a German investor in a newly formed joint venture should insist that the accounting firm and the general counsel are jointly selected, to safeguard the new partner's interest. Also, one has to evaluate thoroughly the economic advantages of a joint venture giving special consideration to the goals and rights of the other party and how to control those.

BRANCH OF A FOREIGN CORPORATION

A branch operation in the United States is a mere extension of the foreign corporation. Except for the registration to do business with the appropriate regulatory agency, no formal formation procedures are required. The foreign corporation is fully responsible for the liabilities of its branch, and there is no mandatory capitalization for the branch itself.

SOLE PROPRIETORSHIP

Any individual may operate as a sole proprietorship and will be required to obtain the applicable state and local permits and licenses to operate. There is no limited liability while operating in this form.

In addition to deciding what legal framework fits one's purposes best, another major consideration for a German investor is where to locate the new business. This of course depends mainly on the nature of the business one is interested in, although some general information is applicable.

While the federal government maintains a policy of neutrality toward attracting foreign investment, state and local governments offer investment incentives to attract foreign investors: Local governments want to create new jobs in their area to enlarge their tax base and the like. The U.S. Department of Commerce is a source of information in general and can also provide the foreign investor with the addresses of industrial development organizations, which in most states are divisions of the Department of Commerce. The forms of incentive include grants and loans as well as tax incentives on federal, state, and local levels.

Below we will highlight some areas of the U.S. regulatory and business environment that contrast significantly with practices in Germany.

LABOR LAW AND EQUAL OPPORTUNITIES

A variety of federal statutes and executive orders prohibit discrimination in employment on the basis of race, color, sex, religion, national origin, age, handicap, or veteran status. These laws apply not only to discrimination in hiring practices but also to discriminatory promotion policies and disparities in pay levels, which may be evidenced by the employment manuals. By contrast with Germany, in the United States employees may obtain evidence contained in the employment manuals fairly easily in a litigation with their employer. The American legal system provides for a so-called pretrial "discovery" wherein the parties can obtain information and documents from the other side to be used as evidence in the lawsuit.

Except for special circumstances (for example, documents being protected by the attorney-client privilege) one has to disclose the information asked for and produce documents. The discovery may be equated with the German "Ausforschungsbeweis," which is explicitly not permissable under German law. The purpose of discovery is to allow each party to find out everything about the other party's case in advance. The aforementioned is applicable not only in labor law disputes but in all kinds of claims under the American legal system. The labor laws are also enforced by numerous government agencies, the more important of which are the Equal Employment Opportunity Commission and the Department of Labor. These agencies have broad investigatory and enforcement powers, which are exerted on employers without regard to the size of their operations. Compliance with equal opportunity laws can be a complicated matter, since the official concept of what constitutes discrimination is a continually evolving one. Moreover, the various agencies have overlapping jurisdictions; each agency may set differing standards of application, making enforcement inconsistent.

The trend over the years has been toward more rigorous enforcement, including the requirement of affirmative action programs to reverse a pattern of systematic discrimination in the past. Penalties for violations can be extremely severe, ranging from fines, injunctions, and back pay awards to loss of government contracts.

Another major difference is that, except for the case of highly paid officers, it is uncommon to have written employment contracts. The basic terms of the employment are usually outlined in a one-page letter or orally.

It is our understanding that especially in these areas a German manager should seek careful advice to remedy a general lack of experience with these issues.

PAID HOLIDAYS, VACATIONS, AND TERMINATION OF EMPLOYMENT

There are about ten holidays in the United States throughout the year. In case they fall on a weekend, either the preceding Friday or the following Monday is given as time off with pay. Commonly, the vacation period is two weeks per year, with longer periods granted after working at the same firm a certain number of years. There is no mandatory law for holidays and vacation; rather, it is a customary development.

Besides the Worker Adjustment and Retraining Act, dealing with large layoffs, plant closings, and the like, there is no specific federal law with respect to the termination of employment in the private area. Customarily, however, a two-week notice or two weeks' severance pay is granted in the event of termination. Termination provisions may be found in contracts with labor unions. With regard to terminations, Equal Opportunity and Fair Employment Practice laws have to be considered as well.

MANAGERS

To supervise their business investment in the United States, German companies often wish to send to the U.S. entity a German manager who is familiar with the business and philosophy of the German parent. In addition to a passport, the foreign manager must obtain a personal immigration visa before being admitted to work in the United States. Application for a visa must be made at U.S. embassies and consulates abroad. Because there exist several non-immigrant visa classifications, some of which require an approved petition from the Immigration and Naturalization Service in order to submit an application at the embassy or consulate, it is advisable to seek professional help from a U.S. law firm in preparing the applications.

In employing U.S. managers, our experience in the past has been that besides looking for experienced professionals, it facilitates matters if the new manager speaks German. This ability helps not only in day-to-day communications and for forwarding documents in German without the need for time-consuming and expensive translation, but also for a better understanding of the different kinds of background and business approaches and for the manager's role as intermediary between German expectations and the U.S. reality.

DISTRIBUTORSHIP AGREEMENT

Here, we describe another pitfall to be avoided by investors already selling their products on the U.S. market by way of distributorship agreements, who then intend to replace those distribution channels by establishing their own U.S. entity. By terminating the distributorship agreements without cause for the mere reason mentioned, the supplying company might be faced with huge damage claims on the part of the distributors. A similar problem occurs in Germany in the context of "Beendigung von Handelsvertreterverträgen/Ausgleichsanspruch." If one does not seek professional advice before negotiating with the distributors and sending a termination letter, one ends up with costly litigation and may be required to pay substantial amounts in damages claimed by the other side.

LEGAL HIGHLIGHTS

We will now highlight some basic characteristics of the United States legal system that are not to be found in Germany and therefore might surprise the German investor.

Attorneys' fees are not regulated by law; there are normally two bases for the billing. The first is a contingency fee under which the lawyers themselves normally pays all expenses and in return get a percentage of the amount recovered, usually ranging between 20 and 40 percent. Contingency fees are mainly agreed on for personal injury cases (e.g., traffic accidents and product liability claims). The advantage for the lawyer working on a contingency fee basis is mainly the prospect of a large monetary recovery of which he will receive a portion.

The second basis for billing is an agreement to work on a fee basis. The fee is based on the amount of time spent working on the case, normally calculated on an hourly basis. The hourly rates vary and are based on the experience and expertise of the attorney. Attorneys for the defendant work only on a fee basis, the reason being that under the U.S. legal system each party has to bear its own costs and expenses so that even the defendant who "wins" is not reimbursed by the plaintiff. An exception hereto exists under Rule 11 of the Federal Rules of Civil Procedure, covering civil litigation in the United States District Courts. This rule holds that if the pleading or motion turns out to have no merit whatsoever, the court may order the attorney and/or its client to pay the expenses of the defendant. The rule basically was adopted in an effort to discourage frivolous litigation, requiring that an attorney undertake reasonable factual and legal research before filing any complaint.

The filing fees with the court are rather low and not related to the claimed amount ("Einheitsgebühr nach Klageart").

Another specialty is the so-called class action, which is a lawsuit brought by a representative member of a large group of persons on behalf of all members of the group. The trial court must specifically certify a lawsuit as a class action. To receive that certification the class must be ascertainable, the members must hold a common interest in the issues of law and fact raised by the plaintiff, and the action must satisfy a variety of special requirements applicable to class actions. If a class action is certified and all members of the class received notice and did not exclude themselves from the class, they are later bound by the judgment.

RESTRICTIONS ON FOREIGN INVESTMENT AND INVESTORS

A number of other federal agencies, including the International Trade Administration, a division of the Department of Commerce, monitor and analyze foreign investments in the United States for information and policy-advisory purposes.

In the United States, there are no exchange controls as commonly experienced by foreign investors in many countries throughout the world. There are also no significant legal restrictions or limitations on the flow of funds into or out of the United States. In that regard one has, therefore, the same conditions as in the Federal Republic of Germany.

In general, there are no government-imposed limitations on investments in the United States by foreign persons, including the acquisition of existing corporations owned by U.S. shareholders;

the policy to date is to admit and treat foreign capital on a basis of equality with domestic capital.

Although the Exon-Florio Act now provides formal authority to the President to restrict foreign acquisitions and takeovers of U.S. companies if deemed harmful to national security, this law is not expected to affect the vast majority of foreign investment.

On the federal level, restrictions on foreign ownership exist in certain fields—for example, communications and defense. Information on this subject can be obtained from the U.S. Department of Commerce.

A number of states prohibit foreign individuals and corporations from directly acquiring real estate. In addition, some states depend the entry of foreign corporations upon fulfillment of certain requirements, which are purely formal in nature. In case a foreign individual or entity acquires or transfers an interest in agricultural land, the Agricultural Foreign Investment Disclosure Act of 1978 requires the submission of a report to the Secretary of Agriculture within 90 days after the date of acquisition or transfer.

There are no requirements in the United States to register the investment of foreign capital or loans; the same applies when agreements of a technological nature are consummated.

Federal government policy directed to foreign investment in the United States is unlikely to change significantly in the near future. Foreign investment has, however, always provided political fodder. Current issues in this area are questions of reciprocity, registration, and reporting requirements, as well as foreign acquisition of prime real estate, especially the concentration of such investment in specific geographic areas.

In the course of advising German clients in cross-border transactions, our experience has taught us a number of principles that we apply in order to achieve the ultimate goal—which is a transaction satisfactory to both parties that each party understands. Our suggested "rules" follow:

1. The first rule in cross-border transactions is patience. It is also the second and the third rule. People negotiating in such transactions often are doing so for the first time or are entering commercial environments previously unfamiliar to them, and business prudence dictates that matters proceed much more slowly than in a domestic transaction or in a transaction whose participants have a long history of past dealings.

2. Explain positions, legal problems, and goals clearly, distinctly, and sometimes repeatedly. Often, cultural differences will allow naive negotiators to assume that the other party has the same general background and perspective on commercial transactions. While the goals of both parties must be similar if there is to be a deal at all, for one of the parties that goal might be a given in any deal, while for the other party it might be a major point requiring substantial negotiation.

3. Language barriers can be serious impediments. Americans in particular assume that the world not only speaks English but also thinks in English. Ideally, the principals of both parties will be fluent in a common tongue, not only socially but also commercially, but usually this is not the case, at least in dealing with Americans or British. If uncertain about the meaning of something, ask.

4. Counterparties have different cultural perspective. Those from some cultures are too polite to express a direct "no." One might be able to discern a negative response to a proposal only from the implications of days of little or no progress on the point. Also, in certain cultures parties will pass over a point, leaving the counterparty with the impression that the point has been agreed upon, only to return to it days or weeks later.

5. Remember the different legal perspectives. The litigious nature of the United States often comes as a shock to the uninitiated, and the voluminous documentation of U.S. transactions is not always comfortable for persons whose business environment is a civil code jurisdiction. Also crucial are the differences in tax systems.

6. Take time to get to know one another. It is important to recognize that cultures differ dramatically in their openness to "foreigners" and "foreign" attitudes, and in approaching the counterparty one never should assume familiarity. While one might want to wrap up the deal in a day, socializing may be far more productive than time spent negotiating.

CHAPTER 5

TAX PLANNING FOR JAPANESE INVESTMENT IN THE UNITED STATES

Hisashi Doi
International Tax Senior Manager
Price Waterhouse, Tokyo

Hiroo Kato
Japanese Tax Partner
Price Waterhouse, Tokyo

Alan S. Woodberry
International Tax Partner
Price Waterhouse, San Francisco

Neal W. Zimmerman
International Tax Partner
Price Waterhouse, Tokyo

INTRODUCTION

Japanese investment in U.S. business is a common and fast-growing phenomenon. Effective tax planning for such investment is vital for a Japanese multinational to maximize after-tax return on its investment. This tax planning requires understanding a Japanese multinational's current and anticipated tax situation in both Japan and the United States. A general review of some of the more important Japanese and U.S. tax rules that affect cross-border investments appears in Table 5–1. Flexibility is an essential component of tax planning because both countries frequently change their tax laws.

TABLE 5–1

Comparison of Major Corporate Japanese and United States Tax Rules in Effect on January 1, 1992

	Japan	United States
Type of system	Japan has a classical double tax system.	The U.S. has a classical double tax stystem.
Corporate tax rates		
	Rate	Rate
	Corporate income tax 37.50%	Federal tax 34%
	Inhabitants tax 7.76%	State tax 0 to 10%+
	Enterprise tax 13.20%	Effective rates (resulting from deductibility of
	58.46%	state taxes) 34% to 40%+
	Effective rate (after deduction for enterprise tax) 51.64%	Some cities levy income taxes that are deductible in computing federal taxable income
	For accounting periods ending during the period April 1, 1991, through March 31, 1992, a surtax is imposed equal to 2.5% of a company's corporate income tax liability in excess of ¥3,000,000.	
Corporate residence	A company incorporated under Japanese law is a Japanese resident.	A company incorporated under the laws of one of the states is a U.S. resident.
Capital gains	Capital gains are taxable at regular tax rates. An additional surtax is imposed on certain real estate transactions.	Capital gains are taxable at regular tax rates.
Group relief	No group relief is permitted.	A group of U.S. corporations may file a consolidated tax return if there is 80% or greater common ownership under a U.S. parent company.
Tax net operating losses	Net operating losses usually can be carried back 1 year and forward for up to 5 years.	Net operating losses usually can be carried back 3 years and forward up to 15 years.

Exposure of foreign income to tax	A Japanese corporation is taxable on its worldwide income, including stock dividends, with worldwide losses available to offset worldwide income.	A U.S. corporation is taxable on its worldwide income with worldwide losses available to offset worldwide income.
Income of foreign subsidiaries	A foreign subsidiary's income is subject to tax when the earnings are distributed as a dividend. Japanese shareholders of certain more than 50% Japanese-owned foreign corporations, either incorporated or managed and controlled in designated low-tax-rate countries, are currently taxable on certain undistributed income.	A foreign subsidiary's income is subject to tax when the earnings are distributed as a dividend. U.S. shareholders of controlled foreign corporations are currently taxable on certain undistributed income (so-called Subpart F income).
Thin capitalization (rule whereby if a subsidiary is capitalized with excessive debt, borrowed from its shareholder, relative to equity, some or all of the debt may be treated as equity for tax purposes)	Japan has no thin capitalization rules.	Generally the tests to avoid thin capitalization are as follows: A loan should be documented by a note; A loan should bear an arm's length rate of interest; The internal debt to equity ratio should not exceed 3 to 1; The total internal and external debt to equity ratio should not exceed 10 to 1; and The borrower should be expected to be able to service the debt.

(continued)

TABLE 5–1
(concluded)

	Japan	United States
Relief from double taxation on foreign income	Avoidance of double taxation is achieved by allowing a foreign tax credit, including a deemed-paid foreign tax credit for underlying foreign company tax for 25% or greater direct corporate shareholders. Generally deemed-paid foreign tax credit is allowable only for foreign taxes incurred by a first-tier subsidiary. The 25% shareholder threshold can be reduced by a tax treaty, e.g., the minimum ownership required under the Japan-U.S. tax treaty is 10%. Use of this credit is subject to a worldwide foreign tax credit limitation. Foreign taxes are deductible but not creditable in computing the enterprise tax. Excess foreign tax credit limitation can be carried back 3 years and forward 3 years. Excess foreign tax credits can be carried back 3 years and forward 3 years. For corporation and inhabitants tax purposes, foreign income taxes may be claimed either as credits or deductions at the annual choice of the taxpayer.	Avoidance of double taxation is achieved by allowing a foreign tax credit, including a deemed-paid foreign tax credit for underlying company tax for 10% or greater corporate shareholders. Deemed-paid foreign tax credit is allowable for foreign taxes incurred by first-, second-, and third-tier subsidiaries. Use of the credit is subject to complex foreign tax credit limitation provisions. No carryback or carryover of excess limitation is permitted. Excess foreign tax credits can be carried back 2 years and forward 5 years. Foreign income taxes may be claimed either as credits or deductions at the annual choice of the taxpayer.

Taxation of a foreign company with local branch	Business income is subject to the same tax rates as corporate profits. No Japanese tax is withheld on repatriation of branch profits.	Business income is subject to the regular federal and state tax rates. The amount of income subject to tax is determined under rules for sourcing income and apportioning deductions. Generally, the states apportion a corporation's net income. Unless reinvested in the U.S., business income is also subject to the U.S. branch profits tax. However, for most Japanese corporations, the Japan-U.S. tax treaty overrides the branch profits tax (IRS Notice 87-56 1987-2 C.B. 367). In certain situations, the U.S. may impose a second-tier withholding tax and the branch tax on interest.
Taxation of income from subsidiaries paid to a recipient in the other country		
Dividends Japan-U.S. tax treaty	15%[a]	15%[a]
Interest Japan-U.S. tax treaty	10%	10%
Royalties Japan-U.S. tax treaty	10%	10%

[a] Reduced to 10% provided that the corporate recipient owned at least 10% of the corporate payor up to the time of the payment and during the entire preceding taxable year and not more than 25% of the paying corporation's gross income consists of interest or dividends (unless received in the banking business or from certain related corporations).

Tax planning is complex because of the many different tax laws, regulations, rulings, and court decisions, and because of the variety of ways in which a company can stucture and conduct its business. This chapter covers certain structural tax issues that a Japanese company should consider when either acquiring or starting a business in the United States. Of course many nontax factors also affect a company's decisions, such as minimizing exposure to legal liabilities and foreign currency fluctuations.

The tax plan of one company will vary from that of another to reflect each company's unique situation, expectations, and nontax considerations. Accordingly, each company must examine the alternatives available to determine its best course of action toward minimizing its overall tax burden over the long term.

SHOULD A JAPANESE CORPORATION OPERATE IN THE UNITED STATES THROUGH A U.S. SUBSIDIARY OR A BRANCH?

U.S. Subsidiary Taxation

A U.S. subsidiary's income is subject to U.S. federal and state tax. Generally, net taxable income differs from net book income as a result of permanent differences, such as tax exempt municipal bond interest, and timing differences, such as use of accelerated methods of depreciation over shorter lives for tax purposes. The United States imposes a witholding tax on payments of income from a U.S. subsidiary to its Japanese parent. Interest and royalty payments are subject to a 10 percent U.S. withholding tax, provided that this income is not effectively connected with the Japanese parent's conduct of a U.S. business. Dividend payments are subject to either a 10 or 15 percent U.S. withholding tax. Payments for goods and services are generally exempt from U.S. withholding tax. All payments between affiliates must be determined on an ''arm's-length'' basis or they may be adjusted by the tax authority if it believes that insufficient taxable income is being reported.

Japan does not tax income of the U.S. subsidiary until earnings are repatriated to Japan as a dividend. Furthermore, when the Japanese parent reports the dividend income in its Japanese tax return, the Japanese parent may claim a foreign tax credit against Japanese tax for the U.S. income taxes associated with the dividend. Creditable U.S. taxes include the U.S. withholding tax imposed on the dividend and the underlying U.S. federal and state income taxes paid by the U.S. subsidiary.

For underlying U.S. income taxes to be creditable in Japan, the Japanese parent company must own at least 10 percent of the U.S. subsidiary's voting stock directly, and only those underlying taxes paid with respect to dividends received for voting stock are creditable. Further, only underlying U.S. and foreign income taxes paid by directly owned U.S. subsidiaries (so-called first-tier subsidiaries) are creditable. No credit is allowed for U.S. income taxes paid by lower-tier subsidiaries. In other words, if a U.S. subsidiary is the U.S. parent of a second-tier U.S. subsidiary, only U.S. and foreign income taxes paid by the U.S. parent can be claimed as foreign tax credits to offset Japanese tax of the Japanese parent when it receives a dividend.

Generally, in a U.S. consolidated tax return group, the Japanese tax authorities accept reasonable allocations of the U.S. federal income tax under the group's tax-sharing agreement in determining the United States parent's U.S. federal income tax liability. For Japanese tax purposes, the allocation of tax to the U.S. parent of the U.S. consolidated tax return group should not exceed the lesser of the tax the company would have paid if it had filed a separate return or the tax actually paid by the group.

In planning for dividends from its U.S. subsidiary, a Japanese parent should be aware of the resulting Japanese tax cost. For example, a Japanese parent may have an effective Japanese tax rate on dividend income of 52 percent. This includes the Japanese enterprise tax (maximum 13.2 percent rate) that cannot be offset by foreign tax credits. The U.S. 10 percent withholding tax and underlying federal and state tax may or may not be sufficient to offset the Japanese corporate and inhabitants taxes (combined 45 percent rate). The U.S. federal and state combined income tax rate before witholding tax are about 40 percent in California (ignoring permanent and timing differences). Including the 10 percent U.S. withholding tax, the U.S. total tax rate increases to 46 percent. However, the effective tax rate for a particular year can vary significantly to reflect various factors such as permanent and timing differences and allowable credits against tax. In some cases, the Japanese parent may prefer that the U.S. subsidiary defer paying dividends and reinvest its earnings in the United States to avoid paying both the U.S. withholding tax and additional Japanese tax.

The Japanese financial reporting system utilizes separate company financial statements, which are the primary financial statements in Japan. Generally, only these statements are mailed to shareholders. Japanese publicly traded companies disclose consolidated financial statements as supplementary financial information in filings with the Ministry of Finance. These statements are available to investors. The earnings of subsidiaries are recognized in the separate company financial statements of the parent only when dividends are distributed.

U.S. Branch Taxation

A Japanese corporation operating directly in the United States is currently subject to both U.S. and Japanese income taxes. Industrial or commercial profits attributable to a Japanese corporation's permanent establishment in the United States are subject to the 34 percent U.S. federal corporate income tax rate. A permanent establishment includes the branch or office of a Japanese parent or the office of a U.S., Japanese, or other partnership engaged in a U.S. trade or business.

In addition to the federal corporate income tax, the United States initiated two new branch taxes beginning in 1987. The new branch profits tax and branch interest tax treat a branch of a foreign corporation, whether operated directly or through a partnership, as if it were a U.S. corporation. The branch profits tax is essentially equivalent to a dividend withholding tax and is imposed on profits of a branch, except to the extent that those profits are reinvested in the U.S. branch. The Internal Revenue Service (IRS) has ruled, however, that generally the Japan-United States tax treaty prevents application of the branch profits tax to a Japanese corporation.

Recognizing that some tax treaties override the branch profits tax, the U.S. tax law has a second method of taxation. Under this alternative method, the United States imposes withholding tax on dividend distributions by a foreign corporation to its shareholders if at least 25 percent of the foreign corporation's gross income for the prior three years was derived from a U.S. business. The Japan-United States tax treaty also provides an exception from this tax for dividends paid by a Japanese corporation to Japanese residents by treating such distributions as foreign source income.

A portion of a Japanese corporation's interest expense is apportioned to the U.S. branch and is deductible in calculating U.S. taxable income under detailed rules. When the U.S. branch's interest deduction exceeds the amount of interest paid by the branch, the branch interest tax can apply. The tax on excess interest is not prohibited by the nondiscrimination provision or any other provision in the Japan-United States tax treaty, but the treaty reduces the tax rate to 10 percent.

A state generally taxes the portion of a corporation's net income apportioned to that state according to a three-factor formula: sales, payroll, and property. Compared with conducting business through a U.S. subsidiary, application of the three-factor apportionment formula may result in higher or lower state tax, depending on the particular circumstances. A few states determine tax liability according to a unitary formula that ignores legal entities in calculating the taxable income derived in a unitary business from a particular state.

California is the best-known state for applying a unitary formula. California allows multinationals to opt out of possible application of the worldwide unitary formula for an annual election fee. This filing method is known as the "water's-edge" election, and is so called because it includes in the unitary group only those related corporations that are incorporated or directly engaged in business in the United States. However, a number of multinationals have filed suit against California, arguing that the worldwide unitary method of taxation should not be permitted. The leading court cases in this matter are *Barclays Bank International, Ltd.* v. *Franchise Tax Board* and *Colgate-Palmolive Co.* v. *Franchise Tax Board*, both of which were decided in favor of the taxpayers by the lower courts. However, the Franchise Tax Board has appealed these decisions to higher courts, which at present have not yet decided these cases. It is likely that final, binding decisions will not be made any sooner than the end of 1992. Until that time, it appears that California will continue to enforce the worldwide unitary method of taxation against those unitary multinational groups that do not choose the "water's-edge" election alternative.

A Japanese corporation is subject to Japanese tax on its world-wide income. The amount of Japanese taxable income or loss generated by a U.S. branch differs from the amount calculated for U.S. tax purposes, because for Japanese tax purposes the computation is made under Japanese tax rules. Japan reduces its tax by giving credit for U.S. federal and state income taxes paid. The amount of foreign tax credit allowed, however, is subject to the Japanese foreign tax credit limitation. To compute the Japanese foreign tax credit limit, an allocation of interest expense is required. Interest on debt specifically identified with a particular investment is allocated against the income from that investment. All other interest is basically allocated on an asset basis.

Because U.S. tax rates are lower than Japanese tax rates, the credit limit may not restrict the ability of a Japanese corporation to claim credit for U.S. federal and state taxes. It is important for a Japanese corporation considering operating in the United States through a branch first to analyze its ability to fully utilize U.S. federal and state taxes as foreign tax credits.

Comparing a U.S. Subsidiary to a U.S. Branch

In general, a U.S. branch does not offer any significant U.S. tax advantages over a U.S. subsidiary. For Japanese tax purposes, whether a U.S. subsidiary or branch is used may significantly affect the tax burden. A U.S. subsidiary allows deferral of Japanese tax on U.S. income until a dividend is paid, and precludes use of a U.S. loss to reduce Japanese tax. Alternatively, the income or loss of a U.S. branch is calculated into the Japanese corporation's world-wide income or loss. In addition, income earned by a foreign branch of a Japanese company is not subject to the enterprise tax (maximum 13.2 percent rate). On the other hand, dividends from a U.S. subsidiary are subject to the enterprise tax, and no foreign tax credit is allowed against the enterprise tax.

In the authors' experience, most Japanese corporations conduct business in the United States through U.S. subsidiaries, thereby allowing deferral of Japanese tax until the earnings are distributed to the Japanese parent. However, there are two principal exceptions: (1) industries that operate through U.S. branches for nontax business reasons, such as airlines, shipping companies, and banks in which the U.S. branches rely on the head office's capital; and (2) investments that are expected to generate tax losses, particularly highly leveraged real estate investments. When U.S. loss activities turn profitable, the U.S. branch may be replaced by a U.S. subsidiary.

SHOULD ASSETS OR STOCK BE ACQUIRED IN A U.S. BUSINESS?

Generally the buyer of a U.S. business prefers to purchase the assets of the business rather than the stock, for two reasons. First, a purchase of assets generally does not involve assuming undisclosed product liabilities, taxes, or other claims against the business that arose prior to the acquisition. Second, a purchase of assets allows the tax basis of tangible and intangible assets to be stepped up to the purchase price, which includes liabilities assumed.

On the other hand, the seller of a U.S. business generally prefers to sell the stock, for two reasons. First, a stock sale relieves the seller of future problems arising from contingent liabilities of the business. Second, the seller can avoid double taxation, which often results when the sales proceeds of an asset disposition are distributed to a shareholder, other than an 80 percent or greater corporate shareholder. When the parties do agree to a stock sale, the buyer often requires that the seller provide certain warranties and guarantees in the sales agreement to protect against contingent liabilities. Sometimes part of the purchase price is withheld for a period of time to partially offset undisclosed liabilities.

Asset Acquisition

The allocation of the purchase price among the assets acquired may significantly affect future tax deductions. For tax purposes, but not necessarily for financial statement purposes, a purchaser generally wants to allocate purchase price to assets that will generate tax deductions at the earliest time, such as inventory and depreciable or amortizable assets with short lives.

The allocation of purchase price in a major acquisition is generally made pursuant to an appraisal obtained from an independent appraisal firm or an accounting firm that has appraisers. While the IRS is not required to accept such an appraisal, a professional appraisal opinion prepared at the time of the acquisition may be difficult for the IRS to challenge.

Generally, a portion of the purchase price is often allocated to intangible assets. For an intangible asset to be amortized for tax purposes, the acquirer must demonstrate both (1) the value of the intangible and (2) the useful life of the intangible. If the acquirer can demonstrate a useful life, estimated with reasonable accuracy, the allocable cost can be amortized over that life. Since goodwill and going concern value do not have lives, they cannot be deducted for tax purposes unless the business that they are attributable to is disposed of or abandoned. Certain intangibles, such as patents, have fixed lives and can be amortized.

Many other intangibles have less certain lives. These assets include customer and subscription lists, the existing core deposits of a bank, the insurance in force of an insurance company, and a work force in place. Advertising relationships and a customer or circulation base in the case of a broadcast, cable, newspaper, or similar business may also be included as intangibles with uncertain lives. U.S. acquirers and their appraisers often carefully evaluate such assets and determine their useful lives based upon statistical information. The IRS, on the other hand, often takes the position that such assets are not depreciable because certain customers may be lost but others can be expected to replace them and, accordingly, such assets may be treated as goodwill or going concern value, having no useful life.

In some cases the courts have flatly refused to allow amortization of such intangibles. In other cases where an intangible, such as a customer list, has been separately valued, with a price put on each customer and a life determined in a statistically valid manner, courts have allowed amortization. The IRS tried to terminate this controversy by proposing legislation for the 1987 Tax Act. This legislation declared that the cost of customer base, market share, or any renewing or similar intangible has an indeterminate life and cannot be amortized. However, in enacting the 1987 Tax Act, the legislature dropped this provision. The controversy between the IRS and taxpayers continues.

Another important asset to consider in the allocation of the purchase price is a covenant not to compete. If the covenant not to compete is included in the sales agreement, any amount allocated to the covenant can be amortized over the useful life specified in the sale agreement, provided that such amount is reasonable and supportable under the circumstances. The only reliable way for a buyer to receive a tax deduction for a covenant not to compete is to include it in the sales agreement.

Special rules applicable to a transfer of a franchise, trademark, or trade name provide a tax planning opportunity. To the extent that payments are contingent on the productivity, use, or disposition of the franchise, trademark, or trade name transferred and are paid as part of a series of payments that are payable at least annually over the period of the transfer agreement and are substantially equal in amount (or payable under a fixed formula), the buyer receives an immediate tax deduction for such payments. If an amount paid on account of a transfer, sale, or other disposition of a franchise, trademark, or trade name is not deductible as a contingent serial payment, generally the taxpayer may elect to amortize the amount ratably over a 25-year period.

The Tax Reform Act of 1986 provided a rule requiring both the seller and the buyer to allocate the sales/purchase price among the various assets in the following order: first, to cash and cash items; second, to marketable securities and other similar items in proportion to their fair market values; third, to all other tangible and intangible assets, except for goodwill and going concern value, in proportion to their fair market values; and fourth, to goodwill and going concern value. Trade receivables would be in the third group. In the case of a bargain purchase, a buyer may be required to allocate an amount to the receivables that is less than the face value of the receivables. When this occurs, the buyer has immediate income recognition upon collection of those receivables at face value.

Before 1987, sellers allocated as much sales price as possible to capital assets to benefit from the lower tax rate for capital gains. Furthermore, buyers would allocate as much purchase price as possible to assets that would result in quick tax deductions. Now that capital gains and ordinary income are subject to the same tax rate for corporations and only slightly different rates for individuals, sellers are less likely to be concerned about the allocation of purchase price. However, there still can be tax consequences to the seller as a result of a particular allocation, because, for example, capital losses cannot offset ordinary income. The buyer and seller should consider including the allocation of the purchase price in the sales agreement to minimize potential problems with the IRS, and they will be bound by such an agreement for tax reporting purposes.

Most book/tax timing differences disappear in an asset acquisition. One example of a difference that survives is deferred compensation that has been accrued as a liability, but cannot be deducted until paid. The buyer cannot deduct the payment when made because the services were provided to the seller. If such a liability is assumed by a buyer in an acquisition, no tax deduction is allowable to either the seller or buyer. Accordingly, it may be preferable to leave such a liability with the seller to pay later. Warranty reserves are also treated like deferred liabilities. If the buyer assumes the warranty reserves, no deduction is allowed when the buyer pays claims related to the assumed warranty obligations.

When assets are acquired, the tax attributes and accounting methods of the seller remain with the seller and do not carry over with the purchased assets. If the buyer does not already have established accounting methods, new ones must be adopted. Such accounting method choices include, among others, the year end, a method to calculate inventory costs—for example, First In, First Out (FIFO) or Last In, First Out (LIFO)—and whether to capitalize or expense research and development costs. Most of these decisions must be made in the first tax return filed.

Finally, there are other sundry matters to consider in an asset acquisition. A buyer should be aware that most states impose sales tax when personal property is sold, though some states exempt bulk asset sales from this tax. Most states or local governments impose real property tax, and in California, a revaluation of that property occurs when the property is transferred to an unrelated person.

If a Japanese company purchases the assets of a U.S. business and operates the business as a branch of the Japanese company, for Japanese tax purposes it may be able to amortize goodwill and other intangibles that it has acquired. For Japanese tax purposes, the purchase price is first allocated to tangible and identifiable intangible assets, including patents, trademarks, and so on. If any excess purchase price remains and it represents excess earning power of the business acquired, this excess will be considered goodwill.

For statutory accounting purposes, Japanese corporations are required to amortize goodwill over not more than five years, although the only penalty for not doing so is a comment in the auditor's opinion on the financial statements. At the time that goodwill is written off for book purposes, whether immediately, over five years, or over some other period, the write-off is allowed as a tax deduction.

Other purchased intangibles are also amortizable by the Japanese company when it operates the acquired business as a branch: trademarks may be amortized over ten years, know-how may be amortized over five years, and patents may be amortized over the shorter of the remaining life of the patent or eight years.

Stock Acquisition

In a stock purchase, the tax basis of the underlying assets in the target company and its accounting methods carry over. The year end of the target company may change to conform with that of a U.S. parent in a U.S. consolidated tax return group. The target company's tax attributes that have not been used, such as net operating losses and various tax credits, also carry over.

The use of net operating loss carryovers or built-in losses is limited when there has been a greater than 50 percent change in ownership of the U.S. loss company during a three-year period. The ownership change can occur in either taxable transfers of ownership or tax-free reorganizations. After the ownership change, the losses can only be offset against future income of the loss company. The amount of loss that can be used annually is limited to the value of the loss company at the time of the ownership change multiplied by the federal long-term tax-exempt rate published by the IRS. For example, if a loss corporation is worth $10,000,000 and the rate is 7 percent, under new ownership the loss corporation could use $700,000 of its preownership change net operating losses or built-in losses annually to offset income. Similar restrictions apply to tax credit carryovers following an ownership change.

The loss corporation is also restricted by the requirement that it continue its historic business or use a significant portion of the old assets in a business during the two-year period after the ownership change. Otherwise, the net operating loss would be disallowed in total.

Future losses of a loss company can be used to offset income of any member of its consolidated tax return. Preacquisition net operating losses can be carried over to offset income only of the company that generated the losses. This restriction does not apply if the acquiring company is the loss company. This restriction may be effectively avoided by merging the loss company into a profitable company or transferring profitable business into the loss company. Similar restrictions apply to tax credit carryovers following an ownership change.

A loss company that acquires a target company with a built-in gain is also subject to a limitation. The loss corporation is not allowed to use its losses to shelter tax on built-in gains of a target company that are recognized within five years of the acquisition. Built-in gains include any income item that was attributable to a preacquisition period.

Stock Acquisition with a Step-Up in Tax Basis of Assets

When 80 percent or more of a U.S. company is acquired in a taxable purchase, the acquiring company can elect to treat the target company as having sold its assets and immediately repurchased them. The target company's current tax liability arising from its deemed sale of the assets at fair market value usually exceeds the future tax benefit to be derived from stepping up the tax basis of the assets. Generally, the target company reports its taxable income from a deemed sale of assets in its own separately filed final tax return and not as part of a selling or acquiring parent's consolidated tax return. This election was far more popular prior to 1987, when a target company's gain on the deemed sale generally was not taxable except for depreciation and investment tax credit recapture.

When a target company has a net operating loss that would be either lost or severely restricted, the above election should be considered. The gain on the deemed sale of the target's assets can be offset by the target's net operating loss. Thus, the net operating loss could be used to obtain a step-up in asset basis, although any unused net operating loss would disappear. Otherwise, if the stock of the target company is purchased and no election is made, the loss is carried over to the buyer, but its use is limited.

If the target company is a member of a United States consolidated tax return group, in a stock acquisition both the selling group and purchasing group can jointly elect to treat the sale as an asset sale. In a Section 338 (h)(10) election, the deemed sale of the assets by the target is treated as a taxable sale in the selling group's consolidated tax return. The seller recognizes no gain or loss on the sale of the target company's stock. In other words, there is only one level of tax on the gain and the buyer acquires a target company whose assets have a stepped-up basis for tax purposes.

The Section 338(h)(10) election can be particularly attractive when the seller has net operating losses to offset gain, because the buyer may be able to obtain a step-up in the tax basis recognized on the deemed asset sale without a significant tax cost to either party. The election also can be very tax effective when the basis of the target company's stock in the hands of the seller is not significantly higher than the tax basis of the assets in the hands of the target company. In this situation a buyer may obtain a step-up in the tax basis of assets without significant additional tax cost to the seller. An illustration of the potential benefit of this election appears in Exhibit 5-1.

HOW SHOULD THE OWNERSHIP OF U.S. SUBSIDIARIES BE STRUCTURED?

Consolidated Tax Return

A U.S. parent company can elect to file a consolidated tax return with members of its affiliated group. Affiliated group members are U.S. corporations in which the U.S. parent owns directly, or indirectly through other U.S. subsidiaries, at least 80 percent of the voting power and 80 percent of the total value of the stock. Japanese corporations cannot be included in U.S. consolidated tax returns. Similarly, U.S. sister companies that are subsidiaries of a Japanese

EXHIBIT 5–1
IRC Section 338 (h)(10) Election

Factual setting:

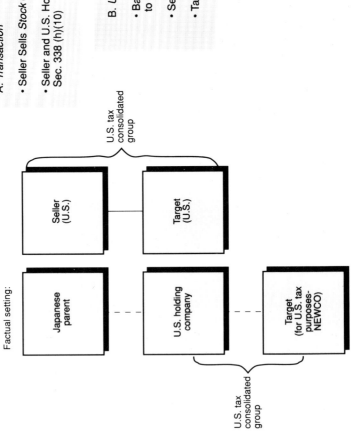

A. *Transaction*

- Seller Sells *Stock* of Target to U.S. Holding Company

- Seller and U.S. Holding Company Jointly Elect IRC Sec. 338 (h)(10)

B. *Useful in situations when:*

- Basis of Target stock in hands of Seller is close to basis of assets in hands of Target

- Seller has net operating losses

- Target has unwanted assets

C. *Results*

- Target is treated as selling its assets to Newco; therefore step up in basis of assets to Newco

- Gain on sale of Target's assets is taxed in Seller's consolidated return

- Only one level of tax

(continued)

Sale of stock

Section 338 (h)(10) election

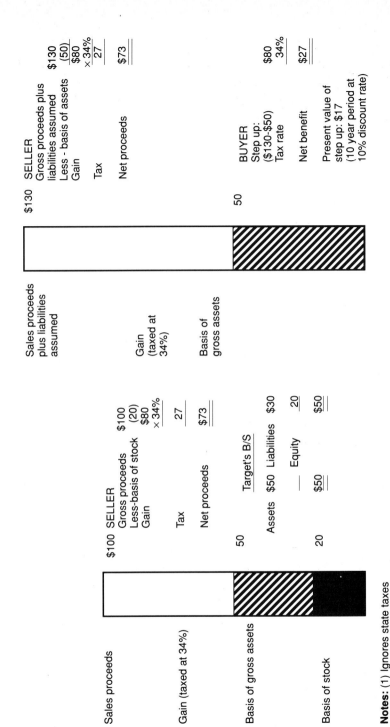

SELLER

Gross proceeds	$100
Less-basis of stock	(20)
Gain	$80
	× 34%
Tax	27
Net proceeds	$73

Target's B/S

Assets	$50	Liabilities	$30
		Equity	20
	$50		$50

SELLER

Gross proceeds plus liabilities assumed	$130
Less - basis of assets	(50)
Gain	$80
	× 34%
Tax	27
Net proceeds	$73

BUYER

Step up: ($130-$50)	$80
Tax rate	34%
Net benefit	$27
Present value of step up: $17 (10 year period at 10% discount rate)	

Sales proceeds

Gain (taxed at 34%)

Basis of gross assets

Basis of stock

$100

50

20

Sales proceeds plus liabilities assumed

Gain (taxed at 34%)

Basis of gross assets

$130

50

Notes: (1) Ignores state taxes
(2) Assumes step-up is attributable to assets that can be deducted for tax purposes

115

parent company cannot file a consolidated return together unless they have a common U.S. parent company (See Exhibit 5-2).

The potential United States tax advantages of filing a consolidated tax return include:

1. The tax loss of one member can offset the taxable income of another member
2. Income derived from sales to members of the consolidated return group is not taxed until the assets giving rise to the gain are disposed of outside the group
3. Dividends can be distributed from one member to another member tax free.

State tax planning can often be implemented within a consolidated tax return group without any adverse U.S. or Japanese tax consequences.

EXHIBIT 5–2
U.S. Consolidated Tax Return

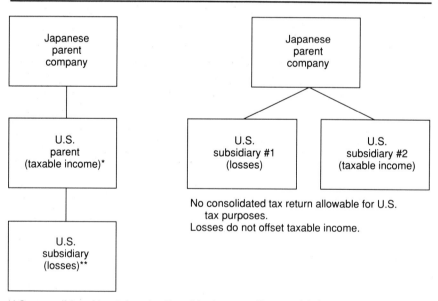

U.S. consolidated tax return is allowable. Losses offset taxable income.

* U.S. parent can be a holding company for many subsidiaries.
** Subsidiary can also have subsidiaries down any number of tiers.

Nearly all United States–owned corporate structures that are eligible to file consolidated tax returns do so in part to benefit from the tax advantages listed previously. One U.S. tax disadvantage of filing a consolidated tax return, however, is that gain recognized from the sale of a subsidiary is subject to U.S. tax. When a corporation is held directly by a foreign shareholder, gain from the sale is generally not subject to U.S. tax provided that the U.S. company is not a U.S. real property holding company. A U.S. company is a U.S. real property holding company if at any time in the five-year period immediately preceding the sale 50 percent or more of the U.S. company's assets consisted of U.S. real estate, natural resources, or both.

Certain disadvantages to filing a consolidated return also exist, particularly if a U.S. subsidiary of a consolidated group is sold at a loss. For Japanese tax purposes, no deduction is allowed when a first-tier U.S. subsidiary sells a second-tier U.S. subsidiary out of a U.S. consolidated group at a loss. Furthermore, it is possible that no loss would be allowed for U.S. purposes in such a situation either. The IRS recently issued regulations that were intended to prevent corporations from using the consolidated return rules to duplicate certain losses; however, the effect of these regulations is that many losses, which in certain circumstances can include true economic losses, may not be recognized upon the sale of a subsidiary from a consolidated group.

Filing a consolidated return triggers several other potentially technical U.S. tax considerations. Changing a U.S. company's structure may or may not be possible without taxation by the United States or Japan, depending on the desired change and the taxpayer's situation.

First-Tier Subsidiaries

As discussed earlier, a Japanese parent receiving a dividend from a U.S. subsidiary can claim a deemed-paid foreign tax credit for U.S., state, and foreign income taxes paid with respect to the earnings distributed as a dividend. For example, assume that a U.S. subsidiary has pre-tax earnings of 100 and federal and state income tax of 40 for a year. If the U.S. subsidiary pays a dividend of 30, the Japanese parent would receive 27 in cash after deducting the 10 percent U.S. withholding tax. The Japanese parent would also report as a dividend the deemed-paid foreign tax credit of 20 that is the U.S. subsidiary's U.S. and state income tax attributable to the 30 of earnings paid in dividends to the Japanese parent. The Japanese parent could claim a foreign tax credit of 23, comprising 3 of direct withholding tax and 20 of deemed-paid foreign tax credit.

Under Japanese tax law only income taxes incurred by first-tier or directly owned U.S. subsidiaries are eligible to be claimed as foreign tax credits by the Japanese parent. In other words, if there is a U.S. consolidated tax return group, only income taxes paid by the U.S. parent are potentially creditable against Japanese tax. Accordingly, many Japanese companies hold their U.S. and other foreign subsidiaries directly to allow maximum potential future deemed-paid foreign tax credit when earnings are repatriated to Japan.

When U.S. subsidiaries are directly held, the U.S. tax advantages of filing a U.S. consolidated tax return are not available. Accordingly, many Japanese companies are rethinking the structure for their U.S. subsidiaries, particularly when earnings of these subsidiaries are largely reinvested in the United States.

When a Japanese parent has a U.S. consolidated tax return group, the U.S. parent is often an operating company because, if the U.S. parent's income is generated only by dividend income from its subsidiaries, the parent's dividend income will not be subject to U.S. tax and thus no deemed-paid foreign tax credits are allowed. The U.S. parent's business and assets should generate sufficient earnings to distribute normal dividends and pay adequate taxes to provide acceptable deemed-paid foreign tax credits with the dividend. Interest income, derived from loans by the U.S. parent to U.S. subsidiaries, can also help to increase the U.S. parent's earnings and U.S. tax burden while reducing the U.S. subsidiaries' share of the U.S. taxes.

For Japanese parents with more than one U.S. subsidiary, combined Japanese and U.S. tax planning opportunities would be enhanced by changing Japanese tax law to allow deemed-paid foreign tax credit for income taxes paid by subsidiaries lower than the first-tier. Under U.S. tax law, deemed-paid foreign tax credits are allowable for foreign taxes paid by first-, second-, and third-tier foreign subsidiaries.

WHERE SHOULD FUNDS BE BORROWED TO FINANCE A U.S. BUSINESS OR ACQUISITION?

The funds to start, expand, or acquire a U.S. business of a Japanese parent could be borrowed in Japan, the United States, elsewhere, or some combination of the three. Alternatively, the funds can be obtained by withdrawing them from existing investments.

When the Japanese parent borrows funds in Japan, the Japanese parent could either invest the funds in a U.S. subsidiary as equity (see Exhibit 5-3) or loan the funds as debt (see Exhibit 5-4). Borrowing by the Japanese parent offers several advantages. First, interest is deductible against Japanese taxable income. Because of the higher effective tax rate in Japan, this can result in a higher tax benefit. Second, an established banking relationship may make borrowing easier and faster. Third, the current interest rate on yen loans from Japanese banks may be lower than on United States dollar loans. On the other hand, a disadvantage is that foreign tax credit utilization may be reduced by interest expense at the Japanese parent level, since interest expense is partially allocated in Japan against foreign source income for purposes of computing the foreign tax credit limitation. One economic issue to consider with this approach to financing is the Japanese parent's exchange risk in holding a U.S. dollar investment funded by what may be a yen obligation. Japanese companies have become very familiar with this issue with the strengthening of the yen since 1985.

Borrowing by a U.S. operating company allows that company to deduct the interest expense to reduce its taxable income (see Exhibit 5-5). This also reduces U.S. profits that could be repatriated to Japan and that would be subject to U.S. withholding tax.

A highly leveraged acquisition of either assets or stock by a U.S. subsidiary or Japanese corporation otherwise subject to U.S. taxation may have unexpected results with respect to the interest paid or accrued on such debt. Legislation enacted in 1989 precludes a corporation that acquires the stock of a target corporation from using net operating losses created by interest deductions on debt incurred in the acquisition to offset the target's income for prior years (i.e., through the carryback of net operating losses). Additional legislation enacted in 1989 restricts an issuer's ability to

EXHIBIT 5–3
Borrow and Deduct Interest in Japan

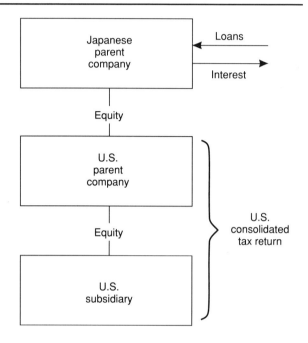

A. Advantages:

    (1) Allows interest to be deducted against higher-taxed Japanese sourced profits.

    (2) Establishes higher cost base for Japanese company's investment in the U.S. parent company

B. Disadvantages:

    (1) Results in U.S. tax on profits before interest expense.

    (2) Interest expense may reduce Japanese parent's foreign tax credit limitation.

deduct interest on certain high-yield, long-term debt instruments with significant amounts of deferred interest (i.e., interest accrued but not paid until a later date) regardless of whether assets or stock is acquired. A portion of such deferred interest is not deductible until paid, while the remaining portion is not deductible at all. The holder of the debt is required to treat the nondeductible portion of the deferred interest as a dividend for certain purposes, but the

EXHIBIT 5–4
Borrow in Japan and Deduct Interest in the United States

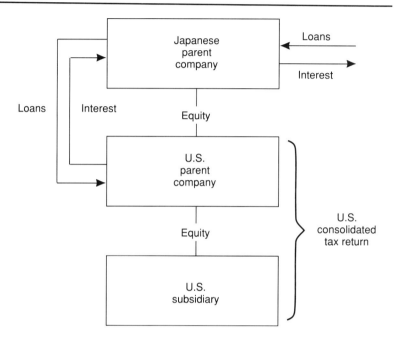

A. Advantages:

(1) Allows interest to be deducted against U.S. profits.

B. Disadvantages:

(1) Results in Japanese tax on interest income.
(2) Interest expense reduces Japanese parent's foreign tax credit limitation.
(3) 10% U.S. withholding tax on interest paid to Japanese parent.
(4) Interest expense deduction by U.S. parent company is subject to earnings stripping limitation.

withholding and deemed-paid foreign tax credit implications of such treatment are unclear.

In purely U.S. structures, a U.S. holding company often borrows funds to acquire a new subsidiary. The parent company's interest expense can offset the subsidiary's income in a consolidated tax return. However, if a U.S. parent is owned by a Japanese parent, this may be undesirable because the U.S. parent's U.S. tax

EXHIBIT 5–5
Borrow and Deduct Interest in the United States

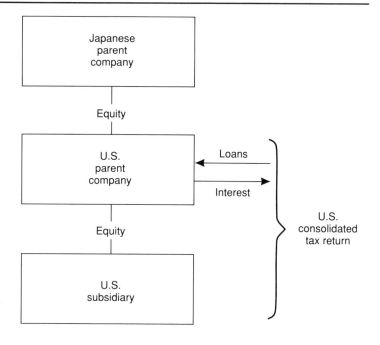

A. Advantages:

(1) Provides a natural hedge against exchange exposure.

(2) Ensures that U.S. tax is paid only on net profit after taking into account interest expense.

B. Disadvantages:

(1) Establishes a lower cost base for the Japanese company's investment in the U.S. parent company.

liability and potential to generate deemed-paid foreign tax credits would be diminished. Accordingly, a Japanese-owned U.S. consolidated return group may do its borrowing through one or more subsidiaries in the U.S. consolidated tax return group.

A U.S. subsidiary may borrow funds from a United States branch or subsidiary of a Japanese bank with the loan guaranteed by the Japanese parent company. No U.S. withholding tax should apply to interest income earned by a U.S. subsidiary or branch of a Japanese bank.

In order to avoid U.S. withholding tax on interest paid to a U.S. branch of a foreign bank, the interest must be effectively connected with the U.S. trade or business of the foreign bank. The key factor in determining whether U.S. source income is effectively connected income is whether the U.S. branch of a foreign bank actively and materially participates in the solicitation, negotiation, and performance of other activities required to arrange the loan. The other activities include soliciting the customer's business, negotiating with the customer concerning the terms of the loan, analyzing the customer's credit-worthiness, preparing and executing loan documentation, and ongoing servicing of the loan. The latter includes performing ongoing credit analyses, disbursement of future advances, and collecting loan interest.

When the Japanese parent loans funds to a United States subsidiary, the interest payments to the Japanese parent are deductible against U.S. taxable income unless the interest expense is disallowed under the earning stripping provision (discussed below). In addition, no deduction is allowed to a U.S. taxpayer with respect to amounts accrued to a related foreign person until such amounts are actually paid. Nevertheless, the Japanese parent must recognize accrued interest income from the U.S. subsidiary. A 10 percent U.S. interest withholding tax will be imposed on interest paid by a U.S. subsidiary to its Japanese parent company.

If a U.S. company borrows funds from a lender located outside the United States, a 30 percent tax may be withheld on interest payments to the foreign lender.

To minimize the interest cost on debt owed to foreign lenders, a U.S. borrower tries to avoid or minimize U.S. withholding tax. There is an exemption from U.S. withholding tax for portfolio interest paid on certain portfolio debt. Portfolio debt can be in either registered or bearer form. In general terms, to qualify a loan as portfolio debt requires the following:

1. Certain procedural requirements must be fulfilled for either bearer or registered debt to ensure that the debt instruments are held by non–U.S. persons and the interest is paid outside the United States.

2. The interest cannot be received by an entity that owns directly, indirectly, or by attribution 10 percent or more of the borrower.
3. The lender cannot be a foreign bank.

Accordingly, a Japanese lender that is not a bank and owns less than 10 percent of the borrower may be able to receive interest income from a U.S. debtor, free of U.S. withholding tax.

Avoiding Thin Capitalization

Thin capitalization exists when an owner of a subsidiary uses so much debt and so little equity to capitalize its subsidiary that the IRS can successfully assert that the debt should be treated as equity. For example, if a Japanese parent capitalized its U.S. subsidiary with $1 million equity and $50 million of debt, the U.S. subsidiary would be thinly capitalized. The U.S. tax consequences to the Japanese parent of a U.S. subsidiary can be severe if the parent chooses to thinly capitalize its subsidiary. If the debt is treated as equity for U.S. tax purposes, no deduction is allowable for interest. Furthermore, both interest and principal payments are treated as dividends subject to U.S. withholding tax to the extent of the payer's current or cumulative earnings.

Japanese tax law does not address the concept of thin capitalization. Therefore, Japanese companies may not be as familiar with the concept as United States taxpayers are. This is a potential trap that should be carefully avoided because of the adverse U.S. tax consequences.

In 1969 Congress directed the IRS to issue regulations with guidelines for determining when thin capitalization exists. The IRS proposed and withdrew various regulations on the subject. There are no official thin capitalization rules other than those outlined in many court cases, which sometimes conflict. In 1989, Congress authorized the Treasury to prescribe regulations as may be necessary to determine whether an interest in a corporation is to be treated as stock or indebtedness for U.S. income tax purposes. Based on past IRS attempts to promulgate regulations, a thin capitalization issue should be avoided if the following guidelines are satisfied:

1. The loan is documented by a note.
2. The loan bears an arm's length interest rate.
3. The inside (or related party) debt to equity ratio does not exceed 3:1.
4. The total (related and unrelated party) debt to equity ratio does not exceed 10:1.
5. The debt is serviced when payments are due.

Proper planning and documentation should allow a Japanese parent to avoid thin capitalization of its U.S. subsidiaries.

Avoiding Earnings Stripping Limitation

The earnings stripping provision in the Revenue Reconciliation Act of 1989 may change some of the conventional financing in connection with related party loans from a Japanese parent company to its U.S. subsidiary. The earnings stripping provision may disallow deductions for interest paid by a U.S. corporation to related foreign corporations when the recipient is not subject to full U.S. tax on the interest received, including a pro-rata disallowance where a tax treaty reduces the otherwise 30 percent U.S. withholding tax.

Interest received by a Japanese corporation that is subject to a 10% withholding tax under the Japan-United States tax treaty is partially treated as disqualified interest. The portion that is disqualified interest is the amount obtained by multiplying the total interest by the ratio that the treaty rate reduction bears to the 30 percent rates. Therefore, in the case of interest received by a Japanese corporation, two-thirds of the interest will be treated as disqualified interest.

A U.S. corporation's interest deductions can be limited with respect to any disqualified interest when that corporation has excess interest expense for the taxable year and the debt to equity ratio of the United States corporation exceeds 1.5:1. Excess interest expense is the excess of a corporation's net interest expense, over the sum of (1) 50 percent of the payer's taxable income excluding net interest expense, net operating loss carryovers, depreciation, amortization, or depletion; and (2) excess limitation. Ex-

EXHIBIT 5–6
Earnings Stripping Limitation

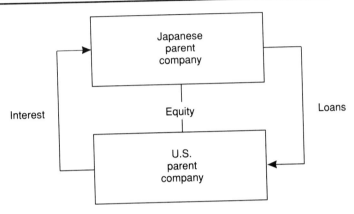

Assume the following:	Year 1	Year 2	Year 3
U.S. company taxable income (loss) before net interest expense, depreciation, amortization	1,000	900	200
Interest paid to Japanese parent	500	700	700
Interest income of U.S. parent	10	10	10

Limitation Calculation:	Year 1	Year 2	Year 3
Disqualified interest (two-thirds)	333	467	467
Adjusted taxable income	1,000	900	200
50% of adjusted taxable income	500	450	100
Add: Limitation carryforward	0	10	0
Subtotal-	500	460	100
Less: Net interest expense	(490)	(690)	(690)
Excess interest expense	0	230	590
Excess limitation	10	0	0
Interest disallowed	0	230	467

cess limitation is the excess, if any, of 50 percent of the corporation's adjusted taxable income over the corporation's net interest expense. An illustration of the earnings stripping calculation is shown in Exhibit 5-6.

The earnings stripping limitation is effective for interest paid or accrued in taxable years beginning after July 10, 1989, except on debt instruments with fixed terms that were outstanding on that day.

The legislative history states that relevant regulations may provide that interest paid to an unrelated third party will be treated as disqualified interest if the use of guaranteed third-party debt is a device for avoiding the operation of the earnings stripping rules.

The earnings stripping limitation on the deduction of interest expense may be minimized or avoided in several ways. When financing would otherwise be obtained from a Japanese bank by the Japanese parent, the U.S. subsidiary could borrow directly from the unrelated party in Japan or from a U.S. branch or U.S. subsidiary of the Japanese bank.

HOW SHOULD JOINT VENTURES WITH U.S. COMPANIES BE STRUCTURED?

In the United States, a joint venture may be structured as either a partnership or a corporation. The partnership form does not exist in Japan and is not always familiar to Japanese companies. U.S. companies often use partnerships. Partnerships do not pay taxes; they function as conduits. This allows partnership losses or income to flow through to the partners, which in turn permits each partner to do its own tax planning. Partnerships can also be used to specially allocate income or deductions among the partners.

The conduit nature of a partnership avoids another level of tax when a partnership is profitable. If a corporate joint venture is used instead of a partnership, the corporation pays regular federal and state taxes on its income. A dividend distribution from the corporate joint venture to a U.S. corporate shareholder would also be taxable to the U.S. corporate shareholder, unless it owns 80 percent or more of the joint venture corporation. If the U.S. corporate shareholder owns less than 20 percent of the corporate joint venture, 30 percent of the dividend is taxable. If the ownership is between 20 and 80 percent, the taxable portion of the dividend is 20 percent.

Partnerships can also have disadvantages. General partners are exposed to unlimited liability for obligations of the partnership. A limited partner can have limited liability but cannot participate in the management of the business. This means that partners in an active business usually will be general partners.

Liability exposure may be restricted by having a separate U.S. subsidiary act as the general partner in the partnership. The liability exposure is limited to the assets of the U.S. subsidiary, in theory, although in many cases, other affiliates and the Japanese parent may remain liable because of the shipment of a product, the transfer of technology, or the need to protect their business reputation.

From a tax standpoint, whether a Japanese corporation should enter into a corporate or partnership joint venture depends largely on whether the interest will be held directly by the Japanese parent or by a U.S. subsidiary.

If a Japanese parent owns a partnership interest directly, the Japanese parent's share of the partnership's income or loss is subject to the same U.S. and Japanese tax treatment as a U.S. branch, which was discussed earlier. Accordingly, the Japanese parent files U.S. federal and state income tax returns. This may not be desirable unless the partnership is expected to generate significant losses that can be used by the Japanese parent to reduce Japanese taxable income.

For Japanese accounting and tax purposes, Japanese companies may select from three alternatives for recording their partnership investment:

- They may record their pro-rata share of each asset and liability of the partnership, and recognize their pro-rata share of each item of income and expense, as if they owned an undivided interest in the assets of the partnership.
- They may record their investment in the partnership as a single line item, but recognize on their income statement their pro-rata share of each item of income and expense.
- They may record their investment in the partnership as a single line item and recognize on their income statement as a single line item their pro-rata share of the partnership's net income or loss.

If the Japanese company selects the first method, it may adopt Japanese depreciation and amortization methods, which may yield a faster write-off than those recognized by the partnership. This would be particularly advantageous if the partnership has purchased intangibles, such as goodwill. Japanese companies may not write off goodwill immediately and are required to write it off over five years. In all three cases, a Japanese company is required to adjust its share of the partnership's income for entertainment expenses, which are not deductible in Japan, and for depreciation and amortization if the partnership is claiming these expenses more rapidly than allowed in Japan.

If either of the first two methods is used, the Japanese companies may claim a foreign tax credit for taxes paid by the partnership. An indirect credit can be claimed in respect of dividends received by the partnership (assuming the Japanese company's proportionate ownership of the distributing U.S. corporation is at least 10%). If the third method is used, no foreign tax credit is available for taxes paid by the partnership or its subsidiaries.

One further complexity is that a U.S. partnership's U.S. business income attributable to foreign partners is subject to U.S. withholding tax. The withholding tax is 31 percent for effectively connected taxable income attributable to individual Japanese partners and 34 percent for Japanese corporate partners. The withholding tax is not a final tax, but rather an estimated tax payment toward the Japanese parent's U.S. tax liability.

On the other hand, a Japanese parent's direct ownership in a U.S. corporate joint venture results in the same tax treatment as ownership of a U.S. subsidiary, assuming that the Japanese parent has a greater than 10 percent interest, which enables it to claim deemed-paid foreign tax credit with respect to dividends. For direct ownership by the Japanese parent of a profitable U.S. joint venture, use of a corporate joint venture is often preferable.

If a U.S. subsidiary holds the interest in the joint venture, generally, from a tax standpoint, a partnership structure is preferable to allow losses to flow through and avoid double taxation of income. Whether the U.S. subsidiary should be directly held by a Japanese parent or by a member of a U.S. consolidated tax return group raises the same issues discussed previously.

CONCLUSION

U.S. Judge Learned Hand observed in 1934 that ''any one may so arrange his affairs that his taxes shall be as low as possible; he is not bound to choose that pattern which will best pay the Treasury; there is not even a patriotic duty to increase one's taxes.'' For a Japanese company investing in the United States, one challenge is developing a tax plan that will minimize combined U.S. and Japanese taxes without unduly disrupting nontax considerations.

PART 2

BANKING, FINANCE, AND INSURANCE

CHAPTER 6

BANKING AND FINANCE IN THE UNITED STATES

Charles H. Eggleston, CPA
Price Waterhouse

OVERVIEW OF THE U.S. BANKING SYSTEM

Nature and Size of the Banking Industry

The commercial banking industry in the United States is composed of approximately 12,500 privately owned banks having combined total assets of $3.4 trillion. However, many of these institutions are small; more than three quarters of all commercial banks in the country have total assets of less than $100 million.

Commercial banks are chartered under either federal or state laws and are regulated by various federal and state supervisory agencies. Federally chartered banks are referred to as national banks and are regulated by the Office of the Comptroller of the Currency, a division of the U.S. Department of the Treasury. National banks, of which there are approximately 4,000, are required to be members of the Federal Reserve System and the Federal Deposit Insurance Corporation (FDIC). Federally chartered banks must include the word *National* or the initials *N.A.* (National Association) as part of the bank's name.

State-chartered banks are regulated by the bank supervisory authorities of the state in which they are headquartered. Of the 8,400 state-chartered banks in the United States, approximately

TABLE 6–1
U.S. Banking Industry as of June 30, 1990 (Amounts in Billions)

	Assets	Loans	Deposits
National banks	$1,983	$1,267	$1,521
State member banks	566	312	401
State nonmember banks	809	491	665
Total	$3,358	$2,070	$2,587

1,000 are members of the Federal Reserve System. All member banks, as they are called, are also insured by the FDIC. State-chartered banks that are not members of the Federal Reserve System, of which there are 7,400, generally have their deposits insured by the FDIC.

Many banks, especially the large banks, are subsidiaries of bank holding companies, which are regulated by the Board of Governors of the Federal Reserve System (Federal Reserve Board) as well as the bank regulatory agencies of the states in which they are incorporated. In addition to traditional loan, deposit, trust, and other banking services, bank holding companies are permitted to engage in certain related financial services. Such services include mortgage banking, consumer and commercial finance, leasing, securities brokerage, factoring accounts receivable, underwriting and dealing in certain securities, insurance, and data processing.

In summary, as of June 30, 1990, total assets, total loans, and total deposits for the principal components of the U.S. banking industry are shown in Table 6–1.

Foreign Banks in the United States

Many foreign banks have banking operations in the United States in the form of representative offices, agencies, branches, or subsidiaries. There are nearly six hundred U.S. branches and agencies of foreign banks, having total assets of approximately $600 billion. These branches and agencies tend to serve foreign customers and tend to be wholesale-oriented. Foreign banking organizations, including U.S.-chartered banks owned by foreigners, account for nearly 30 percent of wholesale banking in the United States. Legally, foreign-owned banks chartered in the United States are subject to the same regulations as domestically owned banks chartered in the United States.

Prior to 1978, foreign banks entering the United States established state-licensed branches or agencies in those states where state law permitted such entities. The International Banking Act of 1978 permitted foreign banks to establish one or more federally licensed branches or agencies in the United States subject to the approval and rules and regulations of the Office of the Comptroller of the Currency. The act provides that the operations of such branches and agencies are to be conducted with the same rights and privileges as those of a national bank. The powers of state-licensed branches are similar, but may vary from state to state.

Representative Offices
Authorized by state law, representative offices of foreign banks are permitted to perform various services for their parent banks such as arranging for loans from the parent or arranging for deposits to be made with the parent. Representative offices may not engage in actual banking activities. A representative office may solicit business for the account of the head office, but it cannot make any commitments on behalf of the head office involving loan transactions and the purchase and sale of funds, notes, and bills of exchange. In addition, a representative office cannot receive payments on behalf of the head office. Consequently, a representative office is not subject to regulation by federal banking regulators. It may be subject to relatively little supervision or regulation by state banking authorities, depending upon the state in which the office is licensed.

Agencies
Agencies may be federally or state-licensed and are permitted to conduct a general banking business in the United States. An agency may lend money or pay checks, but it may not accept deposits. Agencies primarily make commercial and corporate loans and finance international transactions. They can engage in a broad range of banking powers, including making loans; buying, selling, and collecting bills of exchange; issuing letters of credit; paying and collecting activities for the parent foreign bank; and selling or issu-

ing checks, drafts, travelers checks, money orders, and similar instruments.

Branches
A U.S. branch office of a foreign bank may handle payments and settlements, obtain U.S. dollars, invest temporarily excess funds, provide information on local financial and business conditions, and arrange loans and participation in loans and other extensions of credit for the home office and other branches. A U.S. branch office may also provide banking services such as lending, acceptance of deposits, and foreign exchange operations for home office customers, including U.S. subsidiaries of foreign corporate customers.

A branch's lending limit is based on the capital of the parent bank rather than the capital of the branch itself. However, the branch is subject to examination by the licensing state. U.S. branches of foreign banks account for about 15 percent of all commercial and industrial loans in the United States.

Subsidiary Banks
Branches, agencies, and representative offices are viewed as operations of the parent bank. Subsidiary banks are separate legal entities chartered in the United States, the shares of which are owned or controlled by the parent. Bank subsidiaries of foreign banks in the United States are subject to the same restrictions as domestic banks. They have the same powers, including the ability to perform trust functions, to accept deposits, and to obtain deposit insurance from the FDIC.

Federal Reserve System

The Federal Reserve Act of 1913 created the Federal Reserve System, which serves as the central bank of the United States. The Federal Reserve consists of 12 district Federal Reserve Banks and is headed by a 7-member Board of Governors. Members of the Federal Reserve Board are appointed by the President of the United States for a 14-year term.

As the central bank for the United States, the Federal Reserve is responsible for managing monetary policy through the credit and money markets by using the following tools.

Discount Rate

The discount rate is the interest rate charged by the Federal Reserve Banks for borrowings by member banks. Such borrowings from the Federal Reserve Bank must be fully secured by pledged securities or loans satisfying certain terms and conditions. In recent years the discount rate has generally lagged the movements of rates in the money markets. An increase in the discount rate generally signals tighter monetary conditions, while a decrease in the rate generally signals a desire to increase economic activity.

Reserve Requirements

Member and nonmember banks of the Federal Reserve System must maintain reserves against deposits in accordance with Federal Reserve Regulation D. Reserve amounts are determined based upon a percentage of net transaction accounts, nonpersonal time deposits, and Eurocurrency liabilities. An increase in reserve requirements reduces the amount of funds available for loans and investments by banks, and thus inhibits the growth of economic activity. A decline in reserve requirements increases the amount of funds available in the banking system for loans and investments. This action serves as a stimulus to increase economic activity. Changes in reserve requirements are infrequent and are ordinarily used only in correcting serious dislocations in the economy.

Open-Market Activities

The overwhelming majority of open-market transactions by the Federal Reserve are purchases or sales of short-term U.S. government securities, primarily for the purpose of quickly increasing or decreasing total bank reserves and thus the supply of credit available. Purchases of securities on the open market increase bank reserves, while sales of securities reduce bank reserves. Such sales and purchases are carried out daily by the Federal Reserve Bank of New York within the policy directives established by the Federal Open Market Committee. The committee is composed of all 7 members of the Federal Reserve Board and the presidents of 5 of the 12 Federal Reserve Banks. Open-market operations represent the most effective and most commonly used means of influencing the credit and money markets.

Margin Requirements

The Federal Reserve Board has the power to control speculative use of credit by setting margin requirements on the purchase of equity securities. These requirements limit the amounts that may be borrowed to purchase securities. Margin requirements apply to all securities brokers and dealers as well as to all banks. By changing margin requirements, the Federal Reserve Board can significantly change the amount of credit available to purchase and hold securities.

National Clearing House

The Federal Reserve also acts as a national clearing house for payments among banks. Millions of checks and other items are cleared daily through the Federal Reserve System by its member banks, either for their own account or on behalf of their correspondent banks. Since the Federal Reserve charges a fee for the service of clearing checks, banks may also clear items directly with other banks through accounts maintained with those banks or through local clearing houses. Also, as part of its key role in the country's payments system, the Federal Reserve operates the electronic funds transfer system called Fedwire. This system enables banks and their customers to transfer funds electronically among member banks.

Regulation of Banking Organizations

The banking industry in the United States is highly regulated, and banks are subject to periodic supervisory examinations and extensive compliance reporting requirements. The scope of such examinations includes extensive reviews and evaluations of the system of internal control, the quality of bank assets, and the effectiveness of management. Any violations of banking laws or regulations or unsound practices found by regulatory examiners are commented upon in their reports, which demand immediate management attention and action. Typically, formal management responses to each of the exceptions or violations noted in such reports of examination are required by regulatory agencies. Supervisory authorities also have power to grant and revoke charters or licenses previously granted and to liquidate banking institutions that are in a troubled financial condition.

Federal Reserve Board

The Federal Reserve Board is responsible for regulating the activities of state-chartered banks that are members of the Federal Reserve System, bank holding companies, the U.S. operations of foreign banks, and Edge Act and Agreement corporations. In addition, the Board approves or denies applications for mergers, acquisitions, and changes in control by state member banks and bank holding companies, and approves or denies applications for foreign operation of member banks.

In addition, Congress selected the Federal Reserve to write regulations implementing a number of consumer protection laws, such as truth in lending and equal credit opportunity. While the Federal Reserve has the exclusive authority to write such regulations, it can enforce them only with respect to state member banks. The regulations also apply to other depository institutions and are enforced by their principal federal regulator.

Office of the Comptroller of the Currency

The Office of the Comptroller of the Currency (OCC) is the oldest federal banking regulatory agency, having been established as a bureau of the Treasury Department by the National Currency Act of 1863. It is headed by the Comptroller, who is appointed to a five-year term by the President of the United States. The Comptroller also serves on the boards of the Federal Deposit Insurance Corporation and the Resolution Trust Corporation.

The OCC regulates and supervises about 4,000 national banks, with about $2 trillion in combined total assets, which represents about 60 percent of the total assets of all U.S. commercial banks. The OCC has the authority to approve or deny applications for new national bank charters, for the establishment of branches, and for mergers of national banks.

The principal supervisory tools of the OCC are on-site examination and ongoing analysis of national bank operations. The OCC issues rules and regulations concerning bank lending, bank investment, and other aspects of bank operations.

Federal Deposit Insurance Corporation

The Federal Deposit Insurance Corporation (FDIC) was created in 1933 and is headed by a five-member board of directors. The Chairman of the FDIC is designated by the President of the United States for a term of five years.

The FDIC directs two federal deposit insurance programs—the Bank Insurance Fund (BIF) and the Savings Association Insurance Fund (SAIF). The basic insured amount for a depositor is $100,000 at each insured financial institution. The BIF has created an insurance fund through income from investments in U.S. government securities and from annual assessments paid by all insured commercial banks, certain federal and state savings banks, and industrial banks.

The FDIC has the authority to examine insured financial institutions either directly or in cooperation with state or other federal authorities. Its primary regulatory and supervisory authority is confined to insured state-chartered banks that are not members of the Federal Reserve System. The FDIC's supervisory authority has been extended to savings associations in that the FDIC may prohibit activities that pose a serious threat to the SAIF and may limit powers of state-chartered savings associations to those permitted for a federal savings association.

In addition to ruling on applications for deposit insurance coverage, the FDIC protects depositors of failed banks, promotes stability, and maintains public confidence in the banking system. The FDIC acts as the receiver of failed state and national banks and as liquidator of their assets. In conjunction with these responsibilities, the FDIC is authorized to provide various kinds of financial assistance.

State Banking Regulators

Each of the 50 states has a banking supervisor, usually called the bank commissioner or the banking superintendent. The state supervisor is the primary regulator for banks chartered by his or her state; the job's responsibilities are similar in nature to those of the Comptroller of the Currency for regulating national banks. Many state supervisors also regulate state-chartered savings and loan associations or other state-chartered thrift institutions. Most states require their state-chartered banks to maintain federal deposit insurance coverage.

COMMERCIAL BANKING SERVICES

Credit Facilities

The principal service of banks is the extension of credit to individuals, partnerships, corporations, nonprofit organizations, financial institutions, and so on. In general, loans account for about 60 percent of bank assets. Most bank loans are in the form of promissory notes, which are unconditional promises made in writing by the borrower to repay the lender a specific amount of money, usually at some specified date. Bank loans may be secured or unsecured, but most are secured by collateral such as inventory, accounts receivable, plant and equipment, stocks and bonds, and real estate. In addition, the maximum loan to one borrower under national banking laws is 15 percent of capital as defined by the OCC. In the case of loans secured by marketable collateral, the lending limit to one borrower is 25 percent. Individual bank policies, however, may set lending limits lower than the legal maximums.

Following is a description of the principal types of commercial loan commitments and other kinds of bank credit facilities for businesses. There are four principal types of commercial loan commitments: line of credit, revolving credit, term loan, and revolving credit that converts to a term loan. The purpose of the loan commitment is to provide some assurance to the business borrower that funds will be available if and when they are needed.

Line of Credit

A line of credit is an agreement under which a borrower can borrow up to a predetermined limit on a short-term basis, generally one year. Since a line of credit is not a legal commitment, the bank may cancel or change the amount of the limit at any time based on changes in the borrower's financial condition. This arrangement is subject to certain short-term repayment conditions and usually requires a "clean-up" period, generally one or two months each year, during which all funds drawn by the borrower must be repaid. A company does not have to use a line of credit and incurs a cost only for the amount borrowed.

The bank usually establishes the line of credit in a letter to the prospective borrower that states the general terms of the line of credit. The principal terms include the amount of the line, the time during which the line is in effect, and any conditions applicable to the line. Loans made under a line of credit are usually payable either on demand or 90 days after the loan is made.

Revolving Credit

Revolving credit is a formal legal agreement under which a bank agrees to lend up to a certain maximum amount for a specified period of time, generally two to three years. A borrower who is in compliance with the terms of the loan agreement may borrow the difference between the amount of the revolving credit commitment and the total principal amount of all loans outstanding under the commitment. The unique feature of a revolving credit facility is that the borrower has the right to prepay a loan and then reborrow funds up to the amount of the commitment as often as he or she wishes during the term of the agreement. For administrative reasons, it is common to require that each loan under a revolving credit be of a minimum specified amount, or multiples thereof, in order to limit the number of transactions that the bank is required to process.

Typically, such facilities are often used to satisfy a borrower's seasonal needs. As described above for a line of credit, a revolving credit facility generally requires an annual clean-up period during which no loans are outstanding. For example, a bank may require that all loans under the commitment be repaid in full for a period of 30 consecutive days during each of the borrower's fiscal years. This ensures that the loan proceeds under the revolving credit are used to meet seasonal needs.

Term Loan

A term loan is a formal legal agreement under which a bank will lend a certain dollar amount for a specific period exceeding one year. The loan is generally amortized over the life of the loan, but may be paid in a lump sum at maturity. In contrast to a revolving credit facility, a borrower who has repaid any portion of a term loan is not able to reborrow those funds.

In general, the proceeds of a term loan are used for a specific purpose such as to purchase a piece of equipment, renovate a building, redeem stock of the borrower, or refinance existing debt. Since a term loan is typically used for a single purpose, the amount of the loan and the repayment schedule can be matched closely to the specific transaction being financed.

Revolving Credit into Term Loan

A credit arrangement whereby a revolving credit facility is converted into a term loan is commonly referred to as "terming out" a revolving credit. Under this arrangement, which is a very common credit facility, a term loan is made on the date the revolving credit terminates. The amount of the term loan is any amount up to that of the revolving credit commitment. In essence, the term loan is used to repay the revolving credit.

Banker's Acceptances

A banker's acceptance is a time draft drawn on and accepted by a commercial bank. When drafts are accepted, a bank unconditionally promises to pay to the holder the face amount of the draft at maturity, thereby creating a banker's acceptance. Most banker's acceptances arise in international transactions between exporters and importers in different countries. A banker's acceptance is a means of financing a customer's identifiable transactions, such as the shipment of goods by a third party. In essence, the bank substitutes its credit for that of its customer. A banker's acceptance is secured by the customer and the underlying goods in the transaction.

Since there is some tangible security for the bank, acceptance financing is a safer risk for the bank and thus is often slightly less costly overall to the bank customer. However, because of the identifiable transaction requirement, a banker's acceptance is used less frequently than other forms of credit.

Banker's acceptances created by U.S. banks generally finance one of three types of transactions: (1) U.S. imports, (2) U.S. exports, and (3) the storage of goods in a foreign country or shipment of goods between two foreign countries. The maturities of banker's acceptances, which may not exceed 270 days, are generally 30, 60, or 90 days, with 90 days being the most common.

Letters of Credit

Commercial letters of credit are financial instruments issued by a bank in favor of an exporter or other designated beneficiary. The letter of credit obligates the bank to pay the exporter a specified amount of money after certain conditions are fulfilled. In essence, the bank substitutes its credit for that of an importer by guaranteeing payment if the correct documents are submitted. The exporter can usually obtain payment as soon as the necessary documentation has been provided to fulfill the contract.

A standby letter of credit represents a form of bank financial guarantee that a customer will satisfy a financial commitment. It is a contractual agreement issued by a commercial bank that involves three parties: the bank, the bank's customer, and a beneficiary. If the bank's customer fails to comply with the terms and conditions of the commercial contract, the bank guarantees the performance of the contract in accordance with the terms of the standby letter of credit. No funds are advanced by the bank unless the contract is breached by the bank's customer and the bank has to honor its guarantee. A standby letter of credit is payable only upon presentation of evidence of default or nonperformance on the part of the bank's customer. Standby letters of credit are used as backup lines of credit to support the sale of commercial paper, municipal bond offerings, and direct loans such as construction lending. Most standby letters of credit are issued by large, well-known banks that have the highest credit standing.

Leasing

Another form of bank credit is leasing, in which the bank purchases property to be leased to a customer. Leasing is a form of secured lending in which the bank, as lessor, retains actual title to the equipment while the lessee is the user of the equipment. Leasing is viewed by most bankers as an extension of their commercial lending activities. Bank leasing activities involve personal property such as commercial aircraft, ocean-going oil tankers, computers, office equipment, automobiles, trucks, and machinery.

International Banking Activities

The international banking activities of U.S. commercial banks may take place through Edge Act corporations, Agreement corporations, and International Banking Facilities. As is true of foreign banks in the United States, domestic U.S. banks may establish representative offices and branches in foreign countries. In addition, most major banks maintain correspondent banking relationships with local banks in certain foreign markets.

Edge Act and Agreement Corporations
Edge Act and Agreement corporations are special-purpose corporations authorized to engage in specifically defined international banking and financing activities. Edge Act corporations are federally chartered pursuant to the Edge Act, an amendment to the Federal Reserve Act, and the provisions of Regulation K of the Federal Reserve Board. Agreement corporations, which are state chartered, have the same powers and restrictions as Edge Act corporations.

The primary purpose of Edge Act and Agreement corporations, which are subsidiaries of U.S. banks, is to provide financing for the international trading of U.S. importers and exporters. In practice, Edge Act corporations engage in a broad range of activities in the United States, provided that they are "incidental to international foreign business." Edge Act corporations also provide one of the ways by which domestic banks engage in activities outside of the United States.

The International Banking Act of 1978 permits foreign banks and their affiliates to establish Edge Act corporations, subject to prior approval by the Federal Reserve Board. The powers and limitations are similar to those of an agency, except for the limitation that the transactions and activities must have a foreign or international connection.

Subject to the Federal Reserve Act and Federal Reserve Regulation K, Edge Act corporations may receive deposits in the United States from foreign governments, persons conducting business at their foreign offices, and from individuals residing abroad. Edge Act and Agreement corporations may make foreign loans, confirm letters of credit, create banker's acceptances, trade in foreign currencies, receive items for collection from abroad, hold securities for safekeeping, act as a paying agent for securities issued by foreign governments and corporations, and own foreign banking subsidiaries. Edge Act corporations may also engage in financing commercial and industrial projects through long-term loans and equity participations. In addition, the foreign subsidiaries of Edge Act corporations may make equity investments in foreign corporations, particularly foreign banking institutions.

International Banking Facilities

In 1981, the Federal Reserve Board authorized the establishment of International Banking Facilities (IBFs) by U.S. depository institutions, Edge Act and Agreement corporations, and branches and agencies of foreign banks located in the United States. In effect, an IBF is a set of accounts segregated on the books and records of such institutions related to international time deposits, international loans, and the associated expense and income accounts. An IBF may accept deposits from foreign residents or from other IBFs and may extend credit to foreign residents and other IBFs provided that they are used only to support operations outside of the United States. Deposits recorded in an IBF are not subject to reserve requirements under Federal Reserve Regulation D.

Foreign Branches

Branch offices of U.S. banks located throughout the world represent the most important vehicle for U.S. banks to conduct business overseas. A foreign branch is a legal and operational part of the parent U.S. bank. Foreign branches are subject to all legal limitations on U.S. banks and to the banking regulations of the host country. For the most part, the Office of the Comptroller of the Currency and the Federal Reserve Board regulate foreign branches of U.S. banks.

The major advantage of foreign branches is worldwide name identification with the parent U.S. bank and access by customers to the full range of the parent bank's services. In addition, legal loan limits are a function of the parent bank's capital, not the size of the branch.

Correspondent Banks

Services provided to U.S. banks by correspondent banks located in foreign cities include accepting drafts, honoring letters of credit, furnishing credit information, collecting and disbursing international funds, and investing funds in international money markets. Most transactions with correspondent banks involve paying or collecting international funds in connection with international trade.

Other Banking Services

In addition to loans and other credit services, commercial banks provide a wide range of other financial services for businesses, such as accepting deposits, clearing checks, dealing in foreign exchange, corporate trust services, cash management services, electronic transfers of funds domestically and worldwide, capital markets services, and so on.

Foreign Exchange

Large multinational commercial banks make a market in foreign exchange to facilitate international trade and travel. The foreign exchange market provides a mechanism for hedging risks associated with changes in exchange rates, which is particularly important when exchange rates float, as they do now.

There is no single formal foreign exchange market. It is an over-the-counter market in which the participants are linked by telephone, telegraph, cable, and facsimile machines. In the United States, the foreign exchange market is dominated by about 25 large banks, about half of which are located in New York City. The remainder are located in other major financial centers in the country such as Chicago, San Francisco, and Los Angeles. In addition, many investment banking firms have foreign exchange trading operations in the United States.

There are two basic types of foreign exchange quotations—spot and forward. The spot market is the market in which foreign exchange is sold "on the spot." The rate at which currency is exchanged in this market is called the spot rate. While delivery of the currency in the spot market must be made within two business days, it is usually delivered immediately.

In the forward market, the buyer and seller agree to exchange a fixed amount of one currency for a fixed amount of second currency at some time in the future. Forward contracts are written typically for delivery of currency in 30, 60, 90, or 180 days. It is possible to tailor the amount and maturity of the foreign exchange contract. This facilitates international business transactions because it permits the two parties to the forward rate agreement to eliminate uncertainty about the amounts of currency to be delivered in the future.

Foreign exchange markets also include the futures market, in which contracts are traded to buy or sell a standard amount of currency in the future at a particular price. Such contracts are traded on the International Monetary Market of the Chicago Mercantile Exchange.

Foreign exchange rates can also be hedged by using a foreign exchange option contract, which is the right, but not the obligation, to sell currency at a specific price on or before a specific date. The large U.S. banks will write foreign currency options on an individual basis tailored to the needs of the customer. Standardized put and call options on foreign currencies are traded on the Chicago Board Options Exchange and the Philadelphia Stock Exchange.

Corporate Trust

Corporate trust activities include acting as trustee, transfer agent, and registrar for publicly issued and private placements of securities; dividend disbursement agent; and coupon and bond payment agent. The Trust Indenture Act of 1939 requires that bonds and other debt instruments offered for sale to the public must have corporate trustees. As bond trustees, banks maintain legal custody over any property used as security or collateral for a bond issue. As transfer agent, the bank is responsible for the maintenance of records of ownership of corporate stock. Because of the importance of this function, the Securities and Exchange Commission maintains strict control over stock transfer and dividend disbursing activities. Corporate trust activities also include the administration and investment of assets in employee benefit plans such as pension plans, profit sharing accounts, and employee stock ownership plans.

Funds Transfer

International transfers of funds are conducted through the Clearing House Interbank System (CHIPS), which moves funds electronically between New York offices of over 120 financial institutions. Such transfers include more than 90 percent of all foreign exchange trades and nearly all Eurodollar transactions. The Society for Worldwide Interbank Financial Telecommunications (SWIFT) is a system for transferring messages involving foreign exchange, bank transfers, customer transfers, and special messages.

Cash management services provided by commercial banks include the receipt of customer payments through lock boxes, controlled disbursement of funds, automated account reconciliations, and the electronic transfer of funds through the Fedwire transfer system and the Automated Clearing House (ACH) system.

Capital Markets

Investment banking and capital markets services include the underwriting, in certain cases, and the sale of money market securities, U.S. Treasury and federal agency obligations, tax-exempt municipal securities, interest rate swap and option contracts, precious metals, foreign exchange, and so on. Corporate finance activities involve providing merger and acquisition advisory services and arranging private placements of debt.

Deposits

There are various types of deposit accounts available at a commercial bank. A demand deposit account is a checking account in which depositors are entitled to receive their funds on demand and to write checks, which trnsfers legal ownership of funds in the account to others. Banks are prohibited by law from paying interest on demand deposits, which are held primarily for transaction purposes.

Time deposits are the largest source of funds for commercial banks. Unlike demand deposits, time deposits are usually legally due as of a maturity date and funds cannot be transferred to another party by a written check. Time deposits vary widely with respect to maturity, minimum amount, early withdrawal penalties, negotiability, and renewability. The principal type of bank time deposit for businesses is the certificate of deposit. Such deposits are unsecured liabilities of commercial banks, which are issued in denominations of $100,000 or more. They have a fixed maturity date and are negotiable if they meet certain legal specifications. The interest rate on certificates of deposit is competitive with rates on other money market instruments of similar maturity.

OBTAINING BANK FINANCING

Credit Request

Corporate or commercial credits are not normally applied for on an application form. More common is a face-to-face meeting with a commercial loan officer when financial information is requested, including information as to the purpose of the loan, collateral availability, business plan, and so on. The bank loan officer attempts to obtain as much information as possible about the character of the borrower, size and purpose of the loan, sources of loan repayment, and past credit performance of the borrower. It would not be uncommon for the bank to request three years of audited financial statements as well as projections incorporating various degrees of inflation and other cost data. In addition, the loan officer will ask for information about the company such as the principal officers and directors, chief products or services sold, production techniques used, and important competitors.

Credit and Cash Flow Analysis

U.S. financial institutions have traditionally been more "cash flow" lenders than their European or Asian counterparts. In addition, European and Asian banks take a longer-term view of their banking relationships and thus feel more comfortable in taking real estate and plant and equipment as collateral. In the United States, more of this "long-term" financing is provided by insurance companies and pension funds, which have traditionally been the long-term lenders in the United States.

   In general, to evaluate the credit-worthiness of a prospective borrower, the bank credit analyst will consider the following factors: (1) character of the borrower, that is, its integrity and willingness to repay the loan; (2) capacity of the borrower to repay the loan as indicated by its projected cash flow; (3) capital or net worth of the borrower; (4) collateral or assets pledged to secure the loan; and (5) economic conditions at the time of the loan and the borrower's ability to deal with a downturn in the economy.

Prior to granting a loan request, the bank will perform a credit and cash flow analysis of the borrower's audited financial statements in order to assess its creditworthiness. In addition to developing certain financial ratios and comparing them with ratios for similar companies, the bank credit analyst will perform a cash flow analysis to assess the borrower's ability to repay the loan. The credit analyst will pay particular attention to the historical trend and future projections in the borrower's income statement and statement of cash flows. Since principal and interest on loans are generally paid from operating profits, the analyst will focus on the projections of (1) earnings before interest and taxes, and (2) cash flow from operations. Many banks will require that the prospective borrower make such projections to be evaluated by the bank credit analyst.

The basic types of financial ratios commonly used in financial statement analysis include liquidity, management efficiency, leverage, and profitability. Liquidity ratios are the current ratio, which is the ratio of current assets to current liabilities, and the acid-test ratio, which is the same as the current ratio except that inventories are deducted from current assets. Management efficiency ratios measure how well assets are managed to produce sales and profits. Such ratios include the average collection period, which is the ratio of average accounts receivable to sales per day, and the inventory turnover ratio, which is the ratio of cost of goods sold to average inventory. Leverage ratios measure the level of financial risk in the company. Leverage can be measured by the ratio of long-term debt to equity and the ratio of earnings before interest and taxes to interest expense. Profitability can be assessed by the ratio of net income to sales and the ratio of net income to equity. Ratios should be compared with those of similar firms in the same industry and with the company's own ratios over time.

In addition to the financial and cash flow analysis, the bank credit analyst will obtain verification of deposit and loan balances and borrowing history. The analyst will also obtain reports from credit bureaus and other banks. However, in the final analysis, cash flow is the decisive element in credit analysis because cash is the basis for repayment of the loan.

Collateral

Many bank loans made in the United States are secured by collateral as a secondary source of repayment. Assets pledged as collateral may include inventory, accounts receivable, plant and equipment, stocks and bonds, real estate, and personal guarantees. Banks may also secure a lien on the equipment or machinery purchased with the proceeds of the loan.

To ensure their claim to collateral, lenders will carefully document the loan and their claim with appropriate filings with the local courts as required by the Uniform Commercial Code. Should the borrower default on the loan, the bank may sell the collateral to recover the loan amount.

Covenants

It is customary in bank loan agreements to have the borrower agree to comply with covenants. A covenant is an agreement by the borrower to take or not take certain actions. A covenant that specifies actions required to be taken is called an affirmative covenant. Such covenants generally focus on actions that the borrower should take in the normal course of business, such as maintaining corporate existence, complying with laws, carrying proper insurance with a reputable insurance company, and keeping proper records. A covenant that specifies actions not to be taken is called a negative covenant. Such covenants include restrictions on mergers and acquisitions, incurring of debts, granting of liens, and payment of cash dividends.

Financial covenants are based on information contained in the borrower's financial statements and are stated either as a dollar amount or as a ratio. Financial covenants commonly found in loan agreements include minimum working capital, minimum net worth, a minimum current ratio, and a maximum debt-to-equity ratio. Working capital is a measure of the borrower's liquidity and is generally defined as the difference between current assets and current liabilities. Net worth, which is also referred to as shareholders' equity, represents the difference between total assets and total liabilities. Many loan agreements call for the maintenance of a minimum dollar amount of tangible net worth, which is net worth minus intangible assets such as patents, trademarks, franchises, and goodwill. The current ratio is defined to be the ratio of current assets to current liabilities, which is also a measure of the borrower's liquidity. The debt to equity ratio, which is also called the leverage ratio, is the ratio of total liabilities to net worth or tangible net worth.

To monitor compliance with the covenants, the bank will request certain information from the borrower, depending on the amount and type of loan, the borrower's credit-worthiness, its type of business, whether the borrower is a public or private company, and whether any of its securities are traded on a national exchange. In most cases, the borrower provides the bank with its financial statements; filings with the SEC, if it is a public company; and filings with a national securities exchange, if its securities are traded on a national exchange. Financial statements are required to be prepared in accordance with generally accepted accounting principles.

The borrower's failure to comply with a covenant permits the bank to terminate its obligation to make additional loans and may give the bank the right to require the repayment of all outstanding loans.

Loan Agreements

A loan agreement usually provides that specified requirements must be satisfied by the borrower before the bank is obligated to make a loan to the borrower. If the borrower satisfies the conditions in a loan agreement, then the bank is obligated to make the loan. The loan agreement generally requires that the borrower deliver all required documents, obtain all requisite approvals, take all specified actions, comply with the law, verify certain of the bank's assumptions about the borrower, and be in compliance with the terms of the loan agreement.

The items generally required in all loan agreements to be delivered to the bank include the following: the executed note; resolutions of the borrower's board of directors approving the loan agreement, the note, and other documents to be delivered pursuant to the loan agreement; a certificate from the corporate secretary certifying the names and signatures of the officers authorized to sign the loan documents on behalf of the borrower; opinion of counsel to the borrower; and a certificate of no defaults.

Depending on the structure of the loan, other items that may be required by the bank in the loan agreement are as follows: an opinion from counsel to the guarantor, if the loan is guaranteed; a waiver or consent if the borrower's existing agreements restrict it from entering into the loan agreement; approval of a governmental agency that has authority over the borrower; and a security interest or lien in the collateral.

In addition to the conditions of lending and the covenants described above, the loan agreement includes the amount and terms of the loan, the borrower's representations and warranties, and the events of default.

COST OF BANK CREDIT

The cost of bank credit consists of three principal elements: (1) interest rate, (2) origination and commitment fees, and (3) compensating balances.

Interest Rate

The interest rate quoted on a loan by a bank is a function of a number of different factors such as the term and structure of the loan, the bank's assessment of the credit-worthiness of the prospective borrower, and the cost of servicing the loan. In addition, the rate may be fixed for the term of the loan or may be variable and therefore "float" with short-term market rates.

Historically, the prime rate has been generally a bank's lowest interest rate charged on loans to the bank's most credit-worthy customers. Prime rate loans are variable-rate loans because the prime rate will change from time to time based on the cost of short-term sources of bank funds such as negotiable certificates of deposit and federal funds. The prime rate is also influenced by the interest rates on alternative borrowing sources for prime rate customers such as the rate on commercial paper. For customers whose credit-worthiness is judged to be less than the best, the bank will charge the prime rate plus a spread over or a multiple of the prime rate. The size of the spread, or multiple, is a function of the borrower's credit rating.

Over the past few years, variable-rate loans at large banks have been pegged to base rates other than the prime rate. Such rates include the rate on negotiable certificates of deposit, federal funds rate, Treasury Bill rate, or the London Interbank Offered Rate (LIBOR). LIBOR and the U.S. prime rate are the two rates most often used to determine lending rates on negotiated international loans. The prime rate is still a very common base rate for variable rate loans to smaller firms and at smaller banks.

Origination and Commitment Fees

A second element of cost to the borrower are fees for originating the loan and for commitments by the bank to lend money to the borrower. Origination fees may be charged to the borrower upon the initiation of the loan and may also be charged for loan renewals and restructuring. Such fees compensate the bank for the work involved in evaluating the prospective borrower's financial condition; evaluating and recording guarantees, collateral, and other security arrangements; negotiating loan terms; preparing and processing loan documents; and closing the transaction. Such fees may also be referred to as application fees. Restructuring fees are charged for changes in terms or conditions in the loan agreement. These changes may be the result of unfavorable performance by the borrower or by a change in interest rates that necessitates a change in the repayment schedule. The bank may also charge a fee at a renewal date or a fee on draws against a line of credit or commitment.

The bank may agree to make funds available to the borrower in the future or commit to an interest rate in the future. To compensate the bank for assuming these risks, the borrower will pay the bank a commitment fee. The fee for agreeing to provide funds in the future is generally expressed as a percentage on the unused portion of the commitment. These fees are charged on the amount of the commitment that was not used, and may amount to 1/4 to 1/2 of one percent per annum of the total unused commitment.

A facility fee is a form of commitment fee that is based generally on the total amount of the credit facility. It may be charged on both revolving credit and term loan facilities. In the case of revolving credit, the fee is usually based on the amount of the total commitment, regardless of the amount actually outstanding under the revolving credit. In a term loan, the fee is based on the amount of the term loan. The amount of the facility fee is usually between 1/4 and 1/2 of one percent per annum.

Compensating Balances

A third element of the cost of bank credit may take the form of compensating balances. Compensating balances are minimum average deposit balances that borrowers must maintain at the bank, usually in the form of noninterest-bearing demand deposits. Banks can require commercial borrowers to maintain deposit balances in relation to outstanding loans or to unused portions of lines of credit, or both. Such balances effectively raise the rate paid by the borrower on the loan.

While the compensating balance requirements vary, a typical revolving credit requires balances equal to 10 percent of the commitment plus 10 percent of the amount used under the commitment. In a term loan, the balance requirement might be 10 percent of the principal amount of the loan outstanding. If the borrower fails to maintain the required compensating balances, then the borrower is charged a fee. The rate charged on the difference between the balances required and those actually maintained is commonly the bank's prime rate or the rate being charged on the loan.

SPECIALIZED FINANCIAL INSTITUTIONS

In addition to banks, several other types of financial institution are also sources of financing for businesses. Following is a brief description of the types of financing provided by these specialized financial institutions.

Investment Bankers

An investment banker provides a link between a business and the financial markets. With the assistance of an investment banker, a company may be able to obtain long-term financing through the sale of equity securities or debt obligations in the public capital markets or through the private placement of such securities. In general, the investment banker will underwrite, or purchase, an entire block of securities to be issued by a company at a guaranteed price. The securities are then resold by the investment banker to individual investors or institutions. Investment bankers also help prepare prospectuses, select the sale date, and provide general financial advice to the issuer.

While there are about 2,500 investment banking firms involved in securities underwriting in the United States, investment banking is dominated by the 100 largest firms. About half of these firms are headquartered in New York City, with the remainder located in the country's other major financial centers such as Chicago and Los Angeles.

Recent Federal Reserve rulings have allowed certain large New York banks to engage in a limited amount of investment banking activities. Such activities include the placement of commercial paper issued by third parties and underwriting and dealing in municipal revenue bonds, mortgage-related securities, and securities backed by consumer receivables.

Publicly Issued Securities

During the origination of a new security issue, the investment banker can help the issuer determine the amount of money needed, decide on the type of debt or equity financing, design the features of the securities to be issued, and provide advice on the best sale date. The features of debt securities to be determined include maturity, coupon rate, call provisions, and sinking fund. The investment banker can help the company prepare the registration statement to be filed with U.S. Securities and Exchange Commission (SEC). The registration statement contains detailed information about the issuer's financial condition, business activities, management and their experience, the characteristics of the securities to be issued, and a description of how the proceeds of the issue will be used.

In addition to the investment banker, a number of other parties are involved in publicly issuing securities. Generally, credit ratings are obtained from one or more of the credit rating agencies such as Standard & Poor's and Moody's. Legal counsel will issue an opinion on the legality of the security issue and will assist in ensuring compliance with all applicable securities laws. Independent accountants will be required to audit financial statements that are included along with applicable financial disclosures in registration statements filed with the SEC. A trustee must be selected to ensure that the issuer of the securities fulfills its obligations under the security agreement. Other parties involved in the sale of securities to the public include transfer agents, custodians, and financial printers.

Private Placements
The major difference between a private placement and a public offering is that the private placement is made to a small number of professional placement institutions, either directly by the borrower or with the assistance of an investment banker, while the public issue is sold to a syndicate that makes a primary commitment to purchase the securities. In the latter case, the syndicate resells the securities to a large group of investors, which may include private individuals or institutions. Among the advantages of private placements are that a private placement is faster, requiring only a few weeks rather than several months. It entails lower costs, since the underwriters' fee for the public issue is normally three to five times the fee for a private placement of the same size and quality. Also, there are additional legal, insurance, and printing costs for the public issue. Private placement is more personalized because the investment is offered to a limited number of participants who have the ability and experience to analyze documents containing the pertinent data on the securities or debt package being offered. The disadvantages are that the issuer may get a lesser amount for the private placement, because of the bargaining strength of the investors and because privately placed stock may contain severe restrictions on the possibility of resale or redistribution. Furthermore, if large blocks of voting stock end up in a few hands, management may not have as much freedom in the company's direction as it would with a great number of smaller shareholders.

Commercial Paper

Commercial paper is a short-term, unsecured promissory note with a maturity of no more than 270 days. By limiting the maturity to no more than 270 days, the issuer can avoid the registration requirements of the Securities and Exchange Commission. Commercial paper is used to finance short-term working capital needs and generally is issued with an original maturity of between 5 and 45 days, with 30 days being the most common period. Because commercial paper is an unsecured note, issuers tend to be large, well-known companies having the highest credit ratings.

Most issuers back their commercial paper with unused lines of credit from banks. A standard line of credit aggreement allows an issuer to borrow up to 270 days for an annual fee of about 1/8 of one percent of the amount of the line of credit. Smaller and lesser-known companies are able to borrow in the commercial paper market by obtaining a standby letter of credit from a bank. The letter of credit fee ranges from 1/8 of one percent to 1 1/2 percent of the amount guaranteed.

Commercial paper is sold in bearer form on a discount basis—that is, the investor pays less than the face amount for the paper and receives the face amount at maturity. Interest rates on commercial paper are quoted on a discount basis, similar to U.S. Treasury bills. The rate on commercial paper is usually a few basis points higher than the rate on negotiable certificates of deposit issued by banks. Thus, the commercial paper rate is below the bank prime rate. Most commercial paper is sold in denominations of $100,000, $250,000, $500,000, and $1 million.

Almost all companies that issue commercial paper obtain ratings from at least one of the rating agencies. The rating services classify an issuer into one of three basic categories based on the probability of repayment at maturity. For example, the highest rating assigned by Moody's Investors Service is described as follows:

> "Issuers have a superior capacity for repayment of short-term promissory obligations. Repayment capacity will normally be evidenced by the following characteristics: leading market positions in well-established industries; high rates of return on funds employed; conservative capitalization structures with moderate reliance on debt and ample asset protection; broad margins in earnings coverage of

fixed financial charges and high internal cash generation; and well-established access to a range of financial markets and assured sources of alternate liquidity.''

Companies that are not in the highest rating category must pay higher rates to borrow in the commercial paper market because investors will demand an interest rate premium for assuming additional risk.

Most nonfinancial companies sell commercial paper through dealers, primarily investment banks and certain large commercial banks. There are about 30 commercial paper dealers, most of whom are located in New York City. They charge a commission of approximately 1/8 to 1/4 of one percent of the face amount of commercial paper sold.

Insurance Companies

There are two fundamental types of insurance companies in the United States—life and health insurance, and property and casualty insurance. There are approximately 2,300 life and health insurance companies and 3,600 property and casualty insurance companies. Insurance companies invest premiums received for providing insurance coverage into various types of securities and direct investments. As the third-largest private financial intermediary in the U.S. economy, life and health insurance companies are very large investors in corporate debt securities. Because of the long-term nature of life insurance contracts, life insurance companies traditionally invest their funds in long-term investments such as long-term debt instruments, mortgages, and real estate. With the introduction of universal life policies, life insurance companies have shifted their investments to short-term debt instruments and equity securities.

Property and casualty insurance companies issue insurance policies that cover much shorter time periods than life insurance contracts. In addition, the cash inflows and outflows of property and casualty companies are not as predictable because of the nature of risks that they insure. Accordingly, property and casualty insurance companies tend to invest their funds in short-term, highly marketable securities, such as U.S. Treasury securities and corporate debt securities. To offset the lower return typically generated by short-term investments, property and casualty companies will have significant investments in marketable equity securities. In addition, because investment income is taxable, property and casualty insurance companies invest significantly in tax-exempt municipal securities, which typically make up the largest proportion of their investment portfolio.

Insurance companies represent one of the largest investors in the private placement of debt and equity securities. A private placement is a method of issuing securities in which the issuer sells the securities directly to the ultimate investors. The private placement market is used by smaller, lesser-known firms of lower credit quality that generally sell small dollar amounts of securities. In addition, large, well-known companies of higher credit quality may also privately place their securities with insurance companies. In general, private placement agreements contain more restrictive covenants and conditions but may be less expensive than issuing securities publicly.

Commercial Finance Companies

Commercial finance companies generally provide funding that is secured by inventory, receivables, or equipment. Commercial finance companies are often subsidiaries of manufacturing companies that provide financing to facilitate sales of the manufacturer's products. Commercial finance companies have expanded into other business lending areas, including term loans for machinery, equipment, and real estate. Commercial finance companies are almost exclusively secured lenders and are commonly described as asset-based lenders. Asset-based lenders will advance more funds and provide funds to less credit-worthy businesses than commercial banks. Because of greater risks and a higher cost of funds, commercial finance companies charge higher rates than commercial banks, generally from 200 to 600 basis points above the bank prime rate.

Dealing with a commercial finance company involves a thorough approval audit of the assets offered as security and an operational audit of many management areas. During the approval phase, the business will be asked for a deposit to cover the cost of the audit and a commitment fee. These fees vary widely and may be one percent or more of the requested loan. Commercial finance companies continuously and extensively monitor the borrower and the secured asset base.

Commercial finance company loans generally take the form of revolving credit lines. Loan advances are made as requested by the business based on collateral availability. The revolving credit line can increase automatically, within agreed-upon ranges, as the collateral base grows. The term of a revolving credit loan will vary, but rarely exceeds three years. Other significant conditions are definitions of qualifying collateral and extent of personal guarantees.

Floor plan loans are made by finance companies to finance inventory purchased by businesses. Some finance companies make floor plan loans to induce dealers to allow the finance companies to purchase the retail contracts generated from the sales of inventory. Unlike revolving loans collateralized by inventory, floor plan loans generally are collateralized by specific inventory items such as automobiles.

Sales finance companies discount installment sales of vendors, as well as discount or lend on the pledge of installment or other accounts receivable. Finance companies are regulated by the states in which they operate, and are subject to federal regulations.

Leasing Companies

Leasing companies generally finance real estate and personal property and equipment such as machine tools, heavy construction equipment, office furniture and equipment, computers, aircraft, ocean-going oil and liquefied natural gas tankers, automobiles, trucks, and so on. Leasing is a form of secured lending in which the lessor—the leasing company—retains actual title to and is the owner of the equipment while the lessee is the user of the equipment. Leasing requires little or no initial cash investment on the part of the lessee, and leases often cover a longer term than bank loans to fund the purchase of the same equipment. As a result of tax advantages to the leasing company, as well as the expected residual value of the equipment at the end of the lease, lease financing may be less expensive than bank financing for the lessee. Most leasing companies are subsidiaries of bank holding companies and commercial finance companies.

Mortgage Banking Companies

Mortgage banking companies provide financing that is secured by real estate. The mortgage banking company originates mortgage loans and accumulates pools of such loans made to individuals and companies. These pools of loans are then, in turn, sold to institutional investors such as insurance companies and pension funds, or are sold into the secondary mortgage market. Most mortgage banking companies are subsidiaries of bank holding companies and commercial finance companies.

Factoring Companies

Factoring companies provide financing by purchasing trade accounts receivable, usually without recourse. The factoring company purchases the receivables from companies whose customers send their payments directly to the factoring company. Factored accounts receivable are not collateral for loans, but are receivables that have been purchased at a discount. The purchase price is discounted to allow for potential losses and for the time value of money, since payment will not be received by the factor until some time in the future. A factor performs credit reviews, bookkeeping, and collection, and assumes the risks of credit losses. In return for selling its accounts receivable at a discount, the business firm immediately obtains cash from the factoring company.

Factoring usually requires that notification to the customer be placed on the face of invoices indicating that accounts have been sold and that the factoring company is to be paid directly. Factoring companies are usually subsidiaries of bank holding companies and commercial finance companies.

Pension Funds

Pension funds in the United States have total assets of approximately $2 trillion and have been among the fastest-growing financial intermediaries during the past twenty years. Pension funds represent the funds that have been accumulated under pension plans to provide benefits to participants upon their retirement. Private pension plans can be established with a life insurance company or may be managed by a trustee appointed by a sponsoring organization, such as a business or union. The trustee, who is responsible for investment of pension fund contributions and payment of retirement benefits, is usually a commercial bank or trust company. Pension funds consitute more than one third of the assets of commercial bank trust departments. In some cases, particularly with large companies and unions, the sponsoring organization manages the investments of the pension fund.

Because the cash inflow into pension funds is long term and the cash outflow is highly predictable, pension funds are able to invest in higher-yielding, long-term securities. In recent years, pension funds have invested heavily in equity securities to increase earnings of the fund, including direct investments in privately placed securities.

Savings Institutions

While many savings institutions in the United States have failed in the past few years because of mismanagement and credit problems, those thrifts that remain are viable sources of real estate financing for businesses. There are over 3,000 insured thrift institutions, consisting of savings banks and savings and loan associations, that provide commercial real estate financing as well as residential mortgage loans. While it is a small portion of their assets, thrifts also make nonmortgage commercial loans.

Venture Capital Companies

A venture capital investment company is a company whose primary investment objective is capital growth. Such companies invest their capital at above-average risk to form or develop companies. Venture capital investments frequently involve combinations of long-term debt and equity, where the debt may have many equitylike characteristics. Insurance companies and pension funds often participate in the investments of experienced venture capitalists, but will take less of the risk and the return. A venture capital company often provides technical and management assistance to the management of the companies in which it invests. Venture capitalists have traditionally preferred proven growth businesses with potential to go public within three to five years.

Small business investment companies (SBICs) are privately owned corporations that provide equity capital and long-term loans and debt to small businesses. SBICs are licensed by the U.S. Small Business Administration (SBA) under the Small Business Investment Act of 1958. They prefer to invest in established or late-growth-stage businesses in combination with other investment groups. Approximately 300 regular SBICs have about $2 billion of financing outstanding to small business concerns. SBICs may be separate companies or may be subsidiaries of banks and bank holding companies.

Export-Import Bank

The Export-Import Bank of the United States (Eximbank) is a U.S. government-owned corporation that assists in financing and facilitating U.S. exports by making loans and providing guarantees and insurance for loans from commercial sources in connection with the export of U.S. goods and services. To stimulate U.S. exports, Eximbank provides short-, medium-, and long-term financing when this is not available from the private sector on competitive terms. Financing is available for the buyer, seller, or bank involved in the export activity even if the exporter company has foreign ownership; however, the products or services exported must originate in the United States. The Export-Import bank offers international credits without competing with commercial banks.

The Eximbank also works in cooperation with the Private Export Funding Corporation (PEFCO) to make U.S. dollars available to foreign purchasers of American goods and services. While the aim of PEFCO is to stimulate private capital in the United States to support exports, all of its loans are guaranteed by the Eximbank.

In the United States, the unincorporated association of some 51 private insurance companies known as the Foreign Credit Insurance Association (FCIA) provides export credit insurance. Export credit insurance is used by exporters as an alternative to formal letters of credit. Such insurance provides coverage for short-, medium-, and long-term financing arrangements for individual transactions. Political risks can be insured for 100 percent of the loss, but commercial risks are usually insured up to 90 or 95 percent of the loss. FCIA works closely with the Export-Import Bank, but is a private profit-making organization.

CHAPTER 7

COMMERCIAL PROPERTY AND CASUALTY INSURANCE IN THE UNITED STATES

Larry L. Klein
Senior Manager
Price Waterhouse

Jack P. Gibson
President
International Risk Management Institute

INTRODUCTION

Virtually every business enterprise and every financial investment in a business exposes the owners and investors to the risk of economic loss. This chapter will address techniques for managing exposure to fortuitous or accidental injury to tangible property that results in an asset's declining value. In addition, the chapter will address liability loss exposures and their treatment. Insurance is the most commonly recognized technique for managing risk of loss, but before selecting this alternative, managers intuitively or consciously evaluate and employ or discard other options.

The insurance community in the United States has demonstrated its ability to be creative by devising an insurance solution to virtually every conceivable fortuitous loss exposure. An essential element is that the risk of loss must be entirely accidental from the perspective of the insured. Since the insurance business operates in a free enterprise environment, affordable insurance may not be available for all situations. Underwriters are not obligated or may not be willing to assume every risk. As a result, an insurance solution may exist in theory, but in the real world the coverage may not be available.

To illustrate the point in the commercial insurance market, while products liability insurance is generally available to manufacturers of most products, such coverage is unavailable for firms that need protection for claims against the manufacturer concerning products that contain asbestos. In this situation, insurance coverage may be offered subject to an absolute exclusion for products that contain asbestos.

Insurance regulation in the United States falls in the domain of each individual state. Insurance rates are relatively unregulated for commercial insurance coverage. Basic policy forms are prescribed by statute or regulation, although extensive modifications are commonplace. Insurer licensing and solvency, for the present, is regulated by the insurance departments of the various states. Depending on the type of insurance and the particular state, exceptions and special situations may apply. Also, one or more legislative proposals are always under consideration in the U.S. Congress to change the current practice.

Insurers pool their loss experience information among themselves and also across the country in order to develop more credible rates. Insurer organizations have been created to help manage the process, and often they actually submit rate proposals to the separate state insurance departments for approval. The National Council on Compensation Insurance (NCCI) manages the workers compensation statistical gathering and rate filing for all but a few states. The Surety Association of America (SAA) performs similar services for companies that write surety contracts. The Insurance Service Office (ISO) gathers and analyzes statistics for virtually every other property and liability insurance line. In most states, ISO makes rate and form filings that are followed by hundreds of insurance companies.

In each instance, the organization compiles the data and must obtain approval from each state for its member insurers to be authorized to use the rates.

THE RISK MANAGEMENT PROCESS

Despite the broad availability of insurance covering most accidental losses, not every insurable risk of loss is insured. The past decade has seen widespread adoption of the risk management process. The process consists of a series of steps that strive to apply the most cost-effective solution to loss exposures that is consistent with the organization's mission:

- Identify exposures to loss: The types of losses a business can suffer include direct damage to real and personal property, including fixed assets, inventory, and work in process. Indirect losses include loss of revenue and increased expenses necessitated by direct losses. Casualty losses include claims by third parties—such as customers, employees, and the general public—who may be injured due to a firm's negligent behavior.
- Examine feasibility of alternative techniques: Insurance is just one of many alternatives to manage loss exposures. Exposure reduction may be accomplished through loss prevention and control activities. Transferring the exposure and responsibility through contracts with another firm may be a viable option.
- Select "best" apparent technique(s): The technique(s) may not be mutually exclusive, and often a loss control technique will reduce the cost of an insurance technique, making both the "best" solution. Selection is typically based on both financial and business objective criteria.
- Implement the chosen technique(s): The implementation process requires proper sequencing in order to be most effective. Some techniques require technical resources such as loss control engineers and safety specialists, while others require staff with managerial skills necessary to direct technical projects.
- Monitor and improve the risk management program: As the business changes, the risk management program must adapt to the changing risk exposures. In addition, insurance underwriters are constantly reevaluating their positions on price and coverage, so insurance options available to businesses are constantly changing.

PROPERTY LOSS EXPOSURES

Identification

Real and personal property are exposed to damage or destruction from a variety of causes or loss. The obvious direct damage perils that can befall property are fire, explosion, windstorm, and flood. Property is generally insurable against unforeseen types of loss, whereas expected, naturally occurring causes of loss are not insurable. For example, certain property by virtue of its particular characteristics is subject to unusual causes of loss. Fresh fruits and vegetables in their natural state will eventually rot. Similarly, unprotected metal will corrode and disintegrate. Such losses are not normally covered by insurance unless they are caused by some other event that is insured.

For example, a loss of refrigeration that results in unexpected, premature decay of fruits or vegetables is insurable, both for the damage to the refrigeration unit and the resulting loss of perishables. Implicit in nearly every direct damage to property is either a loss of income or extra expenses incurred as a result of lost opportunities that would have been realized by using the asset. Frequently, the indirect damage loss far exceeds the direct damage loss.

Electronically stored data pose special issues. Electronic media are exceptionally sensitive to injury from everyday changes in the environment such as dust, heat, and humidity. Valuating and estimating the cost of records restoration can be exceptionally difficult. Intellectual property—including copyrights, patents, experiments in process, and other research and product development activities—likewise are exposed to a variety of unusual causes of loss.

Property Loss Valuation

Property valuation for insurance purposes uses a different approach from that used by accountants, real estate appraisers, creditors, and the insured's management. Insurable value initially is based on the cost to repair or replace the asset. For real property such as buildings, this is the cost required to rebuild the structure in like kind using similar materials. For inventory valuation, insurance has coined the phrase "Next In, First Out" (NIFO). That is to say, the value of inventory is equal to the cost of replacing the property immediately after a loss.

Buildings and contents are usually insured for their replacement cost or their actual cash value. Replacement cost value (RCV) is the cost to replace the damaged or destroyed property using new materials. Actual cash value (ACV) begins with the replacement cost, but makes a deduction for depreciation. The depreciation deduction is an inexact calculation based on the exhausted percentage of the property's useful life. For example, in the event of loss to a 10-year-old asphalt shingle roof, the claim will be assessed a depreciation of between 33 and 50 percent, to reflect that asphalt shingle roofs have a useful life of between 20 and 30 years. If insured on a replacement cost basis, the full value of a new roof will be covered.

When assessing property loss exposures, professionals should be engaged to estimate four loss scenarios, which follow in descending order of magnitude:

- Maximum Foreseeable Loss—This loss estimate assumes a catastrophic loss situation wherein internal fire protection and fire suppression systems fail, and public or private fire departments are delayed in responding.
- Probable Maximum Loss—This loss estimate assumes that the loss control devices within one fire division are out of service or fail to respond as designed, and public or private departments are delayed in responding. The spread of fire is impeded by fire-resistive partitions.
- Expected Maximum Loss—This loss estimate assumes that the loss control devices within one fire division are out of service or fail to respond as designed, but public and private fire departments are able to respond.
- Normal Loss Expectancy—This loss estimate assumes that all loss control devices are in service and operate according to normal response conditions.

Property Loss Control

Property loss control is attempted through a variety of engineering techniques. Use of automatic sprinkler systems, and halon fire suppression systems are perhaps the two most frequently cited examples. The ultimate objective of property loss control devices is to reduce the likelihood of any loss greater than the Normal Loss Expectancy and to reduce the absolute value of that estimate.

The most common loss control efforts focus on the peril of fire. Depending on the location and use of the property, flood, earthquake, or extremes in temperature or humidity may pose a greater threat to the property than fire. Determining the Maximum Foreseeable Loss should comtemplate a worst case scenario from every conceivable cause of loss.

Property Risk Transfer

Risk transfers are techniques that allow a company to continue business activities yet circumvent exposure to loss of assets. Transfers can apply to the risk of ownership or the cost of financing. Simple examples of risk transfer techniques include leasing property rather than ownership, or contracting with another firm for the distribution of products. While risk transfer techniques may reduce some loss exposures, they may create additional exposures due to the bailment status of the lessee. Furthermore, often the cost of insurance protection purchased by the lessor is passed through to the lessee, making savings illusory. Occasionally, savings can be realized when the lessor can apply greater leverage in the purchase of insurance.

Property Insurance

Commercial property insurance can cover real property, personal property, and net income losses. Generally, real property consists of permanent structures erected on real estate. It also can include permanent attachments affixed to the structure, such as improvements and betterments. Unless specifically described, underground property below footings and foundations may be excluded. This limitation should be amended for manufacturing companies that move work in process through pipes and conduits between structures. Outdoor property such as fences, antennas, and signs may be subject to special limitations.

Personal property consists of all property other than real property. Examples of personal property are furniture, equipment, and inventory. Inventory includes raw materials, work in process, and finished goods. Personal property, because of its portable characteristics, high value-to-size ratio, shorter useful life resulting in more rapid depreciation, and generally higher susceptibility to damage, requires special consideration.

Personal property is exposed to a broader range of causes of loss such as theft and employee pilferage. Its size makes most personal property a greater target for theft than real property. Such furnishings as computer systems rapidly depreciate or become obsolete, thereby necessitating particular attention to their insurable value.

Loss of business income insurance, also known as business interruption insurance, is intended to protect a company for the net loss of income it sustains following a loss to insured property. For example, a commercial printing press may take months for repairs following a loss. Also, the cost to repair, under a crisis situation, may be higher because of express freight charges and overtime for repair workers. During the period of interruption, the printer may subcontract work to friendly competitors. The added cost usually cannot be passed on to the customer, thereby causing a loss of net income to the printer.

Loss of business income insurance claims are calculated by comparing the firm's actual performance, assuming the repairs were made with due diligence and dispatch, to an estimated financial performance that would have been experienced assuming no loss had occurred. The covered period for loss of business income claims is not bounded or limited by the expiration of the insurance policy. This is particularly important, since a catastrophic loss can take several years for restoration to be completed. Naturally, determining and settling loss of business income claims can be complex. A number of public accounting firms have developed specialized practice areas well versed in business interruption losses.

Premium Determination

Fire insurance rates are based on the construction, occupancy, protection, and exposure of the building. Insurance rates for windstorm and flood are based on geographical considerations. The rates and other causes of loss such as vehicle damage, riot, and vandalism are grouped together and priced as a package. The premium is calculated by multiplying the rate by the amount of insurance. Basic rates contemplate the insured retaining a $1,000 deductible. Credits are granted to insureds that will accept higher deductibles.

Classes of construction range from fire resistive, to ordinary masonry, to frame. Fire resistive buildings that have additional fire protection features such as internal fire walls and sprinkler systems can qualify for Highly Protected Risk (HPR) classification. There are three major insurance markets for HPR-constructed properties, the Industrial Risk Insurors (IRI), Factory Mutual (FM), and the Kemper Group. HPR property is characterized by noncombustible construction building techniques, sprinkler systems installed to protect the property, and security systems that detect fires and notify emergency response facilities.

Occupancy materially affects a building's exposure to fire. Certain manufacturing processes are very hazardous; office occupancies are relatively harmless, because most office occupancies have few or no flammables on site and the business activities are not hazardous. Manufacturers frequently have cleaning solvents and other flammable liquids on site and the work processes often create fire hazards. Properties that have multiple occupancies are rated based on the most hazardous individual occupancy within a single fire division.

Protection refers to the type and proximity of fire protection apparatus that is available to respond to a fire. Private fire protection consists of devices such as alarms, sprinkler systems, and hand-held portable fire extinguishers. Protection requirements are based, in part, on the occupancy of the building. Some major facilities maintain a fire department with fire apparatus on site.

Exposure has become less significant with newer constructed buildings, because it reflects the risk associated with the possibility of a fire starting and spreading from adjacent premises. Occasionally, urban property and suburban industrial parks may have an exposure risk.

Changes in occupancy and the resulting necessary structural modifications can adversely affect the fire insurance rate applicable to a building. Relying upon the insurance costs of the current occupant for estimating future insurance costs is not appropriate.

Rates are predicated on the assumption that the insured has

purchased insurance equal to at least 80 percent of the property's value. In the event that insufficient insurance is purchased, the insured will become a coinsurer for every loss in proportion to the deficiency in the amount of insurance purchased. To avoid the possibility of a coinsurance penalty, it is customary to request an "agreed amount of insurance" endorsement that replaces the coinsurance provision in property insurance policies. Most insurers are willing to grant this concession if the insured can furnish a current construction appraisal and agrees to insure the property for at least 90 percent of its value.

The fire insurance rate for personal property starts with the rate for the building and applies a surcharge based on its susceptibility to damage and combustion. Personal property insurance rates also are predicated on the assumption that the insured is carrying sufficient insurance, so the coinsurance provision applies to personal property as well.

An increasing number of companies request the agreed amount of insurance provision or purchase coverage subject to a reporting form condition. The insured purchases an amount of insurance equal to the highest likely values to be on site during the policy period. On a monthly basis, the insured files a report of values with the insurer detailing the actual values on hand as of the date of the report. At the end of the policy period the values are averaged and the final premium is adjusted, based on the average. The insured is assured of having sufficient insurance to cover the maximum foreseeable loss, yet pays a premium based on the actual values at risk during the policy period.

Loss of business income rates are derived from the building rate and based on the coinsurance percentage selected. Since most losses do not cause a prolonged interruption of business, insureds can select a coinsurance percentage as low as 60 percent of the annual net income and continuing expenses.

Property Insurance Covered Losses

Most commercial property insurance policies provide coverage for all causes of loss except those specifically excluded. Insurers avoid use of the term *All Risk* because of adverse judicial interpretation, but coverage can be provided against almost every imaginable cause of loss. Customarily, commercial property insurance policies exclude flood and earthquake causes of loss. Coverage for flood is available through a program reinsured by the U.S. government, and coverage for earthquake is commercially available as a separately purchased extension or endorsement on a property policy. A few insurers issue "Difference in Conditions" policies that normally include coverage for flood and earthquake losses in addition to losses not covered by fire insurance policies.

The current trend for insureds with substantial insurable property values is to purchase coverage using a manuscript insurance form. The property descriptions, valuation provisions, and causes of loss that are covered are specifically developed to suit the particular needs of the insured. Customized insurance programs are most frequently arranged by insureds with over $20 million in total insurance and can assume at least a $10,000 deductible. These amounts may vary depending on the nature of the property insured and the underwriting appetite of the insurer that offers the coverage.

LIABILITY LOSS EXPOSURES

Public Liability

Most organizations are exposed to claims for loss sustained by third parties from a wide range of business operations. Sources of claims include present and past business activities, products previously manufactured or sold, completed operations that subsequently cause injury, and liability for the negligent acts of others for whom the company has assumed responsibility.

Injuries sustained by claimants are not only the obvious bodily injuries and property damage for which there are visible signs, but also include damage to one's reputation and psychic injuries such as emotional stress. Claims for economic loss do not require physical damage or injury, but can consist of loss of profits caused by unfair trade practices such as predatory pricing. Still other claims arise from improper hiring and promotion practices, and rendering erroneous advice to employees concerning their employee benefits and pension plans.

Liability arises not only from the firm's activities, but also from the activities of others. Commonly, one firm will assume responsibility for the negligent acts of its customers, suppliers, landlords, or tenants in an inducement to conduct business affairs. These agreements require careful attention and appropriate insurance to manage the risks. Coverage is customarily arranged by including the required endorsements to a Commercial General Liability (CGL) Insurance Policy. A CGL policy also covers a firm's products and completed operations loss exposures.

Watercraft and Aircraft

The operation, ownership, or use of watercraft and aircraft requires special consideration. Separate policies are necessary to cover the firm for claims that arise from these types of property.

Environmental Injury Liability

In the past few years, concern for environmental damage has exploded. Several major federal laws and state statutes have been enacted to protect land, water, and air from polluters. The thrust of most environmental protection legislation is to protect the environment by penalizing polluters and restore damaged conditions. Potential responsible parties are exposed to joint and several liability for the cost to remediate contaminated property.

Virtually every public liability insurance policy issued since the early 1980s contains a provision intended to exclude coverage for claims alleging that the insured damaged property as a result of the release of pollutants. Few of these recent policies have been tested in the courts. Numerous current legal efforts assert that coverage was provided on policies issued prior to these, some dating back several decades.

Today, a few insurers will provide pollution liability insurance for the company that has exceptionally well-maintained operations. Coverage is limited to sudden and accidental discharges of pollutants that commence and are discovered during the policy period. Comprehensive inspections are required by expert technicians before coverage is offered.

Automobile Loss Exposures

The ownership, operation, or use of automobiles and trucks by companies is similar through the world. In Europe the exposure and insurance is referred to as motor insurance. Losses arise from the negligent operation of the vehicle, causing damage to property or injury to others. Every state requires that vehicle owners demonstrate their financial responsibility for damages or injury they may cause as a result of automobile accidents. Approximately forty states require insurance or qualified self-insurance as the accepted means for demonstrating that ability.

Frequently, an automobile accident also results in a workers compensation claim and occasionally causes substantial damage to the vehicle. Also, if the vehicle is a truck used for transporting goods, a personal property loss is possible. The personal property can be either the insured's or customer's goods.

A Business Automobile Policy (BAP) can provide coverage for third party liability and also physical damage to the insured vehicle. Operation of borrowed, rented, or leased vehicles carries special insurable interest exposures that can be protected by appropriate policy endorsements. Employees who use their own automobiles on behalf of their employer likewise creates exposures that can be protected with an appropriate endorsement.

Worker Injuries

U.S. employers are required by state statute to provide specific benefits to employees who become injured or are killed in the course of employment. Every state's workers compensation statute provides indemnity wage loss and payment of necessary medical expenses resulting from the injury. Most states also require payment for rehabilitation costs and, if applicable, survivor benefits. While the laws in all states are similar, they are not identical. In exchange for guaranteed benefits payable to injured employees, employers are exempt from most common law liability actions.

Despite presumably safer workplace conditions, improved delivery of emergency medical treatment, and countless other risk reduction efforts, workers compensation costs have risen dramatically in the past decade. Recent studies indicate that while the inflation rate of medical treatment is approximately 10 percent annually, the inflation rate for workers compensation medical claims in the same period is 14.9 percent.

Carpal tunnel syndrome claims caused by repeated hand and finger movements over a sustained period of time provide the latest source of workers compensation claim. Muscular, skeletal, and neurological injury caused by prolonged and continuous operation of video display terminals by data processors are commonplace in many firms. Emotional disorders caused by workplace stress are beginning to be claimed by employees in some states.

Supplementing state statutes covering worker injuries are federal laws applicable to a few specific classes of employment. For example, employees of interstate railroads are covered under the Federal Employers Liability Act and workers employed on shipping docks or in harbors, or servicing ocean-going vessels are eligible for benefits provided by the U.S. Longshore and Harbor Workers' Compensation Act.

In addition to workers compensation obligations, firms are subject to safe workplace standards that are enforced in accordance with the Occupational Safety and Health Act (OSHA). The standards adopted as a result of this act provide for inspections and penalties for employers who fail to comply with safe workplace requirements.

Workers Compensation Insurance Programs

Measuring the loss potential for most liability exposures is a formidable task. Workers compensation benefits are determined by state statute, and most commercial workers compensation insurance policies are written without a specified limit; coverage equal to the statutory limit is provided.

In all but 6 states, employers can purchase insurance from private insurance companies. In these 6 states—Ohio, West Virginia, Washington, Nevada, Wyoming, and North Dakota—employers are required to purchase coverage from a state-operated facility. In approximately 12 states, employers have the option of purchasing insurance from a state facility or from private insurers.

Since employers are required by law to purchase workers compensation insurance, every state in which insurance is available only from commercial insurers provides a program that assures every employer a facility to purchase workers compensation insurance coverage. These programs are available regardless of how hazardous the risk is. Most states use an assigned risk plan whereby insurers are arbitrarily assigned applicants in proportion to their share of voluntary insureds. A few states use a reinsurance type plan, which assesses the underwriting losses of the plan against all insurers in proportion to their voluntary written business.

Rates for workers compensation must be approved by the insurance commissioners. In several states, increased workers compensation rates have been rejected or held artificially low despite actuarially sound evidence. As a result, obtaining workers compensation insurance can be difficult, even for employers with good claims experience. Insurers recognize that the more voluntary workers compensation insurance they write, the more assigned risk business they will be forced to assume. In some states, the involuntary business assessment is in excess of 30 percent of the gross voluntary written premium.

More sophisticated insurance buyers that are financially able to qualify elect to be self-insured for workers compensation coverage and purchase excess insurance protection for a specific limit to cover catastrophic claims.

Excess (Umbrella) Liability Insurance

Liability claims occasionally exceed several million dollars. In order to have sufficient limits of coverage for substantial claims, most firms purchase primary liability insurance policies with limits of $1 to $2 million coverage. An excess liability policy is designed to apply higher limits over several primary policies that cover automobile, watercraft, aircraft, public, and products liability exposures. Excess liability insurance limits of $5 million or more are commonplace, with major firms carrying $50 million and higher. Major industries often carry several hundred-million dollars in excess liability insurance.

Loss Sensitive Rating Plans

Large employers that fail to qualify or choose not to self-insure any of their workers compensation exposure often purchase coverage using a loss sensitive retrospective rating plan. The insurer determines a minimum amount premium necessary to administer the coverage. Costs such as underwriting expenses, broker commissions, administrative overhead, and profit constitute the basic premium. The insured's premium is the sum of the basic premium plus all losses, subject to a minimum and a maximum. Losses are loaded with a loss adjustment expense factor, and the total premium is subject to an insurance premium tax.

In effect, the ultimate cost of retrospective rated insurance policies is not determined until after the policy period has ended and claims during the policy are finally resolved. As a result, it is not uncommon for retrospective policies to be adjusted six or more years after the policy has expired. Retrospective policies adjustments can be based on actual paid losses or incurred but not settled losses. If the adjustments are based on paid losses, most insurers require a letter of credit to guarantee that the insurer will be reimbursed when the outstanding claims are settled.

Several insurance companies offer to combine workers compensation, general liability, and automobile liability insurance coverages into a single retrospective rated plan. If the exposures for each line are sufficiently large a "three line retro" will spread losses over a larger base and can result in a lower net insurance cost.

Long "Tail" of Liability Claims

Liability loss exposures and the resulting claims for damages are not always immediately recognized. Some worker injuries develop over a period of years of exposure to harmful conditions. Products manufactured today may not fail and cause injury for several years, and the cause of injury or identity of the manufacturer may take years to determine.

This phenomenon of slowly developed workers compensation and public liability claims is referred to as "Incurred But Not Reported" (IBNR) losses. Manufacturers of machinery with lengthy useful lives are particularly exposed to claims for injuries from products manufactured decades ago. Similarly, because of protracted claims negotiations and lengthy judicial processes, liability claims may be recognized today but not resolved and settled for several years. These claims are known as Incurred But Not Paid (IBNP) losses. When evaluating a company's liability loss exposures, appropriate consideration must be made for these latent exposures.

INSURANCE DISTRIBUTION SYSTEMS

Insurance policies are sold to insurance customers through a variety of different distribution systems. Although many insurance companies adopt a single system, a few insurers use several systems, sometimes in direct competition with themselves.

Direct Writer and Exclusive Agency Insurers

Direct writer insurers employ individuals to sell insurance to prospects. The sales force consists of employees, often under employment contract, who are prohibited from working for or selling insurance for any other insurance company. Exclusive agency insurers contract with individuals to represent the insurance company on an exclusive basis. The agreement establishes an independent contractor relationship rather than an employee-employer relationship.

The major weakness of direct writer and exclusive agency insurance distribution systems is that the agent is limited to a single insurer to furnish a proposal. Insurance buyers need to be aware of this limitation, and if comparative quotations are sought, another agent should be given an opportunity to provide a quotation. The strength of these systems is that the agent usually is more familiar with the underwriting criteria of the insurer, and is therefore presumably more adept at indicating the likely response an underwriter will make to an application.

Independent Agency and Broker Insurers

Unless restricted by contract, an insurance agent can represent more than one insurance company. An agent is licensed by the state insurance commissioner and appointed by the insurer to solicit applicants for insurance on behalf of the insurance company. An insurance broker is licensed by a state insurance commissioner to procure insurance coverage from any admitted insurance company on behalf of the insurance buyer. One advantage of this system is that the agent can submit insurance applications to multiple insurers, thereby obtaining competitive quotations. Frequently, agents are granted authority to bind insurance coverage on behalf of the insurer and collect premium payments from insureds. Some are granted authority to perform other functions including issuing premium quotations, preparing insurance policies, and settling small claims.

An independent agent, unless also licensed as a broker, can place coverage only with insurers that have executed agency appointment contracts. Since there are over 3,800 insurers that write property or casualty insurance in the United States, it is impractical for a single agent to represent every insurer. Even considering that over 900 companies write the vast majority of property and casualty insurance in the United States, very few agents have contracts with more than one percent of these. As a result, most agents that focus on selling insurance to commercial insurance buyers are also licensed as brokers.

The insurance brokerage community is dominated by fewer than a dozen national and international firms. These insurance sales firms have offices located in major cities, enabling them to provide local service to multistate and multinational customers. In addition to insurance sales, major brokers offer ancillary services including claims administration, captive insurance company management (discussed later in this chapter), loss control inspections, actuarial analysis, and loss exposure analysis.

INSURANCE COMPETITION

According to a survey conducted annually by *Business Insurance*, an insurance industry publication, nine insurance brokers each reported over $100 million in gross revenues in 1989. The 100th-largest broker reported over $6 million in gross revenues. Despite the relative size of the major national brokers, competition for customers is keen. There is no merit to generalizations about premium and rate differences, coverage differences, customer service, and claims of professional expertise asserting that one agent, one broker, or even one distribution system is superior to another.

Although standard coverage forms serve as the basic insurance contract, insurers are relatively unrestricted to customize their policies by endorsement. Except in unusual circumstances, such as mass-marketed programs, no producer or insurer has a monopoly on any type of insurance or group of insurance buyers.

Most insurance rating plans are filed and approved by state insurance departments. While automobile insurance and workers compensation insurance rates are closely regulated, often insurers obtain approval for discretionary pricing schedules that permit underwriters to apply credits and surcharges to applicants based on subjective criteria. When combined with objective rate deviation criteria, the range of filed and authorized rates frequently vary from a 70 percent discount to over a 100 percent surcharge from the basic rate. Many states allow insurers to apply excess surcharges beyond the authorized schedule if the insured is aware of and accepts the surcharge.

Insurance professionalism and technical competence in a firm are marked by a large porportion of staff who have earned insurance designations. Chartered Property Casualty Underwriter (CPCU) and Associate in Risk Management (ARM) designations indicate that the individual has a high degree of expertise gained through a formal educational program. Similar designations and certifications exist for other specialists such as actuaries, claims adjusters, and safety and loss prevention engineers.

Insurer Solvency

Since insurance contracts represent payment of a premium today, in exchange for the insurer's promise to fulfill an obligation at some future time, the insurer's financial ability to keep its promise is of paramount importance to the insured. Recent insolvencies by companies that wrote commercial insurance include Mission Insurance Company, Integrity Insurance Company, Mutual Fire, Marine and Inland Insurance Company, Ideal Mutual Insurance Company, Pine Top Insurance Company, and several insurance syndicates that wrote insurance through the now defunct New York Insurance Exchange and the Insurance Exchange of the Americas.

Insurer Ratings

A degree of comfort with the financial condition of an insurance company can be achieved by noting the rating a company has received from an independent organization. While governmental agencies do not issue ratings, insurers are subject to examination by the insurance department of their state of domicile on a triennial basis. Since business strategies and results of an insurance company can change dramatically over a three-year period, reliance on a satisfactory examination by an insurance department may not be adequate for an insurance buyer's needs. Two proprietary organizations have undertaken the role of issuing evaluations of insurers that write a significant amount of insurance in the United States.

A. M. Best Company has issued *Best's Insurance Reports Property-Casualty* on an annual basis since 1900. Although generally accepted as the definitive independent source of information regarding an insurer's conditions, the report contains the following disclaimer:

> Best's Ratings reflect our *opinion* as to the relative financial strength and performance of each insurer in comparison with others, based on our analysis of the information provided to us. These Ratings **are not a warranty** of an insurer's current or future ability to meet its contractual obligations.

A. M. Best Company assigns ratings ranging from A+ (Superior) to C− (Fair) on approximately fifteen hundred insurers. Over eight hundred insurers are reviewed but not assigned a rating for various reasons. In addition, the financial size is categorized in classes from I to XV, based on the reported policyholder's surplus. Pertinent tests and ratios such as profitability, liquidity, and leverage are performed and reported for each insurer. The reader is cautioned against relying exclusively upon the Best's Rating for an indication of an insurer's condition. Over 95 percent of the insurers rated by A. M. Best Company in 1990 received a Superior, Excellent, or Very Good rating.

Standard & Poor's, renowned for their rating of bonds and other financial instruments, recently introduced a "Qualified Solvency Ratings" service. Their ratings are derived from a statistical analysis of data taken from the annual statutory filings insurers make to state insurance departments. On the contrary, A. M. Best Company's rating includes qualitative criteria in the analytical process. The Standard & Poor's service when used in concert with A. M. Best's ratings can serve as a valuable second opinion.

Guarantee Funds

When all efforts fail to avoid buying coverage from an insurer that becomes insolvent, many insureds have some safety net protection available to them from insurance guarantee funds. Commercial insurance buyers are cautioned against relying on guarantee funds, since several state funds set maximum reimbursement limits well below the policy limits they typically purchase. Also, by limiting protection to personal line coverages such as automobile and homeowners insurance and workers compensation and automobile insurance for businesses, some funds will not cover claims for all lines of business.

Other funds do not protect against the insolvency of a surplus line insurer. A surplus line insurer is authorized to write insurance by a state but is not considered an admitted insurer. Surplus line insurers usually specialize in insuring exceptionally hazardous, high-risk, or small-niche business classes or insurance coverages.

Alternatives to Commercial Insurance

Circumstances such as the unacceptable cost of insurance or even the unavailability of desired coverage may prevent traditional commercially purchased insurance from being a viable business decision. Risk financing and risk transfer alternatives have been developed as alternatives. Increasingly, they have become competitive alternatives to insurance.

Self-Insurance

Self-insurance is the most commonly recognized alternative to insurance. The technique requires the company to recognize and quantify its exposure to loss. Ignorance of and blindness to loss exposures are not considered self-insurance. Once the company has assessed the loss exposure, it consciously determines an acceptable level of risk it can withstand. Excess insurance, if necessary, is purchased to cover the loss exposures above the acceptable level of risk, and a financing plan is formulated to cover the acceptable level of risk. Financing plans can include designating cash or near-cash assets to pay for losses, establishing a line of credit to draw against if necessary, or opting to pay for losses out of current income. Self-insurance financing plans must be evaluated on a managerial accounting basis in order to assure that necessary cash will be available, and also on a GAAP basis to assure postloss compliance with balance-sheet-based obligations.

Mandatory insurance coverages such as workers compensation and automobile liability insurance can be self-insured, but the company must demonstrate to the insurance department of each state in which it operates its ability to pay for self-insured losses. Requirements to become a qualified self-insurer include acceptable audited financial statements that meet specified conditions, evidence of reinsurance with an acceptable reinsurer, a bank letter of credit covering the expected losses, and a completed application with the required application fee.

Captive Insurance

A captive insurance company is an insurance company that is owned by a noninsurance company parent. The captive insurance company can insure part or all of the parent's loss exposures, and some captives also issue insurance policies to cover the risks of other companies. Disregarding tax considerations, a captive is very similar to self-insurance. The key differences lie in the fact that a captive provides a formal structure for paying losses, whereas other self-insurance financing techniques are less structured. A buyer considering this alternative should undertake a captive feasibility study.

Risk Retention and Risk Purchasing Groups

As a direct result of insurance companies' unwillingness to provide products liability insurance for many product manufacturers in the late 1970s, the federal government enacted the Products Liability

Risk Retention Act of 1981 (amended in 1984). As amended the act allows industries that are unable to obtain acceptable liability insurance to form their own mutual risk financing organization, or to form an insurance buyers' cooperative to facilitate purchasing insurance as a larger negotiating unit. This federal act was designed to override state insurance laws and regulations that were thought to hamper pooling and financing of these risks.

Numerous innovative programs have emerged, although some have not achieved the promoter's or participant's expectations. Often substantial entry and exit fees are required and the management fees can be sizable. While many RPGs and RRGs have responded to business needs, the relaxed regulatory environment has created an opportunity for deceptive practices.

Cost of Risk

In attempting to evaluate an insurance program's effectiveness, managers can be trapped into simplistic and superficial analysis. Comparing insurance premium changes from year to year, or comparing one company's insurance costs to those of another does not adequately measure a program's effectiveness. While these comparisons can provide useful benchmarks they can also be misleading. Merely looking at insurance premium costs does not indicate whether the most appropriate kinds and limits of insurance were purchased. Clearly, costs alone do not reflect savings realized through safety or loss reduction efforts. A change in deductible or self-insured retention may result in a premium savings but cause an increase in the cost of retained or uninsured losses. The effectiveness of an organization's risk management program can be more accurately measured using these four components:

Insurance Premiums. Insurance premiums should include the full cost of insurance and insurance services purchased from other organizations. Fees to brokers, claims or third party plan administrators, actuarial reports, and risk management information systems data supplied by others should be included. Appropriate allowance should be made for adjustments that can be anticipated as a result of insurance policies being rated as loss-sensitive.

Self-insured Losses. Direct costs incurred for self-insured losses, including the loss or damage to owned property and direct costs relating to clean-up and repairs, should be included. Uninsured loss of net income as a result of a self-insured loss may be included. Some organizations choose not to calculate this because of the inherent difficulties of determining the actual loss sustained. Liability losses should include not only damages paid to third parties but also legal and claims-handling costs that are incurred.

Risk Management Department Overhead Costs. Fully developed departmental costs should be used, including salaries and benefits. Direct expenses include training, travel, and data processing costs.

Loss Control Costs. Capturing the cost of loss prevention and loss reduction expenditures is regarded as the most difficult component to measure accurately. Clearly, the cost to recharge a portable fire extinguisher can be recognized as an expenditure incurred to reduce losses. However, in large organizations nominal purchases such as these are not tracked.

Alternatively, including the cost of installing an automatic sprinkler system in a building can be disputed when this is required by ordinance. Even when amortized over its useful life, such an expenditure can cause distortions. Generally, loss control costs are limited to the labor costs associated with safety and security staff members and the direct costs associated with the performance of their duties.

The sum of these four components should be calculated on an annual basis and tracked over a period of several years. These components should be compared with other business variables—such as gross revenue, total assets net of goodwill, and other intangible assets, or net income before interest and taxes. The effectiveness of an organization's risk management strategy can be monitored on an annual basis by analyzing changes in the ratio of costs of risk to these business variables. Periodically, the Risk and Insurance Management Society, a North America trade association for risk managers, publishes a *Cost of Risk Survey* based on information submitted by its members.

RISK MANAGEMENT ORGANIZATIONS WITHIN COMPANIES

Reporting Relationship

In most organizations the risk management department reports either directly or through a direct chain to the Chief Financial Officer. With the greater use of alternative risk financing options, many risk managers come from the accounting and finance ranks rather than from the insurance industry. The treasurer of one major corporation asserted that he relies on an insurance broker to obtain the most favorable insurance coverage terms and conditions, and relies on the company's risk manager for the quantitative risk evaluations and financial analysis.

Responsibilities and Authorities

Risk manager responsibilities can include a variety of activities beyond procuring insurance coverage. In some companies the risk manager is also responsible for physical facility safety, security, and loss prevention; claims handling, including claims negotiating and settlement; and captive insurance company management.

Rather than assign direct responsibility or authority for these to the risk manager, most organizations assign safety, security, and loss prevention to line management in the plant. Claims handling, particularly for workers compensation, rests with human resources. This enables coordination with other employee benefits and reduces the likelihood of double payment of claims. Claims negotiation and settlement responsibilities are usually assigned to house counsel or legal department.

CHAPTER 8

INVESTMENT INCENTIVES— GOVERNMENT AS A BUSINESS PARTNER

John J. Korbel
Partner
R. Desmond Shaw*
Senior Manager
Price Waterhouse

The United States maintains an open investment environment, with few restrictions on the establishment, acquisition, and ownership of U.S. companies by foreign entities. This, together with the country's long history of political stability, is a key attribute in making the United States an attractive location for foreign investment. Other factors include the large size of the U.S. market, the supply of skilled labor, and the availability of government location incentives.

By the time the foreign investor is evaluating government incentive programs, the question has become not whether to invest in the United States, but where, as illustrated in the flow chart presented in Exhibit 8–1. Incentive programs may not provide the key factor in the planning of new investments or acquisitions, but they do play an important role in the latter stages of the location decision. Everything else being equal, government incentives provide an additional source of support to the foreign investor that may be the ultimate factor in choosing a particular location.

---

* The authors would like to thank Brenda Monroe for her assistance in preparing this chapter.

EXHIBIT 8–1
Flowchart of the Investment Decision-making Process

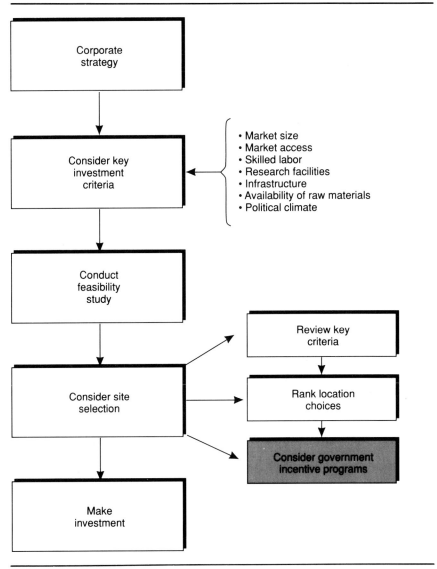

Government agencies, particularly at the state and local levels, are committed to economic diversification and increasing employment and income. In general, their incentive programs tend to target "greenfield" investment rather than acquisitions, and the small investor over the larger one. During the 1980s, states focused much of their attention on attracting new manufacturing plants. In the early 1990s, states appear to be shifting their attention to the retention, expansion, and promotion of current business operations. Foreign investment will, however, continue to play an important role in the efforts of state governments to achieve economic growth and stability.

This chapter discusses the role U.S. government agencies play as your business partner in providing investment incentives. The chapter provides an overview of the types of incentive programs offered by federal, state, and local government agencies; presents some illustrative examples of these incentives; describes recent trends in the evolution of incentive programs; and offers advice on how you can access these incentives.

RELATIVE IMPORTANCE OF FEDERAL AND STATE GOVERNMENTS

It is important to realize that, in the United States, federal, state, and local government agencies play significantly different roles in foreign investment promotion. The federal government tends to play a passive role, neither encouraging nor discouraging foreign investment. It does, however, play an important positive role in maintaining one of the most open investment environments in the world, permitting both domestic and foreign companies to operate without intrusive government involvement. As a consequence, state and local government agencies take the lead in providing specific financial, nonfinancial, and tax incentives in an already fertile investment environment. In the majority of cases, therefore, the federal government will *not* be your first point of contact when evaluating investment incentives.

Federal Programs

By contrast with many other countries, the United States does not utilize a national agency, such as the Invest in Britain Bureau or Ireland's Industrial Development Authority, to actively promote foreign investment. Instead, the federal government takes a neutral approach to foreign investment but maintains an open investment environment.

For example, there are no foreign exchange restrictions, profit repatriation is simple and straightforward, and the tax system does not discriminate between foreign and domestic companies. In only a limited number of sectors (such as defense, communications, air transport, coastal shipping, and nuclear energy) does the U.S. government place restrictions on foreign investment, and this is generally for reasons of national security.

In all other cases, federal government intervention in foreign investment is generally limited to macroeconomic policy and international trade policy, such as the regulation of the money supply and the imposition of import quotas on textiles and steel. Federal incentive programs focus on providing assistance to state and local economic development agencies in order to make their localities more attractive to potential investors, including foreign companies. These programs also provide assistance to private industry to reduce costs associated with capital investment (see Exhibit 8–2).

Federal agencies offering development assistance programs include the following (Appendix A provides additional information):

U.S. Department of Commerce Economic Development Administration (EDA).   Offers assistance to communities (primarily rural) suffering from the poorest economic climate. Cities, states, local nonprofit organizations, and economic development districts (groups of counties using a common economic development plan) may apply for EDA funds. EDA's programs include these types of assistance: public works, technical, economic development planning, economic adjustment, and trade adjustment.

If you are considering specific sites, you should meet with local government officials to determine whether the community will consider applying to EDA to obtain funds for infrastructure improvements. Addresses of the regional EDA offices are included in Appendix B.

Department of Housing and Urban Development (HUD) Community Development Block Grant Program.   Provides housing, public works, and economic development assistance for urban revitalization and improvement. This program provides grants to metropolitan cities and urban counties (approximately 860 communities are currently eligible) and operates a loan guarantee program. It also offers funding for specialized economic development activities, such as initiatives targeted at Native Americans. The vast majority of resources are aimed at the low- and moderate-income segment of the population.

As a foreign company, you should investigate whether a potential site is eligible for HUD grants. If it is, then you should meet with the local government officials and determine whether it is feasible to access HUD funds.

U.S. Department of Agriculture Farmers Home Administration (FmHA).

The Business and Industrial Loans and Grants Program provides loan guarantees to companies establishing operations in rural areas (defined as having a population of less than 50,000, with priority given to communities with fewer than 25,000 people). Eligible companies must be at least 51 percent U.S.-owned. Loans to rural communities are also available through the program.

If your company is eligible, you should apply directly to the local Farmers Home Administration office. The state development agencies listed in Appendix C can provide information on the FmHA offices located within their respective states.

EXHIBIT 8–2
Federal Assistance Programs

Assistance through state and local development agencies	Direct assistance to private industry
• Economic Development Administration	• Farmers Home Administration
• HUD Community Development Block Grant Program	• Small Business Administration
• EPA Office of Water	• Immigration and Naturalization Service
• Employment and Training Administration	• National Science Foundation

Small Business Administration (SBA).   Provides a variety of financial assistance programs, including loan guarantees and long-term loans to small businesses. The definition of a small business varies from industry to industry, based on the company's volume of sales or number of employees. The direct loan program is limited to businesses owned by handicapped persons, Vietnam-era military veterans, disabled veterans, or businesses located in areas of high unemployment. The SBA also operates more than 600 Small Business Development Centers throughout the United States, offering a variety of management and technical assistance to small businesses.

While any small business (foreign- or U.S.-owned) with domestic operations can participate in SBA programs, they have not been used often by foreign companies. You should apply directly to the local SBA office (over 100 exist throughout the country). Contact the state development agencies listed in Appendix C for information on where these offices are located.

Environmental Protection Agency (EPA) Office of Water. Until recently, the EPA directly awarded construction grants for the development of waste-water treatment plants in the United States. Beginning in 1991, the EPA is capitalizing state revolving loan funds (SRFs) for these construction projects. As with the HUD and EDA programs, you should meet with state government officials to discuss whether a potential investment location will consider applying for EPA financial assistance.

Department of Labor Employment and Training Administration.   Under the Job Training Partnership Act (JTPA), which became operational in 1983, the federal government provides funds for job training programs that are managed and administered by state and local governments. Services offered include on-the-job training, remedial education, and job search assistance.

Funds are targeted for Service Delivery Areas, which are designated by the state governors and automatically include units of local government with populations of 200,000 or higher. Almost one half of JTPA funding comes through block grants, providing training for disadvantaged adults and youth in high unemployment areas.

A key component of the JTPA is the "partnership" between the government and the local business community, specifically through State Job Training Coordinating Councils and local-level Private Industry Councils.

Department of Justice Immigration and Naturalization Service (INS).   The Immigration Act of 1990 contains an employment creation provision under which foreign individuals can receive residency visas if they invest more than $1 million in the United States and create at least 10 new full-time jobs. Potential foreign investors should contact the Adjudications Division of the Examinations Office of INS for additional information on how to apply for visas. Petitions for these visas should be filed at an INS regional office, listed in Appendix A. Also, see Chapter 24 for a more detailed discussion of U.S. immigration issues.

National Science Foundation (NSF).   The NSF has established 25 Science and Technology Centers, which support research and educational activities to develop new technology. Many of these centers focus on biotechnology and computer technology, and all are located within U.S. universities. Foreign companies can participate in these activities. Appendix A provides a list of these centers.

The federal government also provides a wide range of detailed information on the U.S. economy, from demographics to consumer costs, infrastructure to interest rates, which can benefit U.S. and foreign companies. Such information allows foreign investors to gain a better understanding of the U.S. market. Major information sources include the following:

The U.S. Department of Commerce, International Trade Adminstration.   Its publications include the annual *U.S. Industrial Outlook,* which includes data on export and imports, competitiveness information, and long-term prospects for over 350 industries.

The Department of Commerce, Bureau of the Census.   Its publications provide information on a wide array of economic and demographic data, including *Current Industry Reports* (information on more than 5,000 manufactured products) *County Business Patterns* (industry information on a state-by-state basis) and the *Census* *of Manufacturers* (information on 83 industries on a national and state-by-state basis).

The Department of Labor, Bureau of Labor Statistics. Its publications include the *Monthly Labor Review,* which includes information on the consumer price index, the producer price index, and the employment cost index; *Employment and Earnings; Current Wage Developments;* and the *Occupation Outlook Quarterly.*

State Programs

In contrast to the federal government, state governments are actively involved in promoting investment. Since the 1930s, states have been using a myriad of economic development programs to attract business from other states and from outside the United States. Prior to 1979, only 10 states committed resources to foreign investment attraction; by 1979, only 3 states did *not* have an active foreign investment attraction program. In the early 1990s, all 50 state governments are actively involved in recruiting companies to locate within their jurisdiction.

Early foreign investment promotion efforts developed from overseas investment missions led by state governors. Overseas offices were subsequently established to follow up on business opportunities developed during these missions. At a later stage, states expanded the breadth and scope of tax and nontax incentive programs available to potential investors, both domestic and foreign. State governments currently maintain more than 150 overseas offices and operate more than 1,060 investment incentive programs. The latter programs are available to both domestic and foreign investors.

State departments of commerce or economic development are typically responsible for foreign investment attraction and for managing the states' overseas offices. Appendix C provides a comprehensive list of these state development agencies.

Initiatives at the Local Level

Local government agencies such as city governments provide additional incentive programs designed to serve the specific needs of the community and to facilitate local private-sector involvement. Other local entities, such as regional development councils, chambers of commerce, and public utilities, also offer incentives to investors. Their programs are many and diverse, and the incentives offered by these local entities should generally be considered by potential investors only after a regional location decision has been made.

Other Initiatives

A variety of other economic development mechanisms under the auspices of federal, state, and local entities are designed to make a location more attractive to the potential investor. Some of these mechanisms act as multipliers, allowing the investments in a specific region to build on one another. They include the following:

Business Incubators.   Provide a variety of services to start-up companies, particularly those in high-technology sectors, and are located throughout the United States. Within the incubator, small companies can access several sources of technical, financial, and management assistance. This ranges from sharing office space and administrative staff to participating in business management workshops and marketing advice. According to the Council of State Policy and Planning Agencies, Pennsylvania has more that 30 incubators—far more than any other state.

Foreign Trade Zones (FTZs).   The U.S. equivalent of international free-trade zones. They are used by both exporters and importers to warehouse, exhibit, package, label, sort, manipulate, and manufacture goods. In these zones (1) import duties are paid on items only when they leave the FTZ and enter the domestic market, (2) the duty paid excludes the cost of processing and the profit realized while the item was in the zone, and (3) the manufacturer can choose to pay the duty on either the finished product or its components, whichever is lower.

By early 1991 there were 167 general-purpose zones and 188 subzones (special purpose facilities typically established for company-specific operations) in the United States. *All* automobile production and most oil refining in the United States are conducted within foreign trade zones. Exhibit 8–3 presents the location of the general-purpose FTZs.

EXHIBIT 8–3
Foreign Trade Zones in the United States

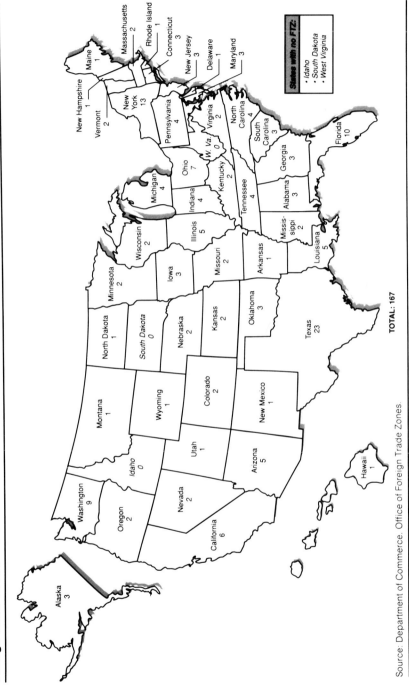

Source: Department of Commerce. Office of Foreign Trade Zones.

States with no FTZ:
- Idaho
- South Dakota
- West Virginia

Maine 1
New Hampshire 1
Vermont 2
Massachusetts 2
Rhode Island 1
Connecticut 3
New York 13
Pennsylvania 4
New Jersey 3
Delaware 1
Maryland 3
Virginia 2
W. Va. 0
North Carolina 4
South Carolina 3
Ohio 7
Kentucky 2
Tennessee 4
Georgia 3
Alabama 3
Florida 10
Michigan 4
Indiana 4
Illinois 5
Wisconsin 2
Minnesota 2
Iowa 3
Missouri 2
Arkansas 2
Mississippi 2
Louisiana 5
North Dakota 1
South Dakota 0
Nebraska 2
Kansas 2
Oklahoma 3
Texas 23
Montana 1
Wyoming 1
Colorado 2
New Mexico 1
Idaho 0
Utah 1
Arizona 5
Washington 9
Oregon 2
Nevada 2
California 6
Alaska 3
Hawaii 1

TOTAL: 167

Enterprise Zones.   Designed to attract businesses to economically depressed areas. Companies operating in these locations are offered a wide range of financial and nonfinancial incentives. These zones are also targeted by many of the federal-level programs offered by EDA and HUD, described previously. Cities, counties, or regions (groups of counties) may be designated as enterprise zones, eligible for a variety of tax inducements ranging from 5 to 20 years. Enterprise zones are operating in 28 states, with an additional 10 states authorized to create zones. In most states, the local government designates zones, but in some, such as Alabama and Louisiana, all localities below a certain economic threshold automatically qualify as an enterprise zone. These two states, therefore, have over 940 and 860 zones, respectively.

Technology Centers.   Usually academic-government-business partnerships designed to stimulate the research and development of new technologies and facilitate their commercial application. These centers work to transfer technology to the state's industrial bases. For example, Ohio's Thomas Edison Program funds six such centers, while Pennsylvania's Ben Franklin Partnership funds four.

If you are interested in initiatives such as incubators and enterprise zones, you should inquire with the respective state development agency as to their location.

TYPES OF GOVERNMENT
INCENTIVE PROGRAM

The number of state incentive programs available to the foreign investor is increasing steadily. The National Association of State Development Agencies (NASDA) reports a 19 percent increase in the number of state incentive programs between 1985 and 1990, to more than 1,060. Of these programs, the most important are tax incentives, which account for more than half. Exhibit 8–4 provides a summary of the major types of incentive programs.

A closer look at the growth in incentive programs reveals that these programs are typically available in most states. For example, programs once considered innovative, such as enterprise zones and technology centers, now exist in more than half the states.

EXHIBIT 8–4

Types of Incentive Program Offered by State Governments

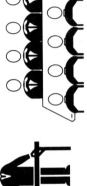

Form 1040   IRS

Name _____
Address _____
City/State _____

Information Provision

- Overseas offices
- Trade and investment missions
- Hosting foreign delegations
- Demographic and site information
- Business consulting

Investment Incentives

- Financial Incentives
  - Grants
  - Loans
  - Loan Guarantees
  - Industrial Development Bonds
  - Equity/Venture Capital Programs
- Employment Incentives
  - Customized Job Training
- Tax Incentives
  - Tax Exemptions and Reductions
  - Tax Credits
  - Abatements

Incentive "Packaging"

State budgets earmarked for trade development/export promotion and foreign investment attraction have also increased in recent years. The average state appropriation for international business development in 1990 was almost $2 million, an increase of 63 percent over the 1988 total. California, Hawaii, Maryland, Michigan, New York, and Oregon had appropriations of $5 million or more each (with California alone appropriating $10.6 million).

One way of determining a state's commitment to attracting foreign investment is by examining the breakdown of each state's budget (see Exhibits 8–5, 8–6, and 8–7). Of the states that provide separate data for trade and investment development in their international appropriations, eight appropriated more than $1 million to investment attraction, and seven appropriated 50 percent or more of their funds for investment attraction.

Incentive programs fall into three main categories: information provision; investment incentives; and investment "packaging." These programs are not mutually exclusive, and foreign investors can take advantage of one or more at the same time. The variety of programs within each of these categories is described in detail below, together with examples of specific programs.

Information Provision

Providing information about their state is one of the most important services offered by state development agencies. A variety of approaches are used to disseminate information. The following is a summary of the kinds of promotional activities currently used:

Overseas Offices.   State governments currently operate more than 150 overseas offices to promote trade and investment. Only seven states—Maine, Nebraska, New Hampshire, New Mexico, South Dakota, Tennessee, and Vermont—do *not* have a direct overseas presence. The states with the largest network of overseas offices are Illinois (11), Minnesota (8), Florida (7), and, with 6 each, Indiana, Maryland, New York, and Texas. The majority of these offices are in Asia (89 offices), followed by Western Europe (37 offices). Table 8–1 provides a list of overseas office locations, while Appendix D provides their addresses.

EXHIBIT 8–5

State Budgets for Investment Attraction: States with More Than $1 Million Budgeted to Foreign Investment Attraction in 1990

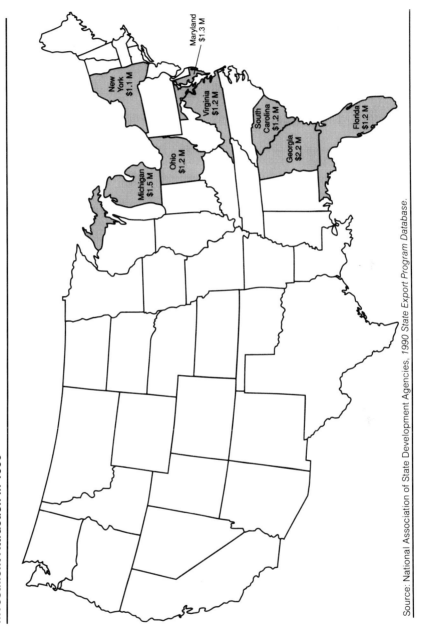

Source: National Association of State Development Agencies, *1990 State Export Program Database.*

EXHIBIT 8–6

State Budgets for Investment Attraction: States with at Least 50 Percent of Their 1990 International Business Development Budget Targeted for Foreign Investment Attraction

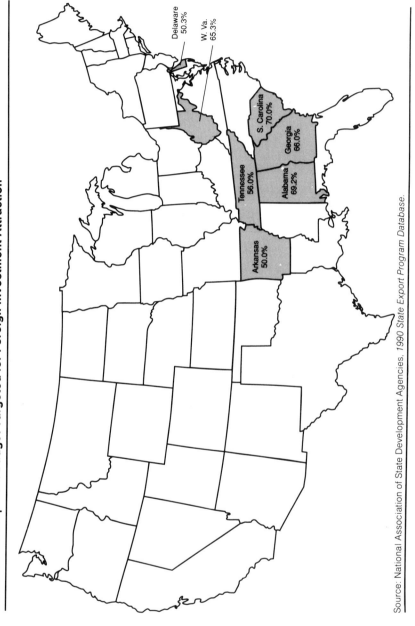

Source: National Association of State Development Agencies, *1990 State Export Program Database.*

EXHIBIT 8–7

State Budgets for Investment Attraction: States That Equally Divide Their Domestic Office Activities Between Trade Development and Foreign Investment Attraction

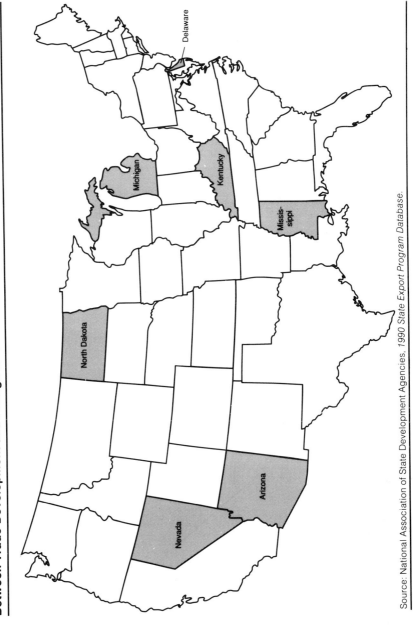

Source: National Association of State Development Agencies. 1990 State Export Program Database.

TABLE 8–1
Location of States' Overseas Offices

State	Japan	Taiwan	Korea	Hong Kong	Belgium	Germany	Canada	Other
Alabama	☐		☐			☐		
Alaska	☐	☐	☐					
Arizona		☐						
Arkansas	☐	☐			☐			
California	☐			☐		☐		UK, Mexico
Colorado	☐	☐	☐					
Connecticut	☐					☐		
Delaware	☐							UK, Netherlands
Florida	☐		☐		☐	☐	☐	UK, Brazil
Georgia	☐	☐	☐		☐		☐	
Hawaii	☐			☐				
Idaho		☐	☐					
Illinois	☐ ☐			☐	☐		☐	China, Mexico, Brazil, Poland, Hungary, USSR
Indiana	☐	☐	☐				☐	China, Netherlands
Iowa	☐			☐		☐		
Kansas	☐							
Kentucky	☐	☐	☐		☐			
Louisiana	☐	☐	☐					
Maryland	☐	☐		☐	☐ ☐ ☐			
Massachusetts	☐							
Michigan	☐			☐	☐ ☐		☐	Nigeria
Minnesota	☐ ☐	☐			☐		☐	Sweden, France, Costa Rica
Mississippi	☐			☐		☐		
Missouri	☐	☐	☐			☐		
Montana	☐	☐						
Nevada	☐	☐	☐					
New Jersey	☐							
New York	☐			☐		☐	☐ ☐	UK
North Carolina	☐		☐	☐		☐		
North Dakota	☐							
Ohio	☐			☐	☐		☐	Nigeria
Oklahoma	☐							India, China, Singapore
Oregon	☐	☐	☐					
Pennsylvania	☐				☐	☐		
Rhode Island		☐		☐	☐			
South Carolina	☐					☐		
Texas	☐	☐	☐			☐		Mexico (2)
Utah	☐	☐	☐		☐			
Virginia	☐				☐			
Washington	☐	☐						
West Virginia	☐							
Wisconsin	☐		☐	☐		☐		
Wyoming		☐						
Total	41	20	16	12	16	13	9	25

Demographic and Site Information.   State development agencies collect and disseminate a wide range of economic and business data. This includes information on the overall economic climate, tax structure, wage rates, infrastructure, energy costs, educational facilities, labor skills, and quality of life. Thirty-eight states publish an international newsletter, and several states publish handbooks on investment opportunities.

Several local governments publish their own investment literature, such as Fulton County, Georgia, which provides a detailed "How To Invest in Fulton County" guide for foreign companies interested in the county. In addition, a question-and-answer booklet, available in five languages, attempts to address all the questions a potential investor might have about the county, from tax structure to transportation, property acquisition to recreational facilities.

Trade and Investment Missions.   The number of overseas missions has increased at both the state and local level. Missions have several objectives: (1) to promote U.S. exports, (2) to encourage foreign investment in the state, and (3) to develop government-private sector and government-government contacts. Delaware, for example, sponsored three "Invest in Delaware" missions to Canada, the United Kingdom, and Japan during 1990.

Business Consulting.   The types of consulting services offered by most states include market studies, export opportunities, and site location studies, many of which are tailored to a specific request. In addition, states are constantly working at improving their data collection to respond to the questions and needs of potential investors. Many states also have programs that tap into the research capabilities of the state's academic institutions, as well as joint programs with local business organizations.

Hosting Foreign Delegations.   In addition to overseas missions, states sponsor visits from foreign business and government representatives. The state overseas offices play an important role in organizing these trips.

Investment Incentives

Investment incentives are broken down into employment incentives, financial incentives, and tax incentives. Of these, tax incentives are still the most commonly used form of government incentive program. Non-financial incentives, however, are becoming increasingly popular. Following is a brief description of each:

Employment Assistance

The most popular incentive program is customized job training, which is offered by almost all states. Most state programs target new or expanding businesses and offer pre-employment training (by the state before the employee begins working) and on-the-job training, as well as the upgrading of worker skills. Several programs also provide funds for training equipment and facilities. In addition, some programs require that a minimum number of jobs be created once training is completed.

Financial Incentives

All 50 states offer programs designed to reduce the cost of establishing a new business facility. These programs include grants, loans, loan guarantees, bond issues, and state-chartered venture capital corporations. Each of these is described in more detail below.

   Grants.   Twenty-three states operate grant programs, which underwrite some of the costs of economic development. They are designed to serve as a catalyst for making a region more attractive to potential investors. The most common of these grants provide funds to improve transportation, encourage research and development, and promote industrial site preparation, such as the construction of water and sewer lines and access roads. Other programs are more specialized, such as Maine's Job Opportunity Grants Program, which provides a new business with $1,250 for each job created in one of the state's four job opportunity zones.

   One of the larger programs is the Tennessee Industrial Infrastructure Program, which provides funds for infrastructure improvements and job training. Unlike many of the other grant programs, the Tennessee program ties eligibility to export or import substitution criteria. One of the more unusual programs is New

York's Secondary Materials Program, which provides financial and technical assistance to companies that are involved in recycling.

Most research and development grant programs fund academic-business partnerships to promote technology transfer. For example, Florida's Applied Research Grant Program funds applied research in seven areas, including biotechnology, microelectronics, computer-integrated engineering and manufacturing, and electro-optics.

Loans.   Most loan programs offer funds directly to companies for the acquisition of fixed assets, although some states also provide loans for working capital. The state rarely provides all of the funds but instead usually offers a low-interest loan that accompanies a conventional commercial loan. For many programs, the state hopes to see a direct correlation between the loan and the number of jobs that will be created as a result of the loan.

While many state direct loan programs target small and minority-owned businesses, some are directed to the large investor. These include the Build Illinois Large Business Development Program and the New York Job Development Authority's Direct Loan Program. For example, the Illinois program provides long-term, fixed-rate, low-interest loans to businesses that are planning to move into the state, are substantially expanding a current operation in the state, or might otherwise leave the state without the loan. To qualify for the loan, a company must be well established and profitable, and employ more than 500 people. The New York Program provides loans to companies that will locate or expand into economically distressed areas of the state. In particular, low-interest rate loans are available for most business development, *except* for retail business, hotels, and apartment buildings.

Loan Guarantees.   Currently, 19 states offer loan guarantee programs, whereby the state guarantees the payment of private commercial loans. As with direct loans, many of these programs target small businesses. Examples of programs that are *not* restricted to small businesses include those of the Missouri Economic Development Export and Infrastructure Board and the Texas Economic Development Fund. The Missouri program is broad and guarantees loans for a variety of projects, ranging from manufacturing plants to facilities for export trade activities. The Texas program guarantees both fixed and working capital loans for businesses located in rural areas.

Industrial Development Bonds. Industrial development bonds (IDBs) are probably the most common form of financing economic development in the United States. Bonds generally cover manufacturing projects and are issued at both the state and local level. While interest is usually exempt from certain local taxes, the Tax Reform Act of 1986 limited the issuance of federal tax-exempt bonds to small-issue IDBs of less than $10 million.

Funds raised from the sale of the IDBs are used to finance major projects with below-market interest rate loans. Currently, 40 states offer locally issued industrial development bonds, 32 states offer state-issued industrial development bonds, and 9 states issue umbrella bonds. All but 2 states (Massachusetts and Wyoming) offer some sort of state-sponsored bond program.

Ohio, for example, issues tax-exempt IDBs through its Pooled Bond Program. Instead of issuing bonds for individual projects, the program pools projects together under a single bond issue, taking advantage of economies of scale. Bond amounts range from $400,000 to $10 million and cover manufacturing projects. Ohio also offers taxable IDBs through the Ohio Enterprise Bond Fund. Bond amounts range from $1 million to $15 million, and the funds can be used for installation, engineering, and other "soft" costs in addition to equipment purchases and construction costs.

Equity/Venture Capital Programs. In addition to the traditional forms of financial assistance—direct loans, grants, and loan guarantees—states are becoming more active in offering venture capital through equity or near-equity investments. Between 1985 and 1990, the number of states offering state-funded or state-chartered equity/venture capital corporations more than doubled, from 8 to 18. In some programs, the state takes an equity position, in others the state provides the necessary start-up capital. A less risky method for providing needed venture capital is for the state to provide tax incentives to privately operated and funded corporations chartered by the state.

Michigan, for example, created a new state agency, the Michigan Strategic Fund (MSF), dedicated to increasing the availability of financing in the state by working with the private sector. Under the Seed Capital Program, the MSF has provided matching funds for several private seed capital companies. Under the Capital Access Program, instead of providing individual loan guarantees, a reserve fund is created within each participating bank to cover future losses from a portfolio of loans.

The MSF matches the borrower's and bank's premium payment to the reserve fund. Under the Business and Industrial Development Corporations (BIDCOs) Investment Program, a new type of financial institution was created, designed to fill the financing gap between traditional bank loans and venture capitalists. The MSF will make initial equity investments but have nonvoting stock in newly created BIDCOs.

Tax Incentives

With financial incentive programs, the state provides companies with funds to develop or expand operations. In the case of tax incentives, the state forgoes certain tax revenues in the short term in the expectation of greater tax returns in the long term. Tax incentives are the more traditional forms of investment incentives and are still the most widely used. These include exemptions, deductions, credits, and abatements. All states utilize at least one of these types of tax incentive.

Tax Exemptions and Deductions.   Every state offers deductions or exemptions from at least one of the state's taxes, such as sales or user taxes. Exemptions are usually applied to various types of purchases including the following:

- Pollution control equipment
- Raw materials
- Industrial fuels
- Transportation equipment (such as rolling stock, trucks, and ships)

Some states have unique tax exemption or deduction programs. New Hampshire, for example, offers an exemption for machinery and other equipment used in ski areas, and Delaware offers deductions for investments in targeted industries and targeted areas.

Tax Credits.   Tax credits are used by many states to offset a company's tax liability. Credits are provided for job creation, new investments, research and development, and the use of alternative energy (solar, wind, and gasohol). Credits are usually granted for 3 years but in some cases may be carried forward for up to 12 years.

Several states have unique tax credit programs. For example, Arkansas offers a tax rebate to motion picture companies that shoot films within the state. California offers credits to companies that implement a ride-sharing program or subsidize mass transportation for their employees. California, Kansas, Mississippi, and Oregon offer credits for companies that provide child care. Connecticut provides credits to companies that develop and expand apprenticeships in the machine tool and metals trades. Kansas, Missouri, and North Dakota offer tax credits for investments into venture capital companies and seed capital programs.

Abatements.   Thirty-two states currently offer some form of property tax abatement, including stabilization of taxes after improvements exemptions of up to 100 percent and exemptions for up to 25 years. In some states, investors receive abatements if industrial development bonds were used to help finance the business, if the property is located in an enterprise zone, or if there was new construction, expansion, or rehabilitation of property. In other states, abatements are offered for investment in specific industries, such as aluminum in Alabama, paper and pulp in Hawaii, mining in Maine, and railroads in New Hampshire.

Incentive "Packaging"

Incentive "packaging" is a combination of tax exemptions, infrastructure improvements, and special training programs, designed as a one-time arrangement to attract very large investments. Probably the largest and best-known packages have been used to attract automotive plants to several Midwest states in the 1980s: the Fuji-Izuzu plant in Indiana, the Toyota plant in Kentucky, the Diamond-

Star Motors Corporation in Illinois, the Mazda plant in Michigan, and the Nissan plant in Tennessee.

It is unlikely, however, that many such packages will be offered in the 1990s. For many public-sector officials, the costs in attracting these investments seem to have outweighed the benefits. Instead, state officials are realizing that it is better to promote several smaller investments than one large one, which in turn will help diversify and improve the local economy.

HOW TO ACCESS GOVERNMENT INVESTMENT INCENTIVES

Government agencies involved in foreign investment attraction, are, by definition, eager to work with foreign companies considering investing in their locality. As a consequence, these agencies are readily accessible to you, the potential investor, and should be consulted early on in the site location process.

Your first point of contact is likely to be the local U.S. embassy in your country. You can also contact a state's overseas office, if accessible (see Table 8–1 for the location of these overseas offices). These offices can offer general advice, but potential investors should speak directly with the state development offices in the United States and visit potential sites before making a location decision. Appendix C lists the relevant state economic development agency contacts (e.g., the state department of economic development or commerce).

In addition to government programs, a number of private-sector organizations can assist you in evaluating locations by comparing the types of incentives offered. These include law firms, accounting firms, plant location consulting firms, real estate developers, public utilities, and chambers of commerce.

CONCLUSION

In the 1980s, states actively promoted themselves to foreign investors, particularly for large investments. In the 1990s, the goals of the state economic development agencies appear to be changing, and so too are their investment incentive programs. The states are moving away from attracting major manufacturing plants and toward business retention and expansion. State and local officials realize that in order to weather business fluctuations, their economies need to be diversified rather than dependent on a single industry or plant. Therefore, development agencies are focusing on small- and medium-sized companies, and working with several smaller investments rather than one large investment.

In addition, budgetary constraints are shifting the emphasis from financial and tax incentive packages to customized job training. States realize that continued job creation and economic diversification will depend on service industries, job training, and the more selective targeting of funds. States are also beginning to work together with neighboring states rather than competing against each other. Finally, there seems to be an interest in creating some new programs, such as the elimination or deferment of the capital gains tax for enterprise zones.

According to a recent NASDA survey, three quarters of the states believe that foreign direct investment is an important part of their investment attraction program, and about half rank foreign investment as "very important," or a top priority. Government incentive programs, therefore, will continue to play a role in attracting foreign investment and influencing the investment site selection process. The advice and support of government at all levels will contribute to an informed and profitable investment decision.

SELECTED BIBLIOGRAPHICAL SOURCES

National Association of State Development Agencies. *Directory of Incentives for Business Investment and Development in the United States.* Washington: NASDA, 1991.

National Association of State Development Agencies. *1990 State Export Program Database.* Washington: NASDA, 1991.

National Council for Urban Economic Development. *Alternative Approaches to Financing Business Development.* Washington: NCUED, 1989.

Price Waterhouse. *Doing Business in the United States.* New York: Price Waterhouse, 1990.

U.S. Department of Commerce, Bureau of Economic Analysis. *Survey of Current Business,* Washington: GPO, various issues.

APPENDIX A
WHERE TO GO FOR ADDITIONAL
INFORMATION ON PROGRAMS
OFFERED BY U.S. FEDERAL AGENCIES
AND OTHER ORGANIZATIONS

Federal

OFFICE OF BLOCK GRANTS
U.S. Department of Housing and Urban Development
451 Seventh Street, SW
Washington, DC 20410
202-708-3587

EMPLOYMENT AND TRAINING ADMINISTRATION
Office of Employment and Training Programs
U.S. Department of Labor
200 Constitution Avenue, NW
Room N 4703
Washington, DC 20210
202-535-0577

OFFICE OF FOREIGN TRADE ZONES
U.S. Department of Commerce
14th and Constitution Avenue, NW
Room 4213
Washington, DC 20230
202-377-2862

ECONOMIC DEVELOPMENT AGENCY
U.S. Department of Commerce
14th and Constitution Avenue, NW
Washington, DC 20230
202-377-5113

Immigration and Naturalization Service Regional Offices

Eastern Regional Office
Federal Building
Elmwood Avenue
Burlington, VT 05401
802-951-6201

Northern Regional Office
Federal Building
Fort Snelling
Twin Cities, MN 55111
612-725-3850

Southern Regional Office
Skyline Center
Building C
311 North Stemmons Freeway
Dallas, TX 75207
214-767-7011

Western Regional Office
P.O. Box 30080
24000 Avila Road
Laguna Niguel, CA 92677-8080
714-643-4739

Other

National Science Foundation's Science and Technology Centers

Center for Biological Timing
Biology Department
Gilmer Hall
University of Virginia
Charlottesville, VA 22901
804-924-4056

Center for Engineering Plants for Resistance Against Pathogens
Plant Pathology
275 Mrak Hall
University of California
Davis, CA 95616
916-752-3474

Center for Development of an Integrated Protein and Nucleic Acid Biotechnology
Division of Biology
139-74
California Institute of Technology
Pasadena, CA 91125
818-397-2765

Center for Research in Cognitive Science
Computer and Information Science
University of Pennsylvania
200 South 33rd Street
Philadelphia, PA 19104-6389
215-898-8540

Center for Magnetic Resonance Technology for Basic Biological Research
Biomedical Magnetic Resonance Laboratory
University of Illinois
West Park Street
Urbana, IL 61801
217-244-0600

Center for Light Microscope Imaging and Biotechnology
Department of Biological Sciences
Carnegie Mellon University
4400 Fifth Avenue
Pittsburgh, PA 15213
412-268-3456

Center for Microbial Ecology
540 Plant and Soil Science Building
Michigan State University
East Lansing, MI 48824
517-353-9021

Center for Computer Graphics and Scientific Visualization
Computer Graphics
120 Rand Hall
Cornell University
Ithaca, NY 14853-5501
607-255-7444

Center for Research on Parallel Computation
Computer and Information Technology Institute
William Marsh Rice University
P.O. Box 1892
Houston, TX 77251-1892
713-285-5188

Southern California Earthquake Center
Department of Geological Sciences
University of Southern California
Los Angeles, CA 90089-0740
213-740-5830

Centers for Clouds, Chemistry, and Climate
Geophysical Sciences Department
University of Chicago
5734 South Ellis Avenue
Chicago, IL 60637
312-702-6194

Center for Astrophysical Research in the Antarctic
Yerkes Observatory
373 West Geneva Street
Williams Bay, WI 53191-0258
414-245-5555

Center for Particle Astrophysics
301 LeConte Hall
University of California
Berkeley, CA 94720
415-642-4705

Center for Analysis and Prediction of Storms
Cooperative Institute for Mesoscale Meteorological Studies
University of Oklahoma
410 E. Boyd Avenue
Norman, OK 73019-0515
405-325-3041

Center for High-Pressure Research
Department of Earth and Space Science
ESS 117
SUNY at Stony Brook
Stony Brook, NY 11794-2100
516-632-8241

Center for Synthesis, Growth, and Analysis of Electronic Materials
Department of Chemistry
University of Texas
Austin, TX 78712-1167
512-471-3702

Center for Photoinduced Charge Transfer
Department of Chemistry
University of Rochester
Hutchison Hall
Rochester, NY 14627
716-275-8286

Center for Advanced Liquid Crystalline Optical Materials
Liquid Crystal Institute
Kent State University
Kent, OH 44242
216-672-2654

Center for Superconductivity Materials Research Laboratory
University of Illinois
104 South Goodwin Avenue
Urbana, IL 61801
217-333-1744

Center for High-Performance Polymeric Adhesives and Composites
Department of Chemistry
Virginia Polytechnic Institute and State University
Blacksburg, VA 24061-0212
703-231-5976

Center for Quantized Electronic Structures (QUEST)
University of California/SB
Santa Barbara, CA 93106
805-893-8600

Center for Advanced Cement-Based Materials
Robert R. McCormick School of Engineering and Applied Science
Northwestern University
1800 Ridge Road
Evanston, IL 60208-4400
708-491-3858

Center for Discrete Mathematics and Theoretical Computer Science
Rutgers University
Busch Campus
P.O. Box 1179
Piscataway, NJ 08855-1179
201-932-5928

Center for Computation and Visualization of Geometric Structures
The Geometry Center
University of Minnesota
1300 Second Avenue South
Minneapolis, MN 55415
612-624-5531

Center for Ultrafast Optical Science
IST Building, Room 1006
Ultrafast Science Laboratory
2200 Bonisteel
University of Michigan
Ann Arbor, MI 48109-2099
313-763-4877

APPENDIX B
REGIONAL OFFICES OF THE
ECONOMIC DEVELOPMENT
AGENCY (EDA)

Austin Regional Office
Grant Building
Suite 201
611 East Sixth Street
Austin, TX 78701
512-482-5461
(Serving Arkansas, Louisiana, New Mexico, Oklahoma, and Texas)

Atlanta Regional Office
401 West Peachtree Street, NW
Suite 1820
Atlanta, GA 30308–3510
404-730-3002
(Serving Alabama, Florida, Georgia, Kentucky, Mississippi, North Caro-
    lina, South Carolina, and Tennessee)

Chicago Regional Office
175 West Jackson Boulevard
Suite A-1630
Chicago, IL 60604
312-353-7706
(Serving Illinois, Indiana, Michigan, Minnesota, Ohio, and Wisconsin)

Denver Regional Office
1244 Speer Boulevard
Room 670
Denver, CO 80204
303-844-4717
(Serving Colorado, Iowa, Kansas, Missouri, Montana, Nebraska, North
    Dakota, South Dakota, Utah, and Wyoming)

Philadelphia Regional Office
Liberty Square Building
105 South Seventh Street
First Floor
Philadelphia, PA 19106
215-597-4603
(Serving Connecticut, Delaware, District of Columbia, Maine, Maryland,
Massachusetts, New Hampshire, New York, Pennsylvania, Rhode
Island, Vermont, Virginia, and West Virginia)

Seattle Regional Office
Jackson Federal Building
915 Second Avenue
Suite 1856
Seattle, WA 98174
206-442-0596
(Serving Alaska, Arizona, California, Hawaii, Idaho, Nevada, Oregon,
and Washington)

APPENDIX C
STATE DEVELOPMENT AGENCIES

Alabama
Alabama Development Office
State Capitol
135 South Union Street
Montgomery, AL 36130
205-263-0048

Alaska
Office of the Commissioner
Department of Commerce and Economic Development
P.O. Box D
Juneau, AK 99811

Arkansas
Arkansas Department of Economic Development
One Capitol Mall
Room 4C 300
Little Rock, AR 72201
501-682-7690

Arkansas Industrial Development Commission
One State Capital Mall
Little, AR 72201
501-682-2052

Arizona
Arizona Department of Commerce
3800 North Central Avenue
Suite 1500
Phoenix, AZ 85012
602-280-1331

California
California Department of Commerce
1121 L Street
Suite 600
Sacramento, CA 95814
916-322-1394

California State World Trade Commission
1121 K Street
Suite 310
Sacramento, CA 95814
916-324-5511

Colorado
State of Colorado
Department of Local Affairs
1313 Sherman Street
Room 518
Denver, CO 80203
303-866-2205

International Trade Office
1625 Broadway
Suite 680
Denver, CO 80202
303-892-3850

Connecticut
Connecticut Department of Economic Development
865 Brook Street
Rocky Hill, CT 06067-3405
203-258-4208

Delaware
Delaware Development Office
99 Kings Highway
P.O. Box 1401
Dover, DE 19903
302-736-4271

Business Development
Delaware Development Office
World Trade Section
820 North French Street
Wilmington, DE 19801
302-739-4271

Florida
Division of Economic Development
Florida Department of Commerce
Collins Building
Tallahassee, FL 32399-2000
904-488-6300

Georgia
Georgia Department of Industry, Trade and Tourism
230 Peachtree Street, NW
P.O. Box 1776
Atlanta, GA 30301
404-656-3556

Georgia Department of Community Affairs
Suite 1200
100 Peachtree Street, NW
Atlanta, GA 30303
404-656-3836

Hawaii

Department of Business and Economic Development
P.O. Box 2359
Honolulu, HA 96804
808-548-8558

Idaho

Division of International Business
Department of Commerce
700 West State Street
Boise, ID 83720
208-334-2470

Illinois

Division of Marketing
Illinois Department of Commerce and Community Affairs
620 East Adams Street
Springfield, IL 62701
217-782-3891

International Business Division
Illinois Department of Commerce and Community Affairs
100 West Randolph Street
Suite C-400
Chicago, IL 60601
312-917-6649

Indiana

International Trade Division
Indiana Department of Commerce
One North Capitol
Suite 700
Indianapolis, IN 46204–2288
317-232-8800

Iowa

International Marketing
Iowa Department of Economic Development
200 East Grand Avenue
Des Moines, IA 50309
515-281-3251

Kansas

Trade Development Division
Kansas Department of Commerce
400 SW 8th Street
Suite 500
Topeka, KS 66603-3957
913-296-3481

Kentucky

Office of International Marketing
Kentucky Cabinet for Economic Development
Capitol Plaza Tower
24th Floor
Frankfort, KY 40601
502-564-7670

Louisiana

Office of International Trade, Finance and Development
State of Louisiana Department of Economic Development
P.O. Box 94185
Baton Rouge, LA 70804-9185
504-342-5361

Maine

Maine Office of Business Development
Department of Economic and Community Development
State House
Station 59
Augusta, ME 04333
207-289-3153

Maryland
Maryland Department of Economic and Employment Development
217 East Redwood Street
Baltimore, MD 21202
301-333-6985

Massachusetts
Massachusetts Office of Business Development
100 Cambridge Street
13th Floor
Boston, MA 02202
617-727-3221

Office of International Trade and Investment
100 Cambridge Street
Room 902
Boston, MA 02202
617-367-1830

Michigan
Michigan Department of Commerce
Manufacturing Development Group
P.O. Box 30225
Lansing, MI 48909
517-373-3530

Minnesota
Minnesota Department of Trade and Economic Development
900 American Center Building
150 Kellogg Boulevard
St. Paul, MN 55101
612-296-5005

Minnesota Trade Office
1000 Minnesota World Trade Center
30 East Seventh Street
St. Paul, MN 55101–4902
612-297-4657

Mississippi
Mississippi Department of Economic Development
P.O. Box 849
Jackson, MS 39205
601-359-3449

Missouri
Missouri Department of Economic Development
P.O. Box 118
Jefferson City, MO 65102
314-751-4241

Montana
Department of Commerce
Capitol Station
Helena, MT 59620
406–444-3494

Nebraska
Nebraska Department of Economic Development
P.O. Box 94666
Lincoln, NE 68509
402-471-3111

Nevada
International Office
Nevada Commission on Economic Development
Capitol Complex
Carson City, NV 89710
702-687-4325

New Hampshire
Office of Industrial Development
Department of Resources and Economic Development
105 Loudon Road
P.O. Box 856
Concord, NH 03302-0856
603-271-2591

New Jersey
New Jersey Department of Commerce and Economic Development
Office of Economic Research
One East State Street, CN-824
Trenton, NJ 08625
609-292-2423

Division of International Trade
Department of Commerce and Economic Development
153 Halsey Street
5th Floor
Newark, NJ 07102
201-648-3518

New Mexico
State of New Mexico
Economic Development Division
Economic Development and Tourism Department
Joseph M. Montoya Building
1100 St. Francis Drive
Santa Fe, NM 87503
505-827-0272

New York
New York State Department of Economic Development
One Commerce Plaza
Albany, NY 12245
518-474-4100

International Division
New York State Department of Economic Development
1515 Broadway
51st Floor
New York, NY 10036
212-827-6224

North Carolina
Business/Industry Development Division
North Carolina Department of Commerce
430 North Salisbury Street
Raleigh, NC 26611
919-733-4151

North Dakota
North Dakota Economic Development Commission
Liberty Memorial Building
604 East Boulevard
Bismarck, ND 58501
701-224-2810

Ohio
Deputy Director for Business Development
Ohio Department of Development
77 South High Street
28th Floor
Columbus, OH 43215
614-644-4551

Oklahoma
Oklahoma Department of Commerce
P.O. Box 26980
Oklahoma City, OK 73126
405–843–9770

Oregon
Oregon Economic Development Department
595 Cottage Street, NE
Salem, OR 97310
503-373-1200

Pennsylvania
Pennsylvania Department of Commerce/Pennsylvania Economic
    Development Partnership
433 Forum Building
Harrisburg, PA 17120
717-787-3003

Rhode Island
State of Rhode Island
Department of Economic Development
7 Jackson Walkway
Providence, RI 02903
401-277-2601

South Carolina
South Carolina State Development Board
P.O. Box 927
Columbia, SC 29202
803-737-0400

South Dakota
Governor's Office of Economic Development
Capitol Lake Plaza
711 Wells
Pierre, SD 57501
605-773-5032

Tennessee
Department of Economic and Community Development
Rachel Jackson Building
8th Floor
320 6th Avenue, North
Nashville, TN 37219
615-741-1888

Texas
Texas Department of Commerce
816 Congress Avenue
P.O. Box 12728
Capitol Station
Austin, TX 78711
512-472–5059

Utah
Division of Business and Economic Development
Department of Community and Economic Development
324 South State Street
Salt Lake City, UT 84111
801-538-8700

Vermont
Vermont Agency of Development and Community Affairs
109 State Street
Montpelier, VT 05602
802-828-3211

Vermont Department of Economic Development
Pavilion Office Building
Montpelier, VT 05602
802-828-3221

Virginia
Virginia Department of Economic Development
Two James Center
P.O. Box 798
Richmond, VA 23206-0798
804-371-8100

Washington
Washington State Department of Trade and Economic Development
312 First Avenue North
Seattle, WA 98109-4598
206-464-6282

Business and Market Development
Department of Trade and Development
2001 6th Avenue
Suite 2600
Seattle, WA 98121
206-464-7143

West Virginia
Governor's Office of Community and Industrial Development
State Capitol
Room M-146
Charleston, WV 24305
304-348-0400

Wisconsin
Wisconsin Department of Development
123 West Washington Avenue
P.O. Box 7970
Madison, WI 53707
608-266-1018

Wyoming
Wyoming Economic and Community Development Division
Herschler Building
2nd Floor West
Cheyenne, WY 82002
307-777-7284

APPENDIX D
LOCATION OF STATES'
OVERSEAS OFFICES

Alabama
State of Alabama Japan Office
8F, Aoki Building
5-32-8 Shiba, Minato-ku
Tokyo 108
JAPAN
(81-3) 5232-3851

State of Alabama
Room 1903, Kukje Center Building
191, 2-ka, Hangang-ro
Yangsan-ku, Seoul
KOREA
(82-2) 798-6838, -6839

State of Alabama
Postfach 5427
Frankfurter Strasse 33-35
D-6326 Eschborn
Frankfort
GERMANY
(49-69) 96-703416

Alaska
Alaska State Office—Tokyo
1-40, 4-chome, Toranomon
Minato-ku, Tokyo 105
JAPAN
(81-3) 436-5285

Alaska State Office—Seoul, South Korea
Kyobo Building, Suite 2112
1, 1-Ka, Changro, Changro-ku
Seoul
KOREA
(82-2) 734-3381

Alaska State Office—Taipei, Taiwan
Taipei World Trade Center, 7B-16
5 Hsin Yi Road, Sec. 5
Taipei
TAIWAN
(886-2) 723-1882

Arizona
Arizona Asia-Pacific Office
Room 7EO1, No. 5
Hsin Yi Road Sec. 5
Taipei
TAIWAN
(886-02) 725-1134

Arkansas
State of Arkansas European Office
Avenue Louise 437, Bte.4
B 1050 Brussels
BELGIUM
(32-2) 649-60-24

State of Arkansas Japan Office
Kowa Building No. 9, 4th Floor
1-8-10, Akasaka, Minato-ku
Tokyo 107
JAPAN
(81-03) 584-7575

State of Arkansas Taipei Office
7D-12 World Trade Center Building
5 Hsin Yi Road, Sec. 5
P.O. Box 109-659
Taipei
TAIWAN
(886-02) 723-2260

California
Asian Office of Trade and Development
State of California
Kowa #35 Building Annex
1-14-15 Akasaka, Minato-ku
Tokyo
JAPAN
(81-3) 583-3140

European Office of Trade & Investment
State of California
14, Curzon Street
London WIY 7FH
UNITED KINGDOM
(44-071) 629-8211

European Office of Trade & Investment at Frankfurt
State of California
Bockenheimer Kandstrasse 98
6000 Frankfurt 1
GERMANY
(49-69) 75-60-06-37

Southeast Asian Trade & Investment Office
State of California
Suite 300 St, George's Building
2 Ice House Street, Central
HONG KONG
(852) 877-3600

Mexico City Office of Trade & Investment
State of California
Paseo de la Reforma 450
Suite 400
06600 Mexico City, D.F.
MEXICO
(905) 208-5161

Colorado

Colorado State Rep. Office—Japan
Izumikan-Sanbancho
3-8 Sanbancho
Chiyoda-ku, Tokyo 102
JAPAN
(81-03) 288-3671

Colorado Taiwan, Trade, Tourism and Investment Office
Taipei World Trade Center
Suite 7D/14, No. 5
Hsin Yi Road, Sec. 5
Taipei
TAIWAN
(886-2) 725-1941, -1946

State of Colorado Rep. Office—Korea
1210 Daewoo Foundation Building
CPO Box 6614
Seoul, 100-095
KOREA
(82-2) 754-2414, -2415, -2443

Connecticut

State of Connecticut
Schutzenstrasse 4
6000 Frankfurt am Main 1
GERMANY
(49-69) 282055

State of Connecticut
Nishishinjuku KB Plaza
Suite 1309
1103 Nishishinjuku, 6 Chome
Shinjuku-ku, Tokyo
JAPAN
(81-03) 342-7070

Delaware
State of Delaware—Japan Office
King Homes #108
1-8-10 Kamimeguro
Meguro-Ku, 153
JAPAN
(81-03) 477-1851

State of Delaware
Monkman-Charron, B.V.
Hoogwerflann 6
2594 BJ Den Haag
NETHERLANDS
(31-70) 852-826

State of Delaware
Heneger House
St. Andrews Road
Coventry, CV5-6SP
ENGLAND
(44-2) 03-712-424

Florida
State of Florida UK Office
18/24 Westbourne Grove
London, W2-5RH
ENGLAND
(44-071) 727-8388

State of Florida
Division of Trade
150 Bloor Street West
Suite 310
Toronto, Ontario M5S ZX9
CANADA
(416) 926-1590

State of Florida European Office
Rue Armand Campenhout 63
1050 Brussels
BELGIUM
(32-2) 537-2900

State of Florida
Xantenerstrasse 8
4000 Dusseldorf 30
GERMANY
(49-211) 43-2542

State of Florida Japan Office
1-48-5 Toshin-cho
Itabashi-ku, Tokyo
JAPAN
(81-03) 974-6620

State of Florida
c/o Shuco International, Inc.
Professional House, 3rd Floor
195-10 Huam Dong
Yangsan-Ku
Seoul 140-190
KOREA
(82-2) 756-6244

State of Florida
c/o Must Executive Services
Alameda Campinas
433-14th Floor
Sao Paulo S.P. 01404
BRAZIL
(55) 289-8325

Georgia

Georgia Department of Industry, Trade and Tourism
380 Avenue Louise
Brussels
BELGIUM
(32-2) 647-7825

State of Georgia Korea Office
c/o IRC Ltd.
5-23 Hyochang-Dong
Yongsan-Ku, Seoul
KOREA
(82-2) 703-9111

Georgia Department of Industry, Trade and Tourism
Kojimachi-Hiraoka Building, 6th Floor
1-3 Kojimachi, Chiyoda-Ku
Tokyo 102
JAPAN
(81-3) 239-5771

Georgia Department of Industry, Trade and Tourism
Toronto Dominion Centre, Suite 2550
P.O. Box 77
Toronto, Ontario M5K 1E7
CANADA
(416) 836-6499

State of Georgia
Taipei Trade Representative
Far East Relations, Inc.
18 Tong Chen Street
Hsin Chu City 3003
TAIWAN
(886) 35-260-713

Hawaii

State of Hawaii Japan Office
Hibiya Kokusai Building
2-2-3, Uchisaiwai-cho, Chiyoda-ku
Tokyo 100
JAPAN
(81-03) 597-7951

State of Hawaii Trade Office
Suite 3702 A, W. Tower
Bond Center
Queensway
HONG KONG
(852-5) 260387

Idaho
State of Idaho
Taipei World Trade Center 7D-15
No. 5, Section 5
Hsin Yi Road
Taipei
TAIWAN
(886-2) 725-2922

State of Idaho
C/O Korean American Business Institute
Room 808, Packman Building
1-KA, Eulji-Ro, Chung-ku
OR-C.P.O. Box 4158
Seoul
KOREA
(82-2) 752-7750

Illinois
State of Illinois European Office
Place du Champ de Mars 5, Bte 14
1050 Brussels
BELGIUM
(32-2) 512-0105

Illinois Bureau de Services, LTDA
CX, Postal 7801
01000 Sao Paulo, S.P.
BRAZIL
(55-11) 257-3355

State of Illinois China Office
You Yuan Hotel, 3rd Floor
No. 4, Section 2
Tai Shan Road
Shenyang, Lioaning Province
PEOPLE'S REPUBLIC OF CHINA
(86-24) 664679

State of Illinois Far East Bureau
Sincere Building—Suite 1304
173 Des Voeux Road Central
HONG KONG
(852-5) 44-3863

Illinois Office In Japan
Ohara No. 3 Building
2-15, Homachi 3-chome
Chuo-ku, Osaka 541
JAPAN
(81-6) 251-4153

State of Illinois Tokyo Office
Sun Kitsukawa Building—7th Floor
1-27-14 Hamamatsu-chu
Minato-ku, Tokyo 105
JAPAN
(81-3) 578-8111

Officia del Estado de Illinois
Paseo de la Reforma 450—Piso 4
Col. Juarez
06600 MEXICO, D.F.
(525) 208-9787/2895/4450

State of Illinois Poland Office
Rutkowskiego 8, Room 309, 310
00-950 Warszawa
POLAND
(48-22) 275961

State of Illinois Canadian Office
123 Front Street W., Suite 900
Toronto, Ontario M5J 2M2
CANADA
(416) 365-9888

State of Illinois Hungary Office
H-1969 Budapest No. 3
Budapest
HUNGARY
(36-1) 115-3417

State of Illinois Moscow Office
Contact Laura Skoko in Chicago, IL at (312) 814-7166 for further infor-
    mation

Indiana
State of Indiana
480 University Place, Suite 602
Toronto, Ontario, M5G 1V2
CANADA
(416) 581-1793/1387

State of Indiana
Suite 1213
China World Tower
No. 1 Jian Guo Men Wai Da Je
Beijing
PEOPLE'S REPUBLIC OF CHINA
(861) 505-3693/0658-0659

State of Indiana
Bouwerij 75
N1—1185 XW Astelveen
NETHERLANDS
(31-2) 043-8217

State of Indiana
Kioicho Residence, Ist Floor
4-5 Kojimachi
Chiyoda-ku, Tokyo 102
JAPAN
(81-3) 230-3526

State of Indiana
Room 608
Hong Woo Building
43-3 Yoido-Dong
Yeongdeungpo-Ku
Seoul 150-010
KOREA
(82-2) 780-0865

State of Indiana
Taipei World Trade Center
Room 7D16
5 Hyinsi Road, Section 5
Taipei 10509
TAIWAN
(886-2) 725-2060

Iowa
State of Iowa European Office
An der Hauptwache 2
6000 Frankfurt/Main 1
GERMANY
(49-69) 28-38-58

State of Iowa Asian Office
1103 Admiralty Centre, Tower 11
18 Harcourt Road
HONG KONG
(852) 861-1777

State of Iowa Japan Office
Kowa Building 31
Shirogaredai 3-Chome
A-1 Minato-Ku, Tokyo
JAPAN
(81-3) 444-1988

Kansas

State of Kansas
c/o International Investment Consultants
Shuwa Kioicho TBR Building 1001
5-7 Kojimachi, Chiyoda-chu
102 Tokyo
JAPAN
(81-3) 239-2844

Kentucky

Far East Representative Office
Commonwealth of Kentucky
4th Floor, Seikosha Building
3-4-10 Azabudai
Minato-ku, Tokyo 106
JAPAN
(81-3) 582-2334

European Representative Office
Commonwealth of Kentucky
149 Avenue Louise
B 1050 Brussels
BELGIUM
(32-2) 534-1730

China Office
Commonwealth of Kentucky
P.O. Box 3075
Taipei
TAIWAN
(886-2) 700-5200

Korean Office
Commonwealth of Kentucky
Ewha Building, Room 202
Seocho-Dong, Seocho-Gu, 1570-5
Seoul 137-070
KOREA
(82-2) 588-3090

Louisiana
State of Louisiana
c/o Asahi Agency
#2 Takachiho Building 2F
1-6-9 Shiba-Daimon
Minato-ku, Tokyo 105
JAPAN
(81-3) 438-3361

State of Louisiana
c/o Sauvage Korea Co., Ltd.
260-199 Itaewon Dong
Yongsan-ku, Seoul
KOREA
(82-2) 796-4296

State of Louisiana
c/o OITFD Taipei Office
7D-13, 5 Hsinyi Road
Section 5
Taipei 10509
TAIWAN
(886-2) 723-1921

Maryland
State of Maryland
Avenue Louise, Bte 14
B-1050 Brussels
BELGIUM
(32-2) 647-5367

State of Maryland
7CO2 World Trade Center
5 Hsin Yi Road, Sec. 5
Taipei
TAIWAN
(886) 725-1554

State of Maryland
Hong Kong Office (FE Trade Office)
803 East Tower
Bond Center
Queensway
HONG KONG
(852) 521-6397

State of Maryland Center
322, Yurakucho Building
1-10-1 Yurakucho
Chiyoda-ku, Tokyo 100
JAPAN
(81-03) 212-0901

State of Maryland
Avenue Louise 222, Bte. 14
B-1050 Brussels
BELGIUM
(32-2) 647-5367

Office of Tourism Development/Baltimore/Washington Airport
State of Maryland
Avenue Louise 222, Bte. 14
B-1050 Brussels
BELGIUM
(32-2) 647-5367

Massachusetts
State of Massachusetts
Homat Rose #201
Oyama-cho 38-14
Shibuya-ku
Tokyo 151
JAPAN
(81-03) 468-5383

Michigan

European Office—Michigan Department of Agriculture
Rue Ducale, 41
B-1000 Brussels
BELGIUM
(32-2) 511-1371

Asian Office, Michigan Department of Agriculture
Jardin House
Connaught Road, Central
HONG KONG
(852-5) 24-4132

African Office/Michigan Department of Commerce
Plot PC 10
Off Idowu Taylor Street
P.O. Box 72192
Victoria Island, Lagos
NIGERIA
(234-1) 613-714/560

Canadian Operations—State of Michigan
One University Avenue, Suite 202
Toronto, Ontario M5J 2P1
CANADA
(416) 369-9630

Japan Operations—Michigan Department of Commerce
San-ei Building 7F
Minato-ku, Tokyo 105
JAPAN
(81-3) 433-3421

European Operations—Michigan Department of Commerce
Rue Ducale, 41
B-1000 Brussels
BELGIUM
(32-2) 511-0732

Minnesota

State of Minnesota
480 University Avenue, Suite 602
Toronto, Ontario M5G 1VG
CANADA
(416) 581-1793

State of Minnesota
c/o Rydin & Carlsten Advokathyra AB
Normalmstorg 1
S-111 46 Stockholm
SWEDEN
(46-8) 24-51-70

State of Minnesota
c/o Oppenheimer Wolff & Donnelly
250 Avenue Louise, Box 31
B-1050 Brussels
BELGIUM
(32-2) 647-4060

State of Minnesota
11 Rue Andre Meynier
"Le Ponthus" Bat. B
35065 Rennes Cedex
FRANCE
(33-99) 25-04-04

State of Minnesota
MTO OSAKA
ECC Open Campus Center
2-4-43, Nakazaki-Nishi, Kita-ku
Osaka 530
JAPAN
(81-6) 359-5586

State of Minnesota
MTO TOKYO
c/o Honeywell Inc.
Nagai International Building
2-12-19, Shibuya, Shibuya-ku
Tokyo 150
JAPAN
(81-3) 409-1611

Minnesota Trade and Investment Office
7G04, Taipei World Trade Center
5, Hsin Yi Road, Sec. 5
Taipei
TAIWAN
(886-2) 723-2075

Minnesota Trade office
APDO 144-1250
Escazu
COSTA RICA
(506) 28-68-61

Mississippi
State of Mississippi Japan Office
Reinanzaka Building, 1st Floor
14-2, Alaska 1-Chome, Minato-ku
Tokyo 100
JAPAN
(81-03) 588-9027/388-9028

State of Mississippi European Office
Bockenheimer Landstrasse 98-100
D-6000 Frankfurt 1
GERMANY
(49-69) 75-60-06-27

State of Mississippi Hong Kong Office
Kamsky Associates Ltd.
c/o Portman Overseas Ltd.
15/F Hop Hing Centre
8-12 Hennessy Road, Wanchai
HONG KONG
(852-5) 27-7837

Missouri

State of Missouri
International Business Office
Heinrichstrasse 169, Eingang B
4000 Dusseldorf 1
GERMANY
(49-211) 631014

State of Missouri
International Business office
Shiba Palace Building, 9th Floor
2-1-15, Hamamatsu-cho
Minato-ku, Tokyo 105
JAPAN
(81-33) 435-8290 or 8299

State of Missouri
International Business Office
Room 7D-09, CETRA
5 Hsin Yi Road, Sec. 5
Taipei
TAIWAN
(886-2) 725-1622

State of Missouri
International Business Office
The Korea Foundation for Advanced Studies Building
Room 600
678-39, Yoksam-Dong
Kangnam-Ku
Seoul
KOREA
(82-2) 566-8395/6

Montana

State of Montana
AIOS Gotanda Building—316
Shingawa-Ku, Tokyo 141
JAPAN
(81-03) 440-9077

State of Montana
Box 109-674 (World Trade Center)
Taipei
TAIWAN
(886-02) 723-1762

Nevada

State of Nevada
Japan Representative Office
IEO Building
6-10, Yotsuya
4-Chome, Shinjuku-ku
Tokyo 160
JAPAN
(81-3) 226-3840

State of Nevada
Korea Representative office
Suite 913, Sang Jee Building
326 Ulgiro 3KA
Chung-ku, Seoul
KOREA
(82-2) 265-0102

State of Nevada
Taiwan Representative Office
7th Floor, D/10
Taipei World Trade Center
5, Hsin Yi Road, Sec. 5
Taipei
TAIWAN
(886-2) 721-6284

New Jersey
Port Authority of New York and New Jersey
701 Kokusai Building
3-1-1, Marunduchi
Chiyoda-ky, Tokyo 100
JAPAN
(81-3) 213-0033

New York
State of New York
Panton House
25 Haymarket
London SW1Y 4EN
UNITED KINGDOM
(44-71) 839-5079

State of New York
Bockheimer Landstrasse 98-100
6000 Frankfurt Main 1
GERMANY
(49-69) 75600620

State of New York
Yurakucho Building, Room 218
10-1 Yuraku-Cho 1 Chome
Chiyoda-Ku, Tokyo 100
JAPAN
(81-3) 213-4387

State of New York
Suite 1133, 11th Floor
Central Building
No. 1 Pedder Street Central
HONG KONG
(852) 841-7764

State of New York
Canada Building Suite 603
455 Rue St. Antoine, West
Montreal, Quebec H2Z 1J1
CANADA
(514) 395-2400

State of New York
Queen's Quay Terminal Building
207 Queen's Quay West—Suite 408
P.O. Box 136
Toronto, Ontario M5J 1A7
CANADA
(416) 868-6935

North Carolina

State of North Carolina European Office
Wasserstrasse 2
4000 Dusseldorf 1
GERMANY
(49-211) 320-533

State of North Carolina
c/o Kenwa Shipping Co. Ltd.
17th Floor
Hing Yip Commercial Centre
272-284 Des Voeux Road Central
HONG KONG
(852-5) 414-877

State of North Carolina Japan Office
Room 208, Shin Yurakucho Building
12-1 Yurakucho
1 chome, Chiyoda Ku
Tokyo 100
JAPAN
(81-3) 284-0656

State of North Carolina
c/o Korean Maritime International, Inc.
4th Floor, Mediterranean Building
43-3, 1-Ka, Pil-Dong, Choong-Ku
Seoul
KOREA
(82-2) 274-78212

North Dakota
North Dakota World Trade, Inc.
c/o Incubator International
1-9-20 Akasaka, Kowa 16 Building
Minato-ku, Tokyo 107
JAPAN
(81-3) 582-2048

Ohio
Ohio Asian Office
7th Floor, Hirakawacho Building
2-6-1 Kirakawacho, Chiyoda-Ku
Tokyo 102
JAPAN
(81-3) 232-1312

Ohio European Office
21 Avenue de la Toison D'Or
B-1060 Brussels
BELGIUM
(32-2) 513-0752

Ohio Office of East/Southeast Asia
Suite 1518, Tower 3
China Hong Kong City
33 Canton Road, Kowloon
HONG KONG
(852) 736-3693

Ohio African Trade office
6 Broad Street
NCR House, 9th Floor
Lagos
NIGERIA
(234-1) 633742, 631758

Ohio Canadian Trade Office
439 University Avenue
Suite 750
Toronto, Ontario M5G 1Y8
CANADA
(416) 351-0060

Oklahoma

State of Oklahoma
E-18 Defence Colony
New Delhi 110024
INDIA
(91-11) 6410494

State of Oklahoma
3-6-2 Nihonbaski Honcho
Chuo-Ku Tokyo 103
JAPAN
(81-3) 665-9600

State of Oklahoma
Ruijin Building, Room 1301
205 Mao Ming Road South
Shanghai
PEOPLE'S REPUBLIC OF CHINA
(86-21) 4333187

State of Oklahoma
36 Level, Hong Leong Building
16 Raffels Quay
REPUBLIC OF SINGAPORE
(65) 321-8918

Oregon

Oregon Economic Development Department
Japan Representative Office
Yurakucho Denki Building
Room 1213, North Tower
1-7-1 Yurakucho, Chiyoda-ku
Tokyo 100
JAPAN
(81-3) 213-3081/4

Oregon Trade & Information Center
Taipei World Trade Center
5 Hsin Yi Lu, Section 5
7th Floor C14
Taipei
TAIWAN
(886-2) 723-2310/11

State of Oklahoma
Korea Liaison Office
Suite 1301, Samkoo Building
Sokong-Dong 70, Chung-KU
Seoul
KOREA
(82-2) 753-1349

Pennsylvania
State of Pennsylvania
Brussels Operations
Rue Montoyer 31, Boite 4
B-1040 Brussels
BELGIUM
(32-2) 5137796/97/98

State of Pennsylvania
Frankfurt Operations
Parkstrasse 12
6000 Frankfurt/Main 1
GERMANY
(49-69) 590365

State of Pennsylvania
Far East Operations
Room 1214, World Trade Center Building
4-1, Hamamatsu-cho, 2-chome
Minato-ku, Tokyo 105
JAPAN
(81-03) 436-5583

Rhode Island
State of Rhode Island
Department of Economic Development
Mier 24
2000 Antwerp
BELGIUM
(32-3) 333-6021

State of Rhode Island
Department of Economic Development
GPD Box 302
Kowloon
HONG KONG
(852-3) 85-1188

State of Rhode Island
Department of Economic Development
6F09/No. 5,
Hsin Yi Road, Sec. 5
World Trade Center
Taipei 10509
TAIWAN
(886-2) 725-1613

South Carolina
State of South Carolina
European Office
Wilhelm-Leuschner-Strasse
D-6000 Frankfurt/Main 1
GERMANY
(49-69) 23-4071

State of South Carolina
Toranomon TBL, Building 902
1-19, 1-Chome, Toranomon Minato-ku
Tokyo 105
JAPAN
(1-3) 591-1604

Texas

State of Texas
Paseo de la Reforma 119-701
Mexico City, D.F.
MEXICO 06500
(525) 566-3532

State of Texas
Dr. Coss No. 843 Sur Desp. "C"
Monterrev, N.L.
MEXICO
(Contact State Office in Austin at 512-472-5059)

State of Texas
Hara Azabu Building 10F
4-18, Higashi-Azuba 3 Chome
Minato-ku, Tokyo 106
JAPAN
(81-3) 589-6627

State of Texas
Taipei World Trade Center
5 Hsin Yi Road, Section 5
Taipei
TAIWAN
(886-2) 723-1914

State of Texas
Bockenheimer Landstrasse 98-100
D-6000 Frankfurt Am Main 1
GERMANY
(49-69) 75-600661

State of Texas
Korea World Trade Center
33rd Floor
159, Samsung-dong
Gangnam-gu
Seoul
KOREA
(Contact: State Office in Austin at 512-472-5059)

Utah

State of Utah
c/o System Science Consultants, Inc.
Silver-Takadanobaba Building
3-18-11 Takada
Toshima-ku, Tokyo 171
JAPAN
(81-03) 986-9361

State of Utah
7C 16 Taipei World Trade Center
#5 HSIN YI Road, Section 5
Taipei
TAIWAN
(886-2) 725-2522

State of Utah
c/o Kim & Chang
Seyang Building
223 Naeja-dong, Chongro-ku
Seoul 110
KOREA
(82-2) 734-4455

State of Utah—European Office
Division of Economic Development
c/o Wang Building
Rue Du Planeur 6
1140 Brussels
BELGIUM
(32-2) 7272946

Virginia

State of Virginia
479 Avenue Louise—Bte 55
B-1050 Brussels
BELGIUM
(32-2) 648-6179

State of Virginia
Fukoku-Seimei Building (1701)
2-2, Uchisaiwai-Cho 2-Chome
Chiyoda-Ku, Tokyo 100
JAPAN
(81-3) 508-2750

Washington
Washington State Department of Trade
Jardine Business Centre—Tokyo
ABS Building
2-4-16, Kudan Minami
Chiyoda-ku, Tokyo 102
JAPAN
(81-3) 221-9709

Washington State Trade Development Office
Room 7-G-01
Taipei World Trade Center
5 Hsin Yi Road, Section 5
Taipei
TAIWAN
(886-2) 725-2499

West Virginia
State of West Virginia
Nihon Seimei Sakaemachi Building
7th Floor
24-17, 3 Chome, Nishiki
Naka-ku, Nagoya 460
JAPAN
(81-52) 953-9798

Wisconsin
Wisconsin Department of Development
European and Middle Eastern Office
Hamburger Allee 2-10
6000 Frankfurt/Main 90
GERMANY
(49-69) 77-20-29

State of Wisconsin
Asian Operations Office
Wisconsin Department of Development
18th Floor, Shun Ho Tower
24-30, Ice House Street Central
HONG KONG
(852) 524-5181

Wisconsin Department of Development
Japan Office
Landic Akasaka 2nd Building, 7F
2-10-9 Akasaka, Minato-ku
Tokyo 107
JAPAN
(81-3) 589-4700

Wisconsin Department of Development
Korea Office
MPO Box 347
Room 1301, Jindo Building
168-5 Dohwa-dong
Mapo-ku, Seoul
KOREA
(82-2) 702-6222

Wyoming
State of Wyoming
Taiwan Trade Office
Taipei World Trade Center, Suite 7D20
5, Hsin Yi Road, Section 5
Taipei
TAIWAN
(886-2) 725-1711

CHAPTER 9

EXPORT FINANCING

John J. Sullivan, Esq.
Walter, Conston, Alexander & Green

Export financing is the basic element in a nation's ability to compete successfully in international trade. With nations striving to achieve favorable balance of payments and companies intensifying efforts to develop global markets, the need for efficient and economical financing of foreign trade is primary. In the United States, trade financing has evolved primarily through direct and indirect government assistance and in part, through overseas expansion by domestic banks, which in turn has contributed to commercial financing of U.S. trade. This chapter will describe the traditional assistance provided by the U.S. government and explore features of commercial bank participation in furnishing international trade credit.

GOVERNMENT FINANCING

The U.S. government, directly and indirectly, finances U.S. trade through a variety of programs. This assistance is designed to support exporters competing with foreign competitors aided by subsidized credit financing. Such assistance is also designed to promote exports to so-called friendly countries where political risks might otherwise preclude such trade activities. This portion of the chapter will describe the uses of these various government programs.

The Export-Import Bank

The Export-Import Bank is the primary U.S. government vehicle for providing financial assistance to U.S. exporters. The purpose of the Eximbank, as defined in its authorizing statute, is "to aid in financing and to facilitate exports and imports and the exchange of commodities between the United States . . . [and] any foreign country." This aid is directed primarily toward assisting export sales to offset any foreign competition that is supported by official export subsidiaries. To a lesser extent, Eximbank aid is also directed toward financing exports that the private sector is unwilling to support because of unacceptable political or commercial risks. For example, Eximbank makes available for major export sales long-term, fixed-rate financing that commercial banks are often reluctant to provide. Generally, Eximbank will not provide credit for sales to developed countries or sales of military goods or services. The Eximbank functions to fulfill its statutory goals in four primary ways: (1) by direct loans, (2) by guaranteeing loans, (3) by discounting loans, and (4) by providing export credit insurance in connection with the Foreign Credit Insurance Association.

Direct Loans

Eximbank provides direct, long-term loans to public or private overseas purchasers for major projects. These loans are generally used to finance high-priced items (such as commercial jet aircraft) or large-scale installations (such as hydro power-generation facilities or telecommunication projects), when commercial lenders would be reluctant to fund such a long-term and sometimes speculative project. Payment is made on behalf of the purchaser by Eximbank directly to the U.S. supplier. The purchasers are generally foreign governments, foreign companies, or U.S. companies operating abroad. Loans and guarantees are available to support exports to almost every area of the world. Expenditures are normally financed on a long-term basis, often up to 15 years. For direct loans to borrowers located abroad, Eximbank will provide up to 65 percent of the export value. A cash payment to the U.S. supplier of at least 15 percent of the export value of the U.S. purchases is required. The balance of the financing is usually provided by private lenders. Eximbank requires that such transactions include some degree of private funding as a condition to its financing. This requirement for private participation is intended to encourage private sector export financing. However, even in connection with such private financing, Eximbank may provide financial guarantees assuring repayment of political and certain commercial risks.

Guarantee

Eximbank also assists export funding by guaranteeing the repayment of small- and medium-term export credit extended by financial institutions to U.S. exporters. The purpose of this program is (1) to facilitate exports by assuming commercial and political risks that U.S. exporters or commercial banks are unwilling or unable to undertake, and (2) to provide guarantees on terms competitive with those offered by foreign-supported export credit agencies. Under this program, the Eximbank guarantee covers up to 85 percent of the commercial risk and 100 percent of the political risk of the financing. Examples of commercial risks include economic deterioration in the market area, changes in demand, shifts in tariffs, technological advances, and national disasters. Political risks include war, civil unrest, insurrection, and revolution. Those financial institutions eligible to participate in this program include commercial banks organized under the laws of the United States or any state, Edge Act corporations, and U.S. branches and agencies of foreign banks. One advantage of this program is that in many situations, the transaction can take place without obtaining approval directly from Eximbank. Financial institutions that have participated in this program may expedite the processing under delegated authority from Eximbank. This allows the exporter to work directly with its traditional commercial lender, which has knowledge of the supplier's business history, financial condition, and operations.

Discounting

Eximbank also provides export credit for small manufacturers through a discount loan program. Small manufacturers are defined as companies having total gross annual sales of $25 million or less. This program enables U.S. commercial banks to extend fixed-rate, medium-term export loans by permitting the banks to borrow from Eximbank against the outstanding value of the indebtedness. This program covers up to 85 percent of the contract price of an export sale funded by a U.S. bank.

Foreign Credit Insurance Association

Private export credit insurance is made available by the Foreign Credit Insurance Association (FCIA), a private corporation comprising U.S. insurance companies. The purpose of this association is to offset the advantage of foreign competitors whose exporting risks are sometimes assumed or lessened by government-affiliated programs and whose payment terms may be more attractive. Working in cooperation with Eximbank, the FCIA permits exporters to insure against political as well as certain commercial risks. Insurance may be obtained through agents or brokers of the member companies or through the FCIA itself.

FCIA insurance may be used as a financial tool in a company's export program. In fact, discounting receivables to obtain financing is a widely used benefit for FCIA customers. Typically, the exporter will assign the promissory note obtained from the foreign purchaser, together with the proceeds of the FCIA policies, to a U.S. commercial bank as collateral against discounted receivables. Because FCIA receivables may be considered equivalent to domestic obligations, commercial banks normally handle these transactions within domestic lending guidelines. The financing provided is thus structured to be considered domestic lending rather than foreign- or country-risk policies. The FCIA also provides insurance directly to commercial banks. Those banks will often have extended credit collateralized by all of the foreign accounts receivable of one or more exporting companies. Such banks are more likely to extend credit to an exporter whose receivables being offered as collateral are insured by the FCIA.

FCIA also provides insurance for the sale of services as well as goods. Coverage is available to management consultants, engineering service firms, and similar companies seeking protection for payments to be made by foreign customers.

The Private Export Funding Corporation

The Private Export Funding Corporation (PEFCO) is a private corporation organized to make loans to public and private borrowers overseas who require medium- and long-term financing. It is owned primarily by commercial banks, although certain financial services companies and industrial companies are also shareholders.

The purpose is to provide loans for the purchase of U.S. goods and services when credit is otherwise unavailable. All its export loans are fully guaranteed by Eximbank. The type of loans made by PEFCO have involved expensive capital goods or large industrial projects, such as mining projects and industrial plants. Often, PEFCO has stepped in where commercial lenders were unwilling to finance large transactions with long-term maturities. PEFCO provides support by either making loans directly to public and private borrowers located outside the United States or by purchasing, under its Note Purchase Facility, medium-term promissory notes without recourse to the seller. As a result, PEFCO's presence as an alternative or supplemental lender is of special assistance to U.S. capital goods suppliers, as well as commercial banks.

The Commodity Credit Corporation

The Commodity Credit Corporation (CCC) is a U.S. government agency whose purpose is to provide credit for farm-product exports by U.S. companies. Generally, commercial banks are unwilling to offer credit assistance involving commodities that will be consumed long before the maturity of the credit. The agency is directed by statute to increase exports of surplus agricultural products by encouraging commercial bank financing of foreign purchases on credit terms of up to three years. Under this program, the exporter will enter into a sales agreement with a foreign importer. After the CCC approves the agreement, the importer will have an irrevocable letter of credit opened on behalf of the CCC that will be confirmed by a U.S. bank. The CCC will assume all of the political risk and 90 percent of the commercial risk for the transaction. When the commodities are shipped, the CCC pays the exporter and then looks to the importer—the foreign bank that opened the letter of credit or the confirming U.S. bank—for payment.

The Overseas Private Investment Corporation

The Overseas Private Investment Corporation (OPIC) is another U.S. government agency involved in export financing. This corporate agency, operated under the Department of the Treasury, is primarily involved in promoting private investments by U.S. companies and loans by U.S. financial institutions in Third World countries. OPIC attempts to encourage such investments by insuring them against political risks. As with other government programs, this agency tries to create a market for American goods by forming a competitive credit arrangement. OPIC differs from Eximbank in that the goods purchased under the assisted program do not have to be imported from the United States.

TRADE FINANCING THROUGH COMMERCIAL BANKS

International trade originating in the United States is financed primarily by large commercial banks. These institutions possess the technological, financial, and human resources essential in properly servicing overseas activities of domestic companies. Through domestic retail operations, U.S. banking organizations are able to reach out to the large numbers of companies, middle-market as well as multinational, that manufacture goods and services capable of export. This is particularly the case with regard to domestic offices of Edge Act corporations, entities formed principally by financial institutions that are organized for the purpose of engaging in foreign banking activities. U.S. banking organizations can thus provide an important introductory link between domestic trading companies and U.S. businesses.

Through overseas banking offices and foreign-correspondent relationships, U.S. banking organizations make available a direct channel to potential foreign clients. Certain major commercial banks have established international networks that reach to most major export markets. This global presence, often long-standing, offers to a trading company a tremendous reservoir of talent and experience in information and sometimes marketing services. For this reason, it is often important for companies that export goods or services to do business with a commercial bank that has an established international division. Personnel at such an institution will either be informed as to local economic conditions, government policies, and business practices or will be able to refer businesses to those who are specialists in a particular area. Banks also have contacts abroad to facilitate introductions and provide business references on which exporters can rely. In addition, in guiding exporters, trained bank personnel can offer advice on currency exchanges and credit information. Thus banks, by virtue of their long-standing international presence and experienced personnel, are valuable as sophisticated information centers, in addition to their role as financiers of international commerce.

The international infrastructure already established by many commercial banks would benefit many exporters or potential exporters who cannot afford the up-front costs of launching an extensive export program. Although there has been some recent contraction, such financial institutions have increasingly expanded overseas operations over the past decade, to the extent that a significant portion of profits is often derived from non-U.S. activities. However, overseas expansion has not significantly benefited small- and medium-sized producers in the United States. Today, a small fraction of all U.S. manufacturers are responsible for the overwhelming majority of exported goods. Congress attempted to change this situation by enacting legislation intended to stimulate the direct involvement of commercial banks in assisting export trading companies.

In general terms, export trading companies function as intermediaries transferring goods and services from domestic producers to foreign consumers. Such companies offer a variety of services, including credit information, market development, freight forwarding, packaging, shipping, and overseas distribution and are often directly involved themselves in the financing of exports. In comparison with certain overseas counterparts, especially the sizable Japanese and Korean trading companies, however, the trading companies in the United States tend to be small, thinly capitalized firms. These organizations have been primarily marketing arms of individual manufacturers, commodities traders, or small independent ventures with limited assets.

Up to now, the lack of close affiliation with financial institutions has been recognized as a major weakness of existing export trade organizations in the United States. An international sales transaction is generally more complicated and, by nature of term, riskier than a comparable domestic arrangement. The difference between purchaser and seller may be measured not only in terms of geography but also in terms of customs, language, and legal traditions. In addition to considering the financial condition of the purchaser and its credit-worthiness, the exporter must assess whether any political problems or exchange controls may affect the purchaser's ability to pay. In evaluating potential loans, banks generally speaking generate lending policy toward areas of lesser risks. Of the categories of businesses seeking bank loans, existing trading companies typically command low loan ratings. In part, this is because such firms are thinly capitalized and are unable to provide the type of financial structure or available collateral that banks would like to see in evaluating credit-worthiness. Banks have been reluctant to advance funds on export trade receivables. Often, banks will lend only against a company's reserves or upon guarantees by its stockholders.

The Export Trading Company Act of 1982 expanded the powers of banking organizations with the specific purpose of encouraging participation in the establishment and development of export trading companies. This legislation altered in some basic ways the potential role of a U.S. commercial bank, by expanding its traditional function as a financier of international transactions to permit it to act as a participant. Banking organizations are permitted under such law to acquire an equity interest in—or even organize their own—export trading companies.

Enacting the Export Trading Company Act, Congress hoped, would increase trade financing provided by banking organizations by removing legal barriers to bank involvement in that area. U.S. banking law, unlike the laws or practices of many other countries, imposes a separation between banks and commercial enterprises. In other countries, the concept of universal banking exists, permitting commercial banks to own nonfinancial institutions, such as manufacturers and service companies.

To better understand this legal separation in the United States, a brief background of the U.S. banking system may be useful. Banking in the United States is subject to a dual regulatory scheme of state and federal supervision. State authorities exercise primary regulatory responsibility for the operation of banks organized under state law, while the activities of national banks chartered under federal law are supervised primarily by federal banking agencies. This scheme of dual regulation can be traced to the historic pattern of development of state and federal government in the United States and the parallel pattern of development of state-chartered and nationally chartered commercial banks. The powers that either a national or state bank may exercise are determined by state or federal law, respectively, except in certain instances when federal law preempts state law. Such powers have generally been limited to activities incidental to the business of banking. The general prohibition on full-scale securities and commercial activities stems, in part, from the practices of and affiliations by and between financial institutions and commercial enterprises that led up to the stock market crash of 1929 and the subsequent bank failures in the early 1930s. Responding to these events, Congress enacted the Banking Act of 1933, popularly known as the Glass-Steagall Act, which created a legal barrier between investment and commercial banking. By enacting this legislation, Congress intended to minimize possible concentrations of power and to eliminate abuses arising from the potential conflicts of interest that existed when banks engaged in the investment banking business.

In the past decade, the restrictions on bank affiliation with commercial enterprises have lessened to some degree. The Export Trading Company Act is an example of one exception to the general principle of the separation of banking and commerce. In specific terms, such legislation permits banks and banking organizations, subject to regulatory approval, to make investments in export trading companies. Bank holding companies may invest up to 5 percent of their capital and surplus in an export trading company.

However, in order to pursue opportunities created by the Export Trading Company Act, banks will have to increase existing knowledge in the export trading company area beyond that existing today. Even though certain large U.S. banks have established general expertise in international commerce, many banks that wish to engage in export trading activities will have to develop more specialized background knowledge. Nonbank export trading companies have marketing skills usually in specific product areas, which banks cannot immediately duplicate. Banks that have entered this field have either acquired ownership of established firms or employed individuals experienced in dealing with the export community. Others have entered into joint ventures with export trading companies in marketing for specific export industries.

In today's economic climate, with many financial institutions reverting to profitable core businesses that provide some historical assurance of earnings, commercial banks are cutting back or abandoning other segments of business whose earnings have not been as certain. One area in which certain U.S. banks have looked to reduce exposure is in their international operations. For certain banks, overseas offices have been downsized and certain business segments have been reduced or eliminated. As a result, the ability of potential exporters to access commercial banks for information, as well as financing, has generally been reduced.

PART 3

LEGAL MATTERS

CHAPTER 10

FORMS OF DOING BUSINESS IN THE UNITED STATES

Howard B. Hill, Esq.
Partner
Pepper, Hamilton, & Scheetz
Donald E. Wilson, Esq.
Partner
Deloitte & Touche

Once the decision has been made to do business in the United States, the form of doing business is usually dictated by business objectives, the investor's resources (both financial and managerial), taxes, legal and other considerations, such as exposure to product liability, environmental risks, and litigation expense.

In this chapter, we will highlight the significant general considerations, the advantages and disadvantages of the principal forms of doing business, major legal issues arising from each form, and the tax considerations in entity selection. Unfortunately, limitations of space do not permit an exhaustive treatment of each subject, but only allow us to heighten the potential investor's awareness and provide a base upon which to pursue more detailed information on a particular situation.

GENERAL CONSIDERATIONS

The way business is done in the United States and certain features of U.S. law can be different from what is normally encountered in, say, Europe and Asia. The investor needs to understand these differences before considering which form best suits its particular needs.

Interplay of Federal and State Laws

Since the formation of the United States, there has been a network of federal and state laws (and in some jurisdictions, significant county and city regulations) that intertwine and sometimes duplicate, sometimes conflict with each other—but in all cases need to be considered. To illustrate this point, one can look at the example of an investor establishing a new company in the United States.

First, unlike most countries and except for specialized industries such as banks, savings and loans, and credit unions, the United States does not incorporate companies on a national basis. Instead, entities are formed and governed by individual state law. Delaware is frequently chosen as the state of incorporation because of the perceived ease in operating the company on the part of management and the well-developed body of corporate law interpreting the relevant statutes. If the proposed business activity will also be performed in other states (i.e., the plant will be built in southern Georgia or the Midwest and sales offices or warehouses will be established around the country), offices of the company may have to be registered to do business in each of those other states.

Once operations begin, certain federal laws must be complied with, such as obtaining a federal tax identification number and paying taxes to the Internal Revenue Service. Likewise, federal and state civil rights laws protect employees against discrimination on the basis of age, race, and sex. If a plant is established, environmental considerations may also arise, and usually there are both federal and state regulations which need to be complied with.

Hence, an awareness of this interplay of federal and state law will help the investor focus on where best to establish its business to limit the ensuing legal complexity and liability.

Greater Amount of Disclosure

Although recent legal changes in the European Common Market have increased reporting requirements for companies over a certain size, most companies in Europe and Japan traditionally face less disclosure than their counterparts in the United States. Foreign entities file limited annual reports that state minimal information such as the company name, the directors and shareholders, the registered office, and perhaps a maximum net sales number. In the United States, extensive public disclosure is required for public companies, which can be both a competitive advantage in finding out about one's competitors and a disadvantage in making the investor equally vulnerable to its competition.

For instance, if the investor were to acquire a publicly held company, there are significant disclosure requirements under U.S. securities laws involving disclosing any material facts that would affect the business, such as future plans and details of ongoing litigation. Acquisitions of U.S. companies could also trigger disclosure and approval mechanisms under the Hart-Scott-Rodino Act and under U.S. Department of Commerce regulations related to foreign investments and acquisitions, particular in defense-related industries. These are discussed in greater detail elsewhere in this book.

Should a company become involved in litigation (and the United States is generally more litigious than other countries), U.S. rules provide for a much greater degree of disclosure of documents (including daily schedules of company officials, telephone records, financial statements, correspondence files and drawings) than is normally the case in many other countries. This sometimes affects the amount of communication that is committed to writing, although the investor should be aware that testimony in the form of depositions and written interrogatories can be used to prove oral communications.

Assertion of U.S. Jurisdiction

Even if a company were not to establish any formal presence in the United States, U.S. federal and state laws are very aggressive in asserting jurisdiction over foreign entities that sell goods or commit some act of negligence with an impact in the United States.

U.S. antitrust laws are now reemerging as a serious concern of foreign companies who in some jurisdictions are used to operating with trade cartels/associations that exchange price and cost information and allocate customers in a manner that would be illegal in the United States. Also, attempts by some foreign companies to minimize taxable income in the United States by manipulating transfer pricing for the products or services being sold in the United States are being met with greater scrutiny by the U.S. Internal Revenue Service, which can impose severe penalties.

Product liability is another area of concern. Goods that either do not meet their stated or implied warranties or that cause injury in the United States will, in fact, submit the foreign investor to greater and greater exposure. Even if the investor and its product were innocent, it might be forced to defend a lawsuit. In the United States, litigation is pursued in a detailed and time-consuming manner. A company will find much of its management talent diverted to the defense of a lawsuit, and the legal costs can be substantial.

TABLE 10–1
Advantages and Disadvantages of Various Forms of Doing Business

Form	Advantages	Disadvantages
Exports	Lower cost and fewer new resources required Complete control of operations by parent Allows trial period 100% of profits Less exposure to liability except for product liability Generally not subject to U.S. tax unless permanent establishment	100% of marketing risk—distant from the market and customers' needs Less timely service since no one is on the scene Less visible commitment to market No access to existing network of customers of another party No local warehouse from which to meet customer emergency (although there are provisions for bonded warehouses in designated free trade zones)

TABLE 10–1
(continued)

Form	Advantages	Disadvantages
Distributor/Sales Representative	Greater presence in market Local party has greater stake and more commitment to success of business Local inventory from which to ship goods Less cost and delay than foreign company establishing distribution for the first time	Must share profit with another party, instead of keeping 100% Potential liability in some states for wrongful termination of distributors Less control over distribution of one's products
Licensing	Create local manufacturing source without cost of building plant Receive passive income (royalties & fees) without bearing the market risks which are best known by the foreign licensee	May put a new competitor in business who will eventually close local market and export to your market at lower cost Less control over quality and product supply Not a long term presence Must share profits
Other Contractual Relationships (Joint Research and Development Joint Product Development Joint Procurement Marketing Consultant)	Split costs of developing new products or adapting U.S. products for local markets can combine complementary technologies Local presence helps avoid mistakes due to ignorance of culture Lower investment than forming company	Less control of technology—a third party may have different agenda Not a long-term presence May educate competitor Must share profits

TABLE 10–1
(continued)

Form	Advantages	Disadvantages
	Business can be terminated without incurring liability for payments/benefits to employees since there are no employees	
Branch Office	Local presence with people loyal to parent company Greater control over distribution network Greater commitment and timelier access to market developments Could limit U.S. tax exposure if simply liaison office and not "permanent establishment"	Increased cost in establishing new office and personnel Greater exposure to liability for products, employees, and taxes Easier for others to assert legal jurisdiction over foreign parent in lawsuits
Joint Venture	Share risks, costs, and financing Knowledgeable local partner More permanent appearance in market Local manufacture with greater control by parent company than license to third party Local partner may have complementary strengths Allows creation of third party independent of business culture of either party—encourage fresh ideas	Must share profit and know-how Less control than 100% ownership Tax losses can't be used by parent companies (important where heavy emphasis on R&D or product development) Efforts and image could be hurt if weak local partner Don't always get best people or undivided loyalty from parent companies
Partnership	Parent company may be able to use tax losses from partnership	Greater liability exposure to parent companies than corporate joint

TABLE 10–1
(concluded)

Form	Advantages	Disadvantages
	No tax at partnership level Appropriate for research and development effort where profits not expected for some time	venture—generally liability stays within a corporation, but flows directly to partners in a partnership Unless limited, one partner can bind the other Do not have 100% of profits and management of entity
Subsidiary	Complete control of profits Complete control of operations and management Can unilaterally withdraw if business is bad	No local partner to advise on local customs and provide complementary strengths Greater cost and liability than acting through agent/distributor Potential start-up delays from "greenfield" operation unless acquire existing business

Principal Forms of Doing Business

The principal forms are:

- Exports
- Distributor/Sales Representative
- Licensing
- Other Contractual Relationships
- Branch Office
- Joint Venture
- Partnership
- Subsidiary

One should keep in mind that no single form may satisfy all of a company's needs. A graduated approach might be adopted such that investment or involvement in the United States can be viewed as a courtship that starts out with limited introductions such as exporting and, if all signs are positive, later evolves into a more permanent investment in the form of establishing a U.S. company, whether newly formed or by acquisition.

Indeed, since many investors may have different product lines, different forms might be employed for different reasons. For instance, the size of the market for a particular product may be so small that exporting alone is satisfactory, while in other areas, overseas transportation costs put the price of the imported goods at a competitive disadvantage and hence make local manufacturing highly desirable.

Further, changes in market conditions and rules and regulations may occur so quickly that the strategy that was suitable last year may have to be revised for the next year. Above all, the foreign investor should remain flexible and knowledgeable of market conditions.

Advantages and Disadvantages of Different Forms

With an awareness of these unique aspects, Table 10-1 examines the specific advantages and disadvantages of different forms of doing business in the United States.

KEY ISSUES TO BE CONSIDERED

Having considered the appropriateness of the various forms, it is necessary to review what is required in organizing particular forms and the key issues that should be considered by the foreign investor.

Exports

Exporting to the United States probably offers relatively few structural differences from exporting to other countries except that the United States has tended to reflect its moral values in laws governing exports and imports into the United States, such as those dealing with the Arab boycott or bribery of foreign officials.

The main laws governing imports are the federal customs regulations, which determine the classification, importability, and duty assessed on various goods. Certain items are forbidden from being imported not because they are inherently dangerous, but because they reflect a particular ethical policy taken by the U.S. government. For instance, ivory and products made from ivory are banned from importation on the theory that this will prevent poaching of African elephants. Certain other goods may be restricted and require import licenses, or may be subject to quotas, as is the case with textiles and Japanese automotive imports.

Individuals making marketing and sales visits to the United States will have to obtain the appropriate visas in advance and, as noted in the tax discussion, should limit the duration of their aggregate annual visits to avoid imposition of individual U.S. income tax.

Because of the enormous geographic size of the United States compared with the relative compactness of Japan and Europe, warehouses may have to be established at various locations to serve emergency needs of customers and overcome any delays in shipment that inevitably occur with overseas shipments. Such warehouses will require lease agreements or if owned, must possess occupancy permits and conform to local zoning rules and safety and fire regulations. If the goods imported will be manufactured or assembled into some other product, a free trade zone and bonded warehouse can be established, which helps cash flow by delaying the payment of customs duties until the goods leave the warehouse. Some states also impose taxes on inventory called use taxes.

The principal difficulty any foreign investor has in establishing a presence in the market by itself is to convince a local customer, particularly for high-priced machinery, that adequate service and spare parts will be readily available to perform warranty and repair service and maintain the products. It is this perceived lack of permanence that frequently leads the foreign investor to a greater presence in the market through an appointment of a distributor/ sales representative.

Distributor/Sales Representative

Another alternative is for a foreign investor to appoint a distributor or sales representative in the United States. This can be an individual or a company. Usually a contract is signed wherein the foreign investor appoints a local party to act on its behalf in conducting sales and marketing efforts.

Finding the right party with the necessary resources and reputable contacts is always a major concern. References should always be sought and checked before entering into any agreement.

An investor should be aware of the differences between a distributor and a sales representative. The distributor buys goods from the foreign company at an agreed-upon discount and resells them at a price the distributor selects. Note that it is illegal in the United States to require a distributor to sell at a specified price (this is also known as resale price maintenance). By contrast, a sales representative simply promotes sales and helps the customer place orders directly with the foreign supplier, who in turn ships directly to the customer and pays the sales agent a commission.

There is nothing particularly unusual about these forms of business in the United States except that companies should be aware that in some states, case law has extended franchise and/or dealer statutes to protect distributors and sales representatives from termination without proper cause and reasonable notice. This protection is similar to what exists in some European countries.

The issues involved in appointing a distributor in the United States are the same as in any other country. Such agreements should expressly state that the distributor/sales representative has no authority to bind the foreign investor; otherwise, the foreign investor could be subject to (1) liability for contracts that the sales agent has signed on unfavorable terms, and (2) the creation of a permanent establishment in the United States that has adverse tax consequences for the foreign company.

The contract should also spell out the specific duties and measures of performance in clear language to avoid future misunderstandings, such as requiring specific annual sales quotas—the failure of which would allow the foreign supplier to terminate the agreement. It is often advisable to provide for minimum inventory, minimum advertising budgets, a specified number of trained competent personnel to perform after-sales service, the submission of regular reports and maintenance of books and records by the distributor.

Likewise, the products included should be defined as well as whether successor or replacement goods are covered. What geographic territory is being granted, and is it granted on an exclusive or nonexclusive basis? If the territorial rights are exclusive, will the foreign supplier be able to sell directly to the national accounts it already has? Will the distributor be required to buy its requirements for the products exclusively from the foreign supplier? If exclusivity is granted, a covenant not to compete should be entered into by the distributor, although these covenants are closely scrutinized by the courts in the United States and must be limited in their scope as to the geographic area, the type of activity covered, and the length of time in effect.

In dealing with compensation, whether it be a discount or commission, it is important to be very specific in defining the basis on which compensation will be calculated. What expense items are deducted from the base? What is expected of the foreign supplier in providing technical assistance, product literature, or translation of labels into English if necessary? On what basis may the agreement be terminated?

A frequent area of discussion involves which law will govern the relationship—those of the foreign supplier's location or those of the state in which the distributor is located. There is no single "U.S. commercial law." While the Uniform Commercial Code is generally present in all 50 states, there can be differences in interpretation by the different states, particularly in Louisiana.

In addition to the considerations mentioned for distributors, the sales representative should be able to pass on to potential customers the foreign supplier's terms and conditions of sale to avoid future misunderstandings. Such terms usually deal with ordering procedures, scheduling, delivery terms, price and payment, warranty language, and the manner in which claims may be asserted. In the United States, there should always be an express disclaimer in bold type of any consequential damage—that is, claims for workers' salaries and lost profits if a faulty product shuts a plant down.

In any case, a written agreement should be entered into to provide certainty to the relationship.

Licensing

If there are inherent advantages in manufacturing locally, (for instance, at the site where the main raw material is available or the location of the principal customer or generally within the country to avoid high freight or labor costs), an investor might consider licensing its know how and technology to a local company to manufacture and/or assemble the product for sale by the foreign company or the U.S. company.

This involves contractually granting the rights to use certain patents, disclosing and explaining the underlying know how and technology, training the licensee's people, being available to trouble shoot problems and pass on improvements in the technology for a specified period of time.

Other than tax issues and the potential need for prior government approvals, the normal considerations applicable to any licensing agreements apply. It is important to be specific as to the technology being supplied, the scope of the rights being granted, the amount of training required and the cost and availability of followup technical assistance. The royalty payments are obviously a business aspect, but are definitely affected by the presence or absence of a tax treaty capping the taxation of royalties or fees.

It is also important to have a detailed timetable and an agreed date by which all technical work is to be completed. Obviously, whether or not improvements are being cross-licensed is also an aspect which needs to be satisfactorily addressed.

The biggest issue is normally whether strategically you want to create another competitor and what patent protections exist and whether the foreign and U.S. laws allow one to restrict where the licensed goods are exported.

As a licensor granting the technology, it is important to define precisely what rights are being granted and to limit what duties of training and technical assistance will be offered so it is not an open-ended obligation.

As a licensee getting the technology it is important to get expansive rights (including exports) and continued access to technical improvements both product and process) as part of the package.

Other Contractual Relationships

This form usually involves establishing a contractual basis by which parties cooperate in a number of ways: research and development, joint product development, joint procurement, or retaining a marketing consultant.

Finding the right local partner is again a major concern. This may be a company already in the business, or in a related industry who would like to be in the business.

An example of where this form is useful is when a foreign investor has a particular innovation used on a foreign automobile that a local U.S. supplier could adapt to the unique structure and requirements of a U.S. vehicle. Perhaps it involves a basic electronics technology that needs to be commercialized into a more practical product that someone is willing to buy. The end result is that the parties agree to develop a product jointly either for a fee or at cost, with profits to be shared in an agreed manner.

Whatever particular type of cooperation is selected, the agreements implementing the relationship should follow the same general rules. The document should spell out the rights and duties of the parties while being clear and concise—understandable by business people, not sources of revenue for lawyers.

With respect to joint product development or research and development arrangements, there is nothing unique about doing business in the United States. The major concerns will be patent protection and copyright issues. Who retains the rights to any technologies or products developed, and the terms and conditions under which each party may use such developments should be clearly delineated in advance. If any underlying patents owned by one party or the other are required to fully use the joint developments, some form of license will also be required. Whether or not improvements are being cross-licensed is also an aspect that needs to be worked out. In short, the foreign partner needs to ensure that its technology is protected from misappropriation by others, since the United States has its own set of laws protecting intellectual property. Ownership rights can be unintentionally lost if these laws are not complied with.

If a marketing consultant is retained, it should be someone knowledgeable in the business who can be of genuine assistance with technical advice and/or contacts with specific customers. The consultant should know the industry contacts on a first-name basis—not simply select names out of a phone book. Experienced consultants are becoming more readily available as a result of several mergers of companies and the efforts by companies to cut costs through offering early retirement packages (both voluntary or involuntary). By contrast with Europe or Japan, where age and experience can be valued and workers have more statutory protections, there are many qualified executives in their early or middle fifties in the United States who have chosen to take a pension package and become independent consultants.

Branch Office

If a company decides to proceed on its own, one method is to establish a branch office instead of a separate corporation. Such an office should be the branch of a newly formed company and not of the parent company itself; otherwise, the entire worldwide assets of the parent company will be exposed to U.S. tax and to assessment of any U.S. legal liability, such as for product liability.

The provisions for registering a branch office are governed by individual state law. Of interest to a foreign investor is the need to register the branch and provide certain information and documents of the foreign company as part of the registration package. In Delaware, for instance, a party must provide a certificate issued by an authorized officer of the jurisdiction of its incorporation evidencing its existence, and if that certificate is in a foreign language, there will have to be a certified translation, with the oath of the translator attached thereto. The name of the branch must be cleared by checking that there is no other legal entity registered under the same name. If there is a conflict, another name must be selected either as the name of the entity or under a "doing business as" format.

Delaware also requires statements filed by an authorized officer of the corporation setting forth (1) the name and address of its registered agent, (2) the assets and liabilities of the corporation as of a date not earlier than six months prior to filing, (3) the business it proposes to do in the state, and (4) its authorization to do business in the jurisdiction of its incorporation. This last statement has to be notarized in accordance with Delaware law and a filing fee must be paid with the Secretary of State in Dover, Delaware.

Thereafter, summary reports and payment of a franchise tax are required annually. In some states, a copy of the incorporating documents (i.e., certificate of corporation and by-laws, known in some countries as the Memorandum and Articles of Association and in others as Statuts) may have to be attached and translated as well.

The appointment of a resident agent in the state for service of process is unfamiliar to some foreign investors. Service on such official agent of a summons and complaint is the method used to commence litigation in the United States. There are service agencies that in fact for an annual fee act as an "official mailbox" to receive notices and summons and forward them to the company headquarters.

Sometimes there is also a requirement that the names and resident addresses of directors be listed. This can create some consternation with foreigners concerned about giving the location of their personal residences to a foreign government.

Finally, as mentioned earlier, if business being conducted in another state exceeds a certain threshold (i.e., an operating plant or an office in which contracts are signed), the foreign investor will also have to register to do business in that state. The procedures for registering, while similar to those described above, do vary by state. In some cases large companies are qualified to do business in all 50 states. There is obviously a certain element of cost and expense incurred in registering and in complying with annual reporting requirements in each state.

Joint Venture

As noted in Table 10-1, a joint venture is frequently desirable when a foreign investor wishes to make a commitment to the U.S. market, but wants to share the risks and liabilities of entering that market with another partner until the foreign partner gains sufficient experience to proceed on its own.

Generically, joint ventures can be done either (1) on an unincorporated basis by merely cooperating, (2) through a newly formed corporation, or (3) through a partnership. The cooperative option was discussed earlier under the Other Contractual Relationship heading, and the partnership route will be discussed in the next section. This section will deal with the issues involved in a joint venture corporation.

Usually the parties negotiate a joint venture or shareholders' agreement that spells out the ownership, division of profits, and management of the joint venture. Frequently attached to this agreement are the various commercial documents applicable to the particular business deal. These can include licensing of patents and trademarks, distribution of the joint venture's products, technical assistance, financing arrangements, and procurement of raw materials, component supplies, or equipment required for the joint venture to operate.

With respect to the ownership issue, control is normally a factor of the percentage of voting shares owned or directed by a party. However, different classes of shares can be created and/or different percentages allocated to give the appearance of control to the local partner while providing equal contractual protections for both parties in the form of equal veto rights on major actions. For accounting purposes, 50 percent is a threshold at which a company is consolidated on a parent company's financial statements or which can trigger many financial covenants in a loan transaction.

While ownership normally governs the amount of dividends to be shared, dividends are not the only way to obtain profit from a joint venture. The foreign investor would be well advised to look at all of the commercial agreements as a whole and to consider how profit is being taken out of the joint venture. Many of the Japanese automotive joint ventures were in loss-making situations while they built the plant and started up operations. The Japanese partners made the majority of their profits from selling the equipment, parts and components imported from Japan used to assemble the cars at the joint venture.

Other sources of revenue for a party can include the interest and fees on direct loans; mark-up for management services provided, particularly for administration of employee benefits and computer services; the profit on supply of raw materials; royalties, fees, and expenses from technology and licensing agreements; fees for managing plant construction; distribution mark-ups or commissions if subsidiaries of the parents resell the joint venture's products; and premiums and charges for insurance and transportation by affiliated companies. These are just a few of the ways in which one party can earn profit disproportionately to the other parties.

Another major issue to address up front is the partners' long-term commitment to the joint venture. Specifically, they should agree not to compete with the joint venture business. This may create difficulties when the local party is someone already in the business and creative draftsmanship may be required. As part of this commitment, each party should also agree to send its best management talent and to treat the joint venture as an independent entity and not simply a subsidiary. A successful joint venture will pursue its aims separate and apart from those of the individual partners.

Another matter to be covered is management control. Who selects the officers and directors? Does one party or the other get to designate certain officers? The foreign partner should try to obtain the right to nominate the chief financial officer since the foreign partner, being at a distance, faces a natural disadvantage in knowing what is going on locally in any detail.

Of importance to all parties is the provision of veto rights over extraordinary actions. This is usually accomplished by giving these parties owning a minimum level of shares (i.e., 25 percent), equal rights to block actions by imposing higher quorum requirements and supermajority voting provisions for board approval. Examples of such actions are commitments over a certain monetary amount, dissolution of the joint venture, issuance of new shares, and/or the purchase, sale, or pledge of significant assets.

Another issue to be addressed is how the joint venture will be financed or capitalized. Will financing be through direct loans by the partners or will the joint venture seek third-party loans from banks, who in turn require a guarantee or comfort letter from the partners?

In organizing the share structure, the foreign partner should request (1) preemptive rights to any additional shares issued—that is, the right to buy sufficient shares to maintain its current ownership percentage; and (2) a right of first refusal to buy the other parties' shares if they either fail to take their allotment of additional shares or wish to get out of the joint venture altogether. There should also be restrictions on the transfer of the shares or any rights or interest therein, such as pledging the shares as collateral to a bank. This avoids one party having a bank or financial institution as an unwanted shareholder in a commercial venture.

In the sale of the shares, whether as a buyout or as a transfer, it is always important to specify the method of valuation as a formula in the agreement and a procedure for sale that is fair to both parties. Related to this is whether (1) one party or another should have a "put," or a right to require the other party to purchase its shares; and/or (2) to give one of the parties an option in which it may require the other party to sell its shares.

Finally, partners should agree on how disputes will be resolved and, if they cannot be resolved, how the joint venture will be broken up and valued. It is advisable to provide for a deadlock notice to be sent to senior management if a dispute arises. This will force the lower staff levels to try to resolve most of the differences before going to their respective chairman or president.

Under Delaware law, a 50-50 joint venture with two partners is entitled to certain termination provisions. Section 273 of Delaware Corporation law provides that in case of deadlock, either partner may file a certificate with the Court of Chancery in Delaware, and the court will order the dissolution of the corporation pursuant to a proposed plan for discontinuance and distribution of the assets. This is a useful procedure if the parties have been unable to resolve their differences and do not wish to resort to costly and extended litigation.

In valuing a joint venture, a variety of formulas and procedures can be used. A formula should be established in advance while the parties are still allies. If a plant is of value to only one party or the other, the formula should value the joint venture as a "going concern" and not simply on the book value of the tangible assets, which can be significantly less.

If there is a breakup, there is almost always a need to provide for some transitional supply arrangements until alternative arrangements can be put into place, such as raw material supply, sale of the output of the plant, or the replacement of existing financial arrangements—all of which cannot be done overnight. These matters are also best addressed prior to a breakup.

Partnership

Partnerships generally involve the same issues as a joint venture, except for a greater exposure to liability, and needs to be worked out and formalized in a written agreement, which may be registered. In the United States, there are generally two types of partnerships: general and limited.

In a general partnership, all partners are liable for the debts and obligations of the other members of the partnership whether or not incurred by them personally. Unless otherwise expressly limited, one partner can bind the actions of the other partners in many areas.

A limited partnership is one in which there is a general partner who is responsible for the management of the partnership and in turn is liable for all the debts of the partnership, and one or more limited partners whose exposure for the obligations of the partnership is restricted to the amount they have contributed. Likewise, the entitlement to profits and voice in the management of the business by limited partners is also restricted, unless otherwise negotiated.

Generally, partnerships need to be registered in particular states, many of which have adopted the Uniform Limited Partnership Act. Delaware law provides for the formation of the partnership, the rights and duties of limited partners and general partners, how the partnerships are financed, how distributions and withdrawals are handled, whether partnership interests can be assigned or pledged, and specific provisions dealing with foreign limited partnerships, including their registration and liability.

As noted in the section on Tax Considerations, a partnership can have significant tax advantages in that anticipated losses can be passed through to shield the income of its partners—but at the same time, so can the liabilities. This problem is sometimes handled by forming a new company that acts as a partner in a partnership—provided, however, that new corporation contains sufficient assets to meet its liability obligations. Frequently, the problem with partnerships is a cultural one of getting foreign investors to understand them and accept them.

Subsidiary

To form a company in the United States is a relatively simple procedure, but one that is done on an individual state basis since no national charters apply except in specialized industries, such as banking.

A company is formed by filing a Certificate (or Articles) of Incorporation with the Secretary of State of the state in question. The certificate usually states the name of the company (including a form of corporate destination); the address of the registered agent; the name of the business to be conducted; the classes and amount of shares; a description of any designations, powers, preferences, rights, qualifications, limitations, or restrictions on the stock; the name and mailing address of the incorporator; and the powers of the incorporator on filing. It may also include certain optional provisions such as indemnifying the directors and limiting the duration of the corporation to a specific term. A company is formed once the certificate is filed with and accepted by the Secretary of State and the appropriate filing fees are paid.

Next, the incorporator takes certain steps or appoints an initial board of directors who take certain actions, such as approving a set of by-laws. By-laws are detailed regulations governing the conduct of the affairs of the company, such as holding shareholders' meetings and electing officers and directors. Of particular interest to many foreign investors is that U.S. law does not provide for proxies for directors or alternate directors. If a director cannot be physically present, no one else can be appointed to act in his or her place, as in England. There are provisions, however, in certain states that permit action by unanimous written consent of all the directors or participation in meetings by telephone. This is of particular value to foreign parties for whom it is not cost-effective to make frequent trips to attend board meetings. Board meetings can usually be held within or outside the state.

Other organization steps taken include ordering a minute book, stock certificates, and stock ledger in which to note the ownership of the shares; opening bank accounts; and applying for federal and state tax identification numbers. If there are to be employees, the company must also register for workmens compensation and set up a payroll system to provide for withholding social security and income taxes on wages paid to employees.

Transfer and proof of ownership of shares are governed by applicable federal and state laws and, if listed on a stock exchange, also by the regulations of that exchange. Generally, ownership is evidenced by a duly signed stock certificate and transfer of ownership by a signed stock power presented to the company, unless transfer restrictions are printed on the face of the certificate. There are no provisions for title to transfer solely by entry in the stock ledger, as in the Netherlands, or for bearer shares, as in Europe, although brokers do hold securities in "street names." However, in order to allow for the orderly conduct of shareholders' meetings and payment of dividends, the by-laws may permit the company only to pay dividends and send notices to shareholders of record as of a certain date.

TAX CONSIDERATIONS IN ENTITY SELECTION

Business Goals

The tax considerations affecting the selection of the proper business entity for conduct of a U.S. business or investment depend on the nature of the investment and the business goals. There is no one perfect strategy for investing in the United States. Planning for a real estate investment has different tax considerations from those for a manufacturing investment. Most importantly, the business strategy of the foreign investor must be taken into account. Investors who wish to repatriate their U.S. earnings would often use a different structure for their U.S. investment than would an investor who desires reinvestment of profit in the U.S. business. Such reinvestment of profit in additional U.S. assets might be preferable to an investor located in a jurisdiction that has a tax rate in excess of the U.S. rate.

   The method of realizing the profit from the U.S. investment is also a factor. Some investments are by their nature short-term and the profit will be realized by a sale of the investment rather than through periodic dividends or other cash flows (e.g., royalties and interest). The proper tax strategy for a U.S. investment cannot be developed in a vacuum. The selection of the appropriate business entity must complement the business goals and commercial strategies of the foreign investor.

Home Country Tax Considerations

The foreign investor must first consider the **tax consequences in the home jurisdiction** in selecting the proper vehicle for U.S. investment. For example, use of a branch operation or partnership in the U.S. may allow for start-up losses to be deducted in the investor's home jurisdiction. However, this is not possible in all countries and may not be beneficial in others. There may be offsetting tax detriments to the use of foreign branch losses, such as loss of foreign tax credits on other foreign income or recapture of the foreign branch losses upon an eventual incorporation of the U.S. branch. Subsequent incorporation of a U.S. branch into a U.S. corporation can also have adverse U.S. tax consequences, such as loss of any U.S. tax loss carryforward. If the investor has other foreign subsidiaries, it might be preferable to have one of these foreign affiliates operate the U.S. branch, particularly when the affiliate's tax jurisdiction allows beneficial use of branch losses or when favorable income tax treaty provisions with the United States may apply (but see Chapter 12 on treaties for a full discussion).

Another home country tax consideration is the **treatment of various types of cash flows** from the U.S. operation. Investors in countries that exempt dividends from foreign subsidiaries, in whole or in part, will want to structure their U.S. investments differently from investors in countries that tax such dividends. If dividends from a U.S. subsidiary are tax free in the investor's home country, use of a U.S. corporation rather than a branch or partnership would generally be preferable for profitable U.S. operations. Investors from countries that do not exempt foreign dividends may wish to use other means of "repatriating" U.S. earnings using tax-deductible royalties, interest, and management charges. Use of a U.S. subsidiary can facilitate the charging of such deductible items to reduce U.S. tax.

The **deductibility of interest on funds borrowed** to invest in the U.S. operation must also be considered. Countries that exempt foreign dividend income often deny a deduction for interest expense related to the investment. Obtaining a tax deduction for interest on funds borrowed for the U.S. investment may influence the choice of U.S. entity and may suggest use of a foreign affiliate of the investor in a third country that has more favorable tax treatment for such investment interest expense.

Finally, the structuring of investment into the United States may depend on the **anti-abuse rules of the investor's home country.** Investment from countries with few restrictions on use of tax haven companies may want to use a holding company in a low tax jurisdiction to hold the shares of the U.S. subsidiary and to receive dividends. This is particularly true when the investor's jurisdiction has a high tax rate and the tax rules do not limit the tax benefits derived from the use of the tax haven holding company.

U.S. Tax Considerations

U.S. tax law initially appears to be a **relatively neutral factor** in determining the choice of entity for most U.S. business operations. U.S. branches of foreign companies and U.S. subsidiaries of foreign parent companies are subject to the same basic corporate tax rates. In addition, the United States has a "branch" tax that is imposed on the "dividend equivalent" amount of the earnings of a U.S. branch of a foreign corporation. This "dividend equivalent" amount basically represents the repatriated profits of the U.S. branch that are not reinvested in the U.S. branch operation. In function, the "branch" tax operates in the same way as the U.S. withholding tax on dividends from a U.S. subsidiary. Both the U.S. "branch" tax and the dividend withholding tax are assessed at a 30 percent rate, and both may be reduced by income tax treaties between the United States and various countries. However, the "branch" tax rules have built-in antitreaty shopping rules that prevent an investment from being routed through a country with a more favorable treaty. Some U.S. income tax treaties have not yet been amended to incorporate similar antitreaty shopping provisions, and dividends paid by a U.S. subsidiary can still qualify for the reduced rate of withholding under such treaties.

Financing arrangements for the U.S. operation are also affected by U.S. tax law. Related party loans to a U.S. subsidiary can result in limitations on the deductibility of interest expense as a result of the so-called earnings stripping rules. If the U.S. subsidiary has a debt-to-equity ratio in excess of 1.5 : 1 and has related party interest expense in excess of 50 percent of adjusted taxable income, U.S. tax law will limit the deductibility of the interest expense. In addition, the rate of interest on such related party loans must be at an arm's length rate. A U.S. branch operation has its own restrictions on the deductibility of interest expense. A branch operation may be able to deduct interest expense it actually pays and interest of the foreign company that is apportioned to the U.S. branch's assets. The regulations for determining the amount of allowable interest deduction for a U.S. branch are quite complex and should be carefully analyzed by the potential foreign investor. The possibility of U.S. withholding tax being imposed on interest paid by the branch or "deemed" paid by the branch should also be considered. Often, the financing requirements for U.S. operations will be determinative of the choice of U.S. business entity. It should be noted that interest is not always currently deductible. In some cases, such as construction period interest, interest must be capitalized and amortized.

Other intercompany transactions can be affected by U.S. tax law. Foreign investors transferring technology and other intangible assets to a U.S. operation will often prefer charging royalties to a U.S. subsidiary rather than attempting to obtain a tax deduction in the U.S. branch for apportioned research and development expenses of the foreign corporation. The introduction of the "super-royalty" standard into U.S. tax law may allow foreign licensors to charge royalties for the use of intangibles by a U.S. subsidiary that are "commensurate" with the income attributable to the intangible. Although the "super-royalty" standard was designed to force U.S. companies to charge higher royalties to their offshore affiliates, the same standard may allow foreign licensors to maximize the royalties they charge their U.S. subsidiaries. Foreign investors selling goods into the United States will often prefer use of U.S. subsidiary over a branch in order to minimize the U.S. taxable income through intercompany pricing (see Chapter 18 on transfer pricing). Care must be exercised in this area, however, because of increased IRS scrutiny of intercompany pricing practices of foreign multi-nationals. Recent tax law changes have greatly enhanced the ability of the IRS to obtain information and litigate perceived abuses in intercompany pricing. Additional legislative proposals to increase the U.S. tax burden of foreign companies operating in the United States have been put forward but not yet approved. Foreign investors should be aware of recent changes that increase the reporting of related party transactions.

Acquisitions

Acquisitions of existing U.S. business operations raise additional tax issues. The foreign investor has the usual issues involving purchase of assets versus purchase of stock, but also has limitations and opportunities not faced by a U.S. resident purchaser. The foreign investor does not have the same ability to engage in tax free liquidations of a U.S. company and cannot generally achieve a tax free spin-off of a subsidiary. Special tax rules governing cross-border transactions restrict the liberal tax free reorganization and liquidation rules that apply in a purely domestic context. Thus, the foreign investor should carefully examine the business assets being purchased and, if possible, consider having a foreign affiliate purchase some types of U.S.-based assets rather than using a U.S. subsidiary to purchase all the assets.

When **purchasing a U.S. business that has foreign subsidiaries,** for example, the foreign investor may wish to separately purchase the foreign subsidiaries to remove future dividend flows from U.S. taxation. Such dividends from foreign subsidiaries paid to a U.S. company are fully taxable in the United States, with an offsetting credit for foreign taxes paid by the foreign subsidiary and any withholding tax paid on the dividend. However, the complex mechanism for calculating the limitation on use of foreign tax credits often results in additional U.S. corporate tax being paid on such dividends. This is particularly true when the U.S. company has significant debt, since the apportionment of U.S. interest expense against foreign income is often the major cause of additional U.S. tax on foreign-source dividends. Thus, a foreign investor planning on leveraging the purchased U.S. operation with acquisition debt may wish first to purchase some of the foreign subsidiaries of the U.S. target company using an offshore company, in order to remove future dividend flows and gains from any eventual disposition from U.S. taxation. This has the added advantage of removing the foreign subsidiaries from the application of the U.S. anti-avoidance rules designed to prevent the build-up of offshore earnings in lower tax foreign jurisdictions. Removal of such foreign subsidiaries from the ownership of the U.S. target company will then allow more flexibility for the remaining U.S. operations to be structured as a branch, partnership, or corporation as best fits the business and tax goals of the foreign investor.

Another situation when the foreign investor may wish to buy assets rather than the stock of an existing U.S. company involves **U.S. companies possessing valuable technology and other intangibles.** U.S. tax law does not allow the tax free transfer of intangibles out of the United States. In addition, the "super-royalty" standard for determining an arm's length royalty between a U.S. licensor and related foreign parties can result in increased royalty income to the U.S. licensor upon an audit by the IRS. The foreign investor may wish to separately purchase certain of the intangible assets of the U.S. target company, using an offshore company that would then license the intangibles back to the U.S. operations and perhaps to other affiliates worldwide. Use of a Swiss licensing company for this purpose may be quite beneficial, but the anti-avoidance rules of the foreign investor's home jurisdiction must also be considered.

There are a **number of special U.S. tax rules** that can come into play in the **acquisition context** and that may have an impact on the structure of the acquisition and the choice of entity. U.S. tax law allows an election to treat a stock purchase as an asset purchase. This is not generally advantageous since the desired step-up in the tax basis of assets usually has a steep tax cost. Generally, the present value of the future tax benefits of the step-up in basis is outweighed by the immediate tax detriment upon electing asset sale treatment. There are also rules that restrict the use of tax loss carryforwards of an acquired company upon a change of ownership. These rules restrict use of the tax loss carryforwards to an annual amount equal to the fair market value of the acquired company times a stated interest rate. The IRS has interpreted these rules to cause such a restriction on the use of a U.S. company's loss carryforwards when there is a change in ownership of the foreign parent company. Thus, the acquisition of a foreign company with a U.S. subsidiary can cause such limitations on the use of the loss carryforward of the U.S. subsidiary because of the change in ultimate ownership. Other tax rules can restrict the use of loss carryforwards when a profitable U.S. company is acquired by a U.S. company with tax loss carryforwards. In some cases, merger of companies may avoid the application of this rule.

Joint Ventures

Joint ventures can take many forms, from mere contractual arrangements to corporate and partnership joint ventures. A foreign investor will often have tax goals that conflict with those of the U.S. joint venture partner. A U.S. company will generally prefer use of a partnership vehicle for a U.S. joint venture. A partnership is not generally a taxable entity for U.S. tax purposes. The income (loss) of the partnership flows through to the partners based on the terms of the partnership agreement, subject to limitations that require the partnership allocations of income (loss) to have "substantial economic effect." The flow-through of partnership income avoids the double taxation that would take place if a corporate joint venture were used. Dividends from a corporate joint venture to a U.S. corporate joint venture partner are taxable but with a dividends-received deduction of 70 or 80 percent, depending on the degree of ownership of the corporate joint venture. Double taxation takes place as a result.

The flow-through of any losses of a partnership joint venture provides another compelling reason for use of a partnership joint venture. The U.S. corporate joint venture partner can insulate itself from the liabilities of the partnership by use of a separate U.S. corporation to hold the partnership investment. Filing a consolidated return with this separate U.S. corporation can consolidate the profits and losses of the partnership for tax purposes with the income (losses) of the entire U.S. consolidated return group of companies.

Often, the foreign joint venture partner will have tax goals adverse to those of the U.S. party. The foreign partner in a U.S. partnership will be deemed to be engaged in a U.S. trade or business as a result of attribution of the partnership's activities. This taxable presence of the foreign partner will require the foreign partner to file a U.S. tax return on its share of the partnership income. In addition, U.S. withholding tax is required on the profits generated by the partnership, even when such profits are not distributed. In some situations, the U.S. "permanent establishment" created by participation in the partnership can cause loss of certain benefits available under income tax treaties. For example, a U.S.-source capital gain of the foreign partner unrelated to the partnership activity can be taxable as a result of having the "permanent establishment" created by participation in the partnership. The foreign joint venture partner can avoid these problems by incorporating a U.S. subsidiary to hold the U.S. partnership interest. In some situations, the foreign partner may want to utilize a separate foreign affiliate to own the U.S. partnership interest. This would be desirable when the losses of the U.S. partnership would flow through for foreign tax purposes and provide a tax benefit for the losses in the tax jurisdiction of the foreign affiliate.

In some special situations, use of a special form of corporate joint venture known as a "cooperative" may be beneficial. Such a cooperative is legally a regular U.S. corporation but one that elects to be taxed as a cooperative (under Subchapter T of the Internal Revenue Code). It is not a flow-through entity like a partnership, but through use of deductible "patronage dividends" it can avoid the double taxation of earnings described above. For the foreign participant, the patronage dividends can be particularly attractive since the qualified earnings of the cooperative paid to the foreign participant may be subject only to the dividend withholding tax rate under an appropriate treaty and may avoid regular U.S. tax at the joint venture cooperative level. An example of a joint venture that might benefit from use of a cooperative structure would be a manufacturing joint venture for automobiles in which both the U.S. and foreign parties will buy the output of the joint venture for sale under their respective brand names. The profits of the manufacturing cooperative joint venture can be paid out in deductible patronage dividends to the parties based on their respective volume of car purchases from the cooperative. So long as each participant's volume of purchases from the cooperative reflects its respective ownership percentages, the payment of patronage dividends will approximate the participants' ownership interests and be equitable. If, however, the volume of purchases does not reflect the equity ownership of the parties, it may be necessary to pay only part of earnings as patronage dividends and to pay out the remainder as regular dividends based on share ownership after payment of tax at the cooperative level on the earnings not distributed as patronage dividends.

While use of such a cooperative arrangement may be very beneficial when all the business of the joint venture is conducted with the shareholder patrons of the cooperative, complex tax issues can arise that may not be clearly addressed by U.S. tax law, particularly as regards the foreign participant's taxability on patronage dividends.

Dispositions of U.S. Investments

As previously mentioned, the selection of the proper U.S. business entity may depend on **how the profit from the investment is realized.** Profit from some investments may, by their nature, only be realized by their sale or disposition. Gain on a commercial real estate development, for example, will generally be realized upon its sale after construction and initial leasing of space to tenants.

In these and other situations wherein the foreign investor intends to realize the profit upon sale of the U.S. investment, it is important that the U.S. tax consequences of disposition be understood. Taxation of gains on U.S. real estate investments are subject to special rules that are described in Part 4 of this book. These tax rules generally take precedence over the more general rules discussed here and should be considered carefully by foreign investors.

Sale of the shares of a U.S. company (other than shares of a U.S. Real Property Holding Company) are generally free of U.S. tax except when held by a nonresident alien individual spending 183 days or more in the United States in the year of sale or, in some cases, when sold by a foreign investor with a "permanent establishment" in the United States. It should be noted that legislative proposals have been introduced in the last couple of years that would change this tax free treatment and impose a 10 percent tax on the gain of sale of shares by foreign persons owning 10 percent or more of a U.S. company. Whether such proposals will eventually be passed into law cannot be predicted. If they are eventually enacted, it is likely that some grace period would be provided for investments from countries with income tax treaties with the United States, since many of these treaties prohibit taxing such stock gains.

Although U.S. tax laws can override treaty obligations, the use of treaty overrides is a controversial topic and some countries have threatened retaliatory legislation if the United States were to proceed with such legislation. However, the foreign investor should obtain advice on the current status of such potential legislation and consider the advisability of structuring share ownership through an appropriate income tax treaty that might prohibit such taxation, at least for some grace period.

Sale of the assets of a U.S. branch or partnership will result in U.S. taxation of the gain on sale of the assets in virtually all cases. Even where payments are deferred to later years when there is no U.S. business presence of the foreign investor, U.S. tax law will result in tax since the taxability of the deferred payments will be determined based on the existence of a taxable presence in the United States in the year of sale.

When the foreign investor will also be subject to tax in the investor's home jurisdiction on the sale of U.S. branch or partnership assets, the imposition of U.S. tax may not be a detriment if a full credit for the U.S. tax can be obtained in the home jurisdiction against the home country tax. In some cases, advance planning can minimize or avoid the U.S. tax through actions such as incorporation of the U.S. branch prior to sale. However, U.S. tax rules can require such steps to be taken well in advance of the subsequent sale in order to be effective.

Individual Foreign Investors

Much of the preceding discussion applies equally to foreign individuals and to foreign corporate investors. However, the foreign individual investor has some special U.S. tax considerations not faced by the foreign corporate investor.

The first consideration is the possible application of the **U.S. estate and gift taxes** to foreign individuals who own U.S. assets. Foreign nationals who own certain U.S. property, including the shares of a U.S. company, will be subject to U.S. estate tax upon their death. U.S. estate tax rates on such U.S. property start at 18 percent and increase in increments to a rate of 50 percent for taxable estates over $2.5 million. Unlike U.S. citizens, such foreign nationals get only a $13,000 estate tax credit unless they qualify under an estate tax treaty for a proration of the $192,800 credit allowed to U.S. citizens. Thus, absent an estate tax treaty, a foreign national will be liable for U.S. estate tax on a U.S. taxable estate over $60,000, while a U.S. citizen only pays tax on a taxable estate over $600,000.

In addition, the deduction for assets passing to one's surviving spouse does not apply to a spouse who is not a U.S. citizen. Similar rules apply to gifts of U.S. property by a foreign national. Foreign nationals will therefore usually want to use an intermediate foreign corporation to hold their interests in U.S. property to avoid the application of these rules, unless the U.S. estate tax can be credited against the estate or inheritance taxes imposed in the investor's home jurisdiction.

A second consideration for individual foreign investors in U.S. property is the possibility that they may become **residents of the U.S. for income tax** purposes if they spend any considerable amount of time in the United States. As resident aliens for U.S. tax purposes, foreign nationals become subject to U.S. income tax on their worldwide income from all sources. Foreign nationals will become resident aliens, regardless of their immigration status, if they spend at least 31 days in the current year and a total of 183 days in the United States over a three-year period calculated in the following manner. The 183-day "substantial presence" test is calculated by adding the days in the current year to one third times the number of U.S. days in the preceding year plus one sixth times the number of U.S. days in the second preceding year. Generally, presence in the

United States for any part of a day and for any reason, including vacations, count as U.S. days in the calculation. Certain exceptions apply for students, teachers, trainees, persons undergoing medical treatment, commuter workers from Canada and Mexico, and persons in transit between international destinations. Foreign nationals are also considered to be resident aliens for U.S. tax purposes if they are lawfully admitted for permanent residence in the United States under the immigration laws (a so-called green card alien).

While becoming a resident alien for U.S. income tax purposes will often have adverse overall tax consequences, in some situations it can be beneficial and allow certain transactions to be accomplished on a tax free basis or result in reduced U.S. taxation. Certain transfers of assets to foreign corporations and cross-border reorganizations can be accomplished tax free by a resident alien that would not be tax free for a nonresident alien. In some cases, taxation in the United States for a resident alien with allowance of certain deductions not allowed to nonresident aliens can result in reduced U.S. taxation.

CONCLUSION

This brief summary of considerations in structuring U.S. investments and selecting the proper business form for U.S. business operations is not an exhaustive analysis of the issues involved. Although the majority of foreign companies probably operate initially in the United States through a distributor and then a subsidiary, this is not always the best form of doing business, particularly from a tax perspective. Indeed, the form and structure may change over time, depending on the evolution and success of its business activities, changes in the market, and regulations related.

The U.S. legal and tax system is probably the most complex tax system of any country, particularly as it affects foreign investors and cross-border transactions. Failure to properly plan for and structure U.S. investment can result in unnecessarily high overall taxation and onerous legal problems—all of which can be very costly to correct at a later date. Foreign investors would be well advised to seek competent professional legal and tax advice before making U.S. investments or commencing U.S. business operations.

CHAPTER 11

FEDERAL LAWS AND REGULATIONS RESTRICTING FOREIGN INVESTMENT IN THE UNITED STATES

Robert A. Skitol, Esq.
Lloyd R. Ziff, Esq.
*Richard B. Nash, Jr., Esq.**
Pepper, Hamilton & Scheetz

INTRODUCTION

Regulation of foreign direct investment and foreign business or commercial activities in the United States is not pervasive, compared with that in some other Western nations. Some aspects of the regulatory regime are changing rapidly, however, in large part because of the clash of two increasingly conflicting governmental policies: a philosophical openness to foreign capital investment on the one hand, and on the other, growing concern that acquisitions by foreigners of certain U.S. assets are undercutting the country's national and "economic" security.

Most regulation of foreign investment, in fact, consists of reporting requirements. Prohibitive restrictions on business or com-

*The authors gratefully acknowledge the valuable assistance of Rebecca Berlow and Diane Ruth Holt.

mercial activities by foreigners chiefly apply to specific sectors such as communications, aviation, or the exploration of natural resources, although restriction on foreign investment in the U.S. airline industry has been somewhat liberalized recently. At the same time, the federal government, prompted largely by Congress, has had to respond to public concern that foreign investment in certain sectors, especially high technology industries such as semiconductors, could erode U.S. national security and economic strength. The Exon-Florio Amendment, which empowers the President to prohibit foreign investments that could threaten national security, broadly defined, is the most visible manifestation of the growing "politicization" of foreign investment. At the time of writing, Congress was considering legislation that would further regulate foreign direct investment, and the following discussion should therefore be reviewed carefully with an eye on possible upcoming developments.

Finally, there may be state statutes or regulations that, although not within the scope of this chapter, may indirectly place restrictions on foreign investment. Among such restrictions are state plant closing laws,[1] which do not place direct limitations on foreign investment (such limitations might be prohibited by the U.S. Constitution's Commerce Clause) but which nevertheless reflect strong local concern about purchasers of U.S. assets "exporting" American jobs overseas. Therefore, a foreign investor should always consider the possible effect of applicable state laws on contemplated investments.

Reporting and Restriction of Foreign Investment for National Security Reasons (The "Exon-Florio" Amendment)

If a merger, acquisition, or takeover by or with a foreign person may threaten national security, it is subject to scrutiny by the Committee on Foreign Investment in the United States (CFIUS) and possible divestment by order of the President. CFIUS comprises members of several executive agencies and is chaired by an official of the Treasury Department.[2] Although the formal statutory authority for CFIUS review and presidential action expired in 1990, Congress permanently reauthorized Exon-Florio in August 1991. The measure also temporarily extended the Defense Production Act retroactively to October 1990, thus confirming CFIUS' full authority to review transactions that may have occurred during the statute's lapse.[3] During that period, the Treasury Department had advised foreign persons to continue to notify CFIUS of such transactions.[4]

Senator Exon and Congressman Florio initially introduced the law allowing the president to interfere with certain transactions to ensure that the president would have authority to prevent important industries and products from becoming foreign-owned or -controlled. The provision they crafted, the "Exon-Florio" Amendment to the Defense Production Act,[5] allows the president to take action to block a merger, acquisition, or takeover if there is "credible evidence" that "the foreign interest exercising control might take action that threatens to impair the national security" and if other laws do not provide adequate protection.[6]

Although Congress first passed Exon-Florio in October 1988, the Treasury Department did not issue final regulations to implement the provision until November 1991.[7] The final regulations, which remain largely unchanged from the proposed regulations under which CFIUS operated since 1989,[8] create three stages of inquiry. First, upon notice by any party to a foreign acquisition, merger, or takeover, CFIUS has 30 days to review the transaction and decide whether to conduct an investigation. Second, if the committee does decide to investigate, it must issue a recommendation to the president within 45 days. Finally, the president then has 15 days to decide whether to suspend or prohibit the acquisition, merger, or takeover. Since Congress first enacted Exon-Florio CFIUS has reviewed over 600 transactions.[9] Thirteen of these were subjected to the 45-day investigation.[10] In only one instance has the president used his authority to order divestment of a foreign-owned company's acquired U.S. subsidiary—the People's Republic of China's takeover of Mamco Manufacturing, Inc., an airline parts supplier to Boeing, Inc.[11]

There is no obligation to notify CFIUS of a transaction;[12] however, if no party gives notice, neither CFIUS nor the president is obligated to act within the statutory period. The president possesses authority indefinitely to make the required findings and to take action, including divestment. In fact, then, the so-called voluntary notice procedures strongly encourage notification for those transactions that may relate to national security. Otherwise, the parties to the transaction may be susceptible to scrutiny or divestment at a time remote from the transaction. If a member of the committee chooses to notify the committee of a transaction that may affect national security, however, this notice will begin the running of the first statutory period.

Neither the Exon-Florio statute nor the final regulations define national security. However, the law sets forth certain factors that raise national security implications:

> (1) domestic production needed for projected national defense requirements,
>
> (2) the capability and capacity of domestic industries to meet national defense requirements, including the availability of human resources, products, technology, materials, and other supplies and services, and
>
> (3) the control of domestic industries and commercial activity by foreign citizens as it affects the capability and capacity of the United States to meet the requirements of national security.[13]

In addition, Congress created the National Critical Technologies Panel in 1990 to identify those technologies important to "future U.S. national security and . . . economic well-being."[14] The Panel identified 22 such technologies in the following areas: materials, manufacturing, information and communications, biotechnology and life sciences, aeronautics and surface transportation, and energy and environment. Although this list carries no legal weight, it may serve as a guide to those areas of investment that will be of some concern to CFIUS and to the president.

The members of Congress who debated the law in conference, however, intended that "national security" be broadly interpreted and not limited to particular industries.[15] Likewise, the authors of the regulations suggest that "notice is appropriate when, for example, a company is being acquired that provides products or key technologies essential to the U.S. defense industrial base."[16] Because the law protects the confidentiality of material submitted to the committee,[17] little information is available about those industries and transactions that CFIUS has chosen to investigate. A study prepared for Congress indicates that among the firms submitting notice to CFIUS were those in the computer, semiconductor, semiconductor equipment, and aerospace industries.[18]

To determine whether a foreign interest is acquiring, taking over, or merging with a domestic interest, the law looks to the nationality of the entity or person with actual control.[19] The regulations likewise employ a functional rather than a mechanical test.[20] If a person has any of the following powers, whether exercised or not, the regulations deem that person to control the entity: the power to sell or transfer the assets of an entity, to dissolve the entity, to relocate the entity's facilities, to make decisions about the entity's contracts, or to amend the articles of incorporation with respect to these decisions.[21] If the holder of control according to this definition is a foreign person, entity, or government, the interest will fall within the statute. Note that, for example, even if an entity is incorporated in the United States and all its business is transacted there, it may be considered to be foreign for purposes of the statute if its outstanding shares are owned by foreign nationals. Likewise, if a foreign national acquires a U.S.-controlled business operating entirely outside the United States, the transaction is outside the scope of the law.

Although Congress reenacted Exon-Florio without substantive changes, legislation currently pending in Congress would expand government authority to limit foreign investment. This bill, called the Technology Preservation Act of 1991,[22] would expand CFIUS's responsibilities in several ways. First, CFIUS could solicit "assurances" or performance requirements that an investment will not "impair the national security."[23] Second, the proposed legislation would require mandatory notification of certain types of transactions.[24] Third, the assistant to the president for science and technology would be empowered to investigate whether a U.S. company being acquired was involved with technology essential to the national security. The legislation, then, not only would force CFIUS to review a broader variety of investments but also is intended to block more foreign purchases than did the 1988 legislation. In addition, the proposed legislation would name the Secretary of Commerce as head of CFIUS. The purpose of this provision is to avoid the conflicting demands placed on the Treasury Secretary, whose overall responsibilities include selling U.S. government securities to foreigners on the one hand and critically reviewing foreign investment on the other. Although both the Reagan and Bush Administrations have opposed greater restrictions on foreign investment, political support in favor of such restrictions has been growing.

International Investment and Trade in Services Survey Act

Congress, in response to a marked increase in foreign investment in this country during the first half of the 1970s, approved the International Investment Survey Act of 1976, which was renamed to incorporate "Trade in Services" in 1984.[25] This act directs the President, by way of the Department of Commerce and the Bureau of Economic Analysis in the Department of Commerce ("BEA"),[26] to collect information relating to foreign acquisitions of U.S. entities, annual surveys of direct investment, and quarterly transactions with foreign parent corporations. This information is gathered by imposition of reporting requirements (a description of which follows) on foreign investors engaging in business and commercial activities in the United States. However, the information reported on all report forms is treated as confidential.[27] The BEA also conducts a comprehensive survey of foreign direct investment in the United States once every five years (the Benchmark survey).[28]

A foreign investor with holdings that constitute "direct investment" for purposes of the act must be a person resident outside of the United States or subject to the jurisdiction of a country other than the United States, who possesses ownership or control, directly or indirectly, of 10 percent or more of the voting securities of a corporation or the equivalent interest in an unincorporated business.[29] The periods of reporting are as follows: upon establishment, acquisition, or purchase of the operating assets of a U.S. business enterprise or real estate (Form BE-13); quarterly (Form BE-605, 606B); annually (Form BE-15); and each five years, in order to enable BEA to compile the Benchmark survey (Form BE-12). A preliminary form, BE-12 (X), is filed to enable BEA to determine the size and extent of foreign investment, since smaller investments may be exempt from reporting requirements, or subject to short-form reporting, if the degree of foreign investment is sufficiently minimal.[30] However, the reporting requirements under BEA regulations are continuous, so that if the applicable exemption levels can no longer be met, reports will have to be filed at a subsequent date.

A report may also be required to be filed by a U.S. person who assists or intervenes in the acquisition of a U.S. business enterprise or who enters into a joint venture with a foreign person. Such a U.S. person may include, without limitation, an intermediary, a business broker, or a brokerage house.[31] Again, certain exemptions are available with respect to real estate held for personal use or if the enterprise that is acquired or disposed of has total assets below a certain level and does not own real estate.

The act was amended in 1990,[32] to permit BEA to exchange the information it gathers with the Census Bureau and the Bureau of Labor Statistics. The information is also available to CFIUS, which is charged with analyzing the effect of foreign investment in certain industries. Violation of the reporting requirements may be penalized with civil fines of up to $10,000 and criminal penalties of up to $10,000 and one year's imprisonment.[33] Under the amended act, the penalties for unlawfully disclosing any submitted information were increased from no more than $10,000[34] to not less than $2,500 and not more than $25,000 or up to five years in prison, or both.[35]

Government Procurement and Benefits

Procurement
The U.S. government is one of the world's largest purchasers of goods and services. Under U.S. law, however, there are certain restrictions on the government's freedom to purchase goods and services from foreign producers in the United States and abroad. Further, there are restrictions on the origin of goods and component parts that are purchased by the government. Although the 1979 GATT Agreement on Government Procurement and the Trade Agreements Act[36] sought to limit the extent to which signatory nations to GATT could accord preferential treatment to their own producers, certain exceptions remained, not least of which are sensitive defense- and national security-related purchases.

Certain federal statutes require that, with some exceptions, federal agencies purchase only items produced in the United States without, however, restricting procurement from a foreign-controlled U.S. corporation that produces the items domestically. For example, the Buy America Act[37] requires government agencies to acquire for public use only materials produced or manufactured in the United States. These provisions do not apply if the agency head determines that it would be "inconsistent with the public interest" or that the cost of the domestic articles is unreasonable. The act does not apply to items purchased for use outside the United States or to items not produced in the United States "in sufficient and reasonably available commercial quantities and of a satisfactory quality." The Buy America Act covers both "unmanufactured articles, materials, and supplies" and "manufactured articles, materials, and supplies."[38]

The Berry Amendment to the Defense Appropriations Act annually restricts the Department of Defense from procuring articles of food, clothing, cotton, silk, synthetic fabric, or specialty metals that are not produced in the United States. There are exceptions for cases in which sufficient quantities cannot be purchased at U.S. market prices, for purchases in support of combat operations, for purchases by vessels in foreign waters, and emergency purchases of perishable foods.[39]

Various special provisions are applicable to producers who are granted government contracts in areas of national defense. Thus, for example, government contract awards in competitions for new aircraft design may not be made to an individual who is not a U.S. citizen, or to a corporation unless 75 percent of its capital stock is owned by and all of its directors are citizens of the United States, or to an individual or corporation that does not have a manufacturing plant in the United States.[40]

Concern about national defense has led to establishing restrictions under the Defense Industrial Security Program (DISP), a regulatory scheme promulgated by the Department of Defense to monitor access by contractors to classified information.[41] Procedures established under this program are set forth in the Department of Defense Industrial Security Regulation (ISR) and the Department of Defense Industrial Security Manual for Safeguarding Classified Information (ISM).[42] Under these regulations, no classified information can flow to a contractor on a DOD project unless the facility of that contractor receives security clearance. Facility clearance is rarely granted for facilities found to be under foreign ownership, control, or influence (FOCI).[43] FOCI is found to obtain when foreign interests hold a significant amount of equity or debt in an organization or when foreign interests control or influence officers, directors, or executives of an organization, or when an organization has interlocking directors with a foreign firm. In such cases, there exists a reasonable likelihood that a "compromise of classified information or adverse impact on performance of a classified contract may result.[44] Security clearance, therefore, poses a formidable obstacle to foreign investors interested in competing with domestic firms for government contracts that are subject to DISP.[45]

Under such regulations, a classified contract is any contract that requires, or will require, access to classified information by the contractor or employees in the performance of the contract.[46] Security clearances are required both for facilities and for individuals occupying key management positions. Foreign ownership, control, or influence of domestic facilities or foreign nationality of such individuals will generally render them ineligible.[47] A modified procedure is available for clearance of facilities if the ownership, control, or influence of such facilities stems from sources with whom the United States has reciprocal industrial security agreements. Such facilities may qualify for clearance.[48]

Subsidies, Insurance, and Other Government Benefits

Foreign-controlled enterprises operating in the United States, whether as branches or subsidiaries, generally (subject to specific exemptions) may not

1. Obtain special government loans for the financing or refinancing of the cost of purchasing, constructing, or operating commercial fishing vessels or gear.[49]
2. Sell obsolete vessels to the Secretary of Commerce in exchange for credit toward new vessels.[50]
3. Obtain construction-differential or operating-differential subsidies for vessel construction or operation.[51]
4. Obtain certain types of vessel insurance unless management restrictions applicable to companies operating vessels in salvage are satisfied.[52]
5. Obtain war-risk insurance for aircraft.[53]
6. Purchase Overseas Private Investment Corporation Insurance or guarantees.[54]

7. Obtain special government emergency loans for agricultural purposes after a natural disaster or government loans to individual farmers or ranchers to purchase and operate family farms.[55]

Political Contributions

Foreign nationals cannot legally make or promise to make a contribution in connection with an election to any political office or in connection with any primary election, convention, or caucus to select candidates for any political office.[56] A *foreign national* means any individual who is neither a U.S. citizen nor a lawfully admitted permanent resident, as well as individuals and organizations that fall within the definition of foreign principal under the Foreign Agents Registration Act (except for individuals who are U.S. citizens).[57] The term *foreign principal* includes (1) a government of a foreign country and a foreign political party; (2) a person (*person* is explained below) outside of the United States, unless it is established that such person is a citizen of and domiciled within the United States or is organized under U.S. law and has its principal place of business in the United States; and (3) a partnership, association, corporation, organization, or other combination of persons organized under the laws of or having its principal place of business in a foreign country.[58]

Foreign Agents Registration Act

The Foreign Agents Registration Act requires public disclosure of the identity and nature of employment of persons acting for foreign principals in connection with political activities. This entails filing a registration statement with the Attorney General of the United States, including comprehensive, detailed statements as to the nature of the registrant's business and activities by any person acting as an agent of a foreign principal.[59] *Person* for these purposes includes any "individual, partnership, association, corporation, organization, or any other combination of individuals," and *agent of a foreign principal* includes all persons who are directly or indirectly subject to the direction or control of a foreign principal. A corporation, partnership, or other organization may be deemed to be a foreign principal unless it is organized under U.S. law and maintains its principal place of business in the United States.[60] The law provides limited exceptions to the registration requirements for diplomats, nations deemed vital to our national defense, and various nonpolitical activities.[61]

In accordance with its focus on disclosure, the Foreign Agents Registration Act requires that all transmitted "political propaganda"[62] be conspicuously labeled or prefaced with a statement setting forth the connection between the foreign agent and the materials labeled as propaganda, the fact of registration, and the availability for inspection of the registration statement.[63] In addition, there must be a notation that registration does not indicate approval of the contents by the U.S. government.[64] In addition, specified books and records must be kept, preserved for a period of three years following termination of registration, and made available for inspection.[65] Content of materials labeled propaganda are not regulated by the act, however.

Trading with the Enemy Act and Other Country-Specific Limitations on Foreign Trade

In 1917, the U.S. Congress enacted the Trading with the Enemy Act as a war measure with automatic applicability to future wars.[66] Broadly speaking, the act allows the President to prohibit transactions involving any property in which a foreign country or national has an interest, and authorizes government seizure of enemy property and administration of that property by the alien property custodian.[67]

Several other statutory enactments also limit transactions with specific foreign nations or governments such as the International Emergency Economic Powers Act,[68] the National Emergencies Act,[69] and the United Nations Participation Act.[70]

Enemy status under the act is determined by reference to residence rather than nationality. Any individual, partnership, corporation, or other entity residing in a nation at war with the United States or resident outside the United States and doing business there is considered an enemy without regard to nationality. Thus, a citizen of a belligerent nation residing in a neutral country has been held not to be an enemy, nor is such a citizen an enemy while residing in the United States, unless the President finds that the safety of the United States or the successful prosecution of the war requires that that citizen be proclaimed an enemy.[71] On the same basis of residence, anyone residing in a belligerent state is deemed to be an enemy, even if that person is a U.S. citizen.[72] The definition of enemy also includes any corporation incorporated in the belligerent nation.[73] In addition to enemy status determined by place of residence or incorporation, the President may designate as an enemy any person or group (other than a U.S. citizen) if the "safety of the United States or the successful prosecution of the war shall so require."[74]

Judicial interpretations of the act have changed the standard from one of strict "place of incorporation" to one of "enemy taint,"[75] and this interpretation has been reaffirmed by the U.S. Supreme Court.[76] Neither case clearly established the elements of enemy taint, thus permitting some flexibility of determination in individual cases. However, such factors as control, domination, and beneficial ownership of stock have been used as critical indicators of the presence of enemy taint.

Nationality or citizenship plays a role in two other areas governed by the Trading with the Enemy Act. First, the act provides that any property sold by the alien property custodian under the act (except when sold to the United States) may be sold only to U.S. citizens in the manner prescribed unless the President directs otherwise.[77] Second, the act empowers the President during time of war or national emergency to regulate commercial transactions by any person subject to the jurisdiction of the United States.[78] The Foreign Assets Control Regulations and Transaction Control Regulations promulgated pursuant to this section include a specific formulation for determining jurisdiction.[79] In determining whether foreign corporations are subject to its regulation, the Treasury Department has focused on the issue of control. For example, the Treasury Department has directed an American corporation in control of a French corporation to order the French corporation to cancel a contract.[80]

Currently, the Treasury Department's Office of Foreign Assets Control administers regulations covering only Cambodia, Cuba, North Korea, and Vietnam pursuant to the Trading with the Enemy

Act.[81] The Office of Foreign Assets Control also administers regulations promulgated pursuant to a variety of other laws. The most important of these is the International Emergency Economic Powers Act, under which authority broad restrictions on trade and travel may be investigated, regulated, and prohibited.[82] In order for an international economic emergency to exist, the president must find an "unusual and extraordinary threat, which has its source in whole or substantial part outside the United States, to the national security, foreign policy, or economy of the United States."[83] Under this authority, the president may control foreign exchange transactions, banking transactions, trade in currency or securities, and disposition of property.[84] The president may not, under this authority, regulate mere communication or limit humanitarian donations or the exchange of informational materials.[85] Currently, at least some relations with the following countries are being curtailed pursuant to this act: Iran, Iraq, Kuwait, and Libya.[86]

The president's authority to interfere with private international transactions derives from other sources as well. The Comprehensive Anti-Apartheid Act makes sector-specific prohibitions on transactions with South Africa.[87] Under the National Emergencies Act, the president may declare a national emergency authorizing the exercise of special or extraordinary authority.[88] Under one section of the International Security and Development Cooperation Act, the president may ban imports of goods and services from any country that supports terrorism.[89] And finally, under a provision of the United Nations Participation Act, the president may implement United Nations Security Council resolutions made pursuant to Article 41 of the United Nations Charter.[90] President Bush relied on this authority together with the National Emergencies Act and the International Emergency Economic Powers Act when he declared sanctions against Iraq and Iraqi-controlled Kuwait during 1990–1991.[91]

Environmental Restrictions

Generally, U.S. environmental laws apply the same standards to citizens and noncitizens. In some cases, such statutes may reflect international treaty obligations. For example, the Federal Ocean Dumping Act was amended to apply standards and criteria binding upon the United States under the Convention on the Prevention of Marine Pollution by Dumping of Wastes and Other Matter.[92] In other cases, treaties prohibit local regulations from discriminating between U.S. and foreign parties.[93]

The Environmental Protection Agency (EPA) is charged with the control of pollution in the areas of air, water, solid waste, noise radiation, and toxic substances. Its environmental regulations and those of other governmental bodies affect domestic and foreign investors equally insofar as they operate, manufacture, sell, or import products used in the United States. Under the Noise Control Act, there are restrictions on the importation into the United States of new products that may violate federal regulations.[94] Foreign investors may be liable as current asset owners for sites that have been polluted with hazardous substances by past owners.[95] The Toxic Substances Control Act (TSCA) regulates chemical substances and mixtures that pose an unreasonable risk of harm to the health of U.S. citizens or the domestic environment.[96] This act applies equally to foreign and domestic manufacture and importation of chemical substances.[97]

Some environmental regulations apply even where the production, manufacture or use of a product is extraterritorial. Under the Federal Insecticide, Fungicide and Rodenticide Act (FIFRA), foreign as well as domestic producers must register their pesticides with the EPA, which is empowered to limit the distribution, sale, or use of any unregistered pesticide.[98] Certain regulations concerning labeling requirements apply even to those pesticides intended solely for export. Foreign governments are notified of any changes in the registration status under U.S. law of the exported pesticide.[99] Chemical substances relevant to TSCA regulation, if produced in the United States solely for export, are still subject to the reporting requirements under that act.[100] For a further example of extraterritorial reach,[101] current U.S. law imposes an excise tax on any item imported into the United States that requires chlorofluorocarbons (CFCs) for its manufacture in the country of origin.[102]

Domestic producers may have some advantages over foreign producers by virtue of their eligibility for tax credits for compliance with environmental laws. Generally, however, the environmental laws, rather than distinguishing between foreign and domestic activities, seek to establish equality of treatment.

Energy and Natural Resources
The field of energy and natural resources is governed by a number of statutes that may affect foreign participation.

Nuclear Energy
The Atomic Energy Act of 1954 applies to the discovery, production, and use of nuclear material and energy. The Nuclear Regulatory Commission (NRC)—charged with ensuring that civilian uses of nuclear materials and facilities are consistent with safeguarding public health and safety, environmental quality, national security, and the antitrust laws—is responsible also for most licensing and related regulatory functions in this area. The 1954 act permits foreigners to apply for and obtain permits or licenses to mine nuclear source material. Once the source material has been located, a permit or license is required for anyone to "transfer or deliver, receive possession of or title to, or import into or export from the United States any source material" and the NRC may not issue a license "if, in the opinion of the commission, the issuance of a license to such person for such purpose would be inimical to the common defense and security or the health and safety of the public."[103]

The act also prohibits the issuance of licenses for the operation of atomic energy utilization or nuclear production facilities to aliens and to foreign corporations or corporations owned, controlled, or dominated by such foreign interests. Determination of what constitutes foreign ownership or control is made on a case-by-case basis.[104]

There are also restrictions on licensing for domestic distribution of special nuclear material.[105] Special regulations have been passed to protect against risk to defense and security interests that may result if classified materials are made available to Department of Energy (DOE) contractors or subcontractors who are owned, controlled, or influenced by foreign governments, individuals, or organizations. All DOE contract solicitations, subject to these regulations, must contain questionnaires seeking to ascertain the extent of foreign ownership, control, or influence.

Other Energy Sources
Under the Natural Gas Act, the importation or exportation of natural gas by any person requires authorization to be secured from the Department of Energy.[106] Such authorization is to be granted unless

the proposed exportation or importation is not consistent with the public interest. The provisions of the act are administered by the Federal Energy Regulatory Commission (FERC), an independent regulatory organization within the Department of Energy. Applications for authorization to import or export natural gas must include information about the citizenship of a corporation's officers, directors, and shareholders.

Under the Federal Power Act, FERC may issue licenses for the construction, operation, or maintenance of facilities for the "development, transmission, and utilization of power" on lands and water over which the federal government has control. Licenses can be granted only to U.S. citizens and to corporations organized under the laws of the United States or any state thereof.[107] There are no limitations on foreign ownership or control of such corporations.

Leases for the development of geothermal steam and associated resources in federal lands administered by the Secretary of Interior may be issued only to U.S. citizens and corporations organized under the laws of the United States or of a state.[108] However, such a domestic U.S. corporation may be foreign-owned or -controlled. Regulations merely require statements disclosing holdings and citizenship of all stockholders with an interest of 10 percent or more in a corporate lessee.

Mining, Pipelines, and Mineral Leasing on Federal Lands

Only U.S. citizens and corporations may acquire rights of way for oil pipelines, leases, or any interests in leases for mining coal, oil, or certain other minerals on federal lands. However, a foreign-controlled domestic corporation may hold such an interest if the country of foreign ownership or control grants reciprocal rights to U.S. corporations.[109]

The Mining and Minerals Policy Act of 1970 provides that mineral deposits on federal lands and the lands on which they are found are not open to exploration and purchase by aliens unless they have declared their intention to become U.S. citizens.[110] Generally, the question of citizenship has been treated as one of fact, with a presumption of citizenship unless evidence to the contrary is presented.[111] In the case of corporations, organization under U.S. law qualifies for citizenship. Therefore, mineral deposits may generally be explored and developed by domestic corporations owned or controlled by aliens.

Public Lands

The acquisition and use of public lands is regulated by various federal statutes that may include citizenship requirements. Under the Desert Land Act, entry onto desert land in the states of California, Colorado, Oregon, Nevada, Washington, Idaho, Montana, Utah, Wyoming, Arizona, New Mexico, and North and South Dakota is similarly restricted. The Desert Land Act also requires that in all such states, with the exception of Nevada, entrants be resident citizens, or persons who have declared their intention to become citizens, of the state or territory in which the land in question is situated.[112]

Acquisition or ownership of public land in U.S. territories is also forbidden to aliens and to persons who are not citizens and have not declared their intention to become citizens.[113] An alien corporation has been deemed to be a person for these purposes[114] but foreign ownership of a U.S. corporation apparently would not be subject to this prohibition. In addition, the statute does not restrict ownership by noncitizens of land in a city, town, or village, or in any mine or mining claim in any of the territories. These provisions governing land in the territories are made applicable to land in the District of Columbia. Alien acquisition of land in Hawaii is further restricted by special citizenship requirements and prohibitions on land transfers to aliens without the written consent of the governor.[115] Citizenship also affects the availability of permits for grazing on public lands. Pursuant to certain statutory requirements, the Secretary of Interior is authorized to issue such permits subject to citizenship restrictions. The Bureau of Land Management of the Department of Interior issues regulations—which include citizenship requirements[116]—with respect to such permits.

Communications

The Federal Communications Act of 1934[117] created the Federal Communications Commission (FCC) and gave it the power to control radio communications.[118] Television is included as a form of radio communication.[119] Under the act, the FCC is authorized to grant or deny licenses as dictated by public convenience, interest, or necessity.[120]

The licensing of foreigners is severely limited. A radio or TV station license may not be granted to or held by any foreign government or its representative, any aliens or their representatives, or any corporation organized under the laws of a foreign government or owned by foreigners.[121] A corporation is deemed to be foreign-owned if any officer or director is an alien or if more than one fifth of its capital stock is owned of record or voted by aliens, by a foreign government, or by a corporation organized under the laws of a foreign country. Futhermore, the FCC is authorized to refuse or revoke a license upon finding that the public interest will be served thereby in the case of a corporation controlled, directly or indirectly, by another corporation of which any officer is an alien or more than one fourth of the capital stock is owned by foreign interests.[122]

The FCC also has the power to prescribe qualifications of station operators and to issue operator licenses, which may be issued only to citizens or nationals of the United States. There are some limited exceptions to this prohibition if the FCC finds this serves the public interest—including one permitting the FCC to waive the citizenship requirement in the case of persons holding U.S. pilot certificates or foreign aircraft pilot certificates valid in the United States on the basis of reciprocal agreements entered into with foreign governments.[123]

The Communications Satellite Act of 1962 was enacted for the purpose of establishing a commercial communications satellite system in cooperation with other countries.[124] It directs that U.S. participation in the system take the form of a private corporation, with a 15-member board of directors, all of whom must be U.S. citizens.[125] Alien ownership is limited to not more than 20 percent of the shares of the corporation offered to the U.S. public.[126] The same license ownership restrictions employed by the Federal Communications Act also apply to the Communications Satellite Act.[127]

Air Transportation

The Federal Aviation Act of 1958[128] presented barriers to foreign participation in the field of aviation, some of which are now, gradually, being eroded. Further deregulation and elimination of some of the impediments to foreign investment are to be expected in the face of the airline industry's financial difficulties and in this age of globalization and multinational investment. Section 401 of the 1958 Act provides that all "air carriers," defined to include only those owned by U.S. citizens,[129] must be certified in order to engage in air transportation. Foreign carriers must obtain permits if they make any domestic flights and, historically, widespread issuance of these permits has been discouraged both by federal law as well as executive policy for reasons related to national security, transportation, and communication needs. Attempts indirectly to procure a significant share of a U.S. air carrier through merger, acquisition, or partial ownership of U.S. air carriers are blocked by the citizenship requirements for certification mentioned above. Finally, registration of foreign-owned air carriers for use in the United States is subject to restrictions. Foreign air carriers must apply to the Department of Transportation (DOT) for permission to engage in air transportation over U.S. air space.[130] In deciding whether to issue a permit, the DOT will consider whether the foreign carrier is "fit, willing, and able", and whether the carrier was designated by its government in connection with an agreement or treaty with the United States, or whether such transportation is "in the public interest."[131] The DOT will also consider more generally how U.S. carriers have been treated in the foreigner's home country, hence it is important that the foreign investor, before submitting an application to the DOT, be apprised of any rights or limitations that exist between the foreigner's home country and the United States.[132]

Neither foreign equity investments in U.S. carriers nor incorporation of U.S. subsidiaries by foreign corporations may serve as indirect channels by which foreign investors can enter the U.S. market of domestic air transportation. In order for an air carrier to receive certification, it must satisfy a two-step citizenship test: First, 75 percent of its outstanding voting stock must be owned or controlled by U.S. citizens, and the president and at least two thirds of the directors must be U.S. citizens;[133] and second, the carrier must be de facto controlled by U.S. citizens.[134] In the past, the DOT has interpreted these requirements broadly, rejecting certification even in cases when foreign participation within the statutory minimum[135] was considered excessive because of the functional control that foreign investors might have exercised. At present, however, the trend seems to be toward interpreting the requirements narrowly to allow for greater foreign participation in certified U.S. air carriers.[136] The foreign investor should note, however, that any merger with or acquisition of U.S. air carriers, even short of a 25 percent voting participation, will be subject to scrutiny by the Federal Trade Commission (FTC) or Department of Justice (DOJ) under the federal antitrust laws.[137]

The citizenship requirements imposed by the 1958 Federal Aviation Act on the registration of foreign aircraft for use in domestic air transportation have been liberalized. Under § 501 (b) of the unamended act, only aircraft owned by U.S. citizens could be registered in the United States. As part of the effort to deregulate the airline industry, an amendment to the Federal Aviation Act in 1977 permitted registration of aircraft by alien owners or by those who could not meet the citizenship requirements.[138] Among the scaled-down requirements are that (1) the aircraft may not be registered under the laws of any foreign country, and (2) it must be "based and primarily used in the United States." The Federal Aeronautics Administration (FAA), under rule-making authority that has been delegated it by the secretary of transportation, has ruled that an aircraft is "based and primarily used in the United States" if its flight hours accumulated in the United States amount to at least 60 percent of its total flight hours during specified six-calendar-month periods.[139]

Finally, citizenship may be a factor in the issuance of airman certificates required for all aircraft operators with the exception of foreign airmen serving on foreign aircraft. The act permits the administrator of the FAA to prohibit or restrict issuance of these certificates to aliens or to make issuance dependent on terms of reciprocal agreements entered into with foreign governments.[140]

Maritime Activities

Congress stated the purpose of the Merchant Marine Act of 1920 in its opening provision:

> It is necessary for the national defense and for the proper growth of its foreign and domestic commerce that the United States shall have a

merchant marine of the best equipped and most suitable types of vessels . . . ultimately to be owned and operated privately by citizens of the United States.[141]

As a general rule, foreigners have been virtually excluded from participation in domestic shipping and are severely hampered in their ability to invest in U.S.-flag vessels engaged in foreign trade. As early as 1789, federal registry legislation restricted ownership of vessels entitled to fly the U.S. flag to U.S. citizens; however, the definition of U.S. citizenship has been subject to repeated revisions. Most recently, Congress closed a loophole in the maritime laws so that foreign ships cannot reflag as U.S. vessels and do business in the domestic fishing industry. Congress also undertook recently to restate the maritime laws in order to streamline their complicated scheme.[142] The shipping laws as enacted, however, contain a variety of changes that harmonize the fishing and vessel documentation laws and eliminate obsolete requirements.

Four categories of maritime law concern the foreign investor. First, certain provisions of the shipping laws prohibit foreign ownership or control of vessels flying the U.S. flag. Second, additional restrictions are placed on vessels engaged in "coastwise trade," meaning maritime activities between points in the United States.[143] Third, when a domestically flagged ship trades internationally, certain restrictions do not apply. And fourth, separate provisions govern fishing within the zone surrounding the United States.[144]

Shipping Requirements for U.S.-Flag Vessels

Foreign participation in domestic shipping is restricted primarily by three statutes: the Vessel Documentation Act of 1980, which became effective on July 1, 1982; the Merchant Marine Act of 1920, better known as the Jones Act; and the Shipping Act of 1916.[145]

In order to fly the U.S. flag, a ship must be "eligible for documentation,"[146] which means that the vessel must meet certain size, status, and citizenship criteria. The ship must weigh at least five tons.[147] It must not be registered under the laws of a foreign country.[148] If an individual owns the ship, that person must be a United States citizen. If an organization owns the ship, it must be owned by (1) an association, trust, joint venture, or other entity in which all members are citizens; (2) a partnership whose general partners are U.S. citizens and the *controlling interest* of which is owned by citizens; (3) a corporation created under U.S. law, whose president or chief executive officer *and* chairman of the board are citizens, *and* whose noncitizen directors do not exceed a minority of the number necessary to constitute a quorum of the board of directors; or (4) the U.S. or state governments.[149]

If a vessel is procured outside the United States, the secretaries of transportation and state must jointly approve the issuance of a certificate of documentation.[150] Such a ship is still subject to the statutory ownership provisions.[151] Once the vessel arrives in the United States, it must be surrendered to the secretary of transportation.[152]

The Vessel Documentation Act requires that a vessel be licensed for the particular trade in which it engages.[153] The licenses, called "certificates of documentation," indicate presumptively the nationality of the ship they certify.[154] The act designates four endorsements that may be placed on certificates of documentation: coastwise, Great Lakes, fishery, and recreational and registry endorsements.[155] Registry endorsements apply to vessels that ply their trade internationally or with Guam, American Samoa, Wake, Midway, or Kingman Reef.[156] All seagoing vessels do not have to be documented; federal law does require, however, that all machine-propelled vessels that are *not* documented must be issued a number by the state in which the vessel principally operates.[157]

Ships flying the U.S. flag must also be operated by a crew that is primarily U.S. citizens. For example, a ship must be commanded by a citizen.[158] If a ship goes out of the command of a citizen, its certificate of documentation becomes invalid.[159] Fraudulent or knowing use of a certificate of documentation constitutes grounds for government seizure and forfeiture of the vessel.[160] The master, chief engineer, and officer in charge of deck watch or engineering watch must also be citizens.[161] Another provision of the maritime laws allows only 25 percent of unlicensed seamen to be noncitizens; this 25 percent must be residents of the United States.[162] This limit does not apply to vessels fishing for certain specified highly migratory species of fish or outside of the exclusive economic zone.[163] The zone sets U.S. boundaries "200 nautical miles from the baseline from which the breadth of the territorial sea is measured" in conformity with international law.[164]

Finally, the Merchant Marine Act limits the alienability of shipping vessels. A vessel of the U.S. merchant marine may be sold or transferred to an alien only if the secretary of transportation has tried and failed to sell the vessel to a citizen.[165] And the secretary may do so only when he or she has determined that the vessel is "unnecessary to the promotion and maintenance of an efficient American merchant marine."[166] The penalty for violation is forfeiture.[167] During time of war or national emergency, another provision of the act expressly prohibits the transfer to noncitizens of control or majority voting power in a corporation owning such vessel without first obtaining the approval of the secretary of transportation.[168]

Certain privileges are not accorded foreigners in the maritime industry. Some subsidies (called construction-differential and operating-differential subsidies) are limited to U.S. citizens. The stricter Shipping Act definition of citizenship (see below) is applicable to such subsidy provisions, with the exception that citizenship for purposes of operating-differential subsidies requires that all directors of a corporation be U.S. citizens.[169] Similarly, the secretary of transportation may guarantee obligations incurred in the construction or reconditioning of vessels only by a citizen as defined in the Shipping Act.[170] Eligibility for war-risk insurance, however, is dependent upon less restrictive citizenship criteria. U.S. vessels and foreign-flag vessels owned by citizens or engaged in transportation in the waterborne commerce of the United States or in other transportation may be insured if the secretary of transportation deems them to be in the interest of the national defense or economy.[171]

Intracoastal Trade

Congress has strictly limited foreign participation in vessels engaging in intracoastal coastwise and Great Lakes trade. Such ships must be built in the United States, captured as a war prize by a U.S. citizen, or rebuilt entirely in the United States.[172] Once a ship is "sold foreign," its owners cannot reacquire the right to engage in coastwise trade.[173] Certain complicated exceptions may apply to the rebuilding requirement for ships that travel through Canadian waterways or the Great Lakes, and for ships previously registered abroad whose countries of registry provide reciprocal privileges.[174] In certain circumstances surrounding the maritime transport of hazardous waste, other exceptions apply.[175]

With respect to ownership, in order to obtain a coastwise or Great Lakes license, a partnership is deemed to be a citizen only if all its general partners are citizens *and* 75 percent of the interest in the partnership is owned by and under the control of citizens.[176] Similarly, to obtain a coastwise or Great Lakes license, a corporation must be created under U.S. law and at least 75 percent owned by U.S. citizens.[177]

The courts have not construed ownership expansively. Devices permitting nominal ownership of stock by citizens while control is retained by noncitizens are prohibited; thus, arrangements such as voting agreements, proxies, or trusts are considered suspect. Furthermore, it has been held that debt holdings by a noncitizen in a thinly capitalized corporation render the corporation a noncitizen.[178] In a case involving a maritime "leaseback" arrangement (known as bareboat charter), one court articulated the test for control as possession by a citizen of "sufficient indicia of ownership" in addition to legal title. So long as a citizen possesses these attributes, the administering agency has some discretion in whether to grant a coastwise license.[179] Hence the courts have looked beyond the legal arrangement to examine de facto ownership.

There are some narrow exceptions to the ownership requirements for engaging in coastwise trade. These include, for example, an exception for the transportation of empty cargo vans, tanks, or barges for use by the owners or operators of the transporting vessel in connection with their cargo in foreign trade, but this exception is available only if the country of the vessel's registry grants reciprocal privileges to U.S. citizens.[180]

Foreign Trade

Alien participation in foreign trade is not as tightly restricted as in domestic trade. Nevertheless, one obstacle to foreign investment is the requirement of the Vessel Documentation Act that a vessel employed in foreign trade be eligible for documentation—although not required to be built—in the United States. However, the 75-percent-ownership requirement discussed above is not applicable to vessels engaging in foreign trade. Thus, documentation may be permitted indirectly through a corporation so long as citizenship requirements for officers and directors are met.

Fishing

U.S. citizenship plays a major role in federal regulation of fishing. Under fishery conservation and management laws,[181] the federal government has fishery-management authority over all fish in the exclusive economic zone contiguous to the territorial sea of the United States, over certain species throughout their migratory range, and over Continental Shelf fishery resources beyond the fishery conservation zone.[182] Foreign fishing vessels (defined as vessels other than those of the United States)[183] may not engage in such regulated fishing unless issued permits to do so. Permits are available only to vessels of those foreign nations with which the United States has entered into an international fishery agreement and that extend substantially the same fishing privileges to U.S. fishing vessels.[184] The secretary of state is authorized to allocate among nations the total allowable level of foreign fishing.[185] In addition, unless otherwise provided by treaty, a foreign-flag vessel may not land in U.S. ports with fish taken on board on the high seas.[186]

A fisheries loan fund was established to upgrade commercial fishing vessels and gear and to provide financial assistance not otherwise available to commercial fishers.[187] However, as in the case of the guaranty and subsidy programs for shipping vessels discussed above, citizenship restrictions apply. For example, since 1970 only a citizen or national of the United States may apply for a fishery loan. For corporations, partnerships, or associations, the citizenship requirements of the Shipping Act applicable to vessels engaging in the coastwise trade must be met, thus necessitating 75 percent ownership by U.S. nationals or citizens to establish eligibility.[188]

In 1988 Congress passed legislation that takes away the incentive to reflag a foreign-built vessel with the U.S. flag and engage in fish processing.[189] As a result, domestically built fishing industry vessels will not be replaced with foreign-built ones. This change was made by expanding the definition of "fisheries," i.e., the cultivation, taking, or processing of forms of marine life or matter within the exclusive economic zone.[190] (Previously, the definition did not include fish processing in reference to vessels built abroad.)[191] Note, however, that while documentation requirements severely limit foreign ownership, the requirement that a vessel be U.S.-built does not.

NOTES

1. See, e.g., [cite to Pennsylvania plant closing law.]
2. In addition to the Treasury Department, CFIUS includes representatives of the departments of Commerce, Defense, Justice, and State; the Office of the U.S. Trade Representative; the Office of Management and Budget; and the White House Council of Economic Advisors. However, at this writing Congress is considering legislation that would change the structure of CFIUS by adding the President's national security advisor and shifting the chair from the Treasury to the Commerce Department.
3. Defense Production Act Extension and Amendments of 1991, Pub. L. No. 102-99, 105 Stat. 487 (1991).
4. The Treasury Department made this announcement on November 6, 1990. See "CFIUS to Continue Reviewing Acquisitions Despite Lapse of Exon-Florio Provisions," 7 *Int'l. Trade Rep.* (BNA), 1739 (1990). (reauthorized by Defense Production Act Extension and Amendments of 1991, Pub. L. No. 102-99, 105 Stat. 487 (August 17, 1991)).
5. Defense Production Act of 1950, § 721, 50 App. U.S.C.A. § 2158 *et seq.* (West 1991) (expired pursuant to 50 App. U.S.C.A. § 2166 (West Supp. 1991) on October 20, 1990). The "Exon-Florio" Amendment appears at 50 App. U.S.C.A. § 2170 (West 1991).
6. 50 App. U.S.C.A. § 2170 (d) (1991).
7. Regulations pertaining to mergers, acquisitions and takeovers by foreign persons, 56 Fed. Reg. 58, 774-58, 788 (Nov. 21, 1991).
8. The proposed regulations are contained in "Regulations Pertaining to Mergers, Acquisitions, and Takeovers by Foreign Persons," 54 Fed. Reg. 29, 744 (1989).
9. Statement of William E. Barreda, Deputy Assistant Secretary of the Treasury for Trade and Investment, before the Subcommittee on Commerce, Consumer Protection, and Competitiveness of the U.S.

House of Representatives, June 12, 1991, at page 6. *See also* ''National Security Review Process Sharply Criticized at House Hearing,'' 8 *Int'l. Trade Rep.* (BNA), 319, 320 (1991).

10. ''Interview with Stephen J. Canner, Director, Office of International Investment, U.S. Treasury Department, and Staff Chairman, CFIUS,'' 2 *Int'l Merger Law* (Feb. 1992) 2.

11. National Security Review Process Sharply Criticized at House Hearing,'' 8 *Int'l. Trade Rep.* (BNA), 319, 320 (1991).

12. 55 Fed. Reg. at 58, 784-85 (to be codified at 31 C.F.R. § 800.401).

13. 50 App. U.S.C.A. § 2170 (e) (West 1991).

14. Statement of William D. Phillips, Chair, National Critical Technologies Panel, before the Subcommittee on Commerce, Consumer Protection, and Competitiveness of the U.S. House of Representatives, June 12, 1991, at page 8. In addition, the Council on Competitiveness has created a comparable list of 26 critical technologies.

15. H.R. Rep. No. 100-576, 100th Cong., 2d Sess., 924, reprinted in 1988 U.S. Code Cong. & Admin. News 1547. See also 56 Fed. Reg. 58, 775 for a discussion of the legislative history contained in the conference report.

16. 54 Fed. Reg. at 29, 746.

17. 50 App. U.S.C.A. § 2170 (b) (West 1991). For the regulations implementing this provision, see 56 Fed. Reg. at 58,787 (to be codified at 31 C.F.R. § 800.702).

18. Dunne, ''US May Extend Foreign Investment Block,'' *Financial Times,* May 14, 1991, at 6.

19. 50 App. U.S.C.A. § 2170 (a) (West 1991).

20. 56 Fed. Reg. at 58, 776.

21. 56 Fed. Reg. at 58, 781 (to be codified at 31 C.F.R. § 800.204).

22. H.R. 2624, 102d Cong., 1st Sess. (1991) (''to amend section 721 of the Defense Production Act of 1950 to clarify and strengthen its provisions pertaining to national security takeovers''). *See also* ''Bill Offer to Strengthen Law Governing Foreign Acquisitions,'' 114 *Daily Rep. for Executives* (BNA), A-13 (June 13, 1991).

23. H.R. 2624 § 1 (b) (2) (B), 102d Cong., 1st Sess. (1991).

24. *See* ''House Energy Committee Approves Tougher Controls on Foreign Takeovers,'' 225 Daily Rep. of Executives (BNA), A-1 (Nov, 21, 1991).

25. The act was renamed by the Trade and Tariff Act of 1984, Pub. L. No. 98-573, § 306 (b) (1), 98 Stat. 2948, 3009.

26. 22 U.S.C.A. §§ 3101-8 (West 1990 and Supp. 1991). See Executive Order No. 11961 (January 19, 1977). See 15 C.F.R. pt. 801 *et seq.* (1991) The BEA prepares and administers the filing of forms pursuant

to these requirements; see 22 U.S.C.A. § 3104 (d) (West Supp. 1991) for the scope of BEA's activities.

27. 22 U.S.C.A. § 3104 (West 1990 and Supp. 1991); 15 C.F.R. § 806.5 (1991).
28. 22 U.S.C.A. § 3103 (b) (West 1990); see 15 C.F.R. Part 806 (1991) (Direct Investment Surveys) and BEA Form BE-12.
29. 15 C.F.R. § 806.7 (1991).
30. Certain exemption tests, with respect to total assets, gross revenues, and net income, can be passed that relieve small, foreign investors of the obligation to comply with these reporting requirements. See 15 C.F.R. pt. 806 *et seq* (1991).
31. BEA Form BE-14; 15 C.F.R. § 806.15 (1991).
32. Pub. L. No. 101-533, 104 Stat. 2344 (1990).
33. 22 U.S.C.A. § 3105 (West 1990 and Supp. 1991); 15 C.F.R. § 806.6 (1991).
34. See 15 C.F.R. § 806.6 (c) (1991).
35. 22 U.S.C.A. 3144 (West Supp. 1991).
36. The United States implemented the Agreement by the Trade Agreements Act of 1979, 19 U.S.C. § 2501 *et seq.*
37. 41 U.S.C. §§ 10a–d; 41 C.F.R. 1–6.104 (1988 and Supp. I. 1989).
38. *Id.*
39. Pub. L. No. 101-165, § 9009, 103 Stat. 1130 (1989).
40. 10 U.S.C. § 2272 (f) (1988).
41. Executive Orders 10865 and 10909 form the basis for Department of Defense's regulations.
42. See 48 C.F.R. subpart 4.402 (1990); Industrial Security Regulation, ISR, 5222.22-R, Industrial Security Manual, ISM, DOD 5220.22-M.
43. ISR § 2-201 (a) 1985.
44. ISR § 2-201 (a), December 1985.
45. See ISR § 2-205 *et seq.* for exceptions to foreclosure from government contracts under FOCI.
46. 48 C.F.R. subpart 4.401 (1990).
47. ISR § 2-201 (a).
48. ISR §§ 2-217, 201 (c).
49. 16 U.S.C. § 742 (c) (7) (1988).
50. 46 App. U.S.C.A. § 1160 (West 1975 and Supp. 1991).
51. 46 App. U.S.C.A. §§ 802, 1151 *et seq.*, 1171 *et seq* (West 1975 and Supp. 1991).
52. 46 App. U.S.C.A. §§ 1281 *et seq* (West 1975 and Supp. 1991).
53. 49 U.S.C. App. §§ 1531, 1533 (1988).
54. 22 U.S.C.A. § 2198 (c) (1990). However, foreign corporations, partnerships, or other associations, wholly owned by one or more U.S.

citizens, corporations, partnerships, or other associations, are eligible (up to 5 percent of the shares may be held by foreigners if required by law without affecting wholly owned status).

55. 7 U.S.C. §§ 1922, 1941 (1988).
56. 2 U.S.C. § 441e (a) (1988).
57. 2 U.S.C. § 441e (b) (1988).
58. 22 U.S.C.A. § 611 (b) (West 1991).
59. 22 U.S.C.A. § 612. The Foreign Agents Registration Act appears at 22 U.S.C.A. §§ 611–21 (West 1991).
60. 22 U.S.C.A. § 611 (West 1991).
61. 22 U.S.C.A. § 613 (West 1991).
62. *Political propaganda* is defined to include any oral, visual, graphic, written, pictorial, or other communication reasonably adapted or intended to indoctrinate or influence with respect to political or public interests, policies, or foreign relations or to promote racial, religious, or social dissension, or such communication that advocates or promotes disorder or violence. 22 U.S.C. § 611 (j) (1988).
63. 22 U.S.C.A. § 614 (b) (West, 1991).
64. *Id.*
65. 22 U.S.C.A. § 615 (West, 1991); 28 C.F.R. § 5.500 (1991).
66. The Trading with the Enemy Act appears at 50 U.S.C. App. §§ 1–44 (1988).
67. 50 U.S.C. App. § 5 (b) (1) (B) (1988). 50 U.S.C. App. §§ 1–44 (1988). 50 U.S.C. App. § 3 governs prohibitions on trade; and 50 U.S.C. App. § 6 governs seizure of property.
68. 50 U.S.C. App. § 1701 *et seq.* (1988).
69. 50 U.S.C. App. § 1601 *et seq.* (1988).
70. 22 U.S.C.A. § 287c (West 1991).
71. *Clemens* v. *Perry*, 29 S.W. 2d 529 (Tex. Civ. App. 1930); *rev'd. on other grounds*, 51 S.W. 2d 267 (Tex. Comm. App. 1932); 50 U.S.C. App. § 2 (c) (1988).
72. *See Miller* v. *Paul*, 237 Ill. App. 166 (1925).
73. 50 U.S.C. App. § 2 (a) (1988).
74. 50 U.S.C. App. § 2 (c) (1988).
75. *See Clark* v. *Uebersee Finanz-Korporation, A.G.*, 332 U.S. 480 (1947).
76. *Kaufman* v. *Societe Internationale pour Participations Industrielles et Commerciales, S.A.*, 343 U.S. 156 (1952).
77. 50 U.S.C. App. § 12 (1988).
78. 50 U.S.C. App. § 5 (b) (1) (1988).
79. 31 C.F.R. § 500.330 (1991). The regulation states that *persons subject to the jurisdiction of the United States*, include

(1) Any person, wheresoever located, who is a citizen or resident of the United States;

(2) Any person actually within the United States;

(3) Any corporation organized under the laws of the United States or of any state, territory, possession, or district of the United States; and

(4) Any partnership, association, corporation, or other organization, wheresoever organized or doing business, that is owned or controlled by persons specified in the above paragraphs.

The Foreign Assets Control Regulations appear at 31 C.F.R. §§ 500.101–.809 (1991); and Transaction Control Regulations at 31 C.F.R. §§ 505.01–.60 (1991).

80. *Fruehauf* v. *Massardy,* [1968] D.S. Jur. 147, [1965], J.C.P. II, 14, 274 bis (Cour d'Appel). This case is discussed in Craig, *Application of the Trading with the Enemy Act to Foreign Corporations Owned by Americans: Reflections on Fruehauf* v. *Massardy,* 83 *Harvard L. Rev.* 579 (1970).

81. 31 C.F.R. § 500.201 (1991).

82. 50 U.S.C. App. § 1702 (1988).

83. 50 U.S.C. App. § 1701 (a) (1988).

84. 50 U.S.C. App. § 1702 (a) (1) (1988).

85. 50 U.S.C. App. § 1702 (b) (1988).

86. 31 C.F.R. § 535.101 *et seq.* (Iran) (1991); 31 C.F.R. § 575.101 *et seq.* (Iraq) (1991); 31 C.F.R. § 570.522 (1991) and 31 C.F.R. § 570.101 *et seq.* (1991) (Kuwait); 31 C.F.R. § 550.101 *et seq.* (1991) (Libya). At the time of writing, the Chief Counsel of the Office of Foreign Assets Control expected all bars on trade with Kuwait to be rescinded. Certain regulations regarding Rhodesia still appear at 31 C.F.R. pt. 530 *et seq.* (1991); these regulations are not enforced.

87. 22 U.S.C.A. § 5001 *et seq* (West 1990).

88. 50 U.S.C. App. § 1601 *et seq* (1988).

89. 22 U.S.C.A. § 2349aa-9 (West 1990).

90. 22 U.S.C.A. § 287c (West 1990).

91. See 31 C.F.R. pt. 575, Appendices A & B (1991); 31 C.F.R. § 575.101 *et seq.* (1991); 31 C.F.R. § 570.101 *et seq.* (1991).

92. The Federal Ocean Dumping Act appears at 33 U.S.C. § 1401 *et seq.* (1988).

93. See *British Airways Board* v. *Port Authority of New York and New Jersey* (the Concorde case), 431 F. Supp. 1216 (S.D.N.Y.), *rev'd on other grounds* 558 F. 2d 75 (2d Cir.), *cert. denied,* 434 U.S. 899 (1977), where the court noted that local regulations limiting aircraft noise may apply to, but not discriminate against, foreigners if the

regulation is to be in compliance with existing treaties between the United States and the home countries of those foreign carriers.

94. 42 U.S.C. § 4909 (a) (5) (1988). The Noise Control Act appears at 42 U.S.C. § 4901 *et seq.* (1988).

95. CERCLA, 42 U.S.C.A. § 9601 *et seq.* (West 1983 and Supp. 1991). Present owner's liability appears at 42 U.S.C. § 9607 (1988).

96. 15 U.S.C.A. § 2601 *et seq.* (West 1982 and Supp. 1991).

97. Foreign importers are brought under the act insofar as the term *manufacture* includes "to import into the customs territory of the United States (as defined in general headnote 2 of the Tariff Schedules of the United States), produce, or manufacture": 15 U.S.C. § 2602 (7) (1988). Regulations requiring importers of such chemicals to comply with TSCA can be found at 40 C.F.R. § 707.20 *et seq.* (1991).

98. FIFRA, 7 U.S.C. § 136a (1988).

99. FIFRA, 7 U.S.C. § 136o (1988).

100. See 15 U.S.C. § 2611, (1988), for statutory requirements concerning exportation of chemical substances under TSCA.

101. Concern for extraterritorial environmental impact of foreign products and their manufacture has led to proposed legislation entitled "Global Environment and Trade Equity Act" (S 2887), which failed to pass in the 1990 Congress. That bill would have required the U.S. Trade Representative to take action against countries that do not enforce environmental regulations. A similar bill entitled the "International Pollution Deterrence Act of 1991" (S 5298), April 25, 1991, would require the EPA to compile a report on the attainment of pollution control standards by the United States's 50 largest trading partners. These bills have had the support of labor and some industries that recognize that the price of imports from countries where environmental regulation is lax fails to internalize the true (environmental) cost of the product, in comparison with the cost to the U.S. counterpart, whose price reflects industry's internalization of environmental costs.

102. 26 C.F.R. pts. 52 and 602 (1991).

103. 42 U.S.C. §§ 2092, 2099 (1988).

104. See Atomic Energy Act, 42 U.S.C.A. § 2011 *et seq.* (West 1973 and Supp. 1991). 10 C.F.R. § 50.2 (1991) contains the definitions of the terms *Production Facilities* and *Utilization Facilities.* 42 U.S.C. § 2133 is the section pertaining to industrial or commercial uses; 42 U.S.C. § 2134 pertains to medical uses and certain research and development activities. Subsection (d) of each of these latter two provisions contain citizenship restrictions.

105. "Special Nuclear Material" is defined at 42 U.S.C. § 2014 (aa) (1988) and 10 C.F.R. § 50.2 (1991). The permit requirement appears at 42 U.S.C. § 2077 (c) (1988). DOE regulations requiring disclosure appear at 10 C.F.R. pts. 10, 11 (1991).

106. 15 U.S.C. § 717b (1988), as amended by the Department of Energy Organization Act of 1977. Regulations requiring disclosure relating to citizenship appear at 18 C.F.R. § 153.

107. 16 U.S.C.A. § 797 (e) (West Supp. 1991), as amended by the Department of Energy Organization Act of 1977. The section was amended to add the requirement that the FERC commissioner consider the environmental impact of the granting the license request. October 16, 1986, Pub. L. No. 99-495 § 3 (a), 100 Stat. 1243. The Federal Power Act appears at 16 U.S.C.A. § 791 (a) *et seq.* (West 1985 and Supp. 1991).

108. 30 U.S.C. § 1015 (1988). The Geothermal Steam Act is enacted at 30 U.S.C. §§ 1001–1025 (1988). The regulation governing disclosure is at 43 C.F.R. § 3202.2–1 (b) (1991).

109. 30 U.S.C.A. §§ 181, 185, 352; see also, 43 C.F.R. §§ 3102.2, 3472.1 (1991). The Mineral Lands Leasing Act is at 30 U.S.C.A. §§ 22, 181 *et seq.* 351 *et seq.* (West 1986 and Supp. 1991).

110. 30 U.S.C. §§ 22, 24 (1988).

111. *Garfield M. & M. Co.* v. *Hammer,* 8 P. 153, 156 (Mont. 1885), *aff'd.,* 130 U.S. 291, 299 (1889).

112. 43 U.S.C. § 325 (1988). The Desert Land Act appears at 43 U.S.C. § 321 *et seq* (1988).

113. 48 U.S.C. § 1501 (1988).

114. *Larkin* v. *Washington Loan & Trust Co.,* 31 F. 2d 635 (D.C. Cir.), *cert. denied* 279 U.S. 867 (1929).

115. 48 U.S.C. § 1508 (1988) relates to the District of Columbia; and 48 U.S.C. §§ 1509–1512 (1988) govern the acquisition of land in Hawaii.

116. 43 U.S.C. § 315 (b) (1988); 43 C.F.R. § 4110.1 (1991).

117. The Federal Communications Act appears at 18 U.S.C.A. §§ 1304, 1464 (West 1984 and Supp. 1991) and 47 U.S.C.A. § 151 *et seq* (West 1991).

118. 47 U.S.C.A. § 151 (West 1991). "Radio communication" is defined as "the transmission by radio of writings, signs, signals, pictures, and sounds of all kinds, including all instrumentalities, facilities, apparatus, and services . . . incidental to such transmission." 47 U.S.C. § 153 (b) (1998).

119. 47 U.S.C. § 153 (b) (1998).

120. 47 U.S.C. § 307 (1998).

121. The FCC's regulatory jurisdiction over cable television is limited to such regulation as is "reasonably ancillary to the effective performance of the commission's various responsibilities for the regulation of television broadcasting." *United States* v. *Southwestern Cable Co.*, 392 U.S. 157, 178 (1968). This leaves cable television largely to state and local regulation. FCC regulations, which relate to such areas as program content, have little impact on foreign participation. See 47 C.F.R. pt. 76 (1991).

122. 47 U.S.C.A. § 310 (West 1991).

123. 47 U.S.C.A. § 303 (West 1991).

124. 47 U.S.C. §§ 701–757 (1988).

125. 47 U.S.C. § 733 (1988).

126. 47 U.S.C. § 734 (d) (1988).

127. 47 U.S.C. § 734 (d) (1988). See 47 U.S.C. § 310 (1988) (license ownership restrictions of the Federal Communications Act).

128. 49 App. U.S.C.A. §§ 1301–1542 (1976 and Supp. 1991).

129. See 49 U.S.C. App. § 1301 (16) (1988): " 'Citizen of the United States' means (a) an individual who is a citizen of the United States or one of its possessions, or (b) a partnership of which each member is such an individual, or (c) a corporation or association created or organized under the laws of the United States, . . . of which the president and two-thirds or more of the board of directors and other managing officers thereof are such individuals and in which at least 75 per centum of the voting interest is owned or controlled by persons who are citizens of the United States."

130. See 49 U.S.C. App. § 1508 (a) (1988), for the statement regarding U.S. supremacy over its air space, and 49 U.S.C. App. §§ 1372, 1551 (b) (1) (B) (1988), which vests the DOT with power over foreign air carriers.

131. 49 U.S.C. App. § 1372 (b) (1988).

132. In a recent move that diminishes some of the restrictions on foreign carriers, the DOT ruled that foreign carriers will have greater access to select U.S. cities under the Expanding International Air Service Opportunities to More U.S. Cities, ("Cities Program"), see DOT Order 90-1-62, January 30, 1990. Under this program, DOT grants a one-year exemption to foreign carriers to provide city-to-city air transportation between a U.S. and foreign city, subject to certain conditions.

133. 49 App. U.S.C.A. § 1371 (a) (West Supp. 1991), for certification requirements, and 49 U.S.C. App. § 1301 (16) (1988) for the act's definition of a U.S. citizen.

134. DOT Order No. 90-9-15, September 12, 1990, p. 6.

135. *Willey Peter Daetwyler dba Interamerican Airfreight Co.*, 58 CAB 118 (1971), where a company with an alien owning (the only non-American) no more than 25 percent voting interest (but who had close ties to holders of the other 75 percent) and where two thirds of the directors were U.S. citizens was found to fail the citizenship test for purposes of being eligible for a certificate.

136. In two recent rulings by the DOT, the status of U.S. citizenship of two U.S. air carriers remained unchallenged, despite active and extensive foreign equity investment in those air carriers. *In the matter of the acquisition of Northwest Airlines, by Wings Holdings Inc.*, DOT Order 91-1-41, January 23, 1991, DOT Secretary Samuel Skinner wrote "We have decided to . . . permit total foreign equity investment in Wings of up to 49% with no restriction other than the 25% voting stock restriction set forth in the Act." This ensures that actual control remains in U.S. citizens' hands. There are no debt restrictions on foreign investments: "Unless the loan agreement provides special rights to the debt holder that imply control, we do not anticipate treating debt as a foreign control issue." This more liberal attitude toward the extent of foreign investment that will be tolerated before a DOT certificate is rescinded appears to be a trend that will persist through the 1990s.

137. The power to approve or disapprove mergers or acquisitions of U.S. carriers, once entrusted to CAB and DOT, ceased on January 1, 1989. That power is now vested in the DOJ, because of amendments to the Federal Aviation Act, by the Civil Aeronautics Board Sunset Act of 1984, Pub. L. No. 98-443, § 3 (a), 98 Stat. 1703.

138. 49 U.S.C. App. § 1401 (b) (1988), as amended by Pub. L. No. 95-163, § 14, 91 Stat. 1278, 1283 (1977).

139. 14 C.F.R. § 47.9 (b)–(c) (1991).

140. 49 U.S.C. App. § 1422 (b) (1988); 14 C.F.R. § 61.13 (b) (1991).

141. 46 U.S.C. App. § 861 (1988).

142. *See, e.g.,* H.R. Rep. No. 338, 98th Cong., 1 Sess. 113 (1983), reprinted in 46 U.S.C.A. Pamphlet 441 (1991).

143. While the act does not define coastwise (or coasting) trade, the shipping regulations describe it to encompass the transportation of cargo between points in the United States and the territories. A *coaster* or *coasting vessel* usually means one engaged in domestic trade as distinguished from vessels engaged in foreign trade or plying between a port of the United States and a port of a foreign country. See 70 Am. Jr. 2d Shipping §§ 32, 34. *Fisheries* is defined in 46 U.S.C.A. Pamphlet § 12101 (a) (1) (West 1991) to include the processing, storing, transporting (except in foreign commerce), planting, cultivation, catching, taking, or harvesting of fish, marine animals, pearls, marine vegetation, etc. at any place within the navigable waters of the United States or in the exclusive economic zone. 46 U.S.C.A. Pamphlet § 2101 (10a) (West 1991). This zone sets U.S. boundaries "200 nautical miles from the baseline from which the breadth of the territorial sea is measured," in conformity with international law. Proclamation 5030. For eligibility for documentation, see 46 U.S.C.A. Pamphlet § 12102 (West 1991).

144. See proclamation No. 5030, 48 Fed. Reg. 10,605 (1983). See also 46 U.S.C.A. Pamphlet § 2101 (10a) (West 1991).

145. The Vessel Documentation Act appears at 46 U.S.C.A. Pamphlet §§ 12101–12122 (West 1991); the Merchant Marine Act at 46 U.S.C. App. § 861 *et seq.;* and the Shipping Act at 46 U.S.C. App. § 801 *et seq* (1988 and Supp. I 1989).

146. See 46 U.S.C.A. Pamphlet § 12102 (West 1991).

147. 46 U.S.C.A. Pamphlet § 12102 (a) (West 1991).

148. *id.*

149. 46 U.S.C.A. Pamphlet § 12102 (West 1991). See also 46 C.F.R. §§ 67.03-1-67.03–13 (1991) (citizenship requirements for vessel documentation).

150. 46 U.S.C.A. Pamphlet § 12112 (a) (West 1991).

151. 46 U.S.C.A. Pamphlet § 12102 (a) (West 1991).

152. 46 U.S.C.A. Pamphlet § 12112 (b) (West 1991). See (regulations promulgated pursuant to this section).

153. 46 U.S.C.A. Pamphlet § 12110 (West 1991).

154. 46 U.S.C.A. Pamphlet § 12104 (West 1991).

155. 46 U.S.C.A. Pamphlet §§ 12105–12109 (West 1991).

156. 46 U.S.C.A. Pamphlet § 12105 (West 1991).

157. 46 U.S.C. § 12301 (1988).

158. 46 U.S.C.A. Pamphlet § 12110 (West 1991).

159. 46 U.S.C. § 12111 (a) (1988).

160. 46 U.S.C. § 12122 (c) (1988).

161. 46 U.S.C.A. Pamphlet § 8103 (a) (West 1991).

162. 46 U.S.C. § 8103 (b) (1988).

163. *id.*

164. Proclamation No. 5030, 48 Fed. Reg. 10,605 (1983).

165. 46 U.S.C. App. § 865 (1988).

166. *id.*

167. 46 U.S.C. App. § 808 (1988 and Supp. I 1989).

168. *id;* see also, *Chemical Bank New York Trust Co.* v. *Steamship West-hampton,* 358 F.2d 574, 583 (4th Cir. 1965), *cert. denied,* 385 U.S. 921 (1966).

169. Provisions relating to construction-differential subsidies appear at 46 U.S.C. App. §§ 1151–1153 (1988). Construction-differential subsidies are available to citizens or shipyards of the United States to aid in the construction of a new vessel to be used in foreign commerce. Once subsidized, the vessel may be sold only to citizens and must remain documented under U.S. law for not less than 25 years. The operating differential subsidies aid citizens in the operation of vessels used in an *essential service,* i.e., one deemed essential for the development of foreign commerce by the secretary of transportation. A contractor receiving an operating-differential subsidy may not own or operate any foreign-flag vessel in competition with any U.S.-flag service deemed essential. Operating-differential subsidies are treated at 46 U.S.C. App. § 1171 (1988). For the meaning of "citizen of the United States" in this context, see 46 U.S.C. App. § 1244 (1988).

170. 46 U.S.C. App. § 1273 (1988).

171. 46 U.S.C. App. § 1283 (1988).

172. 46 U.S.C. App. §§ 883 (1988); 46 U.S.C.A. Pamphlet §§ 12106 (a), & 12107 (a) (West 1991).

173. 46 U.S.C. App. § 883 (1988).

174. *id.*

175. *id.*

176. 46 U.S.C. App. § 802 (1988).

177. The regulations refer to 46 U.S.C. App. § 802 (1988), which defines citizenship for purposes of the Shipping Act. No corporation, partnership, or association is deemed a citizen under the Shipping Act definition, unless the controlling interest is owned by citizens; and to engage in coastwise trade there must be 75 percent U.S. ownership. Additional citizenship requirements under the Shipping Act for a corporation are that (1) the president or chief executive officer is a citizen; (2) the chair of the board is a citizen; (3) no more than a minority of directors needed to constitute a quorum are noncitizens; (4) the corporation is organized under the laws of the United States. 46 U.S.C. App. § 802 (1988).

178. *Meacham Corp.* v. *United States,* 207 F.2d 535 (4th Cir. 1953).

179. *Alaska Excursions* v. *United States,* 608 F. Supp. 1084 (D.c.D.C. 1985). See also *Alaska Excursions* v. *U.S.,* 595 F. Supp. 14 (D.c.D.C. 1984). In this case, the court permitted a bareboat charter to a foreign operator because the owner, a U.S. bank, demonstrated sufficient "indicia of ownership" to be a de facto owner in addition to holding legal title to the ship.

180. 46 U.S.C. App. § 883 (1988).

181. 16 U.S.C.A. § 1801 *et seq* (West 1985 and Supp. 1991).

182. The term *Continental Shelf* means the seabed and subsoil of the submarine areas adjacent to the coast (but outside the area of the territorial sea) of the United States, to a depth of 200 meters or beyond to where the depth of the subjacent waters permits the exploitation of natural sources. These fishery resources are certain anadromous species of fish that spawn in fresh or estuarine waters of the United States and migrate to ocean waters throughout their migratory range and Continental Shelf fishery resources. The species of fish included within the term *Continental Shelf fishery resources* are listed in 16 U.S.C. § 1802 (4) (1988).

183. 16 U.S.C. § 1802 (12) (1988).

184. 16 U.S.C. §§ 1821 (b), (c), and (g) (1988). 16 U.S.C.A. §§ 1821–1827 (West 1985 and Supp. 1991) governs foreign fishing and international fishery agreements.

185. 16 U.S.C.A. § 1821 (e) (West 1985 and Supp. 1991).

186. 46 U.S.C. App. § 251 (1988).

187. 16 U.S.C. § 742c (1988). Citizenship criteria appear in 16 U.S.C. § 742c (b) (7) and (b) (8) (1988).

188. *Id.*

189. 46 U.S.C. App. § 883 (1988).

190. 46 U.S.C.A. Pamphlet §§ 12106, 12107, 12108 (West 1991). For the definition of fisheries, see 46 U.S.C.A. Pamphlet § 12101 (West 1991).

191. See "Commercial Fishing Industry Vessel Anti-Reflagging Act of 1987," H. Rep. No. 423, 100th Cong., 1 Sess. (1987).

CHAPTER 12

U.S. TREATY AGREEMENTS AFFECTING FOREIGN INVESTORS

H. David Rosenbloom, Esq.
Caplin & Drysdale

The legal principles that will influence the economic performance of most investments made by foreign persons in the United States will be substantially affected by international agreements. That may be all that the typical foreign investor needs to know about U.S. treaties. There are, in fact, a large number of such treaties, both bilateral and multilateral in nature, ranging from the vague (in terminology) and general (in subject matter) to precise agreements dealing with narrow issues. The first point for the investor—a point commonly overlooked—is simply that such agreements often alter the rules of U.S. domestic law in important ways.

If foreign investors seek to know more about U.S. treaties, beyond the mere fact of their existence, they will encounter a series of interesting, and in some cases still unresolved, issues. Many of these are a product of the distinctive governmental and legal system of the United States. Because of the insular history of this country, only relatively recently have international agreements begun to rival statutory law in practical importance. Thus, the United States cannot draw upon the long experience with international commitments found, for example, in Europe. And, partly because of the relative newness of international agreements as a source of law, the

United States views such agreements in some ways that may seem strange to the typical foreign investor. It cannot be assumed that the manner in which legal experts in the investor's home country approach an international agreement will be helpful in interpreting such agreements in the United States.

Among the more interesting issues in regard to U.S. treaties are the legal relationship between such treaties and U.S. statutory law, the place of treaties in the U.S. federal system of government, the particular U.S. approach to interpreting treaties, the U.S. view on the availability of treaty rules to foreign persons who have no inherent connection with the country or countries to which treaty commitments were made by the United States, and, of course, the substantive coverage of treaties. Other aspects of treaty process and treaty policy in the United States surely merit analysis, but a review of the foregoing list will provide a basic understanding of the importance of treaties to the typical foreign person who has made, or is contemplating, a U.S. investment.

U.S. TREATIES AND STATUTORY LAW: A SUBTLE AND COMPLEX RELATIONSHIP

In many countries, duly approved international agreements are superior in legal status to domestic statutes. There can be no conflict between the two types of law because the international commitment is entitled to precedence: It can be contradicted only by another international agreement or, in some cases, by constitutional principle. In other countries, the international agreement has no legal force at all until it is enacted as domestic legislation by the national legislature. There may or may not be special rules applied in the process of such enactment, in consideration of the international commitment that is at stake. Having attained binding force through this process, the treaty may then have superior status if it is found to conflict with other domestic statutes.

In the United States, treaties and federal statutes (enacted by the national legislature, or Congress) are brought into force by different processes. Unlike statutes, treaties are considered by only one house of Congress, the Senate; the House of Representatives has no role in the treaty ratification process. Also unlike statutes, which require only a majority vote, treaties require a two-thirds vote of approval—or advice and consent—to permit ratification, following which the treaty enters into force. Once in force, the treaty has status equal to that of the domestic statute; each represents, under the U.S. Constitution, the supreme law of the land.

There is more ambiguity in this concept than meets the eye. Because treaties and federal statutes are equals in status, either type of law can supersede the other. Logically, this implies that, in case of conflict, the more recent law should control—that is, if a treaty was approved after a conflicting piece of statutory law, the treaty should control, and vice versa. For the most part, the American legal system has adopted such a later-in-time rule, giving precedence to the law that has been enacted or ratified more recently.

The question whether a treaty conflicts with a statute is, however, often unclear and open to argument. The courts of the United States, when confronted by such asserted conflicts, follow certain rules, or canons of construction. One of these canons enjoins a court to attempt to avoid conflicts, if possible, and to find a way of reconciling the statute and the treaty if there is any reasonable way of doing so. Another canon holds that specific enactments take precedence over more general ones. The interaction of these rules of construction leaves in place the rule that the later-in-time of enactment governs in direct conflicts. However, courts are often able to sidestep direct conflicts by giving greater weight to the provision that is more specific. Moreover, courts evince a special respect for international agreements, and even in the case of a conflict that cannot be reconciled, they may favor the treaty in instances when the legislative history of the later-in-time statute does not clearly evidence a Congressional intention to override the international agreement.

The following examples should illustrate how the various judicial canons interact. Assume that a general statute states that a rule is X, while the more recent treaty with, say, France states that the rule is Y in the case of France. In such a case it can reasonably be concluded that the rule is Y with respect to persons who are covered by the agreement with France, since the treaty is more recent and more specific than the statute, and since the courts have tended to favor treaties in cases when there is no specific statutory override of the treaty.

Assume next that the more recent enactment is a statute of general application (applicable to everyone), the terms of which are nonetheless more specific than a potentially conflicting treaty rule. For example, the treaty with France states that the rule is Y, but a subsequent statute proclaims that in a specific class of cases, rule Z applies for everyone, including persons covered by the treaty with France. In such a case the rule that the narrow provision takes precedence over the general one points in two different directions. Rule Z has a narrower substantive scope while rule Y applies to fewer people—only persons entitled to claim the benefits of the treaty with France. The canon does not readily permit a judgment as to which provision would prevail. However, the general tendency of the courts to give greater weight to treaties, unless Congress has clearly manifested an intention to supersede or override, suggests that rule Y would prevail.

This tendency of courts to favor treaties has come under attack in the U.S. Congress in recent years. The assault has been greatest in the House of Representatives which has no role in the treaty ratification process. Some members of the House, particularly those on its tax-writing committee, view a treaty as a mechanism by which substantive tax provisions can be altered without their consent. These Congresspersons tend to regard courts' deferential treatment of treaty provisions as usurping their power to write the tax laws of the United States.

Such feelings of resentment, combined with a frustration about the time-consuming and cumbersome nature of renegotiating international agreements, has led to enactment of a series of tax provisions that have specifically overridden treaties. The story begins with the Foreign Investment in Real Property Tax Act, commonly known as FIRPTA, which was enacted by Congress in 1980 to change the tax treatment of foreign persons on their income from the sale of real property located in the United States.

The provisions of FIRPTA conflicted with provisions in many treaties. To deal with these conflicts, Congress provided that the new statute superseded any treaty provision, but only after a period of time. Conflicting provisions in existing treaties were generally to be honored for four years, after which they were to become unenforceable to the extent that they conflicted with FIRPTA. Future treaty provisions conflicting with FIRPTA could become effective only if the FIRPTA statute was specifically amended. Such an amendment would require passage by both houses of Congress. As a result of this provision, the House of Representatives aimed to retain a measure of control over any future changes in the taxation of income from U.S. real property. (Whether a subsequent treaty—as much the supreme law of the land as FIRPTA—could effect such a change despite FIRPTA in the absence of a statutory amendment presents an interesting, if perhaps academic, question.)

Congressional resentment against the tendency of the courts to give greater weight to treaties evidenced itself again in 1986. In that year, Congress enacted a branch profits tax on the unincorporated branches of foreign corporations doing business in the United States. This tax, which does not apply to U.S. corporations, conflicts with the "nondiscrimination" provision found in almost all U.S. tax treaties, barring one country from imposing a tax on the citizens or residents of the other treaty country that it does not impose on its own citizens or residents in comparable circumstances. The branch profits statute limited the effectiveness of the "nondiscrimination" provision by restricting its application to "qualified residents" of the treaty parties. To achieve this result, however, it was necessary for the branch profits statute to override the treaties to the extent that they permit broader application of the nondiscrimination principle.

Congress further dealt with treaty-statute conflicts in 1988, when it formally adopted the later-in-time rule. It enacted a statutory provision deciding that neither statute nor treaty shall have preferential status, and it replaced a section of the Internal Revenue code that explicitly excluded income from taxation to the extent required by any treaty with a provision requiring that the statute be applied "with due regard to any treaty obligation." In formally enacting the later-in-time rule, Congress carved out various substantive exceptions, most of which give precedence to treaties over statutes.

The concern of the Congress about the effect of treaties on U.S. tax law has also led to the enactment of a new provision that generally requires any taxpayer who takes a position that a treaty overrides or modifies a domestic statute to disclose that position to the U.S. Internal Revenue Service. This disclosure does not change substantive U.S. tax law, but it is likely to ensure greater scrutiny of treaty based positions. As a result some foreign persons doing business in the United States will probably be more conservative in their interpretations of treaty provisions. Failure to properly disclose a treaty-based position will subject the noncomplying taxpayer to serious penalties.

None of the foregoing discussion is intended to suggest that Congress cavalierly overrides U.S. treaties. The recent overrides were precipitated by significant economic events, which are not likely to recur often. FIRPTA was enacted after a large increase in foreign acquisitions of U.S. real property. The branch tax in effect responded to the significant growth in direct investment in the United States that occurred in the late 1970s and early 1980s. The 1988 changes were stimulated by the extensive rewriting of U.S. tax law that took place in 1986. After this major overhaul, the tax committees of Congress concluded that many existing treaty provisions were the product of negotiations premised on U.S. laws that had been repealed. These committees believed the massive changes called for a reexamination of the treaties. The preferable method of conducting such a reexamination would have been to renegotiate the treaties, but such a renegotiation is the exclusive province of the executive branch of the U.S. government, and that branch does not always act with the alacrity that Congress would wish. Congress thus took matters into its own hands.

This does not mean that existing treaty provisions are in continuous jeopardy of being overridden. Congress is aware, generally, not only of its legal power to override treaty commitments but of other countries' sensitivities to the exercise of that power. For that reason it usually considers potential overrides with great care and endeavors to avoid unnecessarily provocative actions. Nevertheless, there is a considerable body of federal legislation each year, and the record of Congress in simply remembering the existence of a particular treaty commitment is hardly unblemished; the accidental or inadvertent creation of conflicts between statutes and treaties will doubtless continue, and such cases will ultimately find their way into U.S. courts. In the past, treaties have generally been found to prevail in such situations, but given the new statutory language it is not clear that the courts will continue to give unstated special recognition to international commitments, at least in the tax area. Foreign investors in the United States will have to remain alert for changes in U.S. tax laws that may conflict with existing treaty provisions.

TREATIES AND THE STATES—THE IMPORTANCE OF U.S. FEDERALISM

In the United States, the power to enter into international agreements is vested in the national government; there can be no such agreement between a U.S. state or locality and another country. Furthermore, under the system of federalism that prevails in the United States, national laws—whether domestic statute or treaty—can directly supersede legislation at the state and local levels, provided that the subject matter of such a supervening law falls within the broad (and, at the margins, unclear) domain of national interests. In addition, there are some areas—foreign policy, for example—wherein state laws are a nullity simply because they are preempted by the superior federal interest, even if that interest has not been pursued in the form of a specific statute or treaty.

In light of these principles, it may be hard to see why federalism should bear importantly upon U.S. treaties and treaty policy. Almost by definition, international agreements are the province of sovereign countries; quite apart from the distribution of powers in the U.S. Constitution, it would be unthinkable for the United States to speak internationally through 50 (or more) independent voices. Because both law and practicalities favor the use of the national voice in international affairs, the prerogatives of states arguably should not impinge to any extent upon U.S. treaty policy.

U.S. principles of federalism should not be evaluated in light of views that prevail outside the United States. With some noteworthy exceptions, most countries of the world, including those that have adopted a federalist system, have concluded that their national governments must be able to speak for local components of the system. Accommodation to those components is achieved through frequent consultation, internal laws designed to achieve uniformity and reduce conflicts, or provision for state and local participation in the negotiating process. As a result of such accommodation, the interests of states and localities are not permitted to stifle the achievement of international agreements having effect over a broad range of subject matter—and legally effective not only at the national level but also at the state and local level.

The situation is different in the United States. There are some areas—taxation is a leading example—wherein a strong history of state and local autonomy has led the national government to refrain from exercising to the utmost the powers that it indisputably possesses as a constitutional and legal matter. In a sense, the reluctance is political in nature. Some actions, because they have never been taken by the national government, have a heavy burden of precedent to overcome. The rights of states, vaguely but broadly envisioned in the U.S. Constitution, are still a subject of delicacy in the United States, including the U.S. Congress. The combination of this respect for past practices and a continuing belief that some actions are simply not appropriate at the national level of government sometimes make it impossible—or, at the least, extremely difficult—to achieve international agreements having full sway at the state and local level.

The result may be frustrating for the foreign investor. Legal rules that operate at the state and local levels are certain to bear upon investment. This is especially true in the area of taxation, where state and local governments have enacted substantial taxes, many of which have rules and definitions quite different from those of the national government. Despite the significance of these taxes, U.S. treaties have generally been drafted so as not to supersede or alter them. Since states cannot negotiate their own treaties, the only possibility of obtaining changes in state tax treatment of foreign investors is to persuade Congress to pass a domestic statute that will supersede the offending state and local rules—or, in some cases, by arguing to U.S. courts that the state and local rules trespass on the national government's domain to such an extent that they should be declared null and void as a Constitutional matter. Needless to say, both avenues of potential relief are long, arduous, and expensive. The situation is, moreover, ironic in light of the fact that the United States regularly demands that other countries, in their international commitments, undertake to bind their states and localities.

THE U.S. APPROACH TO
INTERPRETING TREATIES

Largely because the United States does not follow the same approach as many other countries do to interpreting statutes, it does not appear to follow the same approach to interpreting treaties. As a general matter, U.S. courts do not take a strictly literal approach: They look outside the terms of a law that is being construed, seeking the statutory purpose and the intent of the drafter. This practice stands in marked contrast to the approach that prevails in many countries, and it is a source of much international misunderstanding. The foreign investor cannot simply read a U.S. law—statute or treaty—and assume that the dictionary meaning of words will provide a sure guide. The investor must also inquire whether the results of such a reading are consistent with a reasonable view of what Congress or the negotiators of a treaty were probably trying to achieve. This is not to say that the literal meaning of words used in statutes and treaties is entirely irrelevant; in most cases, the reader can probably assume that black will not be interpreted to include white. The point, however, is that black will often include various shades of grey when the issue comes to be adjudged by a U.S. court.

This seems to be just as true when it is a treaty rather than a statute that is being interpreted. The fact that the other party to the treaty may adopt a more literal approach will not affect the basic U.S. approach to the interpretative task. In some cases, the treaty may itself provide a mechanism whereby differing interpretations can be resolved by the countries in question. This does not, of course, preclude the possibility that, in such a resolution, it will be the U.S. view that prevails.

For this reason, the legislative history of a treaty—both the history of the congressional committees (usually the Senate Foreign Relations Committee but, in some cases, others as well) and that of the treaty's negotiators, particularly if formally published, must be consulted. From the standpoint of foreign investors, the process may result in considerably less certainty than they are accustomed to having when they make an investment in their home country.

THE POSSIBILITY OF "SHOPPING" FOR A U.S. TREATY

It should not be assumed that the only U.S. treaties relevant to an investor from, say, Argentina are U.S. bilateral agreements with Argentina or multilateral agreements to which both the United States and Argentina are parties. In many cases, U.S. treaties cover not only citizens and residents of another country but entities formed in that country. In these cases an investor may find it worthwhile to "shop" around for a country that has a treaty with the United States and borrow the provisions of that treaty even though the investor is neither a resident nor a citizen of that country. The practice of structuring business transactions so as to take advantage of another country's tax treaty, commonly referred to as *treaty shopping,* is achieved by forming an entity such as a corporation in a country that has a potentially favorable agreement with the United States.

Because of the use of U.S. tax treaties with low tax jurisdictions, particularly the Netherland Antilles, by persons who are not residents of those jurisdictions, the practice of treaty shopping came under attack from the U.S. Congress and the Treasury in the 1980s. The executive branch has terminated some tax treaties and endeavored to renegotiate others. This is obviously a slow process, but some important changes have resulted.

Most recent U.S. tax treaties contain some form of limitation on who may benefit from the treaty. These limitations take the form of denying the benefits of the treaty to business entities that do not have a sufficient connection, or nexus, with the countries that are the U.S. counterparties. Under these provisions a business entity may be denied the ability to take advantage of a treaty between the country in which it is organized and the United States unless it can show that it is owned mostly by individuals who are residents or citizens of that country, that its stock is traded on a public exchange of that country, or that the principal reason for conducting its operation in that country is something other than obtaining treaty benefits. Thus, a French company that is entirely owned by our Argentine investor but conducts an ongoing business in France may take advantage of the U.S.-France tax treaty. However, a French company formed by an Argentine investor for the purpose of taking advantage of the treaty will not be allowed to benefit from the treaty.

Congress, too, has attempted to limit treaty shopping. In 1986, when Congress enacted the branch profits tax, it provided that only "qualified residents" of countries that have treaties with the United States could use those treaty provisions to achieve reductions of, or exemptions from, this tax. This statutory restriction on who may use a treaty provision to reduce or eliminate the branch profits tax is similar to the "limitation in benefits" provisions found in recent U.S. tax treaties.

Generalizations regarding the extent to which treaty shopping is still feasible are impossible to make: the United States has about 40 tax treaties in force, of different types. There is no substitute for a careful analysis of both the terms of a potentially relevant treaty and the consequences in the other country of forming an entity there to take advantage of a treaty relationship with the United States. Nevertheless, it is indisputable that, even after the recent changes, treaty shopping can be advantageous in some situations.

SUBSTANTIVE COVERAGE: U.S. INCOME TAX TREATIES AS A CASE IN POINT

The foreign investor is likely to find upon examination that, in many areas of substantive law, the treaty rules will be the operative ones. The United States has entered into a wide variety of international agreements, ranging from treaties applicable to particular industries (e.g., air transport or telecommunications) to treaties of potentially general application (e.g., investment treaties or income tax and estate and gift tax treaties). The comments offered thus far in this chapter are intended to apply, at a general level, to all U.S. treaty commitments. When, however, the investor asks what in particular the United States has agreed to by way of treaty commitments, the question must be addressed in light of the otherwise applicable statutory rules. Treaties are, of course, entered into against a background comprising those otherwise applicable rules; it is only by assessing the substantive gap between the two sources of law in any given situation that the investor can reach a judgment regarding the potential benefits of a treaty.

Income tax treaties, which apply to all forms of investment, offer a useful illustration. Such treaties represent an area of current debate and controversy in the United States, and many of the points previously discussed in regard to such treaties have attained an exceptional level of sophistication and public awareness. Moreover, the gap between statutory and treaty law is, in the income tax area, particularly striking.

The United States has a complete statutory scheme governing the taxation of income earned by foreign investors. This scheme, like most other aspects of U.S. tax law, is detailed and complex. It applies in principle to all foreign persons. Although many issues have never been resolved satisfactorily within the scheme, it is fair to observe that there is no need for the United States to enter into tax treaties in order to complete its statutory law.

On the other hand, the United States has employed income tax treaties for almost 60 years now (only slightly less than the 80 years in which the United States has had an income tax system) as a complement to its statutory law and an integral part of its overall tax system. The treaties are generally intended to achieve several goals. First, they are used to fine-tune the statutory rules and permit them to operate harmoniously in conjunction with the laws of other countries in ways that will reduce or eliminate double taxation of income while precluding avoidance or evasion of tax. Second, the treaties create a mechanism whereby individual disputes having an international character can be resolved with the participation of the foreign countries in question. Third, the United States uses tax treaties as a means of deliberately lowering its own—and the other country's—statutory taxes. Finally, such treaties represent, for the United States, a tangible expression of solid economic relations between countries and, therefore, an instrument of general foreign policy.

Tax treaties are always entered into by the United States on a bilateral basis. They are negotiated by the executive branch through officials in the U.S. Treasury Department and are administered, as are all U.S. tax laws, by the Internal Revenue Service. The Revenue Service is, for all practical (although not all legal) purposes, a separate agency, so the U.S. system produces the somewhat peculiar result that the officials who administer a tax treaty are not the ones who negotiated it.

By established U.S. policy—and, arguably, by reason of U.S. constitutional principles—tax treaties are not used to produce for the taxpayer a worse substantive result than the one that would obtain under statutory law. Thus, most U.S. tax treaties state explicitly that none of their provisions shall preclude a taxpayer from invoking the rules of other international agreements or those of domestic law, if those rules should be more generous. The intent of this policy seems clear enough, but its implications can be complicated. It is questionable, for example, whether taxpayers may select certain aspects of a treaty that favor their position while rejecting other closely related aspects in favor of statutory rules. The typical modern U.S. income tax treaty contains highly refined and intricate rules. The issue here is whether the investor must choose one regime or the other—the treaty or the statute—or whether, instead, the investor may elect to treat one transaction under the treaty and another similar or related transaction under domestic law. To date, most observers have assumed that such picking and choosing of rules is available to the taxpayer, but there may be limits, whether articulated in a treaty or merely implicit in its structure.

In any event, the net effect of the policies pursued by the United States by means of tax treaties leads to an often substantial gap between the rules of statutory law and those of the treaties. Like many other countries, the United States does not attempt to establish the ideal set of tax rules in its statute; rather, it comes to the negotiating table with points to concede by negotiation with the other side. In addition, because tax treaties represent a highly developed area of international law, to which many countries throughout the world have contributed, it is perhaps inevitable that a country such as the United States, with a highly refined statutory system, will have to accept changes in terminology and approach in order to achieve international agreements. These changes may not appear large on their face, but in some cases, the gap they create can give rise to important differences in practice when the treaty rules are compared with those of statutory law.

The gap between U.S. statutory law and U.S. treaty commitments has had the effect of reducing U.S. taxation of the foreign investor. There are many manifestations of this effect, of which three have especially broad application. First, the treaties raise the level of presence required in the United States before certain forms of investment, and the foreign investor, are subject to tax at all. Second, the treaties lower the rates of tax applicable to certain forms of investment or, in some cases, provide for outright exemption. Third, treaties generally establish a principal of nondiscrimination—national treatment—designed to ensure that in many, if not all, situations the foreign person will be treated no worse than his or her U.S. counterpart.

Under statutory rules an active investment is subject to U.S. taxation once it attains the status of a trade or business in the United States. This is a somewhat amorphous concept that cannot be defined with precision for all situations. Although U.S. tax laws are far more precise and detailed than U.S. legislation in most other areas, the concepts and criteria that appear in the tax laws do not always contain bright-line tests but instead are left to the long and slow process of interpretation through regulations and rulings by the Revenue Service, and judicial decisions. Some important concepts—trade or business, for example—cannot be articulated in quantitative terms but require, instead, a careful analysis of all relevant facts. Even then, one cannot always be certain that a particular conclusion will be immune from challenge by the Revenue Service or that, if challenged, it will ultimately be upheld in the courts.

The treaties do not clarify the trade or business standard but, rather, erect an entirely different test for active investments, requiring a greater degree of penetration into the U.S. economic system before taxation will attach. Instead of a trade or business, the treaties usually require a permanent establishment: a fixed place of business such as an office or a branch. The precise meaning of this treaty test is probably no clearer than the trade or business standard, but it is clearly possible to be engaged in a trade or business without having a permanent establishment. Investors able to fall within that admittedly ill-defined gap will wish to consider the possibility of benefiting from the treaty rule.

Another basic concept about which similar observations can be made is that of residence. The United States claims the right to tax the worldwide earnings of its citizens and any alien lawfully who is admitted to the United States for permanent residence or who has resided in the United States for a substantial portion of the last three years, as defined by a formula depending on the days present in this country. It is very possible to be considered a U.S. resident for tax purposes during a particular year and also to be a resident of another country, spending most of one's year outside the United States. As a result, there is a significant problem for persons who qualify as residents of two countries and are subject under the statutory laws of both countries to full, residence-basis taxation. Treaties are critical to these individuals because they generally provide relief from double taxation in cases of potential dual residence. The treaties resolve such cases through the application of certain tie-breaker tests. If these tests, which hardly qualify as bright lines, fail, the treaty will usually allow representatives of the treaty parties to resolve the matter through negotiations. Since treaties allow for the possibility of an ultimate resolution in favor of residence in the other country, they clearly raise the threshold for U.S. taxation, and this can be of substantial benefit to the foreign investor.

The foregoing examples relate to U.S. taxation of foreigners who are present in the United States enough to be considered taxable on their income by reason of their presence in this country. In the case of U.S. taxation of passive investments, however, the United States, like most other countries, imposes tax irrespective of U.S. presence, by reason of the source of the tax base. The potential effect of income tax treaties in this area is dramatic. The United States, like many other countries, has deliberately imposed an unrealistically high statutory rate of tax—30 percent, in most cases—with full knowledge that this rate will be reduced in the course of treaty negotiations. The United States follows this practice because it recognizes that most treaty agreements are reciprocal in nature, and the United States has a strong interest in securing reductions in similar taxes for its residents and citizens in their capacity as investors in other countries. The reductions will vary not only according to the specifics of the particular treaty but according to the type of income in question. For example, U.S. taxation of dividends is commonly reduced by treaty from the statutory rate of 30 percent to as low as 15 percent, or even 5 percent in the case of direct investments by corporations. It is current U.S. policy, on the other hand (as reflected in the U.S. model income tax treaty), to seek through treaties to reduce taxation of interest and royalties at source from 30 percent to zero; if the treaty partner is prepared to agree to such a reduction, it will usually find the United States prepared to do the same. Such differences between the statutory rule and a treaty are obviously of a magnitude sufficient to warrant the attention of any foreign investor. It is hardly surprising that the preponderance of foreign passive investment enters the United States through a treaty jurisdiction.

Treaty nondiscrimination provisions are designed to ensure that U.S. law will not discriminate against foreign persons entitled to the coverage of such provisions. Generally, these treaty rules guarantee that all individual U.S. residents will be treated alike, regardless of their citizenship; that foreign corporate residents—U.S. permanent establishments of foreign corporations—will receive the same treatment as similarly situated U.S. corporations; that U.S. corporations owned by foreign persons will be treated in the same way as other U.S. corporations; and that amounts paid to foreign persons will be deductible in the United States to the same extent as amounts paid to U.S. persons. These rules are not mere window dressing: Most countries, including the United States, have a natural tendency toward harsher treatment of persons not represented in the domestic political system than of persons who are so represented. Moreover, the area of nondiscrimination is unique in U.S. tax treaty policy in that there exists here a long history of prohibiting states and localities from discriminating against individuals and businesses from other states.

The foregoing examples of the gap between U.S. statutory and treaty law in the area of income taxation are obviously not comprehensive. Because the United States, like other countries, usually follows a practice of covering the entire range of tax subjects in a treaty, the gap can be found in many specific cases that do not fit, or do not fit precisely, into the molds summarized above. The summaries here should suffice to demonstrate, however, that in contemplating the tax aspects of an investment, the foreign investor will generally have much to gain from analyzing the potential benefits that treaties may offer. And, quite apart from substantive benefits of the type described, treaties will typically contain a mechanism whereby the treaty partners can assemble, through their representatives, to resolve particular disputes. This feature may be as important as the substantive reductions in taxes and lowering of thresholds that the treaties also mandate. The availability of an advocate, in the form of a government official of one of the treaty partners, offers the possibility of resolving contests that may arise, as well as some practical assurance that commitments appearing in a treaty text will, in fact, be respected.

There is, however, a final point to be considered. Most U.S. tax treaties envision that information regarding the taxation of a foreign investor will be shared with the investor's home country. For many foreign investors such information exchange may represent an important negative aspect of tax treaties. Moreover, in light of the growing sophistication of the world's major tax systems, and the more common and regularized use of tax treaties, many countries, including the United States, have been active in perfecting techniques of information exchange. As long as it is possible for foreign investors to borrow a treaty entered into by a country other than the one of their residence, the problem can perhaps be contained. But with increasing limitations on such borrowing, fears of information exchange will become more acute. Whether this issue should lead an investor so far as to forego the potential benefits of a treaty or actually to direct investments elsewhere can only be answered on a case-by-case basis; the concern that some foreign investors evince toward information exchange seems extreme to many Americans, but that may only reflect the confidence of most U.S. persons that tax information, in the U.S. system, will only be put to precisely delineated uses.

CONCLUSION

Obviously, there is much more to be said on the subject of U.S. treaties affecting foreign investors than could possibly be reviewed in the brief compass of this chapter. The subject is intricate in its own right, and its tentacles extend throughout the U.S. legal system. The proper conclusion, therefore, seems to lead right back at the starting point: For many foreign investors, in many situations, the governing legal rules will be treaty rules. This unavoidable fact represents both an opportunity and a potential pitfall.

CHAPTER 13

U.S. EXPORT CONTROLS

David A. Wormser, Esq.
Pepper, Hamilton & Scheetz

The United States limits the exports of goods, technology, and services through a variety of overlapping regulatory regimes administered by numerous government departments and agencies. Most of the restrictions are intended to prevent potential adversaries of the United States from gaining access to technologies that might improve their military capabilities. Others are imposed to influence South Africa's racial policies, isolate governments that foster communism or support terrorism, or to further some other foreign policy objective. Still others attempt to prevent the depletion of scarce natural resources, to limit the shipment of potentially harmful substances, or to protect the market for specific products.

The civil and criminal penalties for ignoring these export controls can be severe. Companies and individuals guilty of violating the regulations discussed in this chapter may face fines ranging between $50 thousand and five times the value of the exports involved, and individuals can be jailed for terms up to 5 years. For "willful" violations, the penalties may increase to $1 million and 10 years in jail. The violator, moreover, risks losing its right to export goods from the United States.

Navigating the U.S. export control system requires the exporter to determine which government agency or agencies exercise jurisdiction over the transaction in question. In most cases, the

Commerce Department will control the export under its Export Administration Regulations (EAR). Depending on the nature of the transaction, though, other agencies may impose additional or different requirements.

This chapter reviews the principal laws and regulations limiting exports of goods, services, and technology from the United States:

- The Export Administration Regulations pursuant to which the U.S. Commerce Department controls exports of commercial goods and technology.
- The International Traffic in Arms Regulations pursuant to which the U.S. State Department regulates exports of military hardware, as well as several categories of commercial items deemed to have important military applications.
- Other regulations limiting exports of narrow categories of items.
- The Foreign Asset Control Regulations, implementing various trade embargoes imposed by the United States to further its foreign policy goals.

In addition, this chapter discusses the steps that companies exporting from the United States should take to ensure compliance with the applicable rules.

EXPORT CONTROL SYSTEMS

Commerce Department Export Administration Regulations

By far the most pervasive of the control systems, the EAR attempt to balance the benefits of exporting goods and technology against the risks to American military security and foreign policy goals. The burdens imposed by the controls have declined in recent years to reflect both an increase in cooperation between the United States and its allies and the decrease in tensions between the United States and its traditional enemies. The regulations nevertheless continue to require that each exporter determine the impact of the EAR on each export transaction.

Reasons for Controlling Exports

The EAR control exports for any of three reasons. "National security" controls are intended to prevent export transactions that would make a significant contribution to the military potential of a foreign country. A few technologies—the most powerful computers, for example, CAD/CAM equipment for designing and producing integrated circuits, and sophisticated telecommunications equipment—require Commerce Department approval for shipment to any destination. Others are restricted for export to a lesser number of countries, while still others are available for export to all but certain embargoed destinations.

"Foreign policy" controls, as the name suggests, attempt to further the foreign policy goals of the United States. The EAR currently support U.S. embargoes against Cambodia, Libya, North Korea, Cuba, and Vietnam. And, although largely replaced as the foreign policy tool of choice by the Foreign Asset Control Regulations (described in a later section), the EAR continue to restrict exports of such items as goods intended for use in nuclear facilities, crime control equipment, and polygraph and fingerprinting equipment to all countries other than the United States's closest allies.

"Short supply" controls attempt to prevent depletion of scarce resources. Examples currently include western red cedar and various chemicals and metals.

Location of the Consignee—Country Groups

A key feature of the EAR is their use of "Country Groups" to determine the level of control applicable to a given transaction. With the exception of Canada, which is subject to no export controls other than those imposed for nuclear nonproliferation purposes, every foreign country falls within a Country Group designated by a letter of the alphabet, roughly as follows:

Country Groups	Countries
Q, W, and Y	The Soviet Union, the Baltic republics, and the members of the former Warsaw Pact (usually, despite world events, referred to as the "Soviet bloc" or "bloc" countries).

| S and Z | Embargoed destinations (currently Cambodia, Cuba, Libya, North Korea, and Vietnam). |
| T and V | All countries (other than the United States and Canada) not included in another group. This group is often referred to as the "Free World" countries. |

While Country Group designations are a rough indicator of a country's treatment under the EAR, they are by no means perfect. Country Group T, for example, nominally includes the People's Republic of China even though individual EAR provisions expose that country to many of the same restrictions applicable to the Soviet Union and others in Group Y. Similarly, Group V included Panama and Nicaragua throughout the years in which U.S. embargoes against these countries precluded most exports.

At the other end of the spectrum, Country Groups T and V also contain the countries benefiting from the most favorable treatment available under the EAR. These include the nations with which the United States has long cooperated in restricting sensitive exports to the Soviet bloc. Among the latter are members of the Coordinating Committee (COCOM)—Japan, Australia, and the NATO countries other than Iceland—as well as various non-COCOM countries that have agreed to adhere to COCOM controls and procedures.

Degree of Control

The EAR provide for two distinct levels of control. The more restrictive level, called a "validated license" requirement, requires the exporter to apply for a certificate authorizing shipment of specific goods or technology to identified consignees in a particular country. The most common form of certificate is the "Individual Validated License," or IVL, authorizing the holder to complete a single export transaction. The IVL is flexible enough to permit multiple shipments to the same consignee over a two-year period. Commerce may also grant a Distribution License to companies making numerous exports of a given commodity to the same region, and other special licenses may replace the IVL under certain limited circumstances.

The lower level of control consists of a set of "general licenses." A general license requires no application or specific Commerce approval; rather, it is a waiver of the application requirements that the EAR grant to all who qualify. The most popular general licenses are "G-DEST" and "GTDR," which apply to militarily insignificant exports of goods and technology, respectively, to non-embargoed destinations. "GFW" authorizes exports of relatively unsophisticated items to Free World countries, "GCT" authorizes exports to more sophisticated goods to other countries participating in COCOM, "G-TEMP" permits temporary exports for trade shows and demonstrations or to support other work performed overseas, a general license designated "BAGGAGE" applies to personal luggage, and any of a wide variety of other licenses may be available for a given transaction.

General license eligibility provides obvious benefits. It permits the exporter to complete a transaction without applying and waiting for Commerce Department approval. It also deprives the Commerce Department of the opportunity to disapprove the transaction.

Whether a given transaction qualifies for a general license depends on the nature of the goods or technology involved, the location and identity of the foreign consignee, and the exporter's compliance with various ministerial requirements. These issues are discussed in the remainder of this section.

Classifying Goods and Technology

The first step in determining whether a given transaction qualifies for a general license is to "classify" the goods or technology to be shipped—that is, to determine first, whether one or more provisions of the EAR describe the item and second, if more than one provision applies, which one is controlling. Once the classification question is resolved, answers to the remaining issues—whether the EAR require a validated license and, if so, whether the Commerce Department is likely to issue one—flow almost automatically.

Classifying an item requires the exporter to review two portions of the regulations. First, the exporter must consider whether the transaction involves "technical data" controlled by EAR Part 779. Second, the exporter must determine whether the commodities involved fall within any of the technical descriptions set forth on the Control List published at EAR Par 799.1.

Technical Data.   The term *technical data* covers virtually the entire range of technical information and know-how other than business and financial data and concepts. "Technical data," according to EAR Section 779.1 (a), means: "information of any kind that can be used, or adapted for use, in the design, production, manufacture, utilization, or reconstruction of articles or materials. The data may take a tangible form, such as a model, prototype, blueprint, or an operating manual (the tangible form may be stored on recording media); or they may take an intangible form such as technical service. All software is technical data." This definition is striking in that it makes no attempt to limit the "technical data" concept to information relating to militarily sensitive items. As a result, manufacturing information falls within the definition whether the good to be manufactured is an airplane or a toothbrush.

The definition also mandates that technical data retain their character even when embodied in some tangible medium. Accordingly, models and blueprints that convey information are governed by the technical data rules. Software remains governed by the technical data controls whether shipped on magnetic tape or disks or burned into so-called programmable read-only memory, or PROM, computer chips, even if these items are also controlled as commodities.

Technical data transactions may be controlled even if completed wholly within the United States. The technical data controls define "export" to include not just shipments overseas, but also the release of information within the United States with the knowledge or intent that it will be transmitted out of the country.

The EAR compensate for the breadth of these definitions by exempting from control information that is "publicly available" or generally accessible to the interested public in any form. EAR Section 779.3 specifically grants general license "GTDA" for all information that has been published in a book, periodical, or electronic bulletin board open to the interested public, made available in a library open to at least a segment of the public, revealed at an open conference or seminar, or made available in the U.S. Patent Office.

Where the information is proprietary, Part 779 effectively requires the exporter to determine whether the data are described by one or more EAR provisions. The location of the applicable description all but dictates the scope of the exporter's licensing obligations. If the data fall within the provisions governing nuclear-related technology, they require a validated license for all destinations *including* Canada. Certain types of technical data, including a great deal of information relating to military aeronautics and navigation, require a validated license for export to any destination other than Canada.

Still other types of data are restricted only for export to the Soviet bloc. These data, including certain types of computer software and a large amount of data related to controlled commodities, may be exported to Free World countries if the consignee provides written assurances that neither the data nor their "direct product" will be reexported without U.S. government approval to a proscribed destination.*

The job of classifying technical data is complicated by the fact that the applicable provisions are spread throughout Part 779 and the Control List. The job is further complicated by the fact that, while the EAR purport to preclude exporters from using general-license GTDR for technical data exports to the Soviet bloc, Congress largely repealed this regulation by statute. The Omnibus Trade and Competitiveness Act of 1988 required the Commerce Department to take certain steps by February 1989 to preserve so-called unilateral national security controls—that is, thosed imposed without the support of other COCOM countries. Rather than taking the required steps, the Commerce Department permitted the unilateral controls to expire.

The challenge is to determine which of the technical data controls are unilateral. The multilateral controls are described in classified documents unavailable to most exporters. The Commerce Department has indicated that most of the multilaterally controlled technical data relate to commodities described on the Control List, but has declined to provide more specific information. Exporters, accordingly, are often required to ask the department to rule in individual cases whether a given control remains in effect, a process

---

* Although the matter is by no means free from doubt, the Commerce Department has unofficially interpreted "direct product" to mean the immediate result of applying the technical data, and has generally refrained from enforcing the restriction unless the direct product is itself a controlled commodity or technical data.

that can approach the licensing regimen in its delays and complexity.

Commodities. The term *commodity* includes any "article, material, or supply except technical data." All of the commodities subject to Commerce Department control appear on a "Control List" that is divided into 10 categories:

Metal working machinery.
Chemical and petroleum equipment.
Electrical and power generating equipment.
General industrial equipment.
Transportation equipment.
Electronics and precision instruments.
Metals, minerals, and their manufacture.
Chemicals, metalloids, petroleum products, and related materials.
Rubber and rubber products.
Miscellaneous.

Each entry on the list has been assigned an export control commodity number (or ECCN) consisting of four digits and a letter (usually *A, D, E, F,* or *G*). The letter provides immediate information about the nature of the controls involved. If the item is controlled by COCOM, the four digits correspond to the COCOM International Control List number and the letter will always be *A*. ECCNs ending in the letter *B* set forth unilateral controls imposed on all or most destinations, in most instances for reasons of foreign policy or short supply. The letters *D,E,* and *F* indicate that the item may usually be exported under general license G-DEST to Free World countries. ECCNs ending in *G* are catch-all items tending to describe commodities within the particular category that are "not elsewhere described." "G" items can usually be exported to any non-embargoed destination under general license G-DEST.

Determining which ECCN, if any, governs a given commodity export requires careful study of the Control List entries that might apply. ECCN 1565A, for example, controls electronic computers and peripheral equipment designed for militarily sensitive uses such as signal processing or meeting certain specific technical thresholds for processing speed and memory. ECCN 6565G, by contrast, controls all computer equipment excepted from control by ECCN 1565A, prohibiting exports to embargoed destinations and for use by the South African police and military and apartheid-enforcing government agencies. Both entries overlap to some degree with ECCNs 1391A (robotic equipment), 1091A (numerically controlled machine tools subject to COCOM restrictions), 5091F (other numerically controlled equipment), 1355A (CAD/CAM equipment for integrated circuits), 1564A (computer components), and any other entry describing equipment into which electronic computers may be incorporated.

Once the classification process is complete, however, it becomes relatively easy to determine if a given transaction is eligible for a general license. The exporter can use the information in the Control List entry to

- Determine whether the transaction is small enough to qualify for general license GLV. Each Control List entry contains a paragraph in the following form:

  GLV $ Value Limit: $5,000 for Country Groups T & V, except $0 for the People's Republic of China; $0 for all other destinations.

  The GLV limit applies to entire transactions, and the EAR specifically prohibit exporters from splitting shipments simply to gain GLV eligibility.
- If the destination is a COCOM country, determine whether general license GCT is available. EAR Part 771 grants GCT for all commodity exports to COCOM countries unless the applicable Control List entry specifies otherwise.
- If the destination is another Free World country, determine whether the transaction qualifies for general license GFW. GFW is available for all Free World exports of commodities that the applicable control list entry indicates are likely to be approved for export to the People's Republic of China.
- Determine whether any of the other general licenses apply. The eligibility requirements are described in Part 771 of the EAR.

If a general license appears to be available for the transaction, the exporter must nevertheless take care to comply with all of the license's requirements, however minimal they may be. General license "GTC," for example, requires the exporter to obtain a written statement from the consignee to the effect that the commodities in question will not be reexported to a non-COCOM country without all required approvals. Many general licenses require the exporter to insert specific language on airbills and other shipping documents.

In addition, the EAR impose a series of other requirements to all general licenses, most of which are intended to ensure that the item will not be diverted to a controlled destination. For example, the exporter must check the EAR listing to ensure that the consignee is not subject to a "denial order" revoking its right to participate in U.S. export transactions. The exporter must also have no reason to believe that the shipment will be diverted to or shipped through a proscribed country.

Classification Requests. Because the entire export control process depends on the public's ability to classify technical data and commodities correctly, the Commerce Department has established procedures for assisting the public. The department invites exporters to submit formal classifications requests to:

Bureau of Export Administration
U.S. Department of Commerce
P.O. Box 273
14th Street & Pennsylvania Ave, N.W.
Washington, D.C. 20044

ATTN: Commodity Classification Requests

The request should include a description of the item, a copy of the marketing materials used to promote sales, and the exporter's analysis of how the item should be classified under the EAR. The department often responds to such requests within two weeks.

The Commerce Department's Office of Exporter Services also provides telephone assistance from offices in Washington, D.C. (202-377-4811), California (714-660-0144), and New Hampshire (603-598-4300). As with most government agencies, the department does not excuse violations that result when the public relies on its staff's oral advice, so questions of interpretation should generally be confirmed in a written classification request. The Exporter Services staff, though, can be extremely helpful in identifying relevant sections of the regulations or directing the exporter to other sources of information.

Applying for a Validated License

If the transaction in question requires a validated license, the exporter must complete and file an application in accordance with the instructions in the regulations. Because the process is complicated, most exporters seek help from the Commerce Department or an experienced professional for the first application with respect to a given item. Most also find that subsequent applications for the same item can be handled with relative ease.

Reexports

The Commerce Department takes the position that U.S.-origin goods and technology remain within the jurisdiction of the United States indefinitely. Therefore, the department purports to limit the ability of foreign consignees to reexport U.S.-origin items to a proscribed destination. The practical impact of this policy tends to be relatively small, because the Commerce Department relies on its COCOM allies to control reexports from within their borders, and EAR impose no restriction on shipments that could have gone directly from the United States under general license. The U.S. reexport controls nevertheless apply to enough transactions to warrant the attention of all of the parties involved.

Recordkeeping

If complying with the EAR is necessary, being able to document compliance is just as important. The EAR require exporters to maintain most EAR-related records for two years, with three- and five-year requirements applicable to certain types of documents. Exporters are well advised to keep their records beyond the required time, because Commerce can bring an enforcement action at any time within five years of a violation.

Further Information

The EAR change often enough that the exporter must regularly consult at least two sources. The first is the Export Administration Bulletin, a loose-leaf set of the regulations published by the Commerce Department through the U.S. Government Printing Office.

Each Bulletin subscriber receives a new set of regulations toward the end of the calendar year and quarterly updates over the following 12 months. These are useful because they track all of the changes to the EAR and incorporates them into the existing body of regulations.

The primary problem with this system is that the quarterly updates may arrive several months after the changes occur. Accordingly, most exporters subscribe to the Federal Register, which publishes changes as they occur.

International Traffic in Arms Regulations

Just as the Commerce Department's EAR govern exports of commercial items, the State Department's International Traffic in Arms Regulations (ITAR) control shipments of military hardware and various other equipment and technology deemed particularly useful in a military context. The ITAR "Munitions List" includes the full range of weaponry from machine guns to fighter airplanes.

It also includes at least two types of items having important commercial uses. First, the ITAR govern all exports of satellites and satellite earth stations. Thus, the State Department rather than the Commerce Department determines whether satellites designed or built in the United States may be launched into orbit by a European, Chinese, or Soviet rocket, and whether their signals can be received by U.S.-origin equipment. In addition, the ITAR control exports of certain encryption hardware and software, including a broad range of systems designed entirely for banking and financial uses.

Commodity Jurisdiction Letters
Whether an item is governed by the EAR or the ITAR can be a matter of great concern, because the ITAR are substantially less flexible. Where the EAR grant general licenses for broad categories of transactions, the ITAR require a license application for all Munitions List exports to any destination. Where the EAR may grant Distribution Licenses permitting shipments from the United States to a large number of customers in a given region, the ITAR require the license application to identify the foreign consignee that will receive the shipment, even if that consignee is merely receiving the shipment for resale to companies within the region. Where the

Commerce Department routinely grants individual validated licenses in a matter of weeks, the State Department may require months to review an application.

These differences occasionally lead exporters to propose that the State Department relinquish jurisdiction over their products to the Commerce Department. The proposal generally takes the form of a "commodity jurisdiction" request to the State Department arguing why the item in question falls or should fall within the purview of Commerce.

ITAR Requirements

The ITAR, if they apply to a given transaction, are substantially less difficult to interpret than the EAR. At the outset, the Munitions List controls exports according to the type of item involved without regard to its sophistication. Thus, the entry for cryptographic equipment theoretically applies equally to all encryption equipment ranging from the most sophisticated device to the least.

The ITAR are also much more stable than the EAR. The fact that the Munitions List takes no account of the sophistication of the weapon in question means that the State Department is not required to adjust the list constantly to reflect technological advances.

The ITAR procedures, as noted, are substantially more burdensome than those imposed by the EAR. At the outset, virtually any export of any item on the Munitions List requires the exporter to apply for specific State Department approval. In order to gain approval, the parties to the export transaction must include in their contract specific language set forth in the ITAR. The required language makes clear that the U.S. government retains the right to disapprove the transaction, and imposes certain duties on the parties.

Further Information. The ITAR appear at 22 C.F.R. Part 123-128. The Munitions List is also reprinted (without the applicable licensing procedures) in a supplement to EAR Part 770.

Industry-Specific Export Controls

In addition to the relatively expansive export controls imposed by the Commerce and State Departments, many other government agencies control international shipments of specific types of goods.

These latter controls are usually part of a broader regulatory scheme affecting the goods in question. The following examples demonstrate the variety of these controls:

Nuclear Materials and Technology
The Department of Energy closely controls exports of all goods and technologies intended for use in nuclear facilities under 10 C.F.R. Part 110. In one case, unresolved at this writing, the Energy Department decreed that Soviet nuclear equipment imported into the United States for demonstration purposes could not leave without an export license. The Energy Department further decreed that U.S. policy precludes licensing nuclear exports for the Soviet Union and, accordingly, the equipment would not be permitted to leave the country.

Narcotics and Dangerous Drugs
The Drug Enforcement Administration, an agency of the Department of Justice, controls exports of controlled substances. The applicable regulations appear at 21 C.F.R. Part 1312.

Natural Gas and Electric Energy
The U.S. Department of Energy controls exports of natural gas and electric power from the United States, as well as the construction, operation, maintenance, and connection at the United States side of the border of facilities for such exports.

Agricultural Products
The Agriculture Department controls exports of agricultural products ranging from grapes to tobacco seeds and live tobacco plants. The reasons for the controls vary, although most by their terms attempt to protect the quality of products shipped to foreign markets.

Endangered Fish and Wildlife
The U.S. Fish and Wildlife Service, an agency of the Department of Interior, governs exports of endangered species of fish and animals.

Foreign Asset Control Regulations

While not generally considered export controls in the traditional sense, trade embargoes are in fact among the bluntest instruments in the U.S. government's export control arsenal. Announced by the president through executive order published in the Federal Register, they are implemented by the Treasury Department's Office of Foreign Asset Control (OFAC) as Foreign Asset Control Regulations.

The president generally orders an embargo to demonstrate the nation's outrage over a particularly egregious act or omission committed by a foreign government. North Korea, Cambodia, Vietnam, and Cuba are the oldest of OFAC's current targets, all as a result of hot or cold wars fought against the United States. OFAC has more recently targeted Iran and Libya as a result of their terrorist activities, South Africa for its apartheid policies, and Iraq for its invasion of Kuwait. Various other countries—Panama, Nicaragua, Rhodesia, and most recently the government of Kuwait—were at one time subject to embargoes that have since been lifted to reflect a change in government.

The scope of OFAC's embargoes can differ widely from country to country. The South African sanctions, for example, reflect the policies set forth in the Anti-Apartheid Act of 1986. Those sanctions attempt to limit U.S. investment in most white-owned South African commercial activities and preclude U.S. imports of key South African commodities, including gold, agricultural products, iron and steel, uranium, coal, and textiles. The Iranian sanctions do not prohibit U.S. companies from exporting goods or services to Iran, but have eliminated all imports. The Iranian sanctions also include provisions implementing the procedures created in 1981 for resolving and paying claims arising from the Iranian revolution.

Several general comments are nevertheless in order. First, most U.S. embargoes have received only passing support from other countries. Few industrialized countries other than the United States view trade as a foreign policy weapon. Even those supporting U.S. goals may view an American embargo as an opportunity to expand their own sales to the target country. Second, recent embargoes have tended to be emotional rather than practical reactions to world events. The president, as noted, generally imposes an embargo to signal U.S. outrage over a particular event such as the Soviet invasion of Afghanistan or the Iranian government's refusal to help resolve the hostage crisis. Until the source of this outrage is eliminated, the president and his successors have generally found it politically difficult to remove the embargo, even in the face of clear evidence that the United States is being hurt worse than the target.

Third, all of the embargoes in force at this writing, in deference to the First Amendment's free speech protections, permit free trade in periodicals, books, films and recordings, and other so-called informational materials, which can be imported and exported without restriction. This exception, though, has its limits: U.S. companies are effectively prevented from investing in the creation of such informational materials in the embargoed country.

MINIMIZING THE BURDEN

Most companies faced with export control issues find it useful, or even necessary, to establish a formal compliance program. Properly constructed, the program ensures that the exporter complies fully with all of the applicable requirements at the minimum cost. The scope of the program will clearly depend on the type of issues the exporter faces. Companies that make occasional exports of garden tools, for example, may simply retain an attorney or consultant to review each transaction for compliance with OFAC embargoes and Commerce Department paperwork rules. Mainframe computer vendors, by contrast, may require a large, well-trained staff to deal with the issues that inevitably arise.

Central to any compliance program is the export compliance officer, or office (ECO). The most effective ECOs have the clear support of management and operate *outside of the sales department* and free of undue pressure to move merchandise at all costs. They also have sufficient resources to educate their colleagues from the sales and shipping departments about the company's export control responsibilities and the lead times required to meet those responsibilities.

The ECO's first mission is to classify all of the goods and technology that the company intends to export, and to obtain any necessary classification rulings. Thereafter, it is the ECO's responsibility to review each export transaction under consideration by the company to (1) confirm that the transaction includes no additional information, technology, or goods that raise new export control questions, or to deal with any additional issues that might be raised by the shipment; (2) confirm that the transaction involves no individual or company specified on the Commerce Department's Table of Denial Orders; (3) apply for any license that may be required to complete the transaction; (4) advise the sales and shipping departments on the progress of the licensing process; and (5) maintain records of the steps taken to comply with the company's export control obligations. The ECO, moreover, may help the exporter cope with embargo-related issues.

The ECO also takes responsibility for preparing and filing the necessary shipping documents. These documents likely include a "Shippers Export Declaration," a form that permits the Commerce Department both to track compliance with its export controls and to estimate the level at which U.S. companies are exporting various types of goods and services. Finally, the ECO tracks all changes in the export control requirements. The EAR in particular are subject to containing revisions and adjustment, often to the exporter's benefit. Few of the changes, though, receive wide publicity. It is accordingly incumbent on every exporter to monitor the Federal Register for new developments.

A FINAL WORD

Even as this book went to press, the Commerce Department was proving the importance of keeping abreast of changes in the export control system. Although most of the principles discussed in this chapter remain intact, Commerce has begun what inevitably will become a total overhaul of its substantive controls. The Department has already published a completely new (and completely renumbered) "Commerce Control List" based largely on agreements reached by COCOM and reflecting the disintegration of the Soviet Bloc. Commerce has also imposed new foreign policy controls intended to impede attempts by various Middle Eastern countries to develop chemical, biological and nuclear weapons, and reduced other controls to reflect changes in South Africa and Cambodia.

These new developments, and each new development occurring in the future, requires every U.S. exporter to reevaluate both the level of control imposed on a given type of export transaction and the effectiveness of its export control compliance program.

CHAPTER 14

ENVIRONMENTAL LAW IN THE UNITED STATES

Carol Dudnick, Esq.
Union Carbide Chemicals and Plastics Company, Inc.

INTRODUCTION

The practice of environmental law in the United States today is a growth industry. The new era of federal environmental law was ushered in during the Nixon Administration with the enactment on January 1, 1970, of the National Environmental Policy Act.[1] In the past five years, significant changes in both direction and scope of major U.S. environmental laws have been made.[2]

This renewed and revitalized interest in environmental issues is not confined to the United States, as evidenced by the increased strength and visibility of the Green Party in Europe, the 1987 Montreal Protocol calling for phasing out the production and use of chlorofluorocarbons (CFCs)[3] and ongoing international negotiations intended to result in treaties to address acid rain, global warming, and the export of hazardous waste. There is growing awareness of the impact that a healthy environment has on the economic well-being of countries. Indeed, appalling environmental conditions in Eastern Europe are considered to be one of the major factors limiting foreign investment in those countries and serve as a reminder that all environmental media (the land we inhabit, the air we breathe, the water we drink) are resources that must be managed and conserved wisely. The process for making these decisions and the decisions themselves (in terms of timing, scope, detail, and stringency) vary considerably among countries.

While environmental issues are of an increasingly global nature and there are greater similarities today among the standards in different countries, environmental law in the United States is unique or at least a bellwether in two main respects. First, while other countries may have stringent environmental statutes, in the United States significant civil and criminal penalties (including jail terms) are *commonly* assessed and penalties have been steadily increasing in size.[4] In this regard, most major federal environmental statutes authorize citizens—in addition to the Department of Justice, U.S. attorneys' offices, and the U.S. Environmental Protection Agency (U.S. EPA)—to file civil lawsuits against individuals and companies for failure to comply with environmental laws. Second, U.S. statutes impose retroactive, strict, joint, and several liability against persons responsible for the release of hazardous substances to the environment. Such persons—including those who arranged for treatment or disposal of hazardous substances, transporters, and owners and operators of the sites at which such substances are located—are liable for costs of investigation, clean-up, government oversight, and damages to natural resources. Courts have held plant managers,[5] corporate officers,[6] shareholders,[7] parent corporations,[8] successor corporations,[9] passive lessors,[10] and lending institutions[11] to be among the liable parties. For sites on the U.S. EPA priority list, clean-up costs currently average $25,000,000.[12]

This chapter provides a brief overview of the environmental regulatory system in the United States, principal federal environmental statutes, and some state environmental initiatives (in particular, statutes providing for disclosure and clean-up as a precondition to the transfer of a property interest). Given the enormous potential financial exposure, not to mention intangibles such as goodwill and good public relations associated with environmental issues, this chapter concludes with the author's view of the steps one should take in making an informed decision on the potential environmental risks associated with a business transaction and the allocation of those risks in the agreement between the parties.

THE ENVIRONMENTAL REGULATORY SYSTEM
IN THE UNITED STATES OF AMERICA

Federal

In the United States, after the legislative branch enacts laws, it is up to the executive branch to execute them and put the meat on the proverbial bones.[13] This task falls in large measure to the U.S. EPA, the agency created by executive order in 1970 with primary jurisdiction for development of regulations and policies necessary to implement and enforce numerous environmental statutes.[14] The Clean Air Act;[15] Clean Water Act;[16] Resource Conservation and Recovery Act;[17] Safe Drinking Water Act;[18] Comprehensive Environmental Response, Compensation and Liability Act (commonly known as Superfund);[19] Toxic Substances Control Act;[20] Federal Insecticide, Fungicide and Rodenticide Act;[21] and Emergency Planning and Community Right-to-Know Act[22] are the major statutes administered by the U.S. EPA. The agency also provides environmental expertise to other federal agencies, including input on environmental consequences of major federal actions that U.S. agencies intend to carry out.[23] The President exerts control over the U.S. EPA through the appointment of its administrator and other high-level officials with the advice and consent of the Senate, through the President's White House staff and through the Office of Management and Budget. The U.S. EPA has grown from an agency of approximately 5,500 employees in 1970, with a budget of $1.289 billion, to one with 17,170 employees in 1990 (the great majority of whom are federal employees *not* subject to presidential appointment), with a budget of $5.145 billion.[24] Congress exerts control over the U.S. EPA through various committees and staff offices that oversee existing legislation and initiate new legislation. Environmental groups and industry trade associations make their interests known through lobbying efforts, commenting on regulations proposed by the U.S. EPA, petitioning the U.S. EPA for rule-making, and in some cases, participating on regulatory negotiation committees intended to make enactment of regulations a faster, less litigious process. While most environmental statutes provide the U.S. EPA with civil enforcement authority, all criminal cases and civil cases involving significant penalties are handled by the Department of Justice and the 97 U.S. attorneys' offices throughout the country.

The rule-making process at the U.S. EPA is open to public comment. The agency's proposals are published in the *Federal Register,* a publication printed each workday and available in many libraries. There are preambles that describe at length the rationale for the proposed regulations, the agency's interpretation of those regulations, and anticipated compliance costs. There is generally a minimum period of 30 days for the public to submit comments. During that time public hearings may be held on major regulatory initiatives. After review and consideration of those comments, the U.S. EPA promulgates final regulations. The regulations as well as discussions of major changes from the proposal and the U.S. EPA's response to comments are published in the *Federal Register.*[25] An opportunity for judicial review is then provided. As a general rule, the agency's regulations may be overturned if they are arbitrary, capricious, an abuse of discretion, or otherwise not in accordance with law.[26] However, it is increasingly rare that courts overturn U.S. EPA rules because of the tremendous deference given to the agency's interpretation of law.[27] It is thus critical to provide comments to the agency *before* rules are finalized. For most major regulations, the U.S. EPA also publishes background and other guidance documents that support and interpret the rules.

The U.S. EPA's headquarters are in Washington, D.C., and it is here that the major policy decisions and rules that are federal in scope are decided. The U.S. EPA also has several technical support centers and 10 regional offices. Each regional office, headed by a regional administrator appointed by the President, has jurisdiction over several states (and territories). While the regional offices must implement the policy decisions made in Washington, D.C., they are also fairly autonomous. In general, it is the regional offices that issue permits to companies, initiate enforcement actions, and work with states within their region to assure that federal environmental laws and regulations are being properly implemented.

Thus, in any due diligence review that a prospective buyer undertakes, obtaining information from U.S. EPA regional offices should be considered. Significant amounts of information, including permits, permit applications, toxic emissions inventories, and monitoring and compliance reports, can be obtained by filing requests for information under the Freedom of Information Act (FOIA).[28] The U.S. EPA has regulations on the procedures to follow in making a FOIA request.[29]

States

In the 1970s, when the U.S. EPA was first created, the general assumption (certainly of legislators in Washington, D.C.) was that states and local governments did not, or could not, address environmental issues with the vigor and uniformity that the federal government could. There was concern that without minimum federal standards too much "forum shopping" would occur. Thus, most federal environmental statutes, particularly those requiring individual plants to obtain permits in order to emit pollutants to the air, water, or land, require the U.S. EPA to promulgate regulations establishing minimum standards,[30] which states in turn must adopt. If states fail to adopt such standards as well as other requirements—such as minimum enforcement authority, procedures for obtaining permits, provision for public disclosure of emissions and other data, and adequate program staffing—they do not obtain authority to implement the federal statutes and the U.S. EPA will do so. Since states generally want to be primarily responsible for the programs affecting their constituents, the tendency has been for most states to seek federal approval or delegation of their programs. For companies, this is beneficial; otherwise, both federal and state permits covering the same discharges would be required—and this is, in fact, the case in some states.

The process for enactment of legislation and promulgation of regulations at the state and local level and the opportunity for lobbying and commenting are similar to those described above with respect to federal legislation. However, enforcement at the state and local level varies widely in number of actions and severity of penalties. While the U.S. Department of Justice and the U.S. EPA have enforcement policies that provide some uniform guidance on the types of violations considered to be significant, as well as the appropriate penalties, this may not be the case within each state and local political subdivision. Given the rather broad scope of most statutory enforcement provisions, there is growing concern within the regulated community that violations that the federal government perceives to be civil in nature may be deemed criminal by local district attorneys' offices and state attorney generals' offices.

Knowing a state's environmental enforcement record and approach is useful for those intending to do business within a jurisdiction.[31] Likewise, identification of "grassroots" environmental organizations is useful since such organizations may play a major role in permitting actions important to a business. Of course, any due diligence effort should entail a review of information in the files of state and local environmental agencies.

In recent years many major environmental initiatives have occurred at the state level. Examples include statutes calling for reduced use of toxic substances, requiring disclosure of environmental conditions in advance of a property transfer (by deed or lease) or upon termination of a leasehold interest, and, as in the case of the New Jersey Environmental Cleanup and Responsibility Act,[32] clean-up or a commitment to clean-up as a precondition to the sale or closure of industrial establishments in the state. Depending on the type of business transaction a buyer or lender is contemplating, knowledge of such laws and trends is critical.

PRINCIPAL FEDERAL ENVIRONMENTAL STATUTES

Obviously, this chapter is not intended to be a treatise on environmental laws and regulations in the United States. However, it is important for owners, executives, and directors of foreign businesses considering doing business in America to understand the basic elements of many of these laws in order to better assess the advantages and disadvantages of a particular business transaction, the form of the transaction (stock or asset sale agreement, licensing agreement, joint venture, etc.), and the offering price. An adequate assessment of environmental issues is often a critical consideration in determining whether to go forward, and if so, in negotiating the allocation of existing and potential environmental costs and liabilities.[33] This assessment includes information on the current compliance status of the business one is considering buying or investing in (and the costs of achieving compliance, if necessary); the current and future personnel, capital, operational, and maintenance costs needed to maintain compliance with environmental statutes and regulations; the ability to expand existing operations or locate new facilities; and the costs associated with site remediation. The latter may include sites formerly or currently owned or operated by the business or by third parties that treated or disposed of the business's hazardous substances. The following brief descriptions of some major federal environmental statutes focus on those provisions of which a purchaser or investor should be cognizant in order to meet these assessment needs.

The Clean Air Act

This statute was substantially amended in 1990 after years of debate focusing principally on acid rain provisions; measures to be implemented by mobile and stationary sources in order to attain national ambient air quality standards (NAAQS), in particular, health-based standards for ozone and carbon monoxide; and controls on day-to-day emissions of hazardous air pollutants. As the debate progressed, new provisions to address CFCs and other stratospheric ozone-depleting chemicals, episodic releases of hazardous air pollutants, operating permits, and enhanced enforcement provisions were also added.

Under the Clean Air Act, the U.S. EPA has established health-based and welfare-based NAAQS for six so-called criteria pollutants: particulate matter, sulfur dioxide, nitrogen oxides, carbon monoxide, ozone, and lead. Areas of the country are classified on the basis of their air quality, as attainment, non-attainment, or unclassifiable for each criterion pollutant. For ozone and carbon monoxide, non-attainment areas are further subdivided into categories based on the degree of non-attainment. Most major urban areas of the United States are classified as non-attainment for ozone (more commonly known as "urban smog"). States and, in some circumstances, local governments submit, for U.S. EPA approval, plans to achieve and maintain the national standards within time frames established by the statute. While the stringency of these plans depends on the air quality of the area covered by a plan, the U.S. EPA establishes minimum requirements that each state or local plan must meet. For example, states seeking EPA approval of their programs for new source review must require businesses that plan to construct new facilities or expand existing ones to meet complex and stringent requirements established by the U.S. EPA as a precondition to project approval. These requirements depend on the amount and type of emissions from the existing facility and the emissions expected from the proposed project. The technology standard to be achieved depends upon the air quality of the area in which the business is located. In non-attainment areas, new construction also depends upon obtaining "offsets"—that is, emission reductions from existing sources in the non-attainment area that equal or exceed the expected increases from the project. Indeed, in the Los Angeles area, a major oil refinery announced a program to purchase older cars lacking catalytic converters in order to obtain approval from the local air pollution control agency for a plant expansion.

In sum, U.S. EPA requirements for state and local plans, the need for U.S. EPA approval of these plans, and U.S. EPA oversight of approved programs all go a long way toward assuring that similar businesses in areas of the country with similar air quality will be subject to fairly uniform treatment.

Consistency with respect to requirements imposed on air pollution sources is also obtained by U.S. EPA's promulgation of certain standards that apply regardless of air quality. These standards have traditionally been "end-of-pipe" requirements, although the 1990 Amendments enhance the agency's authority to establish standards requiring process changes, product reformulation, re-use, and recycling. The U.S. EPA promulgates standards, known as new source performance standards (NSPS), that apply to all emission sources within a designated source category that are newly constructed, reconstructed, or modified. The source categories include such diverse sources of air emissions as petroleum refineries and paper mills as well as residential wood heaters. The standards generally require use of "best demonstrated" technology in the form of a performance, design, equipment, work practice, operational, or work practice standard. Each NSPS also requires notification to the U.S. EPA and/or state or local environmental agency of start-up, emission testing, monitoring results, and noncompliances.

The U.S. EPA also establishes national emission standards to be achieved by sources emitting designated hazardous air pollutants (HAPS). In the past 20 years, the U.S. EPA has promulgated standards covering only seven hazardous air pollutants (arsenic, asbestos, benzene, beryllium, mercury, radionuclides, and vinyl chloride). While most of these National Emission Standards for HAPS apply to manufacturing facilities, some have broader application. For example, the asbestos standard applies to renovation and demolition of commercial property as well. The 1990 Clean Air Act Amendments establish a new and ambitious air toxics program to be phased in within the 90s' that will cover sources of 189 chemicals and compounds. Even small businesses such as dry cleaning establishments are expected to be covered by these regulations.

Under the 1990 Clean Air Act Amendments most major manufacturing and commercial establishments will need to obtain operating permits. Even before enactment of the 1990 Amendments, most states required permits to construct and/or operate that are issued to new plants having air emissions sources or existing plants seeking to make changes that would result in an increase in air emissions. The amendments, however, will require *all* states to have operating permit programs. It is anticipated that by 1995 most plants will have submitted applications for permits to operate. These permits will include monitoring requirements and obligations to pay annual fees, to report achievement of compliance milestones, to report noncompliances, and to provide at least annual certifications of compliance signed by a plant manager or corporate officer. These self-disclosure reports will make it easier for the U.S. EPA, state and local environmental agencies, and members of the general public to assess the compliance status of each permittee.

The Clean Air Act authorizes employees of the U.S. EPA to enter upon the premises of a source or potential source of air emissions in order to assess compliance or for rule-making purposes. The Act has been interpreted in most jurisdictions as authorizing access to government contractors as well.[34] The Act imposes substantial penalties, both civil and criminal, on persons who violate its provisions. The government may also seek injunctive relief, including permanent or temporary cessation of activities. Civil penalties (judicial as well as administrative) may be assessed in amounts up to $25,000 per day per each violation. Knowing violations of virtually every requirement are felonies, and conviction may result in both jail terms and significant criminal penalties. The U.S. EPA takes the position that these penalties may be imposed not just on a business entity but also on the particular employees, including responsible corporate officers, who controlled or could have controlled noncompliant activities. The largest criminal penalties (up to 15 years in jail and $1,000,000 in fines) are reserved for those who knowingly release hazardous air pollutants and who know at the time that they thereby place another person in imminent danger of death or serious bodily injury.

Finally, the Clean Air Act Amendments also establish a new program to prevent and minimize the consequences of accidental releases of extremely hazardous substances. The statute imposes a general duty on owners and operators of stationary sources producing, processing, handling, or storing such substances to identify hazards that may result from releases of such substances and to design and maintain a safe facility, taking necessary steps to prevent releases and to minimize the consequences of accidental releases that do occur. This new program also establishes the independent Chemical Safety and Hazard Investigation Board to investigate accidental releases having serious consequences. The U.S. EPA will also promulgate regulations requiring certain stationary sources to conduct hazard assessments and develop risk management plans.

In sum, the Clean Air Act is a complex statute that, given the recent amendments, will require enactment of many new regulations by both the U.S. EPA and state and local governments. Businesses as well as individuals who drive or buy consumer products will be directly affected.

The Clean Water Act

Under this Act, discharges of any pollutant to waters of the United States are prohibited unless the discharger has a permit. *Waters of the United States* is a term of art which has been broadly defined to impose a permitting obligation on discharges to all waters that are or were used or may be susceptible to use in interstate or foreign commerce as well as those intrastate waters, including wetlands, whose use, degradation, or destruction would or could affect interstate or foreign commerce.[35]

In order to effect this National Pollutant Discharge Elimination System (NPDES) permitting program, the U.S. EPA has established minimum criteria that state programs must meet in order to obtain U.S. EPA approval. Otherwise, the U.S. EPA administers the programs. Some states have programs with greater scope of coverage than that required by federal law. Those provisions (such as New Jersey's requirement for groundwater discharge permits) are not considered part of the federally approved program.[36]

NPDES permits are required by all persons who directly discharge pollutants into waters of the United States through a "point source." Point sources include such conveyances as pipes and ditches as well as landfill leachate collection systems.[37] Thus, a large plant may have a number of point sources, each subject to separate limitations. Those private and public entities that directly discharge pollutants into waters of the United States need to obtain NPDES permits that impose, *inter alia,* limits on flow, discharge limits on specific chemicals or parameters (such as biochemical oxygen demand and total organic compounds), monitoring, and other recording and reporting requirements. The discharge limits are in general the more stringent of technology standards (based on regulations promulgated by the U.S. EPA or, in the absence of such regulations, the best professional judgment of the government permit writer) or water quality standards developed by the state in which the discharge originates. Those businesses that indirectly discharge pollutants into waters of the United States through publicly owned treatment works (POTW) must meet pretreatment requirements and obtain permits or comparable authorization from the POTW specifying discharge limits and other requirements.

As with the Clean Air Act, statutory provisions enacted in the early 1970s' generally imposed end-of-pipe requirements on conventional pollutants and parameters such as total suspended solids and fecal coliform. With each passing amendment, there has been greater emphasis on control of toxic pollutants and, more recently, on pollution prevention.

In November 1990, the U.S. EPA promulgated regulations that will require facilities to submit applications and obtain permits for stormwater discharges associated with industrial activity. This program will apply to facilities now (or in some cases formerly) engaged in a diverse array of industrial activities including petrochemical manufacturing, warehousing, and construction activities. The program will even apply to industrial facilities that discharge to municipal storm sewers.

The one permit program under the Clean Water Act that the U.S. EPA does not directly administer (although its required activities under this program may result in permit denial) is the program requiring permits for the discharge of dredged or fill material into navigable waters. Permits are issued by the Secretary of the Army, acting through the Corps of Engineers. The most controversial issue surrounding this program has been the definition of navigable waters of the United States, which, like the definition of waters of the United States, includes intrastate wetlands and other areas not formerly considered to be "navigable." As the federal government has expanded its jurisdiction, more industrial and commercial activities have been affected by this program.

Finally, the Clean Water Act also requires persons in charge of onshore or offshore facilities to immediately report to the National Response Center or U.S. Coast Guard in the event that certain quantities of oil or hazardous substances (as established by U.S. EPA regulations) are discharged to waters of the United States or the adjoining shoreline. The federal government, in accordance with the National Oil and Hazardous Substances Pollution Contingency Plan[38] will act to remove or mitigate the discharge in the event that the discharger does not do so and will seek reimbursement for such costs, including costs to restore or replace damaged natural resources. This strict liability remedial approach to oil spills in particular was later adopted by Congress to address waste sites. (See discussion of the Comprehensive Environmental Response, Compensation and Liability Act, below.)

In summary, the Clean Water Act requires that those who discharge pollutants into waters of the United States submit permit applications and obtain permits that regulate such discharges. Like the Clean Air Act, no new or different pollutants may be discharged without prior approval of the permitting authority. The inspection and enforcement provisions are similar to those in the Clean Air Act.

The Resource Conservation and Recovery Act

This Act is intended to comprehensively regulate solid waste and its subset, hazardous waste, from cradle to grave. The provisions that most directly affect industrial and commercial enterprises are those addressing hazardous waste and underground storage tanks.

With respect to hazardous waste management, the statute imposes requirements on generators and transporters of hazardous waste, and owners and operators of hazardous waste treatment, storage, and disposal (TSD) facilities. Determining whether one has generated a hazardous waste is the first issue to be resolved and is not an easy task. Some wastes are determined to be hazardous because they meet certain characteristics established by the U.S. EPA; others, because the U.S. EPA has listed them as hazardous. There are procedures for "delisting" a hazardous waste, but, because they are cumbersome and time-consuming, they have not been used with much regularity.

The major obligations on generators of hazardous waste include notification to the U.S. EPA of hazardous waste activity, the use of manifests for off-site shipments (which allows each shipment to be tracked), and the use of only those transporters and TSD facilities that have U.S. EPA identification numbers. Each completed manifest contains a certification that the information provided is accurate and that the generator has a waste minimization program in place. Those who treat, store (generally, for more than 90 days), and dispose of hazardous waste are subject to permitting requirements. Under the Act, existing TSD facilities may obtain interim status, which authorizes them to continue to manage hazardous waste until a final permit decision is made. New plants must obtain permits before commencing hazardous waste management activities. Permitted facilities adding new units for the treatment, storage, or disposal of hazardous waste must obtain permit modifications before such activities may commence.

As with other regulatory programs, the U.S. EPA promulgates minimum permitting requirements, technology and work practice standards, reporting and recordkeeping obligations, and the like, and states are given the opportunity, upon approval by the U.S. EPA, to administer the program. Among the permitting requirements specific to the hazardous waste program are those covering groundwater monitoring, financial assurance, and corrective action. These obligations are intended to ensure that current operations are managed in a manner that minimizes the potential for environmental contamination (in particular, to soil and groundwater) and that action is taken to remediate contamination resulting from prior releases of hazardous waste and constituents from any unit at a plant that does or did manage solid (not just hazardous) waste. The units affected include the typical storage areas and landfills as well as production areas associated with significant spills. Even sewer lines may be included. The financial obligations are intended to assure that the government, and hence, the general public, will not be required to finance these clean-ups under such statutes as the Comprehensive Environmental Response, Compensation and Liability Act (CERCLA), described below. The corrective action program is currently estimated to cost from $10 billion to $60 billion. Indeed, costs may dwarf those associated with CERCLA clean-ups. This remedial program will apply to all plants with TSD permits or interim status. Indeed, some believe it should apply to all facilities at which hazardous waste is generated.

Amendments enacted in 1984 added requirements designed to make the land disposal of hazardous waste the least preferable disposal method. These requirements include restrictions on land disposal of hazardous wastes unless the waste is first "pre treated" to meet EPA standards designed to substantially diminish the toxicity of the waste or the likelihood of hazardous constituents migrating from the waste.

The 1984 Amendments also added a new regulatory program to address underground storage tanks containing petroleum products or hazardous substances. This program establishes technology standards, testing, reporting, financial responsibility, and corrective action requirements with which current and, under certain circumstances, former tank owners and operators must comply.

In summary, the Resource Conservation and Recovery Act establishes a statutory program to follow hazardous waste from its generation until its ultimate disposal through permitting, standard-setting, and manifest requirements, with inspection and enforcement provisions similar to those in the other laws described above. While originally prospective in its approach to waste management, the statute now authorizes a major remedial program to be undertaken by those TSD facilities that seek permits. This remedial corrective action program is intended to assure that those who manage hazardous wastes today remain responsible for cleaning up contamination caused by their current and past activities as well as the past activities of former owners and operators.

As restrictions on ongoing hazardous waste activities become more costly and onerous, the statute is having its intended effect: forcing those subject to its requirements to consider pollution-prevention alternatives to waste generation such as "at-source" reduction, recycling, and product and process reformulation. However, there is concern within the regulated community that the complex regulatory provisions that apply to waste disposal activities will apply to some of these alternative approaches as well (recycling, in particular), thus discouraging their use.

The Comprehensive Environmental Response, Compensation and Liability Act (CERCLA)

Originally enacted in 1980, CERCLA establishes a comprehensive program for the clean-up of sites that release or have the potential to release hazardous substances into the environment. The U.S. EPA has established, through regulations and guidance documents, the methodology for determining which sites to include on a national priority list for clean-ups, obtaining information on these sites from potentially responsible parties, conducting investigations and risk assessments, and choosing a remedial alternative that best protects human health and the environment at a given site. Treatment is the preferred remedial alternative, as opposed to containment of waste or administrative techniques such as deed restrictions. Remedy selections are subject to public comment, as are settlements with responsible parties. Settlements generally contain "reopeners" requiring the settlors to remain liable for additional work in the event the remedy fails or other threats to human health or the environment are later discovered. Those living near sites may obtain technical assistance grants to enable them to better assess the proposed clean-up plan.

As indicated above, clean-up costs are enormous. While the average clean-up may cost about $25 million,[39] there are several sites at which costs may exceed $100 million and others, including federally owned sites, at which clean-up costs may ultimately be in the billions of dollars.[40]

To pay for these clean-ups, CERCLA provides for a Hazardous Substances Superfund financed primarily through taxes on crude oil and chemical feedstocks, a broad-based surtax on corporations, and appropriated general revenues. Additionally, CER-

CLA establishes a strict, retroactive, joint, and several liability scheme pursuant to which liable parties reimburse the Superfund for expended monies or are "encouraged," generally through administrative or judicial proceedings, to pay for clean-ups before and without massive depletion of the Superfund.

CERCLA has spawned a significant amount of litigation, much of which has focused on issues of liability. Given the remedial nature of the statute, the U.S. EPA and the courts have generally taken a broad view as to which companies and individuals are among the four classes of potentially responsible parties, or PRPs (those who arranged for treatment or disposal, transporters who selected the treatment or disposal site, current owners and operators, and owners and operators of the property at the time of disposal) and a narrow view of who is covered by statutory exemptions to liability (the innocent landowner and security interest exemption being the two primary ones).[41]

While litigation certainly occurs among PRPs seeking allocation (in the form of causes of action for indemnification, contribution, and the like), PRPs have also developed alternative dispute mechanisms for allocating liability among themselves. Because of poor information and the problems that arise simply in trying to keep together large groups with divergent interests, most allocations have been based on the relative volume of waste contributed to a site. However, some allocations do take into account equitable factors, such as toxicity and type of transaction (for example, distinguishing between intentional waste disposal at a site and transshipments to an unintended location).

CERCLA contains penalty provisions in addition to the injunctive relief provisions demanded by such a remedial statute. Failure to comply with a clean-up order without a good faith defense may result in treble damages. In addition to clean-up costs, PRPs may also be liable for associated governmental oversight costs and natural resource damages.

While CERCLA does not provide members of the general public with a statutory right to seek damages for personal injuries and property damage alleged to be associated with these hazardous waste sites, principles of common law do provide such redress in appropriate cases. CERCLA's enactment, moreover, has encouraged more of these toxic tort lawsuits to be filed. Also, because of the enormous clean-up and other costs at stake, current property owners have brought actions against previous owners, including direct predecessors in interest from whom they acquired the property, in order to recover all or part of such costs. These cases suggest that the doctrine of caveat emptor will not prevail if environmental conditions are not disclosed in a contract for sale.[42]

Finally, since the Clean Water Act requires immediate reporting to the National Response Center or U.S. Coast Guard of certain releases of hazardous substances only into waters of the United States, CERCLA has expanded upon this concept by requiring reports in the event of releases to *any* environmental media. These notification requirements were further expanded in 1986 with enactment of the Emergency Planning and Community Right-To-Know Act.

Emergency Planning and Community Right-To-Know Act (EPCRA)

New disclosure regulations designed to provide more information to employees about the chemicals to which they are exposed in the workplace, growing fear among the general public of exposure to "cancer-causing chemicals," ever-increasing public involvement in environmental decision-making, and concerns regarding the ability of governmental agencies to respond promptly and soundly in the event of emergencies were all factors that led to the adoption of EPCRA.

As noted above, this statute expands upon the immediate release reporting requirements in the Clean Water Act and CERCLA by requiring oral and written follow-up reports to local and state emergency planning entities as well as to the federal government, and by subjecting additional chemicals to this reporting obligation. Emergency notification is just one of the Act's provisions designed to address emergency planning. Others require states to establish local emergency planning committees to prepare comprehensive emergency response plans for review by the state emergency response commission. The owner or operator of any facility required to prepare or have available material safety data sheets for hazardous chemicals under the Occupational Safety and Health Act[43] is required to provide information on those chemicals to the state and local emergency planning groups as well as the local fire department and, if necessary, health care providers.

In addition to emergency planning requirements, EPCRA imposes a new disclosure obligation on industrial and commercial facilities handling certain toxic chemicals. Each July, these businesses must provide to the U.S. EPA and state a Toxic Chemical Release Inventory Form showing the amounts of such chemicals released into the environment during the previous calendar year. The compilation and disclosure of this information have led many companies to develop internal programs to reduce the amount of these chemicals being released and to communicate with the communities surrounding their plants on what they do and what these reports mean, and has led the current U.S. EPA Administrator, William K. Reilly, to institute an Industrial Toxics Project, a voluntary, multimedia emission reduction program that is part of the U.S. EPA Pollution Prevention Strategy announced in January 1991.

The federal laws summarized above are among the major environmental statutes affecting businesses in the United States. Federal environmental statutes and regulations and the complementary state and local statutes, ordinances, and regulations are interrelated and extremely complex. However, they constitute a four-pronged approach to pollution control:

1. Reducing pollution by requiring compliance with technology standards and/or health and welfare-based limitations.
2. Remediating contamination caused by prior activities regardless of its lawfulness at the time of occurrence.
3. Preventing pollution through the use of a multimedia and enhanced public disclosure approach.
4. Making the polluter pay, through fees required to obtain and maintain permits and especially through a strong enforcement program that places greater emphasis on criminal enforcement and enforcement against those officers, directors, and managers of business entities (regardless of their form) who actively participated in or who controlled or could have controlled the noncompliant activities.

STATE ENVIRONMENTAL INITIATIVES

In addition to the state environmental laws that are modeled after (and, in some cases, were models for[44]) the federal laws summarized above, there are additional state initiatives of which a person interested in doing business in the United States should be aware. These range from laws that prevent or impose restrictions on the use or storage of certain chemicals,[45] laws authorizing liens on property to cover clean-up expenses incurred by the state,[46] laws requiring disclosure of environmental conditions prior to property transfers,[47] and, in New Jersey[48] and Connecticut,[49] laws requiring clean-up or a legally binding commitment to clean up as a condition precedent to property transfer.

In order to provide the reader with a basic understanding of what some of these laws entail, and, concomitantly, some understanding of the issues that may need to be addressed in any transaction in which there are environmental concerns, two of the more demanding of these state laws are described briefly below.

The Indiana Responsible Property Transfer Law

This law,[50] enacted in 1989, requires transferors of real property on which hazardous substances or petroleum products may be located to deliver a disclosure document 30 days prior to the "transfer" to the transferee and lender. The transfers covered by this law include not only conveyances of fee title, but also long-term leases, leases with options to purchase, and mortgages. The form of the disclosure document and the information it must contain are specified in the statute.[51]

The environmental disclosure document advises the transferee of his or her potential liability for environmental clean-up costs and the fact that action other than merely reading the disclosure document will be necessary to meet the "innocent purchaser" provision to avoid CERCLA liability. The document provides information on activities related to management of hazardous substances or wastes and petroleum products as well as information relating to the transferor's compliance with environmental laws.

If a certified disclosure document reveals an "environmental defect" previously unknown to the transferee or lender, the transferee may decide not to accept the property and the lender may decide not to finance the transaction—and the seller will have no legal recourse. An environmental defect is defined as a material violation of an environmental law, a condition requiring remedial action, a condition that would have a material adverse effect on the market value of that property or adjoining property, or a condition that would materially interfere with another party's ability to obtain environmental permits necessary for operations on the property.

After the transfer, the disclosure document must be filed with the Indiana Department of Environmental Management and recorded in the appropriate county office. Should a transfer take place without the transferor having provided the disclosure document, the transferee and lender do not have the right to void the sale under this statute. However, the state may initiate enforcement action against the transferor seeking penalties or a compliance order.

In sum, this state law should encourage a transferor to disclose environmental conditions and material noncompliances in a timely fashion or face severe consequences. One might argue that in today's environmentally conscious times any prudent business person would do so anyhow so that the parties explicitly address the allocation of environmental liabilities in their agreement. Nonetheless, the Indiana Responsible Property Transfer Law goes one step further: By requiring the filing of a disclosure statement with the state environmental agency, the statute alerts that agency to environmental conditions on the property. This sets the stage for potential state action requiring site remediation under the authority of other statutes. It should be noted that Indiana made a conscious decision to not follow the New Jersey approach, discussed below, which essentially mandates state approval of clean-ups under a new law before property transfers may take place and has resulted in the formation of a new bureaucracy (albeit in the existing state environmental agency) to handle the caseload.

The New Jersey Environmental Cleanup Responsibility Act (ECRA)

While the Indiana Responsible Property Transfer Act emphasizes disclosure, ECRA emphasizes state-supervised clean-ups. ECRA[52], enacted in 1983, imposes, as a precondition to the closure, sale, or transfer of certain industrial or commercial property, one of three alternatives: a clean-up plan approved by the New Jersey Department of Environmental Protection and Energy (NJDEPE), a negative declaration approved by the NJDEP essentially stating that no clean-up or further clean-up is necessary, or the execution by the transferor of an administrative consent order with the NJDEPE in which the transferor agrees to comply with ECRA requirements in accordance with a schedule contained in the order. Violation of ECRA by the transferor gives the transferee the right to void the sale and seek damages from the transferor, and renders the transferor strictly liable for clean-up. Failure to submit a clean-up plan or negative declaration to the NJDEPE may also result in NJDEPE voiding the sale as well as other enforcement action.

As with some other environmental statutes, ECRA applicability is not always clear. For example, corporate reorganizations not substantially affecting ownership are exempt from ECRA. Regulations define this exemption in part as the restructuring or reincorporation by the board of directors or shareholders of a corporation that does not diminish the availability of assets for clean-up or diminish NJDEPE's ability to reach the assets. What this means is unclear. Fortunately, NJDEPE does issue applicability determinations on a case-by-case basis to resolve questions of interpretation.

Under ECRA, owners or operators of certain industrial establishments must notify the NJDEPE, by submitting a General Information Submission within five days of a triggering event specified in the regulations. Termination of a lease and the execution of an agreement conveying the sale of the controlling share of assets of an industrial establishment are examples of triggering events. Within 45 days from the triggering event, a Site Evaluation Submission, including a sampling plan, must be submitted for NJDEPE approval. Following these initial notice requirements (and assuming a negative declaration is not an option), a clean-up plan must be submitted for agency approval and then implemented. Financial assurance is required (e.g., surety bond, letters of credit, and self-bonding) in an amount at least equal to the clean-up cost estimate in the approved plan. While the onus of compliance with ECRA is initially on the transferor, the transferee may provide financial assurance and implement the clean-up plan subject to NJDEPE approval.

Because the ECRA deadlines do not necessarily comport with the timing required by most business transactions, the transferor may enter into an administrative consent order so that a transaction may be consumated prior to obtaining NJDEPE approval of a clean-up plan.

New Jersey has more sites than any other state on the U.S. EPA's CERCLA National Priority List, and ECRA was intended to assure that that number does not get much higher. Compliance with this law varies from several months to several years depending on the severity of the contamination that is discovered. In principle, ECRA represents an intelligent, transaction-based approach to solving and paying for contamination problems by striking at an opportune time: when parties are negotiating a business transaction and are addressing the disclosure and allocation of many potential risks. ECRA has been a major impetus to enactment of disclosure and clean-up laws in other states. While the statute places the onus of compliance on the seller, under the theory that the seller should pay for the problems it caused, the parties are free to allocate clean-up costs between themselves as they see fit.

MAKING AN INFORMED DECISION AND ALLOCATING ENVIRONMENTAL RISKS

The overlay of increasingly complex and numerous state and federal environmental statutes; the fact that federal and state environmental agencies or, indeed, different state agencies may issue permits regulating the same activities; the huge expenditures required for remedial activities; the ever-increasing specter of more sizable recoveries in toxic tort cases arising from releases of pollutants; the strict liability standard by which compliance with environmental laws is generally judged; and the increased emphasis on criminal enforcement have all combined to make appropriate inquiry into compliance with environmental laws and past and current uses of property and business activities a necessity in any business transaction.

While the standard for judging the adequacy of such a due diligence inquiry is higher today, such inquiry is, of course, dependent on the transaction being contemplated and the degree to which environmental concerns are an issue. For example, the purchaser of a hotel in Manhattan would most likely place greater emphasis on an assessment of indoor air pollution, such as the presence of radon and asbestos insulation, than an assessment of off-site remedial activities. On the other hand, the inquiry by the purchaser of a chemical manufacturing plant, at which the likely presence of contamination is high and the need for permits clear, would be more comprehensive.

This chapter concludes by discussing the evaluation needed to make an informed decision about environmental risks and how to use that knowledge in addressing and allocating these risks in the business transaction.

Making an Informed Decision: Environmental Due Diligence

Needless to say, the complexity of environmental law in the United States has led to a burgeoning business for technical consultants and attorneys who specialize in the area. Seeking the assistance of such experts is important in any business transaction in which environmental issues must be addressed.

Generally, the prospective parties to a transaction will enter into confidentiality agreements pursuant to which access to property is authorized and business records are made available. Given the numerous disclosure statutes, the desire to avoid rescission of any agreement on the basis of fraud, and the expectation that environmental risks will be allocated, most sellers provide the prospective buyer and his or her consultants with significant amounts of information. In some cases, this may even include analysis of soil and installation of groundwater wells to assess groundwater contamination.

As indicated earlier, most federal, state, and local environmental agencies have a wealth of information that is available through public disclosure acts such as the Federal Freedom of Information Act. Useful information on publicly held companies may also be available in reports filed with the U.S. Securities and Exchange Commission. Obtaining information from sources other than the seller provides an opportunity to assess the reliability of the information provided by the seller and serves as useful background information to any acquisition audit that the purchaser conducts as part of its environmental due diligence activities. A history of owners and lessees of the business to be acquired, of activities conducted and chemicals used at property to be acquired, as well as of properties formerly owned or leased by the business should be reviewed as part of this effort.

While it is necessary for the purchaser to obtain such information, it is the evaluation of the information that is critical. The evaluation should assess:

- The status of the seller's compliance with environmental laws, regulations, and permits.
- The ongoing and projected costs of compliance with existing and expected environmental laws, regulations, and permits (generally anything more than a five-year projection is extremely suspect, and even a five-year projection may prove unreliable. Nonetheless, it is strongly advised).
- Any impediments to plant expansions or continued operation (this may vary from construction bans imposed by the state or federal government on new sources of air pollution or bans on new hookups to a publicly owned treatment works to local community opposition).
- The condition of the property to be acquired as well as the condition of adjacent property and the costs of remediation. (If there is no off-site contamination or if such contamination does not or is not likely to reach or emanate from the property to be acquired, these costs will be lower.)
- Off-site locations at which the business's waste has been treated or disposed of, including property formerly owned or leased by the seller, and information on the current conditions of those sites. (Waste, for purposes of such an inquiry, should be broadly defined to encompass sales of off-specification commercial chemical products, secondary materials, and the like. In the case of properties formerly owned or leased by the seller, information on activities conducted and waste management practices on the properties should be evaluated.)

It is generally easier to determine the status and costs of compliance with environmental laws than it is to determine the cost of remediation, particularly the costs of clean-up at off-site locations historically used by the business. Nonetheless, such an evaluation must be made in order for the person contemplating a transaction to decide whether the benefits of the transaction outweigh the risks and whether the transaction can be restructured to reduce those risks.

Allocating the Environmental Risks

While environmental liabilities are often unknown, contingent, unasserted, and difficult to quantify (especially as they pertain to clean-up), addressing environmental risks is, in general, not that different from addressing numerous other matters critical to a business transaction: One negotiates an agreement that contains terms both parties will accept, and one relies on the advice and counsel of competent technical and legal professionals in order to do so. Contract terms that are important to this endeavor include representations and warranties with respect to compliance with law, pending or threatened claims, litigation and administrative proceedings, and other material matters; terms on included and excluded assets and liabilities, on transfer of permits and licenses, on assumption of certain liabilities by the buyer and retention of certain liabilities by the seller; an indemnification provision; and a condition requiring cooperation between the parties after the closing.

While, in a broad sense, the contract terms that address environmental risks are no different from terms used to address other risks, there are differences, albeit differences of degree. In the environmental area, the erosion of the doctrine of caveat emptor; the imposition of direct and derivative liability on officers, directors, and shareholders; disclosure statutes; clean-up statutes such as CERCLA that impose liability on current and former owners and operators; and the ever-increasing and often unknown costs of remediation have all combined to make clear the need for an indemnification provision[53] specific to environmental liabilities pertaining to clean-up. These same considerations suggest the need for a broader disclosure statement on the conditions of the property and on-site and off-site waste management activities than would otherwise be needed to meet a materiality standard, and, in some situations, would suggest the utility of restrictions on the use of property being sold or leased and the exclusion of certain property from the assets being transferred.

Because environmental liabilities pertaining to remediation are so difficult to quantify and because the time needed for a thorough and extensive acquisition audit may be limited, most purchasers will not accept all such environmental risks. Purchasers will generally seek to adjust the purchase price to take such environmental liabilities into account and also seek indemnification for environmental liabilities arising from conditions existing before the closing. Likewise, sellers will seek indemnification for environmental liabilities arising from conditions after the closing. However, when the transaction involves an ongoing business, it may be difficult, if not impossible, to identify the cause and attribute it to the activities of either party. Hence, some form of risk apportionment or allocation that provides an incentive for a cost-effective approach to site remediation should be considered. Often, such allocations include limitations on the time to assert claims and formulas for allocating costs. For example, one party may be responsible for all costs up to a certain amount, then both parties may share costs up to another amount based on an agreed-upon ratio, and, if costs exceed that amount, then one party may pay the rest.

A range of possible alternatives exists for allocating liabilities for clean-up costs. Obviously, the relative bargaining power of the parties to the transaction and their perception of the environmental risks in light of the benefits to be achieved by the transaction as a whole will play a large part in determining how environmental liabilities are allocated. For the person considering doing business in the United States, it is important to understand that environmental issues may be costly and not conducive to quick and simple solutions, and that appropriate attention to the identification, allocation, and management of those environmental risks must be made.

NOTES

1. 42 U.S.C. 4321 *et seq.* This is not to say that no federal environmental legislation existed earlier. Rather, this represents the start of the current approach to environmental issues and the enhanced role of the federal government in what were before seen principally as local issues (e.g., issuing permits authorizing construction of a plant and having a major enforcement role).

2. Since 1986, new laws and major amendments to existing laws have been enacted addressing air, water, and oil pollution; pollution prevention; clean-up of hazardous waste sites; and emergency planning and community right-to-know. These laws exceed 600 pages. Congress is currently considering major changes to the hazardous waste and water pollution laws.
3. Montreal Protocol on Substances that Deplete the Ozone Layer, adopted and opened for signature September 16, 1987 (entered into force January 1, 1989), reprinted in 26 I.L.M. 1541 (1987). To date, 72 countries including the major CFC-producing countries are parties.
4. A comparison based on statistics for 1983 and 1990, published by the Environmental Crimes Section, Environmental and Natural Resources Division, U.S. Department of Justice, shows that the number of indictments increased from 40 to 134, the criminal penalties imposed from $341,000 to almost $30,000,000, and jail terms from 11 years to almost 72 years. In October 1991 Exxon Corporation agreed to plead guilty to criminal charges resulting from the March 24, 1989, Exxon Valdez spill of 11 million gallons of crude oil into Prince William Sound in Alaska and to pay a criminal fine and restitution of $250 million, of which $125 million was remitted because of Exxon's $42.5 billion clean-up expenditure. While the potential criminal penalties associated with the Exxon Valdez spill may be exceptionally severe, U.S. Department of Justice statistics show that criminal penalties in the six- and seven-figure range are no longer unusual.
5. See, e.g., *United States* v. *Northeastern Pharmaceutical & Chemical Co.*, 579 F. Supp. 823 (W.D. Mo. 1984) (NEPACCO), *aff'd. in part, rev'd. in part,* 810 F. 2d 726 (8th Cir. 1986), *cert. denied,* 108 S. Ct. 146 (1987).
6. See, e.g., *United States* v. *NEPACCO, supra* n. 5; *Kelley* v. *Arco Industries Corp.*, 723 F. Supp. 1214 (W.D. Mich. 1989); *Vermont* v. *Stacco*, 684 F. Supp. 822 (D. Vt. 1988); *United States* v. *Nicolet, Inc.*, 712 F. Supp. 1193 (E.D. Pa. 1986); *United States* v. *Conservation Chemical Co.*, 628 F. Supp. 391 (W.D. Mo. 1985); *United States* v. *Ward*, 618 F. Supp. 884 (E.D.N.C. 1985).
7. See, e.g., *United States* v. *NEPACCO, supra* n. 5; *New York* v. *Shore Realty Corp.*, 759 F. 2d 1032 (2d Cir. 1985); *Conservation Chemical, supra* n. 6; *United States* v. *Ward, supra* n. 5.
8. See, e.g., *United States* v. *Kayser-Roth Corp., Inc.*, 910 F. 2d 24 (1st Cir. 1990), *cert. denied,* 111 S. Ct. 957 (1991); *United States* v. *Nicolet, Inc., supra* n. 6; *State of Idaho* v. *Bunker Hill Co.*, 635 F. Supp. 665 (D. Idaho, 1986); but see *Joslyn Manufacturing Co.* v. *T. L. Jones & Co.*, 893 F. 2d 80 (5th Cir. 1990), *cert. denied,* 111 S. Ct. 1017 (1991).

9. See, e.g., *Anspec Co. v. Johnson Controls, Inc.*, 922 F. 2d 1257 (6th Cir., 1991); *Louisiana-Pacific Corp. v. Asarco, Inc.*, 909 F. 2d 1260 (9th Cir., 1990); *Smith Land & Improvement Corp. v. Celotex Corp.*, 851 F. 2d 86 (3rd Cir. 1988), *cert. denied*, 109 S. Ct. 837 (1989); *in re Achushnet River & New Bedford Harbor*, 712 F. Supp. 1010 (D. Mass. 1989).

10. See, e.g., *United States v. Monsanto*, 858 F. 2d 160 (4th Cir. 1988); *United States v. Argent Corp.*, 21 Ent't. Rep. Cas. (BNA) 1354 (D.N.M. 1984).

11. *In re Bergsoe Metal Corp.*, 910 F. 2d 668 (9th Cir. 1990); *United States v. Fleet Factors Corp.*, 901 F. 2d 1550 (11th Cir. 1990) *cert. denied*, 111 S. Ct. 752 (1991); *Guidice v. BFG Electroplating and Manufacturing Co.*, 732 F. Supp. 356 (W.D. Pa. 1989); *United States v. Maryland Bank & Trust Co.*, 632 F. Supp. 573 (D. Md. 1986); *United States v. Mirabile*, 15 Envt'l. L. Rep. 20994 (E.D. Pa. 1985).

12. *The Wall Street Journal*, April 2, 1991, p. A14.

13. The bones can often be rather meaty. Indeed, the Clean Air Act Amendments of 1990, Pub. L. 101-549, are over 300 pages long!

14. Reganization Plan No. 3 of 1970, 35 *Federal Register* 15623 (1970). Bills have recently been introduced to elevate the U.S. EPA to department status.

15. 42 U.S.C. 7401 *et seq.*

16. 33 U.S.C. 1251 *et seq.*

17. 42 U.S.C. 6901 *et seq.*

18. 42 U.S.C. 3004 *et seq.*

19. 42 U.S.C. 9601 *et seq.*

20. 12 U.S.C. 2601 *et seq.*

21. 7 U.S.C. 136 *et seq.*

22. 42 U.S.C. 11001 *et seq; Title III of the Superfund Amendments and Reauthorization Act of 1986*, Pub. L. 99-499.

23. This authority derives from the National Environmental Policy Act, as amended, 42 U.S.C. 4321 *et seq.*

24. *EPA Journal*, 16:6 (1990): 29. The U.S. EPA budget figures are only part of the picture on government environmental costs. Excluded are costs of administrating environmental programs by other federal, state, and local agencies and costs of compliance by governmental agencies with environmental laws and regulations.

25. Regulations of the executive departments and agencies of the federal government that are published in the *Federal Register* are codified in the Code of Federal Regulations. The Code is divided into 50 titles. Title 40 contains the regulations issued by the U.S. EPA. The Code is revised at least once a year to incorporate regulatory changes pub-

lished in the *Federal Register* since the last Code revision. Title 40 comprises of more than 9,000 pages of U.S. EPA regulations.

26. Judicial review of executive department and agency regulations is generally covered by the provisions of the Administrative Procedures Act, 5 U.S.C. §§701–706. In some cases, environmental statutes provide specific provisions for judicial review. See, e.g., 42 U.S.C. 7607 (d) (9) and 15 U.S.C. 2618 (c).

27. The leading case is *Chevron, U.S.A. Inc.* v. *Natural Resources Defense Council, Inc.*, 467 U.S. 837 (1984). In *Chevron,* the U.S. Supreme Court held that "if . . . Congress has not directly addressed the precise question at issue, courts should accord considerable weight to an executive department's construction of a statutory scheme it is entrusted to administer." *Id.*, at 844.

28. 5 U.S.C. 552.

29. See 40 Code of Federal Regulations Part 2.

30. These standards may be emission standards based on available or the best technology, design, equipment, work practice, or operational standards, or standards based on pollutant-loading.

31. For example, given the complexity of environmental laws and regulations, noncompliances do occur. If, during a due diligence investigation a noncompliance is discovered, parties will want to address the questions of disclosure, who should pay any penalty assessed, and who should bear any costs of achieving compliance. Some states have penalty policies allowing a reduction in the event of self-disclosure or initiation of projects designed to reduce pollution beyond what the law requires. Knowledge of such policies might influence the decisions parties make.

32. N.J.S.A. 13: 1K-6 *et seq.* The transactions subject to this New Jersey statute include multistate or multinational real estate, stock, or asset deals if they directly or indirectly involve even one New Jersey facility.

33. While this chapter does not address ancillary toxic tort lawsuits seeking damages for personal injury and property damage attributable to release of pollutants from plant sites and off-site disposal, these costs are potentially significant and should be considered in any business transaction.

34. See *Bunker Hill Co. Lead and Zinc Smelter* v. *U.S. Environmental Protection Agency,* 658 F. 2d. 1280 (9th Cir. Idaho 1981), but compare *Stauffer Chemical Co.* v. *Environmental Protection Agency,* 647 F. 2d 1075 (10th Cir. 1981) and *U.S.* v. *Stauffer Chemical Co.*, 684 F. 2d 1174 (6th Cir. 1982), *aff'd. without reaching the merits,* 464 U.S. 165 (1983).

35. See 40 CFR 122.2 (1989).
36. Federal preemption is the exception, rather than the rule, with respect to most environmental statutes. Hence, knowledge of state regulatory requirements is critical to assessing compliance.
37. See 40 CFR 122.2 (1989).
38. The National Oil and Hazardous Substances Pollution Contingency Plan (NCP) is a regulation promulgated by the U.S. EPA that "provides the organizational structure and procedures for preparing for and responding to discharges of oil and releases of hazardous substances, pollutants and contaminants." 40 CFR Part 300 (1990). The NCP provides the framework for clean-ups under the Comprehensive Environmental Response, Compensation and Liability Act as well.
39. See p. 378 and n. 12 above.
40. These sites include the Rocky Mountain Arsenal in Colorado, the Savannah River Site in South Carolina, the Stringfellow Site in California, the Bridgeport Rental and Oil Services Site in New Jersey, and the Metamora Landfill in Michigan.
41. 42 U.S.C. §9607(a) and (b) and 42 U.S.C. §9601 (20) and (35). See also p. 378, *supra*, and nn. 5–11, *supra*.
42. See, e.g., *T&E Industries Inc.* v. *Safety Light*, A-93/94, decided March 27, 1991, by the New Jersey Supreme Court.
43. 15 U.S.C. 651 *et seq.*
44. For example, the 1985 New Jersey Toxic Catastrophe Prevention Act, N.J.S.A. 13:1K-19 *et seq.*, was a forerunner to EPCRA and to provisions in the 1990 Clean Air Amendments addressing the prevention of accidental releases of certain regulated substances.
45. See, e.g., City of La Mesa, California Ordinance No. 2511 adopting with some amendments the 1988 Uniform Fire Code.
46. See, e.g., Cal. Admin., Code §13305; and Mass. Gen. Laws Ann. 21E, §13.
47. Calif. Health & Safety Code §25359.7; Ind. Code §13-7-22.5; La. Rev. Stat. Ann. §23.48; N.Y. Admin. Code, Title 6, §373-2.7 (i); W. Va. Code §20-5E-20. Disclosure is generally required to be made to the transferee of property (including a lessee), and often to the state environmental agency.
48. N.J.S.A. 13:1K-6 *et seq.*
49. CT Gen'l. Statutes, §22a-134 *et seq.*
50. Ind. Code §13-7-22.5
51. Ind. Code §13-22.5-15.
52. N.J.S.A. 13: 1K-6 *et seq.*

53. Obviously, the value of an indemnification provision depends on the financial well-being of the indemnitor. If that is in doubt, there are other ways to assure that monies are available if and when needed (e.g., establishment of an escrow account or a parent corporation guarantee).

CHAPTER 15

FUNDAMENTALS OF AMERICAN PRODUCT LIABILITY LAW

Scott L. Gorland, Esq.
John Mucha III*
Pepper, Hamilton & Scheetz

INTRODUCTION

The rapid and continuous growth in the litigation of product liability injury and illness cases is a phenomenon well known to the legal profession in the United States and one with which many business executives, both in America and abroad, are becoming acquainted. As a consequence, insurance coverage for product liability claims has dried up or become so prohibitively expensive that many companies are forced to go without coverage or to maintain substantial layers of so-called self-insured retention coverage, under which the insured company bears the primary risk of liability and the costs of defense. For these reasons, familiarity with the nuances of product liability law and how it is generally applied is critical to the success of any business venture contemplating placing products in the American stream of commerce.

---

* The authors wish to thank Barbara H. Anderson, Judith E. Caliman, and Wallace R. Haley for their valuable assistance in preparing this chapter.

Product liability is a term of relatively recent vintage in American jurisprudence, connoting the liability of a manufacturer, processor, or nonmanufacturing seller for injury to the person or property of a buyer or third party caused by a defective product that has been sold. Although "product liability" is now regarded as a relatively distinct area of law, it shares the basic characteristics of many other types of lawsuits, as it does the legal techniques employed to litigate such cases. One of the most distinctive features to have emerged in product liability law is the doctrine of strict liability, beginning in 1963 with its application in a California case.[1] As will be seen, strict liability is considered a theory of recovery coextensive with traditional theories of negligence or breach of warranty. These theories share common foundational prerequisites that, depending on the product or circumstances, may be more or less difficult for a plaintiff to establish. These include demonstrating that an identifiable product or its accompanying labeling is defective or harmful in some way, that the party sought to be held liable for the injury is identified with the product, and—often the most difficult to establish—that the defective product was the proximate cause of the claimed injury.

Of necessity, there will be no effort here to provide an in-depth discussion of all aspects of product liability laws, theories of recovery, defenses, or other concepts, nor is it possible, for the most part, to relate these issues to specific products or industries. The goal is to provide an overview of the structure of product liability law as it has developed in the United States, and to construct guideposts to foreigners doing business in the United States or considering entering this market. If business executives or their counsel are alerted to the scope and risks of product liability problems potentially associated with marketing or distributing products, our objectives will have been met.

THEORIES OF LIABILITY

The most common theories of liability on which a product liability plaintiff may bring a suit for damages are strict liability, negligence, and breach of express or implied warranty. These theories are not exclusive and may be raised concurrently, depending upon the factual circumstances of the particular case. In addition, a product liability plaintiff may bring suit based upon breach of state or federal statute, if such a statute exists to regulate the particular product area. Other theories and remedies also exist, including imposition of criminal liability in rare cases.

At the outset it should be noted that while much of the law regarding product liability has developed uniformly among the states, some significant variations remain. The reader is advised that only general rules are presented here, not all variations on those rules.

Strict Liability

Strict liability is the leading theory by which manufacturers and those in the chain of distribution are held liable for injuries resulting from a defective product. In essence, strict liability provides that if the product was defective and the defect was the actual and proximate cause of the harm, the defendant will be liable to any person injured or damaged regardless of whether the defendant's conduct was negligent, unless an adequate defense is presented.

The doctrine of strict liability grew out of the recognition that ordinary consumers do not have the ability or sophistication required to evaluate products before purchase, as well as the recognition that traditional theories of negligence often made recovery too difficult for the injured product user. Moreover, strict liability grew out of a policy decision that manufacturers and sellers are better able to bear the costs of injuries caused by defects than are relatively powerless consumers.[2]

The commonly applied definition of strict liability is outlined in the Restatement (Second) of Torts § 402A, which provides

1. One who sells any product in a defective condition unreasonably dangerous to the user or consumer or to his property is subject to liability for physical harm thereby caused to the ultimate user or consumer, or to his property, if:
   a. The seller is engaged in the business of selling such a product, and
   b. It is expected to and does reach the user or consumer without substantial change in the condition in which it is sold.

2. The rule stated in Subsection (1) applies although
   a. The seller has exercised all possible care in the preparation and sale of his product, and
   b. The user or consumer has not bought the product from or entered into any contractual relation with the seller.

Persons Strictly Liable

Strict liability applies to virtually all persons in the chain of manufacture and distribution, including manufacturers, component suppliers, distributors, and retailers. One or all such persons may be named as defendants in a single lawsuit arising out of the same injury.

Where a finished product is composed of component parts, a defect in a specific component may cause the manufacturer of that component, as well as the assembler of the components, to be liable. However, a defect in the finished product does not make the manufacturer of each component strictly liable, but only those component manufacturers responsible for the defect. If the assembler substantially modifies the component part or uses it in an unforeseeable way, the component manufacturer will not be liable.

A difficult question, and one upon which courts are divided, is whether a component manufacturer is liable when the component has been manufactured to meet the specifications of the assembler, but is later determined to be the cause of the injury. While some courts have found the component manufacturer strictly liable, other courts have held that because the component manufacturer faithfully produced what the manufacturer required, the component manufacturer is not liable.

In most jurisdictions, strict liability also extends to those who market goods in the chain of distribution, including distributors, wholesalers, and retailers, even though such sellers did not create the defect, were not aware of it, and could not have reasonably discovered the defect. While imposition of strict liability under these circumstances may seem unfair, the public policy justification for applying strict liability here is premised on the perception that, between the consumer and those responsible for placing a defective product in the stream of commerce, the latter group should bear the burden of any losses because it is in a better position to put pressure on the manufacturer to correct defects and is better able to bear and distribute the costs arising from the injury caused by the defective product.[3]

Proof of Defect
Product defects can take a variety of forms, including defects in product design, manufacturing, and the adequacy of product labeling or warnings. Whether a particular product characteristic is considered a defect depends upon the nature of the product and the type of defect alleged.

Design defects are determined by one of two different tests, sometimes used in combination with one another. The "consumer expectation test" considers a product design to be defective if the product fails to perform as safely as the ordinary consumer would expect when used in an intended or foreseeable manner. The "risk-benefit" test balances the utility of a design against the risks created by the design. In this latter type of analysis, plaintiffs often compare the existing design with an alternative product design, for purposes of showing that a safer alternative was not only feasible, but was as functional and not substantially more expensive to produce. If the alternative design suggested by the plaintiff is not feasible, or would be significantly more expensive to produce, the design will probably not be deemed defective.

Some design defects can involve an entire product line, as when a defective design feature in a specific product is also present in the manufacturer's other products. In such cases, a design defect may affect a significant portion of a manufacturer's assets and may cause the public to be deprived of the product line altogether. Some courts have held that when a product liability claim threatens an entire product line, the plaintiff should be required to show actual fault, grounded in negligence, on the part of the defendant.[4]

Manufacturing defects may occur when a product is not manufactured according to intended or required specifications. These specifications may be ascertained from the particular product design, or may be established industrywide. Manufacturing specifications may also be required for certain products by government regulation. Generally, the failure of a product to meet the applicable specifications will render a manufacturer or seller liable only if the product was defective at the time it left the defendant's possession or control.[5] Proper operation of a product for a substantial period of time may be evidence that the product did not contain a manufacturing defect. When the product has been adulterated after leaving the manufacturer's or seller's hands, the defendant will not be found liable if that subsequent adulteration caused the injury.

Product labeling may also be deemed defective, and can give rise to strict liability. When the risks associated with a product are known (or should have been known) to the manufacturer, the manufacturer and those in the chain of distribution are obligated to warn the consumer. If a label does not adequately advise of the proper use, and does not adequately warn of the risks of improper use, it may be considered defective, even when the product is designed properly and manufactured without defects. Claims of defective labeling are frequently found in cases involving unavoidably unsafe products, such as drugs or chemicals, for which a recognized high degree of risk does not constitute a defect per se unless the consumer is not adequately warned.[6] If the lack of adequate warning was the proximate cause of the injury, the manufacturer may be held strictly liable. The duty to warn is discussed more fully later in this chapter.

Proof of a defect, or the absence of one, regardless of whether the alleged defect relates to design, manufacture, or labeling, will frequently be established through the use of expert witnesses learned in a particular aspect of manufacturing processes, engineering, design, or product labeling. Plaintiffs and defendants typically present competing expert witnesses to establish either liability or a defense. Whether a product will be considered defective in a particular case will hinge upon the sufficiency of the proof presented to the jury.

Proof of Causation

Mere proof of injury and proof of a defective product will not entitle the product liability plaintiff to damages. No liability will attach to the defendant unless the plaintiff can establish that the alleged defect was the actual and proximate cause of the injury. To do this, the plaintiff must show not only that the defect was the cause-in-fact of the injury, but also that "but for" the defect the injury would not have occurred. Once the plaintiff has established that the defect was a substantial factor in the injury, the plaintiff must show that the action leading to the injury was "reasonably foreseeable." As might be expected, courts frequently differ as to what is foreseeable and what is not. In determining foreseeability, courts may consider the remoteness, directness, and natural consequences of the act or injury, among other factors.[7]

While proof of causation may be straightforward in some cases, in others it may be the most complicated aspect. In the case of a punch press or a durable consumer good such as an automobile or a saw, there may be little doubt as to the cause of a traumatic injury. However, plaintiffs in a suit involving a pharmaceutical product or a potentially toxic substance such as a chemical will have the burden of establishing that the particular degree of their exposure to the drug or chemical was capable of causing the injury. They must also establish that, to a reasonable degree of medical or scientific certainty, the drug or chemical was the most likely or probable cause of injury, among what may be a plethora of other possible causes such as congenital defects or exposure to other drugs or chemicals.[8]

Often the proofs required to establish or disprove causation (as well as other aspects of a case) are highly scientific and technical in nature, and outside the knowledge of the average layperson. Parties may, therefore, rely heavily upon expert witnesses to explain the scientific and technical aspects of their case to the jury.[9] In recent years, the number of professional experts appears to have grown, including the number of persons whose "expertise" is not based upon well-recognized methodologies. In turn, there appears to be a proliferation of "expert" opinion based on unscientific and unrecognized methodologies and principles.[10]

Increasingly, the use of such pseudoscientific expert testimony has come under attack, and the testimony of experts is subject to increasing scrutiny.[11] Parties more frequently challenge, and courts more frequently disallow, expert testimony based upon novel or controversial scientific techniques or testimony contrary to the weight of accepted literature in a field. Courts also have rejected expert evidence based upon statistically insignificant data, as well as those opinions that ignore the most trustworthy sources available or are outside the expert's area of expertise. Thus, the ability to identify questionable expert testimony and questionable theories is of increasing significance in proving or disproving causation in the product liability case.

Negligence

Negligence is the traditional theory under which injured plaintiffs seek recovery for their injuries, although it has been eclipsed by the availability of the remedy of strict liability in most jurisdictions. For a defendant to be deemed negligent, that defendent (1) must have owed a duty or obligation to the plaintiff recognized by law, (2) which was breached by the defendant, (3) and which caused the complained-of injury.[12] If the plaintiff cannot identify a recognizable duty, cannot show that such a duty was breached, or cannot show a causal link between the breach and the injury, then the defendant will not be deemed to have been negligent, and no damages will be awarded to the plaintiff.

While all persons in the chain of distribution generally have a duty of reasonable care, the specific duty owed by the defendant will frequently depend upon the role and function of the defendant in the chain of production and distribution. Thus, the legal duties of a manufacturer are usually different from those of a distributor, although they may overlap. A manufacturer's duties may include designing a product that is reasonably safe for its intended or foreseeable use, testing and inspecting the materials used in manufacture, inspecting the finished product for defects, and warning of known defects or hazards. While a distributor typically will not have duties associated directly with the manufacturing process, the distributor will have a duty to warn of known defects and hazards. Distributors and others in the chain of distribution, therefore, face considerably less potential liability under a negligence theory than they do under a strict liability theory.

Regardless of the duty owed, courts will apply a standard of "reasonableness" to determine the extent of the duty and to judge whether the defendant fulfilled that duty. This reasonableness standard is an objective, rather than subjective, test of whether the defendant acted as an average prudent person would have acted under the same or similar circumstances.[13]

However, when the defendant has knowledge or abilities superior to those of the "reasonable" person, courts will expect conduct consistent with such special knowledge and abilities. Because a manufacturer of a product will often have special knowledge of materials, manufacturing processes, and product design, it will frequently be held to the higher standard of an expert in the field.[14]

Even when these higher standards apply, a reasonableness standard continues to determine the extent of the specific duty. For example, while a manufacturer may be under a duty to use reasonable care in designing a safe product, it is not required to design the best possible product, provided that the one it makes is reasonably safe and passes the "risk-utility" test. However, a plaintiff may introduce evidence of safer alternative products to establish that the manufacturer acted unreasonably in not adopting the allegedly safer features of the alternative design, if it could have been done at a reasonable cost.

As with strict liability, no liability can attach without proof of causation. Regardless of whether a strict liability or negligence theory is used, the plaintiff must prove that the act of the defendant (concerning design, manufacture, or warning) was the direct and proximate cause of the injury.

The Duty to Warn

Failure to warn of product risks is actionable under both strict liability and negligence theories. Most actions for failure to warn are brought against the manufacturer, but others in the chain of distribution may also be liable. To state a cause of action for failure to warn, four requirements must be satisfied. First, it must be shown that the manufacturer knew, or should have known of the product's risks. Second, there was no warning or only an inadequate warning given. Third, the absence of an adequate warning made the product unreasonably dangerous. Fourth, the failure to warn was the actual and proximate cause of injury. When the warning is required by government regulation, the failure to warn in keeping with the requirement may be negligence per se, meaning that negligence is conclusively presumed.

The manufacturer must warn about risks actually known and those that should be known. The manufacturer is presumed to know about scientific studies regarding the dangers of the product; a lack of actual knowledge will not provide a defense. If the state of knowledge about a product changes and additional dangers are later identified after the product has been sold, some courts have recognized a duty to warn of the new-found dangers, particularly in the area of drugs, asbestos, or similar products.[15]

In order for warnings to be considered adequate, they should (1) indicate the scope of the danger, (2) adequately communicate the extent or seriousness of the harm that could result from misuse of the product, (3) alert a reasonably prudent person to the danger by making the warning prominent and conspicuous, and (4) indicate the consequences that might result from failure to follow the warning.[16] While each warning must be created with the specific product in mind, it is better to err on the side of caution and provide a warning when in doubt.

For some products, the dangers and risks are obvious, and the manufacturer (or other person in the chain of distribution) has no duty to warn of those risks. Similarly, when products are used by someone fully knowledgeable of the dangers, by virtue of special training or expertise, the manufacturer generally will not have a duty to warn, even though the risks are not obvious to a person without special training or expertise. These defenses are discussed more fully later in this chapter.

The duty to warn requires that adequate warning be provided to all foreseeable users of the product, including intermediate vendors and manufacturers who may use the product as a component in a finished product. A special circumstance arises when potentially hazardous products such as chemicals are sold in bulk and then repackaged and relabeled by the intermediary distributor. As a general rule, the initial manufacturer has no duty to warn the eventual user of the product under these circumstances, provided that it supplied the intermediary with adequate warnings and the intermediary has reasonable expertise and experience to communicate the necessary information to subsequent vendees and users.[17]

Warranty

In addition to theories of negligence and strict liability, a plaintiff in a products liability action may also allege that the product failed to live up to the representations, or warranties, made about the product. Warranties on which plaintiffs may sue can be either express or implied, and may derive from the common law or from statute. Express warranties are written or oral direct representations about the product. Implied warranties are representations imputed from, among other things, advertising, labels, and the circumstances of a sale or transaction.

Suit based on common law breach of implied warranty requires the plaintiff to show that a defect existed that was attributable to the manufacturer or seller, and that the defendant by implication warranted that the product was reasonably safe for the uses that were intended, anticipated, or reasonably foreseeable.[18] By contrast with a suit based on a negligence theory, here the plaintiff need not prove that the defect was caused by the defendant's negligent acts.[19] While the theory of common law breach of implied warranty is legally distinct from negligence and strict liability, the elements of proof may be indistinguishable in some cases, and a court may elect not to submit the common law breach of warranty theory to the jury.[20]

In addition to common law implied warranty, which sounds in tort, a plaintiff may sue for breach of warranty under the Uniform Commercial Code (UCC). The UCC governs both express and implied warranties, including warranty of merchantability and warranty of fitness for a particular purpose, and provides remedies that are contractual in nature. A suit alleging breach of implied warranty of merchantability under the UCC seeks to prove that the defendant failed to provide a product that was merchantable—that is, fit for the ordinary purposes to which such product is normally used—and that the injuries to the plaintiff were proximately caused by the defective nature of the product. A suit alleging breach of implied warranty of fitness, on the other hand, seeks to prove that the defendant failed to provide a product that was fit for the particular purpose contemplated by the plaintiff and that was known to the defendant, and that this defect proximately caused the plaintiff's injury.

Alternative/Market Share/Concert of Action/ Enterprise Liability

Product liability law clearly requires a plaintiff instituting an action to identify whose product caused the alleged injury. However, in product liability litigation, situations often arise wherein the actual manufacturer of the product cannot be identified by the plaintiff.

For example, a generic product, such as a drug or chemical, may have been manufactured by a number of companies and because of the absence of records or labeling or because of the passage of time, the identity of the source of the injury-causing product cannot be ascertained. A classic example of this is diethylstilbestrol (DES) drug litigation, wherein plaintiffs suffered injury because their mothers ingested during pregnancy a drug marketed by numerous manufacturers. In many DES cases, the individual plaintiffs could not identify the drug manufacturer who supplied the DES because of the generic nature of the drug and the lengthy time lapse between the mother's ingestion of the drug and the daughter's contraction of cancer decades later.

Under early negligence and product liability law, a plaintiff who failed to identify the party who manufactured or supplied the product causing the injury was barred from maintaining a lawsuit. Recently, the courts, concerned with this harsh result, have fashioned new remedies that allow the plaintiff to proceed against manufacturers—even if the specific manufacturer who provided the product to the plaintiff cannot be identified. In fact, DES litigation has served as the foundation for many of the remedies discussed below. Because the remedies vary by state, it is critical for the product manufacturer or supplier to understand the law of each state where it does business. The following is a brief overview of these remedies.

Alternative Liability

Alternative liability arises when the plantiff can show that *all* parties were negligent or produced a substantially identical defective product, but that only one party's product could have caused the injury. If a plaintiff can meet the following requirements, then the burden of proof shifts to the defendants and each must show that he or she did not manufacture the injury-causing product. To benefit from alternative liability, plaintiffs must show, first, that all the defendants acted tortiously; second, that all possible defendants are before the court who may have caused the injury and that the plaintiffs were harmed by one of the defendants; and third, that the plaintiffs through no fault of their own, are unable to identify which defendant caused the injury.[21]

Once the burden has shifted to the defendants, they must show that they did not manufacture the product that caused the plantiff's injuries or that the product was not available in the relevant geographical area in which plaintiff (or in the case of DES, the plaintiff's mother) acquired the drug or other product. If they fail to meet their burden, each defendant is held jointly and severally liable for the full amount of the damage award.

Market Share Liability

Market share liability, although not a universally accepted remedy, spreads the burden of loss among the manufacturers participating in the relevant market for the defective product. The theory behind this has been justified in several state courts in situations when the manufacturing and marketing practices involved and the delayed harmful effect make identification of the responsible manufacturer impossible.[22] The policy underlying the theory is that each defendant in some measure shares the culpability in producing or marketing the defective product.

The defendants bear the burden of proving that their product could not have caused the plaintiff's injuries. However, by contrast with alternative liability, if an individual defendant fails to show that his or her product did not cause the injury, then the court will require that defendant to pay a percentage of the judgment that corresponds to the defendant's percentage of the relevant market for that particular product. Thus, if Defendant X establishes a market share of 10 percent of the relevant market and Defendant Y establishes a 70 percent market share, plaintiff would recover $10,000 of a $100,000 judgment from X and $70,000 from Y, with the remaining $20,000 left uncovered if no other defendants are joined. As illustrated in this example, by contrast with alternative liability, the plaintiff does not have to bring before the court all defendants who produced and marketed the product in the relevant area.

Although the market share theory has traditionally been used for DES litigation, it has been applied in other areas. Recently, a federal district court in Florida adopted the market share theory when the plaintiffs were unable to identify the source of supply for a blood component that allegedly contaminated the plaintiffs (two young hemophiliac boys) with AIDS.[23]

Concerted Action Liability

Concerted action liability occurs when defendants act tortiously through some form of joint cooperation. If a plaintiff can establish that *all* defendants acted tortiously under a common plan or design, they will all be held liable for the result. By contrast with the alternative or market share liability theories, under a concerted action, the injured plaintiff may pursue any one joint tort-feasor—regardless of whether the plaintiff knows who caused the injury. The classic example of this is the situation of three cars being involved in a drag race and one car injuring a third party. Under this theory, any one of the cars participating in the race may be held liable because all defendants jointly participated in the negligent activity—the drag race itself.

The concerted action theory has been applied in the product liability area.[24] For example, assume X, Y, and Z all collaborated on the design of a product that they each in turn manufactured. The product is defective and injures the plaintiff. The plaintiff, under a concerted action theory, proves that X provided the product that caused his injury and obtains a judgment of $100,000. If X, Y, and Z are shown to have acted tortiously in collaborating in the design, under a concerted action theory, each defendant is held jointly and severally responsible for the full $100,000.

Enterprise Liability

A variation of the concerted action theory is enterprise liability. Unlike concerted action, enterprise liability is invoked only where the plaintiff cannot identify the manufacturer whose product caused the injury. It was first applied in *Hall* v. *E. I. DuPont de Nemours Co.*,[25] wherein defendants were a group of blasting cap manufacturers who provided a standard industry-wide warning developed from joint participation in a trade association in which all defendants belonged. Because of their joint involvement, the court held each individual defendant jointly and severally liable.[26]

The key to establishing enterprise liability is to show that the defendants jointly controlled their risk through some form of industry wide cooperation—that is, a trade association or a similar rule-making or policy-formulation body.

Statutory Liability

Product liability actions often implicate various statutes, including state and federal acts, ordinances, and regulations, that establish safety standards for industry, transportation, or the environment. The federal government, over the years, has been quite active in advancing legislation intended to ensure or enhance product standards for safety and efficacy. Such legislation often spawns the promulgation of detailed regulations (which have the force of law) by administrative departments or agencies charged with oversight or enforcement of a legislative scheme. In the product area, comprehensive legislation has addressed such products as drugs, pesticides and other chemicals, automobiles, and consumer goods.

These statutes often define a standard of care to be exercised in the manufacture, labeling, and sale of the products, and may expose a manufacturer to civil or criminal liability, or both. A statute providing for criminal penalties subjects the convicted wrongdoer to fine or imprisonment. Criminal actions must be brought by the government, as contrasted with civil liability, which gives the individual a right of action against the wrongdoer.

However, even if the statute is criminal in nature, there are potential advantages to a civil plaintiff if it can be established that the defendant violated the statute. If the court is willing to adopt the legislative standard, or if the statute provides for civil liability, such a violation may be used to establish the standard of care for the common law negligence action. Depending on the jurisdiction, the court may treat the violation as merely evidence of negligence or in jurisdictions subscribing to a harsher dogma, negligence per se.

In a jurisdiction adhering to the negligence per se doctrine, a violation of the statute takes from the jury the question of whether the defendant breached the common law duty of reasonable care to the plaintiff. In these cases, the statute defines the common law duty of reasonable care owed to the plaintiff, and once a violation of the statute is proven, negligence is conclusively presumed.[27] In summary, the products manufacturer should be concerned not only with the common law obligations imposed under negligence, warranty, and strict liability theories, but also with any laws or regulations, both federal and state, that may affect its business.

Federal statutes and regulations affecting the product liability area deal primarily with liability for defective products and product safety, both to the individual consumer and to the environment.[28] The individual consumer is protected under numerous regulations promulgated by various government agencies. Of particular significance in the area of product liability are the Magnuson-Moss Act (setting federal standards for warranty protection);[29] Consumer Product Safety Act (hazardous substances, flammable fabrics, poison prevention packaging, etc.);[30] National Transportation and Motor Vehicle Safety Act;[31] Federal Insecticide, Fungicide and Rodenticide Act (pesticide regulation);[32] and a substantial body of regulations administered by the Food and Drug Administration pursuant to the Federal Food, Drug and Cosmetic Act.[33]

Federal regulations concerning protection of the environment should be of great concern to the products manufacturer or distributor. Over the last 20 years, Americans have become increasingly concerned about their environment, and the federal and state governments have reacted by taking substantial steps to broaden the scope of enforcement and liability for environmental pollution and remediation. Compliance with regulations in this rapidly evolving field is a prime concern to the producer or distributor, especially if the product in any way involves the production and disposal of hazardous waste at any stage of the manufacture or distribution cycle.

Manufacturers should be particularly concerned with the Comprehensive Environmental Response, Compensation and Liability Act (CERCLA)[34] which was enacted in 1980 to establish liability for release of hazardous substances into the environment and to eliminate hazardous waste sites. Under the act, one has a duty to report a hazardous substance release. Furthermore, the act gives the government power to clean up the release and bill all responsible parties, including damages for injury to, destruction of, or loss of natural resources.

Environmental law impinges on the area of product liability particularly when a manufacturer or supplier of primary chemical products is sued by the end users of their products. These end users have usually been sued for improper disposal or spillage of hazardous substances and are subject to response costs for clean-up.

Typically, this type of litigation centers on determining which party or parties are responsible for the release and which party will bear the cost of the clean-up.

Recent litigation has broadened the boundaries of responsibility so far as to suggest that even a primary manufacturer may be held responsible for a later third-party hazardous waste release. A manufacturer could find itself liable for clean-up costs even if it does not maintain title to the product but does exercise some control over subsequent manufacturing processes,[35] or alternatively, has no control over the process but knows that the process will likely generate hazardous waste and fails to adequately warn of these dangers.[36]

The failure to warn of dangers inherent in the disposal of hazardous wastes, even though the primary manufacturer maintains no control and relinquishes title, is particularly troubling in the product liability area. CERCLA imposes liability on those who generate, transport, or "arrange for disposal or treatment."[37] Arguments are currently being advanced in litigation that even a primary generator could be viewed as "arranging for disposal" when it knows the product will lead to generation of hazardous waste and fails to adequately warn of the dangers. Therefore, manufacturers are advised to take the necessary steps to adequately warn downstream manufacturers or suppliers about the dangers of hazardous waste and the necessity for proper disposal.

DEFENDING AGAINST THE PRODUCT LIABILITY LAWSUIT

In addition to rebutting plaintiff's factual proofs, which is the most common means of defending against a lawsuit, numerous defenses are potentially available to the defendant in a product liability lawsuit. Outlined below are several of the key defenses commonly asserted in product liability actions that enable a defendant to avoid or reduce liability. The availability of these defenses, or of other defenses not presented here, will be governed by the circumstances of the particular case.

Statutes of Limitation and Repose

Plaintiffs do not have unlimited time to commence a lawsuit for their injuries, but must bring suit within the time prescribed by the statutes of limitation in the applicable jurisdiction. Failure to do so will bar the claim of liability. Each jurisdiction has its own statutes of limitation for each of the legal theories on which suit may be based (i.e., warranty, negligence, etc.). Consequently, a plaintiff in one jurisdiction may have a longer or shorter period to bring suit than a plaintiff in another jurisdiction, even though the facts and theories may be virtually identical. Typically, statutes of limitation require the plaintiff to commence a product liability action within a period of between one and six years from the date the cause of action arose or "accrued."

Most jurisdictions follow what is known as the "discovery" rule in determining when the statutory period begins to run.[38] Under the discovery rule, once the plaintiff discovers, or *should have discovered*, that he or she is injured and the possible *cause* of the symptoms is displayed, the statutory "clock" begins to run.[39] In other jurisdictions a "manifestation" rule is used, and the statute of limitation begins to run simply upon the outward manifestation of physical symptoms, without regard for the plaintiff's understanding of the cause of the manifestations.

When a product causes immediate and obvious harm, there is no question that the statute of limitation begins to run at the time of the injury. However, in other cases, such as those involving latent injury from pharmaceuticals or chemicals, the outward symptoms of injury may not manifest themselves immediately, and the connection between the product and the injury may not be apparent for months or years after the drug or chemical came into contact with the plaintiff. In such cases, under the discovery rule, the statute of limitation will begin to run from the point when the plaintiff reasonably believed that the product in question caused the injury.[40]

The plaintiff need not know for an absolute fact that the suspected product is the actual cause, but merely must possess a reasonable belief that there was a causal relationship.[41] The plaintiff need not know all the details of the suspected cause of the injury for the statute to begin to run, and the limitations period may start before completion of plaintiff's investigations.[42] If the plaintiff avoids medical diagnosis of the cause of the symptoms, and allows his or her condition to deteriorate, the plaintiff may be deemed to have knowledge of the cause. Further, if knowledge of symptoms similar to plaintiff's and of its causes is widespread among persons similarly situated, a plaintiff may be charged with knowledge of the causal relationship.

Once the statute of limitation period has passed, the plaintiff is absolutely barred from filing suit for damages, and a suit filed late will be dismissed. To avoid this harsh result, the plaintiff may try to establish that the statute of limitation was tolled, or held in abeyance, in some way. The tolling provisions of the various statutes of limitation vary from state to state, and may look to such things as the filing of a worker's compensation claim, bankruptcy, the concealment of the cause of injury, or whether the alleged tort feasor committed what is referred to as a "continuing tort."[43]

In some states, so-called statutes of repose have been enacted that limit the time period within which suit may be brought to a defined period determined not by the date of injury, but by the date of manufacture, sale, or delivery.[44] By limiting the time for filing suit in this way, statutes of repose may serve to bar an action before the injury has occurred or is discovered, even though the statute of limitations period would not have otherwise expired.

Product Misuse

A defendant's duty to use reasonable care in guarding against unreasonable and foreseeable risks generally includes a duty to guard against product misuse or alteration that can be reasonably anticipated. Even if the misuse is substantial, the defendant has a duty to guard against any such misuse that is foreseeable.

Given this standard, product misuse is a defense to a product liability action only when the defendant can show that the misuse was unforeseeable. The question of what is foreseeable will generally be one for the jury, and may focus on anticipated uses of the product, advertising claims, prior history of misuse, and the ease of such misuse or alteration by product users. Product misuse can occur among end users as well as intermediaries, and it has been held that an intermediary's redistribution of a product in unlabeled containers and without warnings constituted misuse of the product precluding recovery against the manufacturer by the injured user.[45] Similarly, an employer's unforeseeable misuse of a product that causes injury to an employee may relieve the manufacturer of liability to that injured employee.[46]

Once it is shown that the misuse was unforeseeable, the defendant may be able to defeat the plaintiff's claims entirely by proving that the misuse was the sole cause of the injury. If the injury was caused by both misuse and a defect in the product, liability may be reduced rather than eliminated. Product misuse that is outrageous or criminal (such as throwing a caustic chemical at another person) generally constitutes a complete defense to claims of liability. Of course, the degree to which product misuse will relieve a defendant from liability will depend upon the specific facts of the case and the law of the jurisdiction.

Assumption of Risk

In some jurisdictions, proof that plaintiffs voluntarily exposed themselves to risks of which they were specifically aware may constitute an absolute defense to liability, particularly where the exposure was unreasonable. In such cases, plaintiffs will be deemed to have "assumed the risk" of the dangerous product, and will be deemed to have relieved the defendant of the duty of care that would have otherwise existed. If the risk which the plaintiffs assumed was not voluntary, or their knowledge of the risks was only general and not specific, then no assumption of risk will be deemed to have occurred.[47]

In the numerous jurisdictions that have adopted a comparative fault standard of apportioning liability, as discussed later in this chapter, assumption of risk has largely been abolished as a defense, and so no longer plays as important a role as it once did in product liability actions.

State of the Art Defense

The so-called state of the art defense has several variations, but in essence, it allows a defendant product manufacturer to escape claims of negligence or strict liability by demonstrating that at the time of manufacture the product (and its attendant warnings) was in accord with existing scientific knowledge and reasonable technical feasibility. A creature of both statute and common law,[48] it is at least partly because of the availability of the defense that strict liability and negligence theories are said to run together in design defect cases.[49]

Design cases generally use the term *state of the art* to relieve the manufacturers of liability when the design conforms to the custom or practice of the industry.[50] The sources used to establish custom and practice of an industry often take the form of written publications by recognized industrial associations[51] and regulations promulgated by governmental entities.[52] When no published standards exist, courts will accept evidence of manufacturing techniques of other manufacturers producing the same or similar products.

More often, compliance with industry custom is not a defense (although considered relevant and admissible to show adherence to a reasonable standard of care). In these instances, the defendant will be relieved of liability only where the product is manufactured to the limits of reasonable scientific or technical feasibility and knowledge.[53] The most extreme view, expressed primarily in asbestos litigation, does not permit application of the defense in strict liability cases, and would impose liability even when no one knew at the time of manufacture that the product posed an unreasonable risk that could have been eliminated by a different design.[54] In these cases, application of state of the art to strict liability has been rejected because of the risk-spreading and accident-avoidance goals of strict liability, with one court "imposing on manufacturers the costs of failure to discover hazards [which creates] an incentive for them to invest more actively in safety research."[55]

In cases involving the adequacy of a warning, strict liability jurisdictions usually consider state of the art evidence in order to establish the adequacy of the warning that should be provided by manufacturers. The nature of the warning to be given about a product depends upon the state of the knowledge of experts in a given professional field. For example, in drug cases or with products such as asbestos, the state of the art is often established by expert testimony concerning the existence of scientific literature documenting the hazards associated with the product.[56] Actual knowledge or imputed knowledge of the scientific literature creates a duty to ensure that information related to hazards associated with the product is disseminated.[57] Such an inquiry focuses on the reasonableness of the manufacturer's conduct, contrary to strict liability concepts, although a manufacturer is held to the knowledge of an expert in the particular field in fashioning an appropriate warning.[58]

Particulary in cases involving prescription drugs, courts impose a duty to warn only of those dangers that are reasonably foreseeable. Comment k to §402A of the Restatement (Second) of Torts (1975) bases the rationale for this distinction on the need to market "unavoidably unsafe products" because of the important benefits flowing from their use. Nevertheless, the seller still retains a duty to adequately warn of the dangers. As should be evident, the state of the art remains a vital defense in many design defect and warning cases, which more often than not will be established through the testimony of experts.

Knowledgeable Purchaser/Learned Intermediary Defenses

The knowledgeable purchaser defense provides that a manufacturer or supplier has no duty to warn the ultimate user of the product when the manufacturer supplies the product to a knowledgeable or sophisticated third party on whom the manufacturer can reasonably rely to warn the ultimate user.[59] The defense is often applied in the context of sales to the employer of the injured party, when the employer has actual knowledge of the specific hazards associated with use of the product.[60]

The defense is sometimes referred to as the bulk supplier defense in situations when the supplier sells its product in bulk, such as chemicals or raw materials, that is used without accompanying labeling or is repackaged for sale. For example, in a silicosis case, the court did not hold the supplier of silica sand liable for injury to a foundry's employees because the foundry was a "knowledgeable purchaser of silica sand and related products."[61] The doctrine has been applied in both negligence and strict liability cases.[62]

There is a split of authority on the issue of whether the purchaser must actually know of the dangers, or whether the fact that the sophisticated user should have known will suffice to eliminate liability of the supplier.[63] Although an actual warning to the purchaser does not seem necessary, some cases hold that providing one would automatically relieve the manufacturer of the duty to warn the ultimate user.[64]

The defense recognizes the fact that modern employers often have professional staffs with health and safety departments, and, charged by law to maintain a safe workplace,[65] are in the best position to ensure that the products used by its workforce are properly handled. Often, such industrial manufacturers, using products in their manufacturing process, are charged with the knowledge of an expert under strict liability concepts, thereby relieving the supplier of a duty to warn.[66]

Related to the sophisticated user defense is the "learned intermediary" doctrine peculiar to the pharmaceutical and medical device industries, where ethical drugs and other products may be dispensed only by a doctor or with his or her prescription. It is well established in most jurisdictions that the manufacturer of an ethical drug has a duty to provide timely and adequate warnings to the medical profession, and not directly to patients, of any risks associated with the use of its product.[67]

The basis of this rule was aptly stated by one Texas court:

> It is unreasonable to demand that the manufacturer of drugs specifically warn each and every patient that received drugs prescribed by the physician or other authorized persons. The entire system of drug distributions in America is set up so as to place the responsibility of distribution and use upon professional people. The laws and regulations prevent prescription type drugs from being purchased by individuals without the advice, guidance and consent of licensed physicians and pharmacists. These professionals are in the best position to evaluate the warnings put out by the drug industry.[68]

Thus, prescription drugs are not sold over the counter because the special expertise of a trained physician is necessary for their safe use.

In this respect, the purchaser's doctor is treated as a learned intermediary between the purchaser and the manufacturer. The physician is able to balance the risks of possible harm against the benefits to be gained by the patient's use of the drug.[69] Thus, when a doctor is not adequately warned, through product information accompanying the drugs or otherwise, the drug manufacturer may, in turn, be liable for breach of duty to the patient.[70]

Defenses Available to Component Suppliers

In addition to the defenses available to any product manufacturer or supplier, the manufacturer or supplier of a product intended for use or assembly in a completed product enjoys the availability of at least two special defenses—namely, the contract specification defense, and the related defense of a component supplier of a nondefective component for defects in the completed product. These defenses are significant in potentially reducing or eliminating the product liability exposure of component suppliers in relation to completed product manufacturers.

Contract Specification Defense

The contract specification defense allows a manufacturer to escape liability when it has built the component product according to the specifications of the purchaser, unless the plans and specifications reveal such an obvious defect or danger that they should not reasonably be followed.[71] In order to apply the contract specifications defense, the component or product in question must be free from any manufacturing defect. The only duty such a manufacturer has is to ensure that it has complied with the plans and specifications.[72]

The manufacturer, be it a component supplier or manufacturer of a completed product, following a purchaser's specifications will be liable, however, if the manufacturer unreasonably relies on the specifications. Two factors influence the reasonableness of the manufacturer's reliance: whether the manufacturer knew or should have known of the design defect, and the knowledge and experience of the person who supplied the specifications.

The manufacturer of a component or product will probably escape liability if the plans and specifications do not reveal an inherent danger in either the component or the overall design.[73] Reliance on the purchaser's specifications is considered even more reasonable when the purchaser is knowledgeable and experienced with respect to the type of product in question.[74]

If the manufacturer reasonably relies on the purchaser's specifications, the manufacturer will have fulfilled its duty to provide a reasonably safe product. Similarly, it will have no duty to warn because it will have no knowledge of the potential danger, which is the "first prerequisite of a duty to warn."[75] In addition, if the manufacturer's reliance on the specifications is reasonable, it does not have a duty to test the specifications. Courts have found that requiring a manufacturer to inspect and test the specifications provided by an experienced purchaser would impose an unfair financial burden, and would amount to holding a nondesigner liable for a design defect.[76]

Accordingly, the contract specification defense and the related "government specifications" or "military contractor" defense,[77] should be very useful to limit the liability of any component supplier or other product manufacturer supplying products specifically called for and pursuant to the plans and specifications of the purchaser. Obviously, the more detailed the specifications and the less latitude accorded the manufacturer, the greater the likelihood of success in asserting this defense.

Limited Duty of a Component Supplier
Related to the contract specification defense is the concept of limited liability of a component supplier for defects in the completed product when the component part itself is not defective. It is a defense that can apply both to "off the shelf" items not made pursuant to a customer's specifications and to specially manufactured component parts.

Some courts have permitted such a defense in situations when the component supplier could not foresee that the manufacturer of the end product would use the component in an unsafe manner. Such cases often entail the situation involving a component, not of unique design, that can be integrated into an end product in many different ways.[78]

In many jurisdictions, a more comprehensive defense is emerging, however, that absolves component manufacturers of a duty to ascertain the safety of the use to which its components are being put in end products, even in situations when the component manufacturer is specifically aware of the end use for which the component is specially made.[79] In these jurisdictions, the liability of a component manufacturer is limited to the design and manufacture of its component part. A component part manufacturer, these courts hold, has no duty, independent of the completed product manufacturer, to analyze the design of the completed product that incorporates its nondefective component part. Thus, knowledge of the component's use on or in the end product is not relevant. The end product manufacturer is solely responsible to design and manufacture a completed product that is safe for reasonably foreseeable uses.

Preemption Defense

In certain situations, federal law may preclude the product liability plaintiff from bringing a state common law tort action against the manufacturer of the product. The U.S. Constitution makes federal law superior to state law where there is a direct conflict between the state law and Congress's objectives in passing the particular federal legislation. Where such conflict exists, the state common law action is "preempted" and cannot be enforced.

Preemption can occur in several different ways. First, preemption can occur through explicit statutory language demonstrating that Congress intends to occupy the particular area in question. The National Childhood Vaccine Injury Compensation Act, for example, provides that "no vaccine manufacturer shall be liable in a civil action for damages arising from a vaccine related injury."[80]

Second, preemption occurs when a state attempts to regulate in a field where Congress intended the federal government to occupy that area exclusively. For example, the federal government has passed the Federal Cigarette Labeling and Advertisement Act regulating the warnings required on the label of a cigarette package.[81] Therefore, state tort actions challenging the adequacy of those warnings are preempted because Congress intended to occupy the field of labeling of cigarette packages.[82] In other areas, courts have held that the Food and Drug Administration's regulations on the labeling, packaging, and marketing of meat occupy the field of meat regulation, thereby preempting actions under a state's consumer protection act.[83]

Third, state law is preempted where the state law actually conflicts with the federal law, making it impossible for a private party to comply with both state and federal requirements. For example, the registration, sale, and use of pesticides is controlled under the Federal Insecticide, Fungicide and Rodenticide Act (FIFRA).[84] Because the act requires the United States Environmental Protection Agency (EPA) to approve the safety and efficacy of the product, and the manufacturers to place a label on their product with the EPA-approved information, state tort actions alleging inadequate labeling or failure to adequately warn of the dangers associated with the product have been found to be preempted.[85] The courts have concluded that a jury award of damages would permit state court juries to do what legislatures and administrative agencies could not do—that is, impose requirements for regulating pesticides.

Therefore, if the federal government has passed legislation preempting an area covered by a state's product liability law, a plaintiff may not bring traditional common law actions such as negligence or strict liability. As indicated above, preemption is more likely to be found in regulatory areas where the federal government is responsible for the evaluation of the safety and effectiveness of a highly regulated product, such as certain drugs or pesticides. Although federal regulation of product safety has expanded drastically over the years, the courts have been reluctant to expand the doctrine of preemption accordingly. The courts fear that such expansion bars plaintiffs from recovering damages for injuries—the cornerstone of negligence concepts.

When the manufacturer produces a product covered under federal law, it should take great care to fully comply with the law and any associated regulations. Such compliance, depending on the jurisdiction, may serve as evidence that the manufacturer has complied with the standard of care required under the common law or it may preclude the state tort action altogether.

PRODUCT LIABILITY DAMAGES

If the plaintiff in a product liability action is successful in establishing liability, the plaintiff may be able, depending upon the facts of the case, to recover compensatory damages from among the several defendants. In some cases, exemplary or punitive damages also may be awarded. While a detailed discussion of the numerous remedies is beyond the scope of this chapter, the following provides an overview of the potential damages that may be imposed upon the product liability defendant.

Compensatory Damages

Compensatory damages represent payment to the plaintiff for actual harm done, whether the harm is in the form of personal injury, property damage, or economic loss (i.e., losses related to the cost of the defective product or those generated as a consequence of the defect, such as lost profits). Compensatory damages may also be awarded to family members who claim some derivative damages related to the plaintiff's injury. Which of these compensatory damages will be available will depend upon the plaintiff's theory of liability and the facts of the case.

The extent of a plaintiff's injuries or harm, and the dollar value of the damages are generally considered questions of fact for the jury after the issue of liability has been decided. Although courts will not generally substitute their own judgment for that of the jury, they have the power to add to or reduce the size and amount of a damage award.

When a defective product has been proven to have caused personal injury, damages designed to compensate the plaintiff for the personal harm will be awarded. Such damages may include medical expenses, cost of future medical care, loss of actual earnings (and other employment benefits), loss of future earning capacity, damages for present and future physical and mental pain and suffering, and damages for emotional distress. Similarly, when the defective product has caused damage to property other than the product itself, the costs of repairing or replacing such damaged property may be awarded.

Plaintiffs also may be entitled to the cost of the defective product itself, particularly if they have brought an action for breach of warranty. In some cases, the failure of a product because of a defect may result in a loss of profits to plaintiffs who have used the defective product in their business, or may cause other consequential economic harm. Courts may allow the recovery of these consequential economic damages in suits premised on warranty or strict liability.[86]

Derivative Damages

In some suits, relatives of the injured plaintiff may sue for derivative damages such as loss of consortium, also described as society, companionship, or services. Typically, the family member plaintiff will be the injured person's spouse, although derivative suits by children and other relatives have been allowed in some courts.[87] Such suits are considered derivative because they are dependant upon the success of the underlying product liability action brought by the injured person. No loss of consortium damages will be awarded unless the plaintiff in the underlying action prevails on the question of liability against the product liability defendant.

Punitive and Exemplary Damages

Punitive damages are sometimes awarded as a means of penalizing a defendant who has engaged in malicious or outrageous conduct, and to deter others from engaging in such conduct. In some jurisdictions the punishment goal has been abandoned, but similar damages, referred to as exemplary damages, are awarded to compensate the plaintiff and to deter others from similar behavior.

For a plaintiff to be entitled to punitive or exemplary damages, the plaintiff generally must show that the defendant acted recklessly, wantonly, or outrageously with conscious or flagrant indifference to the risk of harm. Punitive damages are frequently sought in cases based on negligence or strict liability, but will not usually be awarded for breach of warranty.[88]

The size of punitive or exemplary damages can often be as large, or larger, than the compensatory damages awarded to the plaintiff. Juries may look at the knowledge of the defendant, the nature of the conduct, the wealth of the defendant, and the probable deterrent effect of the award, among other factors, in assessing punitive damages. However, punitive damages that are greatly disproportionate to the actual injury may be deemed to be excessive or against public policy.[89] In some states, legislation has been adopted placing limits on the amount of punitive and exemplary damages.

Attorneys' Fees, Costs, and Interest on Judgments

Under the so-called American Rule, recovery of attorneys' fees by the prevailing party is usually not available, although recovery of costs other than attorneys' fees may be awarded. Frequently, the award of such costs is governed by statute, and must be reasonable to be recoverable. Costs, including attorneys' fees, may also be awarded when a pleading wholly lacking in merit has been filed by opposing counsel, or when the opposing counsel has taken some action for the purpose of harassment or delay.

Damages awarded by a jury are generally subject to interest, including accrual of interest during the period when the judgment may be on appeal. Some courts may also award prejudgment interest, calculated from a triggering date such as date of accrual of a cause of action or date of filing of the complaint. The availability of prejudgment interest varies from state to state, and varies according to the underlying case theory.

Comparative Negligence, Contribution, and Indemnification

The principles of comparative negligence, contribution, and indemnification may be used to reduce the amount of damages a defendant may be required to pay if found liable in a product liability lawsuit. Each principle is distinct but, in certain circumstances, all may operate simultaneously to effect a reduction in damages.

Comparative negligence applies to reduce, but not necessarily entirely eliminate, a defendant's liability for damages when the plaintiff's own negligence is a factor causing the plaintiff's injury.[90] Generally, the doctrine of comparative negligence permits even a negligent plaintiff to recover against a negligent defendant but requires reduction in the amount of the recovery by the plaintiff's proportionate degree of negligence. Jurisdictions adopting a "pure" comparative negligence statute permits a negligent plaintiff to recover regardless of the plaintiff's proportionate degree of fault. Some jurisdictions, however, modify the "pure" rule so that if the plaintiff's contributory negligence is equal to or more than the defendant's negligence, the plaintiff recovers nothing. Thus, under the modified comparative negligence rule, if a plaintiff is charged with 50 percent or more proportionate share of the negligence, the plaintiff would not be able to recover damages from the defendant who was equally (or less) responsible for the plaintiff's injuries. Some other jurisdictions have adopted a rule of comparative negligence that permits an equally negligent plaintiff to recover so long as the plaintiff's proportionate share of the negligence does not exceed that of the defendant.[91]

Jurisdictions also adopt differing views of comparative negligence when there are multiple defendants or tortfeasors. In some jurisdictions, the plaintiff's negligence is compared with the combined negligence attributed to all of the defendants, thereby allowing a negligent plaintiff to recover from a defendant whose fault was less than or equal to the plaintiff's fault as long as the plaintiff's negligence was not greater than that of all the defendants. Other jurisdictions compare the plaintiff's fault with that of each defendant and preclude plaintiff's recovery from the defendants who were less negligent than the plaintiff.

When there are multiple defendants, principles of contribution may also apply to reduce a defendant's liability for damages. Contribution is applied among tort feasor defendants, as distinguished from comparative fault, which is applied between plaintiffs and defendants. An action for contribution against codefendants may be brought either in the original action in which plaintiff sued defendants or in a separate action.

When defendants share a common liability to a plaintiff and one defendant is compelled to bear a disproportionate share of the damages, contribution permits a defendant to recover from other defendants the amount in excess of its pro-rata share of the damages.[92] Contribution is an equitable principle and may be enforced even in the absence of an agreement if a defendant, whether by settlement or judgment, pays an unfair share of the damages.

When there are multiple defendants, principles of indemnity may also apply. Indemnity is generally a contractual principle, either express or implied, or arises out of a special relationship pursuant to which a defendant who has satisfied a judgment is entitled to full reimbursement from another. The right to indemnity may exist if one defendant is subject to tort liability as a result of the negligent acts of another. For example, the vendor of a defective product may be entitled to indemnity from the manufacturer if an injury was caused by the negligence of the manufacturer, assuming the vendor had no opportunity to discover or correct the defect.

In sum, principles of comparative negligence, contribution, and indemnity may *all* be applicable in product liability actions and should be considered as a means of reducing or eliminating the damages a particular defendant would have to pay. Even if there is an allocation of fault among multiple defendants, indemnity may be appropriate if one defendant's liability is based on passive rather than active negligence or is imposed by law.

SUITS AGAINST FOREIGN CORPORATIONS

In addition to fundamental theories of liability, damages, and defenses, the foreign investor who foresees potential involvement in product liability litigation should be generally familiar with the rules that determine whether a court has jurisdiction over a particular suit, as well as the principles governing liability among related entities, such as predecessors and successors, or parents and subsidiaries. While these concepts are not unique to product liability actions, they may play an important role in investment decisions and marketing strategies.

Where the Foreign Corporation Can Be Sued: Personal Jurisdiction

Whether any corporation, including a foreign corporation, can be sued in the courts of a given state depends upon the number and type of contacts that the corporation has in the state. If a corporation has no contact with a state—that is, it owns no property there, does no business there, sells no products there, has no employees there, has no resident agent there, and otherwise has not availed itself of the courts of the state or consented to personal jurisdiction over it—it will not be subject to suit in that state, even though the plaintiff may be located there. To be subject to the personal jurisdiction of the court, absent voluntary consent, the corporation must possess sufficient "minimum contacts" with the state in which the court is located.[93]

Considerable litigation has addressed the question of what constitutes sufficient minimum contacts, and courts have differed somewhat in their conclusions. As a general rule, however, a single or wholly isolated contact with a state does not provide sufficient minimum contacts. For example, a car dealer whose product happens to be driven into another state and causes injury there because of an alleged defect cannot be sued in that state on the basis of that connection alone, since such an isolated contact does not cause the defendant to reasonably anticipate that it would be haled into court there.[94] On the other hand, sufficient minimum contacts have been found from the execution of a single contact in a state, shipping of products into a state, telephone solicitation of customers in a state, or visits to a state.[95] Thus, both foreign and domestic corporations that wish to limit the states in which they can be sued must consciously avoid virtually all contacts with that state.[96]

Predecessor/Successor Liability

Of tremendous concern to an investor who purchases the assets of an existing business entity is whether the successor corporation will be liable for injuries caused by the products made or sold by the predecessor. As a general rule, the successor will not be held liable for the torts of its predecessor, although this rule is subject to a number of very significant common law and statutory exceptions.[97]

If the underlying transaction was a consolidation or merger of the predecessor and successor, then the resulting corporate entity may be held liable for the predecessor's defects.[98] Similarly, if the resulting corporation is a mere continuation of the predecessor, liability may be imposed on the successor, particularly when the successor continues to manufacture or sell the its predecessor's product line.[99] The successor may also be held liable if the transaction between the predecessor and successor is, in truth, merely a fraudulent means of avoiding liability for past defects.[100] Of course, if the successor corporation enters into an express or implied agreement to assume the liabilities of the predecessor, the successor will be held liable. The investor who wishes to avoid liability for past defects with a degree of certainty may wish to obtain an indemnity agreement from the predecessor, if possible.

Parent/Subsidiary Liability

As a general rule, parent and subsidiary corporations are recognized as separate entities. As such, parent corporations are generally not directly liable for the torts of their subsidiary companies. In some circumstances, however, the "corporate veil" will be pierced and liability will be directly imposed upon the parent, with the consequence that the assets of the parent, and not only those of the subsidiary, may be subject to the plaintiff's claims.

Some courts will impose liability upon the parent for the torts of the subsidiary if the parent "dominates" the activities of the subsidiary.[101] In determining whether such domination exists, courts look to factors such as common stock ownership, common officers and directors, responsibility for day-to-day operations, and financing, among others. Other courts have imposed liability on the parent corporation only when there is a showing of fraud or inequity.[102]

A subsidiary is not normally held liable for the actions of the parent unless the subsidiary was involved in the tortious activity. Thus, a subsidiary that has no involvement in the sale or manufacture of a product by the parent or another subsidiary will not itself be liable.[103]

ARBITRATION AND ALTERNATIVE DISPUTE RESOLUTION

Disputes arising out of product liability claims may be resolved by means other than trial before a judge or jury. There are several options available to adverse parties to assist them in resolving their disputes without resort to the costly, often protracted, system of civil jurisprudence in the United States. The alternatives to traditional litigation and trial include negotiation and settlement, mediation, summary trial and mini-hearing, and arbitration.

At the option of the parties, alternative dispute resolution by means of mediation, summary trial, mini-hearing, and arbitration may be governed by court rules, or the rules and recommendations of the American Arbitration Association (AAA), a public service nonprofit organization, or other similar organizations. The AAA typically charges a fee for its services based on a percentage of the amount of the claim.[104] Parties can also agree, however, to their own format for mediation or arbitration; if this occurs, they should consult state statutes and local court rules for guidance.

Negotiation and Settlement

Either before or after the commencement of a lawsuit, the adverse parties can and should confer and discuss their differences. Prior to such a discussion, the parties should engage in some discovery or fact finding in order to better evaluate the merits of their respective claims. A successful negotiation and settlement resolves the dispute privately, amicably, relatively quickly, and without any adjudication or admission of liability.

If negotiations resolve the dispute, a settlement agreement should be drafted to preclude all future claims by the plaintiff or claimant arising out of or related to the controversy at issue. The settlement agreement should require the parties to keep the terms of the agreement confidential, and may provide for the filing of a protective order to ensure confidentiality, if necessary.

Resolution of a controversy by means of settlement must be evaluated in terms of the potential for encouraging the assertion of similar claims by others in the future, particularly involving claims of alleged design defects or inadequate warnings affecting an entire product line. While a confidentiality provision in a settlement agreement will do much to stem the tide of future claims, it is not a fail-safe mechanism, and a consideration should be given in settlement on the possible effect of encouraging other claimants to file suit or assert the same claims. Nonetheless, settlement of claims before or at any time during litigation of product liability claims is usually an attractive alternative to the vagaries and costs of litigation, particularly jury trials.

Mediation

Mediation is another method of settling a dispute without resort to trial. Mediation is an abbreviated, informal proceeding in which each side argues the evidence and supporting law to an unbiased panel of mediators or to a single mediator. The mediators, often experienced attorneys or laypersons, analyze the information and propose a compromise to resolve the case in a manner acceptable to both parties. The mediators may discuss the case with the parties, singly or jointly. The decision of the mediators is not binding on the parties and the parties are free to reject it and resolve the dispute by other means.

Mediation prior to trial is often required under state and federal rules.[105] It may also be invoked under the rules promulgated by the AAA or can be invoked pursuant to a stipulation or contract between the parties.

Summary Trials and Mini-Hearings

Summary trials or mini-hearings may also be used as alternative methods for dispute resolution. In some courts, a case may be selected by the court, or by stipulation of the parties, for a summary jury trial or mini-hearing. The summary jury trial is a half- to full-day proceeding during which the parties' attorneys summarize their cases before a jury. Unless the parties stipulate otherwise, the verdict may be only advisory.[106] A mini-hearing is an abbreviated proceeding in which attorneys for corporate parties present their positions to the parties' senior officials to attempt to settle the dispute. The parties may fashion the procedure that they feel is appropriate, although the court may prescribe certain procedures and time limits.[107]

Under procedures developed by the AAA, a mini-trial requires senior executives of adverse parties to participate, along with legal counsel, in an information exchange in which evidence is presented to a neutral advisor. The senior executives meet after the information exchange and negotiate in an attempt to settle the dispute. If they are unable to settle, the neutral advisor renders an opinion identifying issues of law and fact and giving reasons for the opinion. After the issuance of the advisory opinion, the senior executives meet again in another attempt to resolve the dispute and, absent resolution, they may either abandon the proceeding or submit written offers of settlement to the neutral advisor. The neutral advisor then makes a recommendation of settlement based on those written offers. If the parties reject the advisor's recommendation, the mini-trial is terminated and other methods of dispute resolution may be used.

Arbitration

Arbitration involves the submission of a dispute to one or more impartial persons who, unlike the impartial mediators or the neutral advisor in a mini-trial, have the authority to render a binding decision. Each party may present its case, including evidence, argument, and witnesses, to the arbitrators at a hearing. The hearing is much less formal than a trial and strict rules of evidence do not apply. Opening and closing statements may be given to the arbitrators.

In addition to the rules promulgated by the AAA, arbitration is also governed by the laws of many states. The Model Uniform Arbitration Act has been adopted, with some modifications, in 34 states and the District of Columbia.

The advantages of arbitration as opposed to trial are many. Not only is arbitration swifter and more final, with no extensive appellate process, but it is also more private. Sensitive matters need not become a matter of public record filed in our court system for all to see. Arbitration is somewhat more predictable and reliable than a trial would be to the extent that the arbitrators are selected for their skill and knowledge of the subject matter of the dispute. Finally, arbitration, with its speedy resolution and relaxed rules of evidence, does not inflame the adversary nature of the dispute as much as a trial would.

Bifurcation

In the event settlement or mediation does not resolve the dispute, or in the event that arbitration is not a viable alternative and trial appears inevitable, the parties should consider bifurcation of the trial—that is, a separate trial for separate issues. Bifurcation would allow the liability phase of a products liability suit to be tried separately from the damages portion.[108] Thus, the factual and legal issues relating to liability are kept separate from the often "sympathy-inducing" proof of damages. Resolution of the first phase of the trial may promote settlement of subsequent phases and obviate the need for further trials.

The alternatives to trial are many and varied. Each should be explored to determine which method best suits the needs of the parties. Whether under the auspices of the AAA or pursuant to individually formulated agreements or court rules, alternative dispute resolution is an efficient method to resolve claims.

LEGISLATIVE TRENDS IN PRODUCT LIABILITY

Since the early 1970s there has been a call for uniform product liability legislation.[109] In 1979 the Federal Interagency Task Force on Product Liability issued a draft of a Uniform Product Liability

Act (UPLA), [110] which was intended to be a model for state legislatures to enact. The six goals of UPLA were as follows:

1. To ensure that any person injured receive "reasonable compensation" for the harm.
2. To ensure the availability of "affordable" product liability insurance with "adequate coverage" to protect product manufacturers and sellers.
3. To place the incentive for loss prevention on the party best able to accomplish that end.
4. To expedite the reparations process from the time of injury to the time of payment on claim.
5. To minimize transactions costs.
6. To employ statutory language that would be "comparatively" clear and concise.

Although the UPLA in its original form did not meet with overwhelming success, it has served as the benchmark for other federal and state legislative enactments dealing with product liability. Notwithstanding the noted resistance to the broad, sweeping legislative reform suggested by the UPLA, [111] legislative proposals that were more limited in scope met with much greater success. Early offspring of the Elkind Commission's recommendations that the product liability field was ripe for uniform reform included the Consumer Products Safety Act[112] and the establishment of the Consumer Products Safety Commission in 1973. Thereafter Congress enacted the Magnuson-Moss Warranty Federal Trade Commission Improvement Act.[113] The application, however, of the Consumer Product Safety Act and of the Magnuson-Moss legislation was quite limited in scope, basically covering only consumer products and provisions of express warranty.

More recently the National Childhood Vaccine Injury Compensation Act was adopted, providing no fault compensation for any child injured by a vaccine containing pertussis, diphtheria, tetanus (DTP), polio, measles, mumps, or rubella (MMR).[114] Under this act all claims must be filed with the United States Claims Court. Further, under the provisions of the act no lawsuit can be filed against a vaccine manufacturer or administrator for an injury resulting from DTP, polio, or MMR vaccine until after a claim is filed and litigated under the act.[115] Finally, the act provides compensation even though the child's claim may have been barred by governmental immunity for a state-manufactured vaccine or the statute of limitations.

Notwithstanding the lethargic movement of uniform product liability reform proposals there has been very productive state reform activity. The successes of tort reform by local legislative bodies is based, in part, on the fact that the local movement was supported by service providers, small business, municipalities, charities, and professionals, as well as manufacturers. Product liability reform movement was sponsored almost exclusively by manufacturing firms. Thus, the agenda adopted at the state level was short and simple, focusing on narrowly defined issues such as the reform of the rule of joint and several liability; of the collateral source rule; and of the law of punitive damages; limitations on damages for noneconomic loss; and sanctions for frivolous lawsuits. The success of this coalition has been enormous.

Since 1985, 32 states have abolished or limited joint and several liability, 20 states have either made admissible evidence of collateral source payments or have required reduction of awards of compensatory damages by the amount of collateral source payments, and 27 states have changed the law of punitive damages in one of a number of ways. Also, a number of defenses were legislatively enacted that were designed to assist the manufacturers.[116]

Although the states' efforts have been helpful, they have not resolved the overall problems inherent in the product liability tort litigation system. The legislative enactments of the various states are not comprehensive and do not adequately address the key issues that arise in product liability litigation. Moreover, even if a state enacted a comprehensive product liability statute, the legal rules still would vary from state to state.

The several states cannot effectively address the problems of the present product liability system because reform in one state does little to resolve the tort litigation problems facing those who deal in an interstate market. Product manufacturers and product sellers may be involved in product liability actions governed by the law of any state in which they do business. Thus, an attempt by one state to reform the system cannot alleviate the burden imposed on interstate commerce by the inefficient product liability litigation system.

Despite the efforts of some states to bring order to an often chaotic and complex area, the need for a uniform system is ever present. The responsibility of dealing with the broad policy implications of inconsistent state product liability laws on manufacturers, product sellers, and consumers rests with the Congress. Indeed, during the past two decades, proponents of product liability legislation have continued to champion their cause in Washington, and as a result the most recent version, the Products Liability Reform Act,[117] received committee approval on June 29, 1990. President George Bush expressed his support for such legislation in his January 31, 1990 State of the Union Address. Although the timetable is at best murky, given the attempts of the several states in product liability tort reform and the president's pronouncement that federal product liability reform is a top priority, there are hopeful signs that a federal product liability act will eventually be enacted.

CONCLUSION

Since each state has its own set of statutes or decisional law governing product liability claims within its borders, which may, in turn, be dramatically affected by federal laws or regulations, it would be foolhardy to venture forth from this chapter with the view that it provides sufficient advice to enable the reader to form sound business judgments about a broad spectrum of product liability issues. Each topic presented could alone be the subject of an expansive treatise. Rather, the intent in presenting this outline of the rudiments of product liability issues is that problem areas affecting a particular business or line of products may be recognized, and costly mistakes may be avoided or minimized by obtaining timely and detailed professional advice.

Foreign companies doing business in the United States are as susceptible as domestic companies to the pitfalls of product liability. American jurisdiction in cases when a foreign-made product causes alleged injury has exceedingly "long arms." Also, warnings or product labeling viewed as perfectly acceptable in one's home country may be viewed as woefully inadequate in the United States, particularly if adherence to federal labeling standards, where applicable, is not maintained. A finding of a design defect or defects in labeling can jeopardize the viability of an entire product line or precipitate its recall from the marketplace at tremendous cost. The foreign business executive must be vigilant in considering the product liability ramifications of doing business in America, and must be prepared for them. It is hoped that this chapter has provided insight into this complex realm and presents a first step in the strategic planning that must be undertaken in achieving a desirable level of preparedness.

NOTES

1. *Greenman* v. *Yuba Power Products, Inc.*, 59 Cal. 2d 57, 27 Cal. Rptr. 697, 377 P. 2d 897 (1963).
2. See *Greenman* v. *Yuba Power Products, Inc.*, 59 Cal. 2d 57, 377 P. 2d 897, 27 Cal. Rptr. 697 (1963).
3. Restatement (Second) of Torts § 402A comment c (1965). See also *Wright* v. *Newman*, 735 F. 2d 1073 (8th Cir. 1984).
4. See *Prentis* v. *Yale Manufacturing Co.*, 421 Mich. 670, 365 N.W. 2d 176 (1984).
5. See Restatement (Second) of Tort § 402A comment g (1965).
6. See Restatement (Second) of Torts § 402A comment k (1965).
7. See W. Prosser, *Prosser and Keeton on the Law of Torts*, § 42-3 (W. Keeton, ed., 1984).
8. See *Owens by Owens* v. *Bourns, Inc.*, 766 F. 2d 145 (4th Cir.), *cert. denied*, 474 U.S. 1038, 106 S. Ct. 608 (1985).
9. Rule 702 of the Federal Rules of Evidence permits the trier of fact to receive the testimony of a witness "qualified as an expert by knowledge, skill, experience, training or education" if the expert's specialized knowledge "will assist the trier of fact to understand the evidence or determine a fact in issue."
10. Levin, "Junk Science—And What to Do About It," Drug and Medical Device Seminar (1991). (Available from Pepper, Hamilton & Scheetz).
11. See *Brock* v. *Merrell Dow Pharmaceuticals, Inc.*, 874 F. 2d 307 (5th Cir.), *modified* 884 F. 2d 166 (5th Cir.), *reh'g. denied* 886 F. 2d 1314 (5th Cir.), *cert. denied*, —U.S.—, 110 S. Ct. 1511 (1990); see also *Novak* v. *U.S.*, 865 F. 2d 718 (6th Cir. 1989).
12. See Restatement (Second) of Torts § 281 (1965).
13. See Restatement (Second) of Torts § 283 (1965).
14. *Bradbury* v. *Ford Motor Co.*, 123 Mich. App. 179, 333 N.W. 2d 214 (1983). *modified* 419 Mich 550, 358 N.W. 2d 550 (1984).

15. See *Lindsay* v. *Ortho Pharmaceutical Corp.*, 637 F. 2d 87 (2d Cir. 1980)

16. See *First National Bank* v. *Nor-Am Agricultural Products, Inc.*, 88 N.M. 74, 537 P. 2d 682, 692–693 (1975), *cert. denied New Mexico Mill & Elevator Co.* v. *First National Bank,* 88 N.M. 29, 536 P. 2d 1085 (1985).

17. See *Nigh* v. *Dow,* 634 F. Supp. 1513 (W.D. Wis. 1986).

18. See Restatement (Second) of Torts § 402A comment m (1965). See also *Prentis* v. *Yale Manufacturing Co.*, 421 Mich. 670, 365 N.W. 2d 176 (1984).

19. *Smith* v. *E.R. Squibb & Sons, Inc.*, 405 Mich. 79, 273 N.W. 2d 476 (1979).

20. *Smith,* 405 Mich. at 88.

21. See, e.g. *Abel* v. *Eli Lilly and Co.*, 418 Mich. 311, 343 N.W. 2d 164 (1984), *cert. denied,* 469 U.S. 833, 105 S. Ct. 123 (1984). The Michigan Supreme Court adopted the alternative liability theory in DES actions but restricted it to negligence claims.

22. See *McCormack* v. *Abbott Laboratories,* 617 F. Supp. 1521 (D. Mass. 1985); *Conley* v. *Boyle Drug Co.,* 570 So. 2d. 275 (Fla. 1990); *Sindell* v. *Abbott Laboratories,* 26 Cal. 3d 588, 607 P. 2d 924, 163, Cal. Rptr. 132 (1980), *cert. denied,* 449 U.S. 912, 101 S. Ct. 285 (1980).

23. See *Ray* v. *Cutter Laboratories,* 754 F. Supp. 193 (M.D. Fla. 1991).

24. See e.g. *Abel* v. *Eli Lilly & Co.,* 418 Mich. 311, 343 N.W. 2d 164 (1984), *cert. denied,* 469 U.S. 833, 105 S. Ct. 123 (1984).

25. 345 F. Supp. 353 (E.D.N.Y. 1972).

26. See also *Bichler* v. *Eli Lilly Co.,* 79 A.D. 2d 317, 436 N.Y.S. 2d 625 (1981), *Aff'd,* 55 N.Y. 2d 571, 436 N.E. 2d 182, 450 N.Y.S. 2d 776 (1982).

27. See generally W. Prosser, *Prosser and Keeton on the Law of Torts* § 36 (see *supra* n. 7).

28. Product liability law is also affected by state regulation. However, the treatment of this body of law is beyond the scope of this chapter. Manufacturers or distributors of products should be aware of the laws of the various states in which they do business.

29. 15 U.S.C.A. §§ 2301–2312 (West 1982 & Supp. 1991).

30. 15 U.S.C.A. §§ 2051–2083 (West 1982 & Supp. 1991).

31. 15 U.S.C.A. §§ 1391–1431 (West 1982 & Supp. 1991).

32. 7 U.S.C.A. § 136–136y (West 1980 & Supp. 1991).

33. 21 U.S.C.A. §§ 301–392 (West 1972 & Supp. 1991).

34. 42 U.S.C.A. §§ 9601–9657 (West 1983 & Supp. 1991). CERCLA was amended in 1986 by the Superfund Amendments and Reauthorization Act (SARA), 26 U.S.C. §§ 9501–9602 (West 1989 & Supp. 1991).

35. See *United States* v. *Velsicol Chemical Corp.*, 701 F. Supp. 140 (W.D. Tenn. 1987).
36. See *United States* v. *Aceto Agricultural Chemicals Corp.*, 872 F. 2d 1373 (8th Cir. 1989).
37. 42 U.S.C.A. § 9607(a) (3) (West 1983 & Supp. 1991).
38. *Bonney* v. *Upjohn Co.*, 129 Mich. App. 18, 342 N.W. 2d 551 (1983).
39. See *O'Stricker* v. *Jim Walter Corp.*, 4 Ohio St. 3d 84, 447 N.E. 2d 727 (1983).
40. *Larson* v. *Johns-Manville Sales Corp.*, 427 Mich. 301, 399 N.W. 2d 1 (1986), *reh'g denied*, 428 Mich. 1207 (1987).
41. See *Schiele* v. *Hobart Corp.*, 284 Or. 483, 587 P. 2d 1010 (1978).
42. *Sedlack* v. *Ford Motor Co.*, 64 Mich. App. 61, 235 N.W. 2d 63 (1975).
43. 51 Am. Jur. 2d *Limitation of Action* §§ 138–199 (1970).
44. 63A Am. Jur. 2d Products Liability §§ 921–923 (1984).
45. *Higgins* v. *E. I. DuPont de Nemours & Co.*, 863 F. 2d 1162 (4th Cir. 1988).
46. *Prosky* v. *National Acme Co.*, 404 F. Supp. 852 (E.D. Mich. 1975).
47. See W. Prosser, *Prosser and Keeton on the Law of Torts* § 68 (see supra n. 7).
48. See, e.g., Ariz. Rev. Stat. Ann. §12-683(1) (1990) (provides a defense for products conforming to the state of the art, defined in § 12-681(6) as the knowledge "in existence and reasonably feasible for use at the time of manufacture." *Id*.); N.J. Stat. Ann. § 2A:58 C-3 (West 1987 & Supp. 1990) (defense applies if at the time product left manufacturer's hands, "there was not a practical and technically feasible alternative design that would have prevented the harm without substantially impairing the reasonably anticipated or intended function of the product" unless, through "clear and convincing evidence" it is shown that the product is "egregiously unsafe or ultrahazardous." *Id*.).
49. Culhane, *Possible Effects, Real and Imagined, of Statutes, Restricting the Liability of Non-manufacturing Sellers of Defective Products*, 2 Products Liability L.J. 39, 56 (1990).
50. *Smith* v. *Minster Machine Co.* 669 F. 2d 628 (10th Cir. 1982); Ky. Rev. Stat. Ann. § 411.310 (2) (Michie/Bobbs-Merrill 1979 & Supp. 1990) (which creates a rebuttable presumption of no liability where the design conforms "to the generally recognized and prevailing standards or the state of the art." *Id*.).
51. E.g., American Society for Testing and Materials (ASTM) and the American National Standards Institute (ANSI). Both publish non-mandatory industrial standards for products and materials.
52. *Rexrode* v. *American Laundry Press Co.*, 674 F. 2d 826 (10th Cir.) *cert. denied*, 459 U.S. 862, 103 S. Ct. 137 (1982).

53. See the Model Uniform Pro. Liab. Act, § 107(E) (1979), which adopts this approach.

54. *Johnson* v. *Raybestos Manhattan, Inc.,* 69 Haw. 287, 740 P. 2d 548 (1987); *Beshada* v. *Johns-Manville Product Corp.,* 90 N.J. 191, 447 A. 2d 539 (1982).

55. *Beshada,* 447 A. 2d at 548. But see *O'Brien* v. *Muskin Corp.,* 94 N.J. 169 (1982) and *Feldman* v. *Lederle Laboratories,* 97 N.J. 429, 479 A. 2d 374 (1984) where *Beshada* was limited to its facts.

56. *Borel* v. *Fibreboard Paper Products Corp.,* 493 F. 2d 1076 (5th Cir. 1973), *cert. denied,* 419 U.S. 869, 95 S. Ct. 127 (1974).

57. *Muhlenberg* v. *Upjohn Co.,* 115 Mich. App. 316, 320 N.W. 2d 358 (1982).

58. *Borel,* 493 F. 2d 1076, *Moran* v. *Johns-Manville,* 691 F. 2d 811 (6th Cir. 1982).

59. See Restatement (Second) of Torts, § 388 (1975); *Goodbar* v. *Whitehead Bros.,* 591 F. Supp. 552 (W.D. Va. 1984), *aff'd, Beale* v. *Hardy,* 769 F. 2d 213 (4th Cir. 1985).

60. *Rusin* v. *Glendale Optical Co.,* 805 F. 2d 650 (6th Cir. 1986).

61. *Goodbar,* 591 F. Supp. at 558. See also Restatement (Second) of Torts, § 388, comment n (1975).

62. *Higgins* v. *E. I. DuPont de Nemours Co.,* 671 F. Supp. 1055 (D. Md. 1987), *aff'd,* 863 F. 2d 1162 (4th Cir. 1988).

63. Compare *Strong* v. *E. I. DuPont de Nemours Co.,* 667 F. 2d 682 (8th Cir. 1981) with *Jacobson* v. *Colorado Fuel & Iron Corp.,* 409 F. 2d 1263 (9th Cir. 1969).

64. See *Adams* v. *Union Carbide Corp.,* 737 F. 2d 1453 (6th Cir.), *cert. denied,* 469 U.S. 1062, 105 S. Ct. 545 (1984).

65. See Occupational Safety and Health Act (OSHA), 29 U.S.C.A. § 656 (West 1985 & Supp. 1991).

66. *Dougherty* v. *Hooker Chemical Corp.* 540 F. 2d 174 (3d Cir. 1976). But see *Adkins* v. *GAF Corp.,* 923 F. 2d 1225 (6th Cir. 1991) (a supplier of raw asbestos is not relieved of duty to warn employees of an asbestos product manufacturer since the supplier was familiar with the magnitude of employee exposure to asbestos and was not precluded by the packaging of asbestos from conveying a warning directly to the employees).

67. See, e.g., *Chambers* v. *G. D. Searle & Co.,* 441 F. Supp. 377 (D. Md. 1975), *aff'd,* 567 F. 2d 269 (4th Cir. 1977); *Smith* v. *E. R. Squibb & Sons, Inc.,* 405 Mich. 79, 273 N.W. 2d 476 (1979).

68. *Gravis* v. *Parke-Davis & Co.,* 502 S.W. 2d 863, 870 (Tex. Ct. App. 1973).

69. *Lindsay* v. *Ortho Pharmaceutical Corp.,* 637 F. 2d 87, 91 (2d Cir. 1980).

70. *Muilenberg* v. *The Upjohn Co.*, 115 Mich. App. 316, 320 N.W. 2d 358 (1982).

71. *Garrison* v. *Rohm and Haas Co.*, 492 F. 2d 346 (6th Cir. 1974); *Spangler* v. *Kranco, Inc.*, 481 F. 2d 373 (4th Cir. 1973); Restatement (Second) of Torts § 404 comment a (1965).

72. *Garrison*, 492 F. 2d at 353.

73. *Leahy* v. *Mid-West Conveyor Co.*, 120 A.D. 2d 16, 507 N.Y.S. 2d 514, 516 (1986), *appeal denied*, 69 N.Y. 2d 606, 514, N.Y.S. 2d 1024, 507 N.E. 2d 320 (1987); *Moon* v. *Winger Boss Co.*, 205 Neb. 292, 287 N.W. 2d 430 (1980).

74. *Orion Ins. Co.* v. *United Technologies Corp.*, 502 F. Supp. 173 (E.D. Pa. 1980).

75. *Garrison*, 492 F. 2d at 352.

76. *Orion*, 502 F. Supp. at 178; *Garrison*, 492 F. 2d at 351.

77. In *Boyle* v. *United Technologies Corp.*, 487 U.S. 580, 108 S. Ct. 2510 (1988) the U.S. Supreme Court found that state law that imposes liability for design defects in military equipment is displaced when (1) the United States approved reasonably precise specifications, (2) the equipment conformed to those specifications, and (3) the supplier warned the government about dangers in the use of the equipment known to the supplier but not the United States.

78. See, e.g., *Frazier* v. *Materials Transportation Co.*, 609 F. Supp. 933 (W.D. Pa. 1985).

79. *Childress* v. *Gresen Manufacturing. Co.*, 888 F. 2d 45 (6th Cir. 1989); *Walker* v. *Stauffer Chemical Co.*, 19 Cal. App. 3d 669, 96 Cal. Rptr. 803 (1971).

80. 42 U.S.C.A. §§ 300AA-1 to 300AA-34 (West Supp. 1991).

81. 15 U.S.C.A. § 1334 (West 1982 & Supp. 1991).

82. See *Palmer* v. *Liggett Group, Inc.*, 825 F. 2d 620 (1st Cir. 1987); *Cipollone* v. *Liggett Group, Inc.*, 893 F. 2d 541 (3rd Cir. 1990), *cert. granted* 111 S. Ct. 1386 (1991).

83. See *Animal Defense Fund Boston, Inc.* v. *Provimi Veal Corp.*, 626 F. Supp. 278 (D. Mass.), *aff'd.*, 802 F. 2d 440 (1st Cir. 1986).

84. 7 U.S.C.A. §§ 136–136y (West 1980 & Supp. 1991).

85. See *Papas* v. *The Upjohn Co.*, 926 F. 2d 1019 (11th Cir. 1991).

86. See *Seely* v. *White Motor Co.*, 63 Cal. 2d 9, 403 P. 2d 145 (1965), and its progeny. See also Uniform Commercial Code, Sec. 2-715(2).

87. See *Berger* v. *Weber*, 411 Mich 1, 303 N.W. 2d 424 (1981) (allowing a child's right to recover for loss of parental society and companionship following injury to parent).

88. Uniform Commercial Code, Sec. 1-106.

89. See *Grimshaw* v. *Ford Motor Co.*, 119 Cal. App. 3d 757, 174 Cal. Rptr. 348 (1981).

90. The common law doctrine of contributory negligence, now largely abrogated or modified by state comparative negligence statutes, barred a plaintiff from recovering damages if the plaintiff's own negligence contributed to the plaintiff's injury. Comparative negligence law statutes have softened the harshness of the common law rule by merely reducing the amount of the plaintiff's recovery in proportion to the amount of the plaintiff's negligence. Some states, however, do not permit a plaintiff to recover if the plaintiff's negligence was greater than the negligence of the defendant. Because of the variations in statutory language, each state statute governing the litigation should be examined.

91. For a general discussion of the comparative negligence statutes of the states see 57B Am. Jur. 2d §§ 1140–1154. States adopting the "pure" comparative negligence rule include Alaska, Arizona, California, Florida, Kentucky, Louisiana, Michigan, Mississippi, Missouri, New Mexico, New York, Rhode Island, and Washington. States adopting the modified comparative negligence rule include Arkansas, Colorado, Idaho, Kansas, Maine, North Dakota, Utah, West Virginia, and Wyoming. Finally, those states allowing an equally negligent plaintiff to recover include Connecticut, Hawaii, Illinois, Indiana, Iowa, Massachusetts, Minnesota, Montana, Nevada, New Hampshire, New Jersey, Ohio, Oklahoma, Oregon, Pennsylvania, Texas, Vermont, and Wisconsin.

92. When individual defendants are assigned a proportion of liability pursuant to a verdict under a comparative negligence statute, there would presumably be no right to contribution among codefendants since their individual shares of liability would have already been decided.

93. *International Shoe Co.* v. *Washington,* 326 U.S. 310, 66 S. Ct. 154 (1945).

94. *World-Wide Volkswagen Corp.* v. *Woodson,* 444 U.S. 286, 100 S. Ct. 559 (1980).

95. See generally 36 Am. Jur. 2d *Foreign Corporations* § 472 (1968).

96. *DeMoss* v. *City Market Inc.,* 762 F. Supp. 913, (D. Utah 1991) (Japanese supplier's distribution of a dietary supplement in the United States and its awareness that some of it would be consumed in Utah meant it should not have been surprised to be haled into federal court in Utah).

97. *Kline* v. *Johns-Manville,* 745 F. 2d 1217 (9th Cir. 1984).

98. *Shannon* v. *Samuel Langston Co.,* 379 F. Supp. 797 (W.D. Mich. 1974).

99. *La Fountain* v. *Webb Industries Corp.,* 759 F. Supp. 236 (E.D. Pa. 1991); See also 63 Am. Jur. 2d Products Liability §175 (1984).

100. *Ricciardello* v. *J. W. Gant & Co.*, 717 F. Supp. 56 (D. Conn. 1989).

101. *Phoenix Canada Oil Co. Ltd.* v. *Texaco, Inc.*, 658 F. Supp. 1061 (D. Del. 1987).

102. *Porter* v. *Beloit Corp.*, 667 F. Supp 367 (S.D. Miss. 1987).

103. *Ricker* v. *American Zinser Corp.*, 506 F. Supp. 1 (E.D. Tenn. 1978).

104. For a comprehensive discussion of the rules of the AAA, including mediation, mini-trial, and arbitration, see R. Coulson, *Business Arbitration—What You Need to Know*, 3d ed. (1987).

105. See, e.g., Michigan Court Rules, Rule 2.403; Local Rules 32 and 42 of the U.S. District Courts for the Eastern and Western Districts of Michigan, respectively.

106. See Local Rule 44, U.S. District Court for the Western District of Michigan; M. D. Jacoubovitch & C. Moore, *Summary Jury Trials in Northern District of Ohio* (Federal Judicial Center, 1982).

107. See W.D. Mich. R. 44(c); Parker & Radoff, *The Mini-Hearing: An Alternative to Protracted Litigation of Factually Complex Disputes*, 38 Bus. Law 35 (1982).

108. See, e.g., *Helminski* v. *Ayerst Laboratories*, 766 F. 2d 208 (6th Cir. 1985) (bifurcation appropriate where evidence of liability is wholly unrelated to evidence of damages and evidence of damages could have a prejudicial effect on the determination of liability).

109. In March, 1968 President Lyndon Johnson appointed the Elkind National Commission on Product Safety. The commission issued its findings and conclusions in 1970 with a recommendation that priority be given to legislation that provides consumers protection from "unreasonable product risks." Eginton, *An Overview of Federal and State Legislative Developments in Torts and Products Liability*, 1 Products Liability L.J. 55 (1988). The Elkind Commission concluded that state and local legislation designed to respond to this need amounted to a "hodgepodge of tragedy-inspired responses." *Id.* at 55.

110. The UPLA was published in final form in the Federal Register in 1979.

111. To date, the tort reform legislation that has been offered has failed to satisfy any faction involved in the product liability arena. Criticism to the proposed legislation has come from the plaintiff's bar, manufacturer associations, business and industry groups, insurance counsel, and the defense bar. The most noted concerns have been the clarity of the proposals and uncertainty of the statutory language.

112. 15 U.S.C.A. § 2051–2083 (West 1982 & Supp. 1991).

113. 15 U.S.C.A. § 2301–2312 (West 1982 & Supp. 1991).

114. 42 U.S.C.A. § 300aa-14(a) (West Supp. 1991).

115. 42 U.S.C. § 300aa-11(a) (3) (West Supp. 1991).

116. By way of example, Colorado enacted a statute of repose, Iowa a state of the art defense, and Kansas barred the admission of evidence of subsequent remedial measures. In 1987, California enacted an "inherently dangerous product" defense; Delaware, Georgia, and North Dakota enacted limitations on the liability of product sellers; and Montana enacted a product misuse defense. At the same time, several states made FDA approval a defense to a claim for punitive damages.

117. S. 1400, 101st Cong., 2d Sess. (1990).

PART 4

TAXATION

CHAPTER 16

THE FEDERAL TAX SYSTEM

Bernard M. Shapiro
Managing Partner, Washington National Tax Service
Price Waterhouse
Daniel A. Noakes
Tax Senior Manager
Price Waterhouse

OVERVIEW OF THE TAX SYSTEM

Introduction

Because taxes represent a major cost of doing business, the foreign investor should learn as much as possible about the tax systems of all locations under consideration. Taxation by the U.S. government provides the revenue necessary to operate the government and its many programs. Individual and corporate income taxes provide more than half the government's total revenues. Income tax rules also are responsible for the greatest complexity in the tax laws. Accordingly, this chapter will focus primarily on the income tax.

Legislative Framework of the Tax System

The federal tax system operates through self-assessment, although certain income and payroll taxes are collected largely through withholding, and self-assessment is monitored through information reporting. The basic substantive and procedural tax rules are set forth in statutes passed by Congress. However, the statutes alone do not provide all the information necessary for taxpayers to compute their correct tax liability. Often taxpayers also must consult administrative guidance and judicial interpretations.

The federal tax statutes, with minor exceptions, are compiled and published in the United States Code. The present statutory compilation is known as the Internal Revenue Code of 1986. Previously, the tax statutes were organized as the Internal Revenue Code of 1954 and its predecessor, the Internal Revenue Code of 1939.

The Internal Revenue Code is amended periodically, often several times in a year. Retroactive legislation is permitted and is occurring with increasing frequency. However, legislation rarely provides an effective date for a provision that precedes the date of introduction of the bill proposing the provision.

Statutory tax rules also may be affected by treaties between the United States and other countries. Tax treaties serve to limit double taxation of income from international trade and investment, and provide a framework for an exchange of tax information between the treaty partners and a mechanism for resolution of disputes.

Within the executive branch of the federal government, the Treasury Department has responsibility for implementing the tax statutes. This function specifically is carried out by the Internal Revenue Service (IRS), an agency of the Treasury Department. The duties of the IRS are twofold:

- To interpret the statutes in accordance with the intent of Congress.
- To administer and enforce the statutes.

The interpretive duties of the Treasury Department and the IRS range from the general to the specific. Treasury regulations are written in broad terms to explain and illustrate the provisions of the Internal Revenue Code, and generally are accepted by the courts as authoritative interpretations of the law. On the other hand, revenue rulings, private letter rulings, and technical advice memoranda issued by the IRS interpret the Code only with respect to specific facts or particular taxpayers. Revenue procedures are issued to announce administrative practices that the IRS follows. The IRS uses technical information releases to disseminate important technical information on specific issues.

Taxpayers and the IRS frequently dispute matters of tax law. If not settled through compromise, such disputes may be resolved by federal courts. The decisions of the courts and the opinions expressed therein provide additional interpretations that may provide guidance to taxpayers in the application of the tax laws to their particular situations. Judicial interpretations provide varying degrees of binding precedent, depending upon the nature of the issue and the jurisdictional authority of the court that rendered the opinion.

Principal Taxes

The principal taxes in the federal tax system are income taxes, payroll-related taxes, excise taxes, and estate and gift taxes.

Income Taxes

Under the unitary federal income tax system, income from all sources is aggregated and, after deductions for allowable expenses, is subject to tax at progressive rates.

The principal types of domestic and foreign taxpayers covered by the income tax laws are corporations, individuals, trusts, and estates. Partnerships are not taxpayers since they are treated generally as conduits, whereby the partners, and not the partnership, are taxed on the partnership income.

The income tax system will be covered in greater detail later in the chapter.

Payroll-Related Taxes

Payroll-related taxes represent the second-largest source of revenue for the U.S. government—approximately 37 percent. The two primary taxes in this category are social security taxes and unemployment taxes.

Social Security System.   Federal old-age, survivors, and disability insurance (OASDI), referred to as social security, was inaugurated in 1935 to alleviate financial hardship brought about by the retirement, disability, or death of a wage earner. Another program, Medicare, provides health benefits for the elderly.

The social security and Medicare programs are financed by

taxes on wages, levied at equal rates on both employers and employees. Self-employed individuals pay such taxes on their net earnings from self-employment.

Almost all types of employment and self-employment are covered under social security and Medicare. The only large groups excluded are certain government workers and some religious employees. The railroads have a separate retirement system, but their employees are covered under Medicare. U.S. citizens working abroad are covered if they are working for an American employer or, if coverage has been arranged, for an American employer's foreign affiliate.

Resident aliens are subject to social security tax in the same manner as U.S. citizens. In addition, nonresident aliens may be subject to the social security tax, depending on the type of visa issued to them. For example, temporary business visitors with an incidental business purpose may be subject to social security tax unless exempt from U.S. income tax. Further, temporary workers and alien traders are subject to the social security tax for personal services performed in the United States. Alien employees of a foreign government are exempt from the social security tax, although employers of an instrumentality owned by a foreign government must meet certain criteria to be exempt.

The wage base for these payroll taxes is subject to a dollar limitation. For 1992, the base is $55,500 for the OASDI program tax and $130,200 for the Medicare tax. Employers withhold their employees' portion from wages when paid. Social security taxes (both the employer and the employee portions) must be paid over to the government by employers at least quarterly and, for larger employers, more frequently.

The scheduled rates for 1992 and succeeding years used to compute social security taxes are shown below:

	OASDI	*Medicare*
Employer and employee (each)	6.2%	1.45%
Self-employed	12.4%	2.9%

A self-employed person may reduce self-employment earnings by an amount equal to his or her self-employment earnings multiplied by one half of the rates shown above when computing self-employment tax. This provision roughly parallels the treatment of employer's matching social security payments as nontaxable compensation for employees.

Social security taxes paid by employees are not deductible in computing federal income tax. However, one half of the self-employment tax paid by a self-employed individual is deductible when computing federal taxable income.

The president of the United States has the authority to enter into bilateral agreements with other countries to provide for coordination between the social security systems of the United States and those of other countries. These agreements, appropriately entitled "international social security agreements," are informally referred to as "totalization agreements." Under such an agreement, an employee's periods of coverage under both systems may be combined for the purposes of establishing entitlement to and the amount of old-age, survivor's, disability, or derivative benefits. Totalization agreements are designed to eliminate dual coverage and dual employee and employer taxation for the same work. Since the individual cannot receive credit under both systems, he or she does not have to pay social security taxes under both systems.

Unemployment Insurance. The unemployment insurance program is a joint federal-state undertaking designed to assist those who become unemployed, generally through no fault of their own, for limited periods of total or partial unemployment. The self-employed, agricultural workers on small farms, and some domestic workers are not eligible for unemployment insurance.

For 1992, a federal unemployment tax is levied on employers equal to 6.2 percent of the first $7,000 in wages paid an employee. Because the employer receives a credit of up to 5.4 percent against the federal tax for amounts paid to state unemployment insurance funds, the net federal rate may be 0.8 percent. The federal government pays expenses that the states incur in administering unemployment compensation. To benefit from the credit and financial assistance, a state's compensation system must meet certain standards.

The rate of state unemployment insurance contribution varies from state to state. Within each state, the rates are likely to vary depending on the past history or "experience rating" of the employer with respect to insurance claims of current and former employees.

Excise Taxes
While there are no national, broad-based consumption taxes in the United States, various excise taxes are imposed on goods and services. Depending upon the product, the tax may be collected at the manufacturer, wholesaler, or retailer level. Excise taxes were expected to account for only about 4 percent of the federal government's total 1991 revenues.

Historically, excise taxes have been used as a source of emergency revenue to fund war efforts or as "user fees," as in the case of gasoline taxes used to fund highway construction. In 1990 legislation, Congress significantly increased excise taxes primarily to raise revenue to help offset rising budget deficits. The 1990 legislation extended or increased excise taxes on alcohol products, tobacco products, gasoline, and aviation fuels, and imposed "luxury" excise taxes on automobiles, furs, jewelry, boats, and aircraft costing more than specified amounts.

Estate and Gift Taxes
As discussed below, the U.S. gift and estate tax systems are linked together. The rules applicable to citizens and resident aliens differ from those applicable to nonresident aliens. The following is a discussion of the rules applicable to citizens and resident aliens. The gift and estate tax rules for nonresident aliens are covered in Chapter 20.

Gift Tax.   The federal gift tax applies to all transfers by a U.S. citizen or resident of property by gift, whether in trust or otherwise, whether direct or indirect, and whether the property is real or personal, tangible or intangible. The gift tax is levied at graduated rates on the fair market value of gifts made during any calendar year, less certain exclusions and deductions.

A $10,000 annual exclusion is allowed for gifts of present interests made to any one donee. Accordingly, a donor may make gifts of $10,000 each to several donees every year without incurring gift tax liability. If the gifts are made by a spouse, they may be treated as being made one half by each spouse, in effect allowing for a $20,000 annual exclusion. Deductions allowed from total gifts in a year include an unlimited marital deduction to a U.S. citizen's spouse and all charitable gifts.

The gift tax is cumulative in nature—that is, it is based on the sum of taxable gifts made in the current and prior years. The tax initially is computed at current rates on the total of taxable gifts to date; this amount is reduced by the tax (computed at current rates) on all taxable gifts of previous years. The gift tax rates range from 18 percent on the first $10,000 of taxable gifts to 55 percent on taxable gifts in excess of $3 million. The top rate is scheduled to drop to 50 percent for gifts over $2,500,000 after 1992. A once-in-a-lifetime unified credit of $192,800 is allowed. The allowable credit for each year is reduced by the amount of the credit allowed in prior years.

Estate Tax. The federal estate tax is levied upon the transfer of property of a decedent to his or her heirs or beneficiaries. (The decedent's estate itself usually is treated as a separate taxable entity.) The gross estate of a decedent who was a citizen or resident of the United States consists of all property to the extent of his or her interest therein at the date of death, including real property located outside the United States. Certain lifetime transfers may be includible in the decedent's gross estate if specified interests or powers are retained in or over the property transferred—for example, the retention of a life estate or a general power of appointment. Lifetime gifts made within three years of the date of death are included in the gross estate; however, gifts that are not taxable because of the $10,000 annual exclusion are not subject to this three-year rule.

All items generally are included in the gross estate at fair market value at the date of death or on an alternative valuation date six months after the date of death. Deductions from the gross estate include funeral and estate administration expenses, debts of the decedent and claims against the estate, mortgages and liens, and charitable contributions. In order for transfers to qualify for the marital deduction, the spouse must be a U.S. citizen or the transfer must be to a Qualified Domestic Trust that ensures that federal estate tax will be paid when the surviving spouse dies.

The estate tax is computed by first adding to the taxable estate the amount of taxable gifts made after December 31, 1976, and not otherwise included in the gross estate, and then applying the same rate schedule applicable to the gift tax. This tentative tax is reduced by the amount of gift tax paid on post-1976 gifts. The gross estate tax payable as thus computed is then reduced by the unified credit as outlined above. The unified credit is reduced by the amount of the unified credit claimed by the decedent in prior gift tax returns. Certain other credits are also allowed (subject to limitation), including a credit for state inheritance taxes and foreign death duties.

The United States does not impose an inheritance tax on beneficiaries. However, some states impose an inheritance tax.

Tax on Certain Generation-Skipping Transfers.   A transfer tax is imposed (with certain exceptions) on transfers under trusts and equivalent arrangements between generations of beneficiaries belonging to a generation younger than the grantor's. The tax is imposed on the transferor at a flat rate. A number of significant exemptions exist. Prior to the enactment of this tax, a family could arrange for the transfer of property so that transfer taxes were paid only once every several generations.

Overview of Foreign Tax Concepts

The federal tax system has a number of special tax provisions relating to both inbound and outbound activities. Many of these provisions are covered in detail elsewhere in this book—for example:

- Chapter 8—"Investment Incentives—Government as a Business Partner."
- Chapter 12—"U.S. Treaty Agreements Affecting Foreign Investors."
- Chapter 19—"Taxation of U.S. Investments of Foreign Corporations."
- Chapter 20—"Taxation of Aliens in the United States."

A basic concept in the income taxation of foreign corporations is that income effectively connected with a U.S. trade or business of the foreign corporation is taxed separately from income that is not so connected. In general, effectively connected income is taxed at the rates applicable to a domestic corporation. U.S. source non-effectively connected income is taxed (if at all) at a flat rate of 30 percent on gross income, unless a lower rate is applicable under a treaty. Only certain types of non-effectively connected income are taxable.

Geographical Source of Income

The geographical source of an item of income has a significant impact on the tax liability of both U.S. and foreign taxpayers. Federal tax law sets forth which items of gross income constitute U.S. source income. Certain items of income, although originating from the United States, are specifically treated as foreign source income. The items of gross income that are considered to be from U.S. sources and the exceptions thereto are discussed below.

Interest.   Interest from obligations of the United States and interest on bonds or other obligations of U.S. residents, corporate or otherwise, generally are considered to be from U.S. sources. However, the following types of interest are *not* considered to be from U.S. sources:

- Interest on deposits with foreign branches of U.S. banks.
- Interest received from a U.S. corporation or resident alien if at least 80 percent of the payor's worldwide gross income is attributable to the active conduct of a trade or business in a foreign country or U.S. possession for the three-year period preceding the year of payment. However, an exception to the 80-percent rule applies where interest is paid to a related party.
- Interest received from a foreign corporation not deriving a major portion of its income from a U.S. business
- Certain interest received by nonresident aliens and foreign corporations.

Dividends. Dividends received from a U.S. corporation constitute U.S. source income, *except* for:

- Dividends received by nonresidents and foreign corporations from certain U.S. corporations.
- Dividends received from certain U.S. corporations qualifying as possessions corporations (i.e., a U.S. corporation actively engaged in a trade or business in a U.S. possession that meets certain requirements).
- Dividends from a DISC (domestic international sales corporation) or former DISC, to the extent attributable to qualified export receipts.
- Dividends received from a foreign corporation if less than 25 percent of its gross income is effectively connected with the conduct of a U.S. trade or business for the three-year period preceding the year the dividend was paid. Dividends paid by a foreign corporation deriving 25 percent or more of its gross income from a U.S. business constitute U.S. source income, but only in the same proportion that the foreign corporation's gross income effectively connected with a U.S. trade or business bears to its total gross income. Dividends from a foreign sales corporation (FSC) are not considered to be from U.S. sources.

Compensation for Personal Services. Compensation for labor or personal services (including pensions or other deferred compensation) attributable to services performed in the United States is treated as U.S. source income. Certain compensation for services performed in the United States by a nonresident alien is not considered as U.S. source income.

Rentals and Royalties. Rentals or royalties from property located in the United States, or from any interest in such property, including rents or royalties for the use of patents, copyrights, secret processes, formulas, goodwill, trademarks, and so on, in the United States, are considered to be from U.S. sources.

Sale or Exchange of Real Property. Gains, profits, and income from the sale of real property located in the United States are considered to be from U.S. sources.

Sale or Exchange of Personal Property.   With respect to inventory, income derived from the purchase of personal property outside the United States (other than within a possession of the United States) and subsequent resale in the United States is considered to be from U.S. sources. Similarly, inventory purchased within the United States and sold outside the United States gives rise to foreign source income. However, where inventory produced in the United States is sold outside the United States, an allocation of the income is made between U.S. and foreign sources.

Income from the sale or exchange of personal property other than inventory is generally treated as U.S. source for residents and foreign source for nonresidents. However, there is a special definition of "resident" for this purpose.

Underwriting Income.   Amounts received as underwriting income from the insurance of U.S. risk are considered to be from a U.S. source.

Transportation Income.   Fifty percent of all transportation income, including that from the hire or lease for use of aircraft and vessels, attributable to international transportation that begins or ends in the United States, is U.S. source income.

Income from Sources Within and Without the United States. Items of income not falling in one of the above categories are either from sources without the United States or allocable to sources within and without the United States in accordance with regulations prescribed by the Treasury Department. Items of income that require allocation between U.S. and foreign sources include income derived from the sale of personal property produced within and sold without the United States, or vice versa; and income from the purchase of personal property within a possession of the United States and its sale within the United States.

Other Major Areas of Federal Taxation

Within the federal tax system, there are many specialty areas with complex rules. Some of these areas will be addressed in passing in this chapter. Some, such as employee benefits (Chapter 22), are discussed in greater detail elsewhere in the book.

Also, many industries have their own unique tax rules, such as banks and other financial institutions, discussed in Chapter 6, and insurance companies, discussed in Chapter 7. Other such industries include natural resources and regulated investment companies (mutual funds).

The Internal Revenue Code also sets forth rules applicable to nonprofit organizations, including private foundations. Subject to certain requirements, charitable and similar organizations, trade associations, labor unions, and social clubs are exempt from income tax. However, income from a business activity that is unrelated to the tax-exempt purposes of the organization may be subject to tax.

GENERAL PRINCIPLES OF INCOME TAXATION

Corporate Taxpayers

The United States generally uses the classical system of corporate taxation, in which income is taxed at the corporate level and on distribution to shareholders. However, certain intercompany dividends may be partly or wholly excluded, and a corporate shareholder receiving dividends from a foreign corporate affiliate may be allowed a credit for foreign income taxes paid or accrued by the payor. As mentioned below, special rules apply to certain types of corporations.

The place of incorporation plays an important role in the U.S. taxation of a corporation. Corporations incorporated in the United States are subject to U.S. taxation on their worldwide income, subject to a credit against U.S. tax on foreign income based on foreign income taxes paid with respect to such income; foreign corporations are subject to U.S. tax only on their U.S. source income.

The accounting period used by a corporation for tax purposes is the annual accounting period used in keeping its books, and can be either a calendar or a fiscal year. A change in the accounting period may require the permission of the IRS.

Accounting Methods

In general, accounting for tax purposes follows accounting principles accepted in the United States by accountants and businesses.

The tax law does not specify the type of records that must be maintained, but does require that they clearly reflect income. All income and deductions must be stated in terms of U.S. dollars.

The two overall methods of accounting are the cash and accrual methods. The cash method entails the reporting of income when actually or constructively received, while the accrual method requires the reporting of income when all events have occurred that fix the right to receive such income and the amount can be determined with reasonable accuracy. Deductions are claimed by a cash-basis taxpayer when paid and by an accrual-basis taxpayer when the liability becomes both fixed and determinable. However, certain liabilities are not treated as incurred until economic performance occurs. When the production, purchase, or sale of merchandise is a factor in the production of income, the taxpayer generally must compute income with respect to such activities using the accrual method so that inventories are taken into account at the beginning and end of the year.

The tax law limits the use of the cash method of accounting. In general, corporations other than S corporations may not use the cash method. Certain exceptions are provided for corporations with average annual gross receipts of $5 million or less for the preceding three tax years, certain farming corporations, and qualified personal service corporations.

In addition to the selection of an overall method of tax accounting, there are elections to be made regarding the accounting for special types of income or deductions. For instance, special tax accounting methods are provided for installment sales, bad debts, real property taxes, long-term installation or construction contracts, inventory valuations, depreciation allowances, and certain other items. A change in a method of accounting generally requires IRS permission.

Tax Computation

Corporate net income (taxable income) is computed by subtracting allowable deductions from gross income.

Tax rates for a U.S. corporation cover three brackets and a range of 15, 25, and 34 percent. However, the two lower brackets of 15 and 25 percent are phased out by the imposition of an additional 5-percent tax on taxable income over $100,000, up to $335,000. As a result, corporations with taxable income in excess of $335,000 effectively pay tax at a flat rate of 34 percent. Net long-term gains derived from dispositions of property are taxed at regular corporate rates.

Tax liabilities must be computed under the regular tax system and the alternative minimum tax (AMT) system, with the taxpayer paying the larger amount. The AMT is, in effect, a second tax system parallel to, but separate from, the regular tax. For many corporations, the AMT will be the predominant tax. The AMT increases the burdens placed on taxpayers in the form of complexity, additional recordkeeping, and the acceleration of income tax recognition and payment.

The starting point for computing the AMT is the corporation's regular taxable income. This amount is increased by adding specified tax preferences, and by making other adjustments that substitute a specified deduction or income reporting method for the method used for regular tax purposes. The base then is adjusted by replacing the regular tax net operating loss (NOL) deduction with the AMT NOL deduction (which is computed under a complex set of rules distinct from the regular tax NOL rules). The combination of the regular taxable income, tax preferences, other adjustments, and the appropriate NOL deduction establishes the tentative AMT base. This base is reduced by a $40,000 exemption amount to arrive at alternative minimum taxable income (AMTI), which is taxed at a flat 20-percent rate. The exemption amount is reduced by 25 percent of AMTI above $150,000; thus, a corporation will have no exemption amount if its AMTI exceeds $310,000.

The product determined by the application of the 20-percent rate to AMTI may be reduced by the AMT foreign tax credit, which is determined through a limitation calculation similar to, but separate from, the foreign tax credit limitation calculation used in the regular tax system. The net amount is the corporation's tentative minimum tax (TMT). To the extent that the corporation's TMT exceeds the regular tax liability (before reduction by the regular tax foreign tax credit), the corporation has an AMT liability.

Some or all of the AMT paid may be recouped through a minimum tax credit (MTC). The MTC may not be carried back but may be carried forward indefinitely as an offset against the regular tax liability incurred in future years. The regular tax, however, can be reduced only to an amount equal to the TMT in the carryforward year. The MTC results from the recognition that a portion of the AMT liability may be, in essence, a prepayment of a future year's regular tax liability.

The AMT's importance pertains to its 20-percent tax rate and its broad tax base. The practical effect of the narrow spread between the regular and AMT rates is that a relatively minimal amount of preferences or adjustments can trigger the AMT. Payment of the AMT negates the incentive effect of the special income tax provisions that are characterized as preferences. Because the AMT is so readily triggered, corporations cannot ignore this system in evaluating and structuring their investments.

Tax Credits. Corporations may claim a variety of credits against their tax liability.

To prevent U.S. taxpayers from being taxed twice on their foreign source income—once by the foreign country where the income is earned and again by the United States—U.S. taxpayers are allowed a credit for foreign income taxes, subject to various limitations and special rules. (Possessions income and possessions income taxes are considered foreign, although there are special elective rules for possessions business activities.)

A foreign tax credit (FTC) is available for qualifying direct foreign income taxes that are paid or accrued by a U.S. taxpayer in connection with a branch office or that are withheld on passive income received by the taxpayer. In addition, a U.S. corporation receiving a dividend from a first-tier foreign subsidiary in which it owns 10 percent or more of the voting stock is deemed to have paid the foreign income taxes paid by the distributing corporation on the income from which the distribution is made. A deemed-paid credit also is available for foreign income taxes paid with respect to undistributed income of a controlled foreign corporation that is taxed currently to U.S. shareholders as a deemed dividend.

In claiming a deemed-paid FTC, a taxpayer must add the amount of the deemed credit to the dividend in calculating gross income. This procedure (i.e., the "gross-up") is designed to calculate the tax effect as if the taxpayer received its pro-rata share of pre-tax earnings and profits of the foreign corporation, similar to the treatment of direct income taxes paid on foreign branch income.

If certain ownership tests are met, a U.S. corporation is deemed to have paid all or a portion of the corporate taxes paid by second- or third-tier foreign subsidiaries, as well as a first-tier subsidiary, when dividends are paid through the chain to the parent company through the first-tier affiliate.

The FTC for direct taxes can be claimed by domestic corporations, U.S. citizens, and resident aliens who have income from sources outside the United States. The deemed-paid credit is available only to corporate shareholders. Foreign corporations and nonresident alien individuals engaged in a U.S. business may also be entitled to FTCs under limited circumstances. The amount of the credit a taxpayer may claim in any year is limited to U.S. tax attributable to foreign source taxable income. Excess FTCs may be carried back two years and forward five years.

The following credits are combined into one credit called the general business credit:

- Investment credit (i.e., the regular, energy, and rehabilitation credits).
- Targeted jobs credit.
- Alcohol fuels credit.
- Research credit.
- Low-income housing credit.

In general, the general business credit can be claimed to offset the first $25,000 of net tax liability for the taxable year plus 75 percent of the balance of the tax liability. Excess general business credits may be carried back 3 taxable years and forward 15 taxable years.

Except pursuant to narrowly applicable transition rules, the regular investment tax credit (ITC) no longer is available for assets placed in service after December 31, 1985. However, investments in certain solar energy or geothermal energy properties placed in service by June 30, 1992, are eligible for a 10-percent credit. The tax basis of such energy property for depreciation purposes is reduced by 50 percent of this credit.

A rehabilitation tax credit is allowed for certain structures that are substantially rehabilitated. For nonhistoric buildings originally placed in service before 1936, the credit is 10 percent. For rehabilitations of certified historic buildings, the credit is 20 percent. The basis of the building for depreciation purposes must be reduced by the full amount of the credit. In order to qualify for the rehabilitation credit, various technical rules must be met.

A targeted jobs credit is allowed for a portion of the wages paid to newly hired employees from specified targeted groups, such as economically disadvantaged youths. The employer's wage deduction is reduced by the amount of the credit. The credit is scheduled to expire after June 30, 1992.

A credit is allowed for alcohol (other than that produced from petroleum, natural gas, coal, or peat) used as a fuel of a type suitable for use in an internal combustion engine where the excise tax exemption for alcohol fuels does not apply.

A 20-percent credit is available for qualified expenditures for research (in the United States) in excess of a base amount. The taxpayer's deductions for research expenses are reduced by the credit amount. The credit is scheduled to expire after June 30, 1992.

A low-income housing credit is allowed for qualified low-income rental housing meeting certain requirements. The credit is computed by multiplying the qualified basis of each qualified low-income building by certain percentages and is allowed in annual installments over a 10-year period.

The "orphan drug" credit is allowed for 50 percent of qualified clinical testing expenses. Qualified clinical testing is quite specifically defined and must be carried out for testing a drug for a rare disease or condition. The credit is scheduled to expire after June 30, 1992.

The nonconventional source fuel credit may be claimed against tax, subject to limitations, computed as a multiple of the barrel-of-oil equivalent of qualified fuels sold during the taxable year. The credit applies with respect to "qualified fuels" produced domestically from a well drilled, or facility placed in service, before 1993.

The minimum tax credit has been discussed above in connection with the AMT.

Consolidation.   An affiliated group of companies may elect to file a consolidated income tax return. For this purpose, an affiliated group consists of corporations at least 80 percent of whose voting stock and 80 percent of the total value of the stock is owned directly by one or more of the includible corporations, and a common parent, which owns at least 80 percent of the stock of one of the includible corporations. Certain corporations generally may not be included in a consolidated return– for example, foreign corporations, regulated investment companies, and possessions corporations. Wholly owned Canadian or Mexican subsidiaries may be included in a consolidated return if they are organized to comply with the laws of those countries governing title to, and operation of, property.

Taxable income reported on a consolidated return includes the income or loss of all the affiliated members after the elimination of intragroup dividends and certain intragroup transactions (e.g., the sale of property). Income or loss on intragroup transactions eliminated in consolidation is included in consolidated income when recognized through a transaction with a third party. A net operating loss incurred by a member (other than the parent) in a year prior to its affiliation with the group ("separate return limitation year") may generally be offset only against its own income generated while a member of the consolidated group. The same separate return limitation rules apply to capital losses, investment credits, and certain deductions that economically accrued prior to the affiliate's joining the consolidated group.

As a general rule, certain losses (i.e., dual-consolidated loss) of a dual-resident company may not be used to reduce the taxable income of any other member of the affiliated group with which the dual-resident company files a consolidated tax return. A dual-resident company is one that is a resident of two countries. For example, a company incorporated in the United States is a U.S. company and is subject to U.S. tax on its worldwide income. At the same time, this company may be managed or controlled in the United Kingdom of Australia, under whose law it would be such country's resident.

Other Taxes. An additional 28-percent personal holding company tax is imposed on the undistributed personal holding company income of certain closely held U.S. or foreign corporations. A corporation may be classified as a personal holding company if more than 50 percent in value of its outstanding stock is owned, directly or indirectly, by no more than five individuals. In addition, at least 60 percent of the corporation's adjusted ordinary gross income must generally consist of personal holding company income, which is passive investment income (e.g., dividends and interest), or amounts received for personal services performed by a 25-percent or more shareholder.

An additional 28-percent accumulated earnings tax is imposed on a U.S. or foreign corporation (other than a personal holding company, foreign personal holding company, passive foreign investment company, tax-exempt corporation, or S corporation) avoiding individual income tax with respect to its shareholders by not distributing its accumulated taxable income. A corporation is permitted to reduce accumulated taxable income by the larger of (1) $250,000 in earnings and profits, or (2) earnings retained for the reasonable needs of the business (e.g., working capital and funds for business expansion).

An environmental tax is imposed on corporations, other than S corporations. The environmental tax was enacted to raise revenue to clean up industrial accidents harming the environment. The tax is based on a corporation's AMT income (before net operating loss and environmental tax deductions) in excess of $2 million at a rate of 0.12 percent. The tax is imposed even if the corporation does not pay AMT.

Gross Income

The gross income (before deductions) of a manufacturing, merchandising, or mining business includes its gross receipts from the sale of goods less the cost of goods sold. In a service business, where goods are not a factor, gross profit means gross receipts.

In general, intercompany transactions are accorded the same tax treatment as are transactions with unrelated parties if they are negotiated at arm's length. The IRS is empowered under Internal Revenue Code Section 482 to make whatever adjustment is deemed necessary to clearly reflect the income of the related parties.

Inventory Valuation. The two most commonly recognized methods of inventory valuation are (1) cost and (2) the lower of cost or market. Both methods permit inventory that is unsalable at normal prices to be valued at its selling price less direct costs of disposition, but in no event can it be valued at less than its scrap value. Special valuation methods are available for farmers, securities dealers, and certain other taxpayers. Most importantly, a valuation method must clearly reflect income and conform as nearly as possible to the best accounting practice in the trade or business.

All direct costs (material and labor) and certain indirect costs are included in inventory by using the uniform capitalization rules. Under these rules, most indirect costs (except selling, advertising, and marketing expenses) must be capitalized by manufacturers in the cost of inventory.

Retailers and wholesalers are subject to the same capitalization rules that apply to manufacturers. Costs that must be capitalized include purchasing costs, handling and processing costs, off-site storage costs, and a portion of the general and administrative costs allocable to these activities.

Identifying the cost of inventory items sold may involve matching the goods with specific invoices. If this specific identification method is not possible or practical, an assumption is made as to the order in which goods are used or sold. The two most commonly used inventory identification methods are first-in-first-out (FIFO) and last-in-first-out (LIFO). LIFO may generally be used only where inventory is valued at cost. In addition, the closing inventory of the year preceding the election of the LIFO method must be adjusted to cost. When the LIFO method is used for tax purposes, it must also be used in financial reports to shareholders, partners, or lenders (the LIFO conformity requirement).

Capital Gains. Gains from the sale or exchange of capital assets are generally included in gross income. A capital asset is any property held by a taxpayer other than:

- Inventory held primarily for sale to customers in the ordinary course of business.
- Real or depreciable property used in the business.
- Accounts and notes receivable arising from services rendered or from the sale of inventory assets.
- Certain other assets that are described in the Internal Revenue Code.

The excess of the net gain from all sales and exchanges of capital assets held for more than one year over any net loss from sales or exchange of capital assets held one year or less is termed net long-term capital gain. Currently, net long-term capital gains are taxed at regular corporate rates. Corporate capital losses are deductible only against corporate capital gains. If a corporation's capital losses exceed its capital gains, the losses may be carried back three years and forward five years. Losses must be applied in chronological order, starting with the earliest carryback year.

Special rules generally permit any net recognized losses from the sale or exchange of land or depreciable property used in a business and held for more than one year to be treated as ordinary, and any net gains from the sale or disposition thereof to be treated as capital gains.

Gain from the sale or exchange of "Section 1245 property" is treated as ordinary income rather than capital gain to the extent of depreciation taken after December 31, 1961. Section 1245 property includes depreciable tangible and intangible personal property and other tangible property (other than buildings or structural components thereof) used in the taxpayer's business. Recapture does not apply to the disposition of real property (Section 1250 property) depreciated using the straight-line method that was placed in service after 1986. However, real property placed in service before 1987 is subject to recapture if a depreciation method other than the straight-line method was used.

Gain or loss is deferred if business or investment property is exchanged solely for property of the same character (a like-kind exchange). Real property located outside the United States cannot be considered as property of a like kind as real property located within the U.S. This nonrecognition provision does not apply to inventories, securities, partnership interests, or evidences of indebtedness. In addition, the replacement property must be identified and acquired within certain time limitations. If the taxpayer receives other property in the exchange (e.g., cash) in addition to business or investment property, gain will be recognized to the taxpayer but in an amount not exceeding the value of such other property. Gains from involuntary conversions also may not be taxable. In each case, the gain (or loss) deferred may be recognized in a future transaction. If an exchange takes place between related taxpayers and property subject to the exchange is disposed of within two years, the previously deferred gain must be recognized.

Interest. Interest is includible in gross income, except for interest on obligations of a state, a U.S. possession, or any political subdivision of either of the foregoing. Private-activity bond (industrial development bond) interest also may be exempt. Interest income also may be imputed on certain deferred payment sales, loans with below-market interest rates, original issue discount (OID) obligations, and on certain short-term obligations acquired at a discount.

Dividends. A corporate distribution of earnings and profits to its shareholders generally is includible in gross income as a dividend. However, corporations receiving dividends generally are entitled to a deduction, subject to special limitations in certain cases, with respect to dividends received from certain corporations. A deduction from gross income generally is allowed equal to 70 percent of the dividends received from taxable domestic corporations. A taxpayer receiving dividends from a 20-percent to 79-percent owned corporation (by vote and value) is eligible for a deduction equal to 80 percent of the dividends received from the corporation.

Members of an affiliated group of corporations may elect to exclude 100 percent of the dividends received from another group member. The affiliated group must be qualified to file a consolidated return except that possessions corporations with respect to dividends received therefrom and certain insurance companies may be included. Dividends from a foreign corporation also may qualify for the 100-percent deduction if all of the foreign corporation's gross income was connected with its conduct of a U.S. business.

A distribution of earnings and profits from a corporation organized outside the U.S. is includible in the gross income of shareholders who are subject to U.S. tax. In addition, certain distributions from these foreign corporations require a gross-up amount to be included as dividend income (see discussion of FTC above). In general, dividends received from foreign corporations are not eligible for the deduction for dividends received. However, dividends received from most foreign corporations will qualify for this deduction if at least 10 percent of its stock (by vote and value) is owned by a domestic corporation. The allowable deduction is based on the portion of the foreign corporation's post-1986 earnings subject to U.S. corporate income tax and not previously distributed.

The allowable deduction for certain dividends received from a foreign sales corporation (FSC) is equal to 100 percent of the dividend received that is distributed out of earnings and profits attributable to foreign trade income for a period during which the corporation paying the dividend was an FSC. Dividends distributed out of earnings and profits attributable to qualified interest and carrying charges received or accrued by the distributing corporation while it was an FSC are subject to a 70-percent deduction by the recipient (80 percent in the case of a 20-percent or more owned FSC).

A stock dividend is not included in gross income, with certain exceptions. The basis of the original shares must be apportioned between the old and the new shares.

A dividend in kind (i.e., other than money or obligations of the distributing corporation) received by one U.S. corporation from another U.S. corporation is includible in gross income. The amount of such income is equal to the lesser of the property's fair market value or its adjusted basis to the distributing corporation increased by the amount of gain, if any, recognized to the distributing corporation on the distribution. Dividends paid to or from foreign corporations are subject to special rules.

Generally, dividends received by corporations organized outside the U.S. are subject to withholding of federal income tax at the rate of 30 percent unless otherwise specified by tax treaty.

Royalties.   Royalties are includible in gross income. Certain payments received for the transfer of patent rights, timber, coal, or domestic iron ore royalties may qualify for capital gains treatment.

Service Fees.   Service fees are includible in gross income.

Nontaxable Income.   Nontaxable income items that can be received by a corporation include:

- Interest on certain local government obligations.
- Contributions to the capital of a corporation, with certain exceptions.

- Income that may be exempt by treaty.
- Certain life insurance proceeds.

Deductions

Business Expenses.   Corporations are entitled to deduct ordinary and necessary expenses paid or incurred during the taxable year in the conduct of their business. Some expenses—for instance, illegal bribes and kickbacks—are not allowed as deductions. Other expenses are deductible subject to certain limitations—for instance, charitable contributions and business gifts. Capital expenditures are generally deductible only through depreciation, depletion, or amortization over the useful life of the property, or as the basis of property in determining gain or loss. Payments to affiliates are deductible if they reflect an arm's-length charge.

Depreciation.   For most tangible personal and real property placed in service in the United States after 1980, capital costs are recovered using the Accelerated Cost Recovery System (ACRS), which applies accelerated methods over periods specified by statute. Land is not depreciable.

The cost of depreciable personal property acquired after December 31, 1986, is recovered over a 3-, 5-, 7-, 10-, 15-, or 20-year period, depending on the type of property. The depreciation method for property in the 3-, 5-, 7-, and 10-year classes is 200-percent declining balance, with a switch to the straight-line method to maximize the deduction. The depreciation method for 15- and 20-year property is 150-percent declining balance, with a switch to the straight-line method to maximize the deduction. Residential rental property and nonresidential real property are recovered using the straight-line method over periods of 27.5 and 31.5 years, respectively. Separate methods and periods of cost recovery are specified by statute for tangible personal and real property outside the United States and for special categories of property.

High-priced automobiles and other "listed property" used not more than 50 percent in the taxpayer's trade or business are subject to special rules designed to limit the recovery deduction in any given year.

The cost recovery methods and periods are the same for both new and used property. An election to use the straight-line method over the regular recovery period, or a longer recovery period, also is available. In addition, taxpayers generally may deduct up to $10,000 in a year for the costs of certain depreciable business assets acquired during the year; however, this deduction is phased out if the taxpayer has more than $200,000 of such costs in the year.

For purposes of determining depreciation for leasehold improvements (including buildings erected on leased premises) placed in service after 1986, a lessee's recovery allowance is determined without regard to the lease term even if it is shorter than the ACRS recovery period. If the lease terminates before the end of the property's ACRS recovery period and the lessee does not retain the improvement, the lessee has a loss for the unrecovered basis of the property.

The cost of certain intangibles, such as patents, copyrights, and contracts, the useful life of which is definitely limited in duration, may be amortized under the straight-line method. In general, goodwill and trademarks may not be amortized.

Depletion.   A deduction for depletion is permitted with respect to wasting assets, such as natural resource deposits and timber. There are two general methods of computing depletion, one based on cost and the other (percentage depletion) based on certain specified percentages of the gross income from the property. Percentage depletion rates vary from 22 percent of gross income for uranium to 5 percent for gravel. A percentage depletion deduction in excess of the adjusted cost basis of the property is considered to be an item of tax preference for purposes of computing the AMT.

Interest.   A corporation generally may deduct all interest paid or accrued during the taxable year. However, insufficient capitalization may result in treating instruments designated as debt as equity, with a resulting denial of a deduction for related interest payments. Debt with attendant market discount or acquisition discount may be subject to interest deferral rules. Moreover, deferred payments made for the sale or exchange of property may be recharacterized as between principal and interest if the stated interest in the contract is less than a prescribed statutory interest rate. Interest incurred to purchase or carry securities that yield tax-exempt interest is not deductible. In certain cases, the amount of interest deductible annually with respect to indebtedness incurred to acquire stock or assets of certain corporations is limited to $5 million. Currently, deductible interest (and other carrying charges) with respect to certain properties may be capitalized (at the taxpayer's election)—for instance, mortgage interest on unimproved and unproductive real property or interest incurred in the development of the property. Construction period interest is subject to the uniform capitalization rules.

The earnings stripping rules disallow the deduction for certain corporate interest paid or accrued with respect to a related party if the recipient is not subject to U.S. taxation on such payments, including situations wherein an income tax treaty eliminates or reduces the rate of tax that otherwise would be imposed on a foreign taxpayer.

Interest with respect to OID instruments and payment-in-kind bonds with significant OID, a term of five years or more, and a yield in excess of 5 percentage points over the applicable federal rate is not deductible until actually paid in property other than stock or obligations of the issuer. In addition, if the yield on such instrument exceeds 6 percentage points over the applicable federal rate, then a portion of the OID is to be classified as a dividend rather than interest.

Royalties and Service Fees. Royalties and service fees are deductible.

Employee Remuneration. Reasonable compensation for employee services is deductible. Excessive compensation of an employee-shareholder may be treated as a nondeductible dividend.

Insurance. Insurance premiums generally are deductible. However, insurance premiums on the life of a key employee are not deductible if the corporation is the beneficiary of the policy. Self-insurance reserves are not deductible. Recent court cases have held that insurance premiums paid or accrued by a corporation to a foreign affiliate (captive insurance company) are deductible if a substantial portion of the insurance company's business is attributable to risk unrelated to the parent or affiliates. Premiums paid or accrued to certain multi-owned corporations are deductible. Services income from the insurance of risks of related parties earned by a controlled foreign corporation may be currently taxable to a U.S. shareholder.

Travel and Entertainment.   Special business-connection and substantiation requirements apply to deductions claimed for travel and entertainment expenses (including business meals), business gifts and employee achievement awards, and deductions with respect to certain "listed property" (such as automobiles), as well as various other limitations. No deduction is allowed with respect to an entertainment facility.

Further, only 80 percent of otherwise allowable business meal and other entertainment expenses is deductible, including the cost of meals furnished by an employer to employees on the employer's premises, and the meal costs of employees traveling away from home.

Bad Debts.   The reserve method of deducting debts is available only to certain financial institutions. For other taxpayers, bad debts are deductible only under the specific charge-off method, which allows a deduction for identifiable debts that become wholly or partially worthless during the year.

Taxes.   Taxes generally are deductible, including the environmental tax, payroll taxes, foreign taxes (in lieu of the FTC), and state and local income taxes. However, federal income taxes, including the alternative minimum tax, the personal holding company tax, and the accumulated earnings tax, are not deductible. Deductible taxes (and carrying charges) with respect to certain properties may be capitalized at the election of the taxpayer—for example, real estate taxes on unimproved and unproductive real property. Taxes incurred in the development of the property are subject to the uniform capitalization rules.

Charitable Contributions.   A deduction may be claimed for corporate contributions to certain types of charitable organizations created or organized in the United States, subject to special rules, provided the contribution is to be used within the United States.

However, the deduction is limited to 10 percent of the corporation's taxable income computed before giving effect to the charitable deduction, net operating loss or capital loss carrybacks, and the dividends-received deduction; excess contributions may be carried forward for five years.

Retirement Plans.   Contributions to qualified retirement plans are deductible (within limits) in the year of contribution. The employee is not taxed on his or her share of this contribution or the income earned thereon until it is distributed or made available. (The rules governing qualified retirement plans are extremely complex.) Contributions to nonqualified plans are deductible in the year the compensation attributable to the contribution is included in the employee's gross income.

Organization and Start-up Costs.   A special deduction is allowed for the costs of organizing a corporation or starting up a trade or business. A corporation may elect to amortize such costs on a straight-line basis over a period of not less than 60 months. Expenditures connected with issuing or selling securities do not qualify for this election.

Other.   A taxpayer has the option of deducting currently a variety of expenses that otherwise must be capitalized—for instance, research and development costs, oil and gas intangible drilling and development costs, mine exploration and development costs (other than for oil and gas), and (subject to limitations) farmers' expenditures for land clearing and soil and water conservation.

Nondeductible Items.   Nondeductible items include dividends, goodwill, going-concern value, illegal bribes and kickbacks, penalties for the violation of any law, gifts over $25 per individual per year, certain key-man life insurance premiums, political contributions, and expenses (e.g., interest) relating to tax-exempt income.

Net Operating Loss (NOL).   An NOL is the excess of deductions over gross income in a particular year. An NOL deduction is the deduction of this loss in another year. NOLs generally may be carried back 3 years and foward 15 years; an NOL attributable to a product liability loss may be carried back 10 years. Losses must be applied in chronological sequence, starting with the earliest carryback year. If it is advantageous, a taxpayer may irrevocably elect to forgo the 3-year carryback period.

Restrictions may be imposed on the deductibility of an NOL by a corporation not generating the NOL, for example, the preacquisition loss of a corporation included in a consolidated return. In addition, the deductibility of an NOL by the corporation generating the NOL may be restricted in the event of certain changes in ownership.

Individual Taxpayers

U.S. citizens and aliens resident in the United States are subject to the same tax rules; they are ordinarily taxable on their worldwide income, irrespective of source. Nonresident aliens are taxable only on U.S. (and certain foreign) source business income and certain classes of U.S. source nonbusiness income. For nonresident aliens, business and nonbusiness income are taxed separately, generally in accordance with the same rules that are applicable to foreign corporations. The taxation of aliens is covered in detail in Chapter 20.

Tax Computation
Taxable income for U.S. citizens and resident aliens is computed by subtracting allowable deductions from gross income.

The specific filing categories are as follows:

- Married filing jointly.
- Married filing separately.
- Single.
- Head of household. (This filing status generally is reserved for unmarried individuals who have dependents or who provide a principal place of abode for more than one half of the taxable year to specified individuals.)

Once the taxpayer determines his or her filing status, he or she must refer to tax tables published by the IRS or tax rate schedules to determine the amount of tax before credits. A taxpayer must use the tax tables unless taxable income exceeds $50,000; in the latter case, the tax rate schedules must be used. For 1992, individuals are taxed at 15 percent, 28 percent, and 31 percent.

For 1992, the 31-percent bracket will begin at $86,500 for married individuals filing jointly and $51,900 for single individuals. The 28-percent bracket will begin at $35,800 for married individuals filing jointly and $21,450 for single individuals. The rate brackets are increased annually to reflect inflation.

The AMT system applicable to corporations also applies to individuals. The calculation is nearly identical. Certain adjustments and preferences apply only to individuals. For example, most itemized deductions are not allowed or are limited in computing AMTI. Also, the standard deduction and personal exemptions are not allowed in computing AMTI.

The AMT rate for individuals is 24 percent (compared with the 20-percent rate for corporations). Because of the narrow spread between the regular tax rates and the AMT rate and the broader AMT base, many higher-income individual taxpayers may be subject to the AMT.

Self-employed individuals also need to determine their self-employment tax, as discussed earlier. This tax is included with their individual income tax returns.

Individual taxpayers are permitted certain credits against their income tax, each of which is generally subject to limitation. Most of the credits available to corporations, including the FTC, are available to individuals. Additional credits include:

- A credit for child and dependent care expenses.
- A credit for the elderly, taxpayers 65 or over, and disabled individuals.
- A credit for earned income when adjusted gross income is below certain levels.
- A credit for interest paid on certain qualified home mortgages.

Gross Income
Compensation. U.S. citizens and resident aliens must include in gross income all compensation received (including compensation for services as an employee or as an independent contractor), including living and housing allowances, tax reimbursements, and the

fair market value of many benefits in kind, such as houses and automobiles. Split-employment contracts to compensate U.S. citizens or resident aliens for work performed in and out of the United States do not reduce the individual's U.S. tax liability since such individuals are subject to taxation on their worldwide income.

Certain items of compensation are excludable from gross income, including (1) limited premiums on group term life insurance policies, (2) meals or lodging furnished for the convenience of the employer, and (3) employer contributions to and benefits received under group accident and health plans. In addition, U.S. citizens and residents living outside the United States may qualify to elect to exclude up to $70,000 of foreign-earned income and certain foreign housing amounts.

Capital Gains.   Citizens and residents generally must include all capital gains in gross income. The kinds of gains (and losses) treated as capital in nature are the same for both individuals and corporations. The tax rate on net long-term capital gains is limited to 28 percent.

Capital losses may be deducted only if incurred in business or transactions for profit; thus, a loss on the sale of a personal residence is not deductible. If otherwise allowable, capital losses may be deducted only to the extent of capital gains plus $3,000. Any capital loss in excess of this amount is carried forward indefinitely until it is fully absorbed.

A loss of up to $50,000 ($100,000 in the case of a husband and wife filing a joint return) on the sale or exchange of qualified small business stock may be treated as an ordinary, rather than a capital, loss.

Recognition of gain on the sale of a taxpayer's principal residence is deferred if the taxpayer buys or builds another residence and uses it as his or her principal residence within a specified period of time, and the cost of the new residence equals or exceeds the selling price of the old. If the sales price of the old residence exceeds the cost of the new, gain is recognized to the extent of the difference. If the taxpayer is 55 years of age or older before the date of sale, the taxpayer can exclude up to $125,000 of gain on the sale if he or she owned and used the home as a principal residence for specified periods of time prior to the sale. This $125,000 exemption can be elected only once.

Other Income. Other items included in gross income of a citizen or resident are similar in nature to items included by a corporation, such as dividends, interest, rents, and royalties. Also includible are income from a profession or unincorporated business, pensions, annuities, and certain alimony and separate maintenance payments. The term *income* has a broad meaning and generally may be taken to include all accretions of wealth realized by a taxpayer. However, mere appreciation in the value of an asset is not income until it is recognized by sale, exchange, or other conversion.

Nontaxable Income. The Internal Revenue Code specifically provides for certain exclusions from gross income. The most common of these exclusions are as follows:

- Life insurance proceeds when paid by reason of the death of the insured.
- Interest on obligations of states or political subdivisions thereof, commonly known as municipal bonds.
- Gifts, bequests, and inheritances.
- Social security benefits, up to a limit.

In certain cases, citizens can exclude income from U.S. possessions (other than Puerto Rico, the Virgin Islands, and Guam) received outside the United States. Any individual who is a resident of Puerto Rico for an entire taxable year generally is exempt from U.S. tax on income from Puerto Rican sources.

Deductions

Deductions for individuals fall into two different categories. Some deductions, generally those of a business nature, are subtracted from gross income in arriving at adjusted gross income (AGI). Others are deducted from AGI in arriving at taxable income. AGI is of special significance because certain deductions are subject to limitations expressed as a percentage of AGI. In addition, deductions to determine AGI are allowed even if the standard deduction (discussed below) is elected.

Deductions Allowed in Computing AGI. Certain deductions that are generally of a business nature are allowed in arriving at AGI. The major deductions are as follows:

- Expenses in carrying on a business or profession, other than as an employee, subject to the passive activity rules and the at-risk rules discussed below.
- Expenses attributable to the production of rents or royalties, also subject to the passive activity rules and the at-risk rules.
- Losses from the sale or exchange of investments or income-producing property, except that a net loss from the sale of capital assets is deductible only to the extent of $3,000.
- Contributions to a qualified retirement plan for the self-employed and for other retirement savings under certain circumstances. When deductible, both are subject to annual limitations.
- Certain alimony and separate maintenance payments.

Passive Activities.   The passive activity rules operate to limit the deductibility of passive activity losses in an effort to prevent certain taxpayers from using tax shelter losses to offset taxable income. Generally, passive activity losses and credits may be deducted only to the extent of passive activity income. Portfolio income (dividends, interest, and capital gains) is not treated as income from a passive activity and therefore, in general, may not be offset by passive activity losses. Disallowed losses from a passive activity may be carried forward indefinitely to future tax years. If sufficient passive activity income is not generated in such future years to absorb the losses carried forward, then the losses are allowed in full when the taxpayer disposes of his or her entire interest in the activity creating such losses.

A taxpayer's activities are considered passive unless he or she materially participates in the business. Activities conducted through a limited partnership are considered passive to limited partners. Any rental business (except hotel operations) also is considered a passive activity. However, if an individual actively participates in a rental real estate activity (which may consist of several properties), losses of up to $25,000 a year from that particular activity may be allowed as a deduction against other nonpassive activity income. This $25,000 allowance is phased out for AGI between $100,000 and $150,000.

The passive activity provisions apply to individuals, estates, trusts, personal service corporations, and closely held corporations (other than S corporations). Partnerships and S corporations are not subject to the limits directly since they are treated as conduits and pass their activities through to their owners, who may be subject to the limits.

At-risk Limitations.   The at-risk rules generally prevent taxpayers from deducting business and investment losses in excess of the amount actually at risk. For example, if an individual invests $10,000 in a business, $5,000 of which was obtained through a nonrecourse loan, deductible losses are limited to $5,000. The at-risk rules apply to a lesser extent to real property activities.

Standard Deduction.   Certain deductions (i.e., itemized deductions) may be subtracted from AGI in arriving at taxable income. A blanket deduction, called the standard deduction, is available and may be used when it exceeds the total amount of itemized deductions otherwise allowed. The amount of the standard deduction varies depending on the taxpayer's filing status and is indexed annually for inflation. For 1992, the standard deduction amounts range from $3,600 for single individuals to $6,000 for married individuals filing a joint return. An additional standard deduction is allowed in the amount of $700 for each elderly (age 65 or older) or blind individual filing a joint return; for single taxpayers, the additional amount is $900.

Itemized Deductions.   A taxpayer may elect to itemize certain types of deductions in lieu of claiming the standard deduction. These itemized deductions are:

1. Certain expenses incurred in moving to a new job location.
2. Interest expense, depending on its classification, as follows:
   a. Personal interest—interest incurred for personal purposes, such as for credit cards and automobiles used for personal purposes, is not deductible.
   b. Mortgage interest—consists of interest on the taxpayer's principal and second homes. The interest deduction, in general, is limited to interest paid on loans up to $1 million constituting acquisition indebtedness, and loans up to $100,000 qualifying as home equity debt. A special rule ap-

plies for pre-October 13, 1987, indebtedness. Additional mortgage interest may be deductible if the debt is incurred for educational or medical expenses.

   c. Investment interest—consists of interest incurred on loans to acquire investment assets. Investment interest is deductible to the extent of net investment income. Limited deductions may be carried forward.

   d. Trade or business interest—interest incurred in a taxpayer's trade or business (other than that of being an employee) is fully deductible, subject to the passive activity rules, whether or not the taxpayer itemizes.

3. Certain state, local, and foreign taxes, e.g., income and property taxes. Sales taxes generally are not deductible.

4. Contributions to U.S. charities, subject to certain limitations and special rules.

5. Medical expenses (including medical insurance premiums), to the extent exceeding 7.5 percent of AGI.

6. Casualty or theft losses on nonbusiness property, to the extent exceeding 10 percent of AGI.

7. The miscellaneous itemized deductions listed below are combined and may be deducted only to the extent they exceed in the aggregate 2 percent of AGI. Business meal and entertainment expenses includible in the amount subject to the 2-percent limitation are first subject to the 80-percent limitation also applicable to corporations.

   a. Certain expenses of an employee, including business travel expenses while away from home and business transportation expenses (expenses of commuting are not deductible).

   b. Expenses incurred in connection with the determination, collection, or refund of any tax (such as tax return preparation and consulting fees).

   c. Other expenses incurred for the production of income but not connected with a business (such as investment advisor fees and trustee fees).

For tax years beginning after December 31, 1990, and before January 1, 1996, otherwise allowable itemized deductions (other than medical expenses, casualty and theft losses, and investment interest) are reduced by 3 percent of the amount by which AGI exceeds a certain threshold, which is adjusted annually for inflation. For taxable years beginning in 1992, the threshold is $105,250 ($52,625 for a married person filing separately). In no event, however, will the total of the itemized deductions subject to the reduction be reduced by more than 80 percent. Since an increase in AGI can cause a concurrent loss in itemized deductions, this limitation effectively increases the marginal tax rate of affected taxpayers by one percent.

Personal Exemptions. In addition to those deductions previously discussed, citizens and residents are entitled to deduct personal exemptions. For 1992, exemptions are $2,300 each and are allowed with respect to the taxpayer, his or her spouse, and each dependent. To qualify as a dependent, certain tests regarding relationship, support, and income must be satisfied.

For taxable years beginning after December 31, 1990, and before January 1, 1996, the deduction for personal exemptions is phased out by 2 percent for each $2,500 or fraction thereof ($1,250 for a married person filing separately) by which AGI exceeds the applicable threshold which is adjusted annually for inflation. The 1992 thresholds, are $157,900 for joint returns, $131,550 for a head of household, $105,250 for single filers, and $78,950 for married persons filing separately. Like the limitation on itemized deductions, the amount of the phase-out of personal exemptions increases as AGI increases; thus, the phase-out effectively is an increase in the marginal tax bracket of approximately $\frac{1}{2}$ of one percent per exemption.

Trusts and Estates

Trusts

For tax purposes, a trust is an arrangement, generally created by a will or a lifetime declaration, whereby trustees take title to property to protect or conserve it for beneficiaries. Trusts may be revocable or irrevocable and are used not only for the management of assets but also to achieve tax benefits.

Taxation of Trusts and Beneficiaries. A trust usually is treated as a separate taxable entity. The gross income, deductions, and credits of a trust generally are the same as for individuals.

However, an additional deduction is allowed for income for the taxable year that is required to be currently distributed to beneficiaries and for any other amounts paid or credited or required to be distributed to them. Generally, such amounts are taxed to the beneficiaries and retain the same character as they had in the hands of the trust.

Any amount that, under the terms of the governing instrument, is paid as a gift or bequest of a specific sum of money or of specific property, and is paid in not more than three installments, is neither deductible by the trust nor taxable to the beneficiaries. This provision does not apply to a gift or bequest of a specific sum of money that can be paid only from the income of the trust. The trust generally is treated as a conduit wherein the beneficiaries are taxable on the portion of the income currently distributed and the trust is taxable on the portion accumulated.

Both the deduction for current-year distributions by the trust and the amount taxable to the beneficiaries for the current year are limited to the distributable net income of the trust. If certain trust distributions exceed the distributable net income for the current year, the excess is treated as a taxable distribution of accumulated trust income to the extent thereof. The recipients are required to calculate and pay a tax that approximates the tax that would have been payable if the accumulated amounts had been distributed in the year(s) earned (i.e., "throwback" rules). Subject to limitation, a credit is given for taxes paid by the trust.

Like individuals, trusts pay tax on their taxable income at rates of 15, 28, and 31 percent, although the brackets are narrower than the individual brackets. (Other rates may be applicable to gains on property sold within two years of the initial transfer of the property to the trust.) In arriving at taxable income, a trust is limited to a personal exemption of $100, or $300 for a simple trust. A simple trust is one (1) that is required to distribute all of its income currently, (2) whose trust instrument does not provide for charitable distributions, and (3) that has not made a distribution of principal in the taxable year. A trust is subject to the AMT with limited modifications.

Taxation of Settlors/Grantors.   The tax treatment of a trust settlor depends on whether he or she has retained any power or interest in or over the trust. The retention of certain interests or powers—for instance, an interest in trust income or the power to revoke—will require the settlor to report currently the trust income, deductions, and credits in his or her own return (a so-called grantor trust). The settlor is required to report only those items of income, deduction, and credit that are attributable to the portion of the trust that he or she continues to own.

A U.S. person transferring property to a foreign trust with a U.S. beneficiary may, in certain cases, be required to report the trust income even if the trust is irrevocable and otherwise not a grantor trust. Certain transfers by a U.S. person to a foreign trust also may be subject to an excise tax equal to 35 percent of the excess of the property's fair market value over the sum of its basis and the amount of gain recognized on the transfer.

The irrevocable transfer of an interest in income or property to a trust may be a taxable gift by the settlor. An interest in property that has not been transferred irrevocably to the trust may be included in the settlor's estate for purposes of the estate tax.

Foreign Trusts, Settlors, and Beneficiaries. Although the above discussion generally applies to trusts with foreign elements, the taxation of foreign trusts, settlors, and beneficiaries is subject to the special income, gift, and estate tax limitations applicable to foreign persons. In addition, payments of certain nonconnected U.S. source income to a foreign trust are subject to withholding tax. Moreover, special provisions for the calculation of distributable net income, as well as special throwback rules, are applicable to a foreign trust. A foreign beneficiary is treated as being engaged in a U.S. business if the trust of which he or she is a beneficiary is so engaged.

Estates

An estate is treated as a separate taxable entity. The estate and its heirs or beneficiaries are subject to income tax in generally the same manner and at the same rates as a trust and its beneficiaries. However, estate heirs or beneficiaries are not subject to the throwback rules and the estate is not subject to an alternative rate of tax with respect to gains on property sold within two years of the receipt of the property by the estate. The personal exemption for an estate is $600. The personal exemption is not allowed in the final year of the estate.

Partnerships and Joint Ventures

Partnerships

A partnership generally is treated as a conduit for tax purposes; thus, the partners, not the partnership, are taxed on the partnership income. Although a corporation can be a member of a partnership, a corporation may be required to meet certain standards if a limited partnership in which it is the general partner is to be recognized by the IRS as a partnership, rather than as a corporation.

In general, a partnership may use the same accounting methods as a corporation. However, partnerships with any corporate partners (other than S corporations) may not use the cash method. Exceptions to this rule may apply for partnerships with average annual gross receipts of $5 million or less for the preceding three tax years, certain types of farming partnerships, and partnerships wherein the corporate partner is a qualified personal service corporation. However, if the partnership is a tax shelter, it is prohibited from using the cash method without exception.

The income of a partnership generally is computed in the same manner as that of an individual, except that certain deductions available to individuals are not allowed. Such unallowable deductions include charitable contributions, personal exemptions, foreign income taxes, NOLs, certain itemized deductions, and oil and gas depletion; these items may be deducted only by the partners.

Since certain types of income, deduction, or credit retain their character when passed through to the partners, they must be stated separately from the ordinary business income of the partnership. Such items include capital gains and losses, gains and losses from the sale of business property, charitable contributions, dividends eligible for the corporate dividends received deduction, and foreign income taxes paid.

Each partner is required to report in its income tax return its distributive share of the partnership's ordinary income plus its share of special items, as well as any salary or interest received (without regard to partnership income) from the partnership. A partner's distributive share of ordinary income and special items generally is determined by the partnership agreement. For an allocation under the partnership agreement to be honored by the IRS, it must meet certain regulatory tests establishing that it has substantial economic effect.

A partnership with foreign partners engaged in a U.S. trade or business is required to withhold tax on the amount of its effectively connected income allocable to the foreign partners' distributive shares of such income, whether or not distributions are actually made to them. To the extent that the partnership's effectively connected income is allocable to foreign corporate partners, the withholding tax rate is equal to the highest marginal rate applicable to corporations (currently 34 percent). In the case of distributive shares of effectively connected income allocable to individual partners, the rate is the highest marginal rate for individuals (currently 31 percent). The amount withheld is treated as a distribution to the partner and is a credit in determining the partner's U.S. tax liability.

A partnership also must pay U.S. withholding tax on a foreign partner's distributive share of fixed or determinable annual or periodic income that is not effectively connected with a U.S. trade or business, regardless of whether the amount is distributed. The applicable rate is 30 percent, except where reduced by treaty or statute.

Joint Ventures
A joint venture is generally treated as a partnership and subject to the rules discussed above for partnerships.

Other Entities

The tax law includes special rules for certain categories of corporations and other entities. These provisions may be significant to those contemplating operations in the United States. A discussion of the more important categories follows.

S Corporation
When an election to be treated as an S corporation is made, the corporation is not subject to federal income tax, with limited exceptions for certain gains and passive investment income. This election avoids double taxation—that is, taxation at the corporate level and at the shareholder level—and allows the shareholders to benefit currently from corporate losses. The shareholders include in their individual income tax returns their pro-rata share of the corporation's current taxable income or loss, regardless of whether such income (loss) was actually distributed or retained. The amount of an

S corporation's loss deductible by a shareholder is limited to the shareholder's basis in the stock and the shareholder's loans to the corporation. The at-risk loss limitation rules generally apply to S corporation shareholders.

Only a domestic corporation that is not a member of an affiliated group and that has no more than 35 shareholders (all of whom are individuals) who are residents or citizens may elect to be an S corporation. Estates and certain trusts also may be shareholders.

Foreign Sales Corporation (FSC)
An FSC is the U.S. government's primary tax incentive for exporting goods overseas. The FSC replaced the domestic international sales corporation (DISC). (DISCs are available to a limited extent and require shareholders to pay interest on the deferred tax on DISC income earned after 1984).

An FSC is a foreign corporation located outside the U.S. Customs Zone that is allowed to earn some exempt income on its exports from the United States. The FSC may, as principal or commission agent, engage in exporting U.S.-produced goods to related or unrelated persons. The general effect is that U.S. tax is not imposed on a portion of the FSC's income while the balance is either taxed as U.S. source income to the FSC or taxed to the shareholders of the FSC. An FSC's taxable income is determined by reference either to the arm's-length or administrative-pricing method.

Personal Holding Company
A 28-percent tax is imposed on certain closely held corporations classified as personal holding companies because of the nature of their income and the ownership of their stock. This tax generally does not apply to a foreign corporation if all of its shares are owned by nonresident aliens. A discussion of this tax is contained in the section "Corporate Taxpayers" above.

Foreign Personal Holding Company and Controlled Foreign Corporation
U.S. shareholders (including citizens or residents) of foreign personal holding companies and controlled foreign corporations are taxed on certain undistributed income of such corporations.

Passive Foreign Investment Company (PFIC)
A foreign corporation is a PFIC if 75 percent or more of its gross income is passive income for the tax year, or at least 50 percent of the average value of its assets during the tax year are held for investment. A U.S. shareholder of a PFIC must pay a special tax plus an interest charge on the gain realized from the disposition (including pledging) of stock in a PFIC or upon receipt of an excess distribution from the PFIC.

Regulated Investment Company (RIC) and Real Estate Investment Trust (REIT)
A U.S. corporation that qualifies as a RIC (including a mutual fund or a venture capital company, as defined) or a REIT and complies with certain statutory requirements is subject to special tax rules. The law permits investors to pool their funds in such corporations in order to obtain diversity of investment and professional investment advice without having to pay an additional layer of corporate tax. RICs and REITs can avoid tax if they distribute virtually all of their income. Such income distributed to a foreign corporation or to a nonresident alien individual is subject to a U.S. withholding tax. Net long-term capital gains distributed by RICs or REITs are treated as long-term capital gains in the hands of the owners, and thus are not subject to withholding at source when paid to a foreign corporation or a nonresident alien individual.

Real Estate Mortgage Investment Conduit (REMIC)
A REMIC, usually a trust, is formed to hold pooled mortgages. Much as under the partnership rules, the income of a REMIC is taxed to its owners and not to the REMIC. Accordingly, REMICs avoid the usual double taxation of corporate income.

Possessions Corporation
A U.S. corporation operating in a U.S. possession (i.e., Puerto Rico and the U.S. Virgin Islands) is entitled to a credit equal to the portion of its U.S. tax attributable to certain income derived in the possession. This credit is allowed regardless of whether the possession imposes a tax.

U.S. REAL PROPERTY INTERESTS

The Foreign Investment in Real Property Tax Act of 1980 (FIRPTA) subjects a foreign investor to U.S. tax on gain realized on a disposition of an investment in U.S. real property. A foreign person (a foreign corporation, partnership, estate, trust, or nonresident alien) is treated as being engaged in a trade or business within the United States for purposes of gain or loss from the disposition of a U.S. real property interest (USRPI). Further, such gains or losses are considered to be effectively connected with a U.S. trade or business and taxable at the regular domestic rates.

A USRPI is an interest in real property located in the United States or the Virgin Islands. An interest is an ownership, co-ownership, or option to acquire an ownership or co-ownership. Real property includes land, improvements thereon, leaseholds of land or improvements thereon, and personal property associated with the use of real property.

Any interest, other than solely as a creditor, in a corporation that is a U.S. real property holding corporation (USRPHC) also constitutes a USRPI. A corporation, in general, will be a USRPHC if the fair market value of its U.S. real property equals or exceeds 50 percent of the sum of the fair market values of (1) its U.S. real property interests, (2) its interests in real property located outside the United States, and (3) any other of its assets used or held for use in a trade or business.

Any tax imposed by FIRPTA must be withheld by the buyer of a USRPI from the sale proceeds. The amount of tax that must be withheld upon acquisition of a USRPI from a foreigner is the smaller of (1) 10 percent of the sales price, or (2) the transferor's maximum tax liability. The transferor's maximum liability consists of two elements: (1) the maximum amount of income tax the IRS (upon request) determines could be the liability of the transferor, and (2) any unsatisfied withholding liability, attributable to the foreign transferor's acquisition of the transferred property (or of a predecessor property).

Any buyer or transferee acquiring a USRPI from a foreign person is a withholding agent and is obligated to withhold unless the transaction is exempt. Special rules requiring withholding apply to distributions by domestic and foreign corporations, as well as to partnerships, estates, and trusts, where taxable dispositions of USRPIs and foreign investors are involved.

There are five situations in which the withholding requirement does not apply. These exemptions relieve the transferee from withholding, but do not relieve the transferor from tax. These exemptions apply where:

- The transferor furnishes the transferee with a nonforeign affidavit certifying that the transferor is not a foreign person.
- A U.S. corporation, not publicly traded, furnishes the transferee (of its stock) with an affidavit that it is not a USRPHC.
- The transferee receives a qualifying statement prepared by the IRS certifying that the transferor (1) has made arrangements for payment of its tax, or (2) is exempt from tax and either has satisfied any prior withholding liability or has provided adequate security therefor.
- The transferee acquires realty for use as a residence, at a price of not more than $300,000.
- The USRPI is stock of a corporation traded on an established securities market.

To facilitate the determination of minimum withholding by transferees and withholding agents, the IRS may be requested to calculate the transferor's maximum tax. As noted, the IRS, on request, also is to provide, if applicable, a qualifying statement eliminating the withholding obligation.

ADMINISTRATION OF THE TAX SYSTEM

The following discussion deals with tax administration at the federal level for corporations, individuals, trusts and estates, and partnerships. The discussion of the latter three categories generally describes only those matters administered differently than in the case of corporations.

Corporate Taxpayers

Tax Returns
All domestic corporations are required to file an annual income tax return, even if they have no gross income or no taxable income.

Most domestic corporations must file Form 1120, which is due by the 15th day of the 3rd month following the close of the corporation's taxable year. S corporations file Form 1120S, with the same due date.

Foreign corporations engaged in a U.S. business at any time during the taxable year must file an annual return on Form 1120F, regardless of the amount of gross or taxable income. The return is due by the 15th day of the 6th month following the close of the corporation's taxable year. (Corporations maintaining an office or place of business in the United States and FSCs must file by the 15th day of the 3rd month.) Foreign corporations not engaged in a U.S. business need not file a Form 1120F if their tax liability has been fully satisfied by withholding.

Extensions of time to file a return may be granted. A six-month extension is automatically allowed to a U.S. corporation if it files Form 7004 by the original due date of the return and pays its unpaid, properly estimated tentative tax liability. An extension of time to file does not extend the due date for paying the tax. A penalty for underpayment of tax may be imposed if the corporation has not paid, on or before the due date, at least 90 percent of the amount of tax shown on the income tax return as filed. Interest is charged on any unpaid tax from the original due date to the date of payment.

A three-month extension is allowed automatically (Form 7004 need not be filed) to a U.S. corporation that transacts its business and keeps its records outside the United States and Puerto Rico, and to a foreign corporation with a U.S. office or place of business. This extension also extends the date for payment of the tax; however, interest is charged on any unpaid tax from the original date prescribed for payment to the date of payment. An additional extension (for filing, but not for payment of tax) of three months can be obtained by timely filing of Form 7004 by the 15th day of the 6th month following the close of the corporation's taxable year.

Information Returns

Persons making various types of payment in the course of a trade or business must file information returns with the IRS and send a copy to the payee. Payments covered by these rules include interest, dividends, and royalties (if more than $10 in any calendar year); proceeds from broker transactions; and other fixed or determinable income including non-employee service compensation (if over $600 in any year). Certain exemptions for corporate and foreign recipients apply where appropriate documentation is received (Forms W-9 and W-8). Nominees paying over such payments to investors also must file these returns.

Forms to be filed include the Form 1099 series (for U.S. payees) and 1042S (for foreign payees). Filing deadlines generally are January 31 (payee statements) and February 28 (IRS returns) of the succeeding year, though the filing deadline for Forms 1042S is March 15th. Withholding also may be required in certain circumstances.

A number of special information returns must be filed by U.S. shareholders (and, in certain instances, by citizens or resident officers and directors) of certain foreign corporations. Other special information returns include returns required in connection with the creation of a foreign trust by a U.S. person or a transfer of money or property by a U.S. person to a foreign trust.

Tax Audits

Although the U.S. tax system is based on the principle of self-assessment, all taxpayers and tax returns are subject to audit by the IRS (examination). All income tax returns are checked for mathematical accuracy, with a smaller number selected for further examination. Returns are selected for audit either manually or by computer, based upon various criteria, including type of business, unusually large or small amounts of income or deductions, and random sampling. Computers are used to identify returns having the greatest likelihood of producing significant additional tax. The largest corporations are likely to be audited on an annual basis.

An audit of a corporation's return usually is conducted at the corporation's place of business. Individual returns usually are audited either by correspondence or by an interview at an IRS office. The auditor refers to the corporation's books, records, and other relevant sources of information in order to verify (in varying degrees of detail) the various items included in the return. The taxpayer is entitled to have an accountant, attorney, or certain other persons represent it during the audit. Upon completion of the audit, the auditor will discuss any proposed adjustments with the taxpayer. If the taxpayer consents to the changes, it will sign a consent or agreement and will be billed for the amount owed or receive a refund of any overpayment.

Appeals

If the taxpayer does not agree with an auditor's proposed adjustments, it may request an administrative conference with the IRS Appeals Division, or alternatively, appeal directly to the various courts: the Tax Court of the United States, the U.S. Claims Court, or a federal district (trial) court. The availability of these judicial forums depends upon various criteria. In particular, if the deficiency has been paid, the taxpayer is barred from appealing to the Tax Court; if not paid, the taxpayer is limited to the Tax Court. Decisions of these courts may be subject to appeal. If the proposed adjustment may result in double taxation contrary to the provisions of a tax treaty, the taxpayer may be entitled to present its claim to the competent authority in its country of residence.

Payment and Collection

The three basic methods by which the federal government collects taxes are (1) self-assessment (i.e., payment with the return as filed), (2) withholding at source, and (3) estimated tax payments. The IRS also can collect taxes, when necessary, through enforcement procedures, including liens and levies.

Withholding of tax at source at a rate of 30 percent (or lower treaty rate) is required on certain U.S. source income payments, not connected with a trade or business, made to foreign entities and to nonresident individuals.

Withholding of income tax is required with respect to wages, salaries, and other remuneration paid to employees, taking into account certain deductions to which the employees are entitled. Such withholding is the responsibility of the employer. However, the amount to be withheld each pay period generally is determined by the employee through the filing of Form W-4 with the employer. The employee credits such withholding against his or her final tax liability. The employer also must withhold from wages the employee's share of payroll taxes.

Corporations are required to pay quarterly their estimated tax liability for the current taxable year. This requirement applies to all taxable corporations, except foreign corporations not engaged in a U.S. business. The estimated tax is the amount of tax reasonably estimated for the current year, less the estimated tax credits.

The estimated tax liability normally is payable in four equal installments by the 15th day of the 4th, 6th, 9th, and 12th months of the current taxable year. A penalty is provided for failure to pay the estimated tax liability. This penalty does not apply if the estimated tax paid is at least (1) the tax shown on the corporation's return for the preceding year, or (2) 93 percent of the final tax liability (including the AMT and environmental tax) for the year. Large corporations may base only their first-quarter estimated payment upon the tax shown on the prior year return; subsequent payments must be based upon the actual liability for the year. If there is any reduction in the first-quarter payment by virtue of being based upon the prior-year tax, such reduction must be recaptured by increasing the second-quarter payment. For this purpose, "large corporation" means one that had $1 million or more of taxable income in any one of the three immediately preceding taxable years.

A corporation is required to deposit its tax payments with a Federal Reserve Bank or an authorized commercial bank. The deposit must be accompanied by Form 8109.

Penalties

Certain civil penalties can be imposed for failure or delinquency in filing of a return or payment of the tax or for inaccuracy or for incorrect positions taken on a return. Penalties are not deductible in determining taxable income. In addition, criminal penalties are provided where appropriate.

Statute of Limitations

Normally, the IRS has three years from the due date of the return, or the date of filing, if later, to assess the tax. The IRS may assess the tax or commence a suit at any time in the event that a fraudulent return was filed, or if no return was filed. If a taxpayer has omitted an amount of income that exceeds 25 percent of the gross income reported in a return, the statute of limitations is extended from three to six years.

With respect to claims for refund, a taxpayer normally must file for a refund within three years from the time the return was filed or two years from the date the tax was paid, whichever is later. If no return was filed, the claim must be made within two years from the time the tax was paid. For refunds resulting from FTCs, the statute is extended to 10 years from the date prescribed by law for the filing of the return. There is no statute of limitations for assessments resulting from a claim of excess available FTC.

Individual Taxpayers

Income Tax Returns

An unmarried U.S. citizen or resident alien must file an income tax return for 1992 if he or she has $5,900 or more in gross income (the sum of the personal exemption plus the standard deduction for 1992). The corresponding 1992 filing threshold for a married individual filing a joint return is $10,600. There are three forms for use by individuals—Forms 1040, 1040A and 1040EZ. Form 1040EZ is a relatively simple form that may be used only by certain single taxpayers. Form 1040A is a generalized return format that is simpler than Form 1040; this form may be utilized if the taxpayer's income consists solely of salary income, dividends, and interest and if no itemized deductions are claimed. Generally, individual income tax returns must be filed by the 15th day of the 4th month following the close of the taxable year (April 15).

Nonresident aliens file returns on Form 1040NR if engaged in a U.S. business, if tax liability is not fully satisfied by withholding, or if tax treaty benefits are claimed. Otherwise, no return need be filed. The return is due by the 15th day of the 6th month following the close of the taxable year unless the taxpayer received wages subject to U.S. withholding, in which case the taxpayer's return is due by the 15th day of the 4th month.

Extensions of time to file a return may be granted. A four-month extension is allowed automatically if Form 4868 is filed on or before the original due date of the return. Form 4868 must show the estimated tax liability for the year and must be accompanied by the unpaid portion of the estimated tax. An extension of time does not extend the time for paying the tax. A penalty for underpayment of tax may be imposed if the unpaid tax, as of the due date, is greater than 10 percent of the amount of tax shown on the income tax return as filed. Interest also is charged on amounts not paid by the original due date of the return. A taxpayer may request an additional two-month extension to file beyond the four months through the filing of Form 2688 no later than the extended filing date obtained by filing Form 4868, but the extension is subject to IRS approval.

Assessments

An individual is required to pay the balance of tax due by the due date for the return. However, a taxpayer using Form 1040EZ or

Form 1040A may elect not to compute his or her own tax; in that case, the IRS will compute the tax and so notify the individual, who must pay any balance due within 30 days from the date of the mailing of such notice, or by the due date of the return, whichever is later.

Estimated Tax Payments

Citizens, residents, and nonresident aliens engaged in a U.S. business must pay a specified minimum percentage of tax during the year, by means of withholding and/or estimated tax payments to avoid a penalty for underpayment of estimated tax. An individual whose tax after credit for withholding is less than $500 is exempt from the requirement to make estimated tax payments.

The estimated tax liability normally is payable in four equal installments by the 15th day of the 4th, 6th, and 9th months of the current taxable year and the first month of the succeeding taxable year. Special rules apply to farmers and fishermen. The penalty is not imposed if one of several tests, which are similar to those for corporate taxpayers, is satisfied.

Gift Tax

An individual must file a gift tax return if gifts of present interests made during the year exceed $10,000 in value to one donee or gifts of future interests in any amount are made. Gift tax returns are required to be filed by April 15 following the close of the calendar year during which the gift is made. An extension to file a calendar-year individual income tax return also serves to extend the filing date of a gift tax return.

Estate Tax

Where the gross estate at the death of a citizen or resident exceeds $600,000, an estate tax return must be filed ($60,000 for nonresident aliens). As a result of the unified transfer tax system used for both gift and estate tax purposes, these amounts generally are reduced by the amount of post-1976 taxable gifts not included in the gross estate. Form 706 is used for citizens and residents, and Form 706NA for nonresident aliens. The form must be filed, and the tax paid, within nine months after the date of death. Extensions of time to file a return may be granted on written application (Form 4768) by the fiduciary if good cause is shown. Special extensions of time for payment of the tax may be obtained in certain cases.

Trusts and Estates

A trust is required to file an income tax return if it has any taxable income for the year, has gross income of $600 or more, or has a nonresident alien beneficiary. A decedent's estate, which usually is treated as a separate taxable entity, must file a return if it either has gross income of $600 or more or has a nonresident alien beneficiary.

A domestic trust or estate files Form 1041. A foreign trust or estate files Form 1040NR. If a trust is a grantor trust, income taxable to the grantor must be reported on a separate schedule attached to the return unless the grantor is also the trustee, in which case the grantor reports the income in his or her own return and Form 1041 is not required. The return for a domestic trust or estate must be filed, and the tax paid, by the 15th day of the 4th month after the close of the taxable year. If a foreign trust or estate has a U.S. office or place of business, it files and pays the tax on the same date as a domestic trust; otherwise, it must file and pay the tax by the 15th day of the 6th month. Extensions of time may be granted if good cause is shown. Fiduciaries of trusts and estates must file a special information return for distributions to beneficiaries.

An estate may adopt in its first year either a calendar year or a fiscal year without permission from the IRS. Trusts generally must adopt a calendar year.

Trusts are required to make estimated tax payments in the same manner as individuals. Estates, however, are required to make estimated tax payments only for tax years ending two or more years after the date of the decedent's death. A trust may elect to treat estimated tax payments in excess of the tax shown on its return as paid by the beneficiary. Such excess is considered an estimated tax payment made by the beneficiary on January 15 following the trust's tax year.

Partnerships

A partnership must have the same tax year as that of its majority interest partners unless it establishes to the safisfaction of the IRS a good business reason (other than deferral of tax) for having a different tax year. If the majority owners do not have the same tax year, the partnership must adopt the same tax year as its principal partners. If the principal partners do not have the same tax year and no majority of partners have the same tax year, the partnership must adopt a calendar tax year.

A partnership is required to file an annual return on Form 1065 regardless of the amount of income, except that a partnership carrying on no business in the United States and deriving no U.S. source income need not file a return. The return must be filed by the 15th day of the 4th month after the close of the partnership taxable year. However, if all the partners are nonresident aliens, the return must be filed by the 15th day of the 6th month. Extensions of time to file a return may be granted if good cause is shown.

Special administrative and assessment procedures apply to partnerships. The tax treatment of any partnership item generally is determined at the partnership level, irrespective of the fact that the partnership itself is not a taxable entity. Also, a partner is required to report each partnership item in a manner consistent with the presentation on the partnership return. If a partner treats an item in a manner that is different from its treatment on the partnership return, the partner must file a statement identifying the inconsistency. Otherwise, a negligence penalty may be imposed.

CHAPTER 17

STATE AND LOCAL TAXES IN THE UNITED STATES

Ruurd G. Leegstra
Partner
Philip M. Zinn
Senior Manager
Price Waterhouse

THE U.S. FEDERAL SYSTEM

The Relationship Among Federal, State, and Local Taxes

The relationship between the national government and the states is a product of the system of federalism: The states are considered sovereign in that they have all powers not specifically denied them by the United States Constitution. In this regard, the states are given wide latitude to impose and collect a variety of taxes with no inherent requirement that such taxation be uniform. As a result, the state and local tax environment is extremely diverse and complex, and all taxpayers—be they individuals, partnerships, trusts, or corporations—must carefully review the differing laws, regulations, and practices extant in the jurisdictions where they conduct commercial enterprise in order to make decisions that will afford them the greatest benefits.

Certain taxes have historically been reserved for different levels of government within the governmental system. For example, local governments, including school districts, have almost exclusive rights over real and personal property taxes: taxes that are assessed, collected, and spent by these jurisdictions. States are unique in assessing franchise or privilege taxes: taxes generally measured by net worth and assessed for the privilege of doing business in a state. Further, state and local governments both depend heavily on transaction taxes such as sales and use taxes: taxes that are not imposed at the federal level. Income taxes and various excise taxes, however, are imposed not only by the federal government, but by most state governments and, in a few states, by local governments as well.

The Relationship Among Federal, State, and Local Governments for Constitutional Purposes

While the U.S. Constitution neither requires nor prohibits state and local governments from imposing specific taxes, it does serve to restrict these jurisdictions in specific instances. State and local governments may not impose taxes that violate constitutional principles. The most common violations relate to the restrictions found in the Due Process, Commerce, and Equal Protection Clauses of the U.S. Constitution.

The Due Process Clause will serve to restrict state and local governments from imposing a tax on income or receipts arising from activities that have minimal connection with the taxing jurisdiction: activities for which the jurisdiction has not conferred benefits sufficient to permit it exact something in return. Commerce Clause violations will be found when a tax, on its face or in effect, creates a disparity of treatment between taxpayers that places out-of-state taxpayers at a disadvantage relative to in-state taxpayers. The Equal Protection Clause guarantees that taxing schemes that differentiate between like-situated taxpayers may do so only if the reason for the differentiation or classification is rationally related to a proper state objective.

The Relationship Among Federal, State, and Local Governments for Treaty Purposes

The federal government has the sole right to negotiate and enter into treaties with other countries, under the Foreign Commerce Clause of the U.S. Constitution. Such treaties, however, with the exception of equal treatment protection, are not necessarily binding on the states. This fact can lead to different tax treatments being accorded foreign nationals and foreign businesses at the state and federal levels.

One way in which state and federal treatments differ is in the determination of taxability. Treaty provisions often prohibit a country from imposing a tax on a company that does not have a defined permanent establishment. Goods in a warehouse, for example, will usually not be considered a permanent establishment for treaty purposes. For state purposes, however, the presence of such goods in a state would allow the state to impose tax on the owner thereof. Another example of different treatment can be found in the amount of income taxed. The federal government will tax only that income of a foreign corporation that is "effectively connected." New York State, on the other hand, taxes the income attributable to the state even though such income is not "effectively connected" for federal income tax purposes. Most states will tax only that portion of effectively connected income attributable to that state. Some states, most notably California, may require a group of corporations engaged in a single or "unitary" business to file returns on a worldwide combined basis unless a specific election is made. The constitutionality of applying this methodology to groups with a foreign parent is being tested in the courts at this time. While it is clear that the states are not bound by the treaty provisions that generally provide for use of the separate accounting method to determine the liability of foreign-based corporations, it has not yet been decided whether the worldwide combined reporting method referred to above violates the Constitution by impairing the federal government's ability to speak with one voice in matters of foreign commerce.

THE MAJOR TAXES

Privilege Taxes: Franchise or Capital Stock Taxes Based on Net Worth

A tax is imposed on corporations in many states merely for the privilege of doing business within their borders whether or not such business is actually being conducted. Prior to the imposition of taxes measured by net income, privilege taxes were often considered an extension of property taxes, the most common form of taxing businesses at that time. A privilege tax is generally based on net worth and, therefore, tends to tax the intangible value of the stock of a corporation.

The measure of net worth varies among the states imposing such a tax. The measure may also vary depending on whether the corporation is a domestic corporation (i.e., incorporated within the state) or a foreign corporation (i.e., incorporated elsewhere but registered to do business in the state or doing business in the state).

Some states measure net worth by authorized or issued shares of capital stock, others include surplus in the measure of the tax, while still others include retained earnings and require adjustments for certain reserve accounts. Domestic corporations may be taxed on 100 percent of a lesser measure than that used to determine the net worth of a foreign corporation, but the foreign corporation must be allowed to apportion the tax base in order to pay only on that portion of its net worth attributable to the taxing state.

Income Taxes: Income or Franchise Taxes Based on Net Income

Whereas only 25 states impose a tax measured by net worth, 46 states, plus the District of Columbia, impose either a direct income tax or a franchise tax measured by net income on corporations. These taxes may be imposed in addition to the net worth tax. Forty-four states, plus the District of Columbia, impose a personal income tax on individuals. Some states, including New York, Pennsylvania, and Ohio, also permit certain of their cities to levy taxes on income or earnings. In the case of corporations doing business in more than one state, income is apportioned among the taxing jurisdictions. Individuals generally are taxed on all income by their state of residence but are allowed a credit for taxes properly owed and paid to another jurisdiction.

Almost all states begin their income tax calculations by reference to income for federal tax purposes. Variations among the states, however, exist in this area as in other state and local tax matters. Michigan, for example, taxes all businesses through a tax that begins with federal taxable income but, through a series of additions and subtractions, is in essence designed to be a "value added" tax. A few states tax a percentage of federal tax liability, but the majority tax individuals and corporations on a base derived from federal taxable income.

As will be discussed more fully in the sections on Tax Base and Attribution, the variations among the states in defining and attributing income lead to complexity for taxpayers deriving or earning income from more than one jurisdiction.

Transaction Taxes: Sales, Use, and Other Taxes Based on Gross Receipts

The most common form of transaction tax levied by state and local governments is the sales tax. Very simply, this is a form of consumption tax; it is levied on the sale of goods and certain selected services at ultimate consumption or use. All but four states impose a sales or use tax at the state or local level.

Because a jurisdiction may not levy a sales tax on transactions that occur outside of its borders (interstate sales), a corresponding use tax is generally imposed on the purchase of goods or services used or consumed within the taxing state. This dual system serves the purpose of assuring that the tax cannot be avoided by purchasing goods or services from sellers outside of the purchaser's taxing jurisdiction if they are to be used or consumed in the taxing jurisdiction.

The sales tax is measured by the price at which the goods or services are transferred, whether in money or some other measure of value. Use taxes, similarly, are measured by the purchase price. The states may impose the tax on either the seller or the consumer. This has relevance to the ability to deduct the tax expense for income tax purposes and also to matters of refund. In relation to the actual burden of the tax, it is irrelevant since the tax should be passed on to the ultimate consumer or user. In either instance, the seller is generally charged with the responsibility to collect the sales tax and remit it to the taxing state. The seller may also have the responsibility to collect and remit the use tax if the seller has sufficient contact with the customer's state.

The major differences among the states in the area of sales and use taxation relate to exemptions and the services taxed, if any.

While taxation of services is becoming more common, the majority of states tax only the transfer of tangible personal property and services related to such property. Exemptions will be discussed in more detail in the section on Tax Base.

The other major transaction tax based on gross receipts is levied as a form of business occupation tax. Only one state, Washington, imposes this tax on all businesses operating within the state, but some local jurisdictions in various states also rely on this tax. It is similar to the sales tax except that it is levied on wholesale as well as retail sales and, in Washington, is imposed in lieu of a state income tax.

Property Taxes: Taxes Based on the Value of Real, Tangible, and Intangible Property

Property taxes on real and personal property were the original source of funding for state and local governments. There is no state in which a tax is not imposed on real property. Some states exempt personal property from taxation and others impose a tax on intangible property. In general, as stated above, real and personal property taxes are assessed, collected, and spent at the local level. Intangible property taxes, in contrast, are usually part of the state's taxing system.

The area of greatest controversy in property taxation relates to determining the value (tax base) of the property subject to tax. By definition, this value is generally considered to be what a willing buyer would pay to a willing seller if the property were to be accorded its highest and best use. Under this definition, the value of residential property can generally be determined more easily than can the value of commercial and industrial property. Since residential property within a given assessment district is likely to turn over fairly often and continue to be used for residential purposes, the value of a particular residential property can be determined by comparing actual sales prices of similar properties over a period of time. For commercial and industrial property however, more sophisticated techniques are employed, including the utilization of income production factors, original cost, and obsolescence calculations.

It is common for a state to use a method to equalize assessments for different classes of property in order to achieve uniformity for the class on a local or statewide basis. The equalized value so arrived at may then be reduced by a statutory percentage prior to the application of the local tax rates. Because state constitutions allow for the classification of property but require uniformity of treatment within the class, and because so many local taxing districts are involved in the process within any given state, property tax disputes are very common.

The taxation of intangible property provides its own set of problems. While the value of such property is generally more determinable than is the value of real or tangible personal property, determining the situs of the property presents unique problems. Accounts receivable, for example, are taxed at the booked amount, but a decision must be made as to whether they have a situs in the headquarters state or in the state where the sale giving rise to the receivable was made.

Excise Taxes: Specific Taxes Based on the Cost Price of a Particular Product

State and local governments may impose tax on the sale of specific, as opposed to general, goods. Common examples are the taxes imposed on the sale of motor fuel, liquor, and cigarettes. Such taxes are generally imposed in addition to the sales tax but may be imposed at the distributor rather than the retail level.

Another form of excise tax relates to specific transactions. New York, for example, imposes a gains tax on the transfer of real estate even if the real estate is transferred as an incident to the sale of stock. The sale of realty per se, is not subject to the general sales tax, but by imposing a specific tax on this type of transaction, a state or local government is able to capture greater amounts of revenue.

TAXPAYERS

Individuals

With the exception of the privilege taxes measured by net worth, individuals are subject to, or bear the ultimate burden of, all the taxes discussed above. Most states impose a direct income tax on individuals, follow federal income tax provisions closely, and impose graduated rates. A smaller number of states disallow certain deductions allowed at the federal level, and generally impose a lower, flat rate on the higher income base that results from the disallowance. Several states will tax individuals on a percentage of federal income tax liability.

While states are empowered to tax their individual residents on all income from all sources wherever earned, and to tax nonresidents on all income earned within their jurisdiction, credit mechanisms generally prevent double taxation. Of more concern to many individuals is that the states employ varying definitions of residency. Criteria range from an objective measure based on number of days spent in the state to a subjective determination of intent to establish a domicile.

The obligation to pay sales tax is always passed on to the consumer even though such tax may be imposed on the retailer. Individuals, as well as businesses, however, are directly subject to the use tax. If the retailer does not collect the tax, the state can always assess the individual purchaser. Property taxes are also directly assessed on individual property owners, whereas excise taxes are generally imposed on the business, but passed on to the individual consumer.

Corporations

Corporations are subject to the whole range of state and local taxes. Taxes based on income, gross receipts, net worth, and property values directly affect the bottom line of any corporations. Sales and excise taxes will also affect the bottom line of purchasing corporations but, with the exception of the cost of collection, represent a passed-on cost for selling companies.

Most states will follow the federal treatment of S Corporations for income tax purposes. Quite a number of states, however, require a separate election to be made, and a small number will tax the S Corporation as if it were a C Corporation. In the latter instance, problems can arise for individual shareholders who are taxed on S Corporation income in their state of residence but may not be allowed a credit for taxes paid by the S Corporation in its states of operation.

State taxation of the income of corporations operating in more than one state is complex mainly because of the need to attribute or allocate the income fairly among the taxing states entitled to tax. These complexities will be more fully discussed in the section on State and Local Tax Concepts.

Partnerships and Joint Ventures

The vast majority of states follow the federal treatment of these entities—that is, a partnership is generally exempt from income tax, while the partners are taxed in their individual or corporate capacities. States will generally "flow up" the income and activities of a tiered partnership operating in a state until they reach a taxable entity. Although the partnership may not be subject to tax, many states require the filing of a state partnership return and may impose substantial penalties for failure to file. Also, many states are beginning to impose withholding responsibilities on partnerships that have nonresident partners.

The states may differentiate between individual and corporate partners in their treatment of partnership income. In general, individuals will be taxed only on the partnership income attributable to a state other than the individual's state of residence. Corporate partners, however, are often treated as if they are doing business in the taxing state by virtue of the partnership's activity in the state. As a result, a state may impose its tax on a portion of the entire net income of the corporation rather than merely taxing the partnership income per se. Another distinction made by some states is that between general and limited partners. In these states, general corporate partners will be treated as doing business in the state, while limited partners will be given treatment similar to that accorded individuals.

Estates and Trusts

The state taxation of the fiduciary income of estates and trusts generally follows federal treatment. A few distinctions may exist in particular states relating to the organization of trusts (stock or nonstock) and in the situs of the income distributed to nonresident beneficiaries.

STATE AND LOCAL TAX CONCEPTS

Jurisdiction to Tax

Constitutional Restrictions

As stated above, the Due Process Clause and the Commerce Clause of the U.S. Constitution serve to restrict state and local governments from taxing income that does not have sufficient connection (nexus) with the jurisdiction. As interpreted by the U.S. Supreme Court, the Due Process Clause imposes two requirements on states in relation to the taxation of income generated in interstate commerce: a "minimal connection" between the interstate activities and the taxing state, and a rational relationship between the income attributed to the state and the intrastate values of the enterprise. Under the Commerce Clause the Court has interpreted a state's right to impose a tax on interstate commerce as being limited to taxes that are applied to an activity with a substantial nexus with the taxing state and that are fairly related to the services provided by the state.

Based on various decisions rendered by the Court, it is clear that the states may constitutionally impose a tax on businesses that are engaged in soliciting business through their own employees, through independent contractors or through agents. The Court has also held that exploitation of the market combined with property in the state is sufficient to give rise to nexus. However, the Court has found that a mail-order business that solicits customers without entering the state and ships the goods into the state without personally delivering them does not have sufficient presence to be taxable. At this time, neither the Due Process Clause nor the Commerce Clause would be violated if a state imposed a tax on a business that has a minimal physical presence in the state.

Legislative Restrictions

Under the Constitution, Congress has the right to regulate interstate commerce. In 1959 Congress availed itself of this right and enacted Public Law (P.L.) 86-272. P.L. 86-272 prohibits a state from imposing a tax on or measured by net income if the taxpayer's only activity in the state is "solicitation" of orders for the sale of tangible personal property, the sale is approved outside the state, and the tangible personal property is shipped in from outside the state. It is important to note that a business cannot be immune from a tax on income under P.L. 86-272 in the state under whose laws it is organized.

The immunity from tax provided by P.L. 86-272 is granted solely to sellers of tangible personal property and applies only to income taxes, direct or indirect. It does not apply to the selling of services, nor to the selling, leasing, renting, licensing, or other disposition of real property or intangible property. Furthermore, the immunity does not apply to sales and use tax. As a result, a business may be subject to sales and use tax but immune from income tax in any state.

One major problem faced by those seeking the protection of P.L. 86-272 is determining how each state into which they make sales defines "solicitation." Congress did not define the term in the law but a case is pending before the U.S. Supreme Court. While the states have been left to define solicitation either narrowly or broadly through their own courts it is expected that the Supreme Court will soon provide guidance.

The Tax Base

Because net worth taxes and property taxes vary from state to state, this section will concentrate on corporate income taxes and sales and use taxes.

Income Taxes

In general, most states begin their determination of the income subject to tax with federal taxable income. Depending on state law, this may be taxable income before or after special deductions (i.e., Line 28 or 30 of the federal Form 1120). Many state income tax laws are tied to the federal Internal Revenue Code (IRC). However, significant variations exist with regard to effective dates and specific provisions.

There are several states whose laws are not tied to the IRC, and therefore, technically they do not start from federal taxable income. While in most cases their laws are similar to the IRC, variations can occur that must be taken into consideration. New York, as previously mentioned, uses entire net income as a base rather than federal taxable income. For a corporation organized under the laws

of a foreign (non-U.S.) jurisdiction and paying federal income tax
only on "effectively connected" income, the difference between
the New York tax base and the federal tax base can be significant.

Various modifications are made to federal taxable income to
arrive at a corporation's state tax base. A corporation liable for
income tax in 12 different states very likely could have 12 different
state tax bases.

All states imposing an income tax apply modifications to the
starting point to arrive at the tax base. Although each state has its
own additions and subtractions, several are common to most states.
Following are some of the more common modifications found currently in state law:

Additions	*Subtractions*
State income taxes.	Dividends (general).
Foreign income taxes.	Dividends-controlled corpora-
Local income taxes.	tions.
Interest from state obligations.	Federal jobs credit wages.
Excess ACRS depreciation.	Interest—U.S. obligations.
Excess depletion.	State income tax refunds.
Federal N.O.L. C/O.	Current year capital loss.
Federal capital loss C/O.	Subpart F income.
Federal contribution C/O.	Capital gain from years before
Excluded DISC income.	state law was enacted.
	Federal income tax.
	Partial capital gain deduction.

Dividends.   The states differ in their treatment of dividend
income. However there are some common rules. Some examples
follow.

- Dividends received are excluded in whole or in part if the
  payor is subject to tax in the state.
- Dividends received are reduced in conformity with the
  dividends-received percentage allowed on the federal return.
- Dividends received are reduced by an arbitrary percentage
  fixed by state law.
- The federal IRC Section 78 deemed-paid gross-up on foreign
  (country) dividends is usually excluded from dividend
  income.
- Subpart F income may or may not be treated as dividends.

Net Operating Losses. The state provisions relating to net operating losses vary greatly. Few states allow the same amount of net operating loss claimed on the federal return. Most states allow a deduction for some net operating loss carryover if specific conditions are met.

When a company joins in the filing of a federal consolidated return, but files a separate return for state purposes, net operating loss carryovers for state purposes are determined "as if" the company had filed separate federal income tax returns for all the years involved. Most state laws provide that a company must have been subject to tax in that state in the year a loss is incurred in order to avail itself of a net operating loss carryover in the present year.

Since the state laws vary as to (1) how the amount of the loss is determined. (2) the percentage of loss apportioned to the state, (3) the number of years to which the loss may be carried back or forward, and (4) other specific requirements, the law and regulations of each particular state should be reviewed to determine the amount of net operating loss, if any, that is available.

It is also necessary to look at special laws in relation to the utilization of net operating loss carryovers after mergers and acquisitions. New York recently enacted laws restricting the use of such carryovers in highly leveraged acquisitions.

Depreciation and Depletion. Various states disallow part of the federal deduction for depreciation and depletion because of differences between federal and state laws. The principal reason for the difference results from the enactment of the IRC ACRS provisions in 1981. Certain of the differences relate to the location of the property subject to depreciation. New York, for example, allows an accelerated depreciation deduction only for property placed in service in the state.

Interest on Federal Obligations. The states are prohibited from taxing federal obligations income under the intergovernmental immunity doctrine. However, this doctrine applies only to state taxes imposed *directly on* net income as opposed to those taxes *measured by* net income. States imposing a direct net income tax are required to provide for a subtraction modification for U.S. interest. States levying franchise taxes measured by net income generally tax such income.

Municipal Interest.   Many states require federal income to be increased by the amount of interest received on state and municipal obligations that are exempt from U.S. tax. This income may be reduced by any related expenses that were not allowed as deductions for federal purposes. Some states that require this modification exclude interest received on their own bonds or on bonds issued by their political subdivisions from this provision.

State and Local Taxes on Income.   Most states do not allow a deduction for their own income tax. Many states disallow a deduction for all state and local income taxes. The laws of those states requiring an addback of other states' income taxes must be reviewed to determine which taxes fall within the modification provisions (i.e., income taxes versus franchise taxes based on income). A direct income tax is imposed on net income derived from sources within a state, whereas a tax based on or measured by income is usually imposed for the privilege of doing business in a state.

Federal Income Tax.   A few states allow a deduction or partial deduction for federal income taxes paid. When a corporation seeking to obtain the deduction files on a federal consolidated basis, the computation of the deduction can be complicated.

Sales and Use Taxes

While sales price and cost price are generally used as the base for sales taxes and use taxes, respectively, many deductions are available to retailers and consumers. Most states allow credits for sales and use taxes previously paid to other states with respect to property brought into the state for subsequent use or consumption therein. The sales tax and the use tax exemptions in a given state are usually the same, although not always. Following is an explanation of the most common exemptions or exclusions.

Exemptions/Exclusions Reflecting the Nature of the Seller.

Sales by exempt organizations.
Sales by state governments and their political subdivisions.

Exemptions/Exclusions Reflecting the Nature of the Buyer.

Sales to exempt organizations.

Sales to state governments and their political subdivisions.
Sales to educational institutions.
Sales to the U.S. government.

Exemptions/Exclusions Reflecting the Nature of the Item Transferred.

Periodicals, magazines, and newspapers.
Machinery and equipment used in manufacturing.

Many states grant an exemption applicable to the sale or purchase of machinery and equipment used directly and primarily for manufacturing and processing. The states granting such exemptions often differ as to what constitutes eligible property and/or to what extent it must be used directly and primarily in manufacturing and processing.

Exemptions/Exclusions Reflecting the Purchaser's Intended Use of the Item Transferred.

Sales for resale: Almost universally, states provide exclusions or exemptions from their sales taxes and use taxes for sales for resale. However, as a practical matter, it is presumed that sales of tangible personal property are for consumption rather than for resale. The burden of proving that the sale is for resale rather than for consumption is on the seller. As a general rule, resale certificates should be obtained from the purchaser. Generally, the purchaser must possess a sales tax permit.

Exemptions/Exclusions Reflecting the Nature of the Type of Transaction.

Isolated, occasional or bulk sales: Many jurisdictions grant an exemption applicable to infrequent sales of an isolated, occasional or casual manner and/or to sales involving the transfer of a major portion of a business's assets. Depending upon the particular jurisdiction involved, various statutory and/or regulatory requirements may have to be satisfied in order for the transaction to qualify for exempt status. With regard to bulk sales, it is important to note that some states require notification by the purchaser to the state of the sale. Absent notification, the purchaser may be held liable for any uncollected sales tax due from the seller.

Unitary Theory

The concept of a unitary business is unique to the states and grew out of the nature of a multistate business operation. In general, a multinational company can geographically account for the income generated by its operations in each country. This method, separate accounting, is the standard used to determine the income attributable to each country. Originally, the same method was used by multistate companies to determine the amount of income attributable to each state in which such a company operated. When a company operates as a single business enterprise (a unitary business) it becomes increasingly difficult for profits or income to be geographically sourced to the separate states. The states, therefore, developed the concept of formulary apportionment for such businesses.

As far back as 1920, the U.S. Supreme Court approved Connecticut's use of a formula for income tax purposes, commenting, "The profits of the corporation were largely earned by a series of transactions beginning with manufacture in Connecticut, and ending with the sale in other states." The term *unitary business* itself can be traced to a 1924 case involving New York's imposition of formulary apportionment on the entire income of a foreign-based corporation that brewed its ale in England but sold some of it in New York.

A unitary business may be operated as a single corporation or may be operated through two or more corporations. No "bright line" test has been accepted that will determine the unitary nature of the business. Rather, several tests based on specific facts and circumstances have been developed to help taxpayers and state administrators determine the existence of a unitary business.

The determination of whether a single corporation or group of controlled, affiliated companies is involved in a unitary business was originally developed in two California court decisions that are cited in many other states' court decisions dealing with this issue. The first case describes three elements of a unitary business and is known as the three unities test.

- *Unity of ownership*—A group of companies possesses unity of ownership where affiliated corporations are owned entirely by a parent corporation or controlling shareholders; in practice, the states have required that there be more than 50 percent ownership of an affiliate to satisfy the ownership requirement.

- *Unity of operation*—This is generally evidenced by centralized purchasing, advertising, accounting, and management.
- *Unity of use*—This refers to the use of a centralized executive force or some other asset in the general system of operation.

The second judicial test of unitary businesses is the "contribution" or "dependency" test. Here the court stated, "If the operation of a portion of the business done within the state is dependent upon or contributes to the operation of the business without the state, the operations are unitary; otherwise, if there is no such dependency, the business within the state may be considered to be separate."

Generally, if one of the following situations exists, along with the meeting of the ownership requirements, a unitary group will be found to exist:

Multistate Use of Contiguous Assets.   The business operates through a physical connection of tangible assets. Examples are railroads, telegraph, telephone, and pipeline companies.

Multistate Use of the Same Assets.   The business utilizes the same assets in more than one state: for example, trucks, buses, aircraft, and steamships.

Income Arising from Transactions in More Than One State. The business derives income that arises from a series of transactions in more than one state: for example, the manufacture of a product in one state and its sale in another state.

Local Activities Contribute to Net Income of the Entire Business.—The operations within the state contribute (or are dependent upon) the earnings derived from the entire business. The necessary contribution may be established by a flow of goods, centralized purchasing, advertising, accounting, or management.

The three unities test and the contribution or dependency test have been applied consistently by various state courts in a variety of cases.

The U.S. Supreme Court has alluded to other tests of unity that in reality may be no more than variations on these two standard tests. Specifically, the Court has referred to a unitary business as one that exhibits "contributions to income resulting from functional integration, centralization of management and economies of scale." In addition, the Court has suggested another indication of a unitary business, noting that "the prerequisite to a constitutionally acceptable finding of a unitary business is a flow of value, not a flow of goods." In an alternative approach, the Court has stated that for commonly controlled activities to be nonunitary, they must be part of "unrelated business activity which constitutes a 'discrete business enterprise.' "

It may be possible that one group of companies owned or controlled by the same interest will be engaged in several separate unitary businesses. This is possible, for instance, where management has sought to diversify and hold certain groups of companies as totally autonomous. As an example, one organization might consist of 15 controlled companies. Of these companies 3 may be in one combined group, such as oil drilling or oil-related products (drilling, tooling, marketing, etc.), related to the oil industry. A second group consisting of 7 corporations may be in the outdoor advertising business. The remaining 5 companies may each be in totally unrelated businesses or industries. There are no unitary attributes other than ownership between either of the two groups or the other subsidiaries. Each of the two groups would probably be unitary, and the remaining companies would not. It must be recognized, however, that such combinations of companies are, in fact, unusual, and the diverse nature of the various businesses does not preclude a finding that the businesses are unitary.

In addition, one can argue for different divisions of a single corporate legal entity to be treated as separate unitary businesses. Consider the following example: A conglomerate operates through various divisions. One division is engaged in manufacturing aerospace products, another division is engaged in growing and marketing tobacco and related items, and the third division produces and distributes motion pictures. As long as each division operates independently, one may conclude that the taxpayer is involved in three separate unitary businesses, each of which will have its own tax base and apportionment factors. It may be that no portion of one trade or business of a taxpayer is carried on within a particular state, so that no apportionment is applicable. On the other hand, the separate trade or business may be carried on entirely within a particular state so that all the income or loss is attributable to that particular state. The final measure of tax is the total of all the income of the separate trades or businesses apportioned to this state.

A question often asked is "Which intercorporate connection or unitary attribute is most important?" As is usually the case with such questions, the answer is "It depends." No single factor alone would normally be sufficient. However, a review of the cases that have determined that a unitary business exists would show the two frequently recurring attributes are intercompany product flow and strong centralized management. With the exception of a few cases, the facts have shown some form of intercompany product flow or use. Similarly, integration of top-level, policy-making executives and directors has consistently been considered to weigh heavily in the balance.

Most states provide additional guidance and rules regarding what constitutes a unitary business. Most significantly, they recognize that a single taxpayer may have more than one "trade or business" and set forth three factors, the presence of which creates a "strong presumption" that the activities of the taxpayer constitute a single trade or business:

- *Same type of business:* A taxpayer is almost always engaged in a single trade or business when all of its activities are in the same general line. For example, a taxpayer that operates a chain of retail grocery stores will almost always be engaged in a single trade or business.
- *Steps in a vertical process:* A taxpayer is almost always engaged in a single trade or business when its various divisions or segments are engaged in different steps in a large, vertically structured enterprise. For example, a taxpayer that explores for and mines copper ores; concentrates, smelts, and refines the copper ores; and fabricates the refined copper into consumer products is engaged in a single trade or business, regardless of the fact that the various steps in the process are operated substantially independently of each other, with only general supervision from the taxpayer's executive offices.
- *Strong centralized management:* A taxpayer that might otherwise be considered as engaged in more than one trade or

business is properly considered as engaged in one trade or business when there is strong central management, coupled with the existence of centralized departments for such functions as financing, advertising, research, or purchasing. Thus, some conglomerates may properly be considered as engaged in only one trade or business when the central executive officers are normally involved in the operations of the various divisions and centralized offices perform for the divisions the normal matters that a truly independent business would perform for itself, such as accounting, personnel, insurance, legal, purchasing, advertising, or financing.*

As is clear from the foregoing, the determination of a unitary business depends on many factors and is the subject of much controversy between taxpayers and state tax administrators.

Attribution

Once a determination has been made that nexus exists between an entity and a state, and once the tax base has been defined, the question remaining is the amount of the tax base that should be attributed to the particular taxing jurisdiction. As discussed in the Unitary Theory section, formulary apportionment of a multistate business engaged in a unitary business is the method chosen by the states to attribute income arising from activities conducted both within and without a state. Before looking at the specifics of the formula, certain issues must be addressed.

The first issue relates to the right to apportion. In general, a taxpayer must be taxable in at least two jurisdictions in order to avail itself of the right to apportion income. If no other state has jurisdiction to tax the business, all the income will be attributed to the state in which it does have tax nexus. Some states require a business seeking to apportion its income to actually file tax returns in at least one other state. The validity of such a position is questionable. Most will permit apportionment based on the activities engaged in by the taxpayer is another state irrespective of whether returns are actually filed in that state.

---

* Multistate Tax Commission Regulations, Reg. IV.1.(b), two or more businesses of a single taxpayer.

Once it is established that a taxpayer has the right to apportion, the second issue to be addressed relates to whether the taxpayer's income is considered "business income" or "nonbusiness income." This classification is necessitated by the fact that the majority of the states will subject business income to formulary apportionment and will directly allocate nonbusiness income.

The concepts of business income and unitary business are intertwined. Business income is most often defined as "income arising from transactions and activity in the regular course of the taxpayer's trade or business and includes income from tangible and intangible property if the acquisition, management, and disposition of the property constitute integral parts of the taxpayer's regular trade or business." State regulations generally define "trade or business" in unitary terms—that is, transactions and activities that are dependent upon or contribute to the operations of the taxpayer's economic enterprise as a whole.

Nonbusiness income is generally defined as all income other than business income. Depending on the facts and circumstances, the general types of income that may constitute nonbusiness income are rents and royalties from real or tangible personal property, capital gains, interest, dividends, and patent and copyright royalties. To the extent this income constitutes nonbusiness income, it is generally allocated based either on the commerical situs of the taxpayer or on the business situs of the property giving rise to the income.

Under the generally accepted formula, states use an equally weighted three-factor formula of payroll, property, and sales to apportion business income. "Property" generally includes all real and tangible personal property owned (valued at original cost) or rented (valued at eight times the net annual rental rate) by the taxpayer. In general, "payroll" includes all forms of compensation paid to employees. "Sales" generally includes all gross receipts of the taxpayer from the sale of tangible and intangible property. The property and payroll factors were intended to emphasize the activity of the manufacturing state, while the sales factor was intended to recognize the contribution of the consumer state toward the production of the income of the business.

The amount of business income attributable to a state is determined through the use of the formula that calculates the percentage of the taxpayer's property, payroll, and sales attributable to a state and then averages these three percentages to reach the state appor- tionment factor. It is important to note that while sales are generally attributed to the destination state, many states employ a recapture or "throw-back" rule. The states that have adopted this rule require sales made into a state where the taxpayer is not subject to tax to be attributed, or thrown back, to the state from which the sale origi- nated. The total business income of the taxpayer is then multiplied by the apportionment factor to determine the amount of business income apportioned to the state. Accordingly:

$$\left(\frac{\text{In-State Property}}{\text{Total Property}} + \frac{\text{In-State Payroll}}{\text{Total Payroll}} + \frac{\text{In-State Sales}}{\text{Total Sales}} \right) \div 3 = \text{State Factor}$$

For example, assume a corporation doing business within and with- out the state has the following factors:

	In-State	Everywhere	State Portion
Property	$ 300,000	$3,000,000	10%
Payroll	100,000	400,000	25%
Sales	1,000,000	2,000,000	50%

The average of the property, payroll, and sales attributable to the state is 28.33 percent [(10 + 25 + 50)/3]. Thus, if the corporation's total business income is $500,000, the business income apportion- able to the state is $141,667 (500,000 × 28.33%).

Some states have adopted a modified three-factor formula that consists of 50 percent of the receipts factor, 25 percent of the property factor, and 25 percent of the payroll factor, and certain other states have adopted a one- or two-factor formula instead of the conventional three-factor formula.

COMPLIANCE

Franchise or Capital Stock Taxes Based on Net Worth

These taxes, when assessed on a stand-alone basis, are generally due on the anniversary date of the corporation's qualification or incorporation in the state. In those states that assess them in con- junction with an income tax, they are generally calculated on the income tax return and due a given number of months after the close of the business's fiscal year. Changes in the capital stock will generally be required to be reported as they occur, whereas changes in the amount attributable to the state (apportioned amount) will generally be reported only when the return is due.

Income Taxes

The three common methods of reporting corporate income to the state are separate returns, consolidated returns, and combined unitary returns. Some states require each corporation within their jurisdiction to file a separate return irrespective of the fact that the corporation may be part of a federal consolidated group or part of a unitary group. In these states, income is calculated as if the corporation had no affiliates. Other states will allow affiliated corporations to file a consolidated return similar in nature to the federal consolidated return. Some states allow this methodology only for those corporations that have nexus in the state; others allow a taxpayer to file a consolidated return for the same affiliates included in the federal consolidated return.

Taxpayers that file combined returns or combined reports face the greatest complexity. The purpose of the combined method is to treat a group of taxpayers conducting a unitary business as if they were a single taxpayer for apportionment purposes. California, for example, requires the members of a unitary group to calculate the base income of each member separately subject to certain intercompany eliminations. Each member must account for nonbusiness income separately, but business income is combined prior to being apportioned. The apportionment formula is also subject to combination. Each member of the group uses the total property, payroll, and sales of all members as the denominator and its own property, payroll, and sales as the numerator.

Most states employing the unitary combined reporting method will not include in the numerator the in-state sales of a member of the group that does not have nexus in the state. California, however, following a recent administrative decision, does include such sales and, as a result, a third step is necessary in that state. The total business income apportioned to California through use of the formula is then assigned to the corporations taxable by the state in accordance with the average ratio that the California factors of each such member bears to the total factors of the unitary group.

Transaction Taxes: Sales, Use, and Other Taxes Based on Gross Receipts

The timing and form of return required for these taxes varies from state to state. In general, the timing for sales tax returns is dependent on the dollar amounts collected. For businesses that have fewer receipts, the return may be due annually or quarterly. Businesses generating a great deal of receipts will usually be required to report and remit monthly or quarter-monthly. Electronic filing may be required for the largest retailers in a given state.

The filing of sales and use tax returns is complicated by the fact that most states permit local jurisdictions to impose the tax. A single sale may be subject to tax by the state, the city, the county, and various special taxing districts, for instance transportation districts. The rate may vary from jurisdiction to jurisdiction, and the seller must be aware of the total tax to be collected and remitted for each sale. Generally, the location of the customer will be the determining factor in calculating the rate, but some states require that the rate be used for the jurisdiction where the seller is located.

Property Taxes: Taxes Based on the Value of Real, Tangible, and Intangible Property

In general, real property is assessed by the relevant government assessing authority and a bill is sent to the property owner. The assessment can be protested, however, and the taxpayer can challenge the assessment by providing his or her own appraisal or other measure of worth. Personal property, whether tangible or intangible, is generally self-assessed. The taxpayer is required to submit a form to the assessing jurisdiction listing and valuing the property. Personal property will be valued and listed as of a particular day and if brought into the state at a later date, will not be taxed until the following year.

Excise Taxes: Specific Taxes Based on the Cost Price of a Particular Product

These taxes vary greatly depending on whether they are imposed on a specific item or on a specific transaction. Generally, the taxes on specific goods are taxed in a manner similar to the general sales tax. Taxes on a particular transaction (e.g., real estate transfer taxes) are usually due at the time of the transaction or within a given number of days after the transaction is completed.

PLANNING

Minimizing Liability

In order to minimize liability, a business should consider making changes in operations, changes in structure, or changes in intercompany activities. The opportunity to minimize state and local taxes exists as a result of the diversity in taxing schemes employed by the states. Some of the methods by which this can be accomplished will be briefly explored.

In relation to franchise taxes based on capital stock, a corporation can incorporate in a state such as Delaware and minimize the tax by issuing fewer shares of stock. Because Delaware does not look to the value of the stock but rather to the number of shares issued, a minimum tax can often be ensured.

A corporation should look carefully at the method of accounting required for capital stock tax purposes. In some states an election can be made to use a different method for state franchise tax purposes than is used for financial statement purposes. In this situation, the taxpayer can minimize the tax by using the most advantageous method.

In seeking to minimize income taxes, the business should look to the rate, the base, the apportionment method, and the filing requirements of each state in which business may be conducted. Obviously, it will benefit a taxpayer to place its major operations in a state that has no income tax or one that has a low tax rate. However, since business needs may dictate some other location, a business can benefit from careful examination of the state's treatment of various items of income and expense and from its apportionment and filing requirements.

For example, a number of states do not tax foreign-source income and others do not tax income from intangibles if the only activity of the corporation is the management of such intangibles. As a result, setting up a separate company to hold the stock of foreign subsidiaries or the patents or trademarks giving rise to royalty income, and locating that company in a state that affords such benefits can result in a lower tax burden.

The apportionment formula is also worth examining. If, for example, a business manufactures goods in a state that does not employ the throw-back rule and ensures that its activities in the states into which it sells the goods do not exceed the protection of P.L. 86-272, tax liability will be considerably lessened. In order to obtain the benefit of apportioning income, a business should consider placing property in at least one state other than the headquarters state or assuring that its activities in another state exceed mere solicitation.

The fact that some states require unitary combined reporting while others mandate separate returns can also be turned to the taxpayer's advantage. By properly imposing management fees or otherwise shifting income from one affiliate to another, a taxpayer can create an expense for the affiliate filing in a separate reporting state. If the company receiving the fees is taxable only in a combined reporting state, no concomitant increase in its tax will occur since the income and expense will be eliminated as an intercompany transaction.

Minimizing sales and use taxes depends to a great extent on taking advantage of existing exemptions from the tax. If, for example, a business purchases an item for lease and leases the property to a customer in one of the many states that impose a sales tax on leases, the business may make the original purchase tax free on a sale for resale basis, and collect and remit sales tax on the lease payments.

Many taxpayers overlook the savings that can occur in the property tax area because the tax on real property and improvements is not self-assessed. It is important to be aware of reductions in value sustained for property that is not in use or is obsolete, and the reductions in tax that can be gained by assuring that property is properly classified. In states that exempt personal property, for example, all improvements should be analyzed in relation to the state's rules regarding the classification of certain items as either real or personal.

Minimizing Exposure

Examining the nexus requirements for each state in which business is conducted or into which sales are made is the first step in minimizing exposure to state and local taxes. If, for example, a business will be sending representatives into another state, an analysis should be made of that state's definition of solicitation. If the state is one that takes a very narrow view, care should be taken that the representative's activities do not exceed that view, or consideration should be given to using independent contractors for solicitation purposes. If the needs of the business require greater activity to be undertaken, the company should register to do business and begin filing returns. There is no statute of limitations for nonfilers.

Taxpayers required to collect and remit sales and use tax should be sure to obtain exemption certificates from their customers. While a state may allow proof other than a valid certificate to sustain a claimed exemption, the certificate itself is the safest way to avoid exposure. In a situation involving the acquisition of the assets of an existing company, the buyer must protect itself by carefully following the state's bulk sales provisions. If a portion of the purchase price is not withheld and the proposed purchase is not reported to the state, the buyer may be held responsible for any unpaid liability incurred by the seller prior to the sale.

Acquisitions can also lead to exposure in the area of property taxes. A common problem faced by taxpayers in this regard is caused by negligence in attributing the purchase price to the specific assets purchased. Because many taxing jurisdictions will use the figures so attributed in revaluing the property, it is necessary to correctly attribute the price among the intangible assets, the tangible personal property, and the real property purchased.

In summary, the state and local tax system in the United States is unique. The number of taxing bodies, the variety of taxes, and the absence of uniformity create a complex system that is not instantly understandable. It is, however, workable. Once the basic concepts are understood, the differences among the states become minor. Further, it is these differences themselves that create more opportunities for minimizing the tax burden.

CHAPTER 18

TRANSFER PRICING: SECTION 482

Richard M. Hammer
International Tax Partner
Marylouise Dionne
Manager
Price Waterhouse

INTRODUCTION

The term *transfer pricing* refers to the art (or science) of establishing appropriate charges between commonly owned parties (affiliates) with respect to intercompany transactions taking place between or among the affiliates. In general, intercompany transactions are supposed to be accorded the same tax treatment as if they were transactions with unrelated parties negotiated at arm's length. This is known as the arm's-length standard.

Transfer pricing is generally considered to be an international tax issue. Nonetheless, it should be noted that intercompany pricing concepts apply as well to transactions between domestic companies, but in most cases domestic transactions do not raise issues with the IRS since most U.S. groups file consolidated U.S. tax returns including all their U.S. affiliates. Thus, an adjustment made to one company would be offset by a correlative adjustment to a sister company, with no change in the consolidated U.S. taxable income. Foreign-affiliated corporations, however, are rarely if ever included in U.S. consolidated income tax returns. Accordingly, any adjustments in intercompany pricing between foreign and domestic affiliates (as well as between two or more foreign affiliates in certain cases) will have a direct impact on U.S. taxable income. Consequently, intercompany pricing becomes a much more critical issue when it involves cross-border transactions, both outbound from the United States and inbound into the United States.

Internal Revenue Code Section 482 sets forth the general rule with respect to intercompany transfer pricing. The section is only two sentences long, and, in fact, the second sentence of Section 482 was recently added by the Tax Reform Act of 1986. Regulations have been issued under Section 482 implementing the arm's-length concept contained in the code section. Congress's concern with the inadequate coverage of the language of Section 482 and regulations thereunder, specifically with regard to transfers of intangibles, led to changes made by 1984 and 1986 amendments. The 1984 Act added Section 367(d), which generally requires the recognition of gain on the transfer of intangibles to a foreign affiliate. The 1986 amendment to Section 482, the so-called superroyalty provision, also required a study on intercompany pricing to be performed by the U.S. Treasury Department and the IRS. The main point is that the IRS is empowered by Section 482 (and the regulations) to make whatever adjustments are necessary to ensure the intercompany transactions of any U.S. taxpayer reflect the arm's-length standard.

When the IRS makes a transfer pricing adjustment, the taxpayer has the "burden of proof" on the issue. This is important since the IRS must be proven wrong by the taxpayer in proposing such an adjustment. The IRS is generally sustained by the courts unless the taxpayer can show that the proposed adjustment is arbitrary, capricious, or unreasonable.

In the litigated cases, the courts have the job of deciding whether or not the taxpayer has established an arm's-length price. If the taxpayer sustains its burden of proof on the issue, the IRS adjustment is set aside.

Transfer pricing issues are inherently fact-driven. Increasingly, taxpayers, courts, and the IRS have come to rely on economic analysis and expert economists. In recent years, the courts have expressed great reluctance to embrace either the position of the taxpayer or the IRS. Instead, they make their own determinations of an arm's-length price from the evidence presented to them by both parties.

U.S. courts, particularly the Tax Court, where most transfer pricing cases are heard, have become very sophisticated in deciding transfer pricing issues. A taxpayer that has adopted an overly aggressive methodology (which could border on abuse) is unlikely to escape an adjustment of some magnitude.

More significantly, since 1986, both the Congress and the IRS have been extremely active in stepping up enforcement efforts in the transfer pricing area, particularly with respect to, first, inbound foreign investors and, second, transfer pricing for intangibles (generally outbound). Therefore, foreign investors in the United States must carefully consider the transfer pricing methodologies relevant to their U.S. operations.

This chapter will give a brief history of Section 482, set out the general rules in the area, and then describe the developments since 1986. The last section will briefly examine international transfer pricing.

HISTORY

Before discussing the law and regulations, a brief history of the evolution of these rules affecting intercompany pricing between affiliates is instructive.

The predecessor to Section 482 was enacted in 1923. Regulations adopted in 1935 established the arm's-length standard as the fundamental principle in transfer pricing. In the early 1960s, the U.S. government's concern that profits were being shifted offshore by U.S. multinationals (outbound investors) increased.

In 1962, legislation incorporating a formulary income apportionment among related entities was considered and rejected, deferring intercompany pricing standards to be established by regulations. These were issued in final form in 1968. The regulations provided little guidance for determining an arm's-length price for intangibles; however, the regulations dealt more substantively and realistically with pricing rules applicable to intercompany transfers of tangible property (i.e., sales of goods), intercompany services, intercompany leasing, and intercompany financing.

GENERAL RULES

Section 482 essentially authorizes the IRS to reallocate income, deductions, credits, or allowances among related trades or businesses *in order to clearly reflect income* or to prevent the evasion of taxes. Companies are treated as related, under the IRS regulations, when they are under common control. Control for this purpose includes any kind of control, direct or indirect, whether legally enforceable, and however exercised. In other words, the rules do not provide any percentage ownership threshold to establish a control situation (as is done in other countries and in other areas of U.S. law). Effective control is what counts.

As already noted, the standard governing reallocation under Section 482 is the arm's-length standard; related parties must deal with each other as if they are unrelated. An arm's-length charge is the amount that was charged or would be charged in independent transactions with unrelated parties under the same or similar circumstances. As stated in the regulations, the purpose of Section 482 is to "place a controlled taxpayer on a tax parity with an uncontrolled taxpayer, by determining, according to the standard of an uncontrolled taxpayer, the true taxable income" of the controlled taxpayer. If the controlling interests of a group do not structure internal transactions so that each member of the group derives its true taxable income, then the IRS reserves the right to determine the true taxable income. The standard to be used is "that of a uncontrolled taxpayer dealing at arm's length with another uncontrolled taxpayer."

IRS regulations provide rules on transfer pricing for five specific types of transaction:

- Sales of tangible property (including inventory goods).
- Services.
- Loans.
- Use of tangible property (e.g., rentals).
- Transfer or use of intangible property (e.g., licensing).

The general rules for each type of transaction are summarized below.

Sale of Tangible Property ("Goods")

The regulations set forth *three* methods to be used in determining an arm's-length sales price for sales between related parties. They are the comparable uncontrolled price method (CUP), the resale price method (R−), and the cost plus (C+) method. The regulations establish a priority of application. The first method must be used, if possible, since it is considered to be the most reflective of the arm's-length standard. The resale price method would be used next before the cost plus method. If none of the three prescribed methods is appropriate, then another method must be developed based on facts and circumstances; this is the so-called fourth method.

Each of the three prescribed methods requires the derivation of a comparable product and a comparable set of circumstances from third party transactions against which the transfer price in the intercompany transaction may be tested. Because a comparable may not always be available, the regulations provide the fourth method, thereby sanctioning another approach. Under this method, transfer pricing is established by reference to the particular facts and circumstances of the transaction.

The preferred method, as noted above, is the comparable uncontrolled price method. It *must* be used if proper comparables are available. The CUP method is based on the sales price between unrelated parties. The uncontrolled sales are comparable if the physical property and circumstances are identical, or nearly identical, to the controlled sales. In this regard, it should be noted that a sale to outsiders of a small quantity of products, made primarily to justify a large quantity of intercompany sales, would not qualify as nearly identical and thus such sales would not represent a valid comparable. This is, of course, a necessary anti-avoidance rule. The sales will be nearly identical if the differences either have no effect on price or they can be reflected by a reasonable number of numerical adjustments. But the differences must have a definite and ascertainable effect on the price. Quantifiable differences would include measurable difference in quality of the products, differing terms of sale, differences in the intangible property associated with the product, different times of sale, different market levels, and the variations stemming from different geographic markets in which the product is sold. In certain cases, a lower price may be justified if the primary purpose is to establish or maintain a market for a product, but such lower price has conditions and restrictions on it.

In implementing CUP methodology, a taxpayer may use either its own transactions with third parties (purchases or sales) or prices on third party sales outside the group (e.g., established world prices on primary products, such as oil, minerals, etc.).

The courts will always accept a comparable transaction. The difficulty lies in either finding a comparable or persuading a court that the proposed comparable is sufficiently similar to be treated as such.

The IRS seems to take the position that a comparable product must be an identical product (or almost identical), unless whatever differences that do exist can be demonstrated to have no effect, or no measurable effect, on the price. On the other hand, the courts merely require that a comparable product be a similar product, although it is essential that the differences that exist can be properly quantified so as to arrive at a numerical comparable.

The second of the prescribed methods, the R− method, is based on the uncontrolled retail price of a product sold by a distribution affiliate, *reduced by* an appropriate markup. In order to use the resale price method, there should be no available comparable uncontrolled price to use as the criterion. There must, however, be an applicable resale price within a reasonable time before or after the time of the controlled sale, and the reseller must not have added substantial value to the product either by physically altering the product or by the application of intangible property. The appropriate markup percentage is the percentage of gross profit that would be earned by the reseller on the purchase of a product from an unrelated party and its subsequent resale to an unrelated party, using transactions most similar to the related party purchase and sale transactions. Sometimes industry statistics can be used in determining an appropriate markup percentage when the reseller does not distribute products obtained from third parties.

The third prescribed method, the C+ method, is based on the cost of producing (or purchasing) property, increased by an appropriate gross profit percentage. The appropriate gross profit percentage is the gross profit percentage earned by the seller (or another party) on uncontrolled sales that are most similar to the controlled sale. In determining what is similar, the impact on the gross profit percentage is the key factor. Uncontrolled sales by the seller, where they do exist, take preference over sales made by other parties. Available industry statistics can be used. The C+ method is, in fact, the reciprocal of the R− method.

The fourth method is used when the three prescribed methods (i.e., all of which are variations of the comparable uncontrolled transaction method), are not adaptable to the particular situation because of the absence of proper comparables. Generally, the fourth method is a facts and circumstances approach, using certain selected factors (e.g., comparative rates of return) to apportion the combined income from the manufacture and sale of products between or among the affiliates involved. This approach is sometimes referred to as functional analysis and the result is often called profit split. It is the methodology most frequently used in recent years where significant intangibles are involved, because comparables are almost never available. It has been argued that a profit split, or apportionment, methodology is inconsistent with the arm's-length standard.

Services

The arm's-length rule also applies where one member of a controlled group performs services for the benefit of another member of the controlled group. The definition of services is broad, including (but not limited to), marketing, managerial, administrative, and technical services.

Generally, the service charge (or fee) should be a true arm's-length charge—that is, meeting the third party standard. There is a safe harbor, however, in accord with which a charge equal to the costs incurred by the affiliate in rendering the services is deemed to be arm's length. In other words, a profit margin is not required to be included in the service fee, except where the type of services provided are an integral part of the business of the affiliate performing the services or the affiliate receiving benefit of the services. In that case, the service fee *must* include a profit. Cost of services includes both direct and indirect costs.

There is an important exception to the exception, however. If the service provider is, for example, a parent company that renders similar services to members of its controlled group as one of its principal activities, a profit margin will not be required if the parent's costs of providing such services does not exceed 25 percent of its total costs.

For inbound investors, the biggest risk is that the IRS will assert that service fees paid to the foreign parent are excessive, resulting in a disallowance of the deduction for the excessive portion of the service fee. Furthermore, such excess portion would be regarded as a dividend and subjected to U.S. withholding tax. The foreign investor should be prepared to document its fees by reference to the cost of rendering them (both direct and indirect costs) *or* by reference to an available third party (arm's-length) consideration (e.g., management consultant's fee schedules).

Loans

An inbound investor must carefully review loans made from a foreign member of its group to a controlled domestic U.S. entity. The arm's-length rule, of course, prevails in this area as well. Moreover, the courts tend to be quite supportive of the IRS when non-arm's-length loans exist. The IRS has been successful in litigated cases concerning below-market interest rate loans (generally on outbound loans by U.S. multinationals) as well as cases involving excessive interest rates (generally on inbound loans from foreign multinationals).

The IRS is very aggressive in this area. By reference to cases docketed in the Tax Court, the IRS has indicated that it intends to take a very broad view of what it considers intercompany debt subject to challenge under the transfer pricing rules. In one instance, loans were made from unrelated parties abroad to a foreign multinational's U.S. subsidiary. The debt incurred by the U.S. subsidiary was extremely large. The IRS argued that the debt was really debt of the foreign parent. It reasoned that the foreign parent's credit was used to finance transactions that, in substance, were between the foreign parent and other subsidiaries, as well as to provide favorable credit to customers. If successful, the U.S. subsidiary would be denied a very substantial interest deduction. Admittedly, the IRS would seem to be on rather tenuous grounds in taking such a position, but this example does demonstrate just how aggressive they have become in the area involving intercompany financing.

Generally, the regulations require that if a company makes a loan or advance to a related company with respect to which no interest, or less than an arm's-length rate of interest, is charged, then the IRS may make an adjustment to reflect an arm's-length rate of interest. These rules apply to bona fide indebtedness, including loans and intercompany trade receivables. Interest must be accrued on loans and advances beginning on the day after the loan is made until the day the loan is repaid. Interest is not required to be accrued on intercompany trade receivables until the first day of the third month following the month in which the trade receivable arises. An additional one-month delay is allowed when the debtor is located outside the United States (first day of the fourth month). There are additional exceptions for trade or industry practices *and* for property purchased for resale in a foreign country.

The arm's-length interest rate is defined as an interest rate that would have been charged by an unrelated party. In determining such rate, all relevant factors should be considered, such as the amount of principal, term, security, credit standing of the borrower, and prevailing interest rates at the situs of the borrower or lender. If a lender obtains funds for onlending at the situs of the borrower (i.e., the borrower's country), the proper charge will be the interest rate paid by the lender, increased by other costs incurred by the lender in arranging and executing the loan. In other words, the lender does not need to earn a profit under this scenario, although it may earn a profit commensurate with arm's-length standard if so desired.

The interest regulations provide another of the few safe harbors available under U.S. tax law, although the rules have changed substantially over the years. The safe harbor applies only to *U.S.-dollar-denominated* loans. Generally, if the interest rate charged is between 100 percent and 130 percent of the corresponding applicable federal rate, the interest rate is considered to be arm's length (the applicable federal rate fluctuates with changes in prevailing interest rates). If the interest rate is less than or greater than the safe harbor, then the minimum or maximum rate will apply (and an adjustment is made in accord therewith), unless the taxpayer establishes the appropriateness of another interest rate.

These rules do provide some planning opportunities for inbound investors. In particular, consideration should be given to the maximum safe harbor interest rate if the investor's goal is to maximize the repatriation of U.S. earnings while minimizing U.S. tax costs.

Use of Tangible Property (Rentals)

Consistent with the other types of transactions already discussed, the regulations require that arm's-length rentals be charged to an affiliate using, possessing, or occupying tangible property belonging to another affiliate.

An arm's-length charge is the charge that was or would have been made for the use of the same or similar property between unrelated parties. Again the circumstances surrounding both the related party transaction and the unrelated comparable transaction must be similar, including such circumstances as the period and location of use, the lessor's investment in the property, the expenses of maintaining the property, and the type and condition of the particular property.

As with interest charges for an inbound investor, the IRS would be concerned with excessive rents. Unfortunately, there are no longer any safe harbor rules in this area, since the original safe harbors are applicable only to leases entered into prior to mid-1986. Therefore, the arm's-length standard prevails, meaning that the best defense against a transfer pricing adjustment by the IRS on an intercompany lease transaction would be documentation reflecting a comparable third party transaction.

Sale or Lease of Intangible Property

A major change of the rules in the area of intangibles was brought about by the Tax Reform Act of 1986. Before discussing the impact of this change, however, the old rules will be summarized. After all, they are still applicable to the extent unaffected by the 1986 changes (or implementing regulations to be issued by the IRS).

Again, the overriding rule in the current regulations is that the arm's-length pricing standard prevails. The regulations do acknowledge, however, that as a practical matter, establishing appropriate transfer pricing in this area is difficult because of the lack of comparables. This is in the very nature of intangibles. Therefore, the regulations list 12 factors that are to be considered in attempting to set an arm's-length price for the transfer of an intangible, either by way of a sale or a license. But very little guidance is provided in how to apply these factors to arrive at an appropriate transfer price.

A major exception to the arm's-length rule relating to intangibles is for bona fide cost sharing arrangements. Broadly speaking, such arrangements must establish that each participant therein bears its respective share of the costs and risks in the development of intangibles, with such sharing to reflect the type of arrangement that would be made by unrelated parties. The arrangement must be incorporated into a written agreement.

In 1986, the Congress significantly changed the rules governing the transfer or license of intangibles between or among affiliates. Now, the income with respect to a transfer or license must be "commensurate with the income attributable to the intangible." This rule applies equally to inbound, as well as outbound, investors.

In enacting the new concept (i.e., "superroyalty"), Congress expressed its concern with a particular situation that, they asserted, arose too frequently under pre-1987 law. Such situation involved an outbound license of an intangible for a royalty that, at the time the contract was executed, was presumably arm's length; however, the same royalty would prevail for the life of the agreement, regardless of whether or not the particular intangible yielded significantly higher profits over that period than initially expected. The 1986 change, according to Congress, contemplated that the royalty in such a situation would be increased to reflect these higher profits.

Obviously, the superroyalty provision was aimed at U.S. multinationals transferring technology abroad. But inbound investors need to be aware of (and perhaps concerned with) this as well. For example, if a very successful intangible property right were to be developed from a research and development project conducted jointly by a foreign parent and its U.S. subsidiary, the U.S. subsidiary could not transfer its interest in the new intangible to its foreign parent without giving recognition to the commensurate with income standard. This would necessitate setting a transfer price to be paid to the U.S. subsidiary that would reflect the future income attributable to the intangible, making it perhaps a prohibitively expensive proposition.

From the inbound investor's viewpoint, there may be a potential benefit from the superroyalty (commensurate with income) provision. Since such provision will allow a foreign investor to charge higher than normal royalties to its U.S. affiliates for use of its foreign technology, another means of maximizing repatriation of U.S. profit while minimizing U.S. tax costs is established. This is a planning opportunity that should not be overlooked, particularly by high technology foreign companies investing in the United States. But the right to retroactively increase the royalty to the foreign licensor, in the event of higher than expected profitability, should be written into the original license agreement.

In January 1992, the IRS released proposed regulations reflecting the commensurate with income standard added to Section 482 in 1986. If finalized as drafted, they will replace current rules on transfers of intangible property and modify the rules on tangible property. The cost sharing rules are amplified.

At the outset, it should be noted that the proposed regulations set forth the approach the IRS will take in auditing a taxpayer's transfer pricing, rather than providing effective guidance for taxpayers. This is because the proposed regulations test transfer pricing by reference to third party actual (rather than projected) economic data from the year prior to audit, the audit year and the year following the audit year. This multi-year approach, of course, means that the proposed regulations cannot be used as a planning tool. A taxpayer setting a transfer price today cannot have this year's or next year's third party data.

Moreover, the arm's length standard has been made more stringent. The test to be applied is whether uncontrolled taxpayers exercising sound business judgement would have agreed to the same terms given the actual circumstances under which controlled taxpayers deal. This "prudent businessman" element is new.

The rules for intangible property are entirely new. Highest priority is assigned to the "matching transaction method," i.e., exact comparables. Second is the "comparable adjustable transaction" method, followed by the "comparable profit method." To reflect the commensurate with income standard, periodic adjustments are required, e.g. adjusting a royalty rate paid by a foreign subsidiary to its U.S. parent upwards for high-profit intangibles. Both the comparable adjustable transaction method and the comparable profit method must pass the "comparable profit interval" test, discussed further below.

The rules for sales of tangible property have been modified.

Although the CUP method retains first priority, the resale price and cost plus methods are now coequal. The fourth method remains last in priority. As with intangible property, except for the CUP method, the results under all other methods must pass the comparable profit interval test.

The priority rules for both tangible and intangible property are not rigid. The proposed regulations do not require the IRS or the taxpayer to demonstrate the inapplicability of a higher priority method before applying a lower priority method. Nonetheless, either party may establish that a higher priority method should be applied.

The heart of the proposed regulations is the comparable profit interval. It is designed to identify profit levels of uncontrolled taxpayers and apply those levels to similarly situated controlled taxpayers. A six-step approach is used to determine a comparable profit interval, or range of acceptable profits for the controlled taxpayer, based on profit level indicators applied to uncontrolled taxpayers in the same applicable business classification. Profit level indicators that provide a reliable basis for comparing profits include, but are not limited to, rates of return on assets, ratios of operating income to sales and ratios of gross income to operating expenses. As a practical matter, the CUP and the matching transaction methods will rarely apply, requiring testing under the comparable profit interval in all other cases.

The proposed regulations expand the rules on cost sharing. They provide that such arrangements must reflect certain general principles: (1) developed intangibles must be reasonably expected to be used in each participant's trade or business, (2) the costs of all related intangible development must be shared, (3) each participant's share of the costs of developing the intangible(s) must be proportionate to its share of the income attributable to developed intangibles, and (4) the participants must compensate the owners or developers of existing intangible property at an arm's length rate, unless the property is developed within the cost sharing agreement. Likewise, a participant's share of costs in developing intangibles must be reimbursed by the remaining participants if its abandons or transfers its rights in the intangibles.

As of this writing, these regulations are not yet final. Taxpayers will submit written comments on them, which the IRS will consider in promulgating final regulations. However, the IRS will not change its general approach and is not required, in fact, to change its proposed rules at all.

RECENT DEVELOPMENTS:
HISTORICAL PERSPECTIVE

The IRS needs access to taxpayer information above and beyond what is generally found in a tax return in order to conduct a proper transfer pricing audit. Without detailed information, the IRS just cannot examine a transfer pricing methodology or sustain an adjustment. This has produced an adversarial situation, and the resulting tension has been the cause of all the legislation in the transfer pricing area since the early 1980s', with the exception of the commensurate with income (superroyalty) standard.

Prior to 1982, the IRS had only administrative summons power to require the production of documents held abroad. This summons power was generally unenforceable, because U.S. courts lacked jurisdiction over foreign corporations. However, in 1983, the IRS was victorious in the case of *United States* v. *Toyota Motor Corp.* The court held that a Japanese parent company had such a significant business presence in the United States through its U.S. subsidiary that the court had the jurisdiction to enforce a summons against the Japanese parent. This was a notable decision.

While the case was winding its way through the court system, Congress passed some significant legislation on point. In 1982, it enacted two new provisions. First, Section 982 provided that a taxpayer that refused to comply with a document request from the IRS relating to foreign-maintained documents would be barred from using those documents in any civil court proceeding.

Second, and of greater importance for the IRS, Section 6038A was enacted. This new section required that a domestic corporation or a foreign corporation doing business in the United States (reporting corporation) controlled by a foreign corporation must file Form 5472 with its annual income tax return. Form 5472 is an information return that must include data on various transactions with related foreign parties (i.e., intercompany transactions) (See Exhibit 1 on pp. 565–568). As a practical matter, it functions as a basic roadmap for the IRS in transfer pricing examinations.

Prior to important amendments to Section 6038A in 1989 and 1990 making these rules much more onerous (discussed below), a reporting corporation was subject to this information return requirement if it was 50 percent or more foreign-owned. Transactions carried on by the reporting corporation with related parties had to be reported. Related parties, generally, were those that met a more than 50 percent common control or ownership test. Penalties for failure to comply, however, were not particularly severe. If the required information was not provided, the maximum penalty that could be imposed was $24,000.

The early 1980s' were not all good years for the IRS. Although it won the jurisdictional issue in *Toyota,* it was unable to enforce its summons. The summonses served on Toyota, Japan and its U.S. subsidiary were very broad. The information required included such detail as model numbers of cars sold, direct and indirect costs of manufacture, selling, and so on, as well sweeping requests, for example, for all information relating to the establishment of a transfer price. The court refused to require the production of almost all this information.

The IRS's defeat in the enforcement stages of the *Toyota* litigation is frequently fingered as the cause of the enactment of the amendments to Section 6038A in 1989 and 1990. The IRS expressed its complaint in the White Paper, to the effect that it could not properly carry out its duties because of taxpayer reluctance and resistance in producing necessary documents. This same claim was also made in many speeches by IRS personnel. Of course, these protestations came to the attention of the Congress.

CURRENT SCENE

There have been *four* major developments in the transfer pricing area that happened very recently (1989–1991). The *first* of these is the 1989 and 1990 changes to Section 6038A. The importance of these amendments for inbound investors cannot be overemphasized. Most inbound investors will be affected, and penalties for noncompliance can be extremely severe.

The *second* major development is an increase in penalties for substantial understatements of income in transfer pricing cases. This amendment will have major impact on U.S.-based multinationals, but its applicability to inbound foreign investors should not be overlooked. *Third,* which should be of particular concern to inbound investors, is the perception held by Congress and the IRS that foreign investors in the United States are not paying their fair share of U.S. taxes. Although we do not believe that this assertion is generally valid, it is still something that has to be taken seriously, as the 1990 amendments to Section 6038A can attest. The *fourth* development is a novel IRS procedure designed to permit taxpayers to obtain IRS approval of a transfer pricing methodology on prospective basis. This is of major significance to outbound U.S. multinationals, but it should be of interest to foreign multinationals as well.

Section 6038A Today

The current Section 6038A should be analyzed from two different perspectives, legislative and regulatory. First, legislatively, there were important amendments in 1989 and 1990. Significant changes were made to Section 6038A and a new Section 6038C was added in 1990. New Section 6038C extended the information-reporting and record-keeping rules to all U.S. branches of foreign corporations; previously only foreign corporations with a single 25 percent or more foreign shareholder were covered. Also, the 1990 amendments extended the information-gathering network under Section 6038A and Section 6038C to foreign banks, which were exempt under the pre-1990 rules. Second, 1990 saw the issuance of new regulations interpreting these sections, which impose onerous requirements on inbound investors.

The original (1982) legislation was amended because Congress thought that the IRS would have its hand strengthened in its transfer pricing enforcement efforts aimed at inbound investors if it had access to more information. In summary, Sections 6038A and 6038C impose significant record-keeping requirements and impose significant sanctions for failure to comply with an IRS summons or designate an agent for service of process.

The number of taxpayers required to file a Form 5472 (with their annual returns) has greatly increased. The complexity of the rules, of course, has similarly increased. Now, the reporting requirements apply to U.S. corporations with at least a single 25 percent or more foreign shareholder and generally to any foreign corporation (regardless of the ownership structure) engaging in a U.S. trade or business. Also, the definition of related persons, whose transactions with the reporting corporation must be reported, has been broadened to include 25 percent or more foreign shareholders and other persons that control, are controlled by, or are under common control with either the reporting corporation *or* the 25-percent foreign shareholder of the reporting corporation. The common control threshold is more than 50 percent of voting power or value.

As a result, a U.S. subsidiary of, for example, a Japanese 25 percent or more shareholder will now be required to report information relating to purchases from the Japanese shareholder, as well as other non-U.S. members of the Japanese shareholder's group. Also, a foreign corporation with a U.S. branch would be required to report transactions with other non-U.S. members of its group (i.e., subsidiaries, brothers/sister, etc., as long as connected by more than 50 percent control).

The new rules impose onerous record-keeping requirements. A reporting corporation must maintain the records required by regulations sufficient for the IRS to determine the correct tax treatment of transactions with related parties. The regulations, discussed further below, impose very substantial and onerous record-keeping and even record-creation requirements on reporting corporations.

Monetary penalties for noncompliance have substantially increased. The monetary penalties are applicable if (1) the reporting corporation fails to timely file an accurate Form 5472; and/or (2) the reporting corporation fails to maintain or produce records as required under the regulations. It is important to note that the penalty applies to a failure to *maintain* records as well as produce them.

The amount of the penalty is $10,000 per year for *each* related party. An additional $10,000 penalty per 30-day period is triggered if the reporting corporation fails to comply 90 days after notice to comply is issued by the IRS. There is no limit to the penalty, as under prior law.

Each related foreign party of a reporting corporation must also designate the reporting corporation as its agent for service of process. This designation is made on Form 5472. Of course, this rule is designed to facilitate service of an IRS summons. It only applies to tax matters, however. Therefore, it does not expose foreign related parties to nontax litigation.

The IRS has informally indicated that it will use its summons power judiciously. Therefore, it is not expected that summonses will be routinely issued, for example, to require CEOs resident in foreign countries to testify in the United States.

As a practical matter, both the reporting corporation and related parties will now generally be compelled to comply with an IRS summons. The new rules provide extremely harsh penalties for failure either to designate an agent or to timely comply with a summons. In either event, the IRS, in its sole discretion, may determine the amount of (1) any deductions for amounts paid to a related party and (2) the cost, including portions of the total cost, of any property acquired from the related party. In essence, this means that the IRS could tax a reporting corporation (e.g., a U.S. distribution affiliate) on its gross income, without the benefit of a deduction for its cost of sales if such corporation failed to designate an agent or comply with a summons. This is indeed harsh.

There is limited judicial review of the scope of an IRS summons, which is the sole remedy by which such a summons may be challenged. Moreover, if a taxpayer does not elect to challenge a summons, or is deemed by a court to be in noncompliance, the IRS may impose sanctions for noncompliance. There is very limited judicial review once such a sanction is imposed. Finally, if a taxpayer loses its challenge against the imposition of the noncompliance penalty, there is no further avenue by which to challenge it.

These are rules that cannot be ignored. A word to the wise is sufficient: failure to comply can be serious and potentially devastating to an inbound foreign investor. For example, a deliberate and continued refusal to comply with an IRS summons will invoke the noncompliance penalty discussed immediately above, which, as already noted, could be more expensive than a transfer pricing adjustment. Congress enacted the rules to give the IRS the tools it felt were necessary to force inbound investors to divulge to the IRS all the information it could possibly need in a study of a reporting corporation's transfer pricing. The IRS has been asking for these rules since 1983. It will assuredly use them.

The Regulations

The new regulations under Section 6038A primarily concern record-keeping requirements. They certainly mirror the harsh tone of the 1989 and 1990 statutory amendments. The reporting corporation *must* maintain records of related party transactions generated in the ordinary course of business. Records of a foreign related party, with respect to U.S.-connected transactions with a related party, must be maintained in the U.S. unless they can be produced in English in a timely fashion if the IRS so requests.

The record-keeping requirements are very extensive. Required records include, but are not limited to

- Basic accounting records, such as general ledgers.
- Records sufficient to produce "material profit and loss statements" of the related party group (see below).
- Filings made with foreign governments and banks.
- Organization charts, showing ownership structure and management lines.
- Loan documents and details about guarantees.
- Hedging documents.
- Any documents relevant to the establishment of a transfer price.

There is also what is referred to as a "safe harbor" in the regulations. If the safe harbor records are maintained, the reporting corporation will be deemed to have complied with the record-keeping requirements. However, the record-keeping requirements under the safe harbor are also very extensive. They are so extensive, in fact, that it is not entirely clear what the difference is between the safe harbor and the general rule discussed above (and whether or not it is a true safe harbor). Six categories of safe harbor documents are required:

- Original entry books and transaction records.
- Material profit and loss statements or records from which they can be compiled within a reasonable time.

- Pricing documents.
- Foreign country and third party filings.
- Structure and ownership records.
- Records of loans, services, and other such nonsale transactions.

As stated above, only the monetary penalty attaches to the record-keeping requirement. Nonetheless, these rules too should be treated with respect, since there is no limit to the amount that may be accrued. Because the penalty is $10,000 per taxable year per related party, with additional fines if the taxpayer fails to comply after IRS notice, noncompliance could be quite expensive.

Many foreign investors will understandably be dismayed and perhaps confused by the record-keeping requirements. The IRS has recognized this in its regulations. At the election of the taxpayer, the IRS will hold a conference to determine what records should be maintained and enter into an agreement with the taxpayer concerning the scope of record maintenance. Certain aspects of the safe harbor are so demanding that a taxpayer may want to know in advance what is expected. As a planning matter, therefore, it will generally be better to try to reach agreement with the IRS up front. Certainly this is a better alternative than trying to challenge the IRS when it proposes the imposition of the monetary penalty.

All documents should be retained. Affected companies should be advised not to destroy or discard any materials referring or relating to financial and pricing data.

Perhaps the most controversial of the record-keeping rules is the requirement for the reporting corporation's records to include data sufficient to produce "material profit and loss statements." These statements are, in essence, intended to reflect profitability flow on a particular product or product line from a foreign affiliate into the United States through the reporting corporation. In other words, this product line profit analysis must account for the total product profitability from the very beginning—that is, the manufacture of the product abroad by a foreign affiliate, to its sale to an unrelated customer in the United States through the reporting corporation. As can be seen, this would result in a combined (cross-entity) profit and loss statement incorporating cost data from all the entities in the group involved in the product flow. This requirement also raises serious jurisdictional questions.

Substantial Understatement Penalty

Taxpayers are generally subject to a penalty for an underpayment of tax attributable to a substantial valuation misstatement. The penalty is 20 percent of the underpayment to which it applies.

The 1990 legislation directed that this penalty be applied in transfer pricing cases. The new rules provide that if there is a transfer pricing (Section 482) adjustment, the penalty will apply if

1. The adjustment exceeds $10 million; or
2. The claimed transfer price on the return is 200 percent more than the "correct" price on *inbound* transactions; or
3. The claimed transfer price on the return is 50 percent less than the "correct" price on *outbound* transactions.

The penalty doubles to 40 percent in certain egregious cases where

1. The section 482 adjustment exceeds 20 million; or
2. The claimed transfer price on the return is 400 percent more than the correct price on *inbound* transactions; or
3. The claimed transfer price on the return is 100 percent less than the correct price on *outbound* transactions.

Congressional Climate

In July 1990, a subcommittee of the House Ways and Means Committee held hearings on transfer pricing. The purpose of these hearings was to focus on the amount of taxes paid by foreign corporations operating in the United States and to ascertain whether transfer pricing abuses had led to a substantial reduction in what otherwise should have been the tax liabilities of these foreign multinationals. Preceding the hearings were a number of newspaper stories alleging that foreign multinational corporations had substantially underpaid their U.S. taxes, essentially by means of transfer pricing abuses.

Persons testifying included the Assistant Secretary of Treasury for Tax Policy, the IRS Commissioner, and several IRS field agents, as well as two former IRS commissioners.

Witnesses stated that their statistics showed that foreign-owned companies reported approximately $550 billion in gross sales, but negative taxable income of $1.5 billion. Although the Assistant Treasury Secretary refused to estimate the amount of the deficiency in taxes, the hearing chairman stated that his staff estimated underpayments at $30 billion. Moreover, IRS witnesses testified that the IRS was usually "out-gunned" in larger cases.

Whether or not the government officials are correct, they do believe that foreign corporations distributing foreign-made products in the United States generally do not pay their fair share of U.S. taxes. Accordingly, the IRS has increased audits of inbound investors. With Congressional pressure on the IRS to raise revenue through taxes, it is clear that IRS pressure on inbound investors will continue for quite a while.

Advance Pricing Agreement Procedure

In a novel move, the IRS issued a procedure in 1991 under which a taxpayer can enter into an agreement with the IRS concerning its transfer pricing methodology. This "advance pricing agreement" (APA) will bar the IRS from challenging transfer pricing in a revenue examination providing that the taxpayer complies with the terms of the agreement.

In general, the taxpayer will prepare a formal, written request for submission to the IRS. The APA request will propose a transfer pricing methodology to be applied prospectively, together with documents showing that such methodology produces arm's-length results for transactions covered thereby. The IRS will examine the various materials and documents. If it accepts the taxpayer's proposed transfer pricing methodology, it will enter into an APA covering an agreed-upon number of years into the future. The IRS will also negotiate with fiscal authorities of other countries involved through the competent authority process (see below) to obtain, if possible, their approval of the particular methodology or methodologies.

The list of materials and documents listed in the revenue procedure that must be submitted with the APA request is very extensive. At the election of the taxpayer, however, the IRS will hold one or more prefiling conferences to determine whether an APA would be appropriate for that particular taxpayer. The conference procedure can also be used to clarify and limit the data, documentation, and analyses required to be submitted with the formal APA request. The availability of the prefiling conference(s) will save time and money for both an interested taxpayer and the government.

The few taxpayers that have already obtained APAs reportedly were pleased with both the process and the end results. An APA has decided advantages. First and foremost, there is transfer pricing certainty for the duration of the agreement, provided that the taxpayer lives up to its representations. By entering into an APA, the IRS has agreed that it will *not* propose transfer pricing adjustments to the transactions covered by the APA. This factor alone may outweigh any disadvantages for some taxpayers.

It should be further noted that the taxpayer can select the controlled entities to be covered, with the result that an APA applies only to the companies so selected. By submitting an APA request, a taxpayer is not, therefore, barred from adopting aggressive transfer pricing methodologies in areas not covered by the APA.

Unfortunately, an APA has some distinct disadvantages, as well. First, it will not be useful to a taxpayer that is not audited or is in litigation. Second, the preparation of a formal APA request will require, in whole or in part, the services of attorneys, accountants, and economists, making it a relatively expensive process. Third, competent authority agreement will probably be required, extending the time frame necessary for the completion of the process.

Of more concern to some taxpayers will be the disclosure required to obtain an APA. As noted above, a formal APA request will require very extensive economic and financial data and other documentation concerning the taxpayer. As with virtually all submissions taxpayers make to the IRS, the APA data and documents will be retained even should the request ultimately be withdrawn. Moreover, the District Director with audit jurisdiction over the applicant taxpayer will be notified. If the taxpayer and the IRS cannot agree on an appropriate transfer pricing methodology, the taxpayer has provided a roadmap to the IRS with which to conduct a transfer pricing audit.

Mutual Agreement/Competent Authority

Inbound investors should be aware of the potential to use the mutual agreement/competent authority articles in treaties between their home countries and the United States, if they are not prepared to acquiesce with transfer pricing adjustments proposed by the IRS. These articles generally provide for a negotiation process to be conducted by the IRS and the fiscal authorities of the home countries in an attempt to eliminate any international double taxation. Unfortunately, cross-border transfer pricing adjustments proposed by one fiscal authority generally result in double taxation unless the other fiscal authority agrees to make a correlative adjustment. This is what the mutual agreement/competent authority process is all about—that is, an attempt to reach a symmetrical result to transfer pricing adjustments on both sides of the border.

Unfortunately, the process does not have to come to a successful resolution, in accord with the language in the U.S. tax treaties, since it is only a "best efforts" mandate. Because of this, many taxpayers do not avail themselves of the facility, which is regrettable.

Inbound investors, however, should be on notice that IRS-proposed adjustments do not have to be accepted without first resorting to the mutual agreement/competent authority process. In many instances, the IRS will modify its proposal in order to accommodate the home country fiscal authorities while avoiding international double tax to the taxpayer.

INTERNATIONAL TRANSFER PRICING

This section will briefly discuss the OECD's perspective on transfer pricing, followed by a brief discussion of the transfer pricing rules of Japan, Germany, and the United Kingdom. In general, the arm's-length standard is universal. What is actually meant by the arm's-length standard, of course, may vary from jurisdiction to jurisdiction.

OECD Position

In 1979, the OECD issued a report on transfer pricing called "Transfer Pricing and Multinational Enterprises." In general, it reflected the predominance in the OECD countries of the arm's-length principle (i.e., that prices paid for goods transferred between associated enterprises should reflect prices that would be charged between unrelated parties for the same or similar goods under the same or similar circumstances). The arm's-length rule also prevails for transfers of technology, services, and loans.

Many of the rules in use in the OECD territories are similar to the U.S. rules. For example, the OECD reports that the four methods set forth in the U.S. regulations to determine an appropriate charge for the sale of goods are available and used in other countries.

The OECD report, of course, only mentions practices that are in use in the jurisdictions that are members of the OECD, which, of course, encompasses virtually all of the industrialized nation of the world, including the United States. The report indicates, however, that arm's-length pricing is an international concept, in use beyond only the OECD member states.

The concept of control discussed in the report indicates the widespread use of an actual or effective control concept not necessarily restricted to an ownership percentage. But the report also noted that Japan (an OECD member state) did use a prescribed ownership percentage threshold (50 percent or more) to establish a control situation.

The report was well received when it was issued. Implicit in the report is the acknowledgment that there is no one "right price," but that the arm's-length method contemplates a range of prices that may be appropriate, depending on the particular circumstances.

The report was also criticized for failing to take into account corresponding (correlative) adjustments when a transfer pricing adjustment was made. As noted in the preceding section on mutual agreement/competent authority, where one jurisdiction makes a transfer pricing adjustment, double taxation can result absent a corresponding adjustment by the other jurisdiction involved.

Japan

Japan incorporated the arm's-length standard in its tax law in 1986. To date, no regulations have been issued on the subject, although the statutory provision is more detailed than in most other countries.

Unlike transfer pricing rules in the United States, as discussed above, the Japanese rules apply *only* in the international context. In other words, a transfer pricing adjustment will be made only between a Japanese parent and its foreign subsidiary, or a Japanese subsidiary and its foreign parent.

Moreover, the definition of control is mechanical. A 50 percent or more ownership threshold must be met before a controlled situation exists. Indirect ownership is aggregated in determining whether the control requirement is met. There is an anti-avoidance rule that becomes operative when a Japanese unrelated entity is interposed between related entities for purposes of avoiding a controlled situation and thus avoiding application of the transfer pricing rules. In this situation, control will be deemed to exist.

Although the Japanese law prescribes the same four methods in determining an arm's-length price as are contained in the U.S. regulations, there are no ordering rules as there are in the U.S. rules. Also, there is no guidance under case law. As of this writing, no case has been litigated. The Japanese generally do not litigate such cases, because such litigation is considered dishonorable in Japan.

Japanese law contains a procedure whereby a taxpayer may obtain an advance pricing agreement, similar to the new U.S. procedure described above. But it appears that the Japanese tax administration has not yet issued any rulings under this procedure. Although rulings have been requested, Japan is still in the very beginning stages of implementing its transfer pricing rules, and the tax administration is apparently unwilling to issue such rulings as yet.

Germany

The general rule in Germany also embraces the arm's-length principle. Allocation will be made on intercompany transactions so as to equate such transactions with terms that would be fixed by unrelated parties for transfers of goods and services of the same kind. This is clearly the arm's-length principle in action. In addition to transfer of goods and services, these rules also apply to the intercompany transfer of technology (and other intangible property rights) and intercompany loans.

In an income allocation, many factors are considered, including the structure of the related group and division of risks, functional analysis of each related party, and the capacity in which each member performs these functions, (e.g., whether as agent or principal). These concepts are quite similar to the rules contained in the IRS's White Paper.

German rules established three methods for transfer pricing on goods, which are substantially the same as the U.S. regulations (using comparable uncontrolled transactions as the guide for intercompany transactions). Services are covered as well. There is no priority to the methods, however. A taxpayer must select the method most appropriate under the circumstances. No formal fourth method is provided.

United Kingdom

The United Kingdom also adheres to the arm's-length standard. The statutory rule provides that in computing the income, profit, or losses on intercompany transactions, the result should be the same as would have ensued if the property had been sold or purchased for the price it would have fetched if the transaction had been a transaction between independent persons dealing at arm's length. There is no further guidance as to the meaning of this rule. Regulations have not been issued, and there is very little case law in the United Kingdom (in the United States, there is a very large body of judicial law on transfer pricing).

The U.K. authorities offer no methodology for transfer pricing. Instead, the subject is approached on a facts and circumstances basis, looking to pricing on third party transactions involving identical products under similar circumstances, similarity of geographic regions, similarity of operating conditions, similarity of management structure, and similarity of financing.

The definition of control is similar to that in the United States. In other words, it is the reality of control that is determinative. There is no mechanical test, as in Japan.

It is not entirely clear whether the United Kingdom's transfer pricing rules apply fully to transactions other than the transfer of goods. Although the statute provides that other transactions are covered, such as "rental of property," it is not clear that the transfer pricing rules can be used, for example, to imput interest on below-market loans. This is quite different from the U.S. rules, under which the IRS has invariably been successful in this situation.

EXHIBIT 18–1
Form 5472

Form **5472**	Information Return of a Foreign-Owned U.S. Corporation or a Foreign Corporation Engaged in a U.S. Trade or Business	OMB No. 1545-0805
(Rev. November 1990)	(Under Sections 6038A and 6038C of the Internal Revenue Code)	Expires 10-31-93
Department of the Treasury Internal Revenue Service	For tax year of the reporting corporation beginning , 19 , and ending , 19	

Part I   Reporting Corporation (All information must be written in the English language.)

1a Name of reporting corporation	b Employer Identification Number
Number, street, and room or suite no. (If a P.O. box, see instructions on page 3.)	c Total number of Forms 5472 filed for the tax year
City or town, state, and ZIP code	d Principal Business Activity Code

Part II   25% Foreign Shareholder (Completed Only by U.S. Corporations)

2a Name and address of 25% foreign shareholder	b U.S. identifying number, if any
c Country or countries where business is conducted	d Country of citizenship, creation, or organization

e Country or countries under whose laws the 25% foreign shareholder files an income tax return as a resident

Part III   Related Party (All information must be written in the English language.)

3a Name and address of related party	b U.S. identifying number, if any

c Type of relationship—Check applicable box:
Related party to reporting corporation ☐   Related party to 25% foreign shareholder ☐

d Principal business activity	e Business code number	f Country or countries where business is conducted

g Country or countries under whose laws the related party files an income tax return as a resident

Part IV   Monetary Transactions Between Reporting Corporations and Related Foreign Party (All amounts must be stated in U.S. dollars.) (Reasonable estimates may be used—See Instructions.)

1	Sales of stock in trade (inventory)	1
2	Sales of tangible property other than stock in trade	2
3	Rents and royalties received (for other than intangible property rights)	3
4	Sales, leases, licenses, etc., of intangible property rights (e.g., patents, trademarks, secret formulas)	4
5	Consideration received for technical, managerial, engineering, construction, scientific, or like services	5
6	Commissions received	6
7	Amounts borrowed a Beginning Balance _____ b Ending Balance ▶	7b
8	Interest received	8
9	Premiums received for insurance or reinsurance	9
10	Other amounts received	10
11	**Total.** Add amounts on lines 1 through 10	11
12	Purchases of stock in trade (inventory)	12
13	Purchases of tangible property other than stock in trade	13
14	Rents and royalties paid (for other than intangible property rights)	14
15	Purchases, leases, licenses, etc., of intangible property (e.g., patents, trademarks, secret formulas)	15
16	Consideration paid for technical, managerial, engineering, construction, scientific, or like services	16
17	Commissions paid	17
18	Amounts loaned a Beginning Balance _____ b Ending Balance ▶	18b
19	Interest paid	19
20	Premiums paid for insurance or reinsurance	20
21	Other amounts paid	21
22	**Total.** Add amounts on lines 12 through 21	22

EXHIBIT 18–1
(Continued)

Part V	**Describe All Nonmonetary and Nonconsideration Transactions Between the Reporting Corporation and the Related Foreign Party. (Attach Separate Sheet.) (See Instructions.)**

Part VI	**Additional Information**

1   Does the reporting corporation import goods from a related party?. . . . . ☐ Yes ☐ No

2   If "Yes," is the basis of the goods valued differently than the customs value of the imported goods? . . . . ☐ Yes ☐ No

3   If "Yes," attach a statement to Form 5472 explaining the reason or reasons for such difference

4   Were the documents used to support this treatment of the imported goods in existence and available in the United States at the time of filing Form 5472? . . . . ☐ Yes ☐ No

EXHIBIT 18-1
(Continued)

General Instructions

(References are to the Internal Revenue Code unless otherwise noted.)

Paperwork Reduction Act Notice.—We ask for the information on this form to carry out the Internal Revenue laws of the United States. You are required to give us this information. We need it to ensure that you are complying with these laws and to allow us to figure and collect the right amount of tax.

The time needed to complete and file this form will vary depending on individual circumstances. The estimated average times are:

Recordkeeping	11 hrs., 29 min.
Learning about the form or the law	1 hr., 17 min.
Preparing and sending the form to the IRS	1 hr., 32 min.

If you have comments concerning the accuracy of these time estimates or suggestions for making this form more simple, we would be happy to hear from you. You can write to both the Internal Revenue Service and the Office of Management and Budget at the addresses listed in the instructions for the tax return with which this form is filed. **DO NOT** send the tax form to either of these offices. Instead, see the instructions for the form for information on where to file.

Important Changes.—The Revenue Reconciliation Act of 1990 ("the 1990 Act") made several changes to section 6038A. The information reporting and related requirements have generally been extended to apply to acts (or failures to act) for tax years beginning **on or before July 10, 1989.** Prior to this change, amendments to section 6038A made by the Revenue Reconciliation Act of 1989 ("the 1989 Act") applied to tax years beginning **after** July 10, 1989.

The changes made retroactive to tax years beginning on or before July 10, 1989, include:

• Any requirement to furnish information under section 6038A(a) (as amended by the 1989 Act) if the time for furnishing the information is after November 5, 1990,

• Any requirement under section 6038A(a) to maintain records that existed on or after March 20, 1990,

• Any requirement to authorize the reporting corporation to act as the related party's limited agent in the U.S. under section 6038A(e)(1) (as amended by the 1989 Act) if the time for authorization is after November 5, 1990, and

• Any summons issued after November 5, 1990, without regard to when the tax year (to which the information, records, authorization, or summons relates) began.

The 1990 Act also added new section 6038C. Under section 6038C, **all** foreign corporations engaged in a trade or business within the U.S. must furnish information described in section 6038A(b) relating to related party transactions and any information as the Commissioner may prescribe by regulations relating to any item not directly connected with a related party transaction.

The penalty provisions under section 6038A(d) apply to failures to furnish information or maintain records required under section 6038C(b) or 6038C(a).

In addition, section 6038C(d) provides rules for enforcing requests for certain information.

Purpose of Form 5472.—Form 5472 is used to report information relating to transactions between the reporting corporation (a 25% foreign-owned domestic corporation or a foreign corporation engaged in a trade or business within the U.S.) and any party related to either the domestic or foreign corporation. The 25% foreign shareholder is also considered a related party of the domestic corporation.

Who Must File.—A domestic corporation must file Form 5472 if it is 25% foreign-owned. A foreign corporation must file Form 5472 if it is engaged in a U.S. trade or business.

Corporations Not Required To File.—A corporation is not required to file Form 5472 if during the tax year:

• It had no gross income (determined without reference to losses) subject to United States taxation, other than withholding tax under section 881, or

• Its sole trade or business in the U.S. is banking, financing, or similar business (as defined in Regulations section 1.864-4(c)(5)(i)), or

• It was a foreign corporation and all of its income is exempt from taxation under any provision of the Internal Revenue Code or any applicable tax treaty.

25% Foreign-Owned.—A corporation is 25% foreign-owned if at least 25% of:

a. the total voting power of all classes of stock entitled to vote; **or**

b. the total value of all classes of stock of the corporation

is owned at any time during the tax year by one foreign shareholder.

Total Voting Power.—When determining if one foreign shareholder owns 25% of the total voting power, consider the facts and circumstances of each case, including any arrangements to shift formal voting power away from the foreign shareholder.

Rules of Attribution.—When determining whether a corporation is 25% foreign-owned and whether a person is a related party, the constructive ownership rules of section 318 apply with certain modifications. Substitute "10%" for "50%" in section 318(a)(2)(C). Also, sections 318(a)(3)(A), (B), and (C) shall not be applied so as to consider a U.S. person as owning stock that is owned by a person who is not a U.S. person.

Related Party.—The term **related party** means the 25% foreign shareholder, any person who is related to the reporting corporation, or the 25% foreign shareholder (within the meaning of section 267(b) or 707(b)(1)), or to any other person who is related to the reporting corporation within the meaning of section 482 and the related regulations.

Foreign Person.—The term **foreign person** means:

(1) Any individual who is not a citizen or resident of the U.S., but not including any

individual for whom an election under section 6013(g) or (h) is in effect;

(2) Any individual who is a citizen of a U.S. possession but is not otherwise a citizen of the United States nor a resident;

(3) Any partnership, association, company, or corporation that was not created or organized under the laws of the United States or the laws of any state;

(4) Any foreign trust or foreign estate, as defined in section 7701(a)(31); or

(5) Any foreign government (or agency or instrumentality of a foreign government).

Consolidated Return.—If a consolidated income tax return is filed, a consolidated Form 5472 may be filed. The common parent of the consolidated group must attach a statement to Form 5472 showing which members of the consolidated group would otherwise file a separate Form 5472.

Completing Form 5472.—The reporting corporation must file a separate Form 5472 for each related party with which the reporting corporation had transactions listed in Part IV and Part V. The reporting corporation must show the following information for each related party: the name, address, U.S. identifying number, if applicable, the nature of the related party's business, the principal place or places of business, each country in which the related party is a resident under the laws of that country, and the relationship of the reporting corporation and the related party.

When and Where To File

Attach Form 5472 to the corporation's income tax return. If the corporation does not file its income tax return by the due date (including extensions), it must separately file Form 5472 by the due date (including extensions) with the Service Center where the return will be filed.

Duplicate Filing Required

File a duplicate copy of each Form 5472 (at the same time as the original copy is filed) with the Internal Revenue Service Center, Philadelphia, PA 19255.

Exception.—A reporting corporation is not required to file Form 5472 for a related foreign person if the reporting corporation is controlled by a U.S. person who files **Form 5471**, Information Return of U.S. Persons with Respect to Certain Foreign Corporations, for the tax year and that form contains information regarding the transactions between the reporting corporation and the related foreign person.

Penalties

Penalties for failure to file Form 5472.—A penalty of $10,000 shall be assessed on any reporting corporation that fails to file Form 5472 when required. A similar penalty applies for failure to maintain books and records.

If the failure continues for more than 90 days after notification by IRS, a penalty of $10,000 for each 30-day period (or fraction of a 30-day period) the information remains unfiled or the failure to maintain books and records continues after the 90-day period ends.

EXHIBIT 18–1
(*Continued*)

In addition, criminal penalties under sections 7203, 7206, and 7207 may apply for failure to submit information or for filing false or fraudulent information.

Specific Instructions

Address .— Include the suite, room, or other unit number after the street address. If the Post Office does not deliver mail to the street address and the corporation has a P.O. box, show the P.O. box number instead of the street address.

Part III

Lines 3d and 3e—Principal business activity and business code number.— See the instructions for Form 1120 or Form 1120F for a list of principal business activities and business code numbers.

Part IV

Generally, all of the reportable transactions between the reporting corporation and a related foreign party must be entered on Part IV. However, a transaction does not have to be reported if neither party to the transaction is a United States person (as defined in section 7701(a)(30)) and the transaction:

(1) Does not give rise to any recognized income or gain which is from sources within the United States or which is effectively connected with the conduct of a trade or business within the United States;

(2) Does not give rise to any expense, loss, or other deduction properly allocable or apportionable to such income; and

(3) Does not, in any way, affect any United States income tax obligation of either party to the transaction in any tax year.

Reasonable Estimates

Enter reasonable estimates of the total dollar amount of each of the categories of transactions conducted between the reporting corporation and the related person in which monetary consideration (U.S. currency or foreign currency) was the sole consideration paid or received during the tax year of the reporting corporation.

A reasonable estimate is any amount reported on Form 5472 that is at least 75% but not more than 125% of the actual amount required to be reported. If an actual amount required to be reported does not exceed $66,667 and is reported as "$50,000 or less" then the amount reported is a reasonable estimate.

Part V

For each transaction involving nonmonetary consideration or no consideration, attach a statement describing the substance and the approximate size of the transaction or group of transactions. This description should include all services performed or all property (including monetary consideration), rights, or obligations transferred between the reporting corporation and the foreign related party. The statement should describe the nature and importance of all services performed. Also include a reasonable estimate of the fair market value or a statement of the nature and importance of such property (other than money), rights, obligations, or services. The statement is not required if the related party is a domestic entity.

A transaction for which the entire consideration paid or received by one party was monetary consideration is not required to be described in Part V even though the transaction involved the transfer of both tangible and intangible property, as long as the transfer of the intangible property was related and incidental to the transfer of the tangible property. However, the monetary portion must be reported in Part IV.

CONCLUSION

The U.S. transfer pricing rules are sophisticated in relation to those of other countries. Moreover, the IRS aggressively pursues perceived abuses. It is not possible to conduct business in the United States without a working knowledge of, and compliance with, the U.S. transfer pricing rules.

CHAPTER 19

TAXATION OF
U.S. INVESTMENTS OF
FOREIGN CORPORATIONS

David F. Kleeman
International Tax Partner
Joanne M. Sisk
International Tax Partner
Price Waterhouse

INTRODUCTION

Total foreign investment in the United States rose from $54.5 billion in 1980 to $390.1 billion in 1989, a 22 percent annual rate of increase over the period. The U.S. Congress and Internal Revenue Service (IRS) have been particularly sensitive to the perceived U.S. tax advantage that foreign investors have enjoyed over domestic taxpayers and have recently turned their focus toward the various U.S. tax rules associated with foreign investment. As a result, it is important for foreign investors to understand the recent changes in the U.S. taxing system and the implications for their U.S. operations. Although understanding the relevant foreign country tax rules relating to U.S. investment is also important, such foreign country tax issues are beyond the scope of this chapter.

Within the past several years, there have been a number of significant changes in the U.S. tax rules relating to inbound foreign investment. Congress enacted a new branch profits tax and branch level interest tax in 1986 in order to equalize the taxation of branch earnings with the taxation of a separate U.S. subsidiary. In addition, the 1986 tax legislation added rules that defer a U.S. tax deduction for certain amounts due to related foreign parties until the amounts are actually paid. Recently issued Treasury regulations indicate that although the disallowance applies to interest and royalties payable to a related party, the deduction for management fees may not be disallowed provided certain criteria are met.

The U.S. taxation of foreign investment was further strengthened in 1988 and 1989 with the new "earnings stripping" rules and additional reporting and record keeping requirements that are imposed on U.S. branches and U.S. subsidiaries of foreign corporations. The "earnings stripping" provisions disallow a deduction for interest payable to a related foreign person if such person is not subject to U.S. tax. In addition, these provisions require a pro-rata deduction disallowance on such interest if a tax treaty reduces the 30 percent U.S. withholding tax. Additionally, U.S. taxpayers are now required to disclose any treaty-based tax positions taken on their U.S. tax returns (i.e., situations in which U.S. tax treaties override or modify U.S. tax law). Finally, recent Treasury regulations providing for additional reporting and record keeping requirements are intended to assist the IRS in their review of intercompany transfer pricing.

U.S. TAXATION OF FOREIGN CORPORATIONS

In General

To understand the U.S. tax consequences and planning opportunities available to foreign investors with investments or operations in the U.S., it is necessary to understand the basic U.S. tax rules that apply to such operations. Although the United States taxes domestic corporations on worldwide income, foreign corporations are taxed only on income from U.S. sources unless the foreign-source income relates to the conduct of a U.S. trade or business. A foreign corporation incorporated in a country having a tax treaty with the United States must have a "permanent establishment" in the United States in order to be subject to U.S. taxation on business income related to such permanent establishment. The tax treaty concept of "permanent establishment" is discussed in more detail below.

The United States has two basic methods for taxing the U.S. source income of a foreign corporation. Passive income from U.S. sources is generally subject to a flat 30 percent U.S. withholding tax, while, in general, sales proceeds from the disposition of U.S. real property are subject to 10 percent U.S. withholding. This withholding tax rate can be reduced or eliminated through tax treaties. For flat rate withholding to apply, U.S. source income must *not* be effectively connected with the conduct of a U.S. trade or business.

The other form of U.S. taxation applies to income that is effectively connected with a U.S. trade or business. Such income, which is referred to as effectively connected income (ECI), is taxed at the regular 34 percent corporate tax rate. Unlike passive income, the tax is based on *net* income (i.e., income after deducting all allowable expenses incurred in earning the ECI). U.S. branch or partnership income is subject to U.S. tax on a net basis if it is connected with a U.S. trade or business. If a foreign corporation operates in the United States through a domestic subsidiary, the U.S. subsidiary is subject to U.S. tax on its worldwide income.

Alternative Minimum Tax

Overview
In addition to the regular U.S. corporate tax, the United States also imposes an alternative minimum tax (AMT) on a U.S. corporation or a foreign corporation with ECI. The AMT rules are intended to ensure that every corporation pays at least a minimum amount of U.S. tax. A corporation's annual AMT is equal to the excess, if any, of the tentative minimum tax over the corporation's regular tax liability. The tentative minimum tax is determined by multiplying the excess of the alternative minimum taxable income (AMTI) over the exemption amount (i.e., $40,000) by 20 percent and reducing the result by the corporation's AMT foreign tax credit, if any. It should be noted that the exemption amount must be reduced by 25 percent of the amount by which AMTI exceeds $150,000. Thus, the exemption amount is eliminated when AMTI is equal to $310,000 or more. In addition, a corporation receives a regular tax credit for adjusted

net minimum tax paid, and the credit can be carried indefinitely until utilized to offset the regular U.S. tax liability.

Alternative Minimum Taxable Income (AMTI)

The base for computing AMTI is regular taxable income increased by certain specified tax preference items and other adjustments. Tax preference items and adjustments represent various deductions and income items that have been claimed in computing regular taxable income, and include the use of the installment sales method and certain modifications to the depreciation deduction.

ACE Adjustment

Corporate taxpayers must adjust AMTI by an amount equal to 75 percent of the excess of adjusted current earnings (ACE) over the pre-adjustment AMTI. For this purpose, ACE is equal to AMTI adjusted for certain specified income and expense items and adjustments. The ACE amount is designed to be at least as broad as pre-tax book income computed for financial reporting purposes. Currently, one of the primary components of the ACE adjustment is depreciation computed using the straight line method over asset class lives, which are generally longer than those utilized to compute regular tax depreciation.

INCOME THAT IS NOT EFFECTIVELY CONNECTED INCOME

Passive income paid from the United States to a foreign recipient is taxed at a flat 30 percent on the gross amount of the income, provided the recipient is not engaged in a U.S. trade or business. In other words, no deduction is allowed for any expenses that the recipient may have incurred with respect to the income. Income taxed in this manner includes interest, dividends, rents, annuities and certain compensation. This type of income is generally referred to as fixed, determinable, annual, or periodical income (FDAP). Royalties are usually considered FDAP, although they are not specifically mentioned in the statute.

The 30 percent flat withholding tax applicable to FDAP is reduced or eliminated by the U.S. income tax treaties. For example, dividends paid by a U.S. corporation to a Canadian shareholder are subject to a 15 percent withholding tax under the U.S.-Canada tax treaty (10 percent if the Canadian shareholder owns 10 percent or more of the U.S. corporation).

Tax Treaty Considerations

The taxation of U.S.-source passive income received by a foreign corporation and the level of U.S. activity that subjects a foreign corporation to taxation on U.S. business activities is modified by income tax treaties. For example, the U.S. tax on passive income is ordinarily reduced or eliminated through the provisions of an income tax treaty. In addition, the extent of U.S. business activity necessary to result in U.S. taxation is greater under a treaty than the level necessary under U.S. tax law.

Exceptions to U.S. Withholding Tax Rules

Sections 871 and 881* provide a number of exceptions to the 30 percent U.S. withholding tax requirement. Included in the exceptions are U.S. bank account interest, portfolio interest, dividends paid by a domestic corporation meeting certain foreign business requirements, and dividends from a qualifying mutual fund received by a foreign corporation. It is important to note that the elimination of U.S. withholding tax applies to any interest received from qualifying U.S. portfolio debt earned by a foreign person owning not more than 10 percent of the voting stock of the corporation issuing the debt obligation. The portfolio exception requires that the debt obligation be in registered form and that the beneficial owner be a foreign person. The exception also applies to certain U.S. obligations that are not in registered form if arrangements exist to ensure that the obligations are sold *only* to foreign persons and the interest is payable only outside the United States.

---

* All section references in this chapter refer to the Internal Revenue Code of 1986, as amended.

BRANCH OPERATIONS

U.S. Trade or Business

A foreign corporation engaged in a U.S. trade or business through a branch is generally subject to regular U.S. corporate taxation on net income. The 34 percent U.S. tax is based on the income and expenses allocable to the U.S. operations.

Effectively Connected Income (ECI)

A foreign corporation's ECI is taxed at the regular 34 percent U.S. corporate tax rate. For income of a foreign corporation to be ECI, the foreign corporation must be engaged in a U.S. trade or business. Although there is no specific definition as to what constitutes a trade or business, a continuous and regular U.S. presence will generally be considered to constitute a trade or business if connected with active business operations. The U.S. courts have ruled, on occasion, that even an isolated transaction can result in the taxpayer's being engaged in a trade or business. Since a corporation acts through employees, a foreign corporation may be engaged in a U.S. business due solely to the U.S. activities of an employee.

As previously noted, a foreign corporation is generally taxable in the United States on U.S.-source income. In broad terms, U.S.-source income includes income from the performance of services in the United States, dividends and interest from U.S. corporations, and income from the sale of inventory where title passes in the United States. Foreign-source income of a foreign corporation is also taxed if the U.S. office is a material factor in earning the income. To be considered a material factor, the U.S. office must provide a significant contribution to the realization of such foreign-source income.

With respect to trading in stocks or securities, a foreign corporation can avoid being engaged in a U.S. business by trading through an independent U.S. broker or agent, provided the foreign corporation does not have a U.S. office through which the trades are conducted. In addition, if a foreign corporation is trading for its own account and is not a dealer in securities, U.S. trade or business status can be avoided even if the activity is directed through a U.S. office.

As previously noted, the level of U.S. activity that subjects a foreign corporation to U.S. taxation can be modified by income tax treaties. In order for the U.S. activity of a foreign corporation to qualify for tax treaty protection, the foreign corporation must not have a "permanent establishment" in the United States. The term *permanent establishment* is generally defined in the tax treaties as any fixed place of business (e.g., offices or a factory). Although a permanent establishment requires the existence of a fixed place of business, the use of a facility solely for the storage, display, or delivery of goods will usually not result in a permanent establishment.

Source of Income

Since a foreign corporation is generally subject to taxation on U.S.-source income, it is important to review the rules for sourcing income found in Sections 861 through 865. For example, interest is sourced according to the payor's country of residence or incorporation. Consequently, if a foreign corporation receives interest from a U.S. corporation, the interest is generally U.S.-source income. With respect to gain from the sale of personal property (other than inventory), the general rule is that such income is sourced according to the residence of the seller. Income from the sale of inventory is sourced based on the location of title passage. If depreciable personal property is sold that was used in a U.S. trade or business, any gain will be U.S. source to the extent that depreciation was previously taken on the property for U.S. tax purposes.

A special sourcing rule for intangibles states that any payment made with respect to an intangible contingent upon the use of the intangible is treated as a royalty and is sourced based on the location where the intangible is used. Consequently, a payment received with respect to an intangible used outside the United States is foreign-source income.

There are also prescribed rules for sourcing gain from the sale of the stock of an affiliated company and for income relating to sales through offices or fixed places of business located outside the

United States. It is important to note that the various source rules can be modified by the provisions of an income tax treaty.

Deductions Attributable to ECI

A foreign corporation is entitled to deduct expenses directly related to ECI or related in part to such income. Thus, expenses incurred by a U.S. branch in connection with U.S. operations are generally deductible in computing taxable income. These expenses include office rent, utilities, salaries, travel costs, and similar expenditures. A deduction is considered "definitely related" to ECI if it is incurred as a direct result of the activities from which the ECI was derived.

The process of apportioning expenses to ECI involves the distribution of costs that cannot be specifically allocated to any particular type of gross income. Expenses such as interest expense and foreign head office costs should be apportioned in part to U.S. operations. The following are some head office expenses that may be apportioned to a foreign corporation's U.S. branch income:

- Compensation and other employment costs of general management, senior corporate officers, their deputies, and their immediate assistants.
- Compensation and other employment costs of employees of the international department.
- Rent, supplies, and other support costs applicable to the above items.

Interest allocation rules applicable to U.S. branches set forth in the Treasury regulations provide for the allocation of interest by a multiple step process. This process, which includes a determination of assets that generate ECI and liabilities associated with ECI, is basically an asset allocation.

Disallowance of Deductions

Interest and certain other amounts owed by a U.S. taxpayer to a related foreign person are not deductible until actually paid. This restriction on deductibility does not apply to payments for inventory. A foreign corporation with income effectively connected with a U.S. branch may not be entitled to deduct certain home office charges until such amounts are actually paid by the branch. As a result, both a U.S. branch and a U.S. subsidiary of a foreign corporation are placed on a cash basis for certain expenses payable to related foreign persons.

Joint Venture Partnerships

A foreign corporation can invest in the United States through a joint venture organized as a partnership. If a partnership is actively engaged in a U.S. trade or business through a permanent establishment, there is an imputation of the trade or business income of the partnership to the respective partners. As a result, each foreign partner is required to file a U.S. tax return and report its pro-rata share of the income earned by the partnership. One situation in which investing in a U.S. partnership could result in U.S. taxation, whereas a direct investment might not, is in the area of capital gains. Under many U.S. tax treaties, capital gains realized by a foreign person are exempt from U.S. taxation. Capital gain income earned through a U.S. partnership that conducts a U.S. trade or business, however, would ordinarily be treated as ECI and subjected to U.S. tax.

If a foreign investor located in a jurisdiction having a tax treaty with the United States has an ownership interest in a U.S. partnership, and if the partnership does not have a fixed place of business in the U.S., it may be possible to treat the partnership income as income that is not ECI. This reflects the fact that the relevant tax treaty governs the extent to which the U.S. activity is subject to tax. Thus, if there is no U.S. permanent establishment, the income would not be ECI and would be subject to 30 percent (or reduced treaty rate) U.S. withholding tax.

An investment in a U.S. partnership can result in additional U.S. tax if the partnership investments are passive and generate FDAP income. If a foreign person were to invest directly in passive assets, the resulting dividend and interest income would be subject only to U.S. withholding tax. If FDAP income is earned through a U.S. partnership that, in addition to FDAP income, has ECI, the FDAP income may be treated as related to the ECI and thereby taxed as ECI. This would result in U.S. taxation at the regular graduated tax rates rather than on a flat withholding basis.

The above tax consequences are less clear if the foreign investor is a *limited* partner in a U.S. partnership. An argument can be made that the agency relationship that exists between a partnership and a general partner is not present in the case of a limited partner. Without this agency relationship, a foreign limited partner does not have a permanent establishment in the United States merely as a result of a partnership investment. This is not the position of the IRS, however, since Revenue Ruling 85-60 imputes the existence of a permanent establishment from a partnership to *all* partners, both limited and general.

It is important for foreign investors to realize that the underlying nature of the activities of a U.S. partnership can affect how the partnership income is taxed for U.S. purposes. This is especially true if the foreign investor does not consider the partnership income to be ECI and does not file a U.S. tax return. If it is later determined by the IRS that the income is ECI, the foreign investor may not be able to take deductions against the ECI since a U.S. tax return was not timely filed by the investor.

Withholding on Foreign Partner's Share of Partnership Income

Sections 1441 and 1446 require U.S. withholding at the partnership level on a foreign partner's pro-rata share of certain types of partnership income. Under Section 1441, domestic partnerships with foreign partners are required to withhold 30 percent (or reduced treaty rate) of the partner's pro-rata share of non-effectively connected U.S. source income whether or not such amounts are actually distributed. Under Treasury Regulation Section 1.1441-3(f), such withholding must be made at the time distributions are made to the foreign partners. Distributions are deemed to come first out of non-effectively connected income.

U.S. tax law also provides withholding requirements for ECI earned through a partnership. Section 1446 requires domestic or foreign partnerships engaged in a U.S. trade or business to withhold tax at the highest U.S. marginal rate applicable to the foreign partner. The withholding tax applies to the partner's distributive share of partnership ECI whether or not distributions have actually been made to the partner. The withholding tax rate for ECI allocable to a foreign *corporate* partner is 34 percent and to a foreign *individual* partner, 31 percent. The withholding tax may be used to offset the foreign partner's regular U.S. tax liability if a U.S. tax return is filed that includes the partnership income.

Disposition of Property Used in U.S. Trade or Business

Foreign investors should be aware that Section 864(c)(7) provides that if assets are sold within 10 years after being used in a U.S. trade or business, gain from selling such assets will be treated as ECI even if the foreign corporation is no longer engaged in a U.S. trade or business. For example, equipment used in a U.S. business will be considered a part of that business for 10 years and any gain resulting from sale will be considered ECI. The gain eventually recognized is limited, however, to the fair market value of the equipment at the time it was removed from the United States. If the foreign corporation is generating losses in the United States, it may be advantageous to dispose of U.S. operating assets prior to terminating a U.S. business so that gain from the sale of the assets can be offset by the operating losses.

Branch Profits Tax

Description of Branch Profits Tax

The U.S. branch profits tax (BPT) applies to U.S. branch operations conducted by a foreign corporation and is equal to 30 percent (or lower treaty rate) of the portion of post-1986 branch earnings that a foreign shareholder is deemed to have repatriated from the U.S. business. Those foreign corporations with an investment in U.S. real property that have elected to be taxed on a net income basis are also subject to the BPT. Although the BPT is imposed on the portion of after-tax branch earnings not reinvested in U.S. branch assets, it is also imposed on an actual distribution of prior year branch profits that were previously reinvested.

The BPT is the equivalent of U.S. withholding tax on dividends paid by a U.S. subsidiary to its foreign shareholders. Therefore, the BPT is in addition to the annual 34 percent U.S. corporate tax imposed on branch taxable income. In essence, the BPT places the U.S. branch of a foreign corporation on an equal footing with a U.S. subsidiary with respect to withholding on profit remittances.

Treaty Interaction with BPT

A foreign corporation can claim exemption (or tax rate reduction) with respect to the BPT provided the foreign corporation is a qualified resident of a country having a tax treaty with the United States. Generally, a foreign corporation is a qualified resident if at least 50 percent of the stock of such foreign corporation is owned by residents of the foreign corporation's country of incorporation or by residents of the United States. In the case of holding companies (i.e., companies not engaged in an active trade or business), it is important to note that for BPT purposes, look-through ownership rules do not apply. Thus, if a Swiss holding company is owned by a German operating company, the Swiss company is not a qualified Swiss resident for BPT purposes since its shareholder is not a Swiss resident. To obtain U.S. treaty benefits with regards to BPT, the German shareholder would have to own the U.S. subsidiary directly rather than through a Swiss company.

Branch Level Interest Tax

Description

In addition to the BPT, Section 884 imposes branch level interest tax (BLIT) at a rate of 30 percent (or reduced treaty rate) on interest paid or deemed paid by the U.S. branch of a foreign corporation to the foreign home office. By requiring that interest be treated as though paid by a domestic corporation to a foreign person, branch interest paid to the foreign home office is subjected to U.S. withholding tax. In addition to interest actually paid by a U.S. branch, interest that is "allocated" to the U.S. branch in excess of the interest actually paid is also subject to U.S. withholding tax.

Treaty Interaction

Relief for the BLIT is available provided the foreign corporation receiving the interest is a qualified resident of a treaty country. Therefore, if interest is payable to a qualified treaty resident, the BLIT will either be reduced or eliminated depending upon the terms of the relevant tax treaty.

INVESTMENT THROUGH U.S. CORPORATIONS

In view of the tax consequences of branch operations as discussed previously, a foreign corporation may find it advantageous to operate in the United States through a U.S. subsidiary. For one thing, establishing a subsidiary may result in greater political and cultural acceptance. In addition, incorporating the U.S. operations insulates the foreign profits of the foreign corporation from exposure to U.S. taxation.

Formation of U.S. Subsidiary

It is important to determine whether a U.S. investment will be financed by debt, equity, or some combination of the two. Funding may be accomplished by issuing stock for cash or contributing tangible or intangible property to the capital of the U.S. corporation in exchange for stock. The U.S. tax implications associated with the use of debt versus equity are summarized below.

Equity
A foreign shareholder will frequently receive stock of a U.S. corporation in exchange for cash in order to fund the U.S. business operations. The use of preferred stock having preferential dividend rights, a fixed redemption price, and preferential rights upon liquidation should be considered as an alternative to common stock since this may achieve many of the economic objectives available through the use of a special income allocation in a partnership arrangement.

From a U.S. tax perspective, the use of equity has two primary consequences. First, there is no U.S. tax deduction available for dividends paid by a U.S. corporation to its shareholders. Second, dividend payments to a foreign shareholder will be subject to a flat 30 percent (or lower treaty rate) U.S. withholding tax.

Dividend payments in excess of current and accumulated earnings will be considered for tax purposes to be a nontaxable return of capital. In such a case, foreign shareholders can seek a refund of U.S. tax withheld on the return of capital portion of the distribution. After current and accumulated earnings and capital have been repaid, additional distributions to shareholders will be considered capital gain for U.S. tax purposes. Although Congress recently considered legislation that would have imposed a 34 percent tax on capital gains earned by certain foreign corporate shareholders of U.S. companies by treating such gain as ECI, there is currently no U.S. tax on capital gain income resulting from a sale of the stock of a U.S. company provided the shareholder is not otherwise conducting business in the United States. If the foreign shareholder is engaged in a U.S. trade or business, the capital gain may be considered ECI and be subjected to regular U.S. tax (unless the FIRPTA rules apply, as discussed in Chapter 26).

Debt

The tax benefit of using debt rather than equity is that the payor is entitled to deduct the interest, whereas dividends are not tax deductible. Accordingly, debt financing allows repatriation of U.S. profits to the foreign investor through tax-free debt repayments and tax-deductible interest.

Thin Capitalization

The U.S. tax rules regarding "thin capitalization" come into play when a corporation has a substantial amount of debt and a much smaller amount of equity. The tax advantage of a thinly capitalized U.S. corporation is that the substantial interest expense reduces U.S. taxable income. Since there is no statutory and little regulatory authority regarding when a U.S. company is thinly capitalized, case law provides the primary guidance in this area.

The IRS can disallow the tax deduction for all or a portion of the interest paid to a related person by a thinly capitalized U.S. corporation. In such instances, the IRS will contend that the indebtedness should be treated as an equity investment for tax purposes. As a result, some of the interest will constitute a nondeductible dividend and the debt principal repayments will also be characterized as dividends.

Acquisition of Existing U.S. Corporation

Financing Alternatives

Rather than forming a new U.S. company, a foreign investor may choose to acquire an existing U.S. corporation. Such an acquisition can be accomplished in various ways, including the following:

- Acquire the assets of the U.S. corporation for cash or notes.
- Acquire the assets of the U.S. corporation in exchange for shares of the purchaser.
- Acquire the shares of the U.S. corporation for cash or notes.
- Acquire shares of the U.S. corporation in exchange for shares of the purchaser.
- Acquire newly issued shares of the U.S. corporation.

The method of acquisition will normally have significant U.S. tax consequences for both the buyer and seller. For example, in a cash acquisition it may be preferable to borrow through a U.S. corporation, thereby reducing the U.S. tax liability. U.S. borrowings will generally be preferable if the U.S. tax rate is higher than the effective foreign tax rate of the purchaser. The use of U.S. debt will also reduce or eliminate the amount of dividends that must be paid from the United States to the foreign shareholder in order to service the acquisition debt.

If the foreign purchaser transfers funds to its U.S. subsidiary in order to make the U.S. acquisition, it is often preferable to treat a portion of such funds as interest-bearing loans rather than as share capital since the interest expense will be tax deductible. This is particularly important if the foreign purchaser cannot obtain adequate double tax relief on any dividends received from the U.S. subsidiary.

Tax Basis in Acquired Company

An important consideration in any acquisition is the acquiror's tax basis in the acquired corporation. Under Section 338, a purchaser of stock can increase the tax basis in the underlying assets of the acquired company to reflect the price paid for the stock, provided a qualified stock purchase has occurred. A qualified stock purchase occurs when a corporation purchases at least 80 percent of the voting shares and 80 percent of the total number of shares of any other class of stock within a 12-month period. From the buyer's standpoint, it is frequently preferable to buy assets rather than stock since there can be significant U.S. tax costs associated with obtaining a Section 338 step-up in the asset basis in a stock acquisition.

Section 338 Election

If a normal Section 338 election is made, the acquired company is treated for U.S. tax purposes as having sold its assets on the acquisition date for their fair market value. This deemed sale and any resulting taxable gain is a liability of the purchaser, and is one of the liabilities that must be included in computing the stepped-up tax basis of the assets of the acquired company.

As a result of a Section 338 election, the acquired corporation is treated as having purchased all of its assets on the day following the acquisition. The amount at which the assets are deemed to have been purchased is equal to the purchase price of the acquired corporation's stock plus the amount of any liabilities assumed. Thus, a Section 338 election results in the elimination of the tax attributes of the acquired corporation and a step-up in the basis of its assets. Since the present value of the future tax benefit of this step-up is frequently less than the immediate tax cost resulting from the deemed sale of the assets, a Section 338 election is often not beneficial.

Section 338(h)(10) Election

In General. Section 338(h)(10) provides for a joint election by the buyer and seller to recognize the gain or loss resulting from the deemed sale of the acquired corporation's assets in the seller's consolidated U.S. tax return. The willingness of a seller to join in a Section 338(h)(10) election may depend on such factors as the size of the seller's gain or the seller's ability to offset the tax resulting from the Section 338 election with net operating loss or tax credit carryforwards.

Section 338(h)(10) can only be utilized if both the buyer and the seller agree (and file an election) to treat the stock purchase as a deemed sale of assets. In some cases, the buyer is willing to increase the purchase price in order to induce the seller to make a Section 338(h)(10) election. This would be beneficial for the buyer only if the present value of the tax benefits resulting from the step-up exceed the additional consideration that must be paid to the seller.

Allocation of Stock Purchase Price. The Treasury has issued regulations regarding the procedures for allocating the total purchase price among the various assets of an acquired corporation.

These regulations state that if the purchase price of the stock exceeds the fair market value of the assets, the new tax basis of each asset will be equal to its fair market value and the remaining purchase price will be allocated to goodwill. Presently, since goodwill cannot be amortized for U.S. tax purposes, it is important to identify all of the assets of the target corporation, including intangibles such as supply contracts and computer software. This identification process will serve to minimize the allocation of purchase price to goodwill and/or going-concern value.

U.S. Holding Company

Consideration should be given to structuring the U.S. acquisition so that a consolidated U.S. income tax return can be filed. The ability to file a consolidated return depends upon the existence of a U.S. parent company that directly or indirectly owns at least 80 percent of the voting and nonvoting shares (except for certain nonvoting preferred shares) of each U.S. company to be included in the consolidated return. The interposition of a U.S. holding company between the foreign corporation and one or more separately owned U.S. operating companies will enable a consolidated U.S. return to be filed.

Foreign Holding Company

A reduction in withholding on dividends paid to a foreign parent is possible through the use of an intermediate holding company located in a third country, provided the country has a favorable tax treaty with the United States, and a favorable treaty (or favorable withholding rate) exists between the third country and the shareholder's country. For U.S. tax reasons, an intermediate holding company must be adequately capitalized and have a commercial purpose other than the mere reduction of withholding taxes.

The IRS has taken the position that withholding tax reduction through the use of a U.S. tax treaty will not be allowed if an intermediate foreign holding company has been established for the purpose of taking advantage of a favorable tax treaty. In attacking such "treaty shopping," U.S. tax treaties recently negotiated by Treasury include a provision to eliminate treaty benefits for foreign corporations unless they are at least 75 percent owned by residents of the country of their incorporation.

If the buyer intends to sell the shares of the U.S. corporation within a relatively short period of time, it may be preferable to acquire the shares through a foreign corporation, since a foreign corporation that does not conduct business in the United States is not subject to U.S. tax on capital gain resulting from the eventual sale of the shares (except shares of a U.S. real property holding corporation).

Consolidated U.S. Tax Return

As discussed briefly above, a consolidated U.S. tax return is intended to ensure that commonly owned U.S. corporations do not gain a tax advantage or suffer a tax disadvantage by operating as separate corporations rather than as branches of a single U.S. corporation. The more significant advantages of filing a consolidated U.S. tax return include

- Utilization of operating and/or capital losses of one or more members against income and/or capital gains of other members.
- Full elimination of dividends between members.
- Deferral of any income resulting from transactions between the members.

Some of the disadvantages include

- Current utilization of operating and/or capital losses of one member against the income and/or capital gains of another member where carryback or carryover of such losses would be more beneficial.
- Deferral of losses on deferred intercompany transactions (except to the extent otherwise deferred under related party rules).
- Current or permanent loss of deductions or credits by applying limitations based upon consolidated taxable income where the separate taxable income of the member with such deductions or credits would result in higher limitations.
- Additional level of tax on disposition of consolidated group member.

Since the advantages and disadvantages listed above are by no means all-inclusive, a careful analysis of filing a consolidated U.S. tax return must be made prior to making an election to file such a return.

Incorporation of U.S. Branch

If a foreign corporation incorporates its U.S. branch, certain U.S. tax attributes (e.g., operating losses or tax credits) generally do not carry over to the new U.S. corporation. In addition, income recognition is required to the extent of any depreciation deductions previously claimed with respect to the branch assets.

Operation of U.S. Corporation

Initial Operations
A U.S. corporation has the right to choose between certain methods of tax accounting. For example, in some instances either the cash or accrual method can be used for U.S. tax purposes. In addition, elections are available regarding the methods used for income and expense recognition (e.g., installment sales method, expensing research and development costs, and method used for depreciating fixed assets). A U.S. corporation can also select either a calendar year or fiscal year for U.S. tax purposes.

Related Party Transactions
Reallocation of Income and Deductions. A foreign shareholder may enter into various transactions with a U.S. subsidiary including loans, the sale of inventory or other assets, and providing technical and/or management assistance. The IRS normally reviews transactions between a U.S. corporation and related foreign persons to determine if income has been inappropriately shifted out of the United States. The IRS has the authority under Section 482 to allocate items of income or deduction between the U.S. corporation and related foreign taxpayers if such an allocation better reflects the U.S. corporation's true taxable income. Furthermore, the IRS may reallocate income or deductions whether or not there has been an intent to avoid U.S. tax. The U.S. corporation has the burden of proving that any Section 482 reallocation proposed by the IRS is not appropriate.

The Section 482 regulations provide various safe harbors that can be relied upon by the taxpayer to avoid a Section 482 allocation. In particular, the Treasury regulations discuss safe harbor charges for five types of intercompany transactions including loans and advances, the performance of services, the use of tangible property, the use or transfer of intangible property, and intercompany sales of personal property (including inventory).

The Treasury regulations provide that the charge for the performance of services to a related party must at least equal the cost of rendering such services unless the taxpayer can establish a more appropriate charge. The charge for the use of tangible property must be an arm's-length charge if either party to the transaction is in the leasing business. Otherwise, the rental charge can be based upon the sum of the following:

- Depreciation computed on a straight-line basis.
- 3 percent of the original basis of the asset.
- Current operating expenses

A transfer of intangible property to a related party necessitates that the income received by the transferor with respect to such transfer be commensurate with the income actually realized by the transferee from the property. This is known as the "superroyalty" provision.

The methods set forth in the Treasury regulations to determine the price of inventory include the comparable uncontrolled price method, the resale method, and the cost plus method, in that order of preference. The purpose of these methods is to determine a transfer price that would result if the buyer and seller were unrelated. The first method is basically the price that would result if the buyer and seller were totally unrelated and a comparable product was being sold. The resale method is the actual resale price realized by the purchaser reduced by an appropriate mark-up for the seller. The cost-plus method is the inverse of the resale method in that the cost of production or acquisition is increased by an appropriate mark-up.

Earnings Stripping Rules. Section 163(j) was enacted in 1989 and is intended to disallow a deduction for interest paid to a related person if such person is not subject to U.S. tax on the interest. This provision, which is referred to as the "earnings stripping" provision, also requires a pro-rata deduction disallowance if a tax treaty reduces the otherwise applicable U.S. tax on interest paid to a related foreign recipient. For example, if a treaty provides a 15 percent rate of withholding on interest, one half (15/30) of the interest paid to a related party would not be deductible.

The disallowance of interest expense under Section 163(j) only applies if (1) the net interest expense (excess of interest expense over interest income) exceeds 50 percent of "adjusted taxable income" and (2) the debt-to-equity ratio of the payor at the close of the taxable year exceeds 1.5:1. If only one of these conditions is present, interest expense is not disallowed. The 50 percent limitation must include all related U.S. corporations as defined under Section 1504.

Under recently proposed Treasury regulations, "adjusted taxable income" is defined as taxable income plus various adjustments intended to modify taxable income to more closely reflect cash flow. The interest that is disallowed in a particular taxable year is carried forward and may be deducted, subject to the above limitations, in succeeding taxable years.

Terminating the U.S. Business

A foreign shareholder may terminate its interest in a U.S. corporation in any of the following ways:

- Sell the entire stock interest to a third party.
- Liquidate the U.S. corporation.
- Sell the operating assets and distribute the cash to the shareholders as a liquidating distribution.

In the case of a foreign corporation selling the stock of a U.S. corporation that is not a real property holding company, any gain from the sale of stock would not be subject to current U.S. taxation provided the foreign corporation is not engaged in a U.S. trade or business. As previously noted, Congress has considered, but has not enacted, a tax on such capital gains.

If a consolidated U.S. tax return is filed, recent Treasury regulations disallow the recognition of losses by the parent resulting from the disposition of a member of the consolidated tax return group. In addition, a U.S. parent disposing of a U.S. subsidiary would be required to recognize any gain resulting from the disposition.

If a U.S. corporation is liquidated, the distributing corporation recognizes gain with respect to any assets distributed to the shareholders to the extent that their fair market value exceeds the tax basis of such assets. Capital losses on distributed assets are recognized to the extent of the distributing company's capital gains. The Treasury regulations preclude the recognition of losses on assets that were acquired in a tax-free exchange within five years of the date of liquidation. If assets are sold by the liquidating company prior to liquidation, gain is recognized to the extent that the sales proceeds exceed the tax basis of the assets.

Personal Holding Company

The personal holding company provisions are designed to prevent the use of a closely held corporation to shelter passive income (i.e., dividends, interest, rents, and royalties), which might otherwise be taxed to the shareholders. The personal holding company tax is imposed on the U.S. corporation (rather than its shareholders) and is in addition to the regular 34 percent U.S. corporate tax.

Personal holding company tax status is present only if the corporation meets both the stock ownership and income tests. The stock ownership test is met if more than 50 percent of the outstanding stock is owned, directly or indirectly, by five or fewer U.S. or foreign individuals. Attribution rules are provided whereby an individual is treated as owning the stock of certain related persons.

A corporation meets the income test if at least 60 percent of its adjusted ordinary gross income consists of personal holding company income. Adjusted ordinary gross income is defined as gross income adjusted for certain items such as depreciation and amortization. Personal holding company income includes dividends, interest royalties, certain rents, income from the use of corporate property by a shareholder, and certain personal service income.

If a corporation qualifies as a personal holding company, an additional U.S. tax burden is imposed on the corporation equal to 31 percent of its *undistributed* personal holding company income (excluding capital gain income).

FILING AND RECORD KEEPING
REQUIREMENTS

Foreign corporations are required to file an annual U.S. tax return (Form 1120F) if they carry on a trade or business from an office or other fixed place of business located within the United States. A foreign corporation may also be required to file a U.S. tax return if it has FDAP income only from U.S. sources. There is no requirement for a foreign corporation to file a U.S. tax return if the U.S. tax liability on FDAP income has been satisfied through U.S. withholding and the withholding has been reported on the proper forms (Forms 1042 and 1042S).

Recently enacted Section 6038A provides that any corporation (U.S. or foreign) conducting business in the United States that is 25 percent or more owned by a foreign person must accumulate detailed information pertaining to related-party transactions. In addition, a foreign corporation engaged in a U.S. trade or business is considered a "reporting corporation" and must annually report all monetary and nonmonetary transactions with foreign related parties on Form 5472. This information must be segregated among 10 specified categories (e.g., purchases of inventory, sales of inventory, interest expense, and interest income). Foreign related parties must keep certain specified records relating to intercompany transactions. Failure to furnish the required information or to maintain the proper records can result in substantial penalties and the loss of U.S. tax deductions.

Section 6114 requires that U.S. taxpayers, both U.S. branches and U.S. corporations, disclose treaty-based positions taken on U.S. tax returns. A treaty-based tax return position is taken whenever a tax treaty is used to determine the U.S. tax liability, whether or not the taxpayer actually files a U.S. tax return. These rules generally apply to situations in which a foreign related person is relying upon a tax treaty to reduce or eliminate U.S. withholding tax on payments of FDAP income only if proper reporting of such payments is not made (i.e., filing of Forms 1042 and 1042S). Recently issued Treasury regulations set forth the information that must be reported to the IRS and the areas in which disclosure is required. Penalties may be imposed for failure to disclose treaty-based tax return positions.

CHAPTER 20

TAXATION OF ALIENS IN THE UNITED STATES

Michael Budnick
National Director, International Assignment Tax Services
Price Waterhouse
David K. Grevengoed
Senior Manager, International Assignment Tax Services
Price Waterhouse

INTRODUCTION

A wide variety of taxes, both income and other types, can be imposed on foreign nationals who come to the United States. These taxes are imposed not only by the federal government, but also by a multitude of state and municipal authorities. Federal income taxes are generally of greater significance to foreign nationals in the United States because of the substantially higher tax rates. This is not to suggest that state and municipal taxes are insignificant. In certain states—New York, for example—the additional tax burden imposed under state and local taxing authorities can also be substantial. Therefore, foreign nationals must also consider the state and local taxes that will be imposed where they intend to work or reside.

This chapter is devoted to U.S. federal income tax law as applied to resident and nonresident aliens. For a discussion of state and local taxes in the United States, refer to Chapter 17.

As discussed in Chapter 16, the basic federal revenue law in the United States is the Internal Revenue Code of 1986 (Code), which imposes income taxes, estate and gift taxes, employment taxes, and miscellaneous excise taxes. Frequent changes to the Code are made by Revenue Acts that amend or add sections of the Code. The federal revenue law is augmented by a detailed set of income tax regulations, administrative rulings, and court decisions.

Tax Treaties

U.S. Internal Revenue Code provisions dealing with the taxation of aliens can be modified by income tax treaties that have been negotiated between the United States and other countries. Generally, the benefits provided by income tax treaties are limited to residents of the two countries that have entered into the agreement. Tax treaties are negotiated primarily for the purpose of limiting international double taxation, which may occur when the tax laws of two or more countries provide that each country can tax the same item of income.

While the provisions of each income tax treaty vary, some similar provisions are found in a number of treaties. One benefit that is often found in U.S. tax treaties is the reduction or elimination of withholding tax on various types of income received from one country by individuals or corporations resident in treaty countries. The reduction or elimination of withholding tax is reciprocal in most cases. In addition, income tax treaties may provide special rules for determining residency and may provide an exemption from tax for residents of a treaty country who are temporarily present in the other country. Consequently, it is important for foreign nationals to know whether an income tax treaty will override U.S. tax laws. Appendix I provides a list of countries with which the United States has concluded tax treaties.

Social Taxes

Social Security Taxes
In addition to federal income taxes, another tax is imposed on wages earned in the U.S. under the Federal Insurance Contribu-

tions Act (FICA), a Social Security tax of 6.2 percent and a medicare hospital insurance tax of 1.45 percent are required to be withheld from most U.S. wages. Withholding of FICA taxes from wages is the responsibility of the employer. An employer is also required to pay an amount equivalent to the Social Security and Medicare hospital insurance tax imposed on the employee. The tax is also imposed on self-employed individuals, who are responsible for making the necessary payments.

For 1992, the combined rate of 7.65 percent of FICA withholding is imposed on the first $55,500 of wage or salary income and the Medicare hospital insurance tax of 1.45 percent continues to be imposed on wage or salary income to $130,200. Similarly, the combined rate of tax on self-employed individuals is 15.3 percent on the first $55,500 of self-employment income, while the Medicare hospital insurance tax of 2.9 percent continues to be imposed on income from $55,500 to $130,200.

Resident and nonresident aliens earning U.S. wages are generally subject to FICA taxes regardless of whether they expect to qualify for Social Security benefits. Nonresident aliens who enter the United States on J-1 and F-1 visas, however, are exempt from FICA taxes. In addition, resident and nonresident aliens who are nationals of a country with which the United States has concluded a social security totalization agreement may be entitled to an exemption from U.S. FICA taxes.

Totalization Agreements

Similar to income tax treaties, a social security totalization agreement is entered into by two countries to reduce the incidence of double taxation resulting from the imposition of social security taxes. Totalization agreements also provide another significant benefit. Because of the different social security rules in various countries, an individual may find that social security benefits in the home country are reduced because the individual had worked for a number of years in another country. A totalization agreement will generally provide that the period worked in the other country will be considered in determining the amount of social security benefits.

Under a totalization agreement, social security taxes are generally payable to only one country. The determination of which country is entitled to impose the tax depends on the specific totalization agreement. Totalization agreements are currently in force between the United States and Austria, Belgium, Canada, France, Germany, Italy, the Netherlands, Norway, Portugal, Spain, Sweden, Switzerland, the United Kingdom. Agreements with Finland and Luxembourg are expected to be implemented in 1992. An agreement with Ireland is expected to be signed in 1992 and implemented in 1993. The U.S. has also had discussions or correspondence with Australia, Denmark, Greece, Japan and New Zealand. (Also see Appendix I.)

DETERMINING RESIDENCY IN THE UNITED STATES

Whether or not an alien is a U.S. resident is a crucial determination because U.S. residents are subject to tax on their worldwide income, while nonresidents ordinarily are taxed only on income from U.S. sources. Frequently, when an alien is in the United States for only a short period of time, it may be better to maintain nonresident status, particularly when the alien derives significant income from non-U.S. sources.

It is important to note that an alien can be considered a "nonresident" (or nonimmigrant) for immigration purposes and at the same time be a "resident" for U.S. tax purposes. However, if an alien obtains permanent residency status (i.e., obtains a "green card"), the individual will be considered a U.S. resident for tax purposes regardless of the amount of time the individual is actually in the United States.

An alien individual is treated as a resident of the United States for federal income tax purposes under one of the following two tests:

1. Lawful permanent resident test (i.e., green card test).
2. Substantial presence test.

Lawful Permanent Resident Test

An individual is a resident alien of the United States under the lawful permanent resident test if, at any time during the calendar year, the alien has been lawfully accorded the privilege of residing permanently in the United States as an immigrant (i.e., becomes a green card holder).

An individual who is issued a green card during the year becomes a resident alien of the United States on the first day of being physically present as a "green card" holder. Once an alien acquires resident status under this test, the alien will remain a resident until one of the following events occurs:

1. The alien officially surrenders his or her green card.
2. The green card is revoked by Immigration authorities.
3. There is a judicial determination that the alien has abandoned lawful permanent resident status under the immigration laws.

Substantial Presence Test

An alien individual, even though not admitted lawfully as a permanent resident, may be considered a resident alien for tax purposes under the substantial presence test. In general, substantial presence exists and the alien will be a U.S. resident for tax purposes if

1. The individual is physically present in the United States for 183 days or more during the calendar year; or
2. The individual has been present in the United States for at least 31 days in the current year and has been present in the United States at least 183 "equivalent days" over the current and prior two years. The 183-equivalent-day test is calculated by counting each day in the United States in the current year as a full day and each day in the United States in the first and second prior years as one third and one sixth of a day, respectively.

An individual generally will be treated as present in the United States on any day he or she is physically in the United States at any time during the day. The day of arrival in the United States as well as the day of departure count as full days under this test. If an individual is in transit between two points outside the United States, however, physical presence in the United States for less than 24 hours will be disregarded.

Exempt Days
Days of physical presence in the United States will be disregarded for purposes of applying the substantial presence test in the case of

(1) foreign-government-related individuals (such as a full-time diplomat or consul), (2) teachers or trainees, (3) students (to a maximum of five years), and (4) professional athletes temporarily present to compete in a charitable event. Days of physical presence may be disregarded also by immediate family members accompanying any of these individuals.

Exceptions to the Substantial Presence Test

An individual who would otherwise be classified as a resident under the substantial presence test will be treated as a nonresident alien if one of the following exceptions applies:

1. The 31-day exception.
2. The closer connection/tax home exception.

Thirty-one Day Exception
An individual who is present in the United States for less than 31 days in any calendar year is not treated as a resident alien under the substantial presence test. This is true even if the individual meets the "183-equivalent-day test," which would otherwise treat the individual as a resident.

Closer Connection/Tax Home Exception
An individual who is present in the United States for less than 183 days in the current calendar year but meets the "183-equivalent-day test" is nevertheless treated as a nonresident alien for the current calendar year, provided the following conditions are satisfied:

1. The individual establishes that, for the current calendar year, the "tax home" (see below) is in a foreign country and the individual has a closer connection with that foreign country than with the United States.
2. The individual does not have an application pending for adjustment of immigration status and has not taken other steps to apply for status as a lawful permanent resident of the United States at any time during the year.

The meaning of the term *tax home,* for purposes of this exception, has long been a subject of controversy. The IRS, with concurrence of the Tax Court, has historically (and recently in proposed income tax regulations) taken the position that a taxpayer's "tax home" is the individual's principal place of business. However, several Courts of Appeals have either rejected or limited this interpretation, applying the more customary meaning of "abode" or "residence." In reality, however, since taxpayers will usually live in the vicinity of their principal employment, it generally makes little difference whether a "tax home" is defined as "abode/residence" or "principal place of business."

In order to qualify for the exception, an individual must also establish that a closer connection exists with the country in which the tax home is located than with the United States. The proposed income tax regulations include facts and circumstances that are to be considered in determining whether an individual will be considered to have a closer connection to a foreign country. These facts and circumstances include such items as location of the individual's permanent home; location of the individual's family; location of personal belongings owned by the individual and family; location of social, political, cultural, or religious organizations with which the individual has a current relationship; location of the individual's personal bank accounts; type of driver's license held by the individual; country of residence designated by the individual on forms and documents; and jurisdiction in which the individual votes.

First-Year Election

A nonresident alien may elect to be treated as a resident for the year of arrival in the United States. This election allows the alien to take advantage of certain tax deductions and benefits available only to U.S. residents, such as full itemized deductions and personal exemptions for spouse and dependents. In order to make this election, the individual must satisfy the following conditions:

1. The individual cannot have been a U.S. resident for the previous year.
2. The individual must qualify as a resident under the substantial presence test in the year immediately following the arrival year.
3. The individual must be present in the United States at least 31 consecutive days during the arrival year.

4. The individual must be present in the United States during the arrival year at least 75 percent of the days from the beginning of the 31-day period to year-end. (A 5-day grace period is allowed to meet the 75 percent test.)

The election cannot be made for the arrival year until the substantial presence test is met for the subsequent year. Thus, an individual would have to request the automatic four-month extension of time for filing the initial year's tax return (as discussed later in this chapter).

Married individuals making this election may also qualify to file a joint income tax return in the year of arrival. Under general rules, a joint return is not permitted if either spouse is a nonresident alien at any time during the taxable year. However, an election to file a joint return for the entire year is available where either spouse becomes a resident before the end of the year. This joint return election may be made in connection with the first-year residency election in order to benefit from the more favorable joint return tax rates. (See "Joint Return Election," later in this chapter.)

Beginning and Ending Dates of Residency

Residency Starting Date
An alien who is a U.S. resident under the substantial presence test and who was not a resident in the prior year generally begins U.S. residency in the current taxable year on the first day physically present in the United States. Up to 10 days of "nominal" U.S. presence may be disregarded in determining the date U.S. residency begins if the individual establishes a closer connection to a foreign country than to the United States on such days. In determining the number of days that may be disregarded under this rule, more than one period of physical presence in the United States may be considered. An individual may not disregard, however, any days that occur in a period of consecutive days of presence if all of the days that occur that period cannot be disregarded.

For instance, if an individual was in the United States for two separate seven-day periods for the purpose of finding a house prior to moving to the United States, only the earlier seven-day period can be excluded in determining the residency starting date. If the individual has been in the United States for two separate five-day periods prior to moving to the United States, then both visits could be excluded in determining the residency starting date.

The purpose of the nominal presence exception (also known as the ''10-day *de minimis* rule'') is to permit brief visits to the United States for business or house-hunting without triggering a residency starting date.

An individual who acquires U.S. residency under the lawful permanent resident (green card) test at any time during the calendar year, who does not otherwise meet the substantial presence test, and who was not a U.S. resident during the prior year will begin U.S. residency on the first day present in the U.S. while a lawful permanent resident of the United States. The nominal presence exception does not apply to lawful permanent residents.

If an individual satisfies both the substantial presence and lawful permanent resident tests in a calendar year, the earlier residency starting date will prevail.

An individual who is considered to be a resident as a result of making a qualified first-year election will be deemed to have begun U.S. residence on the first day of the earliest 31-day period that is included in the continuous presence period.

Residency Ending Date

An individual who is a resident alien for the current calendar year under the substantial presence test but who is not a resident in the subsequent year terminates U.S. residency on the last day physically present in the United States during the current calendar year if the alien establishes a closer connection to a foreign country than to the United States for the remainder of the year. A period of nominal presence of up to 10 days, similar to that allowed in determining the residency starting date, will be disregarded for purposes of determining the last day of residency.

An individual who qualifies as a U.S. resident during the current calendar year under the lawful permanent resident (green card) test but who does not qualify in the subsequent year will terminate U.S. residency on the first day the individual ceases to be a lawful permanent resident during the current calendar year if a closer connection can be established with a foreign country.

If an individual satisfies both the lawful permanent resident test and the substantial presence test during the current calendar year, the later residency termination date will prevail.

Effects of Tax Treaties on Residence

Because of the different rules in various countries for determining residence, an individual may be considered a resident for tax purposes in more than one country. If an income tax treaty is in effect between the United States and another country, the determination of residence may be decided by what are referred to as the "tie-breaker" rules set forth in the appropriate treaty.

The legislative history of the 1984 law that defined "residence" and the proposed income tax regulations thereunder provide that an individual who is considered to be a resident of both the United States and a foreign country under the domestic laws of each country may be considered a resident of the foreign country, and not of the United States, under the "tie-breaker" rules contained in the relevant tax treaty. It is the position of the Internal Revenue Service, as stated in proposed Treasury regulations, that when an alien invokes a tie-breaker rule and claims a treaty benefit (as a nonresident of the United States) so as to reduce his or her U.S. income tax liability with respect to *any* item of income covered by an applicable provision of the treaty, such individual shall be treated as a nonresident alien of the United States for *all* purposes of computing his or her U.S. income tax liability for that taxable year. However, the alien would continue to be considered a resident for all other purposes of the Internal Revenue Code (e.g., determining whether the individual is a U.S. person for purposes of the controlled foreign corporation rules).

Unfortunately, a discussion of the application and the potential impact of these treaty provisions is beyond the scope of this chapter. An individual to whom treaty provisions may apply is well advised to consult a tax adviser.

TAXATION OF RESIDENT ALIENS

U.S. citizens and resident aliens are taxed by the United States on their worldwide income, less deductions specifically allowed by the U.S. Internal Revenue Code. Nonresident aliens, on the other hand, are generally subject to U.S. tax on their U.S.-source income and, only under very limited circumstances, on certain foreign-source income.

General Concepts

Alien individuals are required to use the calendar year as their taxable year unless they have previously established a fiscal tax year, either in the United States or in a foreign country. For each taxable year, the tax liability of a U.S. citizen or resident is determined based on the amount of taxable income. Taxable income, as discussed below, consists of gross income less adjustments, deductions, and exemptions. Gross income consists of all income, whether or not from U.S. sources, unless such income is specifically excluded. Individual taxpayers must include all items of income actually or constructively received. A taxpayer is considered to have constructive receipt of income when an item of income becomes available to the taxpayer, although the income may not have been actually received.

Adjustments, deductions, and exemptions are allowed only to the extent specifically prescribed by the Code. Adjustments and deductions are generally allowed only with respect to those expenditures actually paid during the taxable year, without regard to the period to which the deduction relates.

Gross Income

The term *gross income* includes all income derived from any source. Some of the more common items of income that are specifically included in gross income are as follows:

1. Compensation for services, including fees, commissions, fringe benefits, and similar items.
2. Gross income derived from business (i.e., gross receipts less cost of goods sold).
3. Gains derived from dealings in property (i.e., sales proceeds less cost of property, capital improvements, and selling expenses).
4. Interest.
5. Dividends.
6. Rents and royalties.
7. Alimony and separate maintenance payments.
8. Annuities.
9. Pensions.

10. Distributive share of partnership gross income.
11. Income from an interest in an estate or trust.

Certain items that might otherwise be considered gross income are specifically excluded from the definition of gross income for purposes of determining taxable income. Some of the more common exclusions from gross income are listed below:

1. Interest on obligations of states or political subdivisions thereof, generally known as tax-exempt municipal bonds.
2. Gifts, bequests, and inheritances.
3. Life insurance proceeds paid as a result of the death of the insured.
4. Certain amounts received by individuals because of accident or illness.
5. Social security benefits, except that up to one half of such benefits may be subject to tax if adjusted gross income exceeds a certain level.

Special Rules for Certain Types of Gross Income

Employee Stock Options

The tax treatment of a stock option granted to an employee depends on whether the option is a statutory stock option (i.e., an incentive stock option or an option granted under an employee stock purchase plan) or is a nonstatutory option.

Where an employee is granted a nonstatutory stock option that has an ascertainable fair market value at the time the option is granted, the employee must include in gross income at the time of the grant the difference between the fair market value of the option and any amount paid for the option. If the option does not have a readily ascertainable fair market value (which is more likely), income is not realized until the option is exercised or transferred. In either case, if the option is subject to restrictions on transferability or any other substantial risk of forfeiture, income is generally not realized until the restriction is removed. The taxpayer can make an election, however, to recognize income as if the restriction did not exist. The income recognized from the exercise of a nonstatutory stock option is ordinary income. Capital gain or loss treatment will result on the subsequent sale of stock.

There are two types of statutory stock options.

1. Incentive stock options—Options granted pursuant to a plan approved by stockholders and meeting all of the other restrictions imposed by U.S. tax law.
2. Employee stock purchase plans—Options granted pursuant to a plan designed to permit employees to purchase stock at a discount. The plan must be nondiscriminatory and include virtually all employees.

Generally, the recipient of a statutory stock option does not recognize gross income on the granting or exercise of the option. Income is recognized only upon sale of the stock.

In the case of stock received pursuant to the excercise of an incentive stock option, the difference between the fair market value of the stock at the time of exercise and the option price is considered an item of tax preference and may result in the imposition of alternative minimum tax (discussed in this chapter under "Additional Taxes").

Limitations on Losses from Passive Activities

Deductions for losses incurred on investments in activities in which the taxpayer does not materially participate (i.e., passive activities) are limited in the current taxable year to the amount of income generated from such activities in the current taxable year. Losses that are not currently allowed under these provisions may be carried forward to offset passive income in future years or may be recognized when the passive activity property that generated the loss is sold.

Passive activities include, but are not limited to, a limited partner's interest in a business and the rental of real property. A special exception applies, however, that may allow a taxpayer to deduct actual losses of up to $25,000 from the rental of real estate if the taxpayer actively participates in renting the property. Active participation generally requires that the taxpayer make significant and bona fide management decisions with respect to the property. In addition, the full deduction of $25,000 is allowed only if adjusted gross income is less than $100,000. The allowable deduction is ratably reduced when adjusted gross income is between $100,000 and $150,000. No deduction is allowed if adjusted gross income is equal to or greater than $150,000. Also, during any year in which a married individual does not file a joint return with the spouse (see "Election to File a Joint Return," below), the $25,000 allowance is reduced to zero, unless the two spouses live apart during the year.

Gains and Losses from the Sale or Exchange of Property

Prior to 1987, gains derived from dealings in property were, in certain cases, subject to lower tax rates than ordinary income. For taxable years beginning after December 31, 1986, gains from the sale of capital assets have been taxed at the same tax rates as ordinary income. For 1991 and thereafter, the tax rate on capital gains is again lower (28 percent) than the highest ordinary income tax rate (31 percent).

Capital Gains and Losses

Long-term capital gain or loss treatment results from the sale of a capital asset held for more than one year; other gains or losses are treated as short-term capital gains and losses. The maximum amount of net capital loss (computed by aggregating all long and short-term transactions) that may offset taxable income in any one year is $3,000. Losses in excess of this limitation are carried forward indefinitely to offset capital gain income, or ordinary income up to the $3,000 annual limit.

A capital asset is defined as property held by the taxpayer (whether or not connected with a trade or a business), excluding certain assets. The most significant exceptions are the following:

1. Inventory assets or property held primarily for sale to customers in the ordinary course of business.
2. Real property or depreciable property used in a trade or business (see comments below).
3. Accounts and notes receivable arising from services rendered or from the sale of inventory assets.

Depreciable Property

The taxation of gain on the sale of depreciable property used in a taxpayer's trade or business will depend, among other factors, upon the year in which the property was placed in service, the type of property, and the method of depreciation. In general, depreciation allowed on the property may result in a portion of the gain being taxed as ordinary income. The remaining portion of the gain will be capital gain.

Sale of Principal Residence

A special rule allows the gain on the sale of a taxpayer's principal residence to be deferred if the sales proceeds are reinvested in a new principal residence within a two-year period from the date of sale. For sales that occur at a time when the alien taxpayer is treated as a U.S. resident for tax purposes, the replacement residence may be located anywhere in the world. The amount of deferred gain reduces the cost basis of the new principal residence. Consequently, any subsequent sale of the new principal residence will result in the imposition of tax on the deferred gain (and any additional gain) if the sales proceeds are not similarly reinvested in another principal residence.

Taxpayers who are 55 years of age or older as of the date of sale may also make a special one-time election to exclude up to $125,000 of the gain on the sale of principal residence. In order to be eligible for this election, the taxpayers must have owned and used the residence as a principal residence for at least three years during the five-year period ending on the date of the sale. If the property is jointly held by a married couple or is held as community property, only one spouse must meet the age and use requirements in order to make the election on a joint income tax return.

Rent and Royalty Income and Expenses

As noted above, rents and royalties are specifically included in gross income. However, an adjustment to such income is allowed for expenses incurred to carry or maintain property held for the production of rental or royalty income. Such expenses include, but are not limited to, real estate taxes, depreciation or cost recovery deductions, mortgage interest, insurance, utilities, and repairs. In addition, deductions for depletion are allowed for royalty interests in natural resource deposits.

Adjustments to Gross Income

Adjusted gross income (AGI) is determined by reducing total gross income by certain items specifically provided by U.S. tax law. These adjustments normally relate to expenses incurred to generate specific types of gross income. It is important to note that these adjustments reduce gross income prior to the allowance of itemized deductions in determining taxable income. Adjustments to AGI may be taken regardless of whether the standard deduction or itemized deductions are claimed and are generally subject to fewer restrictions than itemized deductions. Thus, it is generally preferable to have an adjustment to gross income rather than an itemized deduction. The determination of AGI is of special significance because certain itemized deductions are limited based on a percentage of AGI. Some of the more significant adjustments to adjusted gross income are set forth below.

Trade and Business Deductions
All ordinary and necessary expenses incurred in carrying on a trade or business are deductible. Trade or business expenses can be incurred by both self-employed individuals and employees, since the performance of services as an employee is considered to be a trade or business. The U.S. tax treatment of expenses incurred by employees is different from the treatment of expenses incurred by self-employed individuals.

An employee's business deductions include expenses incurred while away from home, including travel expenses, in pursuit of business as well as other expenses connected with the performance of services as an employee. When an employer reimburses these expenses under an accountable plan, the reimbursement is not included in the employee's gross income as wages or other compensation. Thus, in effect, the employee is allowed a deduction from gross income. When the expenses are reimbursed under a nonaccountable plan, the reimbursements are included in the employee's gross income as wages or other compensation, and income tax and Social Security tax are required to be withheld from the reimbursement. When the expense reimbursement is included in gross income, the employee is allowed to deduct the actual expenses as miscellaneous itemized deductions subject to a limitation of 2 percent of adjusted gross income.

An employer's expense reimbursement or expense allowance arrangements are treated as paid under an accountable plan if the expenses are incurred in connection with the performances of services by an employee for the employer, the employee is required to substantiate the expenses with an adequate accounting to the employer, and the employee is required to return to the employer any amount paid or advanced under the arrangement in excess of the substantiated expenses.

Special rules apply for meal and entertainment expenses. Generally, only 80 percent of such expenses are deductible. If the employee receives reimbursement for such expenses based on an adequate accounting, the 80 percent limitation applies to the employer. If the expense reimbursement is included in income, the 80-percent limitation applies to the employee.

Self-employed individuals may deduct any ordinary and necessary expenses incurred in the conduct of their trade or business. The 80 percent limitation on meals and entertainment expenses also applies to such individuals. Business expenses of self-employed individuals are taken into account in computing net income from self-employment, which is an element of the individual's AGI.

Exclusions for U.S. Residents Working Abroad
When a U.S. resident alien (i.e., a green card holder) works overseas and is physically present in a foreign country or countries for 330 days out of a consecutive 12-month period, an election may be made to exclude from foreign-earned compensation one or both of the following amounts.

The first of these exclusions relates to housing costs. If the taxpayer's housing expenses exceed a "base amount"—$8,055 for 1991—then the excess is an exclusion that reduces foreign-earned compensation. Housing expenses are the reasonable expenses incurred by the individual in the foreign country, including rent, utilities, and insurance. The second exclusion relates to foreign earned income. The maximum earned income exclusion for 1991 is $70,000. The maximum combined housing and earned income exclusion cannot exceed the individual's total foreign-earned compensation for the taxable year.

Net Operating Losses

Individual taxpayers who incur a net operating loss (NOL) in a given year can use the NOL to reduce taxable income in prior or succeeding years. An NOL is generally defined as the excess of allowable deductions over gross income. Certain adjustments are required to be made, however, in determining the NOL that can be used to offset taxable income in other years. Some of these adjustments are as follows:

1. Capital losses are deductible in determining the offset in other years only to the extent of capital gains.
2. Personal exemptions are not allowed.
3. Nonbusiness deductions are allowed only to the extent of nonbusiness income.

An NOL may be carried back 3 years and forward 15 years. Absent an election to relinquish the 3-year carryback period, the NOL must first be carried back to the third preceding year and then forward to each succeeding year in the carryback and carryover periods until fully utilized. Any portion of the NOL that is unused at the end of the 15-year carryforward period expires.

Deductions and Exemptions

After determining adjusted gross income, taxable income is determined by reducing AGI by deductions and personal exemptions. The taxpayer has the option of using the greater of the standard deduction or actual itemized deductions.

Standard Deduction

The amount of the standard deduction is based upon the filing status of the taxpayer and can be increased if the taxpayer or spouse is 65 or over or is blind. These amounts are adjusted annually for inflation, unless the adjustment is less than $50. Standard deductions for 1992 are summarized in Table 20–1. Additional standard deductions for the elderly or blind are shown in Table 20–2.

Itemized Deductions

Unlike the adjustments to gross income, which normally relate to expenses incurred to generate business income, itemized deduc-

TABLE 20–1
Standard Deductions–1992

Filing Status	$
Married, filing jointly; surviving spouse	6,000
Head of household	5,250
Single	3,600
Married, filing separately	3,000

tions normally relate to nonbusiness expenses. Additionally, itemized deductions are subject to a number of significant restrictions, including limitations based on certain percentages of AGI. Common itemized deductions are described below.

Moving Expenses. Within certain limitations, moving expenses are deductible as an itemized deduction, if incurred in connection with the commencement of work by a taxpayer as an employee or as a self-employed individual at a new principal place of work.

Medical Expenses. The deduction for medical expenses includes amounts paid for doctors, dentists, hospitals, medical insurance, and so on. Medical expenses also include the cost of medicines and drugs that may be obtained only by prescription, and of insulin. The deduction is limited to those expenses that exceed 7.5 percent of AGI.

Taxes. Deductible taxes include state and local personal property taxes; state, local, and foreign income taxes; and state, local, and foreign real property taxes. Foreign income taxes cannot

TABLE 20–2
Additional Standard Deductions

Filing Status	$ Elderly	$ Blind
Single	900	900
Head of household	900	900
Married (joint return)	700	700
Married (separate returns)	700	700
Surviving spouse	700	700

be taken as an itemized deduction if a foreign tax credit (described later in this chapter) is claimed with respect to such foreign taxes.

Interest. The amount of interest that may be deducted depends upon the category in which the interest expense is classified. These categories include qualified residence interest, investment interest, personal interest, interest relating to a trade or business, and interest attributable to acquiring or carrying on an investment in a passive activity. Interest relating to a trade or business is fully deductible, generally in determining AGI. The other categories have specific provisions that limit the amount of deductible interest.

Mortgage interest—Any interest paid on a mortgage entered into on or before October 13, 1987, on a principal or second residence is fully deductible. If the mortgage was entered into after that date or the taxpayer has more than two residences, special rules apply. Interest expense on a mortgage entered into after October 13, 1987, will be deductible if it is qualified residence interest. Generally, qualified residence interest is "acquisition indebtedness" or "home equity indebtedness." Acquisition indebtedness is debt incurred in acquiring, constructing, or substantially improving a taxpayer's principal or second residence up to a maximum indebtedness of $1 million. If a mortgage is being refinanced, the maximum amount of acquisition indebtedness is the amount of debt outstanding immediately prior to the refinancing. Acquisition indebtedness is decreased as loan principal payments are made and may not be increased by subsequent refinancing.

Home equity indebtedness is a loan secured by the primary or second residence other than acquisition indebtedness. The maximum amount of home equity indebtedness is the lesser of $100,000 or the fair market value of the home less the acquisition indebtedness.

Mortgage interest expense incurred on other homes depends on how the properties or loan proceeds are used. For example, interest expense incurred on a third home that is used for personal purposes is considered personal interest which is not deductible.

Investment interest—Investment interest is deductible only to the extent of net investment income. Net investment income includes, but is not limited to, interest, dividends, royalties, and gains from disposition of investment property less related expenses.

Investment interest that is disallowed as a current deduction may be carried forward indefinitely. The carryforward amount may be deducted in subsequent years subject to the net investment income limitation.

Personal interest—Personal interest is consumer interest, including interest on tax deficiencies. Examples of consumer interest are interest incurred on car loans and on purchases made with credit cards. The deduction for personal interest was phased out over a five-year period beginning in 1987. Personal interest is not deductible in 1991 and thereafter.

Passive activity interest—Passive activity interest is subject to the general rules related to passive activities, which were discussed under "Limitations on Losses from Passive Activities" earlier in this chapter.

Charitable Contributions. Contributions of cash and property to recognized U.S. charitable organizations are deductible as itemized deductions. If property is contributed, the amount of the deduction is generally the fair market value of the property. Certain limitations apply in determining the deductible amount of both cash and property contributions.

For contributions to most charitable organizations (e.g., churches, tax-exempt educational institutions, and tax-exempt hospital or medical research organizations), the deduction is limited to 50 percent of a taxpayer's "contribution base." The contribution base is adjusted gross income, excluding any net operating loss carrybacks. For contributions made to certain other charitable organizations (e.g., war veterans' and fraternal organizations, public cemeteries, etc.), the maximum deduction is the lesser of 30 percent of the contribution base or 50 percent of the excess of the contribution base over the amount of charitable contributions qualifying for the 50 percent limitation (see above). These limitations are reduced if capital gain property is contributed. Charitable contributions in excess of these limitations may be carried forward and utilized as charitable contributions in the five succeeding taxable years.

Individuals who make contributions of property valued in excess of $5,000 must substantiate the contributions with a qualified appraisal of the property's value. In addition, a fully completed appraisal summary, on a prescribed form, must be attached to the tax return on which the deduction is claimed. The substantiation requirement applies when an individual donates either an item, or two or more similar items, of property, (such as stamps, coins, or books) whose total value exceeds $5,000.

Casualty or Theft Losses.   A casualty or theft loss is deductible only to the extent that all aggregate losses (after reducing each loss by $100) exceed 10 percent of AGI. A casualty is a sudden event, such as a flood, fire, windstorm, and so on. The loss is measured by the difference between the value of the property before the casualty or theft and the value after. However, the loss cannot exceed the cost of the property, irrespective of its value, reduced by insurance proceeds or any other amount recovered.

Miscellaneous Itemized Deductions.   Miscellaneous itemized deductions include expenses that are related to employment, investments, or taxes. Most types of miscellaneous itemized deductions are deductible only if the sum of the items exceeds 2 percent of AGI. Significant exceptions to the 2 percent limitation are moving expenses (discussed previously) and amortization of bond premium. These expenses are not subject to the 2 percent limitation and are fully deductible to the extent otherwise allowable. Expenses subject to the 2 percent limitation are unreimbursed employee business expenses, business meals and business entertainment, investment counseling fees, and legal and accounting fees. The 80-percent limitation on business meals and business entertainment is applied prior to the 2-percent AGI limit.

Overall Limitation on Itemized Deductions.   For 1991 through 1995, the total of otherwise allowable itemized deductions—excluding medical expenses, investment interest, and casualty and theft losses—must be reduced by an amount equal to 3 percent of the amount of AGI in excess of certain threshold amounts. These threshold amounts for 1992 are $105,250 for married filing jointly, single, and head of household; $52,625 for married filing separately—will be indexed annually for inflation after 1991. In no event is the total of the otherwise allowable deductions to be reduced by more than 80 percent.

Personal Exemptions
In addition to those deductions previously discussed, individual taxpayers are entitled to deduct personal exemptions for them-

selves, their spouses and each dependent. For 1992, each exemption amount is $2,300. Certain tests regarding support, relationship, residence, and income must be satisfied in order to claim an individual as a dependent. Social security identification numbers must be reported for all individuals one year of age or older who are claimed as dependents.

The deduction for personal exemptions is phased out by 2 percent for each $2,500 or fraction thereof (1,250 for married persons filing separate) by which a taxpayer's AGI exceeds a threshold amount. The threshold amounts for 1992, which will be adjusted annually for inflation, are $157,900 for married persons filing jointly, $131,550 for heads of household, $105,250 for single taxpayers, and $78,950 for married persons filing separately.

Computation of Tax Liability

Once taxable income is determined, tax is computed using the applicable tax rates, which are based on the filing status of the taxpayer. The amount of tax determined is then reduced by any available credits to arrive at the net tax liability.

Tax Rates and Filing Status

Individuals are subject to graduated tax rates based on the amount of taxable income. In addition, the filing status of the taxpayer is an important factor in determining the tax liability since there are different tax rate schedules for each filing status. Generally, the determination of filing status depends on whether the taxpayer is married. A brief description of each filing status is set forth below. The 1992 tax rates for each filing status can be found in Appendix II.

1. Married individuals filing joint returns and surviving spouses—The general effect of a married couple filing a joint return is to subject the combined income of the couple to a lower tax liability than if separate returns were filed. In certain circumstances, however, it is possible that a lower combined tax liability will result if a married couple files separate tax returns. The ability to file a joint return is generally denied if either spouse was a nonresident alien at any time during the taxable year. (See the discussion below for the availability of a joint return election.)

A widow or widower whose spouse died within the two immediately preceding tax years, who has not remarried, and who has paid over half the cost of maintaining a home for a dependent child can also utilize the lower married tax rates.

2. Married individuals filing separate returns.
3. Single (unmarried) individuals.
4. Head of household. This status applies to unmarried individuals who maintain a home in which certain relatives live. Generally, this requires that an individual pay more than half the cost of maintaining the home during the tax year. In some cases, the relative does not have to be a dependent of the taxpayer. Use of this status results in a lower tax than would otherwise be imposed on an unmarried taxpayer. The head of household rates are also available to married citizens or residents if the spouse is a nonresident alien and if they otherwise qualify.

Election to File a Joint Return
Notwithstanding the general provisions that deny joint returns for individuals who are nonresident aliens at any time during the year, a U.S. citizen or resident married to a nonresident alien, or a nonresident alien couple that has established U.S. residency by the close of the taxable year may elect to file a joint return in order to use the lower joint return tax rates. As a result of the election, however, the worldwide income of both spouses for the entire year must be included in the joint return (see "Joint Return Election" later in this chapter for more details).

Additional Taxes
Alternative Minimum Tax.   In addition to the regular income tax, the United States has another tax designed to make sure that individuals having substantial income pay a minimum amount of tax. This additional tax, referred to as the Alternative Minimum Tax (AMT), is imposed on "Alternative Minimum Taxable Income" (AMTI) at the rate of 24 percent. Generally, AMTI is calculated by increasing regular taxable income by certain adjustments and tax preference items. See Chapter 16 for more details regarding the AMT.

Self-Employment Tax.   Employees are subject to FICA tax, which is withheld from their wages. Self-employed individuals are also subject to self-employment tax on earned income not subject to FICA withholding. As mentioned earlier in this chapter, self-employment tax is imposed on the "net earnings from self-employment" at a rate of 15.3 percent on a maximum income base of $55,500 for 1992 and the 2.9 percent Medicare hospital insurance tax continues to be imposed on self-employment income to $130,200.

"Net earnings from self-employment" are defined as (1) The excess of gross income from any trade or business over allowable deductions attributable to such trade or business, plus (2) The distributive share of partnership ordinary income (or loss) derived from the partnership's trade or business. Under this definition, director's fees are considered self-employment income.

Nonresident aliens are not subject to the self-employment tax. However, non-U.S. citizens who are residents of Puerto Rico, the Virgin Islands, Guam, or American Samoa are subject to this tax.

Foreign Tax Credit

Under U.S. tax law, certain tax credits are allowed that reduce U.S. tax on a dollar-for-dollar basis in arriving at net U.S. tax liability. The most significant credit that is available is the foreign tax credit.

Foreign income taxes paid or accrued are allowed as a credit, subject to limitation, in computing a taxpayer's U.S. tax liability. Although foreign income taxes can be taken as a deduction, it is usually to a taxpayer's advantage to take a credit for foreign taxes paid.

To claim a credit, the foreign tax paid (or accrued) must qualify as an income tax. In order for the tax to be considered as an income tax, two tests must be satisfied. First, the tax must not be compensation for a specific economic benefit, and second, the tax must be based on realized net income. A tax may meet these requirements even if the provisions for calculation of net income in the foreign taxing jurisdiction "differ substantially" from U.S. tax law. Also, special rules are provided for determining the amount of tax paid or accrued, and for determining when a tax is paid "in lieu of" an income tax. The most common example of an "in lieu of" tax is withholding tax.

The amount of foreign tax which may be credited in any one year is subject to a limitation expressed by the following formula:

$$\frac{\text{Foreign-source taxable income}}{\text{Taxable income from all sources}} \times \text{U.S. tax liability} = \frac{\text{Foreign tax credit}}{\text{before credits limitation}}$$

In determining foreign-source taxable income for purposes of this limitation computation, it is first necessary to determine the source of gross income. The rules for determining the source of gross income are discussed later in this chapter. In computing foreign-source taxable income, deductions are first allocated to classes of gross income to which they directly relate (e.g., rental income is reduced by rental expenses, etc.). Deductions that are not directly allocable to a specific class of income are allocated to foreign source income in the same proportion that foreign-source gross income bears to gross income from all sources.

The foreign tax credit limitation is applied separately to specific categories of income (baskets). Passive income and "high withholding tax interest," for example, will each be treated under limitation baskets separate from trade or business income, such as wages, in determining the foreign tax credit limitation.

If foreign taxes paid (or accrued) in any one year cannot be utilized because of the above limitations, such taxes may be carried back two years and forward five years, subject to the same limitations on utilization.

Returns, Filing, and Payment

Returns

A U.S. resident who has gross income equal to or greater than the exemption amount plus the basic standard deduction applicable to such individual must file an annual income tax return on Form 1040, Form 1040A, or Form 1040EZ. Thus, for example, the minimum gross income threshold for filing a joint married return for the 1992 taxable year is $10,600 ($2,300 × 2 = $4,600 [exemption amount] plus $6,000 [standard deduction]). The determination of which form to use depends generally on the amount and type of income earned, marital status, and whether itemized deductions will be claimed. Form 1040EZ, the simplest return, can be filed only by single taxpayers with no dependents and with taxable income of less than $50,000, consisting of salary income and no more than $400 of interest income. Form 1040A is a short, relatively simple return that may be used by taxpayers who are not required to file any schedules to support the return—that is, they earn salary income, unemployment compensation, no more than $400 of interest or dividend income, and do not itemize deductions. Those not able to use or not wanting to use either of these forms must file Form 1040. Form 1040, for example, must be used if the taxpayer wishes to claim itemized deductions, claim a foreign tax credit, or is self-employed.

Individuals are required to file their annual tax return on or before the 15th day of the 4th month following the close of the taxable year (April 15 for calendar-year taxpayers). The return is filed with the Internal Revenue Service Center for the district in which the legal residence or principal place of business of the taxpayer is located.

Individuals are allowed an automatic extension of four months (to August 15) for filing their returns, provided they file an extension request and pay their expected tax liability by the original due date. An additional extension of time to file may be granted if reasonable cause can be shown. Interest is charged on any unpaid tax from the original due date to the date of payment. The interest rate on tax underpayments is determined by the IRS on a quarterly basis. The interest rate is based on the average of short-term U.S. government obligations plus three percentage points.

Payment and Collection
Generally, the U.S. uses the self-assessment method to collect income taxes. The primary method of enforcing the payment of tax is the filing of annual tax returns. Payments of tax must be made, however, prior to the filing of the annual return. These payments are generally in the form of withholding on wages or payments of estimated tax.

Withholding at Source.   Withholding of tax is required with respect to most wages, salaries, and other remuneration paid to an employee. The withholding amount is computed taking into account an employee's tax credits and personal and dependency exemptions as well as deductions in excess of nonwage income. Such withholding is the responsibility of the employer. The employee credits the withholding against the final tax liability. Withholding at source on payments to nonresident aliens is discussed later in this chapter.

Estimated Tax Payments.   Individuals who earn income that is not subject to withholding tax are required to file estimated tax payment vouchers during the year. Vouchers are required to be filed by a U.S. citizen or resident if the estimated tax liability exceeds withholding by at least $500. Estimated tax payments are generally required to be remitted in four equal installments on or before the following dates, in the case of a calendar-year taxpayer: April 15, June 15, September 15, and January 15. In the event these dates fall on a Saturday, Sunday, or holiday the taxpayer has until the following business day to make the necessary payment.

A husband and wife may file joint vouchers, provided they have the same taxable year. However, joint vouchers may not be filed after a decree of divorce or separate maintenance, or when either spouse is a nonresident alien at any time during the taxable year. Although filing joint vouchers makes the tax liability joint and several (that is, both spouses are liable for the full tax liability), it does not require the filing of a joint tax return.

Estimated tax payments and wage withholding must equal at least 90 percent of the final tax liability or a nondeductible penalty for underpayment of estimated tax is imposed. The amount of the penalty is computed at the same interest rate for late payments of tax on the amount of underpayment from the due date of the appropriate installment to the date actually paid. This penalty does not apply in certain cases when there has not been a substantial increase in income, if the estimated tax paid and/or withholding is equal to the tax liability of the prior year, provided a return reflecting a tax liability was filed for the prior year and the return covered a period of 12 months.

Payment with Tax Return.   The amount of taxes withheld or estimated tax payments are only designed to approximate the final amount of tax due for the year. Each taxpayer is required to file a tax return indicating the actual tax liability for the year. In filing their tax return, taxpayers compute their net tax due, consisting of gross tax liability less tax credits, withholding at source, and estimated tax payments. If there is still an amount due, taxpayers must remit this amount when filing their return.

Withholding or estimated tax payments in excess of a tax-payer's liability may, at the election of the taxpayer, either be refunded or credited against the subsequent year's tax liability.

An individual must pay the balance of the tax due as shown on the return at the filing date of the return, without regard to any extension of time for filing. An individual filing on Form 1040A, however, may elect not to compute the tax, in which case the District Director will compute the tax and so notify the individual. If the taxpayer using Form 1040A elects to compute the tax, the tax must be paid by the date required for filing the return.

Penalties and Interest

The Internal Revenue Code prescribes specific penalties and interest charges for failure to file or delinquency in the filing of various tax returns required by law, and for failure to make timely payment of appropriate taxes. In addition, the law provides an interest charge with respect to underpayment of tax. Under current law, the interest is considered to be nondeductible personal interest. Penalties likewise are not deductible.

Statute of Limitations

The IRS has 3 years from the due date of a particular return, or the date of filing (if later), to start proceedings for assessment and collection of tax. The IRS may assess the tax or commence a suit at any time, in the event a fraudulent return was filed or if no return was filed. If a taxpayer has omitted an amount of income that exceeds 25 percent of the gross income reported in an income tax return, the statute of limitations is extended from 3 to 6 years.

With respect to claims for refund, a taxpayer must file a claim within 3 years from the time the return was filed or within 2 years from the time the tax was paid, whichever is later. For certain refunds or reassessments resulting from foreign tax credits, the statute is extended to 10 years.

TAXATION OF NONRESIDENT ALIENS

The United States generally taxes nonresident aliens only on income from sources within the United States. Under limited circumstances, however, certain foreign source income may be subject to

U.S. tax. A nonresident alien's U.S. source income is divided into two classifications. A nonresident alien may have income from each class in any year. The two classifications are (1) Income not effectively connected with a U.S. trade or business, and (2) Income effectively connected with a U.S. trade or business. The classification of a nonresident's U.S. source income is important because income not effectively connected with a U.S. trade or business is taxed differently from income that is effectively connected with a U.S. trade or business, as discussed below.

Income not Effectively Connected with U.S. Trade or Business

A nonresident is subject to U.S. tax at a flat rate on the gross amount of certain items of income from sources within the United States that are not effectively connected with the conduct of a U.S. trade or business in the year of receipt. The statutory tax rate is 30 percent, but this rate can be reduced pursuant to tax treaties that the United States has with various foreign countries. The rate reduction varies from treaty to treaty, and the applicability of a particular treaty depends upon the recipient's country of citizenship and/or residence. When the recipient is resident in a country other than the country in which the individual is a citizen, a thorough analysis to determine the appropriate income tax treaty should be undertaken.

The collection of the 30 percent flat tax, which is generally imposed on passive or investment income, is effected through a system of withholding at source. It is the responsibility of the payor of the income (or the payor's agent) to withhold the appropriate amount. A nonresident alien whose total U.S. tax liability is attributable to investment or passive income that is subject to withholding tax is not required to file a U.S. tax return unless an election is made to report real property income on a "net basis" (discussed later).

Fixed and Determinable Income
The major classification of income subject to the 30 percent tax is referred to as "fixed and determinable annual or periodic gains, profits and income." This category of income includes U.S.-source

interest, dividends, rent, salaries, wages, premiums, annuities, compensation, remunerations, and emoluments. Other items of income, for example, royalty payments, are also included within this category even though they are not included in the literal wording of the statute.

It should also be noted that this classification includes wages, salaries, and compensation, or similar payments for personal services that are ordinarily considered income effectively connected with a U.S. trade or business (discussed below). The IRS position is that such amounts are subject to the 30 percent withholding tax if paid to a self-employed nonresident, unless reduced or exempted under a tax treaty. Where a nonresident is an employee, the employer is required to withhold tax at the graduated rates applicable to all U.S. employees. Regardless of whether the individual is self-employed or an employee, the alien would file a U.S. tax return reporting the income as effectively connected, claiming appropriate deductions, and crediting the withholding tax against the U.S. tax liability computed at the graduated rates.

Income received or gain realized by a nonresident during a tax year in which the alien was not engaged in a U.S. trade or business may still be treated as effectively connected income. This treatment applies to income or gain realized after 1986 that is attributable to services rendered or to a transaction undertaken in a tax year in which it would have been effectively connected income. Accordingly, a deferred payment such as a bonus, which would be effectively connected income related to the performance of services in the U.S., retains its character as effectively connected income even if paid in a year when the alien is no longer engaged in a U.S. trade or business (e.g., the alien is no longer employed in the United States).

Exceptions

There are important exceptions to the 30-percent gross tax. First, "portfolio interest" earned by a nonresident is exempt from tax. With respect to individuals, "portfolio interest" refers to interest received from certain debt instruments issued after July 18, 1984. The exception to the 30-percent tax does not include (1) interest derived from a corporation or partnership in which the taxpayer has an ownership interest of at least 10 percent, and (2) interest paid to an individual residing in a foreign country where the IRS determines that the exchange of information between the United States and that country is not sufficient to prevent tax evasion by U.S. taxpayers. For obligations issued prior to July 19, 1984, interest continues to be subject to withholding unless the interest income is derived from deposits with U.S. banking institutions.

Second, interest income on U.S. bank deposits is exempt from U.S. withholding tax, provided such interest is not effectively connected with the conduct of a trade or business in the United States.

Third, original issue discount income, provided the original issue discount obligations are payable within 183 days from the date of original issue, is exempt from tax.

A special exception applies to U.S.-source gains from the sale of capital assets by nonresident aliens. Such capital gains are exempt from the 30 percent gross tax if the nonresident alien is present in the United States for less than 183 days during the taxable year in which the sale occurred.

Special Treatment for Rental Real Estate

Because a 30 percent tax on gross rental income would be a prohibitive cost to most foreign nationals investing in U.S. real estate, a special provision is available to nonresident aliens with rental income from U.S. property that is not effectively connected with a U.S. business. This election allows a nonresident alien to be taxed as if the income were effectively connected with a U.S. business. Such an election affords the taxpayer the opportunity to have the rental income taxed (1) on a net basis (i.e., after deducting all expenses related to the rental activity) rather than on gross rental income, and (2) at the graduated tax rates rather than at a flat 30 percent rate.

In cases where nonresident alien realty owner directly engages in managing the property, it is likely that his or her activities would constitute a U.S. trade or business, resulting in taxation at the graduated rates on net income. However, this situation is the exception as most foreign realty owners lease their real estate on a so-called net lease basis, where the lessee operates and manages the property and the foreign taxpayer has little more than a passive investment.

The net basis election has certain disadvantages. First, the election has the effect of characterizing all of the alien's real estate income, whether or not business-related, as effectively connected income. Second, the election treats rents and royalties from U.S. natural resource deposits as real estate income. Third, once the election is made, it remains in effect for all subsequent years and may be revoked only with the consent of the IRS.

In many instances, tax treaties provide for a similar election permitting real estate income to be taxed on a net basis. However, treaty elections are generally structured as annual elections, making the treaty election preferable to the irrevocable election. A treaty election may be made for each year in which the property is producing rental income.

Note: The gain or loss realized by an investor from the disposition of a U.S. real property interest is deemed to be effectively connected income. For a discussion of this topic, see "Gain or Loss from Disposition of U.S. Real Property Interests" later in this chapter.

Income Effectively Connected with U.S. Trade or Business

A nonresident alien's net income derived from the conduct of a U.S. trade or business, and other U.S.-source income that is effectively connected with such U.S. trade or business, is subject to U.S. tax at the regular graduated rates. Deductions are allowed in arriving at the net amount subject to the graduated rates of tax in the same manner as for U.S. citizens and resident aliens, provided such deductions are effectively connected with the U.S. trade or business.

U.S. Trade or Business

The U.S. tax code and regulations do not clearly define the term *U.S. trade or business*. The determination of which activities constitute a U.S. trade or business is a matter of facts and circumstances rather than a matter of clearly defined law. Relevant considerations include the continuity and regularity of the U.S.-based activity, the number of transactions completed in the United States, the amount of income derived from the U.S.-based activities, and the type or nature of the activities.

Specific guidance, however, is provided for certain activities as described below.

Personal Services. The performance of personal services in the United States by a nonresident alien will be considered a U.S. trade or business, unless the nonresident alien meets all of the following criteria:

1. Is an employee of a foreign employer (i.e., nonresident alien, foreign corporation or partnership, or foreign branch of a U.S. business).
2. Is present in the United States for a period not exceeding 90 days.
3. Receives compensation for personal services that is not in excess of $3,000.

Many tax treaties provide a more liberal exclusion than that set forth above. For example, the time period may be increased to 183 days and there may be no dollar limitation on the amount of compensation that may be earned. The nonresident alien must ordinarily be employed by a resident of the other treaty country or, as in several of the most recent treaties, be employed by a U.S. nonresident.

Income earned by a nonresident alien who meets the three general U.S. tax law requirements, or satisfies the treaty provisions, is treated as non-U.S. source income. Accordingly, such income is exempt from U.S. tax since it is neither effectively connected with a U.S. trade or business, nor does it constitute U.S.-source fixed and determinable income.

Trading in Stocks, Securities, or Commodities. Generally, a nonresident alien may trade in stocks, securities, and commodities (that are customarily traded on an organized exchange) through an independent agent resident in the United States (e.g., a resident broker, commission agent, custodian, etc.) without the investment activity constituting a U.S. trade or business. This general rule applies to a nonresident alien who is a dealer (i.e., trading for foreign customers) in stocks or securities, as well as a nonresident who trades for his or her own account. The activity will be a U.S. trade or business if there is a U.S. office through which the security transactions are effected. Although the income may not be effectively connected to a U.S. trade or business, it still may be subject to U.S. withholding tax as fixed and determinable annual or periodic income.

A more liberal rule is available to nonresident aliens (other than a dealer) who desire to trade securities for their own account. Under this rule, nonresident aliens may trade securities in the United States through their own efforts, through the efforts of their employees while present in the United States, or through an agent (whether or not independent) with or without discretionary authority granted to the agent or employee. As long as nonresidents are trading for their own account, the activity will not be regarded as a U.S. trade or business.

Partnerships. A nonresident alien is considered to be engaged in a U.S. trade or business if the individual is a partner in a partnership that is engaged in a U.S. trade or business. The partner's distributive share of effectively connected U.S. partnership income is treated as effectively connected business income and will be subject to withholding tax imposed at the partnership level. The tax is withheld at the highest graduated tax rate based on the type of partner (i.e., individual or corporation). The partner's distributive share of U.S.-source income not effectively connected with a U.S. trade or business (fixed and determinable annual or periodic income) would be subject to withholding tax at the flat 30 percent rate (or lower treaty rate).

Effectively Connected Income

Effectively connected income includes all U.S.-source business income, the gain realized by a foreign investor from the disposition of a U.S. real property interest, and limited categories of foreign-source business income. Also, fixed and determinable income and capital gains that are not typically trade- or business-related can, under certain circumstances, be considered effectively connected income.

U.S. Source Income. All U.S.-source income, other than fixed and determinable income and certain capital gains, is taxed as income effectively connected with a U.S. business, whether or not the income is attributable to the U.S. business activities. Assume, for example, a nonresident alien is engaged in a U.S. business of purchasing and selling electronic equipment. Through an office operating exclusively within the individual's home country, the alien also conducts a business of purchasing and selling vintage wine. If the alien effects a casual sale of wine through this office to a U.S. customer and title passes in the United States, this U.S.-source income will be treated as effectively connected with a U.S. business.

If a nonresident alien has not at any time during the year (i.e., not even for one day) been engaged in a U.S. trade or business, then none of the U.S.-source income for that year can be treated as effectively connected (except for real property dispositions and income or gain that is attributable to a transaction or the performance of services in any other taxable year that would have been effectively connected income had it been taken into account in the prior year).

A nonresident alien who engages in a U.S. trade or business, and who also derives investment income must determine if the investment income is effectively connected and subject to graduated tax as regular business income. An item of fixed or determinable income, or a nonreal property capital gain, is effectively connected with a U.S. trade or business if it meets either of the criteria listed below:

1. The item of income or gain (loss) is derived from an asset or assets used, or held for use, in the U.S. trade or business ("assets use" test).
2. The activity of the business is a material factor in the realization of the item of income or gain (loss) ("business activities" test).

Although a detailed discussion of these tests is beyond the scope of this chapter, a nonresident alien individual who merely performs U.S. personal services would rarely be required to treat investment income as effectively connected.

Gain or Loss from Disposition of U.S. Real Property Interest. Pursuant to the provisions of the Foreign Investment in Real Property Tax Act (FIRPTA), gain or loss realized by a foreign investor from the disposition of a U.S. real property interest is deemed to be effectively connected income, subject to U.S. tax at graduated rates.

A U.S. real property interest includes not only the direct ownership of real property, including any pro-rata interest held through a partnership, trust, or estate, but also stock in a domestic corporation which is a "U.S. real property holding corporation" (RPHC). An RPHC is any U.S. corporation in which the fair market value of U.S. real property interests is, or has been within the last five years, at least 50 percent of the fair market value of the corporation's assets. Only the value of assets used or held by the corporation for use in a trade or business are included in determining the percentage. U.S. real property interests and foreign real property, however, are always included. The FIRPTA regulations contain guidelines and examples of assets used or held for use in a trade or business.

A real property interest includes a mine, well, or other natural deposit, as well as personal property associated with the use of the real property, for instance, furnishings or movable walls. Leaseholds of real property, and options to acquire real property or such leaseholds, are also considered to be real property interests.

FIRPTA does not apply to the sale of shares of any class of stock regularly traded on an established securities market if the seller owned, directly or indirectly, 5 percent or less of such class of stock.

Although gains realized by a foreign investor from the disposition of a U.S. real property interest are automatically considered effectively connected income and subject to graduated tax rates, a portion of the ultimate tax liability is collected through a withholding tax. The purpose of the withholding tax is to assure that the seller pays the required tax. Under the withholding provisions, the transferee is generally required to withhold 10 percent of the gross sales proceeds due to the foreign investor-transferor. There are several exceptions to the 10-percent withholding requirement. For example, withholding is not required on sales of property that were used as a residence if the amount realized for the property does not exceed $300,000.

On the disposition of a U.S. real property interest by a domestic partnership, trust or estate, however, the withholding tax is increased to 34 percent of the gain realized to the extent the gain is allocable to a foreign partner, beneficiary, or grantor (under grantor trust rules) of a trust.

The rules under FIRPTA are very complicated, and aliens with investments in U.S. real property should consult a tax adviser. For more on FIRPTA, refer to Chapter 16.

Foreign Source Income.   Under limited circumstances, as detailed below, foreign source income of a nonresident alien is considered "effectively connected" with a U.S. trade or business and subject to U.S. tax:

1. The nonresident alien has an office or other fixed place of business in the United States.
2. The foreign source income is attributable to that office.
3. The income received is one of the following two types:
   a. Rents or royalties from the foreign use of intangible property or property rights, such as patents, copyrights, secret processes, formulas, goodwill, trademarks, trade names, and like property, and any gain or loss from the sale of such property, provided these items of income are derived from the active conduct of the U.S. trade or business.
   b. Investment income (i.e., dividends, interest, and capital gains) derived from the active conduct of a banking, financing, or similar business in the United States.

In determining whether the nonresident alien has an office or other fixed place of business in the United States, the office of an agent will be treated as the office of the nonresident alien, if the agent has and regularly exercises power to negotiate and conclude contracts or has a stock of merchandise from which the agent regularly fills orders on behalf of the nonresident alien. General commission agents acting in the ordinary course of their own business will not be considered an office of the nonresident alien.

For purposes of determining whether an item of foreign source income is attributable to a U.S. office, the U.S. office must be a "material factor" in the production of such income, and must regularly carry on the business that produced the income.

Determination of Gross Income, Taxable Income, and Tax

As previously discussed, income not effectively connected with a U.S. trade or business is subject to the flat 30 percent rate of tax (or lower treaty rate), without the benefit of any deductions, allowances (including personal exemptions) and credits. Capital gains that are not effectively connected income are not subject to U.S. tax, except for U.S. source gains realized by a nonresident alien who, in the year of sale, is physically present in the United States for at least 183 days.

Income that is effectively connected with a U.S. trade or business is subject to tax on a net basis (after deductions, allowances, and exemptions) at graduated income tax rates.

Exclusions from Gross Income

Certain exclusions from gross income are available to nonresident aliens. First, compensation received by a nonresident alien who is present in the United States as a nonimmigrant for a temporary period under an F visa (student) or J visa (trainee, specialist) is excluded from gross income. The exclusion applies, however, only to compensation paid to the nonresident alien by a foreign employer. A foreign employer includes a foreign office or branch of a U.S. business.

Another gross income exclusion covers amounts received by a nonresident alien from an annuity under a qualified annuity plan, a qualified pension trust, or a profit sharing or stock bonus plan, provided the following two conditions are met:

1. The annuity is paid pursuant to services performed by the alien outside the United States while a nonresident.
2. At the time of the first qualified annuity payment to an alien claiming this exclusion, 90 percent or more of the employees or annuitants in the plan are citizens or residents of the United States.

Deductions

In computing net income, it is necessary for the foreign taxpayer to separate income effectively connected with a U.S. trade or business from total gross income from U.S. sources. Any applicable deductions would then be used to reduce effectively connected income. Nonresident aliens are generally not allowed any of the deductions permitted U.S. citizens or residents. However, they are entitled to claim deductions for expenses that are connected (and only to the extent they are connected) with the derivation of income that is effectively connected with a business carried on in the United States. In other words, all expenses that are ordinary and necessary in relation to activities of a trade or business in the United States by a foreign taxpayer are deductible.

U.S. tax law does not follow the principle of territoriality in determining allowable deductions, and thus it is not the place where an expense is incurred, but rather the nature of the expense and its connection with, or relationship to, the U.S. business activity, that governs deductibility.

In addition to trade or business expenses, a nonresident alien may deduct the following nonbusiness expenses:

1. Casualty and theft losses, provided the property was physically located in the United States when damaged or stolen.
2. Charitable contributions made to U.S. charities.
3. One personal exemption.

Additional personal exemptions may be available in certain circumstances for residents of Mexico, Canada, Japan, and the Republic of Korea.

Credits
Certain credits may also be claimed by a nonresident alien if they relate to income that is effectively connected with a U.S. trade or business. One of the most significant credits that is available is the foreign tax credit.

A nonresident alien engaged in business in the United States may claim a foreign tax credit for foreign taxes paid with respect to foreign-source income effectively connected with the U.S. business so long as such taxes are not levied by virtue of the individual's residency or citizenship in a particular country (i.e., the taxes must be levied by a "third" country). In denying the credit when the income is taxed in the nonresident alien's country of residency or citizenship, the United States is asserting its right to tax income connected with U.S. business activities. Since the imposition of tax in both the United States and country of residency or citizenship would result in double taxation, relief from double taxation would have to be granted in the nonresident alien's country of residency or citizenship.

A foreign tax credit is allowed with respect to income taxes paid to countries other than a nonresident alien's country of residency or citizenship. In such circumstances, the United States recognizes the right of the country in which the income is earned to tax the income. To avoid double taxation, the United States allows a foreign tax credit to offset the U.S. tax on the same income. The limitation on the amount of foreign tax credit is computed in accordance with the rules for U.S. citizens and residents (see "Foreign Tax Credit" earlier in this chapter).

Returns, Tax Rates, and Payment of Tax

Nonresident aliens who do not derive any income that is effectively connected with a U.S. trade or business are generally not required to file a U.S. tax return. This is because their non-effectively connected income is subject to withholding tax, and since such taxpayers are not entitled to any deductions or credits, their tax liability is considered satisfied through the withholding mechanism. If the proper amount of withholding tax is not withheld, however, the taxpayer is required to file a return and pay the balance of U.S. tax that is due.

A nonresident alien engaged in a U.S. trade or business must file a return showing all income subject to U.S. tax, including fixed and determinable income that has been subject to withholding tax. The return should segregate trade or business income, which is taxed on a net basis at graduated rates, from fixed and determinable income, which is subject to a flat 30 percent rate of tax (or lower treaty rate). A nonresident alien is not entitled to claim deductions or credits unless a "true and accurate" tax return is filed. If a tax return is not filed on a timely basis, a nonresident alien taxpayer will be subject to U.S. tax on the entire gross income, and no deductions, exemptions, and credits will be allowed. A return that is filed after the normal due dates of April 15 and June 15 discussed later will be considered to be filed on a timely basis for purposes of allowing a claim for deductions, exemptions, and credits if it is filed before the earlier of 16 months from the original due date or the date IRS mails a notice to the taxpayer advising that a return for the year has not been filed and informing the taxpayer that no deductions or credits may be claimed. Thus, it is very important that a return be filed to avoid loss of allowable deductions, exemptions, and credits.

Nonresident aliens with wages subject to withholding must file a Form 1040NR on or before the 15th day of the 4th month following the close of the taxable year. For an individual with a calendar taxable year, the due date would be April 15. In the case of a nonresident alien who does not have wages subject to withholding, the due date of Form 1040NR is the 15th day of the 6th month following the close of the taxable year: June 15 for an individual with a calendar taxable year.

SOURCE OF INCOME

Generally, nonresident aliens are taxed only on their U.S.-source income. The source of income must also be determined by resident aliens in order to compute the amount of foreign tax credit that may be used to offset their U.S. tax liability.

U.S.-Source Income and Exceptions

U.S. tax law sets forth which items of gross income constitute U.S.-source income. However, certain items of income, although originating from the United States, are treated as non-U.S.-source income. The items of gross income that are considered to be from U.S. sources and the exceptions thereto are discussed below.

Interest
In general, U.S.-source income includes interest from obligations of the United States, any territory, any political subdivision of a territory, and the District of Columbia. Also, interest on bonds or other obligations of U.S. residents, corporate or otherwise, is U.S.-source.

U.S.-source income does not include interest from a resident alien individual or domestic corporation if at least 80 percent of the payor's gross income for the three-year period preceding the year of payment is derived from foreign sources and is attributable to the active conduct of a trade or business in one or more foreign jurisdictions or U.S. possessions.

Dividends

Dividends received from a U.S. corporation constitute U.S. source income, with the following exceptions:

1. Dividends received from certain U.S. corporations qualifying as possessions corporations (i.e., a U.S. corporation actively engaged in a trade or business in a U.S. possession that meets certain requirements).
2. Dividends received from a DISC (Domestic International Sales Corporation) or former DISC, to the extent attributable to qualified export receipts.

Dividends received from a foreign corporation constitute foreign-source income if less than 25 percent of the gross income of the foreign corporation is effectively connected with the conduct of a U.S. trade or business during the three-year period preceding the year the dividend was paid. Dividends paid by a foreign corporation deriving 25 percent or more of its gross income from a U.S. trade or business are partially foreign-source income and partially U.S.-source income. The portion of the dividend that is U.S.-source is based on the ratio of the foreign corporation's gross income effectively connected with a U.S. trade or business to total gross income.

Compensation for Personal Services

Compensation for labor or personal services (including pensions or other deferred compensation) attributable to services performed in the United States is treated as U.S.-source. Compensation for services performed in the United States is not considered as U.S.-source if the conditions shown below are applicable:

1. The services are performed by a nonresident alien temporarily present in the United States for a period not exceeding 90 days in a taxable year.
2. The remuneration is not in excess of $3,000.
3. The remuneration is for services performed as an employee of, or under a contract with, one of the following entities:

   a. A nonresident alien, foreign partnership, or foreign corporation that is not engaged in a trade or a business within the United States; or
   b. A foreign branch or office of a U.S. corporation, partnership, citizen, or resident alien.

Rentals and Royalties
Rentals or royalties from property located in the United States, or from any interest in such property, including rents or royalties for the use of patents, copyrights, secret processes, formulas, goodwill, trademarks, and so on in the United States, are considered to be from U.S. sources.

Sale or Exchange of Real Property
Gains, profits, and income from the sale of real property located in the United States are considered to be from U.S. sources. This is true irrespective of whether an individual is a resident or a nonresident alien.

Sale or Exchange of Personal Property
Income from the sale of tangible and intangible personal property will generally be U.S.- or foreign-source based on the seller's country of residence. For purposes of the sourcing rule, residence is based upon the concept of "tax home." A "tax home" is the individual's home for purposes of determining whether or not traveling expenses are allowed when an individual is "away from home."

   Examples of how this special definition for purposes of the sourcing rules may affect aliens are set forth below:

   Nonresident Aliens.   Although an alien may be a nonresident alien because of failure to meet either the substantial presence or permanent residency test, the "tax home" may still be in the United States. Accordingly, gain on the sale or exchange of personal property by such an individual would be U.S.-source income.

   Such U.S.-source gains may not be subject to U.S. tax, however, under a special rule providing for an exemption from U.S. tax if the alien is physically present in the United States for less than 183 days during the tax year (see page 639). This exemption does not apply if the alien has made a special election to be treated as a resident of the United States.

    Resident Aliens. An alien may be considered a U.S. resident but the "tax home" may be located outside of the United States. In this instance, the general sourcing rule, under which gains from the sale of personal property would be foreign-source, is applicable only if such gains are subject to a foreign tax at a rate of at least 10 percent.

Income from Sources Within and Without the United States

Items of income not falling in to one of the above categories are either from sources without the United States or allocable to sources within and without the United States in accordance with regulations prescribed by the U.S. Treasury Department. For instance, if an alien performs services both in the United States and in foreign countries, then a portion of the income is from U.S. sources and a portion is from foreign sources.

Special Rule for Foreign Tax Credit
For purposes of computing the foreign tax credit limitation, foreign-source income includes only the excess of net foreign-source capital gain over net domestic-source capital losses. Therefore, if a taxpayer has foreign-source capital gains of $20,000 and U.S.-source capital losses of $5,000, foreign-source capital gain income, for purposes of computing the foreign tax credit limitation, is $15,000.

CONSIDERATIONS FOR ALIENS ENTERING OR LEAVING THE UNITED STATES

The previous discussion summarized the U.S. taxation of resident aliens and nonresident aliens, generally under the assumption that the alien is either resident or nonresident in the United States for the entire year. Special considerations arise, however, for foreign nationals who become, or cease to be, residents of the United States during a tax year. These individuals are referred to as "dual-status aliens'' because they are both resident and nonresident within a single taxable year and can be subject to U.S. tax under both resident and nonresident rules. The following discussion deals with special considerations for individuals who will be changing their U.S. residency status. A number of tax planning opportunities will be discussed, as will other special rules and filing requirements. Except as noted otherwise, the rules of U.S. taxation discussed earlier in the chapter are equally applicable to dual-status aliens.

Year of Change in Residence

An alien individual who becomes or ceases to be a U.S. resident during a taxable year is subject to U.S. tax as if the year were divided into two periods, one of residence and one of nonresidence. During the residence period, the dual-status alien is subject to tax on worldwide income. During the period the individual is a nonresident, the alien is subject to U.S. tax only with respect to U.S.-source income. In calculating the tax liability for the year, all of the income earned during the period of residence is combined with all of the income effectively connected with a U.S. trade or business that is earned during the period of nonresidence. This total amount is subject to U.S. tax at the graduated rates. Income that is not effectively connected with a U.S. trade or business and is earned during the period of nonresidence is subject to tax at the flat 30 percent rate or lower treaty rate.

Because individuals are taxed on income when received and not when earned, tax planning opportunities arise with regard to certain items of income that would be exempt from U.S. tax if received during the period of nonresidence, but subject to tax if received during the period of residence. A dual-status alien should consider these opportunities to minimize the U.S. tax liability. As with any tax-planning strategy, the adoption of the plan must be carefully structured and, in most cases, a qualified tax adviser should be consulted. The following tax planning opportunites are based on the more detailed discussions earlier in the chapter.

Personal Service Income
The tax treatment of personal service income earned by a dual-status alien will depend upon its source and whether the income is

received during the period of residence or nonresidence, as outlined below:

1. When an alien becomes a resident during the year, foreign-source personal service income (i.e., from services performed outside the United States) is exempt from U.S. tax if received prior to establishing U.S. residency. Payments received after establishing U.S. residency are subject to U.S. tax regardless of when earned.
2. When an alien becomes a nonresident during the year, foreign-source personal service income is exempt from U.S. tax if received after departure from the United States.

An item of income is considered received and is subject to tax when an individual has effective control over the income. This is referred to as the constructive receipt doctrine. For example, a check received by an alien during the period of U.S. residence but cashed during a period when not a U.S. resident, is considered as being constructively received during the residency period and is subject to tax at the graduated rates. Consequently, care must be exercised in using the above tax-planning opportunities to make sure that the tax treatment desired is not changed by the constructive receipt doctrine.

Deferred Personal Service Income
Personal service income that is received by a nonresident alien during a year subsequent to the year in which it was earned will be treated as U.S.-source effectively connected income (i.e., subject to wage withholding, FICA tax, and income taxation at graduated rates) to the extent it would have been so treated if received in the same year in which it was earned.

Sale of Personal Residence
When a dual-status alien sells a principal residence at a gain, whether the residence is in the United States or a foreign country, the timing of the sale is crucial in determining the U.S. tax consequences.

1. If an alien becomes resident during the year, any gain derived from the sale of the foreign principal residence before

establishing U.S. residency is exempt from U.S. tax. If the principal residence is sold at a gain after establishing U.S. residency, the gain is subject to U.S. tax but may be deferred if an amount equal to the net sales proceeds is reinvested in another principal residence. If the sales proceeds are only partially reinvested in a new residence, the gain is taxed to the extent that the proceeds from the sale are not reinvested. When the proceeds from the sale of the original residence are reinvested and the gain is deferred, the basis in the new residence is reduced by the amount of the gain not recognized. Consequently, the gain could be subject to tax at a later time.

2. If an alien becomes a nonresident during the year and sells a U.S. residence while still a U.S. resident, U.S. tax may be permanently avoided on any gain by reinvesting the net sales proceeds in a new foreign principal residence within the statutory reinvestment period.

3. If an alien does not sell the U.S. principal residence until after the individual has terminated U.S. residency, the gain deferral provisions are applicable only if the replacement residence is purchased in a U.S. location. Obviously, it will be difficult for a nonresident to acquire and occupy a principal residence in the United States.

Gains from Sale of Other Property
The tax treatment of gains derived from the sale of property other than real estate by a dual-status alien will depend upon the status of the individual as a resident or nonresident at the time of sale.

1. An alien who becomes or ceases to be a U.S. resident during the year will be subject to U.S. tax only on foreign-source gains that are realized during the period of U.S. residency. Accordingly, where possible, an alien individual should consider selling property which would give rise to foreign-source income prior to arriving in or after departing from the United States.

2. Even in the case of gains that are U.S.-source income, an alien can avoid U.S. tax if the alien is present in the United States for less than 183 days during the year.

3. When a dual-status alien is present in the United States for 183 days or more during the year, U.S.-source taxable gains realized during the period of nonresidency will be taxed at the flat rate of 30 percent (or lower treaty rate). Taxable gains realized during the period of residency will be subject to tax at graduated rates up to 31 percent (28 percent for capital gains). The taxation of nonresident aliens on sales of U.S. real property, except for principal residences as discussed previously, will be subject to U.S. tax as determined under the FIRPTA rules.

Special Rules

Standard Deduction
The standard deduction is not available to a nonresident alien and therefore may not be claimed by a dual-status alien for the period during which the alien is not a resident of the United States. A dual-status taxpayer must itemize deductions for the period not resident in the United States.

Personal Exemptions
Only one personal exemption is allowed a dual-status alien for the period of nonresidence and residence. However, for the period of residence, a dual-status alien may claim additional exemptions for the alien's spouse and other allowable dependents, provided the total amount of exemptions does not exceed the taxpayer's taxable income (before exemptions) for the period and the spouse and other dependents otherwise qualify for the exemptions.

Filing Requirements

Dual-status aliens are subject to special filing requirements. The exact filing requirements that apply will depend on whether the alien is a U.S. resident or nonresident at the close of the taxable year.

Resident at End of Taxable Year
An alien who establishes resident status by the close of the taxable year must file Form 1040, *U.S. Individual Income Tax Return*, to report income and deductions attributable to the period of resi-

dence. In addition, the alien should file Form 1040NR, *U.S. Non-resident Alien Income Tax Return,* as an attachment to Form 1040, to report income and deductions (if any) attributable to the period of nonresidence. This method of filing applies only to the dual-status year. Only Form 1040 would be filed in subsequent years, until the year in which the alien abandons U.S. residency.

It should be noted that these filing requirements do not apply when an election to file a joint return is made (discussed below).

Nonresident at End of Taxable Year
A resident alien who becomes a nonresident alien before the close of the taxable year must file Form 1040NR, *U.S. Nonresident Alien Income Tax Return,* to report income and deductions (if any) attributable to the period of nonresidence. In addition, the alien should file Form 1040, *U.S. Individual Income Tax Return,* as an attachment for Form 1040NR, to report income and deductions for the period of residence.

Joint Return Election
A joint return is generally not permitted if either spouse is a nonresident alien at any time during the taxable year. However, a nonresident alien married to a U.S. citizen or resident or a nonresident alien couple who have established U.S. residency by the close of the taxable year may elect to file a joint return. Such election is made by attaching a statement to the return for the year in which both taxpayers elect to file a joint return. In making the election, both spouses agree to subject their worldwide income for the entire taxable year to U.S. tax.

By electing to file a joint return, the nonresident alien is treated as a resident alien for the entire taxable year. The various restrictions imposed on dual-status aliens do not apply and the benefit of the lower tax rate schedule for married taxpayers may be obtained. Because the worldwide income of both spouses is included in the joint return, the U.S. tax liability could be substantially increased by making the election if a significant portion of the taxpayers' income is derived during the period of nonresidence. The effect of including worldwide income for the entire taxable year in the return could be mitigated by the foreign tax credit if foreign taxes are imposed on the foreign-source income required to be included in the joint return. Accordingly, the alien should determine the U.S. tax liability with and without the joint return election before determining whether or not to make the election. Because certain aspects of the joint return election may affect future years, the decision on making the election should involve more than the impact on the initial U.S. income tax return.

One additional consideration should be noted in connection with a nonresident alien who elects to file a joint return with a resident alien spouse. Once made, the election generally continues in effect for the current taxable year and for future years, provided one spouse remains a resident of the United States. In certain cases, such as when the nonresident alien spouse anticipates the realization of a significant amount of income, it may be desirable to postpone the election until the year after the nonresident alien spouse realizes the income. As a result of deferring the election, the income would not be subject to U.S. tax. Examples of situations in which deferral of the election might be appropriate include the nonresident alien spouse expecting a large distribution from a foreign trust or a large gain on the sale of business or other property.

Other Filing Requirements

If an alien becomes a U.S. resident, a number of other returns may be required to be filed. Other returns may be required if the alien abandons U.S. residency or departs from the United States. These additional filing requirements are briefly described below.

Departing Alien Filing Requirement
Resident and nonresident aliens, with certain exceptions, must obtain a tax compliance certificate before departing from the United States. A tax compliance certificate, also referred to as an exit permit or a sailing permit, is obtained by filing Form 1040C, *Departing Alien Income Tax Return,* or Form 2063, *Departing Alien Income Tax Statement.* To obtain the certificate, the alien must demonstrate that the entire U.S. tax liability has been satisfied, or pay any remaining liability when applying for the certificate. Alternatively, present IRS procedures allow the alien to attach, to an essentially blank Form 1040C, a letter from the alien's U.S. employer guaranteeing payment of any remaining liability of the indi-

vidual. In any event, a final tax return (Form 1040NR) will still have to be filed for the year of departure. Additional tax due, if any, must be paid with that return.

If the IRS determines that an alien intends to depart quickly from the United States in an effort to defeat the collection of the U.S. income tax, the alien can be immediately assessed for the amount of tax that is calculated to be due for the current and/or immediately preceding year. In such a case, the tax liability for such periods becomes payable immediately even though the due date for filing the return(s) has not yet arrived.

Information Returns

U.S. citizens and resident aliens are required to file certain forms to report foreign bank or financial accounts, acquisition of stock in a foreign (non-U.S.) corporation, and ownership of stock in certain foreign corporations. Since these forms are for information purposes only, no tax is payable upon filing. However, failure to file may result in the imposition of a fine or penalty. Aliens establishing U.S. residency must be aware of these forms and file them where appropriate. A brief description of these forms is set forth below.

Form TD F 90-22.1. A U.S. citizen or resident having signature authority over, or a financial interest in, a foreign (non-U.S.) bank account or financial account during a calendar year must file an annual Form TD F 90-22.1, on or before June 30 of the succeeding year. If the balance in the account did not exceed $10,000 at any time during the year, the requirement to file the form is waived. The form is filed separately from the income tax return.

Form 5471. A U.S. citizen or resident falling into one of the following categories must file Form 5471 with the U.S. tax return for each year, disclosing required information regarding the individual's association and transactions with a foreign corporation:

1. Officer, director, or 10 percent or more shareholder in a foreign personal holding company.
2. Officer or director of a foreign corporation in which a U.S. person acquires a 5 percent or more ownership interest or acquires an additional 5 percent or more ownership interest.

3. Shareholder in a foreign corporation who
   a. Acquires a cumulative 5 percent or more ownership interest, or acquires an additional 5 percent or more ownership interest, in a foreign corporation;
   b. Owns 5 percent or more of the value of the stock of a foreign corporation when it is reorganized; or
   c. Disposes of sufficient stock to reduce ownership interest in a foreign corporation to less than 5 percent.
4. A U.S. person who had control of a foreign corporation for an uninterrupted period of at least 30 days during the annual accounting period of the foreign corporation.
5. A U.S. person who was a 10 percent or more shareholder in a foreign corporation that was a controlled foreign corporation for an uninterrupted period of at least 30 days during the annual accounting period of the foreign corporation, and who owned stock in the controlled foreign corporation on the last day of the annual accounting period of the foreign corporation.

ALIENS ON TEMPORARY ASSIGNMENTS IN THE UNITED STATES

Multinational corporations frequently send foreign executives to the United States on temporary assignments. The length of these assignments can vary from relatively short one- or two-month assignments to assignments that may last as long as two or three years.

The U.S. taxation of foreign executives temporarily assigned to the United States depends upon whether the executive is resident or nonresident in the United States. The factors for determining residence presented earlier in this chapter are applicable in making this determination.

When a foreign executive is on temporary assignment in the United States, the executive may be able to deduct the temporary living expenses (e.g., meals, lodging, transportation, etc.) incurred during the temporary assignment in determining the amount subject to tax in the United States. The deduction for these expenses is available only if the alien is considered to be away from his or her tax home.

Deductibility of "Away from Home" Expenses

Because "away from home" expenses are often a significant deduction in arriving at taxable income, most aliens find it beneficial to qualify for the deduction. To qualify, the following requirements must be satisfied:

1. The expense must be ordinary and necessary.
2. The expense must be incurred in the pursuit of business.
3. The expense must be incurred while "away from home."

It should be noted that these requirements must also be met by U.S. citizens or residents who want to deduct temporary living expenses while "away from home."

Reasonable and Necessary
An expense is "reasonable" if it is not lavish or extravagant under the circumstances, and "necessary" if required by reason of the taxpayer's business. In this regard, personal expenses are not considered necessary "in the pursuit of business" and are therefore nondeductible. Where a taxpayer is accompanied by his or her family, only the expenses attributable to the taxpayer are deductible. Where an expense item is not separately attributable to the taxpayer, an allocation between taxpayer and family must be made.

Pursuit of Business
For an expense to be incurred in pursuit of business, an employee's travel status must be for reasons of employment. Accordingly, expenses incurred by an employee for other reasons (e.g., vacation while on temporary assignment) would not be deductible.

Away from Home
An alien taxpayer may deduct temporary living expenses if "away from home." An alien taxpayer is considered to be "away from home" only if the tax home continues to be in the home country, and the individual is on a short, temporary assignment in the United States.

A 1983 IRS ruling limits the deductibility of travel expenses while on temporary assignment. The ruling states that when the intended or actual length of assignment is two years or more, the assignment will not be considered temporary under any circumstances, and, consequently, temporary living expenses are not deductible. When the originally intended and actual length of assignment is one year or more, but less than two years, "away from home" expenses may be claimed if the individual intends to return to the tax home and is able to meet at least two of the following three tests:

1. The home country abode was used before departing for the assignment, and work contacts have been maintained in the home country.
2. Duplicate living expenses are being incurred in the home country.
3. Family members reside at the home country abode, or the abode is used by the individual for lodging on a frequent basis.

An assignment that was originally intended to be less than two years, but is extended beyond two years probably will not be considered a temporary assignment beyond the date on which the individual is aware of the extension. If an alien's assignment is for less than one year, "away from home" expenses can usually be deducted, depending on individual facts and circumstances.

Deductible Expenses

Representative of expenses that are ordinarily deductible if incurred during a temporary assignment are meals, lodging, utilities, telephone, laundry, and transportation. Of course, other expenses may also be deductible depending on the facts and circumstances.

Again, it must be emphasized that these expenses are deductible only to the extent they are attributable to the taxpayer and not the taxpayer's family. In addition, no deduction will be allowed unless the expense is adequately substantiated. With respect to meals, the IRS has indicated that in cases where substantiation for actual costs is not provided, they will allow a deduction of $26 per day. (In high-cost localities the rate is $34 per day.) For expenses other than meal expenses, receipts should be retained and a log or diary maintained to establish the amount, time, place, and business purpose of each expense. In the case of an employee on a temporary assignment, the temporary assignment is the business purpose for the expense.

Special Rule for J-1 Visas

A well-established principle of U.S. tax law disallows, as a deduction, expenses that would otherwise be deductible, if such expenses are related or allocable to exempt or excluded income. If a foreign executive enters the United States on a J-1 visa, personal service income paid by the foreign employer is specifically exempt from U.S. tax. It is the position of the IRS that in such a case, the foreign executive must allocate a portion of any "away from home" expenses to the exempt income, reducing the deductible amount of such expenses. The allocation is made by multiplying the "away from home" expenses by a fraction, the numerator of which is the exempt personal service income paid by the foreign employer, and the denominator of which is the total personal service income paid by the foreign employer and the U.S. affiliate (including expense reimbursements).

As discussed throughout this chapter, the manner in which an alien is taxed in the United States depends on a wide range of factors including residency, trade or business connections, and treaty considerations, among others. As the number of foreign nationals who live and work in the United States increases, it becomes more important to understand the complex U.S. tax provisions affecting aliens, as well as the interaction between U.S. and foreign tax rules.

APPENDIX I
TAX TREATIES, AS OF JANUARY 1, 1991

Income Tax Treaties

Aruba[1]	Jamaica
Australia	Japan
Austria	Korea, Republic of
Barbados	Luxembourg
Belgium	Malta
Bermuda	Morocco
Canada	Netherlands
China, People's Republic of	Netherlands Antilles[2]

Cyprus
Denmark
Egypt
Finland
France
Germany
Greece
Hungary
Iceland
India
Indonesia
Ireland, Republic of
Italy

New Zealand
Norway
Pakistan
Philippines
Poland
Romania
Spain
Sweden
Switzerland
Trinidad and Tobago
Tunisia
U.S.S.R.
United Kingdom

Estate Tax Treaties

Australia
Austria
Denmark
Finland
France
Germany
Greece
Ireland, Republic of

Italy
Japan
Netherlands
Norway
South Africa
Sweden
Switzerland
United Kingdom

Gift Tax Treaties

Australia
Austria
Denmark
France

Germany
Japan
Sweden
United Kingdom

Social Security Totalization Agreements

Austria
Belgium
Canada
France
Germany
Italy
Netherlands

Norway
Portugal
Spain
Sweden
Switzerland
United Kingdom

NOTES

1. Aruba was covered by the United States-Netherlands treaty, as extended to the Netherlands Antilles. Since that treaty has been terminated, as discussed in n.6 below, the current United States-Aruba treaty also terminated effective January 1, 1988, except for Article VIII and certain ancillary provisions.
2. On June 29, 1987, the United States notified the Netherlands Antilles of its intent to terminate the United States-Netherlands treaty, as extended to the Netherlands Antilles, effective January 1, 1988. A note delivered July 10, 1987, modified the termination to exclude Article VIII (which generally affords a U.S. tax exemption for interest paid from domestic sources to a Netherlands Antilles resident) and certain ancillary provisions.
3. Agreements with Finland and Luxembourg are expected to be implemented in 1992. An agreement with Ireland is expected to be signed in 1992 and implemented in 1993.

APPENDIX II
INDIVIDUAL INCOME TAX RATE SCHEDULES, CALENDAR YEAR 1992

Married Individuals Filing Joint Returns and Surviving Spouses

If Taxable Income Is:	*The Tax Is:*
Not over $35,800	15% of the taxable income.
Over $35,800, but not over $86,500	$5,370 plus 28% of the excess over $35,800.
Over $86,500	$19,566 plus 31% of the excess over $86,500.

Heads of Household

If Taxable Income is:	*The Tax Is:*
Not over $28,750	15% of the taxable income.
Over $28,750, but not over $74,150	$4,312.50 plus 28% of the excess over $28,750.
Over $74,150	$17,024.50 plus 31% of the excess over $74,150.

Unmarried Individuals

If Taxable Income Is:	*The Tax Is:*
Not over $21,450	15% of the taxable income.
Over $21,450, but not over $51,900	$3,217.50 plus 28% of the excess over $21,450.
Over $51,900	$11,743.50 plus 31% of the excess over $51,900.

Married Individuals Filing Separate Returns

If Taxable Income Is:	*The Tax Is:*
Not over $17,900	15% of the taxable income.
Over $17,900, but not over $43,250	$2,685 plus 28% of the excess over $17,900.
Over $43,250	$9,783 plus 31% of the excess over $43,250.

CHAPTER 21

FINANCIAL REPORTING IN THE UNITED STATES

R. Lawrence Soares
Partner
Gail T. Rold
International Business Specialist
Price Waterhouse

The process by which accounting standards and practices are established in the United States is complex and time-consuming. By law, the standard-setting authority rests with the Securities and Exchange Commission (SEC). In practice, however, the responsibility for establishing accounting standards, interpretations, and definitions has been delegated to boards and committees composed of accounting experts in the private sector. Accounting policies are continuously evolving as existing pronouncements are adapted to satisfy new needs for information in ever-changing investment and business environments. This chapter provides background regarding the process of establishing accounting standards in the United States and explores the fundamental financial reporting and auditing requirements applicable to both public and private enterprises.

ESTABLISHMENT OF FINANCIAL REPORTING STANDARDS IN THE UNITED STATES

When the U.S. Congress passed the Securities Act of 1933 and the Securities Exchange Act of 1934, the SEC was born. The SEC is an independent, quasi-judicial governmental agency. It is responsible for the administration and enforcement of the several laws that govern the process by which companies raise capital through the issuance of securities to the public and that regulate the markets for securities after their initial issuance.

The SEC is administered from its Washington, D.C., headquarters and has regional and branch offices throughout the United States. SEC staff includes accountants, engineers, examiners, lawyers, and security analysts. There are four operating divisions through which the SEC administers its regulatory responsibilities:

Division of Corporation Finance.

Division of Market Regulation.

Division of Investment Management.

Division of Enforcement.

The Division of Corporation Finance has the primary responsibility for administering the registration and reporting requirements of the securities laws. The division interacts with registrants seeking to comply with the requirements of the SEC by means of (1) prefiling conferences with management, attorneys, and/or accountants; (2) issuance of no-action letters, and (3) issuance of letters of comment (deficiency letters) on registration statements and other documents filed with the SEC.

As the highest-ranking accounting officer of the Commission, the Chief Accountant is ultimately responsible to the Commission for all accounting and auditing matters arising under the Securities Acts administered by the Commission. In this powerful role, the Office of the Chief Accountant:

- Advises the Commission on accounting issues, where new policies are under consideration or existing policies are being administered, and supervises the preparation of SEC pronouncements on those issues.
- Establishes standards of accounting for highly regulated entities such as stock exchanges, broker/dealers, and investment advisers.
- Establishes precedents in accounting matters based on matters referred by the Division of Corporation Finance and advises registrants on accounting-related issues that arise during the securities registration process.

- Supervises investigations where accounting or auditing practices are in question and works closely with the Division of Enforcement on criminal, civil, and administrative actions involving financial reporting and auditing issues.

Although it has the sole statutory authority to establish financial accounting standards for publicly owned companies in the United States, the SEC has delegated much of its responsibility for the establishment and interpretation of generally accepted accounting principles to other privately funded organizations. Because no single reference source exists to define generally accepted accounting principles, the SEC's staff has stated that it will accept accounting methods that have substantial authoritative support in the literature issued by those organizations. There are no statutory reporting or statutory audit requirements for companies whose shares are not publicly held. Financial institutions that provide funds to nonpublic companies, however, often require audited financial statements that must be prepared in accordance with generally accepted accounting principles. The bodies whose literature provides the substantial authoritative support recognized by the SEC also have the power and responsibility to define generally accepted accounting principles to be followed by closely held, nonpublic companies.

The American Institute of Certified Public Accountants (AICPA) has played a vital role in establishing financial accounting standards in the United States. The AICPA, the national professional organization of practicing Certified Public Accountants (CPAs), initially established the Accounting Research Committee and the Accounting Principles Board, both of which issued official pronouncements, called Accounting Research Bulletins and APB Opinions. These organizations, whose membership consisted largely of practicing professional accountants, endeavored to define appropriate accounting practices and narrow areas of difference in the application of accounting principles.

In 1973, under pressure to avoid governmental intervention, the AICPA dissolved the APB and replaced it with a new structure composed of the Financial Accounting Foundation (FAF), the Financial Accounting Standards Board (FASB), and the Financial Accounting Standards Advisory Council (FASAC). The FAF selects the members of the FASB and its Advisory Council, provides funding for their activities and generally administers and oversees the activities conducted by the FASB. The FASB has been effective in its role as the primary financial accounting standards-setting body in the United States largely because of its composition. The Board consists of seven full-time members who hold no other private positions with firms, companies, or institutions. Their substantial backgrounds in business, moreover, are not necessarily limited to financial accounting and reporting. Since its formation, the FASB has issued 106 Statements of Financial Accounting Standards and numerous interpretations of those statements.

At the present time, the sources of substantial authoritative support are

- Accounting principles promulgated by bodies designated by the AICPA to establish those principles. Originally this was the Accounting Research Committee followed by the APB, which was subsequently replaced by the FASB. Pronouncements issued by these bodies consist of FASB Statements and Interpretations, APB Opinions, and AICPA Accounting Research Bulletins.
- Pronouncements of AICPA and FASB committees composed of expert accountants. These committees follow due process procedures, including broad distribution of their proposals for public comment, for the intended purposes of recommending changes to accounting principles or describing existing practices that are generally accepted. This literature includes AICPA Industry Audit Guides that contain recommendations as to the most appropriate accounting principles and practices to be followed by companies in a particular industry, as well as FASB Technical Bulletins and AICPA Statements of Position (SOPs). SOPs are issued by the Accounting Standards Executive Committee (AcSEC), a body designated by the AICPA as the senior technical committee with authority to represent the AICPA on financial accounting and reporting issues.
- Practices or pronouncements widely recognized as being generally accepted because they represent prevalent practice in a particular industry, generally as set forth in AICPA Accounting Interpretations.

- Other accounting literature, which includes minutes of the FASB's Emerging Issues Task Force (EITF), APB Statements, FASB Concept Statements, and AICPA Issues Papers.

The EITF, formed in 1984 as an advisory group, assists the FASB in identifying implementation and emerging issues on a timely basis that might require action by the FASB. Members of the EITF include representatives of the public accounting profession and of industry. In addition, the Chief Accountant of the SEC or a representative participates in EITF meetings. Although the EITF is a discussion group and not a standard-setting body, through its deliberations and the public comments received at its open meetings, the FASB determines the courses of action to pursue. Where there is a divergence of views on a given issue, the FASB may take further action. If a consensus of EITF members is reached, the issue is generally considered to have been resolved and there is no need for additional formal guidance from the FASB.

DISCLOSURE AND REPORTING GUIDELINES
FOR FOREIGN ISSUERS

According to the guidelines set forth in the Securities Acts of 1933 and 1934, a public offering of securities in the United States requires the filing of a detailed and comprehensive registration statement with the SEC by the issuer prior to the commencement of the offering. The SEC has tried to ensure that foreign issuers supply information equivalent to the information provided by U.S. companies, a difficult task given the differences in national laws, accounting principles, and business customs.

In an effort to balance their responsibilities to protect investors by insisting on full disclosure with the need to maintain an open environment in which foreign investors may participate, the SEC has reduced its reporting and disclosure requirements for foreign issuers under the Securities Exchange Act of 1934, the act that controls the post-distribution trading of securities on national securities exchanges and in the over-the-counter market. The disclosure requirements under the 1933 act, which governs the initial sale and distribution of publicly offered securities, are virtually the same for U.S. and foreign issuers, although different forms are filed.

A foreign company that wishes to offer its securities in the United States should take a number of preliminary steps. Management should consider the feasibility of making such an offering and develop a strategy to deal with the various legal, regulatory, accounting, and marketing issues to be considered in making a public offering. Other preliminary actions that may be necessary include structural corporate changes, such as a reorganization or recapitalization. For example, it may be necessary to amend the charter documents of the corporation to permit the issuance of additional ordinary shares or registered share certificates. It may also be necessary to choose a transfer agent and registrar to be responsible for the transfer of shares in the United States.

The SEC has an integrated disclosure system in that requirements for general disclosures about the issuer are the same for documents that must be filed under both the 1933 and 1934 Acts. There are four forms for registration of securities of foreign issuers under the 1933 act—F-1, F-2, F-3, and F-4, that specify disclosure and reporting requirements. The determination of the appropriate form to be filed is based on the legal structure of the foreign issuer and the securities being offered.

The 1933 act registration statement consists of two parts. Part I is the information included in the prospectus, which is the selling document provided to prospective investors. The prospectus contains information about the offering, including the type and amount of securities being offered and the expected use of the proceeds; information about the issuer, including a description of its business and properties; and a discussion and analysis of its financial condition and results of operations for the company for each period for which financial statements are required to be filed. Audited financial statements are to be included in the prospectus, including a balance sheet as of the end of the two most recent fiscal years and statements of operations and cash flows for each of the three most recent fiscal years. These statements must be audited by an independent auditor in accordance with generally accepted U.S. auditing standards; however, foreign issuers may present their financial statements in accordance with foreign accounting principles, provided they quantify and reconcile material differences from generally accepted U.S. accounting principles.

Part II of the registration statement requires other technical information, such as supplemental financial schedules and exhibits that must be filed with the SEC. These schedules and exhibits include expenses associated with the offering as well as detailed support for selected caption balances in the audited financial statements. The form and content of the supplemental schedules to be presented are set forth in SEC Regulation S-X.

If, upon completion of the public offering, the issuer intends to list its securities on a U.S. securities exchange or to have them traded over the counter and quoted on the NASDAQ system, or if the issuer's securities are held of record by more than 300 persons resident in the United States, then the issuer is also registered under and subject to the 1934 Act.

Registration under the 1934 Act is accomplished by filing Form 20-F. The information required by Form 20-F is generally the same as the information included in the 1933 Act registration statement, with only minor modifications. Unlike other SEC forms, Form 20-F is both a registration and annual report form. The instructions to the form identify those items that must be answered if used as an initial 1934 Act registration statement (Parts I, II, and IV) and those that must be answered if filed as an annual report (Parts I, III, and IV). Annual reports on Form 20-F are to be filed within six months after the fiscal year end.

Foreign companies are not subject to SEC proxy rules and are not required to file quarterly financial statements as are domestic U.S. companies. Instead, foreign registrants may be required to furnish periodically Form 6-K reports to the SEC when circumstances warrant. Form 6-K contains significant information that the issuer is required to make public in its country of domicile pursuant to foreign law, or that has been publicly filed with a foreign stock exchange or distributed to its securities holders.

INTERNATIONAL ACCOUNTING AND REPORTING STANDARDS

The International Accounting Standards Committee (IASC) was established in 1973 by agreement among professional accounting bodies of its nine founding nations. As a private-sector body founded to promulgate international accounting standards, IASC now has a supporting membership of nearly 100 professional accounting organizations from more than 70 countries. Interest in and support of IASC activities is growing as more and more enterprises seek access to broader capital markets to maintain their competetiveness in an environment of rapid globalization.

A board made up of representatives of up to 13 countries and up to 4 organizations from each country having an interest in financial reporting conducts the business of the IASC. Its efforts are supported by the Council of the International Federation of Accountants (IFAC), formed in 1977 with the broader objectives of developing and harmonizing accounting standards worldwide.

Many Statements of International Accounting Standards previously issued by IASC will be affected when IASC's current proposals to harmonize accounting standards are finally adopted. These proposals are intended to establish preferred accounting principles and will probably require disclosure of a reconciliation to these principles where other accounting alternatives are permitted. An important first step has been taken by establishing and obtaining worldwide support for the IASC. However, the issue of fixing responsibility for interpreting the standards and assisting in their implementation has not yet been addressed. Considering the existing variety of interpretations from different countries and accounting professionals, this is the critical next step.

The AICPA has agreed to support IASC standards and, as stated in paragraph 4 of the Preface to Statements of International Accounting Standards, use its best endeavors "to ensure that published financial statements comply with these standards or that there is disclosure of the extent to which they do not." Currently, however, responsibility for setting accounting standards in the United States rests primarily with the FASB, and no binding reporting, accounting, or disclosure requirement of any kind arises directly in the United States from IASC pronouncements.

RESPONSIBILITIES IN THE UNITED STATES OF MANAGEMENT, AUDIT COMMITTEES, AND THE INDEPENDENT AUDITOR

Among the numerous business and accounting professionals involved in the financial reporting process in the United States are corporate management, members of boards of directors and audit committees, and independent auditors, each of whom plays a unique and vital role in administering and reporting the financial results of a business enterprise.

Management

Management of a company is accountable to the board of directors, which ultimately reports to the company's owners. Among its other duties, management is responsible for accumulating and recording financial information that constitutes the financial statements. Recently, the AICPA focused on clarifying management's responsibilities compared with those of the independent auditor. As stated in the AICPA's Professional Standards:

> The financial statements are management's responsibility. The auditor's responsibility is to express an opinion on the financial statements. Management is responsible for adopting sound accounting policies and for establishing and maintaining an internal control structure that will, among other things, record, process, summarize, and report financial data that is consistent with management's assertions embodied in the financial statements. The internal control structure should include an accounting system to identify, assemble, analyze, classify, record, and report an entity's transactions and to maintain accountability for the related assets and liabilities. The entity's transactions and the related assets and liabilities are within the direct knowledge and control of management. The auditor's knowledge of these matters is limited to that acquired through the audit. Thus, the fair presentation of financial position, results of operations, and cash flows in conformity with generally accepted accounting principles is an implicit and integral part of management's responsibility. The independent auditor may make suggestions about the form or content of the financial statements or draft them, in whole or in part, based on information from management's accounting system. However, the auditor's responsibility for the financial statements he has audited is confined to the expression of his opinion on them.

Audit Committees of Boards of Directors

The board of directors of a company is generally responsible for ensuring that management's actions and decisions are in the best interests of the company. These responsibilities typically include establishing basic objectives and broad policies of the company, electing members of management and monitoring their performance, approving important management decisions and authorizing management to execute them, and ascertaining that proper annual and interim reports are furnished to shareholders and applicable regulatory agencies.

Audit committees have been established by substantially all boards of public companies and many nonprofit organizations. The responsibilities and duties assigned to the audit committee are determined by the board of directors; there are no statutory requirements. In the broadest sense, the two primary responsibilities usually assigned to an audit committee are:

- Assisting the board of directors in fulfilling its responsibilities as they relate to the company's accounting policies and controls, financial reporting practices, and business ethics policies.
- Maintaining, by way of regularly scheduled meetings, lines of communication among the directors and financial management, the internal auditors, and the company's independent auditors.

Audit committees are often asked to recommend the appointment of independent auditors. Current practice of many companies assigns responsibility for the selection of independent auditors to the board, with subsequent approval by a majority of the shareholders. Because of its day-to-day dealings with the independent auditors, management is typically in the best position to evaluate the quality of services provided, and the views of management are usually carefully considered when the appointment of independent auditors is being reviewed by the board.

The Independent Auditor

The AICPA, through its Auditing Standards Division, develops and administers the standards that govern the role and conduct of the independent auditor.

According to the AICPA's Professional Standards:

The objective of the ordinary audit of financial statements by the independent auditor is the expression of an opinion on the fairness with which they present fairly, in all material respects, financial position, results of operations, and its cash flows in conformity with generally accepted accounting principles. The auditor's report is the medium through which he expresses his opinion or, if circumstances require, disclaims an opinion. In either case, he states whether his audit has been made in accordance with generally accepted auditing standards. These standards require him to state whether, in his opinion, the financial statements are presented in conformity with generally accepted accounting principles and to identify those circumstances in which such principles have not been consistently observed in the preparation of the financial statements of the current period in relation to those of the preceding period.

All publicly held companies are required by the SEC to file annually audited financial statements accompanied by a report of the independent auditor. For nonpublic companies, there are no similar statutory requirements and an audit may not necessarily be the most appropriate level of service provided by the independent auditor. Alternatives, such as a review or compilation of the financial statements, may be more appropriate based on the individual needs of a company.

Review engagements are more limited than audits in the scope and depth of testing procedures. A review does not include a study and evaluation of internal control, tests of accounting records, independent confirmation, or physical examination. Rather, review procedures focus on obtaining knowledge of the accounting principles and practices of the client and its industry, and information regarding the nature of the client's business transactions, accounting records, and employees. The independent accountant inquires of management as to actions taken at board of directors and stockholder meetings, as well as procedures employed for recording, classifying, and disclosing transactions in the financial statements and obtains from management written representations that the financial statements have been prepared in conformity with generally accepted accounting principles. Additionally, analytical review procedures are performed by the independent accountant to identify relationships and individual items that appear to be unusual.

If the owners of a business are very active in the day-to-day management of an enterprise and have first-hand knowledge and direct control over the business, they may not require an audit but may desire some degree of assurance on the financial statements. Typically, these enterprises do not need financial statements for third parties or, where third parties are involved, they find review reports acceptable. The review report issued by the independent accountant expresses no opinion as to the fair presentation of the financial statements. It does, however, provide limited assurance that the independent accountant is not aware of any material modifications that should be made to the financial statements in order for them to be in conformity with generally accepted accounting principles.

Compilations of financial statements are performed primarily for individuals with minimal or no third party financing requirements. The accountant performing a compilation provides no assurance as to the fair presentation of financial information that has been provided by management, since testing procedures are not normally undertaken. Under normal circumstances, compilation engagements are advantageous only when performed as an adjunct to other professional services such as tax return preparation.

The higher level of assurance associated with an audit benefits most businesses through the evaluation of the internal control structure and the issuance of recommendations to improve controls or operating efficiencies. When financial statements are expected to be used in the foreseeable future to obtain debt or equity funds or where a fiduciary responsibility exists, an audit performed in conformity with generally accepted auditing standards (GAAS) is advisable.

THE NATURE OF THE AUDIT

The independent auditor's report states that an audit is planned and performed to obtain reasonable assurance about whether the financial statements are free of material misstatement. The audit includes examining, on a test basis, evidence that supports the amounts and disclosures in the financial statements, assessing the accounting principles used and significant estimates made by management, and evaluating the overall financial statement presentation.

The quality of the performance of these procedures is prescribed by generally accepted auditing standards adopted by the AICPA. These standards are categorized into three groups: general standards, standards of field work, and standards of reporting.

General Standards

- The audit is to be performed by a person or persons having adequate technical training and proficiency as an auditor.
- In all matters relating to the assignment, an independence in mental attitude is to be maintained by the auditor or auditors.
- Due professional care is to be exercised in the performance of the audit and the preparation of the report.

Standards of Field Work

- The work is to be adequately planned and assistants, if any, are to be properly supervised.
- A sufficient understanding of the internal control structure is to be obtained to plan the audit and to determine the nature, timing, and extent of tests to be performed.
- Sufficient competent evidential matter is to be obtained through inspection, observation, inquiries, and confirmations to afford a reasonable basis for an opinion regarding the financial statements under audit.

Standards of Reporting

- The report shall state whether the financial statements are presented in accordance with generally accepted accounting principles.
- The report shall identify those circumstances in which such principles have not been consistently observed in the current period in relation to the preceding period.
- Informative disclosures in the financial statements are to be regarded as reasonably adequate unless otherwise stated in the report.
- The report shall either contain an expression of opinion re-

garding the financial statements, taken as a whole, or an assertion to the effect that an opinion cannot be expressed. When an overall opinion cannot be expressed, the reasons therefore shall be stated. In all cases where an auditor's name is associated with financial statements, the report should contain a clear-cut indication of the character of the auditor's work, if any, and the degree of responsibility the auditor is taking.

Independence

Generally accepted auditing standards are highly interrelated; however, one standard—that concerning independence—serves as a fundamental underpinning of the accounting profession in the United States. Independence has traditionally been defined by the profession as the ability to act with integrity and to maintain an impartial attitude on all matters that come under review. Independence makes it possible for persons with diverse interests in the financial statements of an enterprise to rely on the opinion of the independent auditor. According to the AICPA Statements on Auditing Standards, "Independence does not imply the attitude of a prosecutor, but rather a judicial impartiality that recognizes an obligation for fairness not only to management and owners of a business but also to creditors and those who may otherwise rely upon the independent auditor's report."

The types of relationships or situations that may impair independence or the appearance of independence include financial interests in clients, certain business relationships, family or personal relationships, and occupations with conflicting interests as well as such other situations as contingent or past due fees and litigation involving clients and the independent auditor.

Materiality

Another concept that underlies both the reports issued by the independent auditor and the nature, timing, and extent of procedures performed in an audit is materiality. While materiality is difficult to define because of the complex interaction of various factors such as audit risk and the size and complexity of the business, financial statements are generally considered to be materially misstated when they contain misstatements whose effect, individually or in the aggregate, is important enough to change or influence the judgment of a reasonable user of the financial statements. Misstatements that cause the communication of unreliable information to the users of financial statements can result from misapplications of accounting principles, departures from fact, or omissions of necessary information.

The concept of materiality also recognizes that some matters are important for the fair presentation of financial statements in conformity with generally accepted accounting principles, while other matters are not important. As discussed in AICPA Statements on Auditing Standards, "The auditor's consideration of materiality is a matter of professional judgment and is influenced by his perception of the needs of a reasonable person who will rely on the financial statements."

The decision as to whether material misstatements exist necessarily involves both quantitative and qualitative considerations. If it is probable that the judgment of a reasonable person relying on the information would be changed or influenced by the omission or misstatement in light of surrounding circumstances, then the omission or misstatement is generally considered to be material. The primary objective of the independent auditor, therefore, is to obtain reasonable assurance that the financial statements are free of material misstatement. As outlined below, there are various conclusions that can be reached, and independent auditors can issue differing opinions based on the nature of the circumstances.

THE AUDITOR'S REPORT

The four types of reports generally issued by an independent auditor based on the results of an audit are:

- An unqualified opinion.
- A qualified opinion.
- An adverse opinion.
- A disclaimer of opinion.

There are numerous variations of each depending upon, for example, the time period covered by the audit and special circumstances that might require explanatory paragraphs.

In general, an unqualified opinion is issued when an auditor has accumulated sufficient evidence to support his or her opinion that the financial statements are fairly presented in conformity with generally accepted accounting principles. An example of the standard unqualified opinion is as follows:

Report of Independent Auditors

To the Board of Directors and
Shareholders of X Company

We have audited the accompanying consolidated balance sheet(s) of X Company and its subsidiaries as of December 31 19X2 and 19X1, and the related consolidated statements of income and retained earnings and of cash flows for each of the three years in the period ended December 31, 19X2. These financial statements are the responsibility of the Company's management. Our responsibility is to express an opinion on these financial statements based on our audits.

We conducted our audits in accordance with generally accepted auditing standards. Those standards require that we plan and perform the audit to obtain reasonable assurance about whether the financial statements are free of material misstatement. An audit includes examining, on a test basis, evidence supporting the amounts and disclosures in the financial statements. An audit also includes assessing the accounting principles used and significant estimates made by management, as well as evaluating the overall financial statement presentation. We believe that our audits provide a reasonable basis for our opinion.

In our opinion, the consolidated financial statements audited by us present fairly, in all material respects, the financial position of X Company and its subsidiaries at December 31, 19X2 and 19X1, and the results of their operations and their cash flows for each of the three years in the period ended December 31, 19X2, in conformity with generally accepted accounting principles.

Guidance issued by the AICPA allows the independent auditor to express an unqualified opinion on financial statements but requires the report to include an additional explanatory paragraph for material uncertainties or for a lack of consistency in the application of generally accepted accounting principles. There remain, however, other circumstances wherein the independent auditor may not be able to attest to the fair presentation of financial statements, in which case a qualified or adverse opinion would be required.

Qualified Opinions

A qualified opinion is issued when:

- There is a lack of sufficient competent evidential matter or there are restrictions on the scope of the audit that have led the auditor to conclude that he or she cannot express an unqualified opinion and that he or she does not need to disclaim an opinion.
- The auditor believes, on the basis of the audit, that the financial statements contain a departure(s) from generally accepted accounting principles, the effect of which is material, and the auditor has concluded not to express an adverse opinion.

When the auditor expresses a qualified opinion, all of the substantive reasons for the qualification must be disclosed in the report.

Audit scope limitations resulting in the omission of significant auditing procedures believed necessary by the independent auditor can result in a qualified opinion or disclaimer of opinion. The decision to qualify or disclaim depends on the independent auditor's assessment of the importance of the omitted procedure(s) to the auditor's ability to form an opinion on the financial statements taken as a whole.

Adverse Opinions

An adverse opinion on the financial statements taken as a whole may be expressed only when the independent auditor has completed the examination in accordance with generally accepted auditing standards, and has concluded that the financial statements do not present fairly the financial position or results of operations or cash flows in conformity with generally accepted accounting principles. This is a situation in which, typically, disputes concerning the proper accounting treatment for certain transactions are not resolved between management and the independent auditor.

Disclaimers of Opinion

A disclaimer of opinion generally results from scope limitations of which the effects cannot be readily identified or quantified and, in exceptional circumstances, from the existence of material uncertainties. The auditor is required to state in a separate explanatory paragraph of the report all of the reasons for the disclaimer. Disclaimers of opinion are also issued in connection with an independent auditor's performance of review and compilation engagements and for special reports or agreed-upon procedures that do not constitute an audit.

FINANCIAL STATEMENTS IN THE UNITED STATES

Financial statements generally issued in the United States by commercial enterprises are the balance sheet, the statement of operations (income or loss), the statement of changes in shareholders' equity (or a statement of changes in retained earnings, often combined with the statement of operations), and the statement of cash flows. Financial statement footnotes are considered an integral part of the statements. Additional requirements exist for SEC registered companies, which must present a comparative balance sheet, three years of results of operations and cash flows, earnings per share data, and additional supporting schedules to specified financial statement components. Generalized examples of basic statements for a publicly held company are presented in Exhibits 21–1 through 21–4.

Balance Sheet (Exhibit 21–1). The balance sheet of nonfinancial enterprises is usually classified—that is, presents assets and liabilities expected to be realized or liquidated within one year as current assets and liabilities and all others as long term. The account form of the balance sheet is also commonly used. Assets are listed together in the order of liquidity. Liabilities and stockholders' equity are shown together, and the sum of liabilities and stockholders' equity equals total assets.

EXHIBIT 21–1
ABC Company
Consolidated Balance Sheet

Assets	Year Ended December 31, 19___	19___
Current assets:		
Cash and cash equivalents	$xxx,xxx	$xxx,xxx
Marketable equity securities	xxx,xxx	xxx,xxx
Accounts receivable, net	xxx,xxx	xxx,xxx
Inventories	xxx,xxx	xxx,xxx
Prepaid expenses	xxx,xxx	xxx,xxx
Total current assets	xxx,xxx	xxx,xxx
Property, plant, and equipment:		
Land	xxx,xxx	xxx,xxx
Buildings	xxx,xxx	xxx,xxx
Machinery, equipment, and furniture and fixtures	xxx,xxx	xxx,xxx
	xxx,xxx	xxx,xxx
Less—accumulated depreciation	xxx,xxx	xxx,xxx
	xxx,xxx	xxx,xxx
Intangibles and other assets	xxx,xxx	xxx,xxx
Total assets	$xxx,xxx	$xxx,xxx

Liabilities and Shareholders' Equity

Current Liabilities:		
Notes payable, current portion	$xxx,xxx	$xxx,xxx
Accounts payable—trade	xxx,xxx	xxx,xxx
Dividends payable	xxx,xxx	xxx,xxx
Income taxes	xxx,xxx	xxx,xxx
Other accounts payable and accrued expenses	xxx,xxx	xxx,xxx
Total current liabilities	xxx,xxx	xxx,xxx
Long-term debt	xxx,xxx	xxx,xxx
Deferred income taxes	xxx,xxx	xxx,xxx
Total liabilities	xxx,xxx	xxx,xxx

(continued)

EXHIBIT 21–1
(continued)

Assets	Year Ended December 31,	
	19____	19____
Stockholders' equity:		
Common stock, without par value— xxx shares authorized; xxx shares issued at stated value of $xx a share	xxx,xxx	xxx,xxx
Capital in excess of par value	xxx,xxx	xxx,xxx
Retained earnings	xxx,xxx	xxx,xxx
Total stockholders' equity	xxx,xxx	xxx,xxx
Total liabilities and stockholders' equity	$xxx,xxx	$xxx,xxx

Statement of Operations (Exhibit 21–2). The statement of operations, commonly referred to as the income statement, can be presented in various forms. Substantially all variations, however, include at a minimum sales and other revenues; cost of goods sold; selling, general, and administrative expenses; interest expense; income taxes; and net income (or loss). Extraordinary items, the results of discontinued operations, and cumulative effects of accounting changes are also separately disclosed before net income on the face of the statement of operations.

Statement of Changes in Stockholders' Equity (Exhibit 21–3). The primary purpose of this statement is to reconcile equity account balances at the beginning of the year to year-end balances. Changes in outstanding capital stock, net income or loss, and dividends declared during the year are the most significant reconciling items.

Statement of Cash Flows (Exhibit 21–4). A statement of cash flows is presented for each period for which a statement of operations is presented. The statement is divided into three categories: cash provided by (or used in) operating activities, in investing ac-

EXHIBIT 21–2
ABC Company
Consolidated Statement of Income

	Year Ended December 31,	
	19____	*19____*
Sales	$xxx,xxx	$xxx,xxx
Other operating revenue	xxx,xxx	xxx,xxx
	xxx,xxx	xxx,xxx
Expenses:		
Cost of goods sold	xxx,xxx	xxx,xxx
Selling and administrative expenses	xxx,xxx	xxx,xxx
Depreciation and amortization	xxx,xxx	xxx,xxx
Other costs and operating expenses	xxx,xxx	xxx,xxx
	xxx,xxx	xxx,xxx
Income from operations	xxx,xxx	xxx,xxx
Other income:		
Interest income	xxx,xxx	xxx,xxx
Miscellaneous	xxx,xxx	xxx,xxx
	xxx,xxx	xxx,xxx
Other expenses:		
Interest expense	xxx,xxx	xxx,xxx
Miscellaneous	xxx,xxx	xxx,xxx
	xxx,xxx	xxx,xxx
Income before taxes	xxx,xxx	xxx,xxx
Provision for taxes on income	xxx,xxx	xxx,xxx
Net income	$xxx,xxx	$xxx,xxx
Earnings per common share	$ x.xx	$ x.xx

EXHIBIT 21–3
ABC Company
Consolidated Statement of Changes in Stockholders' Equity

	Year Ended December 31,	
	19____	*19____*
Balance at beginning of year	$xxx,xxx	$xxx,xxx
Net income for the year	xxx,xxx	xxx,xxx
Dividends declared	(xxx,xxx)	(xxx,xxx)
Balance at end of year	$xxx,xxx	$xxx,xxx

EXHIBIT 21–4
ABC Company
Consolidated Statement of Cash Flows

	Year Ended December 31,	
	19____	*19____*
Cash flows from operating activities:		
Net income	$xxx,xxx	$xxx,xxx
Adjustments to reconcile net income to net cash provided by operating activities:		
Depreciation and amortization	xxx,xxx	xxx,xxx
Provision for losses on accounts receivable	xxx,xxx	xxx,xxx
Gain on sale of facility	xxx,xxx	xxx,xxx
Payment received on installment note receivable for sale of inventory	xxx,xxx	xxx,xxx
Change in assets and liabilities net of effects from purchase of Company S:		
Increase in accounts receivable	xxx,xxx	xxx,xxx

Decrease in inventory	xxx,xxx	xxx,xxx
Increase in prepaid expenses	xxx,xxx	xxx,xxx
Decrease in accounts payable and accrued expenses	xxx,xxx	xxx,xxx
Increase in interest and income taxes payable	xxx,xxx	xxx,xxx
Increase in deferred taxes	xxx,xxx	xxx,xxx
Increase in other liabilities	xxx,xxx	xxx,xxx
Total adjustments	xxx,xxx	xxx,xxx
Net cash provided by operating activities	$xxx,xxx	$xxx,xxx
Cash flows from investing activities:		
Proceeds from sale of facility		$xxx,xxx
Payment received on note for sale of plant	$xxx,xxx	
Capital expenditures	(xxx,xxx)	(xxx,xxx)
Payment for purchase of Company S, net of cash required	(xxx,xxx)	(xxx,xxx)
Net cash used in investing activities	(xxx,xxx)	(xxx,xxx)
Cash flows from financing activities:		
Net borrowings under line-of-credit	xxx,xxx	xxx,xxx
Proceeds from issuance of long-term debt	xxx,xxx	xxx,xxx
Dividends paid	(xxx,xxx)	(xxx,xxx)
Net cash provided by financing activities	xxx,xxx	xxx,xxx
Net increase in cash and cash equivalents	xxx,xxx	xxx,xxx

(continued)

EXHIBIT 21–4
(continued)

	Year Ended December 31,	
	19___	19___
Cash and cash equivalents at beginning of year	xxx,xxx	xxx,xxx
Cash and cash equivalents at end of year	$xxx,xxx	$xxx,xxx

Supplemental schedule of noncash investing and financing activities:

The company purchased all of the capital stock of Company S for $xxx,xxx. In conjunction with the acquisition, liabilities were assumed as follows:

Fair value of assets acquired	$xxx,xxx
Cash paid for the capital stock	(xxx,xxx)
Liabilities assumed	$xxx,xxx

A capital lease obligation of $xxx,xxx was incurred when the company entered into a lease for new equipment.

Additional common stock was issued upon the conversion of $xxx,xxx of long-term debt.

tivities, and in financing activities. Supplemental disclosures of significant noncash investing and financing activities—for example, the conversion of debt to equity—is also required. An illustration of the Statement of Cash Flows is presented in Exhibit 21–4.

Disclosure Requirements

Generally accepted auditing standards require that information essential for a clear understanding of financial statements be set forth in the statements or the footnotes to the statements. This information is basically that which is required by generally accepted accounting principles and which might affect the conclusions drawn by a reasonably informed reader. The methods of disclosing this information include the following:

- Classification and segregation of data in the body of the financial statements.
- Captions and parenthetical comments on the face of the statements.
- Notes to the statements that present information and explanations that cannot readily be incorporated in the body of the financial statements.
- Separate schedules of financial data that would be contained in the basic financial statements or notes, except for the bulk of the information or completely distinct types of data, such as segment and geographic information.

The actual information disclosed in the notes to the financial statements may vary significantly from company to company. The following footnotes, however, are standard and are usually present:

- Summary of significant accounting policies—the summary should describe all principles and methods that have a significant effect on financial position, cash flows, and results of operations. It should not, however, duplicate information or details presented elsewhere in the financial statements. Examples of items that are typically included in the summary of accounting policies follow.
  - A description of the reporting entity or basis of financial statements (e.g., principles of consolidation, accounting for less than majority-owned investments).
  - A description of the basis for computing earnings per share data in complex situations or when not evident from a table.
  - The accounting principles and methods for recognizing each major element of revenue or expenditure. The description should include when revenue is recognized, which costs are carried forward to be matched against future operations, and the method and basis for allocating items between current and future periods.
  - Peculiar accounting principles, methods, and financial statement classifications relating to a particular industry; significant nonrecurring transactions.

- Accounting principles and methods followed in areas in which substantial authoritative support for two or more alternatives may exist or in which principles and methods are not clearly established in practice.
- Where appropriate, reasons for the use of a particular principle or method and any inconsistency arising from a change in accounting principle or method during the period for which statements are presented.
- Analyses of property, plant and equipment, investments and inventory, if not given in the basic statements.
- Details of long-term debt, including a five-year repayment schedule.
- Outstanding commitments such as leases, compensation arrangements, pensions, stock options, and postretirement benefits other than pensions.
- Components of income tax expense and deferred taxes, including a reconciliation of the statutory tax rate to the effective tax rate.
- Related party transactions.
- Significant contingencies, such as pending litigation and unresolved tax issues.
- Off-balance sheet risks and financial concentrations.
- Material events or occurences arising subsequent to the date of the most recent balance sheet.

SOME FUNDAMENTAL ACCOUNTING PRINCIPLES

Historical Cost

Financial statements of nonfinancial companies in the United States are generally based on the historical cost concept. A business entity operating in the United States need not consider or disclose current replacement cost or the effect of inflation on the recorded value of its assets or the results of its operations. Exceptions to the historical cost principle do nevertheless occur, most frequently in valuing current assets, such as marketable equity securities and inventories. These are recorded at the lower of cost or market value.

Revenue and Expense Recognition

In principle, the recognition of expense is matched with the recording of revenue where a reasonable relationship between the expense and related revenue can be established or assumed. In practice, however, the timing of recognition of revenue and expense is one of the most complex accounting issues in the United States. Numerous pronouncements and interpretations have been issued by the FASB and AICPA regarding specialized industry or other specific concerns relating to revenue recognition. Generally, the recognition of revenue is based on the accrual method of accounting and requires the consideration of three broad criteria: Revenue has been realized, assets associated with revenue are realizable, and the earnings process has been completed. Realized revenue results when products, merchandise, or other assets are exchanged for cash or claims to cash. Realizable revenue is recognized when related assets received or held are readily convertible to cash in a specified amount. Finally, revenue is considered to be earned when the business entity has substantially accomplished what it must do to be entitled to the benefits represented by the revenue.* In determining whether revenue recognition is appropriate in a given situation, several issues must be considered, including delivery of the product, customer acceptance, additional performance obligations of the seller, and the customer's right of return.

In accordance with the accrual method of accounting, expenses are recorded not when paid, but rather when they have been incurred.

Losses, Contingencies, and Reserves

General reserves are not permitted under generally accepted accounting principles in the United States. However, if it is probable that a loss has been incurred or an asset has been impaired and such loss can be reasonably estimated, it must be recorded. For those loss contingencies that are probable but not reasonably estimable or

---

* "Recognition and Measurement in Financial Statements of Business Enterprises," Statement of Financial Accounting Concepts No. 5 (Stamford, CT: FASB, December 1984), par. 83-84.

those that are reasonably possible but not probable, the nature of the contingency must be disclosed. Remote loss contingencies, except for financial guarantees, need not be disclosed in the financial statements or the accompanying notes. Gain contingencies are not recorded until realized; however, adequate disclosure of the nature of the contingencies should be presented.

Consolidation

To achieve the fair presentation of financial information, all majority-owned subsidiaries—that is, those companies in which a parent has a controlling financial interest through direct or indirect ownership of a majority voting interest—must be consolidated unless control is likely to be temporary or control does not rest with the majority owner, as in cases of legal reorganization or bankruptcy. The usual condition for a controlling financial interest is ownership of over 50 percent of the outstanding voting shares. Consolidation might also be appropriate if a controlling financial interest has been achieved through management and financial support agreements coupled with the ability to obtain over 50 percent of the voting shares, such as through conversion of notes or exercise of options. In accounting for less than majority-owned companies, the equity method of recognizing the investor's pro-rata share of the investee's income or loss is required when the investor has the ability to exercise significant influence over the financial and operating policies of the investee. This is generally presumed to be the case if 20 percent or more of an investee's outstanding voting shares is directly or indirectly owned by the investor.

Business Combinations

There are two methods of accounting in the United States for business combinations: the pooling of interests method and the purchase method. A pooling of interests assumes that two companies, rather than transact a purchase and a sale, have combined their managerial and financial resources to create a new single entity. To qualify as a pooling of interests, 12 conditions must be met that relate to the characteristics of the merging entities, the terms and conditions of the combination itself, and prohibitions on transactions subsequent to the formation of the new enterprise. A business combination that meets all of the specified conditions must be accounted for using the pooling of interests method of accounting; all other business combinations must be accounted for as purchases.

Under the pooling of interests method, assets and liabilities of the combined entities are recorded at book value and the basis of accounting does not change. In a business combination accounted for as a purchase, assets and liabilities purchased by the acquiring company are recorded at their fair values and any excess of the purchase price over the fair value of the tangible net assets acquired is recorded as goodwill, an intangible asset that must be amortized over a period of not more than 40 years.

SPECIFIC ACCOUNTING PRINCIPLES

Many accounting principles that are generally accepted in the United States may not be as widely accepted elsewhere in the world. Although the authoritative sources that define these principles in the United States are too numerous to thoroughly explore here, the following discussion highlights certain important U.S. accounting principles.

Property, Plant, and Equipment

These assets are recorded at cost and are depreciated over the estimated useful lives of the assets based on a systematic depreciation method. An accumulated depreciation account offsets gross asset costs in the balance sheet, and depreciation charges are reflected in the statement of operations on a periodic basis. Depreciation methods commonly found in practice include straight-line and accelerated methods, such as the sum-of-years-digits and declining balance methods, all of which are acceptable provided they are used consistently from year to year.

Accounting for Leases

A lease with terms that effectively transfers the risks and rewards of property ownership from the lessor to the lessee is considered a capital lease and is recorded as an asset and corresponding liability in the financial statements of the entity leasing the property. This transaction is substantively the same as if the lessee had borrowed funds to purchase the property. Instead of recording periodic rental expense, charges consisting of amortization of the capital lease asset and related interest expense are recorded in the income statement. Lease payments less the interest component reduce the recorded liability amount.

Inventories

Inventory costs are composed of material, labor, and fixed and variable overhead costs that can be calculated using various methods. The most frequently used methods of determining cost are the first-in, first-out (FIFO), weighted average, and last-in, first-out (LIFO) methods. If the market value of inventory is less than its recorded cost, then it must be reduced to market value, which is generally the net realizable value of the inventory less costs of completion or disposal.

Foreign Currency Transactions

If transactions occur that are denominated in a currency other than the entity's functional currency and result in exchange gains or losses, these gains or losses are recorded in the statement of operations in the period in which the transaction occurs. If financial statements are translated from a reporting currency into a functional currency, unrealized gains or losses resulting from the translation are accumulated in an equity account in the balance sheet.

Intangible Assets

Business start-up and organizational costs, patents and trademarks, and other intangible assets such as good will may be capitalized, if recoverable, and charged to income periodically over varying time periods. Research and development costs must be expensed as incurred.

Deferred Taxes

At the present time there are two pronouncements governing the accounting for income taxes: Accounting Principles Board Opinion No. 11 (APB 11) and Statement of Financial Accounting Standards No. 96 (FAS 96). FAS 96, which supersedes APB 11, was issued in 1987. Under APB 11, comprehensive interperiod tax allocation is required that recognizes total tax expense based on pretax income adjusted for permanent differences. The difference between the total tax expense and the current amount due is the deferred tax provision. FAS 96 changes the form of interperiod tax allocation to a liability method. This method focuses the determination of deferred taxes on the differences between the book and tax bases of assets and liabilities (temporary differences) in the balance sheet. The FASB is currently deliberating an amendment to FAS 96 that, while maintaining a liability method of interperiod tax allocation, will simplify the complex calculations required under FAS 96 and provide for less restrictive recognition of deferred tax assets. In light of these deliberations the FASB has delayed the required adoption date of FAS 96 to fiscal years beginning after December 15, 1992.

CONCLUSION

As the functional language of business, accounting is a dynamic and evolving medium through which information is effectively and thoroughly communicated to the financial statement user in the United States. The complex interaction of numerous authorities on accounting, auditing, and financial reporting matters with the professionals practicing in the field results in pronouncements and principles designed to best meet the informational needs of the financial statement user. Through statutory regulation governed by the SEC and the accounting profession's internal mechanisms of developing policy, a strong foundational structure of financial reporting has been established. The true test, however, will be in the ability of these policymaking bodies to grow with the global marketplace and facilitate international commerce.

PART 5

EMPLOYEE RELATIONS

CHAPTER 22

EMPLOYEE BENEFITS: AN OVERVIEW OF THE LEGAL AND TAX IMPLICATIONS

Marc R. Garber, Esq.*
Pepper, Hamilton & Scheetz

INTRODUCTION

Employee benefits is best described as that part of an employee's compensation package that is not current salary. These benefits take many forms, such as profit sharing, deferred compensation, retirement and savings, sickness and accident, disability, company cars, country club fees, equity participation, and severance plans. Employee benefits serve the interests of employees and their families, as well as employers and the government. As a result, employee benefits have great social and economic impact.

Employees place great importance on the benefits made available to them. In fact, employees are as concerned about their benefits as they are about their salaries. A primary reason for their concern is that employee benefits provide to employees necessary services they may otherwise be unable to afford. An obvious example of such a benefit is employer-provided health insurance. Health care costs have skyrocketed over the past few years, and health

* The author gratefully acknowledges the assistance and encouragement of Sumi C. Chong and Lori D. Kettering (both, as is the author, are associates of Pepper, Hamilton & Scheetz) in preparing and editing this chapter.

insurance policies, particularly individual policies, are prohibitively expensive for most individuals. Employer-provided health benefits may be the only way these individuals can obtain health coverage. Provision of health insurance by private employers grants individuals access to the health care system, and also reduces the amount of societal resources that would otherwise be dedicated to the care of individuals not covered by private insurance.

Employers, however, increasingly view benefits as a growing cost burden that they are unwilling to shoulder alone. Although benefit programs can help an employer attract and retain better workers, the cost of providing benefits is increasing dramatically. Typically, employee benefits account for 15 to 25 percent or more of an employer's total compensation for many U.S. corporations. In light of the skyrocketing cost of benefits, corporations are under constant pressure to design plans that are cost-effective; to shift part of the cost burden to employees, where possible; and to eliminate certain programs altogether. Judicial decisions and statutory changes, however, are making it increasingly difficult for employers to eliminate or reduce existing benefits programs. Thus, employers are re-evaluating their policies and positions on employee benefits.

The U.S. government also derives a benefit from the existence of a private employee benefit system. Although the government loses revenue by providing tax incentives to private employers to encourage their establishing benefit plans and by regulating and enforcing the federal laws relating to these plans, it also, by relying on the existence of employee benefits provided by the private sector, has never had to develop or subsidize national benefit programs to help all employees. Thus, the government relies on the private benefit system either to provide benefits it does not provide or to supplement benefits it does provide.

The benefits provided directly by the federal government include Social Security old age and disability benefits, unemployment compensation, and other similar benefits. The government is also aware that without the private pension system, many individuals would not have the financial resources to retire, reflecting the increasingly high cost of living and relatively low benefit provided by the federal Social Security retirement system. To reduce the risk of insufficient income for retirees, U.S. laws encourage the establishment of employee benefit plans. This encouragement takes the form of tax and other incentives. Indeed, the traditional sources that constitute retirement income have often been referred to as a "three-legged stool," or the combination of government-provided Social Security income, individual savings, and private employer-paid pension income. Consideration of government-provided benefits and individual savings, while important to employees, is beyond the scope of this chapter, which instead focuses on employee benefits provided by employers in the private sector.

Because employee benefits affect the interests of so many diverse parties, take such a wide variety of forms, and have become an integral form of compensation, they influence an expanding range of issues, from business to law to economics. Accordingly, any discussion of employee benefits is necessarily broad in scope, and the legal and tax analysis is technical and complex; an exhaustive analysis of the subject could fill many volumes. This chapter, however, is intended to provide simply an overview of the legal, tax, financial, and human resource considerations involved with employer-provided employee benefits in the United States. The next section sets forth a general description of the federal laws that govern employee benefits. The third section discusses welfare benefits, and finally, the last section explains executive compensation.

FEDERAL REGULATION OF PENSION AND WELFARE BENEFITS

For the most part, employee benefits in the United States are subject to federal rather than state laws. This arrangement ensures that benefits provided to employees in different states generally are subject to uniform legal considerations. The federal laws that first applied to employee benefits were contained in earlier versions of the Internal Revenue Code (Code) and in the judicial law that developed from the common law of trusts, which governed fiduciary relationships, among other things. The early tax laws that applied to employee benefits applied almost exclusively to retirement plans and established minimum standards that plans had to satisfy in order to receive favorable tax treatment. These standards were designed to protect participants.

It was not, however, until 1974 that the United States Congress passed comprehensive legislation specifically regulating employee benefits. On September 2, 1974, President Ford signed into law the

Employee Retirement Income Security Act of 1974 (ERISA). The law falls under the joint jurisdiction of the Treasury Department and the Department of Labor (DOL), as well as the Pension Benefit Guaranty Corporation (PBGC), an agency within the DOL specially created by the statute itself. ERISA was designed to govern welfare and pension plans maintained by the private sector. ERISA's emphasis is on pension plans and not welfare plans, largely because the concerns that led to the enactment of ERISA principally involved pension plan issues. Accordingly, many of the rules in ERISA apply to pension plans only.

The Employee Retirement Income Security Act

ERISA was designed to protect the interests of plan participants and their beneficiaries. The statute provides for the enforcement of the obligations arising under benefit plans, and guarantees access to and remedies in the federal court system. To ensure that participants are fully and fairly informed about their plan participation, ERISA contains specific reporting and disclosure requirements. ERISA also regulates the design and operation of employee benefit plans. This is accomplished through the imposition of minimum standards regarding eligibility to participate, vesting rules, funding rules, and rules respecting plan distributions, among others. Some of these rules were taken from earlier versions of the Code. ERISA also implemented a government insurance system that covers certain benefits provided under qualified defined benefit pension plans. The purpose of this insurance system is to enhance the security a participant has in the private pension system.

ERISA is divided into four titles:

Title I—Labor Provisions.

Title II—Tax Provisions.

Title III—Jurisdictional and Administrative Provisions.

Title IV—Plan Termination Provisions.

ERISA's reach is very broad, as best demonstrated by the definitional section. The terms *Employee Pension Benefit Plan* and *Employee Welfare Benefit Plan* are defined broadly:

". . . employee pension benefit plan" and "pension plan" mean any plan, fund or program which . . . is . . . established or maintained by an employer or by an employee organization, or by both, to the extent . . . such plan, fund, or program-(i) provides retirement income to employees, or (ii) results in a deferral of income by employees for periods extending to the termination of covered employment or beyond. [ERISA § 3 (2)(A), 29 U.S.C. § 1002(2)(A)]

"employee welfare benefit plan" and "welfare plan" mean any [employer-sponsored or employee organization-sponsored benefit plan that provides] . . . medical, surgical, or hospital care or benefits, or benefits in the event of sickness, accident, disability, death or unemployment, or vacation benefits, apprenticeship or other training programs, or day care centers, scholarship funds, or pre-paid legal services, or . . . any benefit described in Section 302(c) of the Labor Management Relations Act [of] 1947 (other than [a retirement or death benefit]). [ERISA § 3(1), 29 U.S.C. § 1002(1)]

The breadth of these defined terms, in combination with other provisions, subjects most employee benefit plans and programs sponsored by U.S. employers to regulation under ERISA, regardless of the formality of the plan or arrangement, whether or not the plan or arrangement is maintained pursuant to the collective bargaining process, and whether or not the plan or arrangement is in writing.

Title I: The Labor Provisions

Title I of ERISA contains the "labor provisions," regulated by the DOL. This title contains a comprehensive set of rules governing the operation and, to a lesser extent, the design of employee benefit plans. Title I also creates rights in participants and beneficiaries that may be enforced in federal court to ensure fair treatment by the fiduciaries of the employee benefit plans. Title I's application is not limited to so-called qualified plans (as described in the discussion on Title II, below). Title I also covers many welfare benefit plans and certain executive arrangements (as described in the third and fourth sections, respectively, below).

Reporting and Disclosure.   The disclosure provisions require the plan sponsor or plan administrator to distribute information to participants and their beneficiaries regarding the design of a plan and their rights under the plan. The reporting provisions require plan fiduciaries and sponsors to file with the DOL, the Internal Revenue Service (IRS), and the PBGC certain annual and periodic reports. Participants and their beneficiaries are entitled to receive copies of the annual financial reports for certain plans. Moreover, for plans that cover at least 100 participants, an annual independent audit is required. Both civil and criminal penalties, enforceable in some instances against individual fiduciaries, are provided for failure to comply with the reporting and disclosure provisions.

Plan Design. Title I also contains minimum plan design standards that almost all pension plans must satisfy. These standards, however, which are not as rigorous as the similar provisions in the Code that many pension plans must satisfy, relate to eligibility to participate, vesting of benefits, the rate at which benefits accrue, rules regarding how employment service is credited, and protective features that do not permit the alienation of benefits, among others. In addition, Title I establishes rules related to businesses that are under common control. Subsequent legislation and judicial decisions have made clear the importance of carefully analyzing these common control requirements because an employer may be responsible for certain plan liabilities of a related employer without regard to whether the employer sponsors or makes contributions to the plan involved. Furthermore, from the perspective of satisfying the various nondiscrimination rules and coverage requirements (as discussed below), employees of all members of a controlled group of businesses must be considered as employed by a single employer. This rule has significant impact on plan design and operational matters.

Funding Standards. The funding standards of ERISA require annual funding of pension plans in an amount at least equal to an established minimum determined by an actuary. These funding rules are designed to encourage full funding of pension plans. The IRS imposes an excise tax if a pension plan fails to satisfy the minimum funding standard. This excise tax is equal to 10 percent of the funding deficiency, and is imposed each year until the deficiency is corrected. Every member of the controlled group of corporations could be jointly and severally liable for payment of this excise tax. An additional 100 percent excise tax may also be imposed in certain instances.

Funding waivers are available from the IRS under certain circumstances. In order to obtain such a waiver, the employer must demonstrate that a temporary business condition makes it extremely difficult to fund the plan without jeopardizing the viability of the business. However, as a bit of a paradox, the employer must also demonstrate, when requesting such a waiver, that it will recover quickly from its temporary setback and be in a position to make required contributions shortly thereafter. The waived amount is amortized over a five-year period, which increases the annual employer costs of the plan over the succeeding five years.

Fiduciary Provisions.   Title I of ERISA also contains rules concerning fiduciaries of pension and welfare plans. Many of these rules have their origin in the common law of trusts. These rules require that all plans be in writing and name at least one fiduciary. In addition to the named fiduciary, any individual or entity that has discretionary authority or power over the administration of the plan or the investment of the plan's assets is deemed to be a fiduciary. Thus, the definition of fiduciary is fairly expansive.

The statute also dictates that plan assets be held in trust, except for certain insured plans. ERISA requires that plan fiduciaries satisfy a duty of loyalty. The duty of loyalty requires that a fiduciary act for the exclusive purpose of providing benefits to participants and beneficiaries, and solely in the interests of participants and beneficiaries. In addition, a fiduciary is subject to the duty of prudence. The statute requires that assets be invested in a diversified fashion so as to minimize the risk of loss. Finally, to the extent consistent with ERISA, a fiduciary is required to act in accordance with the documents that govern the plan.

ERISA also contains rules prohibiting a fiduciary or plan sponsor from causing a plan to enter into transactions directly or indirectly with certain parties-in-interest to the plan. For example, unless specifically permitted by some other provision of ERISA or the Code, the trustee of a plan cannot invest plan assets in securities of the sponsoring employer. The fact that none of the general fiduciary provisions, such as the duty of loyalty or the duty of prudence, are violated with respect to a transaction does not preclude the imposition of liability under this provision. Breach of the prohibited transaction rules results in the imposition of an excise tax. Specific statutory and administrative exemptions to these prohibitions exist for common situations that would otherwise technically constitute a breach. Parties may also request a private exemption from the DOL with respect to these provisions. Generally, in order to gain a private exemption, the proposed transaction must be administratively feasible, protective of rights of participants, and in the interests of the plan and its participants. It typically takes six to eight months to secure a private exemption from the DOL.

A substantial body of regulatory and judicial law has developed with respect to ERISA's fiduciary standards. In many instances, these regulations and judicial decisions are very fact-sensitive. Liability for a breach of the rules could be substantial. Issues under these rules arise in the day-to-day operation of a plan as well as in transactional matters such as investment decisions and decisions involving the payment of benefits.

Enforcement. The enforcement provisions of Title I of ERISA are equitable in nature and broad in scope. They permit participants, the DOL, and fiduciaries to seek redress for legal violations concerning benefit plans. The statute also permits the grieving party to recover attorneys' fees in certain circumstances. Congressional intent for the uniform federal regulation of employee benefits is made manifest in ERISA's broad pre-emptive provision that results in federal law controlling over state laws in most cases. Thus, although state and federal courts exercise concurrent jurisdiction over ERISA disputes, parties tend to choose the federal forum for most benefits-related litigation. In fact, even when a suit is initiated in state court, the defending party can easily remove the action to federal court. Exceptions to federal preemption exist, however, for state laws that regulate banking, insurance, or securities, and that are directly at issue in a particular matter.

ERISA also requires pension and welfare plans to follow stated claims procedure in determining whether benefits should be paid in a particular instance. The plan sponsor must disclose this claims procedure to employees participating in the plan. With regard to disputed claims, the administrative process must be exhausted before a case is appropriately brought to court. This general rule applies in most instances with few exceptions.

COBRA. A new section was added to Title I of ERISA (along with a mirror-image section added to the Code) known as COBRA, effective for plan years beginning after July 1, 1986. COBRA requires the continuation of medical and other health-related benefits for certain qualified employees and their family members following certain events that otherwise would result in a loss of coverage. Employees and their covered beneficiaries are provided continuation coverage at their cost without having to prove good health (and therefore, insurability) or satisfy a pre-existing condition exception. The type and level of continuation coverage is generally the same as the coverage in effect at the time the qualifying event occurs. Although participants must pay for continuation coverage, it is offered at group rates that are substantially lower than individual rates for private insurance.

The events that require continuation coverage under COBRA include employment termination (for reasons other than gross misconduct), reduction in employment hours, the death of a covered employee, or separation or divorce from the covered employee, entitlement to Medicare under the federal system, and the employer's filing for bankruptcy. The right to continuation coverage lasts generally for 18 months when the termination is for reasons other than death, and 36 months for death and other circumstances. The 18- or 36-month period begins as of the first of the month following the date in which coverage would otherwise cease. The rules provide for notification to participants and their eligible dependents, and require a minimum election period during which affected individuals may select the benefits offered. Plans and employers may incur penalties for noncompliance with the provisions of COBRA. This penalty is an excise tax in the amount of $100 per day for the period of noncompliance.

Title II: The Tax Provisions

Title II of ERISA contains the tax rules. These rules have been incorporated into the Code, have been amended and supplemented substantially since the adoption of ERISA, and have been explained and expanded upon through Treasury Department regulations. The Code provisions govern, among other things, the deductibility of contributions made to fund plans, the tax-deferred status of contributions held in trust or through insurance with respect to plans, and the favorable tax rules that apply to distributions from plans. In order to be eligible for favorable tax treatment, plans must satisfy certain qualification requirements. These rules require, among other things, nondiscrimination as to coverage, and contributions and benefits, and mandate vesting of benefits within established time frames. The Code also contains rules regarding the tax treatment of contributions made to fund or pay welfare benefits. These tax rules are covered separately under the discussion of welfare plans. This analysis of Title II will focus on the rules that apply to pension benefits.

Most U.S. employers, and virtually all large employers, sponsor "qualified plans," which are employee pension benefit plans that meet the tax-qualification requirements of the Code. Under a qualified plan, the employer, or plan sponsor, makes contributions to a trust, and benefits are later paid from the trust to plan participants. The employer receives a current tax deduction for the amount of its contributions in the year in which the contributions are made (up to a certain limit, as discussed below), but employees do not recognize income on the contributions made or benefits accrued on their behalf until they receive benefit payments from the trust. In addition, the contributions grow tax-deferred in the trust: neither the employer nor the participants are taxed on the income, and the participants are not taxed until they actually receive a distribution.

A qualified plan can be either a defined benefit plan or a defined contribution plan. In a defined benefit plan retirement income is expressed as a promised or defined benefit. The plan document guarantees a fixed amount of benefit to be paid to the employee at retirement (or termination of employment, or other events as specified by the plan). The amount is defined in that the plan sets forth a specific formula for calculating the benefit. The formula usually takes into account factors such as the participant's compensation and years of service. For example, a typical defined benefit plan guarantees a participant a certain number of dollars of monthly benefit for each year of service the employee has completed at retirement. In a defined benefit plan, all contributions and earnings are held together in a single fund, and benefits are paid from this single pool of assets.

Historically, most large employer plans and most collectively bargained plans have been defined benefit plans. Because the amount of benefit is guaranteed, however, the employer or plan sponsor bears the investment risk in these types of plan. If the trust's actual income is lower than projected, the employer will have to make additional contributions. The converse to this is also true. Thus, if investment gains are in excess of assumed gains, the subsequent year's contribution requirements will be less than originally projected. Also, a defined benefit plan generally can be terminated only at a time when trust assets are sufficient to pay benefit obligations (as defined in ERISA). In fact, as discussed below, a defined benefit plan with insufficient assets can be terminated only in limited circumstances.

In recent years, many sponsors have begun terminating their defined benefit plans and replacing them with defined contribution plans, especially salary deferral plans (401 (k) plans). Defined contribution plans are often less costly than defined benefit plans, depending on the comparative benefit and contribution formulae and on the demographics of the employer's work force, and clearly pose less risk to the employer, both because the employee bears the investment risk and because the employer can terminate the plan much more easily.

In a defined contribution plan, the amount of annual contribution rather than the amount of retirement benefit is defined in the plan. For example, a plan may require an employer to contribute to the plan 5 percent of total compensation of all participating employees for each plan year. A defined contribution plan may be either a money purchase plan, in which the plan requires a set amount of contribution each year, or a profit sharing plan, under which the contribution is discretionary. The advantage to a money purchase plan is that the employer is permitted to contribute up to 25 percent of covered compensation, whereas contributions to a profit sharing plan are limited to 15 percent of covered compensation. In a defined contribution plan, each participant has a separate account to which contributions and earnings are credited. This account is not required to be physically segregated from other participants' accounts, but must be accounted for separately.

Two examples of profit sharing plans are the salary deferral plan, also known as a cash or deferred compensation arrangement, and the employee stock ownership plan (ESOP). A salary deferral plan (or 401 (k) plan, named for the Code section governing these types of plans) is a type of profit sharing plan under which employees elect to take a portion of their compensation either as immediate cash salary or as a contribution to the plan. An ESOP is a defined contribution plan that invests primarily in employer securities. ESOPs must meet strict rules under the Code and federal securities laws. Recently, ESOPs have been used and have been attempted to be used as antitakeover devices.

Finally, more employers recently have begun implementing target benefit plans, which are defined contribution plans that use a defined benefit-type formula. Under a target plan, the plan contains a benefit expressed as a certain amount per years of service. An actuary then estimates the amount of annual contributions necessary to provide this amount of benefit to participants at retirement. Although the plan sponsor makes its contributions based on the actuary's recommendations, because the plan is a defined contribution plan, and the benefit formula is only a target, the participants bear the risk if the contributions and earnings thereon ultimately are insufficient to pay the target benefit. This type of plan combines the advantages of a defined contribution plan—no investment risk to the employer, and no liability at termination for insufficient assets—with the appearance of a traditional retirement-type benefit. Of course the expression of the retirement benefit is more in the nature of a projection than a defined benefit, because the benefit actually payable at retirement is equal to each participant's account balance.

The Code sets forth several sets of rules governing the design and administration of qualified plans. The following is an overview of these qualification rules.

Eligibility. Although employers are not required to cover any specific category of employees under any benefit plan, (and, in fact, are not required to sponsor any plan at all), the Code contains specific rules on exclusion of employees based on age and service. Generally, plans may require that employees reach age 21 and complete one year of service with the employer before they are eligible to participate in the plan. A two-year eligibility period is permitted in certain circumstances. This rule permits employers to save administrative costs associated with covering employees in positions with historically high turnover (such as the retail sales industry), while ensuring that employees participate promptly. Employers may also exclude certain classes of employees, such as employees covered by a collective bargaining agreement that does not provide for plan participation, or employees at a specific plant, as long as the plan otherwise meets the participation, coverage, and nondiscrimination requirements described below.

Coverage/Participation.   The Code also contains an interrelated set of requirements concerning plan participation and nondiscrimination in the provision of benefits. The Tax Reform Act of 1986 and the Treasury Department regulations issued with respect to that act made substantial changes in these areas.

First, each qualified plan generally must cover a minimum number of employees, which is the lesser of 50 employees or 40 percent of the work force. For purposes of this requirement, and most other requirements associated with qualified plans, the "employer" includes all members of a controlled group of corporations, of a group of trades or businesses under common control, and of any affiliated service group. A controlled group of corporations covers parent/subsidiary companies and certain brother/sister groups. The effect, for purposes of the minimum coverage requirement, is that a plan sponsored by one member of the group must cover the lesser of 50 employees or 40 percent of the entire controlled group work force, regardless of whether employees of the related corporations are eligible to participate in the plan. The legislature has provided some relief by permitting "separate lines of business" within the controlled group to satisfy this requirement separately, but new Treasury Department regulations on the definition of separate lines appear to be too restrictive to be of use to most employers.

Each qualified plan must also cover a minimum percentage of employees. Generally, a plan must cover at least 70 percent of non-highly compensated employees (determined on a controlled group basis), or a percentage of non-highly compensated employees that is at least 70 percent of the percentage of highly compensated employees covered (again, determined on a controlled group basis). If the plan does not meet one of these percentage coverage tests, it must instead satisfy an average benefits test. The average benefits test has two parts. First, the plan must cover a reasonable classification of employees. Although the IRS will determine reasonableness based on the facts and circumstances of each case, regulations suggest that reasonable classifications include plans covering only hourly or only salaried employees, or plans based on specified job categories. The second part of the test requires the average benefit percentage of non-highly compensated employees (calculated as benefits or contributions as a percentage of compensation) to be at least a certain percentage of the average benefit percentage of highly compensated employees. Certain plans of a single employer may be aggregated to satisfy the participation tests, and certain portions of plans may be considered as separate plans. As with the minimum coverage rules, discussed above, employees of all members of a controlled group are considered as employed by one employer for purposes of this test, although the separate lines of business rules may offer some relief.

Nondiscrimination/Social Security Integration. The final component of the participation/coverage rules is the requirement that a plan not discriminate in favor of highly compensated employees. Generally, no highly compensated employee may have a greater contribution rate or greater benefit accrual rate under a plan than any non-highly compensated employee. Recent regulations issued by the Treasury Department set forth several safe harbors for satisfying this general rule.

The regulations also set forth new rules for permissible integration of plan benefits with Social Security payments, an exception to the general nondiscrimination rules. The federal government's calculation of old-age Social Security payments is based on earnings up to a limited dollar amount for each year; therefore, Social Security payments replace a greater proportion of salary for employees who earn less than or equal to the limit on which benefits are calculated than for highly paid people, who accrue no additional Social Security benefits with respect to salary over a certain amount. The Code permits qualified plans to take into account estimated Social Security benefits in structuring benefit formulas. The theory is that when employer-provided and government-provided benefits are considered together, employees will receive approximately the same level of benefits when expressed as a percentage of compensation.

For a defined contribution plan, an integrated contribution formula usually provides that the employer will contribute an amount equal to a certain percentage of compensation up to the amount of an employee's covered compensation (the amount on which Social Security benefits are calculated), plus an additional percentage of compensation in excess of the employee's covered compensation. A defined benefit plan can use one of two basic formulae, a step-rate excess formula or an offset formula. A step-rate excess formula works in a similar manner as integration in a defined contribution plan: Employees accrue a benefit equal to a certain percentage of their compensation up to covered compensation, plus an additional percentage of compensation in excess of covered compensation. In an offset formula, the plan sets forth a benefit formula, then subtracts from that benefit the amount of an employee's estimated Social Security benefits. The IRS has issued copious rules governing the percentages and limitations permitted in connection with Social Security integration.

In addition to the general nondiscrimination rules, 401(k) plans must satisfy special rules as to both salary deferral contributions and employer matching contributions (if available under the plan). These rules set the parameters for permitted disparity in contribution between highly compensated and non-highly compensated employees. The average salary deferral percentage for eligible highly compensated employees may not be more than 1.25 times the deferral percentage for non-highly compensated employees, or, alternatively, may not be more than two times the deferral percentage for non-highly compensated employees and may not exceed the non-highly compensated employee percentage by more than two percentage points. The deferral percentages are averaged for all eligible employees; therefore, employees who are eligible to participate but do not elect to defer part of their salary are counted as a zero percent deferral percentage in calculating the average. Since lower-paid people are generally less able, and less likely, to elect to defer part of their salary, employers must monitor their plans to be sure the plans meet the nondiscrimination requirements. Employers commonly install safeguards in their plans to prevent the plan's inadvertently failing the test.

Also, in addition to the other nondiscrimination rules, special rules apply to top-heavy plans, plans under which key employees' benefits or account balances exceed 60 percent of the total benefits or account balances under the plan. If a plan is top-heavy for a year, special, more rapid, vesting and minimum benefit contribution or accrual rules apply for that year. Top-heavy considerations generally affect only smaller and some mid-sized employers.

Deductions/Funding. The amount that an employer may deduct for tax purposes for contributions to a qualified plan is limited. For a defined contribution plan, an employer may deduct an amount equal to only 15 percent of participants' compensation for contributions to a profit sharing or stock bonus plan, and up to 25 percent of participants' compensation for contributions to a money purchase plan. Since profit sharing contributions may be discretionary, many employers adopt both a profit sharing plan and a money purchase plan, to permit a higher deduction while maintaining some flexibility in the amount of contribution required. Also, the Code permits certain carryforwards permitting employers to take deductions in a later year attributable to contributions made in an earlier year.

For contributions to a defined benefit plan, the employer may deduct up to the amount necessary to satisfy the minimum funding standard for that year for the plan, as determined by an actuary. Because a defined benefit plan's benefits are defined, rather than based on accumulated annual contributions and earnings thereon, an actuary must estimate the amount of contributions required for each year to accumulate the promised amount of benefits at the end of the year. The plan's funding standard account must include the normal cost of the plan for the year plus amounts necessary to amortize the cost of unfunded past service liabilities and experience losses. The Code sets forth detailed requirements governing funding of defined benefit plans and maintenance of the funding standard account.

Limitations on Contributions and Benefits. The Code also limits the amount of contributions or benefits that a plan participant may be credited with in each year, or that may be paid as an accrued benefit at retirement. Generally, for each plan year, the annual additions to a participant's account in a defined contribution plan (profit sharing or money purchase plan) are limited to the lesser of $30,000 or 25 percent of the participant's compensation. Annual additions include employer contributions, employee contributions, and forfeitures allocated to the participant's account.

Under a defined benefit plan, a participant's accrued benefit, expressed as an annual retirement benefit, is limited to the lesser of $108,963 (adjusted for cost of living) or 100 percent of the participant's compensation averaged over the three highest-paid years.

These defined benefit limitations, normally calculated based on benefits payments beginning on a participant's Social Security retirement age, as defined in the Social Security Act, are adjusted if the participant begins receiving benefits before or after his or her Social Security retirement age.

These limitations apply to all benefit plans sponsored by the employer. Therefore, if an employee participates in both a profit-sharing plan and a money purchase plan, the employee's total annual additions under both plans combined may total only $30,000 or 25 percent of his or her compensation. If an employee participates in a defined contribution plan and a defined benefit plan, Treasury Department regulations prescribe a special equation for calculating the employee's limitations under each plan.

A plan, either a defined contribution plan or a defined benefit plan (although less commonly in defined benefit plans), may permit employees to make after-tax employee contributions to be held in the plan's trust fund. In a defined contribution plan, these contributions count toward the employee's annual additions for the year. Because compliance with the annual additions limitation is a condition for qualification of the plan, the plan document usually limits the amount an employee may contribute. Salary deferral contributions under a 401(k) plan count as employer contributions, rather than employee contributions.

Vesting. Although employees must be permitted to participate in the plan after meeting the plan's age and service requirements, that does not necessarily mean that they will receive a benefit when they leave the company. The Code permits a plan to provide that participants forfeit all or part of their benefit according to a stated vesting schedule. An employer may not use a vesting schedule more restrictive than either five-year cliff vesting or seven-year graded vesting. Under five-year cliff vesting, if employees terminate employment before completing five years of service, they forfeit their entire benefit or account balance under the plan. Under seven-year graded vesting, employees are 20 percent vested (they forfeit 80 percent) if they leave after completing three or fewer years of service, and become vested in 20 percent more per year until they become fully vested after seven years of service. Special rules govern crediting service if employees leave and are later rehired.

Generally, if employees return to the employer within five years of the date they left, their prior service and vesting credit will be restored.

The vesting rules also provide that participants must become fully vested in their benefits at the plan's defined normal retirement age, and at termination of the plan. Once participants become vested in a portion of their benefit, that amount is absolutely nonforfeitable. Therefore, the Code prevents an employer from amending or changing a plan to reduce benefits already accrued under the plan.

Distributions.   Although pension plans commonly are thought of as retirement income plans, participants can receive distributions earlier, such as at termination of employment. To ensure that qualified plans do provide retirement income, however, rather than merely a tax-favored investment opportunity, the Code contains rules governing the timing and form of benefit payments.

Normally, unless a participant elects a later commencement date, benefit payments must begin by the later of the participant's 65th birthday (or the plan's defined normal retirement age, if earlier), the 10th anniversary of the date the participant commenced participation in the plan, or the participant's termination of service. Under this provision, a plan may require a participant who terminates at age 35 to wait until age 65 to begin receiving payments. Most plans permit payment soon after termination, primarily for administrative efficiency reasons. Participants must in any event, however, begin receiving their benefits by no later than the April 15 following the calendar year in which they reach age $70\frac{1}{2}$, even if they are still working.

Payments from a defined benefit plan or a money purchase plan must be made in the form of an annuity, unless both the participant and, if married, his or her spouse, elect another form of benefit. The normal form of benefit for an unmarried participant is a single life annuity, and the normal form for a married participant is a joint and 50 percent survivor annuity. Certain profit sharing plans under which employees cannot elect an annuity payment option are exempt from the rules requiring annuity payments in the absence of a spousal consent. Also, if the participant's account balance, or the present value of the participant's accrued benefit, is less than $3,500, the plan may pay the benefit in a lump sum, regardless of applicable annuity rules and without securing the participants consent.

In-Service Distributions: Loans and Withdrawals

Under certain limited circumstances, a plan may permit employees to receive payments from the plan while still working. Generally, a plan may permit participants to borrow from their accounts in a savings, 401(k), or profit sharing plan up to the lesser of $50,000 or one half of their vested account balance. A plan may require a minimum loan amount, for reasons of administrative simplicity, as long as the minimum is not so high as to preclude lower-income participants from using the loan program. A loan, other than a loan to buy a principal residence, must be required to be repaid within five years, and must bear a reasonable rate of interest. If the participant is married, generally his or her spouse must consent to the loan.

A 401(k) plan may permit employees to make in-service hardship withdrawals from the amount of their salary deferral contributions (not from the interest on those contributions accrued after December 31, 1988). To demonstrate a hardship, the Code requires that an employee show an immediate and heavy financial need, such as medical expenses or purchase of a primary residence, and show that the money is not available from other sources. A plan is not required to offer this feature, although many do. A 401(k) plan may also permit employees to withdraw the amount of their salary deferral contributions after reaching age $59\frac{1}{2}$, even without showing any hardship. Profit-sharing plans also may permit in-service withdrawals of certain amounts.

Plans that permit employees to make after-tax employee contributions may permit participants to withdraw these amounts at any time. The plan probably will want to place some limit on this feature for administrative reasons.

Taxation of Distributions.   Distributions to participants from qualified plans may qualify for special favorable tax treatment. Rather than being treated as ordinary income in the year received, a certain type of distribution is eligible for five-year forward averaging. Five-year forward averaging permits the recipient to pay tax at a rate as though the distribution were received over five years rather than in a single year, although the tax, after it is calculated, is still payable for the year of receipt.

In addition, a participant may be able to rollover without any current tax liability all or part of the otherwise taxable distribution to an individual retirement account or another qualified plan. To be eligible for a rollover, the distribution must be made on account of retirement, separation from service, death, or disability, or must be received after the participant reaches age $59\frac{1}{2}$. The Code sets forth comprehensive rules governing eligibility for rollover treatment.

Termination of the Plan. Just as an employer is not required to maintain a plan, an employer generally may terminate its plan at any time. As discussed above, all account balances or accrued benefits must become fully vested at termination. For a defined contribution plan, the plan administrator may then proceed to pay benefits to participants. A defined benefit plan, however, is covered by Title IV of ERISA (as discussed below) and, to be terminated by the employer, must meet the requirements for either a distress or standard termination. A fully funded plan, with adequate benefits to pay all benefit obligations at termination, files the required filing paperwork with the PBGC, and then may distribute its assets. Generally, the employer wishes to make distributions fairly quickly, to relieve itself of ongoing reporting and administrative requirements, and so either purchases annuities or pays lump sums, with appropriate participant and spousal consents.

If a defined benefit plan terminates and is overfunded, the trust holds assets in excess of those necessary to satisfy all of the plan's benefit obligations. Such excess assets may revert to the employer after all benefits are paid. Under a recently enacted law, the amount of the reversion is subject to a 50 percent tax. This 50 percent tax is reduced to 20 percent if the sponsor either (1) transfers 25 percent of the reversion to a qualified replacement plan, which can be either a new or existing plan, or (2) uses 20 percent of the reversion to increase benefits ratably for all qualified participants in the terminating plan.

Title III: The Administrative Provisions
Title III of ERISA concerns juridical and administrative matters. It facilitates the coordination of activities between the government agencies involved: DOL, IRS, and PBGC. It also provides guidelines that apply to actuaries who desire to be enrolled. Only enrolled

actuaries may sign the actuarial reports that must be filed pursuant to the requirements of these agencies.

Title IV: The Plan Termination and Multiemployer Plan Provisions

Plan Termination Provisions. The plan termination provisions of Title IV of ERISA are designed to ensure that certain vested benefits accrued by participants are paid if a pension plan is terminated. This title of ERISA covers single employer pension plans and multiemployer pension plans (discussed separately below). The insurance program with respect to single employer pension plans requires the payment of an annual premium of at least $16 per participant and as much as $34 per participant for underfunded plans. If a single employer pension plan is terminated with insufficient assets to pay benefits, the PBGC will cover certain vested benefits that have already accrued. There is a limit on the guaranteed monthly benefit limitation of $2,028.41 (adjusted for cost of living changes).

Under rules that took effect in 1986, an underfunded plan can be terminated only in one of the following situations: (1) when the employer has either filed a petition for liquidation or is in the process of bankruptcy reorganization, and the court determines that the plan must terminate to enable the employer to pay debts and survive the reorganization process; (2) when the PBGC determines that an employer will not be able to continue in business without the termination of the plan; or (3) when the PBGC makes a determination that the cost of maintaining the plan has become too burdensome to the employer because of a decline in the employer's work force. Any benefits paid by the PBGC are recoverable against the sponsoring employer and members of the corporate control group. In addition, the PBGC may establish a lien pursuant to ERISA.

Multiemployer Plans and Withdrawal Liability. On September 26, 1980, Congress passed the Multiemployer Pension Plan Amendments Act (MPPAA), which amended ERISA.

MPPAA applies if the employer or any business under common control with the employer has an obligation to contribute to a "multiemployer plan" covered by Title IV of ERISA, and if that plan has "unfunded vested benefits" (UVBs).

A multiemployer plan covered by Title IV of ERISA has the following characteristics:

1. The plan is maintained by more than one employer pursuant to an agreement with one or more labor organizations.
2. The plan is not an individual account plan (such as a 401(k) plan or profit sharing plan).
3. The plan provides retirement benefits (not health and welfare benefits).

Generally, an employer with an obligation to contribute to a multiemployer plan has signed a collective bargaining agreement. That agreement will contain a provision requiring the employer to make contributions to a multiemployer benefit plan sponsored by the union, or by a group of unions in conjunction with an employer group. The contributions are usually based on hours or days worked by covered employees, but some plans measure contributions as a percentage of covered payroll, or are based on a measure of output (such as tons of coal or containers handled by covered employees).

Not all plans maintained by union/employer groups are subject to the MPPAA. If the plan provides only health and welfare benefits, for example, it is not subject to the MPPAA. However, some plans have names that sound like welfare plans, but in fact are pension plans. If the plan is a pension plan, it is covered by the MPPAA only if it is not an individual account plan. An individual account plan is a plan that maintains separate employee investment accounts for each participant. Very few multiemployer plans are individual account plans.

Each employer contributing to a multiemployer plan is allocated a "share" of the plan's unfunded vested benefits. The UVBs represent the difference between the present value of the nonforfeitable benefits accrued by plan participants and the assets of the plan, as of a given date. If the plan's assets exceed its vested benefits, generally, there will be no withdrawal liability. If, as is more common, the plan's vested benefits exceed the assets, the plan must adopt a method to allocate the UVBs among the contributing employers. MPPAA prescribes four methods for allocating the UVBs; a plan may design its own method subject to government approval.

Under MPPAA, all plans are required to provide employers with the general information necessary to allow them to estimate their withdrawal liability exposure without regard to the method used in determining the amount of withdrawal liability. In most cases, this will include a description of the allocation method used by the plan, the UVB values for each relevant year, and the total plan contributions used to determine the employer's share. The employer then must determine the contributions it made for the relevant years, and insert those values in the plan's calculation. Most plans will perform this calculation for the employer, either without charge or upon payment of a modest fee.

Many small employers are reluctant to ask multiemployer plans about potential withdrawal liability. However, this information is essential for a purchaser of a U.S. business who wants to be in a position to make rational decisions concerning the acquisition. In such cases, it is recommended that the seller ask the multiemployer plans for an estimate of withdrawal liability for use by the seller's accountants in the preparation of the seller's annual audit. This explanation should not alert the plan as to the impending sale.

Withdrawal liability could be triggered as follows. Let us assume that a purchaser of a U.S. business has determined that the employer is contributing to a multiemployer plan, and that it is exposed to considerable withdrawal liability. That exposure is of no consequence so long as the employer does not incur a "withdrawal."

A complete withdrawal occurs whenever an employer ceases to have an obligation to contribute to the plan, or terminates all covered operations under the plan. A partial withdrawal can be one of two types: a facility take-out or a 70 percent decline. A "facility take-out" occurs when the employer ceases to have an obligation to contribute to the plan or terminates covered operations at one or more (but not all) facilities or collective bargaining units subject to the plan, *and* either continues operations at that location or in that unit of the type for which contributions were previously required, or transfers the covered work to another noncontributing facility. A "70 percent decline" occurs when the employer's annual contribution base units (usually hours or days by which contributions are measured) in each year of a three-year testing period fall below 30 percent of the employer's highest two-year average for the five-year period preceding the testing period. Plans in the retail food industry may substitute 65 percent for the 30 percent figure.

In the event of a partial withdrawal, the employer's liability is a fraction of the potential complete withdrawal liability, determined by the employer's contribution base units for the year after the partial withdrawal divided by the employer's average contribution base units for the five years prior to the withdrawal or prior to the testing period. In the case of a facility take-out, it is quite common for the partial liability to be considerably greater than the portion of the employer's contributions represented by the affected facility. This is because the employer may well have been experiencing an overall decline in covered employment that did not trigger any liability, but that will count in determining the partial withdrawal fraction.

Special rules exist for employers in certain industries. For example, if substantially all of the covered employees of an employer are engaged in construction industry work, and if the plan covers primarily construction industry employees or adopts the construction industry rule, the employer will be deemed to have withdrawn only if the employer continues to perform work in the jurisdiction of the plan within the five-year period after the cessation of covered operations. A construction industry plan also cannot assess partial withdrawal liability unless the employer's obligation to contribute is continued for only an insubstantial portion of its work in the jurisdiction of the plan. The entertainment industry has rules very similar to those for the construction industry.

The MPPAA also contains a narrow relief provision for "trucking industry" plans. Unfortunately, the definition is so narrowly drawn that only a handful of small plans meet the standard.

In addition to the direct employer, ERISA imposes joint and several liability on all members of a group of trades or businesses under common control as of the date of withdrawal. In some cases, when a member of the group is unincorporated, this will result in personal liability on the part of business owners.

In general, withdrawal liability can be reduced in a number of ways: first, by taking advantage of a statutory reduction or liability avoidance provision; second, by arranging to withdraw in an advantageous year; and third, by successfully challenging some aspect of the plan's assessment. Once all of these possibilities have been explored and exhausted, the only alternative is for the employer to pay the assessment.

MPPAA contains a number of provisions that allow an employer to modify or eliminate its contribution obligation without triggering a withdrawal. For example, a reorganization of the corporate employer (such as a transfer of operations within a controlled group of corporations) will not trigger a withdrawal. Similarly, the sale of stock of a business will not trigger a withdrawal, so long as the contribution obligation does not cease.

The most useful liability avoidance provision is Section 4204 of ERISA. That section allows the seller to avoid complete or partial withdrawal liability if the withdrawal is due to a sale of assets that satisfies certain requirements. In this regard, the complying asset sale is treated like a stock sale for MPPAA purposes. The purchaser must agree to contribute to the plan for substantially the same number of contribution base units as the seller had been obliged to contribute for, and the asset purchase agreement must contain certain "magic" indemnity and secondary liability provisions. The seller must also either provide a bond or escrow to the plan for the five plan years after the sale, or more commonly apply for and satisfy the regulatory requirements for waiver of the bonding requirement. If the selling business is substantially liquidated before the secondary liability provision expires, the seller must also satisfy a bonding requirement.

An important side effect of Section 4204 sales is that the purchaser acquires only the seller's last five years of contribution history. Generally, this can be very beneficial. However, if the seller has other contributing operations that are *not* being sold, a transfer of the last five years of contribution history for some of the seller's operations may well *increase* the seller's exposure for the remaining business.

The most commonly applicable relief provision is Section 4225(a). That provision limits an employer's liability to a portion of its liquidation value—30 percent for employers with a value of $2 million or less. However, a number of limitations apply to this rule:

1. The withdrawal must be caused by an arm's-length sale of assets of the employer's entire business.
2. The employer's liability will in any event be at least the value of UVBs attributable to its own employees and retirees.

In the event a single sale of assets under Section 4225(a) results in a withdrawal from two or more multiemployer plans, the plans must share the employer's 4225(a) limit on a pro-rata basis, in proportion to the relative value of UVBs assessed by each plan.

If the employer is insolvent at the date of withdrawal, Section 4225(b) may apply, but only if the employer is being liquidated or dissolved. This section is actually a relief provision for other general creditors, and provides that 50 percent of the employer's withdrawal liability is given priority *behind* other general creditors.

Another way of reducing an employer's exposure to withdrawal liability is to take advantage of relief provisions designed to minimize liability for smaller employers. For example, if the employer's share of the plan's UVBs is less than $150,000, the statute provides for a *de minimis* deductible. If the UVB share is less than $100,000, the deductible is the lesser of $50,000 or $\frac{3}{4}$ percent of the plan's total UVBs. If the UVB share is between $100,000 and $150,000, the deductible may be increased to $100,000 by plan amendment. If a small seller is selling the business to a larger purchaser, it may be advisable to trigger a withdrawal upon the sale (within the *de minimis* deductible) and allow the purchaser to come in as a new contributor.

Other Federal Laws

In addition to ERISA and the Code, other federal laws, primarily securities and employment discrimination laws, affect employee benefit plans. An analysis of these laws is beyond the scope of this chapter; however, certain of these laws are identified below:

1. The Securities Act of 1933.
2. The Securities Exchange Act of 1934.
3. The Investment Company Act of 1940.
4. The Investment Advisors Act of 1940.

5. The National Labor Relations Act.
6. The Age Discrimination in Employment Act.

WELFARE BENEFITS

As set forth above, ERISA defines employee welfare benefit plans expansively. Despite the seemingly comprehensive list of benefits that fall within the definition of *welfare benefit* under ERISA, welfare benefit plans are subject to little substantive regulation by ERISA other than the fiduciary duty and reporting and disclosure rules, as discussed above.

In contrast to the treatment of welfare plans under ERISA, welfare plans are regulated extensively under the Code. The general rule of taxability is that employer-provided welfare benefits are taxable to an employee as compensation unless the Code excludes a particular benefit from the employee's gross income. Accordingly, if an employer provides a welfare benefit to employees that is not explicitly excluded from income by the Code, then the employees must include the dollar value of the benefit in their gross income in the taxable year in which they receive the benefit. Because of the separate tax treatment of each category of benefit, individual welfare benefits must be considered separately.

Most of the benefits listed in the ERISA definition of welfare benefits are statutorily excluded from income. Benefits such as health and group life programs are generally excluded from employee income, within limits and, in certain cases, subject to satisfaction of specific nondiscrimination requirements set by the Code. Some benefits, however, such as educational assistance programs are given favorable tax treatment on a year-to-year basis only. Thus, while employer contributions for an educational assistance program are excluded from a participating employee's income this year, no guarantee exists that the U.S. Congress will renew the statutory exclusion for such a benefit to allow for favorable tax treatment in succeeding years. In essence, both the employer and the employee take an annual risk that the statutory exclusion will be renewed from year to year when offering and participating in such programs. Congress tends to renew the favorable tax status of such programs as a general matter, but it need not do so.

Health Plans. Employer-provided health benefits—either in the form of employer premium contributions for a health insurance policy, known as an insured plan, or in the form of contributions to a self-insured plan—are excluded from an employee's gross income. A self-insured health plan may lose such favorable tax treatment, however, if it discriminates in favor of highly compensated employees in either their eligibility to participate in the plan or in the benefits provided. Also, special rules apply to the tax treatment of health benefits provided to self-employed individuals.

Group-Term Life Insurance. Pursuant to the Code, the cost of the first $50,000 of employer-provided life insurance is excluded from employee income if the following requirements are satisfied: (1) the insurance policy provides a death benefit excludable from income under the Code; (2) the policy, which must be owned either directly or indirectly by the employer, is provided to a group of employees; and (3) the policy must set forth the amount of insurance available to the employee in such a way as to preclude individual selection. Nevertheless, highly compensated employees can lose the exclusion if their employer discriminates against the rank-and-file employees in their favor. Thus, if an employer discriminates in favor of a highly compensated employee as to eligibility or benefits on any day in a given year, group-term life insurance coverage is taxable for any highly compensated employee in that year.

Disability Benefits. Like health and group-term life insurance benefits, employer-provided disability benefits are also given favorable tax treatment under the Code. As an employer-provided benefit, the company contributions for disability insurance are tax deductible to the employer and not included as income to the employee. The drawback to the disability exclusion, however, is that if the employee incurs a disability and receives disability payments from the insurance policy, such payments are fully taxable as income.

A more tax-efficient approach, from the employees' perspective, entails allowing them to pay for the cost of disability coverage with dollars already subject to income taxes or after-tax dollars. Basically, employees would pay the premium cost with after-tax dollars so that should they ever become disabled, the benefits paid out from the policy would be tax free. Disabled employees would then realize a tax savings at a time they would need it most.

Cafeteria Plans.   A cafeteria plan is an employer plan under which employees may choose from among two or more benefits consisting of cash and certain qualified welfare benefits. Qualified welfare benefits means that such benefits are given statutory exclusions from gross income under the Code. Structurally, a cafeteria plan is the framework by which an employer offers its employees the freedom to select from benefit programs available under the cafeteria plan. Without using the cafeteria plan vehicle, employees could recognize current income for benefits not selected under the constructive receipt doctrine discussed below. Employers may choose which benefits they will offer to the employees under the plan. Similarly, subject to restrictions contained in the plan, the employees have the option of choosing from among the benefits offered which benefits they will use.

Pursuant to regulations under the Code, a cafeteria plan must meet the following requirements. It must have a written plan document that describes each of the benefits available. The plan document must also explain, among other things, the time periods and procedures for making the benefit elections, and the duration and expiration of such elections. Finally, a cafeteria plan may offer only qualified welfare benefits. Nonqualified benefits include scholarships and educational assistance programs, among others.

The manner by which a cafeteria plan operates depends on its design. One design is known as the flexible benefits plan. Under this kind of plan, the employer gives an eligible employee a stated amount of benefit dollars with which the employee may purchase some, all, or none of the available benefits. The calculation of the amount of benefit dollars allocated to each employee may be a function of the current year's actual benefit cost per employee or an average cost of all employees. In addition, employees are often permitted to contribute their own money on a pre-tax basis to supplement the employer's allocation of benefit dollars in order to purchase benefits. Moreover, if the employee finds that he has excess benefit dollars after he makes his benefit selections, he may receive the excess as additional cash compensation. A simpler design is one that allows eligible employees to pay their benefit costs with pre-tax dollars. Participants of such a plan realize significant tax savings which is quite an advantage over a standard welfare benefit program where participants pay their benefit costs with after-tax dollars.

Each year, employees must elect the benefits they desire for that year in accordance with the cafeteria plan procedures as set forth in the plan document. Such selection, by law, must stay in effect for at least one year. Plans may be drafted to permit no changes in the employee's selection or to permit changes only under circumstances prescribed by the relevant Code regulations. A change in family circumstances, for instance, may warrant a review and change of an employee's benefit selection. Absent new elections for subsequent years, however, the prior elections usually stay in effect.

Cafeteria plans appear to be the welfare benefit program of choice in recent years. Aside from the tax advantages available to both employers and employees, cafeteria plans provide great flexibility. Moreover, in light of the skyrocketing cost of providing welfare benefits to employees, cafeteria plans help implement a fair system of cost-sharing between employers and employees.

VEBAs. Voluntary employees' beneficiary associations, or VEBAs, are organizations that are generally exempt from tax under the Code. A VEBA is an entity, usually a trust or a corporation, that is independent of both the employees and the employer, and provides life, sickness, accident, or other benefits. Tax exempt VEBAs are usually collectively bargained associations, although they need not be collectively bargained in order to remain tax exempt if they meet certain other requirements. VEBAs must be submitted to the IRS for recognition of exempt status under the Code. Indeed, the IRS will not treat them as a tax exempt association before such application is made.

Generally, membership in a VEBA must be voluntary. Membership is deemed voluntary if employees join by some affirmative act; if membership is a condition of employment where the employee incurs no detriment, such as mandatory contributions to the VEBA; or if membership is required as the result of a collective bargaining agreement. In addition, only the membership, an independent trustee or trustees, or trustees who are appointed by or on behalf of the membership may control a VEBA.

Finally, VEBAs may provide only life, sickness, accident, or other benefits. Other qualified benefits are described as those benefits similar to life, sickness, or accident benefits or benefits intended to protect or improve the health or the earning power of members or their dependents. These benefits include severance benefits, vacation benefits, education or training benefits, and personal legal service benefits through a group legal service program. Nonqualifying benefits include commuting expenses, homeowner's insurance for property damage, and loans.

One key advantage to a VEBA is the ability to pre-fund benefits with currently deductible contributions. The amount of pre-funding is equal to current year's costs and a reserve contribution for future costs. The Code limits the amount of reserve contributions. Depending on the specific welfare benefit at issue, different limitations apply.

EXECUTIVE COMPENSATION

Many U.S. employers provide special retirement plans and equity-based compensation programs for their key employees and outside directors. As noted above, ERISA and the Code limit the amount of benefits that may be provided under qualified plans to highly compensated employees. In the usual circumstance, a gap exists between the benefits that can be provided pursuant to qualified plans and the level and type of benefits employers desire to offer to key employees. Further, under the qualification rules (described above), outside directors are not permitted to participate in qualified plans. Hence, if an employer wishes to offer benefits to outside directors, it must be done through nonqualified plans. Many techniques are utilized in providing executive benefits. Some of the arrangements are not subject to the requirements of ERISA; others are. If designed properly, however, such plans or programs are not subject to the somewhat onerous participation, vesting, and funding rules of ERISA, but may be subject to the enforcement provisions and fiduciary rules.

Nonqualified Deferred Compensation

Supplemental Executive Retirement Plans

Nonqualified deferred compensation plans come in many forms. One such plan is known commonly as a Supplemental Executive Retirement Plan (SERP). Under a SERP, the company promises to pay from its general assets a certain level of retirement income to the key employee. Payment is usually made at retirement, either in a one-time payment or in annual installments. The plan may provide a death benefit and a disability benefit. The retirement income can be measured in a number of ways: a percentage of final compensation, a stated dollar amount, the sum of annual phantom allocations made during the key employee's working career, or an amount based on company performance. It is also possible to coordinate a SERP with one or more qualified plans. For example the ultimate benefit payable under the SERP can be reduced by amounts payable under some or all of the company's qualified plans, as well as by benefits payable under Social Security. SERPs are also used with respect to outside directors who are not permitted to participate in the corporation's qualified plans since they are not employees of the company. This type of SERP can be the mirror image of a qualified plan, but cover outside directors.

In practice, most SERPs cover only key employees—that is, employees who are either highly compensated or key policymakers. These plans are also known as "top-hat" plans. Coverage of employees other than key employees could result in the plan's being subject to all of ERISA's requirements, including the participation, vesting, and funding rules. Compliance with these provisions would make a SERP far too costly to maintain in almost all circumstances.

Yet another type of SERP is one used in conjunction with early retirement incentive programs. Such a nonqualified deferred compensation arrangement provides benefits in addition to those provided under qualified plans. This type of SERP benefit is viewed as an incentive for individuals to retire voluntarily, which may be essential for the continued viability of a company, especially in recessionary times. In addition to complying with ERISA and the Code, such early retirement incentive programs must comply with other laws such as the Age Discrimination in Employment Act and the Older Workers Benefit Protection Act. An analysis of these laws is beyond the scope of this chapter.

Another reason to use a SERP is to replace benefits lost by key employees who are hired after spending a substantial part of their career with another employer. Generally, under qualified retirement plans, a participant will have an ultimate benefit under two plans that is less than it would have been had all service been rendered under one plan. Accordingly, a need may arise to provide a benefit enhancement through a SERP in order to attract a seasoned executive who is concerned about his or her retirement income.

Finally, a U.S. employer may offer a special enhanced benefit through a SERP to retain a key employee. In order to be effective, these plans usually have a stringent vesting schedule that far exceeds the maximum permissible schedule under ERISA (which does not apply in this instance). This is sometimes known as a "golden handcuff."

"Rabbi Trusts" and Other Deferred Income

Many U.S. employers also maintain a form of elective cash-based deferred compensation. This type of program is tax-driven and allows a key employee to elect to defer receipt of compensation or bonus income to a later date when the recipient's tax rate may be lower. These plans involve no cost to the employer other than design and administrative expenses.

Under all of the above-mentioned programs and others that have not been described above, no trust is established for the benefit of the participants. Because no trust has been established, the covered key employee has no security other than the company's unsecured promise to pay the benefit. This arrangement entails an obvious element of risk. Devices exist to help mitigate such risks. One device is known as a settlor trust or rabbi trust. Under a settlor trust, however, the employer remains the settlor, and, to retain the tax deferral, the assets of the trust must be subject to the claims of creditors of the corporation.

From an income tax perspective, if properly designed, the key employee covered by a nonqualified deferred compensation plan is not deemed to be in receipt of income until the benefits are paid from the company with respect to the plan. At this time, the employer is entitled to a deduction with respect to the amount of such payment. Careful attention must be given to the design of the plan to ensure this favorable tax result. The IRS may apply certain doctrines, known as the economic benefit doctrine and constructive receipt doctrine, that could result in the acceleration of income recognition to a time before the benefit is payable. This result would be attained if the key employee has rights to receive the benefit at a date before the distribution date. The tension here is that from a general design perspective there are usually many reasons why a key employee may need or desire access to funds at an earlier date.

Equity-Based Compensation

In addition to cash-based nonqualified deferred compensation plans, many U.S. employers sponsor equity or equity-based compensation arrangements for their key employees. These arrangements take many forms such as stock option plans, phantom stock plans, restrictive stock arrangements, and the like. The theory behind establishing such plans and arrangements is to provide economic rewards to key employees based on the increase in value of the company. While not necessarily directly related to the contributions of the company's key employees, a benefit measured in increased value of the stock of the company is a fairly common way of designing such a program. Equity and equity-based arrangements can also contain mechanisms that have the purpose of retaining the executive, the so-called golden handcuff approach.

Restrictive Stock
U.S. corporations will often convey or sell to their key employees shares of stock of the company. The shares typically contain restrictions regarding their transferability and forfeitability. Thus, the shares are only transferrable back to the company (except in the case of death, in which event they are transferrable to the estate), and do not become vested unless the key employee remains an employee for a stated period of time. Under the U.S. tax rules, the key employee is not subject to income tax until the first year in which the property becomes transferrable or when there is no

longer a risk of forfeiture. The delay in taxation could represent a significant benefit to the key employee. Additionally, the company will receive a deduction for the amount includable in income by the key employee for its taxable year in which the key employee recognizes income. In order to receive the deduction, the employer is required to withhold tax for the year in which income is recognized by the key employee.

Since the stock is restricted, until the restrictions lapse, the key employee is not treated as the owner of the shares for tax purposes. Accordingly, any "dividends" on the shares that are paid to the key employee are treated as compensation payments and are therefore deductible. This is advantageous to the company because dividend payments on unrestricted shares are generally not deductible. A key employee is entitled to make an election to be taxed before the restrictions on the stock lapse. Such an election must be made within six months from the date of the purchase or conveyance of the stock. Since the tax is based on the difference between the fair market value at the time of determination and any purchase price, if any, for the shares, the key employee who believes the value of the shares will rise substantially may wish to make the election when the tax liability may be quite low, with the thought of holding on to the shares for a time thereafter. Without making the election, the tax would be payable upon the shares' becoming vested, at which time the value might be considerably higher than on the date of grant or conveyance.

Stock Options

Another form of equity-based compensation for key employees is stock options. A stock option is a contractual right granted to a key employee to purchase stock of the employer during a stated period of time for an established price. In the United States, stock options take the form of either nonqualified stock options (NQSOs) or incentive stock options (ISOs). Usually, three events are involved with respect to stock options: the grant of the stock option, the vesting of the stock option, and the exercise of the stock option. To the extent that the efforts of a key employee contribute to the enhanced value of the company, the stock option becomes more valuable as the value of the underlying stock exceeds the price of the stock option. ISOs and NQSOs are subject to different rules and sections of the Code and the tax treatment differs under each type of option.

The following is an analysis of each type of stock option.

Nonqualified Stock Options. A NQSO provides much more flexibility than an ISO. However, the tax treatment with respect to the key employee is less beneficial under a NQSO than under an ISO. NQSOs can have any exercise price (however, a nominal exercise price may result in immediate taxation to the employee), may extend for any stated exercise period and vesting period, and may be issued in any amount. The key employee does not recognize income on account of the grant of a NQSO provided the options are issued for more than nominal value. Moreover, there is no tax recognition at the time of vesting of the option. The key employee does recognize ordinary income at the time the NQSO is exercised. The amount of income recognized is the difference between the current fair market of the stock and the key employee's exercise price for the NQSO. The company receives a tax deduction based on the difference between fair market value and the exercise price. With corporate tax rates being higher than individual tax rates, an overall tax efficiency is achieved through the use of NQSOs at this time. NQSOs may be granted to employees as well as outside directors.

From an accounting perspective, the company need not be concerned about the financial accounting at the time of grant or exercise of a NQSO if the option price is at least equal to the fair market value of the stock as of the date of grant. If the option price is less than fair market value, that difference is a compensation expense that must be charged to earnings for financial accounting purposes over the time period of the option.

Incentive Stock Options. ISOs must satisfy certain technical requirements to be eligible for special favorable tax treatment. ISOs are, therefore, less flexible than NQSOs. One of these technical rules is that no more than $100,000 worth of the employer's stock may become first exercisable in any one year after the grant of the option. Under another rule, ISOs may be granted only to employees. Thus, they cannot be used to compensate outside directors.

Under yet another rule, ISOs may be granted only within the 10 years following the adoption of the option plan. Last, ISOs must be issued for at least the fair market value of the stock at the time they are granted (110 percent of fair market value with respect to 10 percent or greater shareholders).

By contrast with NQSOs, the tax treatment of an ISO is more favorable to the key employee but less favorable to the employer. The key employee recognizes no taxable income at the grant (although alternative minimum tax liability may arise), vesting, or excercise dates. In order to defer income recognition at the exercise date, the shares received must not be disposed of within two years of the grant date or one year of the date of exercise. No financial accounting considerations exist with regard to ISOs.

Phantom Equity Plans

Many U.S. companies do not issue stock to key employees in the company. Some of these companies do, however, wish to reward key employees with cash compensation based on the performance of the company as measured by increase in the value of the stock. This objective may be attained by using certain devices described below. One device is known as stock appreciation rights plan (SAR) and another is known as a phantom stock plan (Phantom Plan). They are similar in nature. The difference between an SAR and a Phantom Plan is that in an SAR the key employee only receives payment equal to the increase in value from the date of grant in the shares of underlying stock, whereas in a Phantom Plan the key employee receives not only payment equal to such increase in value but also a payment equal to the initial value of the underlying shares. Furthermore, an employer may use an SAR plan in conjunction with an option plan. This is not the case with respect to Phantom Plans. In a combined option/SAR plan the key employee has the election of exercising the stock option and receiving the shares of stock, instead of exercising the SAR and simply receiving a cash payment equal to the increased value of the underlying shares and forgoing any possible further appreciation in the value of the shares. The following is a description of SARs and Phantom Plans.

Stock Appreciation Rights.   The grant of an SAR provides a key employee with a contractual right to receive payment equal to the appreciation in value in the company's stock. This appreciation is measured from the date of grant to the date of exercise, and can be calculated in different ways. One method is to use the fair market value of the stock. Other methods include increase in earnings or a multiple of earnings, or increase in book value and the like. Upon exercise of a SAR, payments can be made, depending on the design of the plan, in either cash or shares of stock of the employer.

The key employee does not recognize income on the grant of an SAR. Amounts received in either cash or stock upon the exercise of an SAR are taxed as ordinary income. These amounts are subject to withholding tax, which withholding facilitates a deduction by the company at the time the SAR is exercised in an amount equal to the amount of income recognized by the key employee. From a financial accounting perspective, the employer must recognize compensation expense during the years in which the key employee performed services related to the SAR. This compensation expense measures the increase in value of the SAR units. Decreases in value may also be taken into account.

Phantom Plans. Phantom Plans are very similar to SARs. The distinguishing factors are that Phantom Plans are not combined with options, they provide a benefit based on future appreciation, and the initial value of the underlying stock and benefits are paid in cash only. Generally, the tax and accounting treatment is the same for phantom stock as for SARs.

U.S. companies that are subject to the Securities Exchange Act of 1934 (the "Act") must carefully design and administer their equity and equity-based plans in compliance with specific rules. These rules include registration and exemption matters as well as the short-swing profits recovery rules applicable to insiders of the issuing employer. This subject is beyond the scope of this chapter, but must be carefully considered whenever dealing with a company subject to the Act.

In addition, SAR and Phantom Plans must be designed carefully in order to avoid the application of ERISA. Generally, this is achieved by providing for a payment on maturity date that is not the date of employment termination. For example, maturity could occur after a stated number of years pass or on a certain date. This approach results in the plan's not deferring income to termination of employment, one of the tests used to determine if a plan is a pension plan covered by ERISA. If an SAR or Phantom Plan is subject to ERISA, then the somewhat onerous participation, vesting, funding, and trust rules would apply. The tax consequences could also differ.

CHAPTER 23

COMPENSATION AND EMPLOYEE BENEFITS IN THE UNITED STATES: A PRIMER ON DESIGN AND HUMAN RESOURCE IMPLICATIONS

Louis L. Joseph
Senior Manager, Employee Benefits Services
Richard B. Stanger
Managing Partner and National Director, Employee Benefits Services
Price Waterhouse

INTRODUCTION

The term *pension plan* encompasses a vast range of alternatives. There are defined benefit plans and defined contribution plans, from which further distinctions are made including single-employer and multiemployer plans; profit sharing plans and employee stock ownership plans; money purchase plans; thrift plans; executive compensation plans; and tax-qualified and non-tax-qualified plans.

A tax-qualified pension plan is one of the best tax shelters available. An employer is allowed a current deduction for its contributions to the plan. The employee pays no tax on money contributed for his or her benefit until a distribution is made, earnings from investments made with funds in the plan accumulate tax free, and distributions from the plan may be afforded favorable income tax treatment. The nontax reasons for adopting a tax-qualified pension plan include attracting employees, reducing employee turnover, increasing employee incentive, and accumulating funds for retirement.

If a plan is not qualified, the deduction for employer contributions is deferred until benefits are taxed to the employee. The employee is taxed when benefits are vested and earnings on plan investments are taxed currently.

The rules for qualified plans are basically the same for corporate employers and nonincorporated trades or businesses. A tax-qualified pension plan is especially attractive to working owners of closely held corporations and to self-employed persons. Their long-term service gives them the best opportunity to accumulate large sums through the tax-free build-up of capital. Although benefits must be provided for other employees as well, the owner-employees usually receive a much larger benefit than the other employees.

There are two distinct elements embodied in the term *qualified pension plan*. The first element is the term *pension plan*. A pension plan means any plan or program maintained by an employer or an employee organization (or both) that (1) provides retirement income to employees or (2) results in a deferral of income of employees for periods extending generally to the end of employment or beyond, regardless of how plan contributions or benefits are calculated or how benefits are distributed.

The second element is the term *qualified,* which means that the pension plan is afforded special tax treatment for meeting a host of requirements of the Internal Revenue Code. These requirements have four fundamental underpinnings. The plan must be a definite written program, it must be communicated to the employees, it must be permanent, and it must prohibit the use or diversion of funds for purposes other than the exclusive benefit of employees or their beneficiaries.

There are numerous additional requirements that must be met before a plan qualifies for favorable tax treatment. The plan must not discriminate in favor of employees who are highly compensated. With few exceptions, the plan must provide for the payment of benefits in the form of a joint and survivor life annuity and death benefits in the form of a preretirement survivor annuity. The plan must provide that benefits may not be "assigned or alienated" (e.g., to creditors). The plan also must comply with rules regarding vesting of benefits, commencement of benefit payments, and limitations on the amount of benefits payable to a participant.

Additional requirements apply to top-heavy plans, under which benefits are provided largely for key employees—officers, directors, and certain highly compensated employees. These additional requirements include more rapid vesting and minimum benefits for non-key employees.

TYPES OF EMPLOYEE BENEFIT PLANS

Qualified pension plans are divided into two basic categories: defined contribution plans and defined benefit plans. Some tax-qualification rules apply equally to both categories. Other tax-qualification rules apply solely to one category.

Defined Benefit Plans

General Characteristics
A defined benefit plan provides employees definitely determinable retirement benefits based on a formula typically taking into account both compensation and length of service. A general pool of assets is maintained in trust to provide the promised benefits.

Funding a Defined Benefit Plan
To ensure that sufficient money will be available to pay the promised retirement benefit, defined benefit plans are subject to minimum funding requirements. Employers maintaining a defined benefit plan are required each year to fund the pension benefits earned that year. In addition, there are certain circumstances in which there may be additional funding requirements beyond the required

minimum contribution. This situation can arise when a plan has assets that are less than the liabilities it owes to its employees and their beneficiaries for the plan year.

Single-Employer Plans and Multiemployer Plans

A single-employer plan is a plan that is sponsored by one employer. That employer is responsible for meeting the minimum funding requirements and for administering the plan. A plan that has been established under a collective bargaining agreement and to which more than one employer is required to contribute is referred to as a multiemployer plan. In contrast to the single-employer plan, responsibility for a multiemployer plan lies with a board or trustees comprising both union and employer representatives. The minimum funding requirements are designed so that the benefits will be funded over the working lives of the participants. An actuary determines the amount that must be contributed each year so that the participants benefits will be funded upon retirement.

Multiemployer plans are subject to a different set of rules from those for single-employer plans. For example, hours of service that are credited to participating employees for purposes of eligibility, vesting, and accrual of benefits are determined under different rules; there are different minimum funding requirements, and the provisions governing plan terminations are different.

The concept of multiemployer plans was developed to meet the needs of industries such as construction, transportation and mining. Employers that participate in such plans usually employ craftsmen and draw their employees from a limited pool of workers within a specific georgraphical area. A multiemployer plan can benefit a particular industry because it permits employees to take their pension benefits with them when they move from one participating employer to another within the same industry. Such a plan stabilizes pension costs among participating employers; reduces competition for a limited number of employees; provides economies of scale because of the pooling of pension resources, which, in theory, results in either increased benefits or reduced employer costs; and reduces administrative costs because there is only one plan sponsored by several employees.

ERISA and the PBGC

Whether a defined benefit plan is a single-employer plan or a multi-employer plan, it is subject to the rules of the Employee Retirement Income Security Act of 1974 (ERISA). ERISA was enacted to regulate pension plans from inception to termination. Title I of ERISA contains administrative and enforcement provisions including rules on reporting and disclosure of pension information; employee coverage requirements such as participation and vesting; and funding requirements. Title I is administered by the Pension and Welfare Benefits Administration (PWBA) of the Department of Labor (DOL). Title II addresses the relationship between ERISA and the Internal Revenue Code. Title II is administered by the Department of the Treasury and the Internal Revenue Service. Jurisdiction, administration, and enforcement are dealt with under Title III.

Finally, Title IV governs the termination of most defined benefit plans. In addition, it establishes an insurance program to guarantee that employees and their beneficiaries will receive their pension benefits in the event the plan is terminated and does not have sufficient assets to pay benefits. This program, designed to be self-financed, is funded with premiums paid by covered plans. ERISA established the Pension Benefit Guranty Corporation (PBGC) as a wholly owned government corporation to administer the plan termination rules and to establish the mechanisms for insuring benefits. Benefits under most single-employer defined benefit pension plans and multiemployer pension plans are insured by the PBGC.

Plan Terminations

A single-employer plan covered by the PBGC can be voluntarily terminated by the employer that sponsors the plan only if certain conditions are met. A plan can be voluntarily terminated by the employer under either a standard termination or a distress termination. A plan administrator is required to give employees who participate in the plan (and the PBGC, in the case of a distress termination) 60 days' notice in advance of a plan termination.

A standard termination is permitted only for a plan that has sufficient assets to cover all vested and nonvested plan benefits, including contingent benefits such as early retirement supplements or subsidies and plant closing benefits.

Once the procedural requirements for a standard termination have been met, the plan administrator must distribute the plan assets. This generally is accomplished by purchasing annuity contracts to provide benefits payable in annuity form or by paying a lump-sum amount to those employees who have so elected.

If any assets remain after providing for all accrued benefits of plan participants, the excess assets generally may be returned to the employer, if the plan so provides and has so provided for five years. When residual assets cannot be returned to the employer, such assets are allocated to employees who had participated in the plan based on the ratio of the present value of each participating employee's accrued benefit to the present value of all participating employees' accrued benefits.

A distress termination can occur only if an employer's plan can satisfy certain tests to demonstrate financial hardship as outlined by the PBGC. These tests are extremely difficult to meet outside a bankruptcy or reorganization proceeding. The PBGC pays guaranteed vested benefits upon a distress termination. The PBGC also has a claim against all controlled group members for the excess of plan benefits over plan assets, which can be very large.

An involuntary termination will occur if the plan is terminated by action of the PBGC. The PBGC is authorized to seek a court order terminating a covered plan if (1) the employer has not satisfied the minimum funding standards, (2) the plan is unable to pay benefits when due, (3) certain distributions have been made to substantial owners by a plan with unfunded vested benefits, or (4) the possible long-run loss to PBGC under the plan can be expected to increase unreasonably.

A partial termination of a single-employer or multiemployer plan may occur when a significant group of employees covered by a plan is excluded from coverage as a result of either an amendment to the plan or their discharge by the employer. Similarly, a partial termination may occur when benefits or employer contributions are reduced, or the eligibility or vesting requirements under the plan are made more restrictive. If a partial termination of a qualified plan occurs, the termination requirements of the Internal Revenue Code (e.g., accelerated vesting) apply only to the portion of the plan that is terminated.

Withdrawal Liability

Multiemployer plans are rarely terminated either voluntarily or involuntarily. However, an employer that contributes to a multiemployer plan may be subject to withdrawal liability, upon a "complete withdrawal" or a "partial withdrawal" from the plan.

A complete or partial withdrawal may result from a wide variety of corporate actions, including but not limited to a major decrease in operations covered by a plan, a complete cessation of operations, the employer's bargaining out of a plan, a transfer of operations, or a sale of assets. If a withdrawal has occurred, the employer's liability is based on a share of the plan's unfunded vested benefits. This amount is adjusted in the case of a partial withdrawal, and also may be reduced or limited under one or more relief provisions. However, the liability can be large, and all controlled group members are liable.

Defined Contribution Plans

General Characteristics

A defined contribution plan is a pension plan that provides for an individual account for each participant and for benefits based solely upon the amount contributed to the participant's account, and any income, expenses, gains and losses, and any forfeitures of accounts of other participants that may be allocated to such participant's account. Profit sharing, money purchase pension, and stock bonus plans are examples of defined contribution plans.

There are three distinguishing attributes of a defined contribution plan: plan contributions are determined by a formula (either definite, discretionary, or both) and not by actuarial requirements; plan earnings and losses are allocated to participants' accounts and do not affect the employer's retirement plan costs; and plan benefits are not insured by the PBGC.

The Internal Revenue Code sets limits on contributions and other allocations to participants' accounts in a defined contribution plan. Contributions and other additions are referred to as "annual additions" to a participating employee's account. For years beginning after 1986, the annual addition is the sum of employer contributions, employee contributions, and forfeitures. (Forfeitures are those amounts in the account of a participating employee that have not yet vested upon that employee's termination. Such forfeitures are either reallocated among the accounts of the remaining participants or used to reduce employer contributions.)

Profit Sharing Plan

A profit sharing plan is a defined contribution plan to which an employer agrees to make "substantial and recurring" though generally discretionary contributions. Amounts contributed to the plan are invested and accumulate tax-free for distribution generally upon disability, death, or termination of employment.

Contributions to a profit sharing plan are usually keyed to the existence of profits. However, neither current nor accumulated profits are required for employer contributions.

Although many employers adopt a discretionary contribution formula, others adopt a fixed formula. For example, an employer may obligate itself to contribute to its profit sharing plan a specified percentage of each participating employee's compensation if profits exceed a specified level. Similar to other defined contribution plans, a participant's retirement benefits are based on the amount in his or her account at retirement. Also, forfeitures arising from employee turnover may be reallocated among the remaining participants in the plan.

Stock Bonus Plan

A stock bonus plan is similar to a profit sharing plan except that benefit payments must be offered in the stock of the employer. Thus, stock bonus plan may distribute cash to an employee subject to the employee's right to demand a distribution of employer stock. Further, if the plan permits cash distributions and the employer securities are not readily tradable on an established market, the participants must have the right to require the employer to repurchase the distributed stock under a fair valuation formula.

Employee Stock Ownership Plan

An employee stock ownership plan (an ESOP) is a special type of stock bonus plan. A stock bonus plan permits but does not require current investments in employer stock. An ESOP on the other hand, must invest primarily in employer securities. Also, an ESOP may borrow from the employer or use the employer's credit to purchase employer securities from the employer or shareholders.

Generally, the lending of money to a plan is considered a prohibited transaction. However, a loan to an ESOP or the guarantee by the employer of a loan to an ESOP by a commercial lender will not be a prohibited transaction if the loan satisfies certain requirements. A stock bonus plan that is not an ESOP generally is prohibited from engaging in such transactions.

An ESOP loan to purchase employer securities is repaid with deductible employer contributions to the ESOP. The deduction allowed for contributions to repay loan principal can be as high as 25 percent of the compensation paid to the ESOP participants. Contributions to pay loan interest are deductible without limitation.

Employer securities are held in trust under the ESOP and allocated to participants' accounts as an ESOP loan is repaid. When a participant terminates, the participant is paid his or her vested interest in the plan in the form of employer securities or, upon demand, a cash distribution. However, an ESOP may preclude a participant from obtaining a distribution of securities if the employer's corporate charter or by-laws restricts the ownership of substantially all employer securities to employees or the ESOP.

A terminated ESOP participant can "put" the securities back to the employer at fair market value if the securities are not readily tradable on an established market. To keep the securities from falling into the hand of competitors, either the ESOP or the employer may be given the right of first refusal of the securities. However, participating employees cannot be required to sell their securities back to the employer.

ESOPs are capable of doing much more than simply providing retirement benefits for employees. An ESOP can be used as a market for employer stock, as a method of increasing an employer's cash flow, as a means of financing an employer's growth, and as an estate planning tool.

401(k) Plan

A profit sharing or stock bonus plan that includes a cash-or-deferred arrangement for participants is one of the most popular and widely offered employee benefit plans. They are commonly known as "401(k) plans," after the applicable section of the Internal Revenue Code. A 401(k) plan permits a participant to elect to have the employer make a contribution to the plan on his or her behalf or to pay an equivalent amount to the employee in cash. Most 401(k) plans operate on the basis of a salary reduction election, although the rules also permit participants an election between current or deferred profit-sharing.

Subject to certain limitations, a participant's elective contributions under a 401(k) plan are excluded from income when made and are not taxed until distributed. For purposes of many of the rules applicable to qualified plans, elective contributions are considered employer contributions.

A 401(k) plan may be a stand-alone plan (permit elective contributions only) or may also permit other types of employer contributions and/or voluntary employee after-tax contributions. However, a 401(k) plan is the only method available under which employees may defer compensation on an elective, pretax basis under a qualified plan.

Money Purchase Pension Plan

A money purchase pension plan is a defined contribution plan under which an employer's contributions are mandatory and are usually based on the compensation of participating employees.

The obligation to fund the plan distinguishes a money purchase pension plan from a profit sharing or stock bonus plan.

Contributions must be made to a money purchase pension plan even if an employer has no profits. A failure to contribute to a money purchase pension plan can result in the imposition of a penalty tax.

Forfeitures that occur because of employee turnover may reduce future contributions of an employer or may be used to increase the benefits of remaining participants. Retirement benefits for a participant are based on the balance in his or her account at retirement.

Thrift or Savings Plan

A thrift or savings plan is a defined contribution plan under which employees contribute toward the ultimate benefits that will be provided. The plan may be a money purchase pension plan, or a profit sharing plan, or a stock bonus plan.

These plans are contributory in the sense that the employer contributions on behalf of a particular employee are based on mandatory contributions by the employee. An employee contributes a part of his or her compensation to the plan in order to participate in the plan.

Employer contributions typically are made on a matching basis. For example, a plan might provide for an employer contribution equal to 50 percent of the total contribution made by the employee. Thrift or savings plans may also include an additional voluntary employee contribution feature. The employer does not make a matching contribution for these voluntary employee contributions.

Executive Compensation Plans

Generally, executive compensation plans are nonqualified deferred compensation arrangements. Historically, it was believed that executives would be in a lower tax bracket when they received their money from the plan than when it was deferred. Today, tax rates have been leveled, and the role of the nonqualified deferred compensation plan, as a tax shelter, has been somewhat diminished. However, the compounding effect of the pre-tax earnings continues to provide significant tax savings. Moreover, nonqualified plans have become increasingly popular as a means of supplementing an executive's retirement benefit in light of the more restrictive limitations imposed on benefits under qualified retirement plans.

The major advantage of nonqualified deferred compensation plans is that they are not covered by many of the requirements of ERISA. The funding requirements of ERISA do not apply to nonqualified plans, and certain nondiscrimination, participation, and vesting requirements also do not apply.

A disadvantage, from the executive's standpoint, is the lack of security of the deferred compensation arrangement. Most nonqualified deferred compensation plans are unfunded and employers pay benefits on a pay-as-you go basis. Therefore, executives participating in such a plan may not perceive their deferred compensation as adequately secured. In order to address this perception and provide a systematic method of accumulating assets to pay benefits, many employers consider informally funding their deferred benefit obligations. For example, an employer may purchase corporate-owned life insurance or establish rabbi trust as a means of ensuring that the benefits will be paid. A rabbi trust is a trust under which the assets are at all times available to pay the employer's creditors in the event of the employer's bankruptcy. An employer must be careful in using such financing arrangements in order to avoid current taxation to the executive.

Supplemental Executive Retirement Plans

Supplemental Executive Retirement Plans, or SERPs, are non-qualified arrangements intended to accomplish a number of objectives. These objectives can include one or more of the following: (1) provide retirement income based on total compensation, including bonus payments, incentive awards, and deferred compensation not taken into account under the qualified plan formula; (2) provide greater benefits to select executives that would be provided under the qualified plan; (3) provide meaningful benefits for executives with fewer years of service resulting, for example, from a mid- or late career job change; and (4) make up for benefits forfeited by a newly hired executive for leaving a former employer.

The form of benefit payments under a SERP usually parallels the payout method from the employer's qualified plan. However, where the benefits from a qualified plan may not be forfeitable once vested, SERP payments may. For example, SERP benefits may be conditioned upon the executive's not competing, or on being available to consult, with the employer after retirement.

Unlike qualified plan benefits, which are paid out of a trust and are protected from claims of the employer's creditors, benefits under a SERP are typically paid out of the employer's general assets and are not protected from creditors' claims. Therefore, whether the employer will be able to fulfill its deferred compensation obligations in the future (e.g., in the event of financial difficulty) can be an issue of real concern for the executive.

Excess Benefit Plans

The Internal Revenue Code has significantly limited the benefits of qualified plans. As a result, many employers have adopted what are referred to as excess benefit plans. These plans provide for contributions or benefits for executives in amounts that, when aggregated with the contributions or benefits from the employer's qualified plans, equal the amounts called for by the qualified plan formula, irrespective of the Internal Revenue Code limitations.

Under a defined benefit excess benefit plan the executive is provided with an annuity in an amount equal to the excess of the executive's computed benefits over the Internal Revenue Code limitations. Under a defined contribution excess benefit plan, contributions are credited to a memorandum account, in the executive's name, in the amount of the annual contribution that cannot be made to the tax-qualified plan because of the limitation imposed by the Internal Revenue Code. These memorandum accounts are generally credited with interest during the deferral period to simulate the earnings of the employer's qualified plan.

This type of nonqualified arrangement is frequently confused with the SERPs discussed above. Although SERPs commonly make up the reduction caused by the Internal Revenue Code limitation, the basic benefit payable under a SERP is usually dependent upon some other factor or formula.

Stock Acquisition Plan

Many employers use stock acquisition plans to supplement cash and other compensation arrangements for their executives because such plans benefit both the executive and the employer.

Stock acquisition plans give the key executive a capital accumulation program, establish a common interest between shareholders and key executives, enhance the employer's ability to attract and retain top executives, minimize the use of corporate funds for the payment of compensation, and provide a limited vehicle for raising capital for the employer through sale of stock to executives.

Unfortunately, there are two serious drawbacks to the use of stock acquisition plans as long-term incentives. First, newly issued shares of the employer's stock can dilute the ownership interests and voting power of existing shareholders (a problem of special concern for smaller companies). Second, stock market fluctuations could mean that the selling price of the employer's stock would not reflect the performance of the employer or the executive. In any event, stock acquisition plans can still serve the interests of a particular employer, its shareholders, and its executives.

There are various alternative plan designs for stock acquisition plans. Different plans may have different economic, tax and financial reporting results, which need to be weighed against an employer's objectives in adopting such a plan. Areas of concern for the employer are the size of compensation expense and resulting pretax charge to earnings, the cash benefit of the corporate tax deduction (related to the inclusion of income by executives), the net corporate cash flow, and incremental shares outstanding (whether the new shares will dilute earnings per share).

SOCIAL SECURITY BENEFITS

Financing of Social Security Benefits

Integration Overview
The Social Security Act plays an important role in the life of every American employer and employee. An employee must pay Social Security tax each year on wages earned that year. The employer also must pay Social Security tax based on its employees' wages. Social Security provides retirement benefits to the retiree, survivor benefits to certain of the retiree's family members upon the retiree's death, Medicare benefits, and in certain cases, disability benefits.

An employer can make its qualified plan part of an overall retirement scheme that includes Social Security benefits. This combination is called integration. Integration can provide an employer a means for obtaining a substantial savings because the cost of an employer's pension or profit sharing plan can be reduced. Many employers take Social Security benefits into account in the benefits provided to employees under a qualified plan.

Through Social Security, every employer is already paying a portion of a retirement benefit for its employees. By integrating, or combining, the employer's private pension or profit sharing plan with Social Security, the employer gets the benefit of its Social Security tax payments. The employer in effect makes its plan part of an overall program that combines both Social Security and the employer's private plan.

Technically, an integrated plan means a plan that is not considered discriminatory in favor of highly compensated employees, as long as the difference in the plan benefits of employees is attributable to what the Internal Revenue Service refers to as "permitted disparity." Permitted disparity, or integration, can, as mentioned above, mean a substantial savings for the employer because the cost of the employer's pension or profit sharing plan can be reduced.

HEALTH AND WELFARE PLANS

Types of Plans

Medical Plans
A comprehensive medical plan is usually an essential part of an adequate employee benefits program. There are four basic principles to consider in the design of a medical care program: cost sharing, cost control, coordination of benefits, and postretirement coverage.

With cost sharing, employees contribute to the cost of the medical care program; for example, the employees would pay a portion of the health insurance premiums. The employee contribution amount is usually a fixed percentage of the total cost of coverage (e.g., 20 percent) for both the employee and his or her dependent(s).

Cost control features are usually built into the design of the medical care plan to encourage employees to take an active role in controlling medical costs. These features include the use of deductible amounts (i.e., no amount is paid under the plan until the employee's expenses exceed a specified amount, such as $200), coinsurance on certain services (i.e., once the deductible is met, the employee pays a portion of each expense and the plan pays the remaining expense, reimbursement based on fixed fee schedules, mandatory second surgical opinion programs, and precertification for hospital admissions. First-dollar coverage may be provided only as an incentive for the use of less costly but medically acceptable alternatives or the use of preventive services.

Coordination of benefits is necessary to preclude employees from obtaining double reimbursement for the same medical expenses from multiple plans. For example, the employee may be covered under the employer's plan and under a plan maintained by the spouse's employer or a government plan.

Basic Health Insurance

Basic health insurance generally provides for first-dollar coverage (no deductibles) on a paid-in-full service basis or, less commonly, a fixed dollar indemnity schedule. Service benefits are expressed in terms of services covered rather than dollar limits. Indemnity benefits pay in full for each service, up to the limits set by the coverage for each such service. The two major categories of basic health insurance are basic hospitalization (including outpatient services) and basic medical/surgical (physical coverage) programs.

Major Medical Insurance

Major medical insurance is based on reimbursing insured persons for out-of-pocket expenses incurred for covered services, minus deductible amounts and coinsurance payments. Major medical coverage can either supplement basic insurance, picking up where the basic coverage ends for particular services, and providing coverage for services not in the basic program, or it can be the whole insurance program, with no first-dollar basic coverage at all. The latter is called comprehensive major medical.

Typical major medical programs cover a significantly wider range of benefits than basic hospitalization and medical/surgical programs, especially with respect to out-of-hospital services. Most types of medical expenses are routinely covered, except for dental care, long-term institutional care, and the services of certain non-physician practitioners, such as chiropractors.

There are various types of major medical programs. For example, a supplemental program is one that is added to a plan offering both basic hospitalization and medical/surgical benefits. A wrap-around major medical program is sometimes added to a plan of basic hospitalization benefits in lieu of basic medical/surgical benefits, thus providing the advantages of first-dollar coverage and service benefits for necessary expensive institutional health services. A comprehensive major medical program provides an alternative to programs combining basic hospitalization and medical/surgical coverage. Usually, all covered benefits in a comprehensive program are melded into a single package, with one set of deductibles and coinsurances. There is no first-dollar coverage in this kind of program.

Health Maintenance Organizations

Health maintenance organizations (HMOs) are alternatives to traditional health insurance. An HMO is an organization that provides comprehensive health care at a predetermined price. The employee must receive all nonemergency covered services from only those physicians employed by, and facilities provided by, the HMO. The benefit of an HMO is that the employee usually receives a broader set of benefits than under a typical basic hospitalization/major medical plan and with lower copayments and deductibles. HMOs have two distinct functions: to insure the cost of the care needed by their subscribing members and to provide most of that care, either directly through group practice clinics or by contractual arrangements with local physicians and hospitals.

Employees usually have a choice between traditional health insurance benefits and one or more HMOs. Employees generally may change their elections annually during a limited period of time.

Cafeteria Plans

Traditional employee health benefits programs give all covered persons identical benefits. Individual needs differ, however, based upon medical history, age, sex, health habits, and health profiles. Moreover, the importance different individuals attach to financial security as related to risks of varying magnitude differs markedly. In addition, the risks of incurring such high costs are not totally unpredictable or randomly distributed.

These facts coupled with an employer's desire to contain medical costs have led to cafeteria plans, or flexible benefits plans, in which employees may select from a menu of different health insurance options often including traditional health insurance, HMOs, and dental insurance. Cafeteria plans are often used to allow employees to pay their share of medical benefits on a pre-tax basis. For example, employees may be given the choice to reduce their compensation by a specified amount and have that amount applied to pay the employees' deductibles and coinsurance on a pre-tax basis.

Preferred Provider Organizations

The preferred provider organization (PPO) is an organization established by physicians, hospitals, or both. This organization provides services to beneficiaries of group buyers at favorable prices in return for receiving preferred consideration from the plan. For example, a physician PPO may offer services to employees and dependents covered by an employer plan at a 15 percent discount from the doctor's usual fees. An employee who uses the PPO physician might also pay a 10 percent copayment instead of the usual 20 percent when a non-PPO physician is used.

Dental Programs

Dental insurance is another popular option. There are basically three types of dental plans: Free-standing programs, programs integrated within major medical programs, and per capita plans.

Free-standing dental programs are provided through commercial insurance companies or nonprofit service plans, and are generally administered with little or no reference to other coverages. They usually pay dentists and oral surgeons through (1) a dollar indemnity schedule, with or without deductibles and coinsurance, or (2) payment systems similar to medical/surgical payment systems, with or without deductibles or coinsurance. In addition, a free-standing dental insurance plan may set overall yearly dollar maximums for the dental program as a whole, and may set yearly and lifetime dollar maximums for specific areas of benefits, such as orthodontics.

The principal feature of a dental plan that is integrated with a major medical program feature is a common deductible for medical and dental expenses. Under a per capita plan, the dentists provide total primary dental care as needed by the subscribers and are paid a monthly amount per employee rather than paid on a fee-for-service basis.

Benefit Plans Beyond Medical Care

In addition to various forms of medical and dental care, some employers offer additional benefit packages to their employees including group legal services, group automobile insurance, and extraordinary and catastrophic insurance.

These programs provide various tax advantages for the employers that implement such programs and their employees. Generally, these programs are not subject to the participation, vesting, and funding requirements of ERISA. They are, however, subject to the ERISA reporting requirements.

REPORTING REQUIREMENTS FOR EMPLOYEE BENEFIT PLANS

The Internal Revenue Code

Each employer that maintains a defined benefit plan or a defined contribution plan is required to file an annual report with the Internal Revenue Service. A Form 5500 is used for this purpose. The appropriate Form 5500 (Form 5500, 5500 C/R, or 5500EZ) must be filed for each plan, including plans under which benefits have ceased to accrue or contributions have been discontinued.

Plans with 100 or more participants must file Form 5500 each year. Plans with fewer than 100 participants must file the C version of the Form 5500-C/R for the first plan year, at least once every three years thereafter, and for the final plan year. For the years that the C version is not required, the R version of Form 5500-C/R, a brief registration statement, is filed.

A one-participant plan may file a Form 5500EZ. A one-participant plan is a plan that covers only (1) the owner of a business and the owner's spouse (provided the business, whether or not incorporated, is wholly owned by the owner or the owner and the owner's spouse), or (2) partners (or the partners and their spouses) in a business partnership.

Department of Labor

ERISA contains several reporting requirements. For example, a qualified plan and certain funded nonqualified plans must file an annual report with the Department of Labor. The Form 5500 is also used for this purpose. The Form 5500 is filed with the Internal Revenue Service and a copy is supplied to the Department of Labor by the Internal Revenue Service. In addition, a summary plan description (SPD) must be filed with the DOL and a copy given to each participant. An SPD is a description of the major provisions of the plan written in a clear manner to be understood by participants. When changes are made to a plan, the SPD must be revised and reissued or, instead, a description of the changes, referred to as a summary of material modifications, may be distributed to participants. Penalties may be imposed for the failure to comply with the reporting requirements under ERISA and the Internal Revenue Code.

CONCLUSION

This chapter has provided you with a broad overview of a very complex area in hopes that you can extract a general understanding of the employee benefit plans available and be alerted to various issues surrounding employee benefit plans. In implementing a plan, it is important to consider detailed information on your specific needs.

CHAPTER 24

INTRODUCTION TO THE EMPLOYMENT AND IMMIGRATION LAWS OF THE UNITED STATES FOR THE FOREIGN INVESTOR

Anthony B. Haller, Esq.
S. Sandile Ngcobo
Pepper, Hamilton & Scheetz

INTRODUCTION

There is a familiar phrase that says, "When in Rome, do as the Romans do." In the business world, this saying becomes: A foreign-based investor must do in a foreign country what domestic-based investors do. To do as domestic investors do, it is imperative for a foreign-based investor to possess a basic familiarity with the employment laws of the country where business is to be done. Likewise, a foreign-based employer seeking to do business in the United States must be familiar with basic American employment law. This need has been underscored by the U.S. Supreme Court in *Sumitomo Shoji Americana, Inc.,* v. *Avagliana* (455 U.S. 933 [1982]), where the highest court ruled that foreign corporations doing business through "local subsidiaries are considered . . . to be companies of the country in which they are incorporated; *they are entitled to the rights and subject to the responsibilities of other domestic corporations*" (emphasis added).

The employment law in the United States is complex. It is impossible to comprehensively discuss it in a single chapter. Employers face a complicated maze of federal, state, and local laws that regulate employment relationships. In addition to the U.S. employment law, the foreign employer needs to be familiar with immigration laws as they relate to importing foreign executives or technical staff to supervise the initial stages of a new business venture in the United States. In view of the complexity of the employment regulation in the United States, it is imperative for a foreign-based employer to understand the scope and content of its legal obligations. The purpose of this chapter is to give a foreign-based employer a basic familiarity with the United States employment and immigration laws as they affect the conduct of business in the United States.

COLLECTIVE BARGAINING PROCESS

The level of union organization in the United States is extemely low compared with most Western countries. As a result, less than 20 percent of the work force in the United States is represented by labor unions. Despite this low percentage, trade unions are extremely strong in major industrial sectors such as car manufacturing, steel, coal mining, and transportation.

The Nature of the Bargaining Process and the Legal Framework Within Which It is Conducted

Industrial relations in the unionized sector are conducted within the system of collective bargaining. This system is essentially adversarial in nature. The unions, as representatives of the employees, have the responsibility to bargain the basic terms and conditions of employment. The primary aim is to reach a privately regulated, enforceable agreement that embodies the terms and conditions of employment for a definite period. "An agreement resulting from collective bargaining 'is essentially an instrument of government, not merely an instrument of exchange.' It is more than a contract; it is an attempt of self-government" (*Hendricks* v. *Airline Pilots Ass'n International*, 696 F. 2d 673, 676 [9th Cir. 1983]). This is considered to be a key factor to ensure certainty and predictability in employment relations. As a general matter, these labor agreements generally restrict the right to resort to self-help and provide for private settlement and arbitration of disputes.

The primary labor statute that governs the process of collective bargaining agreement is the National Labor Relations (Wagner) Act of 1935 (NLRA) (29 U.S.C. §151, *et seq.*), as amended by the Labor Management Relations (Taft-Hartley) Act of 1947 (29 U.S.C. §141, *et seq.*). This statute provides the basic framework within which all collective bargaining relations are to be conducted. Its primary aim is to promote collective bargaining and foster industrial peace.

The NLRA is enforced by the National Labor Relations Board (NLRB) in Washington, D.C., which is aided by its regional offices throughout the country.

The Right to Belong to a Trade Union

The right of employees to form, join, and participate in trade union organizations is guaranteed by Section 7 of the NLRA. This section provides:

> Employees shall have the right of self organization; to form, join, or assist labor organizations, to bargain collectively through representatives of their own choosing, and to engage in other concerted activities for the purposes of collective bargaining or other mutual aid or protection. [29 U.S.C. §157]

The rights guaranteed to employees in Section 7 are affirmatively protected by Section 8 of the NLRA (29 U.S.C. §158). This section makes it unfair labor practice to interfere with, restrain, or coerce employees in the exercise of their Section 7 rights (29 U.S.C. §158 [a] [1]). The effect of these two sections is to prohibit employers from taking any action against prospective or current employees that discriminates against them because of their membership in a union.

The NLRA, however, also guarantees the right of an individual not to join a union or take part in union activities. Thus any attempt by either a union or an employer to coerce an individual to join a trade union is prohibited by the Act. As a consequence, closed shop agreements, which provide that only union members may be considered or retained for employment, are illegal under the Act. However, in limited cases, Section 7 permits so-called union security agreements. Such agreements generally provide that employees may be required, as a condition of employment, either to join the union as a full member or to pay to the union a sum equivalent to initiation fees and periodic dues paid by full union members. As will be discussed later on, once the union is certified as a bargaining representative of the employees, it becomes the sole representative, representing not only its members, but nonmembers also. The object of a union security agreement is to ensure that non-union members do not obtain all the benefits of union representation without making any financial contribution. Non-union members, however, are not obliged to become active members or to make any contribution to political funds.

Determination of the Representative of the Employees and the Appropriate Bargaining

Section 9 of the NLRA guarantees to employees the right to bargain through representatives of their own choice. Employees can choose their representative either by signing union authorization cards or by voting for the union in an official election conducted by the NLRB. This choice, however, must be made by a majority of employees. Thus, a union can achieve voluntary recognition from the employer by presenting the employer with authorization cards signed by a majority of employees for a particular group that seeks representation. When the employer challenges the majority support of the union, the union's right to representation can be established only through a secret ballot election supervised by the NLRB.

Before an election is held, it is necessary for the NLRB to determine the proper constituency of employees entitled to vote in such an election. This constituency is called "the appropriate bargaining unit." Employees with a sufficient community of interest generally constitute an appropriate bargaining unit. In determining the appropriate bargaining unit, the NLRB considers a variety of factors to establish whether the employees in the particular proposed bargaining unit have a sufficient "community of interest." Such determinations are made on a case-by-case basis. It is thus possible to have several bargaining units in one plant, separated along craft lines, single plantwide, or even industrywide bargaining units. However, as a general rule the NLRB prefers plant units. Once the appropriate bargaining unit has been designated, only employees in that unit may cast their ballots and express their choice.

Apart from determining the appropriate bargaining unit, the NLRB will also supervise the balloting and enforce standards during the election campaign to ensure that employees exercise their free and rational choice. Misconduct, interference, or intimidation by either side during the campaign may result in the election being set aside. Thus it is advisable for an employer who is faced with a union organizational campaign to seek legal advice on its legal rights in mounting a campaign to dissuade employees from voting for the union.

If a majority of employees in the appropriate bargaining unit vote for the union, the union then becomes the exclusive representative of all the employees, including non-union members, in that unit. An employer who enters into separate agreements with individual or rival unions commits an unfair labor practice. In return, the union has a duty of fair representation, which requires the union to represent all union members and non-union members in the bargaining unit without acting arbitrarily, discriminatorily or in bad faith (*Vaca* v. *Sipes,* 386 U.S. 171 [1967]). The doctrine of fair representation generally requires the union to process diligently and faithfully any grievance raised by an individual employee. While the duty of fair representation provides safeguards against abuses of majority power, it recognizes that the individual employee interests may, at times, have to yield in favor of the collective interest, provided, of course, that a decision is made honestly and in good faith.

The Union and the Employer Have a Duty to Bargain in Good Faith

Once the union has been certified as the exclusive bargaining representative, both the union and the employer are under a reciprocal obligation to meet with each other at reasonable times and confer in good faith with respect to "wages, hours and other terms and conditions of employment" (29 U.S.C. §158 [d]). The obligation to meet and confer in good faith is referred to as the duty to bargain in good faith. This duty, however, does not mean that the employer is obliged to reach an agreement with the union. The NLRA specifically provides that neither side is required to make concessions or reach agreement (*Id.*) The primary purpose of this duty is to encourage the employer and the union to reach an agreement without dictating the substantive terms of the agreement. In practice, however, the enforcement of the duty to bargain in good faith has enabled the NLRB and the courts to monitor and control bargaining table conduct and, even indirectly, the content of the agreements.

This duty requires the employer and the union to approach the negotiations with open minds, and demonstrate a sincere effort to reach an agreement. Thus, going through the motions of bargaining through ''surface bargaining'' is insufficient to discharge the obligation. The question of whether an employer has bargained in good faith is, of course, a question of fact. As a general matter, an employer should make a genuine effort to resolve its differences with the union. This includes listening to union proposals regardless of whether they are predictably unacceptable. In some cases, this may also entail providing the union with some information that will enable the union to determine the genuineness of the proposals made by the employer. The obligation to provide the union with information may exist even though the information is confidential.

It is very important for the employer to bargain in good faith since this may ultimately determine whether the employer can unilaterally impose terms and conditions, should the negotiations reach an impasse. An employer who has negotiated in good faith may lawfully and unilaterally impose terms and conditions contained in the last offer to the union, in the event negotiations result in a deadlock. By contrast, an employer who has not negotiated in good faith may face unfair labor charges. These charges may result in the terms and conditions of employment imposed by the employer after impasse being rescinded and the employer being ordered to resume bargaining. Therefore, it is very important for the employer to negotiate with the incumbent union and to do so in good faith.

The employer's right to unilaterally impose terms and conditions of employment at the point of impasse is matched by the union's right to engage in a strike in order to obtain its demands.

The union may even engage in a strike during the negotiations. Thus, while the statutory restrictions to a certain extent influence the content of the collective bargaining agreements, the relative economic bargaining power of the parties determines the existence and the content of the collective bargaining agreements.

What to Bargain About: Mandatory and Nonmandatory Subjects

The NLRA only requires the employer and the union "to confer in good faith with respect to *wages, hours and other terms and conditions of employment*" (29 U.S.C. §158 [d]). Over the years the courts and the Board have defined the subjects over which the parties are obliged to bargain by making a distinction between "mandatory" and "permissive" or nonmandatory subjects of bargaining. The distinction between mandatory and permissive subjects of bargaining is crucial for three main reasons:

1. The parties have a statutory obligation to bargain only with regard to mandatory subjects of bargaining. Consequently the employer may refuse to bargain over a permissive subject of bargaining.
2. It is a violation of the NLRA to insist to impasse over a permissive subject of bargaining; this is tantamount to refusal to bargain over mandatory subjects of bargaining.
3. A mandatory subject of bargaining may not be unilaterally changed unless the employer has bargained in good faith to impasse and the change is contained in the last offer to the union. (See Charles J. Morris, *The Developing Labor Law,* 2nd ed., vol. 1, pp. 770–771.)

The NLRB has the primary function to determine whether a particular subject is a mandatory or permissive subject of bargaining. In making its determination, the NLRB will generally consider whether the topic "vitally affects the terms and conditions of employment" (*Allied Chemical & Alkali Workers Local 1* v. *Pittsburgh Plate Glass Co.,* 404 U.S. 157, 179 [1971]) and will also look at the bargaining practice in the industry concerned (*Ford Motor Co.* v. *NLRB,* 441 U.S. 488, 551 [1979]). The Supreme Court has recognized that there are a number of management decisions concerning commitment of investment capital and the basic scope of the enterprise, over which the employer has no duty to bargain (*Fibreboard Paper Products Corporation* v. *NLRB*, 379 U.S. 203 [1964]). These include decisions on introduction or elimination of product lines, capital investment, new equipment, mergers, acquisitions, and plant closures. Despite the fact that these decisions "vitally affect" the job security of employees, the employer may unilaterally make them since they "lie at the core of entrepreneurial control" (*Fibreboard Paper Products Corp.* v. *NLRB, supra,* at 202). In *First National Maintenance Corporation* v. *NLRB* (492 U.S. 666 [1981]), the U.S. Supreme Court ruled that an employer need not bargain over its economically motivated decision to close all or part of its business, but must bargain over the effects of that decision. Thus, a decision to transfer and consolidate operations that turns upon a change in the nature and direction of a significant facet of business has been considered by the Board as a managerial decision over which the employer has no duty to bargain (*Otis Elevator Co.* [*Otis II*], 116 LRRM 1075 [1984]).

The NLRB has interpreted *First National Maintenance Corporation* v. *NLRB (supra)* to provide that relocation, subcontracting, and reorganization decisions are subject to mandatory bargaining only when they "turn on labor costs" *(Otis II, supra).* Where the employer has a duty to bargain over the effects of its decision, it is necessary that the employer give the union a notice of its decision for the purposes of bargaining on the effects of such a decision. Effects bargaining will include subjects such as severance pay, seniority, pensions, vacation pay, and early retirement programs. Failure to bargain over the effects of a decision may result in the employer being ordered to bargain over the effects, including payment of limited backpay (*Transmarine Navigation Corp.,* 67 LRRM 1419 [1968]). In some cases the employer may even be enjoined from implementing its decision until it has bargained on the effects of such a decision.

The Collective Bargaining Agreement

The bargaining process normally results in a collective bargaining agreement, which is a legally enforceable contract. A collective bargaining agreement embodies the terms and conditions of employment that will govern the employees covered for a definite period of time. These agreements cover wages, hours, work schedules, overtime rates, premium rates for weekend and holiday work, job descriptions and classifications, terminations, promotions, layoffs, transfers, medical insurance, pensions, dues checkoff, seniority provisions, grievance procedures, and discipline and discharge for cause. It is also common to include a no-strike and arbitration clause in these agreements. These clauses prohibit the union from striking during the time of the agreement over the issues that are subject to arbitration. It is also common to have a management rights clause that reserves to management the right to act unilaterally in regard to certain specified topics, including what may otherwise be mandatory subjects of bargaining, during the term of the agreement. Except where specified, the terms of the agreement are frozen and may not be changed without an agreement during the contract period.

An important provision in collective bargaining agreements is the termination for just cause provision. Such a provision provides that an employee may be discharged only for just cause, which at times is defined in the agreement. Such a provision constitutes an exception to the employer's common law right to discharge an employee at will.

Although collective bargaining agreements are essentially a contract, they are treated as contracts of a different kind. The courts and the Board have cautioned against the wholesale application of the general contract principles to collective bargaining agreements as likely to undermine the purpose that collective bargaining agreements were designed to achieve (*Hendricks v. Airline Ass'n. International,* 596 F. 2d 673, 676 [9th Cir. 1983]).

Enforcing the Collective Bargaining Agreement

As a general matter there are three modes of enforcing collective bargaining agreements. First, collective bargaining agreements normally establish formal procedures for resolving grievances under the agreements. Grievances are normally resolved by the union at different levels of the management hierarchy, culminating in binding arbitration. This enables the parties not only to administer their collective bargaining agreement, but also to ensure its continued application to the work environment. Labor arbitrators, who are entrusted with the obligation of interpreting collective bargaining agreements, have developed the so-called law of the shop, which is that body of the custom and practice that exists in every employment relationship. Because of their expertise in interpreting collective bargaining agreements, they enjoy deference from federal courts and the NLRB. Awards of arbitrators will always be upheld if they draw their essence from the agreement.

Second, under Section 301 of the LMRA, federal courts have jurisdiction to entertain suits for breach of collective bargaining agreements. However, federal courts will not hear a case unless the internal remedies under the grievance and arbitration procedures have been exhausted. Courts are more willing to enjoin strikes or work stoppages in breach of collective bargaining agreements that provide for binding arbitration. However, because injunctions interfere with industrial action by the union, courts will only issue an injunction in limited circumstances.

Third, under Section 10 of the NLRA, the Board has wide powers "to prevent any person from engaging in any unfair labor practice." Because this power is not "affected by any other means of adjustment or prevention that has been or may be established by agreement, law or otherwise", the Board plays a role in interpreting and enforcing labor agreements. Thus, the NLRB may be required to construe a collective bargaining agreement to determine whether an unfair labor practice has been committed (*NLRB* v. *C&C Plywood Corp.*, 389 US 421, 430 [1967]). The policy of the Board, however, is to defer to arbitration procedures where there is an overlap between an unfair labor practice charge and a question of contract interpretation (*Speilberg Manufacturing Company*, 112 NLRB 1080 [1955]; see also, *Collyer Insulated Wire, a Gulf and Western Systems Company*, 192 NLRB 837 [1971]).

Thus, both the courts and the NLRB have a policy of deferring to arbitration any dispute involving the interpretation of collective bargaining agreements. In this manner, the law of the shop, as developed by arbitrators, has become very important in regulating employment relations in the United States. Arbitration awards are enforceable by court order, and failure to comply with the remedies provided by the arbitrator may result in civil contempt, with penalties such as fines and imprisonment.

Collective Bargaining Agreement and Change in Enterprise Ownership

The primary employment issue, once there is a change in the ownership of the enterprise, concerns the obligation, if any, that the new employer has to the incumbent union. The obligations of the new employer toward the incumbent union depend, generally, on whether the new employer is a successor or an alter ego employer.

Generally, successor employer status exists where there is substantial continuity in the identity of the employing enterprise, work force and in the appropriateness of the bargaining unit. This will be present where there is a continuation of the same business operation, the same plant is being used, the same supervisors are present, the same product is being manufactured or the same services are being rendered, with the same work force, machinery, equipment, and methods of production (*Premium Foods, Inc.,* 260 NLRB 708 [1932], *enforced,* 709 F 2d 623 [9th Cir. 1983]). A successor employer has a duty to recognize and bargain with the union (*NLRB* v. *Burns International Detective Agency, Inc.,* 406 U.S. 272 [1978]). It does not, however, have the obligation to assume the predecessor's collective bargaining agreement and is ordinarily free to set, unilaterally, the initial terms and conditions on which predecessor's employees will be hired *(Id.).* In determining successorship status the most important factor is the continuity in the identity of the work force. If a majority of the employees of a successor are former employees of a predecessor, the successor employer will be obliged to bargain with the employees bargaining representative. Where, however, the new employer replaces the majority of the work force, it does not have the duty to bargain with the incumbent union. A successor employer, however, may not refuse to hire the employees of its predecessor for the reasons that they are union members in order to avoid bargaining with the incumbent union (*Howard Johnson Co.* v. *Detroit Local Joint Executive Board,* 467 U.S. 249 [1974]). However, there is no obligation on the successor employer to hire the employees of its predecessor *(Id.).*

The alter ego or single employer status exists where the former and present employer are, in reality, the same or substantially indentical entity. An alter ego employer status is generally found where the new employer is so related to the first employer by common ownership, centralized control of labor relations, management, operations, equipment, customers, and supervision (*Crawford Door Sales Co.*, 226 NLRB 1144 [1976]). In such a case the new employer is not only obliged to bargain with the union but is also bound by the predecessor's collective bargaining agreement (*Bellingham Frozen Foods* v. *NLRB*, 626 F. 2d 674, 105 LRRM 2404 [9th Cir. 1980]), enforcing in part 237 NLRB 1450 (1978).

The Use of Economic Pressure

The right of employees to engage in a strike in support of their bargaining demands has long been recognized in the United States. As early as 1921, Chief Justice Taft of the U.S. Supreme Court stated:

> Is interference of a labor organization by persuasion and appeal to induce a strike against low wages under such circumstances without lawful excuse and malicious? We think not. . . . [T]he right to combine for such a lawful purpose has in many years not been denied by any court. The strike became a lawful instrument in the lawful economic struggle or competition between employer and employees as to the share or division between them of the joint product of labor and capital.
>
> [*American Steel Foundries* v. *Tri-City Council*, 257 U.S. 184, 208–209 (1921)]

This right is now enshrined in Section 7 of the NLRA.

While the right to engage in an industrial action is essential to the employees' bargaining power, there are certain limitations on the right to strike. The right to engage in strike activity is limited by the NLRA and may also be limited by a collective bargaining agreement. As a general matter, prohibited or unprotected strikes are those that employ unlawful or wrongful means such as taking possession of the property of the employer and excluding others from entry, and those that have an unlawful purpose, such as those that violate the NLRA and the collective bargaining agreement. It is common for collective bargaining agreements to contain no-strike clauses. A no-strike clause effectively prevents the union from engaging in a strike during the term of the collective bargaining agreement and an employer may obtain an injunction to prevent a strike action in violation of a no-strike clause. In addition, a strike in the face of a no-strike clause exposes the union to damages for loss of production. In the case of a wild cat strike, where employees simply walk out of their jobs, the law imposes an obligation on the union to stop the strike, failing which the union may be liable for loss occasioned by the strike.

The NLRA imposes certain limitations on the right to engage in a strike depending on the objectives of the striking workers. For instance, a strike whose purpose is to compel an employer to assign particular work or jobs to employees belonging to the striking union is prohibited by Section 8(b)(4)(D) of the NLRA. Another example is a strike for recognition where another union is already certified. The NLRA also prevents hasty strike action by requiring unions to comply with certain procedural requirements in certain instances. In this regard, Section 8(d) of the NLRA provides that the union may not engage in a strike to enforce its demands or to modify or terminate an existing collective bargaining agreement before going through certain notice requirements.

In addition to statutory limitations on the right to strike, there are practical limitations on the right to engage in concerted activity. An employer may replace employees who are engaged in an economic strike with temporary replacements or permanent replacements. Strikers who have been permanently replaced have no right to immediate reinstatement but merely possess preferential hiring rights for a reasonable period should vacancies occur. When an employer decides to reinstate the employees who had been engaged in a strike, the decision to reinstate them may not be based on their degree of participation in the strike because this tends to discourage participation in union activities and is thus an unfair labor practice.

It is important to bear in mind that strikers who have been engaged in an unfair labor practice strike are entitled to reinstatement to their former jobs upon an unconditional offer to return to work (*Pecheur Lozenge Company,* 98 NLRB 496, 29 LRRM 1367 [1952]). An unfair labor practice strike is a strike activity generally initiated in response to an unfair labor practice committed by the employer (*NLRB* v. *Mackay Radio & Tel. Co.,* 304 U.S. 333 [1938]). Unfair labor practice strikes are entitled to reinstatement even if the employer has hired permanent replacements and even if the replacements have to be discharged (*NLRB* v. *Mackay Radio & Tel. Co., supra,* see also, *NLRB* v. *Efco Mfg., Inc.,* 227 F. 2d 675 [1st Cir. 1955], *cert. denied,* 350 U.S. 1007 [1956]).

Another most common form of concerted activity in the United States is picketing, which occurs where there is a deployment of pickets at business premises. While picketing may be a form of free speech, protected by the First Amendment to the U.S. Constitution, there are certain limitations on the right to picket. State courts, for example, in the exercise of their police powers, may enjoin violent and mass picketing. In addition, Section 8(b)(4)(B) of the NLRA deals with secondary boycotts by prohibiting picketing that has an unlawful secondary object. A union may not, for example, picket a neutral employer if the object of picketing is to force the neutral employer to cease doing business with the employer with whom the union is engaged in a dispute (Section 8[b][4][i]). Under Section 303 of the LMRA, the neutral employer may recover any loss resulting from illegal secondary activity by a union.

Enforcement of the Collective Bargaining Process

The primary function of the NLRB is to enforce the NLRA. This it does by investigating, processing, and adjudicating charges of unfair labor practices. An unfair labor practice charge is made, in the first instance, to the regional office of the NLRB, which will inquire into the substance of the charge in order to determine whether a formal complaint should be issued. If a formal complaint is issued, a hearing is subsequently conducted before an Administrative Law Judge. After hearing the evidence, the Administrative Law Judge issues a recommendation to the NLRB in Washington, D.C. A panel of the NLRB will then review or adopt the findings of the Administrative Law Judge. Parties have the right to challenge the findings and the recommendations of the Administrative Law Judge by way of exceptions filed with the NLRB. Where exceptions have been filed, the Board will review or adopt the findings of the Administrative Law Judge in the light of the exceptions.

Where the NLRB determines that a violation of the Act has occurred, it may order the offending party to cease and desist from such unlawful conduct and take appropriate affirmative action to correct its conduct. Depending on the nature of the violation, the

NLRB orders may include backpay, reinstatement, and resumption of negotiations. A party who is not satisfied with the decision of the NLRB may take an appeal to the appropriate circuit Court of Appeals. On appeal, the NLRB's order may be enforced, reversed, or remanded back to the NLRB. Failure to comply with a court-enforced NLRB decision may expose the party to penalties for civil contempt, including fines and imprisonment.

In addition to the above, the NLRB may, in limited circumstances, intervene to resolve a jurisdictional dispute between the unions over entitlement to particular work and to seek a court injunction against any union engaged in prohibited secondary activity. In appropriate cases, while a dispute is pending before the NLRB, the NLRB may seek temporary relief so that the dispute will not escalate before a decision is made (29 U.S.C. §160 [j]).

THE AIRLINE AND RAILROAD INDUSTRIES

The airline and the railroad industries are governed by a separate statute, namely, the Railway Labor Act, 45 U.S.C. §151-188. Collective bargaining agreements in these industries are concluded at conferences that are mandatory under the Railway Labor Act. As a general matter, the Railway Labor Act provides for the obligation to meet and confer with representatives of employees and prohibits any change in the collective bargaining agreement without any negotiations. This statute provides an elaborate procedure for the resolution of disputes. As a general matter, there are two modes of resolving disputes under the Railway Labor Act, namely, the minor dispute procedures and the major dispute procedures. A minor dispute is one that can be resolved by reference to the parties' collective bargaining agreement, while a major dispute is one that concerns the creation of terms and conditions of employment (*Consolidated Rail Corp.* v. *RLEA*, 109 S. Ct. 2477, 2481 [1989]). Minor disputes are required to be resolved by the parties, failing which through arbitration. There is a general prohibition against the use of strikes in minor disputes. An employer may unilaterally impose its own interpretation of the agreement (*Id.* at 2480–81). On the other hand, the major dispute resolution procedures are very lengthy, "almost interminable" (*Detroit & Toledo Shore Line Railroad* v.

United Transp. Union, 396 U.S. 142, 149 [1960]). New conditions may end up being imposed by Congress. On April 18, 1991, the U.S. Congress imposed conditions of employment on railway employers and railway unions in response to a national railroad strike that threatened essential transportation services (H. J. Res. 222, Pub. L. No. 102-29 [April 18, 1991]).

INDIVIDUAL EMPLOYMENT CONTRACT AND THE TERMS AND CONDITIONS OF EMPLOYMENT

As indicated earlier on, a significant number of employees in the private sector are not covered by collective bargaining agreements. The employment terms covering such employees are generally set or negotiated on an individual basis. Within the past decade, an increasing number of employers have prepared and distributed handbooks or personnel policies that describe the rules and regulations of the workplace. In addition, these handbooks may include other terms of employment including benefits offered by employers. Employers generally offer various benefits to their employees, including health, medical, life, and temporary disability insurance; pension plans; and, in some cases, stock ownership plans. These terms and conditions of employment are generally not open to negotiation except for with highest-paid executive contracts.

Apart from individual employment contracts, terms, and conditions of employer are, to a certain extent, regulated by various statutory provisions, including both federal and state legislation.

Generally, there are two forms of the individual employment relationship. The first is for employment of an indefinite term, the so-called employment-at-will relationship. Most employees enter into an oral understanding providing that they will be employed for an indefinite period of time and that they will be paid on an hourly basis pursuant to a weekly or biweekly wage or annual salary. Under this kind of relationship, an employee may leave at any time and the employer may discharge the employee at any time with or without notice, and with or without cause. However, the employer's right to discharge is to some degree limited by the employer's other obligations contained in state and federal antidiscrimination and anti-retaliatory laws. In addition, as discussed later on, the employers' right to discharge an employee at will, has recently, in many states, been severely limited by exceptions based on public policy, common law tort, and contract theories.

The second form of employment relationship is the fixed term contract. Under this kind of employment relationship a contract is entered into for a specified period of time. The need to enter into these contracts generally varies with the interest sought to be protected. Normally, written contracts are entered into with executive and managerial personnel because of the complex compensation plans that may involve salary, bonuses, stock options, and retirement benefits. It is common for these contracts to include provisions dealing with termination of the contract, protection of trade secrets or confidential information, restrictions on postemployment competition, and methods of resolving disputes, including selecting the law that will govern the contract and selecting forums where legal actions may be brought. For these contracts to be valid, they must comply with the general requirements of a valid contract.

Terms and Conditions of Employment

Apart from the NLRA, labor relations in the United States are governed by various state and federal laws, including the U.S. Constitution. As a general matter, federal law reaches all businesses engaged in interstate commerce and covers a wide range of employment issues such as wages and hours, safety in the work place, and employment discrimination. State laws often cover the same areas and generally supplement federal law. As a general rule, where there is a conflict between federal and state laws, federal law, under the Supremacy Clause of the U.S. Constitution, will prevail provided Congress has expressed an interest to control the area. Because the state laws are too diverse for detailed analysis, this section will focus on some of the important federal statutes that regulate terms and conditions of employment.

Working Hours and Compensation

The basic statute that regulates working hours and wages is the Fair Labor Standard Act of 1938 (FLSA) (29 U.S.C. §201 *et seq.*).

Although this statute is broad, executive, administrative and professional employees are exempt from its minimum wage and maximum hour requirements (29 U.S.C. §213). FLSA is enforced by the Wage and Hour Division of the Department of Labor, which investigates alleged violations. The Secretary of Labor has the authority to bring lawsuits to ensure compliance with FLSA. In addition to FLSA, there are state laws that regulate hours and wages on a limited scale. The statutes that regulate wages and hours generally lay down the minimum wage and the maximum hours. Actual hours and wages are regulated by individual employment agreements or collective bargaining agreements.

FLSA regulates working hours by providing a penalty wage for work done in excess of 40 hours a week (29 U.S.C. §207). It requires that hours worked in excess of 40 hours in a week be compensated at a rate of $1\frac{1}{2}$ times the regular rate of pay. However, the Act does not prevent employees from working hours that are either less or more than 40 hours in a week. An employee may thus work as many hours as she or he likes, as long as she or he is paid overtime pay for all hours worked in excess of 40 hours in a work week. FLSA does not specify how these hours are to be spaced out in a week, nor does it say how many hours may be worked in a day. The generally recognized work week consists of five days with the sixth and seventh day being recognized as rest days.

In addition, FLSA sets the minimum wage below which wages cannot fall. The primary purpose of minimum wage laws is to ensure that the wages paid provide a minimally acceptable standard of living and also to ensure that employers compete without engaging in wage busting. Section 6 of FLSA sets the minimum wage at $4.25 an hour (29 U.S.C. §206). The time and manner of payment is generally regulated by state law. Normally compensation is paid weekly, biweekly, or monthly. Payment is normally made in cash or check. In addition, however, there are other federal and state statutes that regulate wages. The Davis-Bacon Act, Welsh-Healy Act and Service Contract Acts generally require employers who are federal government contractors to pay the wage determined by the Secretary of Labor as the prevailing wage for persons employed on the work covered by the contract that employers perform. In addition, the Equal Pay Act of 1963 prohibits discrimination in compensation on the basis of sex.

In addition to regulating hours and wages, FLSA also requires employers to keep records of their employee compensation practices. Employers are obliged to furnish their employees with cards reflecting all deductions made from their wages. Failure to comply with the provisions of FLSA may expose the employer to a suit for amounts due under FLSA, attorneys' fees, and double the amount owing under the statute. Under FLSA, however, the liability of the employer for back pay is limited to two years, except in a case of willful violation. In some cases, criminal penalties, including fines and imprisonment, may result from failure to comply with FLSA (29 U.S.C. §216). The Act prohibits the discharge of an employee for filing a complaint under its provision (29 U.S.C. §215).

The Duty to Provide a Safe Work Place

Compensation for Injury at Work

Under common law, an employer has a duty to provide a safe work environment for its employees. Failure by the employer to comply with this obligation exposes the employer to liability for injuries sustained as a result of the neglect of the duty. The common law liability has since been replaced by a system of no-fault insurance. A number of states have enacted workers' compensation statutes that largely follow a similar pattern. Under these statutes, employers are required to undertake a comprehensive insurance either privately or through a state administered fund. Claims are presented to a workers' compensation bureau that will determine whether compensation is payable. Payment is made according to predetermined schedules based on the type and permanency of the injury. Some states now provide compensation for certain occupational diseases, including those resulting from exposure to toxic substances. The workers' compensation statutes generally provide exclusive compensation to an injured employee and the employer is not liable in a civil action to an injured employee.

The Duty to Provide a Safe and Healthy Working Environment

The primary federal statute that governs safety and health matters in the work place is the Occupational Safety and Health Act (29 U.S.C. §651, *et. seq.*). Section 5(a)(1) requires employers to keep their work places free from "recognized hazards that are causing or likely to cause death or serious harm." It covers any person who has employees and who is engaged in business affecting commerce. "Person" is defined to include corporations, partnerships, associations, legal representatives, and any organized group of persons (29 U.S.C. §652 [4]). The Act extends beyond interstate commerce, covering all activities that affect commerce, even if such an activity is within a state. (29 CFR § 1975.2). In addition, it includes activities such as conducting business through the U.S. airmail and activity in preparation for or winding up interstate business (*Godwin* v. *OSHRC*, 540 F.2d 1013 [9th Cir. 1976]; *American Company*, 5 BNA OSHC 1491 [1977]). An employer with one employee is also covered by the Act (*Elma Vath, Printing Contractors*, 2 BNA OSHC 1091 [1974]). However, there are certain exemptions for smaller employers (29 CFR § 1904.15).

This statute is enforced by the Occupational Safety and Health Administration (OSHA), which falls within the Department of Labor. Apart from conducting inspections of work places, OSHA promulgates safety and health standards that impose specific obligations on employers. It has rules of procedure for promulgating, modifying, or revoking its standards. The rule-making procedures of OSHA allows public participation before proposed standards become mandatory standards. In addition, OSHA provides guidance on maintaining safe working places. OSHA has issued general industry work place safety and health standards. These standards include providing a clean work place, fixed industrial stairways, means of egress, fire prevention equipment, and records indicating work-related death or injuries. There is, however provision for exemption from the OSHA standards. An employer who is complying with a state-mandated safety standard that has been approved by OSHA can apply to the Assistant Secretary of Labor for exemption from OSHA's general industry standards.

To ensure compliance with health and safety standards, OSHA conducts inspections of work places. Where there are violations, OSHA will issue citations for civil violations and will propose monetary penalties for such violations. The Occupational Safety and Health Review Commission adjudicates violations of the OSHA standards. In the first instance, a formal hearing is held before an Administrative Law Judge, who decides whether to affirm, vacate, or modify findings of the agency and its proposed penalty. The Administrative Law Judge's decision is subject to a discretionary review by the Occupational Safety and Health Review Commission (OSHRC). The decision of the OSHRC is subject to review by the appropriate circuit Court of Appeals.

Violations of OSHA standards may also result in criminal violations rendering the employer liable for fines of up to $10,000 for a first offense. In addition, special procedures are available to OSHA in dealing with extremely hazardous conditions that may cause death or serious injury before standard OSHA methods for correcting the hazard can be put into effect. If an employer fails to remove the hazard despite notice, OSHA may file a petition with the federal district court for injunctive relief including a request for a temporary restraining order in cases of imminent danger. The court will normally grant this relief pending the outcome of OSHA's enforcement proceedings relating to the hazard (29 U.S.C. § 662[a][b]).

Termination of Employment

As indicated previously, most employees are not covered by collective bargaining agreements and most do not have written employment contracts. They are employed on the basis of oral understandings for an indefinite period. The traditional rule in the United States is that an employee who is employed for an indefinite period can be discharged at any time with or without cause. However, this unlimited power of an employer to discharge an employee at will has been severely eroded by various exceptions based on statutes, judicially recognized public policy exceptions, and common law tort and contract theories.

Statutory Limitations
A growing number of states have directly abolished the employment-at-will rule. The State of Montana has enacted the Wrongful Discharge From Employment Act, which prohibits, among other things, a discharge without good cause. In addition, there are various antidiscrimination statutes, both federal and state, that indirectly limit an employer's right to discharge at will by prohibiting discharges based on race, sex, color, religion, national

origin, age, disability, handicap, or status as a veteran. The antidiscrimination statutes are discussed later on. Furthermore, a number of federal and state statutes protect employees from discharge in retaliation for exercising their statutory rights to assert claims to vindicate statutory rights or engage in protected activity. In addition, the right of an employer to discharge an employee at-will is limited by the so-called whistle blowing statutes. These statutes prohibit employers from discharging employees who bring to the attention of state or federal authorities an employer's violation of a statute (*Garibaldi* v. *Luck Food Stores*, 726 F. 2d 1367 [9th Cir. 1984]).

Public Policy Exceptions

More recently, a growing number of state courts have recognized exceptions to the traditional employment-at-will rule based upon public policy considerations. These exceptions are premised on the theory that the law should not be used to countenance employee dismissal for reasons that violate a fundamental public policy. For instance, it is considered to be against public policy to dismiss an employee for exercising his or her legal right to file for workers' compensation. (*Frampton* v. *Central Indiana Gas Co.,* [1973] 260 Ind. 249, 297 N.E. 2d 429). In addition, a few state courts have recognized public policy exceptions based upon an implied covenant of good faith and fair dealing in the employment contract that restricts an employer's ability to discharge at-will employees (*Cloutier* v. *Great Atl. & Pac. Tea Co.,* [1981] 121 NH 915, 436 A. 2d 1140). This exception views the employment relationship as contractual, and recognizes an implied contractual right to job security as necessary to ensure stability. According to this exception, there is an implied obligation to deal freely and in good faith with employees that requires an employer not to discharge employees for unjust reasons (*Cleary* v. *American Airlines*, [1980] 111 Cal. App. 3d 443, 168, Cal. Rptr 722).

Exceptions Based on Contract and Tort Theories

Where circumstances surrounding a discharge amount to tortious conduct, most states have allowed an employee to recover damages flowing from the employer's conduct. Such conduct includes the employer's prying into or exposing an employee's private affairs, intentionally inflicting emotional distress upon the employee, intentionally interfering with an employee's contractual relationship with others, or falsely accusing an employee of wrongdoing.

There is a growing trend by state courts to find a limitation on the right to discharge an at-will employee based on the employer's oral statements or written procedures contained in employee handbooks. Statements suggesting that an employee is being offered permanent employment, or employment until retirement, may be sufficient to restrict the employer's right to discharge at will. These statements may require the employer to have good cause before discharging an employee. Similarly, statements in employee handbooks that establish discipline and discharge procedures are sometimes given contractual significance. Courts, however, permit an employer to avoid the contractual effect of such statements by including in the employee handbook a prominent and clear disclaimer. Collective bargaining agreements generally provide comprehensive grievance procedures aimed at establishing the existence of "good cause" for discharge. It is necessary that these procedures be followed to avoid violation of the agreement.

Remedies for Unlawful Discharge

As a general matter, all of the remedies normally available to a plaintiff in a state court contract or tort action are available in an unlawful dismissal case. These may include a full range of equitable remedies such as injunctions and specific performance decrees. An employee may also recover monetary compensation. In contract suits, remedies can include compensation damages calculated to make up the employee's loss as a result of the breach or liquidated damages if the written contract spells out consequences of a breach. In tort actions, an employee can recover compensatory damages, which may include compensation for pain and suffering and emotional distress. In addition, most states will allow exemplary or punitive damages in tort actions where the employer acted in a wanton, reckless, malicious, or oppressive way.

Due to the financial implications that an unlawful discharge may have to an employer, it is very important for an employer to ensure that discharges are not arbitrary. In addition, the employer ought to avoid discharge involving any kind of discrimination.

Layoffs and Termination of Employment

Owing to a variety of factors, it may be necessary for an employer to lay off some of its work force. The layoffs result in the termination of the employees involved in the layoffs. The primary issues raised by a layoff include the obligation to negotiate with the employees to be laid off, the criteria for selecting employees to be laid off, and severance pay to the employees to be laid off. Under the U.S. employment laws, an employer has no general obligation to pay severance as a result of a layoff. For those employees who are covered by collective bargaining agreements, layoffs are governed by the collective bargaining agreements. These agreements often cover a whole range of issues such as payment of severance pay and procedures to be followed in case of layoff. As indicated previously, while the employer is not obliged to negotiate with an incumbent union on its decision to lay off workers, it is nonetheless obliged to negotiate with the union on the effects of such a layoff. In addition, the right of employer to lay off its employees is circumscribed by federal statutes requiring notice to the union and those prohibiting discrimination.

The Worker Adjustment Retraining and Notification Act (WARN) is perhaps the most significant restriction on the employer's right to lay off its employees (29 U.S.C. 2101 *et seq.*). WARN requires employers who employ 100 or more employees to provide a 60-day advance notice before they carry out plant closings or mass layoffs that result in an employment loss for a certain number of employees. In the case of a plant closing, notice is required if 50 or more employees will lose employment. A plant closing is the shutdown of a single site of employment, or one or more facilities of operating units within a single site of employment. In the case of a mass layoff, notice is required if 33 percent of the full-time employees lose their employment, where the total number of employees is at least 50. A mass layoff is defined as the reduction of the work force by one third (and more than 50 employees) or by 500 employees. Under WARN, the employer is required to give a detailed written notice to the affected employees or their representative, the state dislocated workers unit, and the chief elected official of the local government where the facility is located. The Act provides for certain exceptions to the 60-day notice requirement. An employer is not required to give notice if it closes a temporary facility, if the closing or layoff results from completion of a temporary project and employees were hired with the understanding that their employment was of a temporary nature, or where a closing or layoff constitutes a strike or lockout. In addition, where a layoff results from unforeseen business circumstances or a natural disaster, less than 60 days' advance notice is permitted. Furthermore, where a company is in economic difficulty, and notice will prevent the company from procuring needed capital, reduced notice is permissible.

WARN provides remedies for its violation, which include payment of back pay and benefits for up to the full 60-day violation period, to employees who did not receive notice, and payment of a penalty of not more than $500 per day, up to a maximum of $30,000 for a full 60-day violation period, where no notice was given to local communities. In addition, attorneys' fees are available to a successful plaintiff. In view of the high costs that may result from failure to comply with the notice requirements, it is very important for employers to comply with the notice requirements.

Outside of the notice requirement, an employer is generally free to make a reduction in its work force in a manner consistent with its business needs. However, the employer's right to lay off workers is, of course, limited by the antidiscrimination laws. Thus, in laying off workers, the employer should avoid decisions that have a disparate impact on employees in protected groups such as minorities, handicapped persons, and older workers. It is necessary to scrutinize carefully any early retirement plans or other inducements to reduce the work force, to ensure compliance with the Age Discrimination in Employment Act (ADEA).

Unemployment Compensation

Employees who lose their employment through no fault of their own are protected by state unemployment compensation laws. These laws generally provide for compensation for a fixed period of time unless the employee is in some way disqualified. To qualify for compensation, the employee must establish, among other things, that he or she is able and available to perform work. The unemployment fund is financed by employers through taxes or contributions based on their payroll. While the Federal Unemployment Tax Act also imposes a levy on employers for unemployment compensation, it permits a credit against employers' liability for contributions paid under state law.

Benefits may be denied where the employee has refused to accept work, has been discharged for willful misconduct, or has left voluntarily without a compelling or just reason. As a general matter, employees who are out of work as a result of a strike are similarly disqualified from receiving benefits. However, in some states strikers are entitled to unemployment benefits if they did not precipitate the strike. There is a right of appeal to an unemployment compensation referee against the decision of a hearing officer. The final appeal lies to an unemployment compensation board of review. The decision of the board may be taken on appeal to a state court.

Pension and Welfare Benefits

Employers offer various pension and welfare benefits to their employees. The primary statute that regulates benefits is the Employee Retirement Income Security Act (29 U.S.C., §§ 3301–3311) (ERISA). This statute generally prescribes the minimum standards for the regulation of pension and welfare schemes and seeks to protect the interests of the individual participants by regulating the administration of benefit plans. The requirements of ERISA are discussed in detail elsewhere in this book.

THE EQUAL EMPLOYMENT OPPORTUNITY LAWS

A number of statutes ensure that all individuals have equal employment opportunities. These statutes generally prohibit the denial of employment opportunities solely on the basis of sex, race, national origin, age, handicap, or disability. They are premised on the notion that all persons are born equal and, as such, are entitled to the equal pursuit of happiness. In addition to federal antidiscrimination laws, state legislatures have enacted a number of antidiscrimination statutes that usually supplement federal statutes.

The Civil Rights Act of 1964: Title VII

The earliest statute that prohibits discrimination against formation of contracts on the basis of race is Section 1981 of the Civil Rights Act of 1866. Section 1981 has been interpreted to prohibit employers from refusing to hire persons because of their race. In 1964, Congress enacted the Civil Rights Act of 1964, which was a comprehensive piece of legislation directed at eradicating economic, social, and political discrimination in the United States. Title VII of this statute was specifically directed at discrimination in employment (42 U.S.C §2000e-2).

Title VII prohibits employers from discriminating in hiring, discharge, compensation, terms, conditions, or privileges of employment against a person on account of race, color, religion, sex, or national origin. It has been extended to cover discrimination on the basis of pregnancy as well. Title VII defines the employer broadly to include "a person engaged in an industry affecting commerce who has 15 or more employees for each working day in each of 20 or more calendar weeks in the current or preceding calendar year" (42 U.S.C. § 2000e[b]). Therefore, the statute covers virtually every employer.

In a Title VII suit, an employee can prevail in two ways: (1) by proving that he or she was treated differently on the basis of one of the impermissible criteria, or (2) by establishing that the employer's policy has a disparate impact on persons of a particular race, color, religion, sex, or national origin, unless the policy in question is reasonably necessary to the employer's business. In a disparate treatment case, the employee must initially show that (1) he or she belongs to a protected class, (2) that he or she applied for and was qualified for the job, (3) that he or she was rejected despite possessing the requisite qualifications, and (4) that after he or she was rejected, the employer continued to provide applications to persons with similar qualifications. These factors, unless explained by some legitimate business reason, will lead to the inference that the individual concerned was discriminated against. Where the employer has offered a legitimate business reason for its decision, an employee can succeed only if he or she proves that the business reason offered is merely pretext for an underlying discrimination.

In order to avoid discrimination charges based on disparate impact, the employer must avoid employment practices that, though neutral on their face, have an adverse impact on protected groups. Where a disparate impact has been demonstrated, the employer can only avoid discrimination charges by showing that its policies are justified by business necessity.

Title VII provides for specific defenses to employers. Thus, if different treatment can be justified on the basis of a genuine occupational qualification, charges of discrimination will not succeed. Similarly, disparate treatment or impact is justified if made pursuant to a bona fide seniority or merit system, provided the scheme was established without any intention to discriminate and is equitably administered. In addition, an employer may rely on the results of a professionally developed ability test, as long as it is not used with the intention to discriminate.

Title VII is enforced by the Equal Employment Opportunity Commission (EEOC). The EEOC has wide powers of enforcement, including compelling maintenance and production of employment records and statistics, promulgating its own guidelines and regulations, and investigating individual complaints to determine whether there has been any unlawful discrimination. Guidelines and regulations promulgated by the EEOC are accorded great deference by the courts. Victims of discrimination bring charges to the EEOC. The EEOC will in turn investigate the charges, and, if it believes that they have merit, it will first attempt a reconciliation between the parties. If there is no reconciliation, the EEOC may bring suit in federal court against the employer. If the EEOC does not bring suit, the employee may bring suit on his or her own behalf. There is no right to a jury trial under Title VII. In general, Title VII allows an employee to recover back pay for up to two years before the date the original charge was filed. Back pay may also include compensation for lost overtime and fringe benefits. In addition, the court may issue an order for injunctive and affirmative relief, including reinstatement, promotion, and crediting of seniority and other benefits to make the employee whole. No punitive or compensatory damages are recoverable under Title VII suits (See *John C. McCarthy: Punitive Damages in Wrongful Discharge Cases*, p. 281 [1985]). In addition, the employee may be awarded front pay to compensate for losses caused by discrimination. In Title VII suits, the court may award costs to the prevailing party, including attorneys' fees. Attorneys' fees are not limited to fees in connection with filing the suit itself, but also include fees for work performed in connection with the required administrative proceedings that preceded the suit (*New York Gas Light Club* v. *Carey,* 447 U.S. 54 [1980]). Under Title VII, an employee may also bring a class action on behalf of a whole group of individuals similarly situated. Pending in Congress is a new Civil Rights Act that may have a significant impact on some of the rules described in this section.

Age Discrimination in Employment

In 1967, Congress enacted the Age Discrimination in Employment Act (ADEA), which prohibits discrimination against employees on the basis of age. This statute applies to employees who are at least 40 years old (29 U.S.C. § 621). In an age discrimination case involving a layoff or discharge, the employee must show that he or she (1) was within the protected age group, (2) was discharged, (3) was replaced with a person not within the protected group, and (4) was qualified to do the job (*Price* v. *Maryland Casualty Co.,* 561 F. 2d 609 [5th Cir. 1977]). As with Title VII, the employer may defend its otherwise discriminatory practice on the ground that the age is a bona fide occupational qualification, or that the discrimination is the result of a bona fide seniority or merit system. Where, however, an employee demonstrates that age was the determining factor in the employment decision, it is not necessary for him or her to show that he was replaced by an employee outside of the protected age group (*McCuen* v. *Home Ins.,* 663 F. 2d 1150 [5th Cir. 1981]). A bona fide occupational qualification must amount to a business necessity. Age is a bona fide occupational qualification only if there is a factual basis for believing that all or almost all people beyond a certain age could not perform the job in question. (See *John C. McCarthy: Punitive Damages in Wrongful Discharge Cases, supra,* at 288).

As with Title VII, ADEA is enforced by the EEOC. Where the unlawful discrimination occurs in a state that prohibits the act in question and has enforcement capabilities, the employee must first file a charge with the state agency (29 U.S.C. §§ 262 [d][2], 633[b]). Where there is no appropriate state or local enforcement procedure the complaint must be filed with the EEOC Secretary within 180 days after the alleged discriminatory violation occurs (29 U.S.C.

§ 626 [d][1]). The plaintiff under the ADEA, however, is entitled to a jury trial. A civil action under the ADEA must be brought within two years from the date of the alleged violation. A successful employee can obtain lost wages, overtime, and other job-related benefits. In addition, an employee may also seek liquidated damages of an amount equal to the pecuniary loss in cases of willful violation. Equitable relief, such as reinstatement or an injunction against age discrimination, is also available under the Act. A successful employee may recover attorneys' fees.

Equal Pay for Equal Work

Another significant federal antidiscrimination statute is the Equal Pay Act of 1963 (29 U.S.C. § 2006) (the EPA). This statute basically makes it illegal to make any unequal payment of compensation between sexes for work that demands equal skill, effort, and responsibility and that is performed under similar working conditions. The Act, however, permits differences in pay where differentiation is based on (1) a seniority system, (2) a merit system, (3) a system that measures pay by quality or quantity of production, or (4) any other factor not based on sex. An employee who has been discriminated against on the basis of sex in relation to pay may sue under both Title VII or the EPA.

Pregnancy Discrimination Act

The Pregnancy Discrimination Act of 1978 (42 U.S.C. § 2000e) supplements the other antidiscrimination legislation. While this statute does not provide for the right to maternity leave, it nevertheless adopts a policy of providing the same benefits to the pregnant woman as are available for any temporary disability. This statute generally requires employers to treat any pregnancy, childbirth, and related medical conditions exactly like any other temporary disability. The Act makes it unlawful discrimination to require females to take maternity leave in any certain month in the pregnancy. In addition, work rules that prevent pregnant women from doing certain hazardous jobs are legitimate only when there is evidence of potential harm to the fetus.

Americans With Disabilities Act of 1990

As a result of congressional findings that 43 million Americans have one or more physical or mental disabilities, on July 26, 1990, Congress enacted the Americans With Disabilities Act of 1990 (ADA). The ADA has as its mission the provision of "a clear and comprehensive national mandate for the elimination of discrimination against individuals with disabilities" and "clear, strong, consistent, enforceable standards addressing discrimination against individuals with disabilities" (§ 2[b][1][2]).

Title I of the ADA prohibits discrimination in employment. The effective date of Title I is July 26, 1992. This title prohibits discrimination on the basis of disability by covered employers with respect to hiring, job application procedures, compensation, promotion, training and other terms, conditions, and privileges of employment. Employers who are covered by Title I are those who are engaged in industries affecting commerce and who have 15 or more employees for each working day in each of 20 or more calendar weeks in the current or preceding calendar year. However, for two years following July 26, 1992, the effective date of Title I, an employer means a person who has 25 or more employees.

The underlying premise of this title is that persons with disabilities should not be excluded from job opportunities unless they are actually unable to do the job. The Act requires that job criteria should measure skills required by the job. To ensure that there is a match between the job criteria and the applicant's actual ability to do the job, the ADA requires that (1) persons with disabilities not be disqualified because of their inability to perform nonessential or marginal functions of the job, (2) any selection criteria that screens out or tends to screen out people with disabilities should be job-related and consistent with business necessities, and (3) reasonable accommodations be provided to assist persons with disabilities to meet the job criteria. Thus, where a person with a disability meets all selection criteria except for one that the person cannot meet owing to a disability, such a criterion must relate to an essential aspect of the job. Such a criterion must be tailored to measure the actual ability of a person to perform the essential functions of the job. If the legitimate selection criteria can be satisfied by the prospective employee with reasonable accommodation, then reasonable accommodation must be provided.

The ADA provides examples of reasonable accommodations that may have to be made, such as job restructuring, part-time and modified work schedules, reassignment to a vacant position, acquisition or modification of equipment or devices, appropriate adjustment or modification of examination, and training materials or policies, including the provision of qualified readers or interpreters. An employer, however, is relieved from its duty to accommodate a disability if doing so would impose an "undue hardship." To escape its duty to accommodate a disability, an employer will be required to show significant difficulty or expense in providing reasonable accommodations. In addition, the ADA permits discrimination against individuals whose disabilities impose a "direct threat" to the health or safety of others in the workplace, if the threat cannot be reasonably accommodated.

The ADA does not define "disability." However, the following are likely to constitute disability: blindness, impaired hearing, multiple sclerosis, diabetes, epilepsy, heart disease, dyslexia, hypertension, hepatitis-B, lack of index finger on the right hand, Huntington's chorea, post-traumatic stress disorder, recovered alcoholism, former drug abuse, AIDS, and tuberculosis. The ADA, however, specifically excludes certain conditions as disabilities, such as homosexuality, bisexuality, transexuality, exhibitionism and compulsive gambling, kleptomania, and pyromania.

Under the ADA, an employer may require a medical examination only after an offer of employment has been made to a job applicant and prior to the commencement of employment duties. However, an employer may reject the applicant based on the results of the medical examination only if all applicants for the job are required to take the examination and the information obtained is treated as confidential. The employer may not reject an applicant based on the results of the medical examination if the individual is qualified to perform the essential functions of the job with reasonable accommodation.

The requirement of reasonable accommodation thus requires that when making structural alterations, employers should keep in mind the most common forms of disabilities such as paraplegism, quadriplegism, blindness, and deafness. In the case of employees with communicable diseases, employers will have to routinely review requirements of OSHA and recommendations from the Surgeon General and the Center for Disease Control so as to inform themselves about what diseases are communicable and the circumstances under which such diseases may be transmitted, as well as the precautions that may be taken to safeguard the health of other employees.

In addition to prohibiting discrimination in employment, the ADA has three general prohibitions that cover areas such as public accommodations, commercial facilities, and public transportation services provided by private entities. Under Title III, employers who provide public accommodations and public transportation services are prohibited from discriminating on the basis of disability and are required to provide to disabled individuals full and equal enjoyment of goods, services, facilities, privileges, advantages, and accommodations. Commercial facilities and places of accommodation are required to be made accessible to individuals with disabilities in a new building built for occupancy more than 30 months after January 26, 1992, the effective date of Title III. Finally, common carriers of wire or radio services are required to provide hearing-impaired individuals with the functional equivalent of telephone service.

The EEOC is charged with the enforcement of the ADA. The EEOC has the same powers as are available to it under Title VII of the Civil Rights Act of 1964. Thus, the powers, remedies, and procedures available to persons discriminated against based on disability are the same as, and parallel to, the powers, remedies, and procedures available to persons discriminated against on the basis of race, color, religion, sex, or national origin. Title III is enforceable through a private right of action. The applicable remedies are those available under the Civil Rights Act of 1964, including an application for a permanent or temporary injunction, or restraining order. Enforcement remedies can include an order to alter facilities to make them accessible to individuals with disabilities, removing barriers in existing facilities where readily achievable, and in constructing or altering public accommodations and commercial facilities. A violation of Title III may expose an employer to a civil penalty of up to a maximum of $50,000 for a first violation and $100,000 for any subsequent violation.

Sexual Harassment

Sexual harassment is generally defined as unwelcome sexual advances, requests for sexual favors, and other unwelcome verbal, visual, or physical conduct of a sexual nature. In particular no executive, manager, supervisor, or other employee may threaten or suggest that another employee's refusal to submit to unwanted sexual advances will adversely affect that person's employment or any other term or condition of employment. Employers are generally under a duty to ensure that no sexual harassment occur in the workplace. Thus failure by an employer to investigate and prevent sexual harassment may expose the employer to charges of sex discrimination under Title VII.

In addition to the above antidiscrimination laws, there is a substantial body of law holding that sexual harassment is a form of sex discrimination and a violation of Title VII. In 1980, the EEOC issued specific guidelines to this effect. According to these guidelines, it is illegal to make submission to unwanted sexual advances a basis for hiring, promotion, or discharge decisions.

Affirmative Action

One of the legacies of racial discrimination in the United States has been the exclusion of blacks from certain occupations. Prior to 1964 blacks were largely relegated to unskilled or semiskilled jobs (*Steelworkers* v. *Weber*, 443 U.S. 193, 202 [1978]). As of 1962, the nonwhite unemployment rate was 124 percent higher than the white rate (*Id.*). In 1964, Congress recognized that "the crux of the problem was to open employment opportunities for blacks in occupations which have been traditionally closed to them." Title VII of the Civil Rights Act of 1964 prohibits racial discrimination in employment with this objective in mind. Because it was recognized that outlawing racial discrimination in employment will not break down the old patterns of racial segregation and hierarchy, it was considered necessary to take affirmative steps to break down these old patterns. That marked the emergence of affirmative action plans, which are plans primarily aimed at ensuring that minorities are utilized at all levels and in all segments of the work force. Affirmative action programs have been extended to other minorities.

Compulsory Affirmative Action Programs

Consistent with the goal of promoting equal opportunities in employment, it has become national policy to require those employers who do business with the federal government to actively assist minorities in the job market. In 1965, President Johnson issued Executive Order 1246, which prohibited every government contractor or subcontractor with 50 or more employees and government contracts with $10,000 or more from discriminating against any employee or applicant for employment because of race, religion, sex, or national origin. Those contractors and subcontractors with 50 or more employees and with contracts of $50,000 or more are required to develop a written affirmative action plan every year for each of their establishments. In the plan, the employer is required to set goals and timetables for the full utilization of minorities in all job categories. However, the employer is required only to make a good faith effort to achieve its goals, but is not required to achieve its goals.

The Executive Order is enforced by an agency of the Department of Labor, the Office of Federal Contract Compliance Programs (OFCCP). This agency monitors contractors' compliance with the requirements of the Executive Order. Failure to comply with the Executive Order may result in the termination, cancellation, or suspension of an existing government contract or subcontract. In addition, it may result in the particular employer being barred from future government contracts. Back pay can also be recovered where a particular class has been adversely affected by past or present discrimination (See 416 C.F.R. §61-1.26 [1977]). An individual has no remedy against the employer under the Executive Order but can institute an action against the OFCCP to enforce the Executive Order (Schlei & Grossman: *Employment Discrimination,* p. 203 [1979 Supp.]) Public interest or advocate organizations may file complaints without identifying employees discriminated against.

The OFCCP compliance procedures have been utilized by Congress to provide affirmative action for the handicapped and the Vietnam veterans. It will probably be extended to apply to those who have served in the Gulf War as well. The Vocational Rehabilitation Act of 1973 (VRA) requires federal contractors in connection with any contract in excess of $2,500 to have affirmative action for mentally and physically handicapped individuals (29 U.S.C. §701-794). The VRA defines a handicapped individual, generally, to mean any person who has physical or mental impairment that substantially limits one or more of such person's major life activities. In addition, the Vietnam Era Veterans Readjustment Act of 1974 promotes affirmative action plans for military verterans who once served in Vietnam, and were discharged within four years preceding their application owing to a disability that occurred in the line of duty. They must have at least 30 percent or greater disability. This act covers federal contractors with contracts of $10,000 or more.

Voluntary Affirmative Action
Employers in the private sector who desire to adopt affirmative action plans to eliminate conspicuous racial imbalance in traditionally segregated job categories may do so voluntarily. Such plans are not prohibited by Title VII of the Civil Rights Act of 1964. Voluntary affirmative action plans were endorsed by the U.S. Supreme Court in *Steelworkers* v. *Weber, supra,* where the Court had the following to say:

> We cannot agree . . . that Congress intended to prohibit the private sector from taking active steps to accomplish the goal that Congress designed Title VII to achieve. The very statutory words intended as spur or catalyst to cause employers and unions to examine and to self evaluate their employment practices and to endeavor to eliminate, so far as possible, the last vestiges of an unfortunate and ignominious page in this Country's history, . . . cannot be interpreted as an absolute prohibition against all private, voluntary, race conscious affirmative action effort to hasten the elimination of such vestiges. It would be ironic indeed if a law triggered by a nation's concern over centuries of racial injustice and intended to improve the lot of those who have been excluded from the American Dream for so long, constituted the first legislative provision of all voluntary, private, race-conscious effort to abolish traditional patterns of racial segregation and hierarchy. [*Id.* at 204]

For an affirmative action plan to survive the statutory challenge, such plan (1) must be designed to open employment opportunities for minorities in occupations that have been traditionally closed to them, (2) must not unnecessarily trammel the interest of other employees, (3) must not create an absolute bar to the advancement of other employees, and (4) must be temporary, that is, must be designed to eliminate a manifest imbalance and not maintain any balance (*Id.* at 208). An employer who voluntarily adopts affirmative action need not point to past discriminatory practices (*Id.* at 213).

Because of the potential suit by nonminority employees, it is essential that an employer who adopts a voluntary affirmative action shows that it complies with the law.

EMPLOYMENT OF ALIENS

Introduction

At times it may be necessary for an employer to import its executive or technical staff to supervise the initial stages of a new business venture in the United States. Only aliens who are in possession of valid work authorization documents may be lawfully employed within the United States. It is unlawful for an employer to employ an alien who is not in possession of valid work authorization documents. Thus, employers are under a duty to verify the work authorization documents of their employees before hiring them. This duty will generally entail ensuring that the alien is in possession of a valid visa allowing the alien to be employed in the United States. Therefore, knowledge of the types of visas that permit employment in the United States is essential.

The employment of foreigners in the United States is governed by the Immigration and Nationality Act, as amended (8 U.S.C. §§1101-1525) (INA). This statute makes provision for two categories of aliens, namely (1) nonimmigrant, those desiring to remain in the United States temporarily; and (2) immigrants, those aliens desiring to remain permanently in the United States. The INA is administered by the Immigration and Naturalization Service (INS) through its regional and district offices in the United States, and the Department of State through its consular offices abroad.

Immigration law in the United States is a highly specialized practice. This section is intended only to provide a foreign investor with a general outline of the types of visas that are available to foreign investors and business personnel as well as the requirements for such visas.

B-1 Temporary Visitor For Business

This visa is normally issued to a visitor for business who desires to visit the United States for a relatively short period. It is usually given for a period of entry that is necessary to conduct an alien's business (8 U.S.C. §1101[a][15][B]). The B Visa Category is valid for six months, and may be extended for a further period of six months. In practice, business visitors are granted only a period of entry that is necessary to conduct their business. Such visits range from three months to six months (*1991 Immigration Procedures Handbook* at 1.1). To be eligible for a B Visa, the alien must meet the following requirements: (1) The alien must enter the United States for a limited duration; (2) the alien must intend to depart at the expiration of the stay period; (3) during the stay in the United States, the alien must maintain a foreign residence without an intention of abandoning such residence; (4) the alien must have adequate financial arrangements to travel to and from the United States; and (5) the alien must intend to engage in legitimate business activities. Should a stay beyond three months be necessary, the period of stay can be extended by making an application for an extension of stay to an INS office in the United States. The holder of a B-1 Visa may be accompanied by his or her spouse and children. The spouse and the children are usually issued with a B-2 Visa, which is issued to visitors for pleasure. Holders of B-1 or B-2 visas may not accept employment in the United States.

Visa Waiver Program for Tourists and Business Visitors from Certain Countries

In 1986, the U.S. Congress authorized a visa waiver program, under which nationals of designated countries may enter the United States for up to 90 days for the purposes acceptable under the B-1 and B-2 visa categories, but without being required to obtain a visa before coming to the United States. The countries that participate in this program are France, Germany, Italy, Japan, the Netherlands, Sweden, Switzerland, and the United Kingdom. This program has recently been extended and is due to expire on September 30, 1994. To participate in this program, the alien must (1) be in possession of a nontransferable round-trip ticket that is valid for one year, refundable only in the country that issued it or the alien's home country, and issued by a carrier that has entered into an agreement with the U.S. government to participate in the program; and (2) the alien must arrive on an airline or other transportation line that has signed an agreement to participate in the program. Most major airlines have entered into such agreements. In addition, the alien will be required to sign a waiver to contest a finding of excludability at the border.

Under this program, an alien can be admitted to the United States only for a period of 90 days, and this period cannot be extended. In addition, an alien cannot change to other status. Foreign investors must carefully assess whether the 90-day period is sufficient for the purposes of their trip. Thus, it is advisable for business travelers to obtain B-1 visas if they anticipate the need to change status or extend their stay.

Once admitted to the United States under the program, an alien may travel to Canada, Mexico, Bermuda, and most Caribbean Islands during the U.S. visit and still be readmitted to the United States with the original entry documentation. However, the period of admission would still be subject to the original 90-day limit imposed on the initial admission.

TC Visa Category for Canadian Business and Professional Persons

The United States and Canada have entered into a Free Trade Agreement (FTA), which provides for an expedited admission of business persons from each country into the other. Pursuant to the FTA, Canadian professionals and business persons may now be admitted to the United States under the new TC nonimmigrant category. The FTA provides for a far more liberal admission of business visitors who qualify under the B-1 visa category, professionals who qualify under the H-1B visa category, and those aliens who qualify under the E visa category.

Under the TC category, professionals who qualify can work for U.S. companies on a temporary basis. In addition, qualifying professionals who are independent business persons can open U.S. operations or undertake U.S. assignments for clients (*Immigration*

Procedures Handbook, p. 1-67). To qualify for the TC visa category, the Canadian professional must be engaged in one of the occupations mentioned in Schedule 2 of the FTA. Schedule 2 includes the following occupations: accountant, engineer, scientist, research assistant, medical/allied professional, architect, lawyer, teacher, economist, social worker, mathematician, hotel manager, librarian, animal breeder, sylviculturist (forestry specialist), range manager, forester, graphic designer, land surveyor, landscape architect, nutritionist, dietician, computer assistant analyst, psychologist, scientific technician/technologist, disaster relief insurance claims adjuster, and management consultant.

In order to be admitted under the FTA, a business visitor must be engaged in any of the activities set out in Schedule 1. These activities include research and design, growth, manufacture and production, marketing, sales, and general service.

The application for admission under the FTA is made at the port of entry, usually at the Canadian airports. Application is made by presenting proof of Canadian citizenship, a description of purpose of the entry, and proof that the individual is engaged in one of the activities or occupations listed in Schedule 1 or Schedule 2, as the case may be. As with all Canadians, no visa is necessary, the alien simply presents the application to the INS inspectors at the port of entry, usually at INS preflight clearance post at the port (*Procedures Handbook,* 1-71). An INS inspector at the border will admit the Canadian alien for a period requested subject to maximum period of one year. The TC status can be renewed by simply presenting a new application at a port of entry and being admitted to the United States for a new one-year period. A professional who is working in the United States on a long-term but temporary assignment can make a formal extension of stay to the appropriate regional office of the INS.

Aliens under TC status are allowed to bring their families into the United States.

E-1 and E-2 Treaty Visas

The E Visa category is available to business personnel who wish to enter the United States for a longer period of time to work (1) in an enterprise engaged in trade between the United States and a foreign state, or (2) an enterprise that has made a substantial investment in the United States (INA §101 [8][15][E]). The primary purpose of this category is to give effect to those treaties between the United States and foreign countries that make provision for reciprocal benefits to nationals of each country who invest in the other country or who conduct trade in between the two countries (*1991 Immigration Procedure's Handbook*, 3-1). Two types of visas are issued under the E Visa Category: (1) the E-1 Visa, which can be used for the purposes of conducting trade between the United States and a foreign company whose majority stock owners are nationals of a country that has a treaty of commerce and navigation with the United States; and (2) the E-2 Visa, which is issued to foreign nationals coming to the United States to oversee investments in the United States.

Before considering an E-Visa category, it is necessary first to establish whether the country of the foreign investor has a treaty of commerce and navigation with the United States. The information concerning the existence of such a treaty can be obtained either from the investor's country or from the U.S. Consulate Office in the foreign country. As of 1991, the United States had treaties of commerce and navigation with the following countries:

Trade and Investment (E-1 and E-2 Status):

Argentina	Iran	Philippines
Austria	Italy	Spain
Belgium	Japan	Suriname
Canada	Korea	Switzerland
China	Liberia	Thailand
Colombia	Luxembourg	Togo
Costa Rica	Netherlands	Turkey
Ethiopia	Norway	United Kingdom
France	Oman	Yugoslavia
Germany	Pakistan	
Honduras	Paraguay	

E-1 Treaty-Trader Status Exist Only:

Bolivia	Estonia	Ireland
Burnei	Finland	Israel
Denmark	Greece	Latvia

E-2 Treaty-Investor Status Only:

Bangladesh	Cameroon
Grenada	Zaire

(Reproduced from *1991 Immigration Procedure Handbook*, pp. 3-3 and 3-4.)

Because the treaties of commerce and navigation confer different status, it is also necessary to establish whether the treaty in question provides for trade and investment (E-1 and E-2 status), or whether it confers E-1 treaty-trader status only.

The company engaged in trade or investment in the United States must have the same nationality as the treaty country. The nationality of the country engaged in trade or investment is determined by the nationality of the persons who owned at least 50 percent of the stock of the company. The nationality of the persons owning the company stock is their country of citizenship. The nationality of a company that holds company stock is determined by the citizenship of its shareholders. In addition, the company or principal who will be entering the United States must also be the nationality of the same treaty country through which the investing or trading company qualifies.

In addition to the above requirements, which apply generally to the E Visa category, the E-1 and E-2 Visas have different requirements.

E-1 Visa

An applicant for an E-1 Visa must show that the trading company is engaged in substantial trade principally with the United States and that he or she will serve the company in either managerial capacity or the capacity that involves essential skills. Trade has been widely defined and includes almost any business activity, including exchange, purchase, or sale of goods or services. Services also includes economic activities that do not involve tangible goods such as data processing, advertising, accounting, design and engineering, and management consulting.

The substantiality of trade is usually measured by the volume of trade, the number of transactions, and the continued course of trade (*1991 Immigration Procedures Handbook*, 3-11). To determine whether trade is substantial, it is useful to consider factors such as how many companies demand the type of product manufactured by the trading company and how many products are sold in a year, as well as the percentage of U.S. cities as compared to worldwide cities (*1991 Immigration Procedures Handbook,* 3-12).

The trade would be considered to be principally with the United States if at least 51 percent of the total volume of business of the U.S. office consists of trade between the United States and the treaty country. It is, however, not necessary that the parent or affiliated company, which is situated outside the United States, be principally engaged in trade with the United States (*Id.*, 3-13).

Two types of employees may enter the United States under an E-1 treaty-trader visa, namely (1) an employee who performs supervisory or executive duties and (2) an employee who possesses specific qualifications that will make his or her services essential to the efficient operation of the company's enterprise. Generally, an employee who is closer to the top level of management will satisfy the requirement of supervisory observative duties. Nonexecutive and nonsupervisory employees will generally qualify if they are highly trained technicians who are (1) familiar with the product of the company and are engaged in training and supervision of persons in the manufacturing, maintenance, or repair of the product; and (2) performing the manufacturing, maintenance, or repair of the product owing to the unavailability of the United States workers (*Id.*, 3-15). It is necessary that the skills of a technician be essential to the company's operation. In addition, the technician's qualifications must be demonstrated by prior experience and the skills must be relatively rare.

E-2 Treaty-Investor Visa

An applicant for an E-2 treaty-investor visa must generally show that there is an active and substantial investment in the United States that is likely to create job opportunities for United States workers. In addition, the persons on whose behalf the visa is being sought must play an essential role in the enterprise, such as developing and directing the investment, or be a qualified manager or specially trained and highly qualified employee necessary for the development of the investment (*Id.* at 3-16, 3-17). An investment will be considered active if the business enterprise that underlies the investment represents a real operating enterprise productive of some service or commodity (*Id.* at 3-17). There is no minimum dollar amount necessary before an investment can be considered substantial. As a general matter, an investment will be considered substantial where (1) it is proportional to the total value of the particular company, or (2) it is an amount usually considered necessary to establish a viable enterprise of the kind contemplated by the investor (*Id.* at 3-19). The investment, however, must not be marginal. It must have a potential of creating jobs in the United States.

A principal investor will generally qualify for a visa if his or her responsibilities involve the development and direction of the investment. Aliens who are coming to the United States as employees of the investing company must be either people who are serving in a managerial capacity or people who serve in technical capacities that require special training and qualifications. The purpose of importing these employees must generally be to establish the enterprise, to train employees who are employed in technical positions, including manufacturing, maintenance, or repair, or to monitor and improve on the quality of the product.

E-Category Visa, Application Process and Duration of Stay

An application for an E-Visa category is made to the United States Consulate Office of the foreign country. The initial validity period of an E-Visa category is five years, unless the treaty in question specifies a lesser period. However, the period of the visa is generally determined by the needs of the company. Upon being issued with a visa, the holder is entitled to travel to the United States and make an application for admission into the country to the INS. The INS will generally admit holders of E-Visa category to stay for periods ranging from one to two years in the United States. This they will do even though the visa itself is valid for a period of five years. The period of stay can be extended for further periods of two years for almost indefinitely. Each time the holder leaves the country, he or she will be given a new period of one year. When the period of one year expires while the holder is in the United States an application for an extension can be made to the local office of the INS. The extension of the stay period will be determined by the existence of further needs for services of the holder. Upon the expiration of the visa, a new visa must be applied for in the same manner as the original application. If the visa expires during the validity of the period of stay, the holder need not leave the United States until the period for which he or she was admitted expires.

An E-Visa category will entitle the holder to be accompanied by the spouse and unmarried children. The spouse and unmarried children, however, may not accept employment in the United States without any change in their status.

H-1B Visa Category

A foreign investor who wishes to employ, temporarily, a foreign employee may make use of the H-1B Visa category. This visa category is limited to the foreign nationals in "specialty occupations." The position to be filled by the foreign national can either be temporary or permanent. However, the employer's intention must be to employ the foreign national temporarily in that position and the foreign national must have an intention of remaining temporarily in the United States. The new act restricts the number of individuals who can enter to 65,000 annually.

A "specialty occupation" is an occupation that involves "theoretical and practical application of highly specialized knowledge," and whose minimum entry level requirement is a bachelor's degree or higher degree. In addition, the new act states that to be considered a "specialty occupation," it must require state license to practice and completion of a bachelor's or higher degree or its equivalent or experience in the field equivalent to a degree and expertise in the field acquired through holding responsible positions. Thus, professionals will include persons who are engineers, accountants, lawyers, scientists, financial analysts, system analysts, architects, management consultants, and market research analysts.

Since the definition of "specialty occupation" in the new act is almost the same as the INS's definition of professional under the amended act, the present INS regulations provide some useful guidelines to the factors that the INS is likely to consider in determining whether a particular position is a "specialty occupation." In determining whether a position is a professional one, the INS generally considers factors such as whether a bachelor's or higher degree is a minimum entry-level requirement, whether the industry practice requires a degree in parallel positions, whether the position is so complex or unusual that a degree is a requirement, whether the employer's normal requirement for the position is a degree, or whether the level of responsibility and authority involved in the position is normally associated with professional standing.

To apply for this visa, the employer must first file an H-1B visa petition with the INS in the United States. The petition must be accompanied by documents that establish the need for the foreign employee, including the qualifications of the foreign employee. The Immigration Act of 1990 has for the first time introduced a requirement that the petitioning employer must file a special labor attestation. The act provides that no alien may be admitted in the status as an H-1B nonimmigrant unless the employer has filed with the Secretary of Labor a "labor condition application." In the application, the employer must state that it will pay the prevailing wage to the alien and to other employees in the same occupation, and that the working conditions of the alien will not adversely affect working conditions of other workers. A copy of the labor condition application must be publicized by the employer at its principal place of business or worksite. Penalty procedures including up to a $1,000 fine and a minimum of one-year bar on the importation of alien workers may be imposed for misrepresentation in the process.

Once the visa petition is approved by the INS, the alien employee can then apply for an H-1B visa at the U.S. Consulate in the foreign country. The maximum period for which an alien employee may be admitted to the United States is six years. However, the period of stay will be determined by the needs of the employer. The period of stay can be extended, based on further needs, subject to the maximum period of stay of six years. In extraordinary circumstances, the period of stay can be extended beyond the six-year maximum limitation period. The application for an extension of an H-1B Visa can be made to the appropriate INS Regional Office. An employer who dismisses an employee before the expiration of an H-1B status must pay the employee's return transportation costs.

The holder of an H-1B Visa is entitled to bring along the spouse and unmarried children. However, the spouse and the children may not be employed without a change in their status.

H-2B Visa Category

An employer wishing to employ temporarily skilled or unskilled foreign nationals in positions that are temporary in nature and for which unemployed United States workers are not available, may use the H-2B visa category. It is essential that the employer should intend employing the alien for a temporary period and that the employer's need for the alien's skills be temporary. Thus, what distinguishes an H-2B visa from an H-1B visa is that the former emphasizes the temporary nature of the employer's need for the alien's skills and not just the temporary nature of the employer's need for the particular alien. In the case of an H-1B visa, the employer's need for an alien's skills can be permanent, even though the employer only intends employing the alien temporarily. An employer seeking to bring an employer under the H-2B visa category must first seek a labor certification from the Department of Labor indicating that the alien will not displace unemployed U.S. workers and that the proposed employment will not adversely affect the employment conditions of other U.S. workers. The period of stay largely depends on the period for which the services of the alien are needed. The period of stay initially granted may be extended upon demonstrating that the initial period is insufficient for the completion of the duties to be performed and that the unavailability of U.S. workers persists. The application process begins by filing a request for a labor certification; upon approval of labor certification, petition for an H-2B visa is filed with the INS. Once the petition has been approved, the alien must then apply for the H-2B visa at the U.S. Consulate Office abroad. A holder of an H-2B visa may bring along the spouse and unmarried children. Under the new act the number of aliens who may be admitted under the H-2B visa category is restricted to a figure of 36,000 annually.

L-1 Intracompany Transferees

The L-1 Visa category is very useful to a foreign investor who wishes to bring foreign employees to the United States (Section 101[a][15][L] of the INA, 8 U.S.C. §1101 [a][15][L]). It has relatively few basic requirements: (1) the employee must have worked for the overseas company for at least one year, (2) the company abroad must be the same employer or a subsidiary or affiliate of the U.S. company, (3) the U.S. or foreign company must continue to do business abroad during the entire period of the employee's stay in the United States, (4) the employee must have been employed by the overseas company in an executive or managerial or a position that involves specialized knowledge, (5) the transferee must be coming to the United States to fill the position of an executive or manage or a position involving specialized knowledge, and (6) the transfer must be temporary in nature, although the position filled by the employee can be a permanent one. In addition, the transferee must be qualified for the position to which he or she is being transferred and must be able to produce proof of qualification for the job. It is not necessary, however, that the transferee fill the same capacity in the United States that he or she filled abroad.

To qualify as an executive, the primary duties of the transferee must include directing the management of the enterprise or a major section of the enterprise, establishment of goals and policies, the exercise of a wide latitude of discretionary decision-making, and receiving only general supervision or direction from higher level of executive, board of directors, or shareholders. To qualify as a manager, the primary duties of the transferee must involve the management of a department, subdivision, function, or component of the organization; control of other professional, supervisory, or managerial employees or the management of an essential function within the organization at a senior level; and the exercise of discretionary authority over the activity or function involved. As a general matter, knowledge of the company product and its application in international markets or an advanced level of knowledge of processes and procedures of the company will satisfy the "specialized knowledge" requirement. Thus, an employee with a high level of expertise and experience in the company's techniques and management policies may qualify for the "specialized knowledge" classification. However, such knowledge must have been acquired through extensive prior experience with the employer.

As a general rule, one of the companies involved in the transfer must have effective control of the other. Effective control would be established by proof of majority ownership. However, the emphasis is on common control of the companies involved in the transfer.

Affiliate companies controlled by a common parent will qualify for an L-1 visa petition.

To obtain an L Visa category, the prospective U.S. employer must file an L-1 Petition with the appropriate regional office of the INS. The petition must be accompanied by all of the documents demonstrating that the prospective employee qualifies for an L-1 Visa status. Upon the approval of the L-1 petition, the transferee may then approach the foreign U.S. consulate to make an application for a L-1 Visa. Executives and managers may stay for up to seven consecutive years in the United States. The L-1 "specialized knowledge" alien can only stay up to five consecutive years. However, the actual period of stay will be determined by the needs of the company, subject to the maximum of seven or five years, as the case may be. The initial period of stay is usually three years and can be renewed for an additional period subject to the maximum allowed for the employee in question.

The holder of the L-1 Visa is entitled to bring the spouse and unmarried children to the United States. However, the spouse and the children may not be employed without altering their status to permit employment.

O Visa Category

The Immigration Act of 1990 has created a new nonimmigrant category, the O-1 visa category. This category generally applies to aliens with "extraordinary ability" in sciences, arts, education, business, or athletics. It encompasses some, but not necessarily all who previously qualified as "pre-eminent" aliens under the H-1B visa category on the basis of their exceptional business achievements.

The act does not define "extraordinary ability." There are some indications in the act that Congress intended that the "extraordinary ability" standard should be higher than the exceptional ability standard. In another context, the INS has indicated that "exceptional ability" is more difficult to meet than the "pre-eminence test." It can thus be expected that the "extraordinary ability" standard will even be more difficult to meet. Given the difficulty that may exist in satisfying the "extraordinary ability" standard, it is advisable that aliens who can qualify in the E or L visa categories should consider these as viable options to an O visa. However, aliens in the motion picture and television industries need show only a "demonstrated record of extraordinary achievement . . . recognized through extensive documentation."

In addition to the O-1 visa category, the act creates the O-2 visa category, available to accompanying aliens. To be admitted as an "accompanying alien," the alien must be entering the United States on a temporary basis to accompany and assist the principal for a specific event, the alien must be an "integral part of such actual performance," and the alien must have critical skills and experience that are not of a general nature and cannot generally be performed by other individuals.

The act does not specify any maximum period for which an O nonimmigrant alien can be admitted to the United States. The period of admission is subject to "such period as the Attorney General may specify in order to provide for the event."

Immigrant Visa

One of the ways in which permanent resident status in the United States can be achieved is by means of a visa petition filed by a prospective employer in the United States. The permanent resident status, the so-called green card, entitles foreign nationals to live and work in the United States without time limitations. The INA prescribes a somewhat elaborate procedure to qualify for a permanent resident status. This system is partly based on preferences that are given to certain groups of aliens. In addition, there is a limitation on the number of immigrant visas that may be issued under various categories. The Immigration Act of 1990 has increased the number of immigrant visas available for employment-based immigration from the current 54,000 to 140,000. Furthermore, it has created new preference categories. This act has significantly improved immigration opportunities for business persons, professionals, and skilled workers. Under this act, the following categories have been established.

Priority Workers: The New First Preference

This category involves aliens with extraordinary ability, outstanding professors and researchers, and certain multinational executives and managers. Of particular importance for multinational corporations, the priority worker category appears to relieve the employer of the old obligation of proving that executives and managers are "professionals" within the meaning of the regulations. Practitioners have for many years grappled with the problem of proving that business people are professionals within the meaning of INS regulations, particularly with respect to individuals who do not possess degree qualifications. A manager includes an individual who manages a function or component of the organization. Under the new law, it should not be necessary to show that the manager actually supervises and controls other professional employees. This means that an individual who has purely functional responsibilities can qualify as a priority worker.

Professionals with Advanced Degrees and Aliens of Exceptional Ability: The New Second Preference

The second preference category is for aliens who are members of the professions holding advanced degrees (or their equivalent) or who are of exceptional ability in the sciences, arts, or business. A bachelor degree plus at least five years of progressive experience in the professions should be considered the equivalent of an advanced degree. The new second preference category is subject to the labor certification requirement.

Skilled Workers, Entry-Level Professionals, and Unskilled Workers: The New Third Preference

The third preference category, which is also subject to labor certification procedures, consists of three groups: entry-level professionals, skilled workers, and unskilled workers. Professionals are defined as immigrants who hold baccalaureate degrees and who are members of a profession. There is no provision for proving professional status based upon work experience amounting to degree equivalency. A skilled worker is defined as an individual working in a position that requires a minimum of two years training or experience. The unskilled worker portion of the third preference cannot exceed 10,000 visas annually.

Investors

The act creates a new fourth preference category for investors, with 10,000 immigrant visas allotted annually. To qualify under this section, a foreign investor must invest, after November 29,1990, at least $1 million in a "new commercial enterprise" that creates full-time employment for at least 10 U.S. workers. The status of an investor visa holder is conditional for two years; at the end of the two years the investor status can be terminated if the INS determines that the enterprise was established to evade the immigration laws or that the alien has not actively invested or sustained the investment throughout the required two-year period.

The Attorney General is authorized to adjust the amount of the standard investment from time to time in consultation with the Secretary of Labor and the Secretary of State. In addition, special provisions relate to investments in so-called targeted employment areas, defined as rural areas, or areas that have experienced unemployment of at least 150 percent of the national average. At least 3,000 visas under the 10,000 annual allocation are reserved for investors in targeted areas. Such investors may qualify on the basis of a smaller than standard investment amount but not less than $500,000. Criminal penalties are also established for fraudulent investments.

Application Procedure

The application procedure for permanent resident status generally involves three stages: (1) the application for labor certification, (2) the visa petition, and (3) an application for an immigrant visa. It is possible to change from a nonimmigrant visa status to an immigrant visa status. A condition necessary for an application for a permanent resident status is an offer of employment. However, before the permanent position is offered to an alien, the employer must demonstrate that there are no U.S. citizens who are able, willing, and qualified to occupy the position offered to the alien. In addition, it must be demonstrated that employment of the alien will not adversely affect the wages and the working conditions of other workers in the United States. These factors are demonstrated through a procedure called labor certification, which involves advertising the position and obtaining certification from the Department of Labor demonstrating that these factors have been satisfied. In addition, it must be demonstrated that the person to be employed fits in within the preference categories. A labor certification is *not* required for individuals who qualify as priority workers.

Upon the issue of labor certification, or in the case of priority workers, the prospective employer may proceed to file a petition with the INS to have the employee classified as a qualified immigrant, including the information that the alien falls within one of the preference categories. Once the INS classifies the alien as a qualified immigrant, the final step is to apply for permanent residence status at a U.S. Consulate abroad. When an alien who seeks permanent residence status is already in the United States, it is possible to make an application to the INS for adjustment of status, from nonimmigrant to immigrant status. However, the granting of adjustment by the INS is discretionary, and it may still require the alien to go through the normal procedures.

The decision as to which visa is appropriate must be made based on the needs as well as the advantages that each visa has. In view of the sometimes complex procedure involved in applying for a visa, including the impact that a formal denial of a visa might have on future visa applications, it is advisable to seek legal advice on the appropriate visa as well as the procedure to be followed.

CONCLUSION

What has been said in this chapter demonstrates that foreign employers operating in the United States are subject to a myriad of employment-related legal obligations as well as restrictions. The purpose of this chapter was merely to introduce the foreign investor to the U.S. employment and immigration laws and to highlight some but not all of the issues involved in conducting business in the United States. Therefore, this chapter should not be considered to be the final word on the issues it has covered but rather the basis for obtaining detailed professional advice.

CHAPTER 25

EXECUTIVE RECRUITMENT IN THE UNITED STATES

Howard M. Fischer
President
Joellen Mazor
Consultant
Howard Fischer Associates, Inc.

INTRODUCTION

The demand for innovative leaders has never been greater than in today's highly competitive global marketplace. After a wave of mergers, corporate restructurings, and continuing layoff programs (euphemistically called "downsizings"), the resultant companies find themselves in need of a new breed of executive to deal with more complex business problems. These new multicultural executives have been christened the supermanagers of the 1990s. Increasingly, as we close out the twentieth century, a company's assets will be measured, not in traditional terms of equipment, property, and capital, but rather in human capital—the people capable of making these assets perform.

Unlike elsewhere in the world, for today's U.S. executive, climbing the corporate ladder rarely means a gradual ascension to the throne of a single company. On the contrary, it is viewed by many as "de rigueur" to have gained a broader perspective from exposure to a variety of corporate environments. Changing companies is seen as a way to gain greater responsibility more quickly, not to mention a significant increase in compensation. Loyalty to one's employer has been greatly diminished in light of the ever-present possibility of corporate restructurings or mergers. Recent statistics indicate that 1 out of 4 chief executives have been with their companies less than five years. This is in contrast to the 1 out of 12 who fit that category in the late 1960s.[1]

At the other end of the spectrum are the Japanese, in whose country 95 percent of high-potential recruits, "sogoshoku," from the top universities, remain with their original employer until retirement. This makes it worth the 13 months and ¥6 million typically spent by a Japanese firm to recruit just one university graduate.[2]

Although less pronounced in European countries, "cradle to grave" employment is certainly far more prevalent there than in the United States. This phenomena, however, is fast eroding everywhere, with rapid overseas expansion and diversification leaving companies with a new kind of challenge that their existing executives cannot always meet. According to a survey conducted jointly in 1990 by Columbia University and a major U.S.-based executive search firm, business will experience the highest level of executive turnover in history over the next decade.

As companies evolve, so do their staffing needs. As management consultant Peter Drucker once said, "There is no such thing as a good executive; good for what is the question." It is important to match an executive's capabilities with the particular needs of the company at a given time in the company's life cycle. Establishing a company on U.S. soil requires an unusual blend of executive talents—an entrepreneur, yet a team player; someone who has the drive to operate autonomously, yet cooperative enough to do so within the company's cultural guidelines. Building a business in the United States will require the skillful use of executive recruitment tools to help the leaders of non-U.S. companies attract and select the right executive to suit their particular situation.

What follows is a discussion of the various executive recruitment options available in the United States, their benefits, and their drawbacks, as well as related issues. For the purposes of this book, we will define "executive" as three levels down from the chief executive officer—at a minimum, director or vice presidential level—and earning a total compensation package (base plus bonus) of at least $100,000.

EXECUTIVE SEARCH—RETAINER-BASED AND CONTINGENCY

By far the fastest-growing form of recruitment at the senior level in the United States, executive search dates back to the 1940s, when a severe shortage of managers in an expanding war economy required the help of a recruitment intermediary. Initially, generalist management consulting firms would charge their client companies an hourly fee for recruitment consulting services. Eventually, some of those generalist consultants left to establish firms of their own, specializing in recruitment at the highest levels. Still maintaining a consulting approach to the recruitment process, these firms were exclusively retained by an employer, with a nonrefundable fee being paid over the course of the search. Another fee arrangement evolved simultaneously with retained search; employers paid a fee "contingent" on the hire of an executive. Such firms came to be known as contingency recruiters.

For the most part, both kinds of firms charge about one third of the estimated cash compensation (base salary plus bonus) for the executive's first year of employment, although many contingency recruiters work off a lesser percentage. Retainer firms will frequently reduce the fee if several searches are given to them at the same time. All retainer firms charge for expenses they incur on behalf of their client companies, as do many contingency recruiters.

Although the executive search concept exists elsewhere around the world, nowhere is it as accepted and recognized as in the United States. In most countries, few firms will admit to using their services, since it may be viewed as an admission of failure. In Germany, until the late 1970s, it was even illegal to solicit an individual for employment because the government alone was allowed to offer employment services. This antiquated law was originally designed to protect job seekers from being exploited by agencies charging them fees. In actual fact, the value of search firms has been recognized and the government has given its tacit approval.[3]

Today, contingency search is a very popular method of recruiting executives at the junior and middle-management level. Almost half of the executive search firms in the United States fall into this category, and clients use them almost half the time, according to statistics collected in 1989 by *Executive Recruiter News.*[4] However, the emphasis on completing an assignment, rather than finding the right person, may not be in the best interests of the client.

While the contingency approach may prove satisfactory in the recruitment of executives below the $100,000 total compensation range, most American companies prefer to use the broader-based services of the retainer firm to fill their critical senior positions. The cost of a hiring mistake has been calculated at as much as two to three times the executive's annual compensation, not to mention the intangible costs of executive turnover—lost productivity, low morale on the part of subordinates who felt they should have gotten the job, embarrassment on the part of the hiring parties responsible for the mistake, and on the part of the executive, plus the general stress and tension felt by all involved.

Only the retained search firm has the expertise and the time to scour the country for the most qualified and talented individuals, and then evaluate their fit in the hiring organization's environment. The available pool of candidates may be roughly broken down as shown in Exhibit 25–1. Being able to access that 10 percent who make things happen can help give your company the competitive edge.

Search firms come in all sizes, from one-man operations to huge international firms. According to the Fifth Annual survey conducted by the International Association of Corporate and Professional Recruiters (IACPR, formerly the NACPR), the trend is toward smaller firms, with a majority of them consisting of four or fewer members.[5] Many companies choose to hire a large national or multinational firm for its far-reaching network, if the position in question calls for a broad geographic search. There is a perception that the large firm can draw on greater computer resources and will activate researchers in all of their offices. In point of fact, however, most of the largest firms run their offices as profit centers, which leaves little motivation for cooperation from one location to the next. Statistics confirm that the vast majority of searches are completed regionally.

Another precaution, relative to the big versus small issue, is that the larger a search firm gets, the longer the list of "off-limits" companies and the narrower the field of qualified candidates.[6] Many smaller firms have established international affiliations to lengthen

EXHIBIT 25–1
Candidate Pool

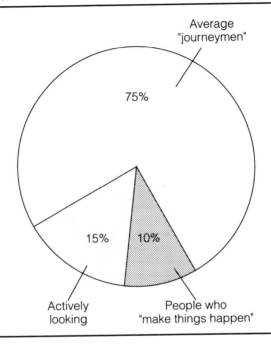

their reach, all the while avoiding being hampered by an extensive "hands-off" list. A third precaution when using a large firm is to make sure that the consultant who sold you the business will actually stay involved in the search process. Smaller firms are often selected precisely for the personal attention given by senior members of the firm, as well as their smaller client base and, inversely, larger potential universe of candidates.

U.S. companies will typically interview several search firms before awarding one the assignment. This is known in the industry as a "shoot-out." It is prudent to check the search firm's references if you haven't worked with them previously. Frequent users of search generally draw from a short list of preferred firms, although an increasing number of corporations are establishing a close partnership with one or perhaps two firms with proven track records. This saves time at the outset of the search because the recruiter is already familiar with the history, culture, and special needs of the client company.

Some executive search firms specialize in only one industry, but the majority specialize in at least three. Still others describe themselves as generalists and argue that their effectiveness is partially derived from the broader perspective they bring to the mission. (The Appendix at the end of the chapter provides a list of directories and reference sources that will help identify specialists in each field.)

EXECUTIVE SEARCH PROCESS

Since executive search is the primary method used by U.S. companies to fill their top jobs, a basic description of the process is in order. Exhibit 25–2 provides an overview and comparison of the various recruitment methods relative to a five-step search process: Identification, Evaluation, Selection, Attraction, and Transition.

At the outset of the search, the executive search consultant(s) will visit the client organization to gain an in-depth understanding not only of the position requirements, but also of the company's culture and management philosophy. A candidate profile is developed, compensation parameters are outlined, and a search schedule is planned. (Most searches take a minimum of three months to complete, with an industry average closer to four.) Armed with this information, the recruiter will start to hone in on the best and the brightest in the field. This is accomplished through a variety of methods that are a mixture of original research and elaborate networking techniques.

Although identifying that 10 percent who will "make a difference" in your organization is the sine qua non of the executive search profession, it is only a small portion of the service provided. It is arguably in the management of the other steps of the process where the search firm truly adds its value. (See Table 25–1 "Retainer versus Contingency Recruitment.") Throughout the process, the client company is kept informed of the progress of the search through frequent oral and written reports. All candidates are interviewed in person prior to being sent to the hiring company for further selection. Search firms limit the number of candidates actually presented to the client to a handful of qualified finalists. By the time the finalists are presented, the client is in possession of not only

EXHIBIT 25–2
5 Vis-à-vis the Search Process

	"Old Boy" network	Advertising	Personnel agencies	Electronic databases
Identification	Limited to people you know (or your people know), not always best you can attract.	Quick response. Limited to unemployed and those actively seeking a change.	Limited to unemployed.	Targeted candidate pool. Quick. The best & the brightest may not be on file.
Evaluation	Candidates are know or come recommended. Success in one company culture not a guarantee in another.	Responsibility of hiring company. Time consuming to sort through unqualified candidates.	Geared toward finding candidate a job—little thought to proper fit.	Overabundance of resumes. Little, if any, pre-screening.
Selection	Can damage goodwill with peers and candidates not selected.	Onus on hiring company. Candidate references suspect.	High risk; rarely check references. Onus placed on hiring company.	Left to hiring company.
Attraction	May be costly to attract them. May leave ill feelings.	Hiring company responsible.	Interested in "selling"both candidate and client. Easier to attract unemployed candidates at lower compensation.	Left to hiring company, in most cases.
Transition	Managed by the hiring company. Typically, little is done to facilitate executive's transition.	Managed by the hiring company. Typically, little is done to facilitate executive's transition.	Managed by the hiring company. Typically, little is done to facilitate executive's transition.	Managed by the hiring company. Typically, little is done to facilitate executive's transition.

EXHIBIT 25-2
(continued)

Executive temporaries	Contingency recruiting	Executive search	Outplacement firms
Limited to unemployed or retired executives. Includes executives who have chosen short-term assignments as "permanent" employment.	Access primarily to the 20% who are actively looking or unemployed.	Access to all candidates, particularly those NOT looking, i.e., usually the best quality.	Small universe of candidates from firms who have let them go.
Candidates screened by phone and/or in person. Some reference checking.	Candidates screened by phone, rarely in person. Greater margin for error.	All candidates screened in person. Better chance of good fit.	Groom candidates to perform well in an interview. Not geared to best interests of employer.
In hands of hiring company, with recommendations from executive temporary firm.	Lacks objectivity, as fee is contingent on hire. Infrequent and cursory reference checks.	Greater objectivity, as fee is guaranteed. In-depth reference audits (psychological testing may be administered).	Not involved in selection process.
Relatively easy attraction, as commitment not long-term.	Employer usually handles compensation and removal of obstacles. May leave ill feelings.	Responsibility for attraction and compensation negotiation. Search firm acts as buffer and ferrets out problems.	Not involved in attraction phase.
Managed by the hiring company. Typically little is done to facilitate executive's transition.	Step out of process once hire is made. Managed by hiring company.	Search firm deals with relocation and family issues. Frequent communication subsequent to hire and monitors potential problems.	Not involved in transition.

TABLE 25–1

Retainer versus Contingency Recruitment

Retainer	Contingency
Fee paid for consulting services usually resulting in a hire Benefit—guaranteed to work on assignment until filled Drawback—fee non-refundable if a decision is made not to fill position	**Fee paid contingent on hire** Benefit—no fees until a candidate is hired Drawback—limited commitment on difficult assignments; salespersons versus consultants
Exclusive contract Benefit—focus on the "best" fit for client as opposed to getting someone hired. Greater likelihood of making successful placement Drawback—takes longer	**Several firms competing to fill spot** Benefit—speed and sense of urgency on recruiter's part Drawback—less objectivity and greater risk; emphasis on "selling" candidate
Multiple client visits to understand the company culture, people, and personal fit Benefit—better understanding of environment and better able to assess candidate fit Drawback—none	**Typically, recruiter does not meet client** Benefit—none Drawback—less of an appreciation of culture, people, and manager's specific needs. No basis to assess fit
Access to those not looking Benefit—larger candidate pool and more high-quality candidates Drawback—generally more difficult to lure away employed candidate. May be more costly	**Access primarily to those actively looking or unemployed** Benefit—can attract at lower salary Drawback—access only to 20% of the market who are actively seeking jobs—usually not the best performers
Candidates screened in person Benefit—search firm knocks out interpersonally inappropriate candidates Drawback—may result in additional expense for hiring company	**Candidates screened by phone, rarely in person** Benefit—none, may save time in short term only Drawback—more mismatches leading to more turnover

Comprehensive candidate evaluation and search progress reports
Benefit—provides market intelligence and insights into candidate's weaknesses and motivations
Drawback—none

3–5 finalist candidates typically presented
Benefit—less time on hiring company's part spent interviewing
Drawback—none

In-depth reference audits
Benefit—greater likelihood of identifying problems or weaknesses. Enables hiring manager to better plan new executive's responsibilities and development
Drawback—none

Attraction and compensation negotiation of chosen candidate
Benefit—third party to help candidate see the benefits of client's opportunity; more credibility. Avoids an adversarial relationship between client and candidate over compensation negotiations
Drawback—none

Standard one-year guarantee on hiree (replacement free of charge)
Benefit—ample time to assess candidate's performance on the job. Eliminates the risk to client of a bad hire
Drawback—none

Candidate resume only is provided
Benefit—none
Drawback—doesn't prepare company interviewer. Weaknesses are hidden

Numerous candidates are presented
Benefit—none, except for a feeling of greater selection
Drawback—takes up more of hiring manager's time

Few and cursory references provided
Benefit—none
Drawback—greater possibility of overlooking problem areas—resulting in turnover

Employer usually handles compensation negotiation
Benefit—none
Drawback—heavily motivated to sell candidate since fee contingent on hire. May leave some ill feelings between candidate and employer

30- to 60-day guarantee on new hire
Benefit—none
Drawback—usually not long enough to determine if it was a good hire, thereby increasing risk to client

their résumés, but also a written evaluation that generally includes the candidates' strengths and weaknesses, as well as motivations for considering the position.

Key to the final selection process should be in-depth reference audits. Properly conducted, they will often turn up "red flags" on an apparently blemish-free candidate. A reputable search firm will perform a thorough and balanced audit of past positions held by the candidates and speak not only with the candidate's superiors, but with peers and subordinates as well. (Some companies will also administer psychological testing at this time.)

The point at which most searches derail is in the attraction process. A whole host of issues that have surfaced in recent years make it increasingly difficult to actually land the chosen executive. Not the least of these is the advent of the dual-career couple. Women around the world have for a long time worked outside the home, but nowhere have they climbed the corporate ladder as fast and as far as in the United States. Consequently, they have become significant contributors to household income, the loss of which would result in substantial hardship. Relocation for career advancement has, therefore, become much more than an unpleasant undertaking. It opens up a veritable Pandora's box of financial, social, and psychological nightmares. This is especially true given the recent and growing phenomenon of the wife's career equalling or even surpassing that of her husband.

In an attempt to avoid this knotty problem, dual executive couples will sometimes undertake a commuter marriage—working in separate cities and traveling to be with the spouse on weekends. This is, quite obviously, far from an ideal solution. Therefore, more and more companies, or their search firms, provide job assistance to the trailing spouse.

The instability of America's corporate world today has added to the difficulty of attracting candidates of choice. While no one these days dare talk of job security, making a move is a much riskier situation than it once was. Despite good performance on the part of new executives, in the event of a merger, takeover, or change in leadership, they are liable to find themselves out on the street. To counteract this possibility, executives are demanding and receiving employment contracts. This can be likened to the ever more popular prenuptial agreement that, well before the wedding bells chime, provides for the division of wealth between wife and husband in the event of a break-up. In the corporate world, the contract takes the form of a prenegotiated severance package in accordance with the stature of the executive. This provides a modicum of insurance that the executive, if forced to bail out, at least will glide down on a "golden parachute."

To prevent their valued executives from jumping ship, U.S. companies have devised an effective safeguard to outside recruitment efforts. Stock options, vesting at some future date, and long-term incentive payments are the "golden handcuffs" that invisibly bind their leaders to the helm. Few will walk away from lucrative promised rewards that will be theirs only if they are around to collect them! Breaking these bonds requires that the hiring company "buy out" chosen candidates to make up for the loss they will incur, whether it be in the form of cash or similar long-term incentive programs. Finding an effective leader, however, is so critical today, that the investment is often felt to be worth it.

Recognizing that having the right leaders in place is a necessity for survival in today's competitive marketplace, the senior management of many American companies has taken to calling on outside search consultants to help them evaluate internal candidates for promotion. Executive search firms are increasingly being asked to find the best possible candidates on the outside and compare them with internal candidates. This stems from a desire to optimize each position; even if the insiders are good, the hope remains that the ideal person for the opportunity just may be out there. Then too, with the fallout from mergers and acquisitions in the 1980s, many senior executives find themselves in the position of having to assess subordinates they hardly know, and therefore, are more comfortable with an outside opinion. Other companies use search firms to evaluate their own candidates for political reasons. Top management can shift the blame to the search firm if the internal candidate who is next in line does not get the nod. In the case of joint ventures, neither side can be accused of favoritism if an impartial consultant makes the candidate recommendation.

One out of every five top-level searches now entails the assessment of executives who already work for the client company.[7] The outside candidate must be markedly superior to overcome the risk of damaging company morale or chancing the unknown.

Once the executive is on board, a reputable search firm will provide a kind of "post-hire" guarantee, for up to one year. If, during that time period, the candidate leaves or is fired, the search firm will replace the candidate at no extra fee, just out-of-pocket expenses. To ensure that this eventuality never occurs, proper management of the transition period may well prove critical. This includes spousal employment help; lining up schools, physicians, and other support systems; and generally providing the transplants with an introduction to the new community. If no relocation is involved, the search consultant should, at the very least, stay in touch with the hiring manager and the new employee for at least six months to monitor their satisfaction quotient. This will enable the consultant to act as an impartial intermediary and hopefully nip any nascent problems in the bud.

Although executive search is the recruitment option of choice for the most senior positions, a variety of other alternatives are employed either alone, or in conjunction with one another, to recruit executives at other levels.

ALTERNATIVES TO EXECUTIVE SEARCH

The "Old Boy" Network

This is perhaps the oldest method of recruitment, and consists of contacting people known to you or your colleagues. The name *old boy* connotes an informal clique of fellows of a similar rank and station in life, and implies the traditional absence of women at the executive level.

Although this can be a quick and inexpensive way to identify a qualified candidate, the process has its limitations, as well as its pitfalls. Not the least of these may be that there are better people, "unknowns," you may be able to attract. There is also the issue of differing company cultures, which is left unassessed: The candidate's success in one company environment is no guarantee of success in another. Most sensitive of all is the handling of friends or colleagues *not* selected; goodwill may be damaged. Therefore, most companies prefer to augment this method with others.

Advertising

The benefit of advertising in newspapers and trade publications, much like the networking method, lies in its low cost and rapid response. While this recruitment option will allow you to reach a broader public, it is circumscribed by those who are unemployed or actively seeking a job. You may be left with an avalanche of résumés and curriculum vitae to sift through, the end result of which will very likely be few, if any, qualified potential candidates. Selecting from this universe of individuals is at high risk, since candidates will undoubtedly have prepared a few friendly references in advance. Therefore, at the executive level we are discussing, this method alone is infrequently used.

Personnel or Employment Agencies

These firms are geared toward out-of-work individuals seeking employment, and, infrequently, those wishing to make a job change. The candidates themselves are sometimes required to pay the fee; with the exception of some public access databases, this is not the case with other recruitment options. As mentioned above, with the development of computerized pools of candidates, employment agencies are able to offer the employer a greater and more focused list of potential candidates. They cannot, however, afford to take the time to assess the candidate fit in the client company environment or do reference audits that might uncover problem areas. Their focus is primarily on selling the candidate and the client on one another, and quickly. Personnel agencies guarantee a placement for a limited time—generally 30–45 days. Therefore, executives in the compensation bracket we are discussing are rarely, if ever, recruited by this method, let alone listed with these organizations in the first place.

Outplacement Firms

According to the Association of Outplacement Consulting Firms, the concept of providing formalized job assistance to terminated executives originated in the United States in the late 1960s. The need for this service became acute in the wake of a period of overexpansion earlier in the decade.

The popularity of outplacement firms is of relatively recent vintage, however, spawned once again by the flood of unloaded executives from newly slimmed-down companies. Through the use of these outplacement firms, corporate conscience seeks to provide the exiting executive with career-counseling and support services, such as résumé writing and interview coaching, as well as temporary office space from which he or she can pursue the job search. The goal of these firms, as their name denotes, is to counsel the executives to increase their probabilities of being successful at finding a job, and is a service provided predominately to high-ranking managers. Since outplacement firms are paid by the executive's former employer, they will provide their list of available candidates free of charge to anyone. Some routinely forward capsule descriptions of outplaced executives to recruitment firms.

Whereas in the past, being separated from one's company bore the stigma of failure, today we are witnessing an influx of high-caliber executives into the marketplace who, unfortunately, find themselves on the wrong side of a merger or takeover. Therefore, it is certainly advisable to at least take a look at the outplacement firm's roster of available candidates.

Although this is a no-cost way of recruiting, the universe of candidates the outplacement firms provide is still too small to offer a truly satisfactory selection. Beware, too, of these professionally coached candidates; their evaluation is particularly difficult. Trained to steer clear of their weak points, these candidates are frequently better equipped to control the flow of the interview than the hiring manager!

Electronic Database

Until recently, recruitment databases, which house a collection of information on potential employment candidates, were used by corporations for internal promotion purposes or were the proprietary resource of executive search firms. Now, employment agencies, university alumni services, government employment offices, and private database companies are offering on-line résumé services at a relatively low cost to the user. This form of recruiting is especially popular at middle-management levels and in the high-tech field. Prospecting companies either buy the data outright or are charged to tap into the database on a per-hour basis. Still others provide a mixture of database search and telephone search. The databases vary significantly. Some are limited to job seekers, while others include listings of individuals wishing to hear about other opportunities in their field. Executive search firms, whose databases can be accessed only by the firm's (or their affiliates) recruiters, will also include résumés of executives who have earned a good reputation within their specialty.

The proprietary nature of search firm databases notwithstanding, there appears to be a slight trend on the part of some recruitment firms to do "targeted searches" for middle managers, principally making use of their computerized databases. Instead of the usual percentage of the candidate's total compensation, a flat fee is charged, based on the complexity of the search. And, at least one major search firm has compiled a separate database of candidates at middle-management level that, for a fee, is available to anyone.

Large employment agencies have long used recruitment databases to fill positions, and more recently, agencies of all sizes have begun to pool their candidates in a "networked" job bank. The average network includes between 50 and 200 members.[8] Some are general in nature, but the majority are germane to a specific industry or function. While some electronic databases will provide lists of names, others will make available only a brief résumé of the candidate's background. Names are revealed only after the client firm has narrowed the choice to a handful of candidates.

Although recruiting via database may be an appropriate and cost-effective alternative at lower levels, its usefulness is minimal in hunting for an upper-echelon executive. The "creme de la creme" are generally not actively seeking a change nor would they want it known that they might be willing to listen to outside opportunities.

Executive Temporaries

The use of interim executives is more widely accepted in Europe and Japan, where the active market for such temporaries is supported by cultural variations, work attitudes, and a lack of management consultants. With an eye to the 1992 unification of Europe, a heightened need for executive temporaries has been felt especially in planning and strategy departments. Particularly in Eastern Europe, a real dearth of executive talent has led to a burgeoning demand on firms that specialize in short-term assignments.

Although slow to catch on here, the "Executive Temporary" niche is the fastest-growing portion of the multibillion-dollar market for temporary employees in the United States. The oldest of the established firms dates back only to 1986, and, as of this writing, the industry totals approximately 40 firms. None of them offer conventional executive search services. These firms are typically founded and staffed by senior-level executives, the majority of whom have come from other consulting organizations, corporate positions, or, more rarely, executive search firms.

Speed is the primary selling point of this type of service. Interim executive positions are typically filled in 5 to 15 days for assignments that average 3 to 9 months in duration. Three quarters of these positions involve temporary relocation for the executive. Going the executive temporary route is one path taken by victims of corporate consolidation and restructuring. In fact, 50 percent are between jobs or hoping to clarify their own career goals through experience working in a variety of corporate climates. Of the estimated 70 percent who turn temporary work into permanent assignments, most are senior-level professionals whose compensation packages exceed $100,000. The typical candidate is a 52-year-old chief executive officer (CEO), chief operating officer (COO), chief financial officer (CFO), or marketing, human resources, or operations professional. Most earn in excess of $100,000. Many of these executives contact temporary placement firms directly. To expand their databases and enhance the caliber of executives within those databases, the firms themselves often cultivate executive interest through advertisements, networking, or direct telephone contact originating from prequalified referrals. A handful of these firms place executives in specific fields or in nontraditional work situations. One firm specializes in representing women hoping to return to the work force while raising their children, and another, in executives who have chosen the life style of temporary employment as a "full-time" occupation.

Whether specializing in a certain field or bringing generalist skills to an organization, these temporaries are hired on a project basis for some specific expertise, or to fill in during the search for a permanent manager. Interim executives are particularly needed by small companies with no succession planning, by a corporation whose downsizing has left it without the requisite talent, or by companies looking for special assistance on a short-term project.

Although estimated at a $50–75MM market, with as many as 200,000 temporary executives in the field, there is no established fee or billing structure. Some firms work on a retainer basis; others bill separately for the employee's compensation and the firm's fee. Still others place the executive on their own payroll and "rent" that individual to a client organization. Generally, this averages 20–30 percent of the interim manager's compensation.[9]

ADVISORY BOARDS—A SPECIAL USE FOR EXECUTIVE SEARCH

Foreign companies wishing to establish a strong presence in the American marketplace should consider the benefits of establishing an advisory board staffed by leading American business people. Such a board can provide the company with advice and insight into how business is conducted in the United States as well as the political system and its leaders, banking contacts, and so on, which might otherwise take years to understand and cultivate. It is important that these directors be carefully selected to add value to the company's efforts by bringing to the table some functional area of expertise, geographic knowledge, or industry specialization. Their strengths and experiences should complement one another, and redundancy should be kept to a minimum.

Since these directors serve not as traditional board members, but rather as advisors without legal voting rights, their appointment entails no legal liability, which might otherwise create problems of control for the host company and liability for the directors. Serving as a panel of experts at the pleasure of the CEO, its members can be periodically rotated based on the strategic needs of the company at any given time.

The search for ideal board candidates is perhaps best conducted on two fronts simultaneously. Your own board members should be asked to participate in deciding what type of background and experience would add strength to the board and, if appropriate, suggest candidates whom they find worthy of consideration.

Also, a growing number of companies are finding it extremely worthwhile to seek the assistance of search firms that have experience assisting chairmen and nominating committees with director searches. These search firms bring objectivity to the evaluation of candidates recommended by board members, as well as the ability to introduce highly qualified candidates who may not be currently known to the board.[10]

A valuable by-product of the process of getting to know prospective director candidates as part of a targeted search is the education the chairman and fellow board members receive from meeting outstanding people with experience that may not currently exist on the board. Even if the chairperson decides not to invite a particular director candidate to join the board, he or she will have learned a great deal and established new personal contacts that can prove of ongoing value to the firm.

Putting together an effective advisory board can be a matter of great strategic importance to the company's future. By analyzing where the firm is headed, and looking far and wide for CEOs whose experience is in line with its strategic goals, the advisory board can become an extremely valuable asset to growing companies in the United States.

CONCLUSION

No longer insulated from the world marketplace, U.S. firms have realized the bottom-line importance of hiring the right executives. To prosper in today's international marketplace, and particularly in the United States, companies will need more than just good managers; they will need leaders who possess vision and the communications skills to disseminate their vision down through the organization. Companies have finally become aware of the importance of optimizing each executive-hiring opportunity and are relying on innovative methods to identify, select, and attract these transcultural leaders.

NOTES

1. Byrne, John A., "The New Headhunters," *Business Week*, 2/6/89, p. 65.
2. Logan, F. J., "Executive Recruitment Japanese Style" *Across the Board*, 9/90, p. 26.
3. Goodman, Susan, *On Target* 2, no. 1 (Spring 1990), p. 4.
4. Kennedy, James H., "Executive Recruiter News," Fitzwilliam, New Hampshire.
5. "The Fifth Annual Membership Survey Results", The national Association of Corporate & Professional Recruiters; Louisville, Kentucky, p. 3.
6. This refers to the policy of not recruiting from client companies for a two-year period.
7. Byrne, John A., "The New Headhunters," *Business Week*, 2/6/89, p. 71.
8. Willis, Rod, *Personnel*, May 1990, p. 28.
9. Statistical information provided by Kennedy Publications, "Head-Renting: Hot New Executive Search Niche," October 1990.
10. Howard Fischer Associates, Philadelphia; Spencer Stuart; and Korn Ferry, New York City are three such firms with a specialty in this area.

APPENDIX: PARTIAL BIBLIOGRAPHY OF RECRUITMENT ASSOCIATIONS AND PUBLICATIONS

The Association of Outplacement Consulting Firms
365 Parsippany Road
Parsippany, NJ 07054
(201)887-6667, FAX (201)887-8145
(40 members as of Spring 1991)

Directory of Outplacement Firms
Templeton Road
Fitzwilliam, NH 03447
(603)585-6544

International Association of Corporate & Professional Recruiters, Inc.
4000 Woodstone Way
Louisville, KY 40241
(502)228-4500, FAX (502)228-8955

National Association of Executive Recruiters
222 South Westmonte Drive, Suite 101
Altamonte Springs, FL 32714
(407)774-7880, FAX (407)774-6440

Association of Executive Search Consultants, Inc.
230 Park Avenue, Suite 1549
New York, NY 10169
(212)949-9556, FAX (212)949-9560
(Approximately 108 members)

"Executive Recruiter News"
Kennedy Publications
Templeton Road
Fitzwilliam, NH 03447
(603)585-6544, FAX (603)585-9221
(Published monthly)

Directory of Executive Temporary Placement Firms
(See October 1990 issue of "Executive Recruiter News")

The Directory of Executive Recruiters
James H. Kennedy, Editor & Publisher
Templeton Road
Fitzwilliam, NH 03447
(603)585-6544
(Published annually since 1971)

A. Robert Taylor
How to Select and Use an Executive Search Firm
New York: McGraw-Hill, 1984

William Lewis & Carol Milano
The Directory of Executive Search Firms
New York: Simon & Schuster, 1986

PART 6

REAL ESTATE AND CONSTRUCTION

CHAPTER 26

TAXATION OF FOREIGN INVESTMENT IN U.S. REAL ESTATE

Robert L. Anderson
Partner
Price Waterhouse

INTRODUCTION

The U.S. tax treatment of foreign investment in U.S. real estate has undergone numerous changes beginning with the enactment of the Foreign Investment and Real Property Tax Act of 1980 (FIRPTA). In the years before FIRPTA, the foreign investor could usually eliminate U.S. income and capital gains taxes through the use of several proven tax structures widely known within the professional community. These structures were simple to form and relatively inexpensive to maintain. In those days, any U.S. income tax paid by a foreign investor from an investment in U.S. real estate was essentially a voluntary contribution to the U.S. Treasury.

Since FIRPTA, Congress has revisited the taxation of the foreign investor on several occasions. Many of the tax bills introduced into the Congress since 1980 have contained provisions seeking to further restrict the flexibility of foreign investors in U.S. real estate, and increase their U.S. tax burden. While most proposals have not survived the legislative process, several have found their way into law. For example, in 1986, the Branch Profits Tax was added to the U.S. tax law. Its impact, which will be discussed in more detail later in this chapter, was particularly troubling to the foreign investor. Virtually all investment structures needed to be modified to accommodate its provisions. Similarly, in 1988, the U.S. estate tax (death tax) virtually doubled from its prior levels. Once again, almost every existing investment structure had to be analyzed and, in many cases, adjusted to accommodate the change in the law. Finally, in 1989 and again in 1990, some in Congress sought to pass legislation that would impose a U.S. tax on the foreign investor's capital gains from sales of certain closely held stocks. To date, those provisions have been defeated through the joint efforts of foreign governments and leaders in the U.S. business and professional communities. The lesson from these historical developments is that change in the tax structure applicable to the foreign investor is probably inevitable. Where possible, structures should be established with a view to potential change in the U.S. tax law.

The laws of most foreign jurisdictions have also changed over the years. Since the obvious objective for the foreign investor is to minimize his or her worldwide tax burden, changes in the laws of all relevant jurisdictions must be considered. Proper U.S. tax planning for the foreign investor cannot be limited to the U.S. rules alone. Similarly, the planning cannot be limited to only the income tax. Since the U.S. and home country estate, gift, or death taxes may exceed the income tax, the additional taxes must be properly taken into account in any structure. Finally, the planner must compare not only income tax rates, but also any nuances in the foreign law, such as property valuation methodologies for foreign estate taxes, that may differ from established U.S. principles.

REGIMEN OF U.S. TAXES APPLICABLE TO THE FOREIGN INVESTOR

Federal Income Taxes

The U.S. federal government taxes the net income of its citizens and residents at graduated rates. In 1991 those rates for individuals range from 15 to 31 percent for ordinary income, with a maximum rate of 28 percent for any applicable capital gains. Taxable income is defined as gross income from all sources, less allowed deductions and exemptions. In general, all income is taxable unless specifically exempted, and nothing is deductible unless specifically allowed.

Foreign non-resident individuals are taxed in the United States on two types of U.S.-source income. U.S.-source income that is effectively connected with a U.S. trade or business is taxed on a net basis, i.e., gross income less allowable deductions, by the federal government at the same graduated rates applicable to U.S. resident taxpayers. U.S.-source income that is not effectively connected with a U.S. trade or business is taxed by the federal government on a gross basis at a flat rate of 30 percent, unless the rate has been reduced by an applicable tax treaty to which the U.S. is a party.

U.S. corporations are generally taxed in a manner similar to individuals. An exception is that the top federal tax rate in 1991 was 34 percent rather than the 31 percent maximum applicable to individuals. Also, there is no reduced federal tax rate for the capital gains of U.S. corporations. In the United States, except in special instances, distributed profits are not a deduction from corporate taxable income. Distribution of net profits of the corporation as reduced by the corporate tax are taxed again at the shareholder level as ordinary income. This double taxation cannot be avoided by a corporate distribution of appreciated assets. In that case, the corporation must recognize taxable income as if it had sold the asset to an unrelated purchaser for a price equal to its fair market value. This rule also applies to corporate liquidations. Exceptions to these general rules apply for certain special corporations and are generally unavailable to the foreign investor. However, one such exception, the real estate investment trust (REIT), is available for foreign investors' use and will be discussed later in this chapter.

Foreign corporations are taxed on their U.S.-source trade or business income in a manner similar to U.S. corporations. U.S.-source income that is effectively connected with a U.S. trade or business is taxed by the federal government on a net basis at the same rates applicable to U.S. corporations. U.S.-source income that is not effectively connected with a U.S. trade or business is taxed by the federal government on a gross basis at a flat 30 percent or lower treaty tax rate. A foreign corporation operating a trade or business in the United States will also be subject to the federal Branch Profits Tax, as discussed later in this chapter, unless exempted or reduced under the provisions of a relevant tax treaty.

The federal income tax law also includes Alternative Minimum Tax (AMT) provisions. These AMT provisions create a minimum tax level by disallowing certain excess rental losses and extending depreciable lives of property along with other adjustments. Although a credit for prior AMT is usually available when the regular tax provisions apply, these accelerated tax payments could alter the economic return of an investment.

State and Local Income Taxes

Individuals and corporations are also subject to income and other taxes of the U.S. states and their subdivisions. State income tax rates typically vary from zero to more than 10 percent, depending on the jurisdiction. The amount of income subject to tax is usually derived by principles similar to those employed in determining federal taxable income, with certain modifications. These modifications typically include differences in calculating income and deductions for state purposes and differences in determining the source of the income or expense item. For example, California is a high-tax state but does not tax "like-kind" exchanges of real property even when the property received is located outside of California. Other states do not allow tax-free like-kind exchanges if the property received is located outside of the state. Income taxes may be imposed by cities in certain states and some states impose a net worth tax on corporations. Since the laws of the various states differ, a detailed discussion of their various consequences is, by necessity, beyond the scope of this chapter. Although it is possible to reduce or eliminate state income taxes through proper planning, experience indicates that state tax planning is too often overlooked for real estate investments.

Federal Withholding Taxes

Foreign corporations and nonresident alien individuals are subject to a federal tax on their gross U.S.-source income that is not effectively connected with a U.S. trade or business at a flat 30 percent or reduced treaty tax rate. The mechanism for collection of this tax is withholding. Under the federal system, if a U.S. payor knows that the payee is a foreign corporation or individual, he or she is required to withhold and remit to the U.S. Treasury 30 percent from all payments of interest, dividends, rents, and other payments made to the foreign person. The payor is liable for the withholding of the tax unless the payee provides satisfactory written evidence that the withholding tax does not apply. Failure to properly withhold can subject the payor to substantial penalties, including but not limited to payment of the tax on behalf of the foreign recipient. With certain exceptions, most notably in the partnership and real estate sales areas, the withholding of tax does not apply when the income is effectively connected with a U.S. trade or business. Also, many income tax treaties to which the United States is a party either reduce or eliminate the necessity of withholding for certain classes of income. A discussion of some of the mechanics of the withholding process is contained later in this chapter.

Estate and Gift Taxes

The U.S. estate and gift tax applies only to individuals. Estates of U.S. citizens and U.S. resident individuals are subject to estate tax on the fair market value of the decedent worldwide holdings at the date of death. Each state in the U.S. may also impose estate and gift tax. Generally, the state tax is creditable against the U.S. tax. Nonresidents pay U.S. estate tax based on the fair market value of their U.S. situs property. The estate and gift tax is a unified tax imposed on a graduated rate system. The 1991 tax rates vary between 18 and 55 percent of the taxable value. To determine the current estate or gift tax, all prior gifts are included in the tax base. Prior gift tax payments are credited against the current calculation of tax.

A special generation skipping transfer tax may be applied in addition to the estate and gift tax, if the property is transferred to a beneficiary more than one generation after the decedent/donor. The effect of the generation skipping transfer tax is to effectively impose a tax on each generation, as if the middle generation had received the property and passed it on to the third generation.

Real estate located in the United States, stock of U.S. corporations, and notes receivable from U.S. persons are all U.S. situs property. Accordingly, these investments are subject to the U.S. estate and gift taxes. In addition, a U.S. partnership that holds these types of assets will increase a foreign individual's exposure to U.S. estate tax since the partnership interest will likely be treated as U.S. situs property in the hands of the foreign individual. One of the most direct techniques to avoid the U.S. estate and gift tax is to eliminate any direct ownership of the U.S. situs assets by the foreign individual. Perhaps the least complex way of doing this is to insert a foreign corporation between the individual and the U.S. situs property. Indeed, that is one of the major reasons most foreign individuals use a foreign corporation somewhere in their U.S. real estate investment structure.

Planning for estate and gift taxes is important. The tax is based on the gross value of the investment without regard to the investment's cost. This feature of the tax could have a devastating effect on the beneficiaries of the foreign investor. For example, assuming a 50 percent estate tax rate, an initial investment of $5 million could be followed with a U.S. estate tax liability of $2.5 million the very next day, if the investor were to meet with an untimely demise. If the home country estate tax rate were only 30 percent, the investment in the U.S. real property would cost this individual's beneficiaries an additional and unnecessary $1 million in worldwide tax.

Branch Taxes

In order to correct a perceived inequity in the U.S. tax system, Congress added the Branch Profits Tax provisions to the Internal Revenue Code. Prior to enactment in 1986, most shareholders were exempted from the withholding of U.S. tax on dividends they received from foreign corporations. On the other hand, U.S. corporations that paid dividends to foreign shareholders generally were required to withhold 30 percent from the payment. A foreign corporation that operated in the United States as a branch could thereby repatriate funds to the home country without incurring any U.S. tax on the "dividend." A majority in Congress believed that this diversity of treatment worked to the competitive disadvantage of U.S. corporations. The mechanism for correction of this inequity is a 30 percent tax on the "dividend equivalent amount" of the foreign corporation. The dividend equivalent amount approximates U.S. earnings and profits removed from the U.S. branch.

Branch Level Profits Tax
The dividend equivalent amount is basically defined as the current year's earnings and profits, as adjusted for changes in U.S. net equity. If U.S. net equity increases during the year, the dividend

equivalent amount is decreased, dollar for dollar, but not below zero. If U.S. net equity decreases, the dividend equivalent amount is increased on a dollar-for-dollar basis. Any increase in the dividend equivalent amount due to a reduction in U.S. net equity is limited to previously accumulated effectively connected earnings and profits that have not been previously taxed under these rules.

U.S. net equity is U.S. assets reduced by U.S. liabilities and can be a negative amount. U.S. assets are money and the aggregate adjusted basis of property of the foreign corporation treated as effectively connected with the conduct of a U.S. trade or business. U.S. liabilities are the liabilities of the foreign corporation treated as effectively connected with the U.S. trade or business. Regulations provide specific examples of assets considered to be effectively connected with a U.S. trade or business and are meant to be consistent with the general "effectively connected income" rules contained in Section 882 of the Internal Revenue Code.

The Branch Profits Tax has only limited application to residents of most countries having an income tax treaty with the United States. If a treaty applies, the maximum rate of the Branch Profits Tax is limited to the specified Branch Profits Tax rate, if any, contained in the applicable treaty. If a rate of tax is not specified, the treaty withholding rate on dividends paid by a wholly-owned domestic corporation to a parent company resident in the treaty country is applied. In most instances, the dividend withholding rate is reduced to 15 percent or less. Congress has required that these treaty provisions be limited to qualified residents of the treaty country. For a corporation to be a qualified resident, more than 50 percent of the stock of the foreign corporation must be held by residents of the treaty country or the United States. So called treaty shopping is unavailable in the Branch Profits Tax area.

The Branch Profits Tax can be indefinitely deferred by continually reinvesting the earnings of the U.S. trade or business in U.S. assets. For a typical real estate investment, this might be easily accomplished by using earnings to pay down any acquisition debt on the real property. Once the real property is sold, the Branch Profits Tax can be completely avoided if all U.S. earnings and profits are withdrawn from the United States and the corporation completely terminates its U.S. trade or business. To qualify for the termination exception, Regulation 1.884-2T(a)(2) provides that the foreign corporation:

1. Must have no U.S. assets at the end of the terminating year (or the shareholders must have adopted an irrevocable resolution in the taxable year to completely liquidate and dissolve the corporation and before the close of the succeeding year, all U.S. assets are either distributed, used to pay off liabilities, or cease to be U.S. assets);

2. Must not use, directly or indirectly through a related corporation, any of the U.S. assets or the terminated trade or business in the conduct of a trade or business in the U.S. at any time during a period of three years from the close of the year of complete termination;

3. Must have no income that is, or is treated as, effectively connected with the conduct of a trade or business in the U.S. during the period of three years from the close of the year of complete termination; and

4. Must attach to its income tax return for each year of complete termination a waiver of the period of limitations extending the statue of limitations to a date not earlier than six years after the close of the termination year.

The termination exemption is applied on a company-by-company basis. By using a separate corporation for each U.S. real property investment, the Branch Profits Tax can be avoided by properly planning interim cash flow and completely terminating the U.S. business upon disposition of the real estate. This ''deferral/ exemption'' technique can provide a viable alternative for foreign corporations who cannot avail themselves of an income tax treaty exemption from the Branch Profits Tax.

Branch Level Interest Tax

The Tax Reform Act of 1986 added a corollary to the Branch Profits Tax in the form of the Branch Level Interest Tax. Generally, a foreign corporation is allowed a deduction against its U.S. taxable income for an allocable percentage of interest expense relating to its U.S. trade or business income. The allocation is determined under specific formulas found in Internal Revenue Code Section 882 and Regulation Section 1.882-5. Under these rules it is possible for a deduction to be permitted that is in excess of the amount of interest actually paid by the U.S. branch of the business. To the extent of that excess, Congress believed there was a possibility for a foreign corporation to withdraw earnings from the United States without bearing the proper level of withholding tax.

Under the Branch Level Interest Tax, the excess of the allowed interest deduction over the amount paid by the U.S. trade or business is deemed to be interest paid by a domestic corporation to a foreign corporation. This deemed payment requires that a withholding tax of 30 percent be "collected" unless an income tax treaty provides for reduced withholding. As with the Branch Profits Tax, the benefits of a treaty are not available unless the foreign corporation is a qualified resident of the treaty country.

Planning for the Branch Level Interest Tax involves a pro forma calculation of interest expense allocable to the U.S. trade or business and the amount of interest to be paid by that trade or business. To avoid the Branch Level Interest Tax when an imbalance occurs, the amount of expense allocated to the U.S. trade or business must be reduced, or the amount paid by the U.S. trade or business increased. The allocations are mechanical in nature and require an understanding of the foreign corporation's worldwide assets and liabilities.

TAXATION OF REAL PROPERTY INCOME

Under U.S. tax law, gains from the sale of U.S. real estate are taxed as U.S. trade or business income. Since the gain is taxed as U.S. trade or business income, it is to the advantage of most investors to have the rental income or loss of their U.S. real property treated as trade or business income.

As noted previously, foreign individuals and corporations are taxed on a net basis and can deduct expenses only to the extent they are effectively connected with a U.S. trade or business. Real estate investors usually incur real property taxes, interest expense, and administrative costs. If the property is classified as investment rather than trade or business property, foreign corporations and individuals will be unable to deduct those expenses in the United States. Most rental income from U.S. real property is considered U.S. trade or business income, with the exception of certain long-term triple net lease property. In the rare instance of a triple net lease type of arrangement, the foreign investor should consider making the election available under the Code and many treaties to treat the income as effectively connected with a U.S. trade or business. That election allows the expenses to be deducted against the gross real property income.

The deductions allowable to foreign investors must be allocated between all income types, including U.S. trade or business income based on the regulations under Internal Revenue Code Sections 861, 862, and 863. Generally, the regulations require that deductions, other than interest, be apportioned based on classes of gross income and/or other reasonable methods. The deduction allowed for interest expense is calculated differently for foreign individuals and foreign corporations. Foreign individuals have more opportunity to allocate interest expense to U.S. trade or business activities. All that is required of foreign individuals is that the interest be borrowed for, reflected on the books of, and paid by, the U.S. trade or business. Foreign corporations must follow an apportionment formula established in Regulation Section 1.882-5. The corporate allocation formula is based on a ratio of U.S. to worldwide trade or business assets.

In the case of real estate that is investment property rather than trade or business property, the deduction of expenses can be particularly troublesome. Unfortunately deduction of expenses is possible only when there is gross income being produced from the property. Indeed, Sections 871(d) and 882(d) of the Code clearly state that a foreign individual or corporation, "which during the taxable year derives any income . . . may elect for such taxable year to treat all such income as income which is effectively connected with the conduct of a trade or business within the United States." If there is no real property income for a given year, the election is not effective even though it theoretically remains in force for years that have real property income.

This point was clarified in Revenue Ruling 91-7, 1991-1 C.B.110, which dealt with A foreign investor's use of Section 266. This Section allows a taxpayer to elect to capitalize taxes and carrying charges on certain types of land. However, the expenses must be otherwise deductible before they can be capitalized under Section 266. The ruling held that foreign investors cannot use Section 266 in years they have no real property income, because under the Code, the foreign investor could not be engaged in a trade or business. Since trade or business status is required for expenses to be deductible by foreign investors, and since Section 266 only applies to amounts otherwise deductible under the Code, the ruling held that Section 266 did not apply. As a result, foreign investors can neither deduct nor capitalize interest expense or taxes on investment property that does not generate income. This can be particularly burdensome since debt is often used to acquire U.S. real property. Often the only solution is to place the property inside a taxable U.S. entity to obtain the benefits provided U.S. taxpayers.

PLANNING FOR INVESTMENT IN U.S. REAL ESTATE

General

For the individual U.S. investor, the optimum tax strategy is usually to hold an investment directly or through a pass-through entity in order to avoid the double taxation that occurs with corporations. Those forms of ownership also entitle the U.S. investor to use the reduced capital gains tax rate that may be applicable to the disposition of most real estate. Perhaps most importantly, direct ownership and partnerships allow the investor access to operating cash flow, often without any income tax, since depreciation and other noncash deductions usually exceed mortgage amortization in the first 5 to 10 years of a U.S. real estate investment. Excess proceeds from refinancing would also be available on a tax free basis.

The holding of U.S. real property by foreign investors requires much forethought and planning in order to maintain a U.S. income tax burden comparable to that which would be incurred by a similarly situated U.S. investor. For example, it is generally impossible to reduce the U.S. tax burden of a foreign pension fund investing in U.S. real estate to either that of a U.S. pension fund, a real estate investment in the home country of the foreign pension fund, or a real estate investment in many industrialized countries. U.S. pension funds do not pay any income tax on their unleveraged real estate investments. However, a foreign pension fund is treated as A taxable entity in the U.S.

The position of the U.S. Department of Treasury is that any special tax treatment accorded foreign pensions funds should be covered by tax treaties rather than the Internal Revenue Code.

There is not a universal structure for either the foreign individual, pension fund, or other taxable entity investing in U.S. real estate. Rather, there are a number of building blocks—foreign corporations, real estate investment trusts, portfolio debt, participating debt, hybrid entities, and so on—that are used to build a structure that produces an acceptable U.S. and home country tax burden. There is no single structure that can be used for U.S. real estate, even by the same investor. While many of the blocks will be similar, the facts are rarely the same, resulting in the inclusion or exclusion of some specific item.

The next section of this chapter is devoted to a discussion of specialized building blocks. A discussion of complete structures is impossible because of the many facts that must be considered. The concepts presented are unique blocks that can be part of most real estate structures.

Real Estate Investment Trusts

The real estate investment trust (REIT) provisions were enacted to allow a large number of small investors to invest in real estate on an equal basis with large investors but have wider applications, especially for foreign pension funds. REITs are U.S. corporations taxable as corporations trusts or associations, that (1) specialize in investments in real estate and real estate mortgages, (2) meet certain requirements as to ownership and (3) meet the gross income, asset diversification, and distribution requirements. The benefit of REIT status is the reduction of corporate level income tax.

REIT Requirements

To qualify as a REIT, an entity must elect REIT status; meet certain asset, income and distribution tests, and meet certain ownership tests.

A REIT must have at least 75 percent of the value of total assets represented by real estate assets, cash, cash equivalent items including receivables, and government securities. However, securities cannot represent more than 25 percent of the total assets of the company. Any one security cannot represent more than 5 percent in value of the assets of the REIT and cannot more than 10 percent of the outstanding voting securities of the issuer. Constitute also earn 75 percent or more of its income comes from

- Rents from real property,
- Interest on obligations secured by mortgages on real property or on interests in real property,
- Gains from the sale or disposition of real property (including mortgages but excluding property held for sale as a dealer), dividends, or other distributions on and gain from the sale of stock in other REITs, and
- Other real-estate-related income.

In addition, at least 95 percent of gross income must include the above real estate income items, along with dividends and interest, while less than 30 percent can come from the sale or disposition of stock or securities held one year or less, property in prohibited transactions, or real property held less than four years unless involuntarily converted or foreclosure property.

The ownership rules require that there be 100 or more shareholders, and this requirement unnecessarily stops many foreign investors from considering a REIT. The actual value of shares owned need not be material. For example, a widely held foreign corporation could meet this requirement by giving one share of stock to 100 different U.S. or foreign charities. These shareholders could own less than 1 percent of the capital value and the company could still qualify as a REIT.

The limiting factor to ownership is that 5 or fewer individuals cannot directly or indirectly own more than 50 percent of the value of a REIT. In addition, there are extensive rules for attribution of ownership among family members and related parties. A U.S. pension fund is treated as an individual for this test; however, a foreign pension fund is treated as a corporation. Since the ownership rules provide for a look-through to the shareholders or beneficial owners of a corporation, a foreign pension fund should be able to establish a REIT.

Finally an entity must elect to be a REIT. The election is made for the first year an entity desires REIT status by computing its income as a REIT and filing Form 1120-REIT. No other method of election is acceptable. The election is effective until properly revoked or until REIT status is terminated by disqualification.

Because of the ownership requirements, REITs must comply with regulations prescribed for ascertaining the ownership of the outstanding shares. The REIT must keep written records within the Internal Revenue District in which it files its return. The REIT must demand written statements from the shareholders of record disclosing those persons required to include the dividends in gross income in their returns. Statements are to be demanded as follows:

> For 2,000 or more shareholders of record, from each record holder of 5 percent or more of the stock,
> For 200 but less than 2,000 shareholders of record, from each record holder of one percent or more of the stock, or
> For less than 200 shareholders of record, from each record holder of 1/2 percent or more of the stock.

The regulations instruct the REIT to inform shareholders that if they fail to provide the written statement requested by the REIT, they must disclose the information in his or her personal return. The information must disclose the name, the number of shares owned, and the amount of dividends for the actual owner or owners of stock held by the shareholder.

Taxation of REITs
Generally, taxable income of REITs is computed in the same manner as a corporation but dividends paid by a REIT are deductible in computing its taxable income. A REIT must distribute at least 95 percent of its taxable income, as adjusted. This requirement excludes capital gains, but a portion of a distribution may be designated as coming from capital gains. Undistributed REIT income, undistributed capital gain income, and all other classes of income remain taxable at the corporate rates. These provisions intend for most of the income to be from passive income sources and not the active conduct of a business.

The other classes of income are primarily foreclosure property and prohibited transaction income. These income types are taxable to the REIT regardless of the distributions to shareholders. Foreclosure income is taxed at the standard U.S. corporate tax rates while the net income from prohibited transactions is taxed at 100 percent. Prohibited transactions consist primarily of the sale of dealer property in the ordinary course of a business.

If all current earnings are distributed, REITs generally pay little or no federal income tax although state income tax treatment varies by state. Therefore, there is substantially only one layer of tax.

Taxation of REIT Shareholders

A REIT is a corporation for U.S. tax purposes and the dividends are taxed to the recipient in the normal manner. For the most part, the distributions are also treated as dividends for income tax treaty purposes. For example, assume a company in the United Kingdom invests in a U.S. REIT. The U.S. income tax treaty with the United Kingdom limits the U.S. tax on dividend distributions to 5 percent. The total U.S. federal income tax on the U.K. company's share of the distributed REIT taxable income is only 5 percent.

The new German treaty, on the other hand, does not allow a reduction in withholding taxes for distributions of REIT income unless the recipient owns less than 10 percent of the voting shares of the REIT. If 10 percent or more of the voting stock is held, the standard 30 percent rate applies. If less than 10 percent of the voting stock is held, the withholding rate is reduced to 15 percent. While relatively high by U.S. standards, the flat 30 percent tax rate is still lower than the higher German tax rates.

REITs may distribute capital gain income. A capital gain distribution is treated as a gain from the sale or exchange of a capital asset held more than one year and realized in the taxable year the dividend was received. However, there are special withholding rules for dividends designated as capital gain distributions. Section 897(h) enacted by FIRPTA generally provides that a distribution by a REIT to a nonresident individual or corporation shall, to the extent attributable to sales or exchanges of real property interests, be treated as gain recognized from the sale or exchange of a U.S. real property interest. Regulation Section 1.1445-8(a) and (c) treat capital gain distributions from REITs as gain from the disposition of U.S. real property and require tax withholding equal to 34 percent of the capital gain distribution to foreign shareholders.

Since the FIRPTA provisions treat capital gain distributions as gain from U.S. real property interests, the gain is taxed at the U.S.

graduated tax rates as if effectively connected with a U.S. trade or business. Preferential treaty withholding rates for dividends are not available, and an income tax return must be filed to obtain any refund of overwithheld tax. Undistributed capital gain income remains taxable to the REIT.

The REIT must designate a capital gain distribution within 30 days following the end of the year in which the distribution occurred. Without the proper designation, all distributions are deemed distributions of ordinary REIT income. Section 1445 withholding (34 percent rate) does not apply to ordinary REIT dividends paid to foreign investors. Since capital gain distributions are usually beneficial to U.S. citizens because of the 1991 maximum capital gain rate of 28 percent, some discretion must be exercised by a REIT with both domestic and foreign investors when designating distributions as from capital gains.

Like-Kind Exchanges

If the REIT desires to reinvest its capital gains rather than make a distribution, the capital gain tax can be deferred through use of like-kind exchanges. Like-kind exchanges provide investors in real estate the opportunity to exchange one property for another while deferring the gain usually recognized upon the sale of a property. Like-kind exchanges would be appropriate where the REIT wishes to reinvest the proceeds in U.S. real estate rather than make a distribution of the proceeds or pay the capital gains tax itself.

Section 1031 provides an exception to the general rule requiring the current recognition of gain or loss on the sale or exchange of property. Under Section 1031, no gain or loss is recognized if property held for productive use in trade or business or for investment is exchanged solely for property of a like kind to be held either for productive use in trade or business or for investment. Any gain is deferred until the "exchange property" is disposed of in a subsequent taxable transaction. The property to be received in the exchange must be of greater value than the property relinquished to defer the entire gain. Gain will be recognized to the extent of any money received (including net relief of liabilities) in the transaction.

Certain statutory requirements must be met in order for an exchange to qualify for like-kind treatment. Qualifying property is limited to property held for productive use in trade or business or for investment. Qualifying property does not include stock in trade or other property held primarily for sale, stocks, bonds, notes, other securities or evidences of indebtedness or interest, interests in a partnership, certificates of trust or beneficial interest, or choses in action.

In addition, qualifying property must be identified within 45 days after the date the relinquished property is transferred and received within the earlier of 180 days from the date of the initial transfer or the due date of the taxpayer's tax return, including extensions. Failure to meet these requirements will result in the transaction being taxed currently even though the proceeds were reinvested in real estate.

Like-kind exchanges need not be straight two-party swaps. Multiple-party exchanges can qualify for like-kind treatment under the statutory guidelines. Properly structured, like-kind exchanges allow REITs to reinvest in property of greater value without current tax consequences.

Portfolio Indebtedness

Interest income has had a generally favorable position in the international regime of U.S. taxes. Most income tax treaties to which the United States is a party either partially or fully exempt interest income from the U.S. withholding tax. Historically, residents of countries not having an income tax treaty with the United States could use the U.S. tax treaty network through use of an entity properly organized and operated under the laws of an appropriate treaty country.

The U.S. Treasury has challenged and continues to challenge the use of treaties by nonresidents of a treaty country. Their reasoning is that only residents of the specified treaty country should receive the benefits the treaty intends. When the U.S. Treasury successfully concludes its campaign against "treaty shopping," the flexibility of foreign debt financing, will be seriously impaired.

Fortunately, the Internal Revenue Code contains provisions that can allow the foreign investor a way to earn interest without the imposition of the U.S. withholding tax. The Tax Reform Act of 1984 created this possibility by adding the "portfolio indebtedness" provisions to the Code. While this exception was originally designed to

allow U.S. borrowers access to funds in the Eurodollar market
without establishing a foreign finance subsidiary, it can, if properly
utilized, allow foreign lenders to achieve their objective of repatriating interest income free of withholding.

Portfolio interest is interest not effectively connected with a
U.S. trade or business received by nonresident aliens or foreign
corporations on qualified obligations issued after July 18, 1984. Two
types of obligations qualify for portfolio indebtedness: bearer obligations described in Section 163(f)(2)(B) and registered obligations
with respect to which the U.S. withholding agent has received a
statement that the beneficial owner is not a U.S. person. Several
restrictions and requirements must be fulfilled to ensure that the
interest will be received only by a non-U.S. person who does not
own 10 percent or more of the U.S. borrower.

With respect to bearer obligations, Section 163(f)(2)(B) has
three requirements. First, there must be arrangements reasonably
designed to ensure that such obligation will be sold (or resold in
connection with the original issue) only to a person who is not a
U.S. person. Second, in the case of an obligation not in registered
form, interest on the obligations must be payable only outside the
United States and its possessions. Third, on the face of the obligation, there must be a statement that any U.S. person who holds such
obligation will be subject to limitations under U.S. income tax laws.
The statement must be in English, as follows:

> ANY UNITED STATES PERSON WHO HOLDS THIS OBLIGA-
> TION WILL BE SUBJECT TO LIMITATIONS UNDER THE
> UNITED STATES INCOME TAX LAWS, INCLUDING THE
> LIMITATIONS PROVIDED FOR IN SECTIONS 165(j) AND
> 1287(a) OF THE INTERNAL REVENUE CODE.

Payments must be made outside the United States and not to a U.S.
person. Interest payments made by transfer of funds into an account maintained by the payee in the United States or mailed to an
address in the United States will not be considered to be made
outside the United States for this purpose.

The other source of portfolio interest is an obligation in registered form and with respect to which the U.S. withholding agent has
received a statement that the beneficial owner of the obligation is
not a U.S. person. A registration required obligation is any obliga-

tion (including any obligation issued by a governmental entity) other than an obligation that

1. Is issued by a natural person,
2. Is not of a type offered to the public,
3. Has a maturity (at issue) of not more than one year, or
4. Is a bearer obligation described in Section 163(f)(2)(B).

To be in registered form, an obligation must be registered as to both principal and interest. Transfer of the obligation may be accomplished only through the surrender of the old instrument and the issuance or reissuance to the new holder, or through a book-entry system. In general, a book-entry system is a record of ownership of an obligation wherein the transfer of ownership is required to be reflected in a book entry, whether or not physical securities are issued.

The exemption for registered securities is available only if the U.S. withholding agent receives a statement that the beneficial owner is not a U.S. person. Such a statement may be made either by the beneficial owner of the obligation or by a securities clearing organization, bank, or other financial institution that holds customers' securities in the ordinary course of its trade or business. The required statement must be signed by the beneficial owner under penalties of perjury, must certify that the beneficial owner is neither a U.S. citizen nor a resident, and must provide the name and address of the beneficial owner. The statement may be made on Form W-8 or on a substitute form that is similar to Form W-8.

Exempt portfolio interest does not include interest paid on an obligation held by a *10 percent shareholder*. The term *10 percent shareholder* means in the case of an obligation issued by a corporation, any person who owns 10 percent or more of the total combined voting power of all classes of stock of such corporation entitled to vote. In the case of an obligation issued by a partnership, *10 percent shareholder* means any person who owns 10 percent or more of the capital or profits interest in such partnership. The attribution rules of Section 318(a) apply with some modifications for corporate shareholders. Partnership ownership rules are to be prescribed in regulations. These rules are sufficiently broad in scope to make it difficult for any family relationship or common ownership structure not to be counted toward the 10 percent limitation.

Certain foreign bank loans and loans from controlled foreign corporations do not qualify for the portfolio interest exemption. Additionally, arrangements that are determined to be back-to-back loans could be excluded from portfolio interest status. Back-to-back loans could be used to circumvent the 10 percent shareholder and foreign bank exclusions. For example, a foreign shareholder of a U.S. taxpayer or a foreign bank may lend money to an unrelated foreign party who in turn lends that money at a discount to the U.S. taxpayer. In such cases, the legislative history of this provision directs the IRS to use means at its disposal to determine whether back-to-back loans exist. Back-to-back loans are more commonly used to obtain favorable treaty benefits. As discussed later in the chapter, it is important to understand when back-to-back loans will be considered to exist.

Participating Portfolio Indebtedness

Properly structured, the portfolio interest exception should be available to minimize U.S. taxes on foreign investment in U.S. real estate. One possible structure is the "participating portfolio loan." Recall that the ownership interest cannot exceed 10 percent for the portfolio exception to apply. This would include parties related to the foreign lender. Participating debt is a means by which the foreign lender can participate in the upside of U.S. real estate while maintaining the benefits of the portfolio interest exception.

Participating debt usually takes the form of debt that has a fixed interest feature plus a contingent interest feature. The contingent interest can be a percentage of property cash flow, a percentage of the sales proceeds, a percentage of the net gain from sale, and so on. The participation feature must be carefully structured to avoid a recharacterization of the debt as equity, thereby defeating the advantages of a portfolio loan.

The courts have ruled that the business and legal characteristics of lending should be present in order for a transaction featuring participating financing to qualify as debt for tax purposes. Additionally, the courts have considered several factors in determining whether participating loans are debt or equity. These factors include

1. The intent of the parties,

2. The name given to the document evidencing the advance,
3. A fixed and adequate interest rate,
4. The presence or absence of a maturity date,
5. The right to enforce the payment and interest, including remedies for default,
6. The source of payment,
7. Participation in management,
8. A status equal to or inferior to that of regular creditors,
9. Capitalization of the borrower,
10. Identity of interest between creditor and stockholder,
11. Whether or not the entity could have obtained loans from outside lending institutions, and
12. Fair market value of the collateral in excess of the debt.

No one factor is conclusive; rather, all the facts will be examined before the determination of debt or equity is made. With these factors in mind, there are some general guidelines for the structure of a participating loan. These guidelines are as follows:

1. The borrower is personally liable for some or all of the debt or has substantial equity excluding the borrowed funds.
2. The debt should have a fixed maturity date.
3. The participation is in gross operating income as opposed to net income.
4. The participation in asset appreciation is a participation in sale proceeds or appraised value over original cost.
5. No participation should survive the maturity date of the debt. The asset appreciation should be due and payable at maturity, even if appraisals are necessary to determine the amount of participation.
6. Credit standards similar to those used by a U.S. lender should be observed.
7. Debt terminology is used in the loan documents.

Participation levels should generally be no greater than the participation levels that unrelated U.S. lenders are obtaining in the market at the time of the transaction. Participation levels over the current U.S. standards are more likely to be scrutinized for equity characteristics.

Care must be exercised in the future treatment of the participating loan even if it successfully passes the "debt versus equity" test.

Under the FIRPTA Regulations, a participating loan is to be treated as a U.S. real property interest. Gain, if any, on the sale of such an instrument is to be treated as gain from the disposition of a U.S. real property interest and is subject to the FIRPTA tax. An exception to the FIRPTA tax currently applies if the note is merely repaid by the maker. In that case the note payments are generally respected as principal and interest, and accordingly should continue to have their taxability determined under the rules applicable to interest. In short, a sale or other disposition of such a note could completely negate the tax benefit the participating loan was intended to provide.

In a related area, the IRS has recently issued a notice of proposed rulemaking (FI-189-84) that discusses the tax treatment to be accorded to certain participating debt instruments currently offered on Wall Street. The IRS intent from this pronouncement is clearly to split the instrument into its multiple parts, with different tax treatment accorded each feature. The fixed interest "lending" piece will continue to be treated as interest, while the riskier contingent interest piece is to be considered as an equity return. It is unclear whether the position of the Treasury can be sustained in the long run. It is also not clear whether the Treasury would attempt to expand its position to include participating real estate loans. In any event, the planner must consider the possibility of future challenge by Treasury when using a participating loan.

Other Lending Considerations

Favorable tax treaties can exempt interest income from U.S. taxation when paid to persons or corporations based in the treaty country. In an effort to limit the availability of these treaty benefits, Congress has enacted provisions that, if applicable, could limit an investor's use of some tax treaties in a "back-to-back loan" situation. Other provisions known as the "earnings stripping" rule could disallow or defer interest expense deductions for persons who pay interest to related foreign persons not subject to U.S. tax on the interest received. Additionally, there are now reporting requirements regarding treaty positions taken that are intended to uncover transactions between related parties that are "treaty shopping."

Back-to-Back Loans

Congress has long been concerned about the potential for abuse of tax treaty provisions by taxpayers who involve foreign entities in transactions. In the years 1984–1987, Congress began to focus its attention on the use of "back-to-back" loans to avoid the U.S. withholding tax. The term *back-to-back* is undefined in the Code and regulations. Guidance in this area must be obtained from court cases, committee reports, and revenue rulings.

The first major attack on back-to-back loans came with the Deficit Reduction Act of 1984. It was here that Congress specifically directed the IRS to control the use of back-to-back loans. The latest relevant pronouncement comes from the House Committee Report on the Revenue Reconciliation Act of 1989, which provides the following example of back-to-back loans:

> A U.S. corporation borrows money from a Dutch bank that has borrowed money from the foreign parent corporation of the U.S. corporation. Interest payments to the Dutch bank may be treated as payments to the foreign corporation. Similarly, where a U.S. corporation borrows money from a Dutch bank, which loan is guaranteed by the foreign parent corporation of the U.S. corporation, interest payments to the Dutch bank may be treated as payments to the foreign parent corporation.

This extract indicates the continued interest of Congress.

Most of the available information on back-to-back loans comes from revenue rulings issued by the IRS. Many of the positions taken in the revenue rulings are supported by the language in the congressional committee reports of various revenue acts from 1984 to date.

The first revenue rulings coinciding with the Congressional attention to back-to-back loans were 84-152 (1984-2 C.B. 236) and 84-153 (1984-2 C.B. 238). Both revenue rulings dealt with the issue of related party financing. In Revenue Ruling 84-152 *(supra),* a foreign parent corporation had loaned money to a Netherlands Antilles subsidiary at 10 percent. The Netherlands Antilles subsidiary loaned a slightly smaller amount at 11 percent to a domestic subsidiary of the common foreign parent. The domestic corporation deducted the interest expense, while the Netherlands Antilles Corporation paid no tax on the interest income by claiming an exemption from U.S. tax under the U.S.-Netherlands Antilles Income Tax Convention.

Under this fact pattern, the IRS ruled that the interest payments from the domestic subsidiary to the Netherlands Antilles subsidiary did not qualify for an exemption under the treaty. Its logic was that the loans could be "collapsed" into a direct loan from the foreign parent to the domestic subsidiary. Two main points were stressed in this ruling. First, the Antilles subsidiary acted as a conduit in that there was never "dominion and control" over the interest payments. This ruling relied upon the case law precedent set in *Aiken Industries Inc.* v. *Commissioner*, 56 TC 925 (1971). There, the Court ruled that a Honduras subsidiary was merely a conduit because it never exercised "dominion and control" over the payments. The second point of the ruling was that the primary reason to involve a Netherlands Antilles subsidiary in the transaction was merely "the avoidance of United States Tax."

Revenue Ruling 84-153 *(supra)* reiterated the concept of "dominion and control" over interest payments. In this ruling, a domestic parent attempted to finance the manufacturing activities of a wholly owned subsidiary domiciled in a nontreaty country. The parent arranged for a separate wholly owned Netherlands Antilles subsidiary to issue bonds to foreign investors. Then, the funds were loaned from the Netherlands Antilles subsidiary to the nontreaty country subsidiary at one percentage point higher than the rate on the bonds.

Again, the IRS ruled that the interest was not subject to the exemption provided in the treaty. The main point of the ruling was that interest income had not been "derived . . . by" the Netherlands Antilles subsidiary from the nontreaty country subsidiary because there was never dominion and control over the payments. Another relevant factor was the business purpose of the transactions. The explanation of the revenue ruling states: "This use of X lacks sufficient business or economic purpose to overcome the conduit nature of the transaction, even though it can be demonstrated that the transaction may serve some business purpose."

When explaining the intent of certain provisions of the Tax Reform Act of 1986, Congress once again echoed fears of an increase in the use of back-to-back financing. The committee reports on this area specifically state: "The conferees wish to emphasize that back-to-back loans, as generally provided under present law, will be collapsed by the IRS and the ultimate recipient, if not treaty protected, will be subject to U.S. tax."

The IRS replied with Revenue Ruling 87-89 (1987-2 C.B. 195), which expanded on the related party precedents set in Revenue Ruling 84-152 *(supra)*. Example 1 of this ruling describes a foreign parent depositing money in an unrelated bank domiciled in a country with a tax treaty. The unrelated bank then lends a slightly lower amount to a domestic subsidiary of the foreign corporation. For its role in the transaction, the bank receives a spread on the interest received versus the interest paid of less that one percentage point.

In ruling on this case, the IRS left itself plenty of latitude. First, the wording was quite broad and advised the use of a "facts and circumstances" test. Second, no reliable guidance was provided on what a properly structured transaction would be. The ruling does, however, provide that the form of the loan would be respected if the same loan would have been advanced to the subsidiary on the same terms in the absence of a deposit by the parent. A key point was that if the lender has the ability to offset the parent's deposit against the subsidiary's deposit, it will be interpreted as presumptive evidence that the lender would not have made the same loan in the absence of the deposit.

These revenue rulings can be summarized into six major factors that appear to be used in determining whether a loan structure is a back-to-back loan subject to collapse. The determination of whether the loans could be collapsed will be based upon all the relevant facts and circumstances. Therefore, these factors are critical:

1. *Interdependency of transactions.* In cases where the deposit and the loan are two "independent transactions" such that the loan would be made on the same terms irrespective of the deposit, taxpayers should be able to avoid the back-to-back loan classification.

2. *Ability of intermediary to offset the subsidiary's liabilities with the parent's deposits.* In Revenue Ruling 87-89 *(supra)*, the IRS listed this ability as presumptive evidence that the loan to the subsidiary would not have been made in the absence of the parent's deposit.

3. *Dominion and control over interest.* If an intermediary receives the interest income from a subsidiary and then makes an immediate payment to the lending source, the intermediary will have the appearance of being a conduit. The loan

would less resemble a back-to-back transaction in cases where the intermediary receives the interest payment and has independent "dominion and control" over it.

4. *Interest rate differential.* Revenue Ruling 87-89 *(supra)* also implied that a differential in the interest rates of less than one percent could be construed as evidence that the intermediary was acting as a conduit. Interest rate spreads that mirror common banking practices would lend support to the assertion that a loan is not back-to-back.

5. *Loan terms.* The IRS considers loan terms that are substantially different from normal lending practices as indicative of a back-to-back loan. For example, loans that lack maturity dates, market interest, or adequate collateral are suspect.

6. *Legitimate purpose for involving third party.* This may be the least subjective of all the factors. If it is determined that the intermediary is involved in the transaction mainly to avoid U.S. tax, the structure will probably be collapsed. Structures having legitimate business purposes are less likely to be considered back-to-back.

Loans arrangements must therefore be structured with the back-to-back loan rules in mind in order to qualify for exemptions from withholding tax.

Earnings Stripping

The Revenue Reconciliation Act of 1989 added the "earnings stripping" rule to the Internal Revenue Code. This rule disallows or defers deductions for certain interest payments to related foreign persons who are not subject to U.S. tax on the interest received. Any interest that is disallowed may be carried over indefinitely. A related person is defined as a person who is related to the taxpayer within the meaning of Section 267(b) or 707(b)(1). These sections are broad in scope and include, among other relationships, family members, as well as an individual and a corporation if the individual owns, directly or indirectly, 50 percent or more of the outstanding stock of the corporation. Back-to-back loans could result in an otherwise unrelated person being considered related.

The mechanics of the disallowance are complex. The amount of the disallowed interest deduction is limited to "excess interest expense." Excess interest expense is the excess of the net interest expense over 50 percent of adjusted taxable income. Adjusted taxable income is taxable income computed without regard to net interest expense, net operating loss carryover, or any deduction allowable for depreciation, amortization, or depletion. Net interest expense is equal to the total interest paid or accrued during the year reduced by any interest income received. Any interest that is disallowed for any taxable year is treated as paid or accrued in the succeeding taxable year and is subject to the overall limitation for the succeeding taxable year. In addition, if a taxpayer has an extraordinary gain in a given year and has an excess amount of limitation available, (i.e. 50 percent of adjusted taxable income exceeds net interest expense), the excess limitation may be carried over for three years.

The interest deduction disallowance does not apply to any corporation that satisfies a 1.5:1 debt-to-equity ratio. Equity for this purpose equals the corporation's cash funds plus the adjusted tax basis of all its assets, reduced by total indebtedness. The earnings stripping provision is generally effective for interest paid or accrued in taxable years beginning after July 10, 1989. Fixed term loans that were issued on or before July 10, 1989, are grandfathered and not subject to disallowance.

Disclosure of Treaty-based Positions

The Technical and Miscellaneous Revenue Act of 1988 enacted Internal Revenue Code Section 6114, which requires taxpayers to disclose tax return positions if a tax treaty modifies or overrides general U.S. tax law. In addition, Section 6712 imposes a penalty for failure to make the required disclosures. Regulations under these sections set forth the rules for determining when there is a treaty-based return position and the penalties for failure to file the required disclosure statement. The primary purpose of these reporting requirements is to assist the IRS in uncovering transactions between related parties that are "treaty shopping."

It is important to note that reporting of a treaty-based position is required whether or not the taxpayer is required to file a U.S. income tax return. Regulations describe the disclosure statement and requirements. An entity that would not otherwise file a tax return must now file a partial return if it is required to disclose a treaty-based position. The penalty for failure to disclose the treaty-based position is $10,000 for corporations and $1,000 for all other taxpayers. These penalties are for each failure to disclose and can be imposed more than once in any taxable year.

WITHHOLDING AND REPORTING REQUIREMENTS

In general, Section 1441(b) states that U.S.-source interest, dividends, rent, compensation, remunerations, and so on are subject to tax withholding at a 30 percent rate. Tax treaties and other provisions may modify the rate at which tax is imposed or may exempt the individual or corporation from tax altogether. One important provision that should be noted is set out in Section 1445. This section provides that 10 percent of the amount realized (gross proceeds) on the disposition of a U.S. real property interest by a foreign person must be withheld as tax.

Not all income paid to a foreign corporation or nonresident individual is subject to withholding. Non-U.S.-source income and income effectively connected with a U.S. trade or business are not subject to withholding. Also, general capital gains that are subject to tax in the hands of a foreign individual are not subject to withholding.

The Section 1441 regulations provide that nontaxable distributions of stock are not subject to withholding. Also, a distribution treated as a distribution in part or full payment in exchange for stock is not subject to withholding (Reg. Section 1.1441-[3][b][ii]).

Section 1441(c)(9) provides that interest classified as "portfolio interest" is not subject to withholding when a U.S. person pays such interest to a foreign person. The use of portfolio debt can be a very effective planning tool and is discussed in detail in the Tax Planning Section.

Many times it is difficult for the withholding agent to accurately determine whether a person in question is a nonresident alien for purposes of computing tax. Regulations under Section 1441 have been set forth to give guidance to withholding agents. Since a U.S. citizen or resident is not subject to the 30 percent tax, a withholding agent can rely on a written statement filed with the withholding agent by the individual payee that the payee is a U.S. citizen or resident. The payee can also claim U.S. residency by filing Form 1078. A corporation or partnership may also file a written statement with the withholding agent stating that the entity is a domestic entity. The statement should give the entity's U.S. address or place of business and be signed by an officer of the corporation or a partner in the partnership.

With regard to dividends paid to a shareholder, Reg. Section 1.1441-(3)(b)(3) states that tax is to be withheld if the shareholder's address is outside the United States. Likewise, if the shareholder has a U.S. address, it can be assumed the shareholder is a U.S citizen or resident. If a shareholder changes addresses from a non-U.S. address to a U.S. address, the withholding agent is to continue withholding until the shareholder provides a written statement or the withholding agent is otherwise satisfied that the shareholder is not subject to tax.

Code Section 1446 provides that partnerships must make estimated tax payments for foreign partners. The amount of estimated tax to be paid is based upon each foreign partner's allocated share of U.S trade or business income. The estimated tax is computed based on the maximum rates for individual or corporate partners and must be paid regardless of whether the partnership distributes the earnings to its partners.

Tax on U.S. trade or business income of individuals and corporations is payable in quarterly estimated tax payments. There are penalties for failure to properly pay estimated taxes.

The regulations under Section 6302 provide certain procedural rules for the administration of foreign tax withholding. A withholding agent and/or foreign person should be aware of the numerous forms required to be filed regarding withholding or exemption from withholding. The withholding agent is required to file Form 1042, "Annual Withholding Tax Return for U.S. Source Income of Foreign Persons," by March 15 of each year. This form should be accompanied by any Forms 1042S, "Foreign Person's U.S. Source Income Subject to Withholding."

Form 1042 reports income that may be taxable even if no tax is required to be withheld. Form 1001, "Ownership, Exemption, or Reduced Rate Certificate" may be filed by the payee with the withholding agent in order to obtain an exemption from withholding or a reduced treaty rate. Also, once Proposed Regulations Section 1.1441-6(b) and (c) become final, the payee will be required to submit Form 8306, Certificate of Residence, in order to be eligible to use the desired tax treaty.

Section 1445 provides that a transferee of a U.S. real property interest is required to withhold 10 percent of the amount realized by the foreign transferor on the sale. Some states also have their own withholding rules with regard to sales of U.S. real property interests. For example, California imposes a tax of one third of the federal rate on the disposition of California real estate.

As is the case with withholding on U.S.-source income, no tax need be withheld if there is proof that the transferor is not a foreign person. However, since the purchaser is responsible for any withholding of tax on the transaction, the purchaser is at risk if he or she fails to obtain proof of does not withhold tax. With most sales, the seller will deliver to the purchaser a certificate signed under the penalty of perjury that the transferor is not a foreign person. A sample Certificate of Non-Foreign Status, which should include the seller's U.S. taxpayer identification number, is found in Reg. Section 1.1445-2(b)(2)(iii).

Tax Returns for Foreign Taxpayers

In recent years, the United States has stepped up its efforts to obtain tax returns from foreign taxpayers. Additional penalties and disallowance of deductions have been added recently through the regulations under Section 874. Now more than ever, a foreign taxpayer should be aware of U.S. filing requirements and the potential implications for not filing or paying tax.

A nonresident alien is required to file Form 1040NR (U.S. Nonresident Alien Income Tax Return) if one of the following conditions are met:

1. He or she is engaged in a trade or business in the United States at any time during the taxable year even though
   a. He or she has no income effectively connected with a trade or business in the United States,
   b. He or she has no U.S.-source income, or
   c. His or her income is otherwise exempt from tax.

2. He or she has made the net basis election for reporting income.
3. He or she is underwithheld on U.S. source annual or periodic income.

Through the regulations under Section 874, the IRS can deny the benefits of deductions and credits if the taxpayer fails to file a timely return. Also, under Section 6712 the IRS can impose a $1,000 penalty on an individual for failure to disclose a treaty-based position in a tax return.

Foreign corporations engaged in a U.S. trade or business at any time during the taxable year must file Form 1120F if a return would be required had the corporation been a U.S. corporation. As was the case with nonresident aliens, the returns must be filed even if

1. The corporation has no U.S. trade or business effectively connected income,
2. The corporation has no U.S.-source income, or
3. The corporation's income is otherwise exempt from U.S. tax.

If the corporation does not have any gross income, a statement should be attached to the tax return describing the amount and type of exclusions claimed. Finally, if a foreign corporation with U.S.-source income does not file a tax return, the IRS can prepare a return for that corporation and then assess and collect the tax.

Reporting Related Party Transactions

Section 6038A, which was recently amended by the Revenue Reconciliation Act of 1990, requires a 25 percent foreign-owned domestic corporation or a foreign corporation engaged in a trade or business within the United States to report information relating to transactions between the corporation and any party related to the corporation. For Section 6038A purposes, a 25 percent foreign shareholder of a domestic corporation is considered a related party. There are numerous attribution rules used to determine who are 25% shareholders.

The potential penalties set forth by Section 6038A are extremely severe. Before this section was amended by the 1990 Act, failure to file the required information carried a $1,000 penalty with a potential maximum penalty of $24,000. The penalty provisions of

Section 6038A(d) now provide for a $10,000 penalty for failure to file. Once the Service notifies the reporting corporation of failure to file, the corporation has 90 days to file the necessary information or be subject to a penalty of $10,000 for every 30-day period thereafter for which the corporation is not in compliance.

CHAPTER 27

MANAGING THE COMMERCIAL PROPERTY IN THE UNITED STATES

Kenneth A. Shearer
Executive Director
Donald I. Feiner
Senior Director
Cushman & Wakefield, Inc.

When a property is purchased the new owner is faced with a decision, namely, how to manage and lease the property. Unless the owner has a large portfolio of properties, the necessary infrastructure, and market knowledge to manage and lease the property, consideration should be given to the use of a fee management and leasing company. The decision to hire a fee manager is particularly important if the owner is in a business in which he or she is not normally involved in property management or if he or she is not located close to the property.

The selection of a particular managing agent should be based upon the agent's experience, depth of personnel expertise, and reputation for functional quality. The latter can easily be determined by interviewing their clients, and the former can be evaluated by reviewing the types of properties managed—that is, large or small, new or old, complicated or simple mechanical systems—and reviewing résumés of their personnel's experience. It is not only important to know which other owners have hired the managing agent recently, but also who has terminated the agent recently and for what reason. Hiring a local firm should result in local market knowledge, while hiring a national firm with a local branch office should provide not only local knowledge but an opportunity for national marketing.

In addition, the national firm would most likely have a larger technical base of expertise to apply to the property. In any event, the managing/leasing agent must cooperate with other local brokers to take advantage of all leasing opportunities. This is accomplished by paying the cooperating broker a full commission and paying the managing agent a half commission. Paying one commission to split between the two parties is counterproductive and will result in noncooperation between the brokerage community and the managing/leasing agent.

A "Request for Proposal" (RFP) should be developed. The more information can be provided in the RFP, the less the requirement for a bidder to include extra costs to offset unknown contingencies. The RFP should require the following information:

A. Business background.
   1. Description of the company.
   2. Ownership of company.
   3. Financial statements.
   4. Description of existing management and leasing portfolio.
   5. Description of types of buildings managed in terms of technical sophistication of mechanical, electrical, and building management systems.
B. Reporting requirements (required reports).
   1. Accounting (monthly reports).
      a. Income analysis.
      b. Arrears report.
      c. Expense analysis.
      d. Budget analysis (comparison of actual versus budget).
      e. Lease abstracts.
      f. Deferred conditions (contained in leases).
      g. Any additional special reports required by the ownership.
   2. Operations.
      a. Monthly inspection reports.
      b. Status reports of major projects.
      c. Contractor performance report.

       d. Analysis of labor utilization and costs.

       e. Analysis of service orders.

       f. Energy consumption analysis.

C. Supervision.

Experience of agent's staff: Identify personnel who will be assigned to supervise building operations—for instance, agent's property manager, on-site building manager, and chief engineer. It is important to determine what other assignments and responsibilities are assigned to the agent's property manager and what percentage of his or her time will be devoted to this assignment.

D. Building staff.

Provide a table of organization for the staffing of the building (showing, in the case of a new building, when the staff will be hired).

E. Leasing.

1. Outline how the building will be marketed (a general statement of what types of tenants should be targeted and the perceived marketability of the building).
2. Identify leasing staff, experience, and any other present assignments.

F. Fee structure.

1. Management fee.
2. Construction management fees.
3. Leasing fees.
4. In the case of a new building, the fee and a budget estimate of the capital costs likely to be incurred during the start-up period should be provided.

G. Term of contract.

Minimum contract term and early cancellation penalties, if any, should be requested.

The agent's management fee may be based upon a fixed fee or a percentage of rental income. It is usually beneficial for the owner to use a fixed fee since a percentage of rent has no relationship to actual cost of performing the service; the incentive to increase the rental income is in the commissions paid. It is preferable for the broker to be completely compensated on a commission basis rather than salaried so that a maximum effort is exerted by the broker. Sometimes an advance against future commissions is provided if the broker's total efforts are limited to this property.

The basic objective of the managing and leasing agent is to produce maximum occupancy, profitability, and efficiency in the most economical way, without compromising the quality of the services provided or the environment in which the tenants function.

ASSUMPTION OF
MANAGEMENT PREREQUISITES

In order to assume the management of a property in an orderly manner, and not to create any interruption or delay in tenant services, an initial research analysis must be performed and a checklist developed. All this must be done prior to the closing of a building sale, and before assumption of management by a new owner or managing agent. Of primary importance, besides the normal due diligence analysis, is an in-depth investigation of the presence of hazardous substances. This investigation must also include examining any documentation concerning the previous removal of any hazardous materials.

The types of materials involved are

1. Asbestos.
2. Industrial, radioactive, or chemical waste.
3. Urea formaldehyde insulation.
4. Lead-based paints.
5. PCB's and PCB-containing electrical transformers, capacitors, or other equipment.
6. Underground storage tanks.
7. Waste disposal areas (e.g., former waste dump).
8. Other toxic, hazardous, or contaminated substances (or present or past use at the property).

Liability for environmental damage for people with real estate interests affects all parties involved in the transfer of an interest in the property. The Comprehensive Environmental Response Compensation and Liability Act (CERCLA) has created a vast framework for liability of purchasers, sellers, landlords, tenants, brokers, and managing agents in connection with the discovery and disposal of hazardous waste. CERCLA gives the Environmental Protection Agency (EPA) two choices of enforcement: (1) it can use Superfund money for clean-up and sue the current owner or other responsible parties (including former owners) for reimbursement; or (2) it can seek injunctive relief to compel the current owner to clean up the site at its cost. As discussed below, ignorance of the hazardous materials, like "ignorance of the law," is no excuse.

Purchaser Liability

A purchaser of real estate can be held liable for all hazardous waste on the premises, regardless of culpability. CERCLA requires owners of property containing hazardous substances to bear the cost of clean-up—even if the owner did not place the substances on the property and did not know of their existence at the time of purchase. Thus, in order to avoid potential EPA action and the resulting clean-up costs, a purchaser should investigate the previous ownership of the property. If the past ownership indicates activity likely to have produced or handled waste, then the purchaser should investigate for contaminated conditions. A prudent purchaser will address this issue in negotiations with the seller by insisting upon an environmental audit of the property and, if hazardous materials are found to exist, by having the purchase price reflect the clean-up costs. If the purchaser elects to proceed without addressing this issue, and is later charged by the EPA with the cost of clean-up, its only recourse is to seek reimbursement, voluntary or otherwise, from the seller and/or other parties involved in the transaction.

Seller Liability

Under CERCLA, an owner of contaminated real estate cannot escape liability by selling. The person who owned the property at the time of the improper disposal or release of hazardous waste remains liable. Sellers are in the same position as purchasers—they are presumed responsible "by law." Consequently, a seller may wish to conduct an environmental audit to establish the extent of contamination prior to closing.

Landlord Liability

A tenant's action that produces hazardous conditions can create liability for the absent or unwary landlord. In order to minimize the risk of being held responsible for the acts of its tenant, a landlord should periodically inspect the tenant's use of the property. Additionally, lease provisions should require the tenant to comply with laws regulating storage or disposal of hazardous waste and provide for appropriate remedies for any violation of such laws.

Tenant Liability

Tenants can be held liable under CERCLA when governmental agencies cannot locate the owner of the premises. In this instance, the EPA will look to former as well as existing tenants for responsibility. To be held liable, tenants do not have to be the cause of the contamination. Liability is based on the simple assumption that a person leasing a site over a period of years learns of any hazardous conditions. In not terminating the lease and reporting the conditions to governmental agencies, the tenant is deemed to have accepted the hazardous condition.

Broker Liability

To date, no court has held a broker responsible for the costs of clean-up of contaminated property. However, a purchaser facing millions of dollars in removal and treatment costs will likely seek to drag the brokers involved in its purchase into litigation. A broker could be held liable on the following theories: (1) fraud based on intentional misrepresentation or failure to disclose known defects, (2) negligent misrepresentation for failing to exercise reasonable care to discover the hazardous waste, and (3) strict liability for an innocent misrepresentation made to a purchaser (i.e., passing on inaccurate information provided by the seller).

Property Management Liability

CERCLA identifies "owners or operators" as parties responsible for hazardous waste disposal. As such, property managers fall within the definition of an "operator." Liability extends not only to the corporation acting as the property manager but also to the individual managers themselves. The reasoning behind CERCLA's individual liability is that the property manager has the capacity to prevent or abate the damage caused by the disposal of hazardous substances.

CERCLA requires owners or operators of property containing hazardous substances to bear the cost of clean-up, even if the operator did not place the substances on the property and did not know of their existence during the property management engagement.

The following is a checklist of other items that should be researched:

A. General management information
  1. Establish exact description of asset (address, block and lot number, etc.).
  2. Obtain building telephone numbers.
  3. Interview all employees to evaluate experience and function and to introduce new management personnel.
  4. Evaluate on-site manager and chief engineer for retention or replacement.
  5. Prepare a tenant change of management/ownership letter and a tenant information kit.
  6. Review all building office clerical functions including tenant charge and purchase order procedures and prepare all necessary changes where required.
B. Operations management information
  1. Review and analyze all service contracts for:
     a. Form and type of agreement.
     b. Insurance requirements and vendor insurance certificates.
     c. Cancellation and expiration provisions.
     d. Unusual provisions.
  2. Prepare notification letters of management change to:
     a. All utility companies.
     b. All vendor contractors with cancellations where appropriate.
  3. Review all utility bills for:
     a. Correct application of rate.
     b. Correct computation of invoices for past 12 months.
     c. Any unpaid water and sewer tax invoices.
  4. Conduct violation search at local building department.
  5. Review list of tenants' contractors and their insurance certificates.

6. Review tenants' insurance certificates.
7. Compare directory board listings against leases.
8. Review keying system and location of all master keys.
9. Review all building plans, architectural, mechanical, alterations, and leasing.
10. Secure copy of the Certificate of Occupancy and all modifications of same.
11. Determine total legal compliance with:
    a. Fire safety.
    b. Exterior inspections.
    c. Elevator inspections, testing, and so forth.
    d. Tenant alteration procedures and compliance with filing procedures.
12. Inventory of all building equipment, furniture, tools, spare parts, and so forth.
13. Inspect the building including roof, exterior, mechanical, and elevator systems.
14. Review all preventive maintenance procedures.
15. Review whether existing management has taken advantage of any utility company retrofit rebates and whether any opportunities for future rebates exist.
16. Prepare a list of initial recommendations and possible capital expense requirements.

C. Financial management information
   1. Secure payroll data.
   2. Search tax department for unpaid bills. Obtain signed copy, in triplicate, or current rent roll, showing in detail office or store number, tenant's name, annual rental, monthly rental, and commencement and expiration dates.
   3. Obtain copies of leases, agreements, modifications, assignments, sublease approvals, letters modifying leases, and so forth. Review and abstract all necessary information to establish current billings and deferred conditions. Establish fixed-charge billings for condenser water, utilities, and so forth.
   4. Obtain list of occupants other than those under lease, showing space occupied, term, and agreement.

5. Obtain a signed list of security or deposits made by tenants showing whether such security deposit is interest-bearing. If so, at what percent?

6. Obtain a signed list of current conditions of each tenant's account for rent, sundry charges, or advance payments showing which months are in arrears or are prepaid.

7. Develop a list of charges to be billed other than those in leases.

8. Develop a schedule for special billing arrangements such as address, duplicate bills, special dates for billing, billing rates, and so forth.

9. Obtain a signed detailed report of all cases in the hands of an attorney or marshal, including vacated tenants.

10. Obtain a list of vacancies showing office and store number, area, rental, and possession date.

11. Obtain a list of approved subtenants, if any.

12. Obtain a copy of the last meter list if space is submetered, name of company reading meters, and dates of readings.

13. Obtain a list of tenants identified for close collection attention and a list showing each tenant's paying habits or billing peculiarities. Make thorough investigation of all delinquent accounts.

14. Identify owner's monthly statement requirements.

15. Obtain the sales tax registry number, if applicable.

16. Obtain the utility tax registry number, city, and state.

17. Obtain employer's federal I.D. number.

18. Secure copies of approved unpaid bills and commitments.

19. Obtain a blank lease form, review, and comment.

20. Obtain a copy of ground lease if leasehold property.

21. Obtain a copy of last sales and use tax return.

22. Obtain a copy of any air-rights leases.

23. Obtain a copy of the mortgage encumbrance, if applicable.

24. Obtain or develop tenant escalation information, workpapers, and invoices.

D. Risk management (insurance) information
   1. Obtain information on building insurance policies, procedures, and costs.
   2. Obtain all Tenant Insurance Certificates.
   3. Arrange for risk management department or insurance broker to take over all insurance policies and render report.
   4. Have the owner's insurance representatives supply certificates for the foregoing forms of insurance.
   5. Arrange to have managing agent's (if applicable) name included in policies, workmen's compensation, public liability, and any other forms of legal liability coverage.

In order to create the tools that will produce the desired result, a full range of skills and knowledge must be applied to the leasing and physical operation of the property. The primary tools include a "Leasing Plan," a "Management Plan," "Building Operating Manuals," and monthly and quarterly inspection reports, financial reports, and budget reviews. Periodic interdiscipline meetings must be held between the owner's representative and the leasing and management agents. The frequency of these meetings depends upon the specific requirements of a particular property.

THE LEASING OR MARKETING PLAN

The following is a typical outline of a marketing plan:

I. Market Overview.
   A. Description of the district in which the building is located, what changes have occurred in the previous year, the average vacancy rate, and the addition of any major blocks of space that have become available.
   B. A discussion of the general tenant interest in the district, the trend of vacancies and effective rental rates, the trend of competition between landlords and the general trend in concessions given by landlords to attract new tenants and retain existing tenants.

C. A general discussion of existing and anticipated business conditions and how it is anticipated this will affect the existing and near future vacancy rate.
D. A discussion of the perceived advantages and disadvantages that for the next decade will affect the district in which the building is located. The following are examples of assumed advantages and disadvantages that could easily be interchanged for different districts.
  1. Advantages.
     a. Access to and from the district.
     b. Anticipated environmental improvements.
     c. Level of interest by other owners in renovations to improve quality of existing buildings.
     d. Image of district compared with other districts.
  2. Disadvantages.
     a. Construction activity over next few years.
     b. Anticipated future competition between similar buildings in the district.
     c. Quality of existing space in the district, for instance, a decline in the quality of the inventory could cause tenants to look for space in another district perceived to present newer and more efficient space.
II. Leasing performance.
   This section would describe recent leases concluded in the building, currently available space, and space becoming available in the next one to two years. For example:
   A. During the past year the following leases were signed at (address of building):
      (Name of Tenant)
      Floor: _____
      Area: _____sq. ft.
      Rent: _____/sq. ft.
   B. The following space will be available in (year):
      Date Available:
      Floor: _____
      Area: _____sq. ft.
      Asking Rent _____/sq. ft.
      List each space separately.

   C. Current status of the building.
   This section lists interest in space, current transactions, their status of negotiation, design, construction, and date of completion. This section also lists latest recommendations of competitive rental rates, work letters, escalation terms, and any concessions that should be offered.
III. Strengths and weakness of project.
   A. Changes in marketplace.
   This paragraph should discuss in detail any positive or negative area events that would affect the leasing effort. This would include any public agency improvements, quality of security and sanitation, and renovation of competitive buildings, their lobbies, and/or exterior. The latter is of particular interest if you are dealing with an existing building, and comparably aged buildings in the area are being upgraded.
   B. Analysis of the Market for this Particular Building.
   This section describes the basic floor sizes, suitability for subdivision, and how they would appeal to various types of tenants. High windows-to-floor areas for example would occur on smaller tower floors and this would be of particular interest to small attorneys or investment companies who require many private offices. On the other hand, larger floors in the building base with a smaller perimeter-to-interior area ratio would be more attractive to larger tenants such as insurance companies, service companies, and advertising or publishing firms. The rental rate, of course, is of importance to all of these tenants, as is the perceived "prestige" of the building location and its importance to tenant's clients.
   C. Comparison with Competition.
   This paragraph should contain an objective review of the perception of this building by other brokers in comparison to comparable buildings in this marketplace. It should indicate how the other rental rates and lease escalation clauses compare with this building—whether they are higher or lower and why. A comparison should be made of such features as loss factor, curb appeal, tenant amenities, lobbies, housekeeping, elevator service (waiting time), air

conditioning charges, electrical cost, electrical capacity, and, last but not least, the tenant mix. This section should also describe what is being done or has been recommended to eliminate any negative perceptions.

IV. Leasing strategy.

This paragraph should describe which space is becoming available in the near term, who the leasing team is, and their prior experience and successes.

   A. Canvassing.

   The canvassing strategy and agenda should be described. The canvassing effort is crucial to the successful leasing of the building. The procedure includes exhaustive foot canvassing, follow-up telephone calls, mailings, brochures, and targeting companies that are particularly suited for various types of space—for example, large occupancy, small occupancy, retail, and special occupancies such as data processing.

   B. Broker cooperation.

   A teamwork approach is essential to the successful marketing of the space. To maximize exposure and interest in the property, the entire brokerage community must cooperate.

   Canvassing. If canvassing efforts uncover companies with genuine requirements who are already represented by another broker, this broker must be immediately contacted to inform him or her of availabilities in the building and explore if this property is a viable option for their customer. A follow-up letter should then be sent to the particular company's decision-maker describing conversations with its broker and a complete descriptive package of the building.

   Inquiries and Proposals. All inquiries and proposals must be recorded and given an immediate response. In addition, any prospective tenants and/or their brokers who visit the premises must be accompanied by a member of the leasing team. This ensures that any questions are properly answered and any mechanical or engineering information can be provided by the appropriate building personnel.

   Negotiations. The leasing team must represent the owner's interest by assembling the best professionals, achieving the highest value through positive encouragement, and seeking creative solutions to potential problems and conflicts.

Commissions. The positive image of the ownership should be reinforced by being timely and competitive in all commission payouts to the brokerage community.

C. Competitiveness.

The property's ultimate success depends on the employment of the most effective use of the leasing strategies coupled with the economic competitiveness of the property. The market must be continuously reviewed to determine such changes in marketing trends as types of escalation, up-front concessions, free rent, and work letter allowances. Decisions must then be made with the owner as to whether these changes will cause a modification of the leasing plan.

D. Tenant retention program.

A tenant retention program must be established. This program depends upon the establishment of a positive relationship with the tenant. The most important thing is to provide the tenant with the quality of service required by the lease.

This is not always just the provision of service but providing it in a timely manner by demonstrating a level of response and follow-up that assures tenant satisfaction. A written tenant questionnaire to monitor performance of the building personnel response is also helpful. Conduct monthly or bimonthly breakfast meetings with all tenant office managers to discuss building performance and to monitor their needs for services and future additional space.

The provision of other tenant amentities should be considered, such as

A concierge desk to arrange for services such as:
Theater tickets.
Limousine services.
Restaurant services.
A monthly newsletter—"What's happening in the building and the district" (shows, plays, etc.).
Valet services.
A health club, preferably in the building.

Delivering flowers or a plant to tenants on lease anniversaries.
Annual tenant Christmas party.
Building bootblack.
Controlled messenger service.
A conspicuous level of security.

V. Advertising focus.
Development of a comprehensive advertising campaign that includes

1. Brochures.
2. Placement of advertisements in the media.
3. Direct mailing campaigns.
4. Promotional giveaway items—for instance, pens, alarm clocks, coasters, candy, and so on. (These promotional items work only if they are something that is lasting and will not be thrown into a drawer; this is why small candy in a jar etched with the leasing program logo is a popular item.)
5. Broker mailings.
6. Broker meetings at the building to show the space, with a cocktail reception afterward.

VI. Goals.
Establish leasing goals for the coming year by identifying which floors are anticipated to be leased.

THE MANAGEMENT PLAN

Regardless of who is managing the property, it is essential that a plan be developed to enumerate how the building will be managed.

The initial plan, an "Interim Management Plan," establishes the objectives to be accomplished during the first three months after the assumption of management. The objectives must consider the competitive rental market, the owner's financial goals, and the efficient use and preservation of the building structure and equipment.

In order to provide both effective management and benchmarks against which this management can be measured, management goals must be established. The Interim Management Plan defines these initial goals.

In the start-up of a new building or the assumption of management of an existing building, a management plan is essential so that the procedures can be immediately established to ensure the development of an efficient operation in the shortest amount of time. Any new building that is started up in an inefficient manner will be inefficient for many years. Starting up a new building or accepting transfer of management of an existing building involves too little knowledge to establish a final management plan. Therefore an Interim Management Plan must be developed until the occupancy of the building and the experience gained is sufficient to establish a final management plan.

The following is an outline of the format of an Interim Management Plan.

Objective for the Project

For an existing building this section describes exactly what is anticipated to be accomplished—for example, initial leasing efforts, changes in staffing, initial reductions in operating costs and anticipated rebidding of existing contracts.

In a new building a checklist of what will be done prior to and during initial occupancy should be enumerated. In both cases dates should be established so that a schedule of events is developed. This schedule establishes milestones by which property management performance is evaluated. Adhering to this schedule assures efficient performance.

Building Operating Manual

Depending upon the sophistication of the building mechanical systems, this section of the management plan may not be accomplished during the interim period. The best way of assuring the establishment and continuation of efficient building operational procedures is to eliminate oral tradition as a method of conveying information.

In order to accomplish this, all information pertinent to the administrative and mechanical operation of a building is reduced to a logical written form, which serves as a manual of operation. Immediately upon assumption of management, the engineering staff will assemble all the necessary information to start developing the mechanical portion of the operations manual.

The development of emergency procedures will be given priority, including fire and evacuation plans.

The following pages describe the administrative and emergency procedures portion of the manual; this can be used in part as an outline in the management plan.

Labor

This section lists the staff required for the operation of the building for the next three months, taking into account the anticipated level of occupancy. The plan should also indicate the intent for future levels of staffing.

When an existing fully staffed building is to be purchased, it is essential that prior to the closing decisions be made as to whether the new owner will assume the existing building staff.

This is particularly important where labor union contracts exist because assuming the existing staff will also result in accepting obligations such as staffing levels, termination benefits, vacation schedules, and salary levels.

The preferred method to reduce the labor cost obligations is to have the employees terminated by the existing owner at the time of closing; then the new owner will hire only those employees who have been prescreened and determined to be necessary to the operation. This procedure will require the seller to settle all termination payment obligations with the personnel prior to closing and permit the new owner to restaff the building at a level that is not dependent upon historical practices or based upon a possibly difficult union negotiation.

At the same time a new schedule of benefits not based upon prior employment longevity or prior commitments can be established. Depending upon the election of the new employees, either the same union, a different union, or no union representation at all may occur.

Training

This section is a statement such as the following: "Our objectives for personnel training will be as follows:" (the methods should then be listed).

Organization

This section describes the interfacing of on-site and off-site staff and contains job descriptions of all personnel involved in the project.

Administration

This is probably the most important section of the Management Plan because it provides in detail all the information necessary to establish a functioning management system. The following is an example of a list of administrative systems that would be established for the takeover of an existing building. A similar list should be developed for a new building, which would include the initiation of contracts, punchlist procedures, and so forth. For example:

Purchase order procedures.
    Purchase Order Log.
    Acceptance and delivery tickets.
    Approval of invoices.
    Payment.
Budget.
    Reconstruct present budget in manager's/owner's format.
    Verify cost.
Recap all annual purchase orders for contract services.
    Perform contract abstracts for existing contracts.
Office procedures.
    Tenant and lease files.
    Names of important representatives of tenants.
    Directory board listings.
    Tenant signs.
    Work order system.
    Preventive maintenance system.
    Complaint log, security log, contractors log, cleaning log, elevator maintenance log, and so on.
    Purchase order system.
    Material receiving documentation.
    Payment procedure.
    Emergency plans.
    Asbestos abatement and other environmental procedures.

Personnel procedures.
  Evaluation procedures for new hires and annual reviews.
  Vacations (allowances and schedules).
  Uniforms.
  Sickness (allowances and procedures).
  Hiring (interview procedures).
  Termination (methods and causes for same).
  Union affiliation, if any.
  Benefits (description of health insurance, life insurance, and retirement, IRA, or 401K plans).
Energy consumption records.
Contract files for:
  Cleaning.
  Security.
  Unions.
  Elevators.
  Chemical treatment (cooling tower and closed systems).
  Window washing and scaffold maintenance.
  Centrifugal chillers (maintenance contractor).
  Piped-in music.
  Plant maintenance.
  Building automation system.
  Building HVAC control system.
  Trash removal.
  Fire protection systems (including sprinklers and alarms).
  Emergency generator (maintenance and fuel).
  Switch gear maintenance.
Insurance certificates files for contractors and tenants.
Building passes.
  List of building employees and type of identification issued.
Sign rules and directory board use.
Forms for periodical reports to owner.
List of insurance agent, accountants, and other consultants.
Building rules and regulations.
  Assurance that employees are familiar with rules for:
    Tenants.
    Lobby area.

Loading dock area use.

Hours of use of elevators.

Additional charges for extra services.

Reporting system for parking lot operators.

Additional services.

Develop procedures to accept, document, follow up, and invoice tenant requests for additional services, for example:

1. Additional janitorial services.
2. Additional maintenance services.
3. Additional elevator services.
4. After-hours or special air conditioning services.

Building inventory.

Lobby furniture.

Restroom furniture.

Lobby ashtrays.

Trash receptacles.

Maintenance and engineering office furniture.

Special equipment and tools.

Tenant improvement plan.

Establish written procedures for the following:

1. Tenant requests to proceed with alterations.
2. Landlord requirements and approval.
3. Local filing requirements.
4. Scheduling deliveries and construction work.
5. Acceptance and permit write-offs.

Tenant Move-in.

Coordination of move-in with tenant and movers.

Coordination of

Telephones.

Security.

Elevator use.

Mail.

Trash removal.

Keys (access cards).

Cleaning.

Directory listings.

Janitorial.
> Tenant area precleaning and postmove cleaning.
> Follow-up for such items as tenant space clean-up (special).
> Restroom cleaning.
> Restroom supplies.
> Tenant complaints.

Operations newsletters: These are narrative-form descriptions of significant events that have occurred during the past month. These include operational and leasing items.

Interface with leasing group: Interface with leasing group to establish and coordinate procedures to estimate, construct, and accept tenant alterations.

Develop management's office space, and employees and cleaning contractor's locker and storage space requirements.

EMERGENCY PROCEDURES

Emergency manual—Tenants.
> Fire.
> Bomb threats.
> Severe weather—hurricanes, tornadoes.
> Blackouts.
> Earthquake.

Emergency personnel list with telephone numbers (management and tenant).

Emergency Manual—Employees.
> Fire.
> Bomb Threats.
> Severe weather—hurricanes, tornadoes.
> Blackouts.
> Earthquake.
> Flooding.
> Oil spill.
> Gas leaks.
> Elevator (evacuation of passengers).

Fire protection during tenant improvements and after occupancy.

Name of person responsible for enforcing compliance by tenant improvement contractor.

Inspection schedule and log.

Fire extinguishers.

Quantity.

Types.

Locations.

Federal and local fire codes and record-keeping for:

Type of portable fire extinguishers and extinguishing systems.

Locations.

Inspection frequencies and schedule.

Recharging discharged extinguishers.

Test schedule and log for standpipe and sprinkler systems.

Security.

Outline of building security basic coverage and procedures to be used during the above-listed types of emergencies.

It is obvious from the foregoing that the key to the successful management of a commercial property is the application of operational knowledge in an organized manner. Operational procedures should be constantly monitored and compared. The operating personnel should be aware of all costs and be an integral part of budget preparation.

The more the operators are involved, the more they are motivated. The supervisors should have operational backgrounds; otherwise, they cannot motivate by asking "what if" and being able to distinguish whether the reaction is logical and positive.

Personal computers should be used to manage the workload efficiently; manual tracking of work orders, tenant requests, labor utilization, preventive maintenance, cleaning functions, and budgeting should be eliminated.

In the past years, many owners have not given enough attention to maximizing the efficiency of the management of their commercial property assets. With the changes in the tax laws, buildings that depended on depreciation to provide investor income are now required to generate a net operating income (NOI) based upon the efficient leasing and management of the property. As the economy has slowed, vacancies have increased and the rental rates have become highly competitive. As a result, the only way the NOI can be positively influenced is by operating the property more efficiently. In the same way, when an investor is considering the purchase of a property, it makes sense to have experts in property management review the building operations to determine if a potential for operating cost reduction exists.

It is normal to retain the services of an engineer to review the physical condition of a property prior to purchase. However, it is just as important that the mechanical systems and total operation be reviewed from an operational perspective since any identified operational savings that are identified, when capitalized, can have an important effect on the value of the property.

CHAPTER 28

DEVELOPMENT AND CONSTRUCTION IN THE UNITED STATES

Robert D. Lane, Jr., Esq.
Robert F. Cushman, Esq.*
Pepper, Hamilton & Scheetz

INTRODUCTION

If the late 1970s and 1980s have taught us anything about real estate development and construction in the United States, it is that land will be bought, projects will be developed, and buildings will be constructed whenever financing is available. The market demand for particular real estate development appears to be relevant only insofar as it affects the availability of financing, not a developer's willingness to build the project.

The unprecedented boom in real estate development and construction in the United States during the 1980s occurred primarily because of the confluence of a number of factors making capital

---

* The authors wish to acknowledge, with deep appreciation, the contribution of G. Ralph Guthrie, Chairman and Chief Executive Officer of the Urban Investment and Development Company in Chicago, Illinois with regard to portions of the Construction sections of this chapter, which he coauthored with Mr. Cushman in the 1984 edition of this book. Furthermore, the authors gratefully recognize the substantial contribution of Brad A. Molotsky, Esquire, an associate at Pepper, Hamilton & Scheetz, on the Foreign Developer Disclosure/Reporting Obligations section of this chapter.

plentiful and readily available for real estate development. The high inflation of the late 1970s made real estate appear to be a "no-lose" proposition for just about anyone who could finance a project (which meant virtually everyone). The tax incentives in place following the recession of 1973–1974, already a powerful motivation for the investment of private capital into real estate ventures, was significantly enhanced in 1981 when the tax laws were changed to allow investors to depreciate real estate over 15 years instead of 30 to 40. By the beginning of the 1980s, investment real estate became a powerful tax shelter.

A second factor was the deregulation of the lending industry in 1982, purportedly to permit savings and loans to compete in an environment of unprecedentedly high interest rates, which impelled savings and loans, commercial banks, and even insurance companies and pension plans to finance real estate ventures.

By the time the 1986 Tax Reform Act burst the domestic investors' balloon, the United States's foreign trade imbalance combined with the infusion of petrodollars to bring new investment money from Japan, the Middle East, the Netherlands, the United Kingdom, and other foreign sources.

The "crash" of the U.S. real estate market in 1990–1991—largely reflecting the long-expected impact of the 1986 Tax Reform Act, which eliminated the tax-subsidized portion of owner's equity in real estate, together with a generally overbuilt national market—gave many foreign real estate investors pause; nevertheless, many others see the 1990s as an excellent time to begin, or expand, their ownership of U.S. real estate. This chapter addresses the question of how new projects in the United States can be developed and constructed.

BENEFITS AND RISKS OF U.S. REAL ESTATE DEVELOPMENT

Benefits

Investors with an eye to opportunities in the United States typically identify a number of especially attractive characteristics of real estate development and ownership there.

The first and foremost of these characteristics is political stability. The U.S. government—its dollar, the economy, and the American system of laws—is among the most stable in the world, particularly when contrasted with the volatility of the "new" markets of China, the Soviet Union, eastern Europe, and the Third World countries, and even the unpredictability of the eagerly anticipated European Community. Property rights are thoroughly defined and protected by federal, state, and local laws throughout the United States.

Diversity, opportunity, and prospects for growth in America are also marked benefits of U.S. real estate development. Most investors seek diversification in their investment portfolios including real estate, which is diversified both geographically and characteristically. The enormous breadth of different development opportunities, types, and geographical areas make the United States unique throughout the world.

The other advantages of real estate investment generally apply with equal force in the U.S. market, including the advantages of leveraging investment with borrowed funds, real estate's traditional hedge against inflation, and the opportunity to combine cash flow, tax benefits, and appreciation, as well as the significant psychological rewards inherent in real estate ownership.

Risks

Prospective developers must, however, balance the many benefits of U.S. real estate with several meaningful risks. Currently, the most worrisome risk relates to the basic principles of supply and demand. Many U.S. markets are perceived as having an oversupply of various types of real estate. These types might include office buildings, retail shopping centers, and apartments. An oversupply of office space in a particular market can result in high vacancies, leading to decreases in the rental rates obtainable. If the generally beneficial principle of leveraging was pursued too aggressively, rentals in a depreciating market might be insufficient to meet debt service and/or operating expenses, thereby leading to the danger of foreclosure.

Another risk inherent in real estate is its lack of liquidity. Especially in times of a perceived oversupply of a particular class of real estate, the time required to sell or refinance a property can be substantial. Even under the best of circumstances, transactional requirements generally require weeks or months to complete.

Yet another risk present in any foreign investment in real estate relates to the extensive system of federal, state, and local laws and regulations and the danger of a foreigner's failure to recognize or appreciate the nuances, the highly diverse requirements, and/or the hidden expectations of varying local jurisdictions. To the extent that the foreign developer relies on local professional guidance in this regard, the investor risks a diminution of control.

Somewhat as a reaction to the unbridled growth and development during the 1980s, many American local governments and communities have greatly expanded their roles in the development process. An ignorance of the political aspects of local real estate development, whether in a major metropolis such as New York City or a small suburban municipality in the Midwest, can be deadly to a foreign investor. These concerns will be explored in detail later in this chapter.

DEVELOPMENT AND CONSTRUCTION GENERALLY

Development Phases

Generally speaking, real estate development occurs in five phases: (1) site selection and acquisition, (2) pursuit and processing of governmental and other approvals for development, (3) construction, (4) marketing, and (5) management. Financing is not considered a "phase," but rather a factor related to how the project will be structured and what objectives are held by the investor.

Frequently, some or all of these five phases are performed by different parties, each with the requisite expertise and wherewithal relevant to the phase to be performed. For example, land speculators may obtain an option on a site that they believe is prime for future development. They may market or sell their option to a developer who has the experience and skills necessary to obtain the extensive zoning, subdivision, environmental, and other approvals necessary to permit the development. The developer may then sell the "package" of development-approved land to a builder who might contract with a long-term owner prospect, such as a pension fund or insurance company, who will ultimately own the project. The pension fund or insurance company might joint venture with a real estate company experienced and skilled in management. Of course, it can also happen that one single entity conceives, creates, and implements a project from start to finish. The message for foreign investors, however, is that they need not commit to the entire "soup-to-nuts" process, but rather can limit their participation to one or more of the phases depending upon their investment objectives. These objectives will primarily relate to a weighing of acceptable risk against desired reward. In the arena of U.S. real estate development and construction, the earlier phases clearly represent higher risk but can also bring greater reward (i.e., profit). Since marketing and management are treated in particular depth elsewhere in this book, only the first three phases—acquisition, development, and construction—will be discussed further in this chapter.

Kinds of Real Estate Projects

Deciding upon the specific real estate product to be developed is an essential precondition to choosing location. If one anticipates engaging solely in land speculation, it might be possible to search a geographical area for well-located land and then decide upon its use. Nevertheless, someone interested in developing a real estate product must have a requisite level of experience, training, and expertise in that kind of real estate. The ability to develop a retail shopping center successfully is wholly different from the ability to develop an office building or a residential project. Even within the residential subcategory, home-building is a very different business from apartment development. These varying kinds of real estate products include the following:

- Residential—for sale.
- Residential—for lease.
- Urban high-rise office building.
- Suburban office park.
- Strip shopping center.

- Regional retail mall.
- Warehouse and/or flex office/warehouse.
- Manufacturing—light and heavy.
- Hotel.
- Resort/recreational.
- Mixed use.
- Healthcare facility.

Of course, a whole host of specialty properties can also be added to the list.

The Acquisition Phase: Alternatives

How properties should be owned or acquired will generally depend upon the objectives of the investor. Land can be entitled in individuals, corporations, partnerships, trusts, or unincorporated associations, or in joint ventures between or among any combination of these. The chosen entity can control or own an interest in real estate in a variety of ways including fee simple (outright) ownership, leasehold, option, easement, or agreement of sale.

How the foreign investor chooses to structure itself for purposes of holding its interest in the real estate to be developed will depend upon the number of parties involved and what attributes of ownership the varying parties require. The ramifications to be considered include tax implications, economics, control issues, liability, relative liquidity, and psychological benefits.

The nature of the interest held may depend upon which phases of real estate development and construction the parties anticipate and what risks are expected to be undertaken. For example, if relatively little capital is to be risked while obtaining governmental approvals for a particular development, an individual person or corporation might seek an option interest in a particular property, generally in return for the payment of an option fee, which gives the prospective developer the right to buy the property at a previously agreed-upon price at a later time. While holding the option, the developer can try to obtain the requisite development approvals, and possibly financing as well.

Alternatively, the prospective developer might wish to place the property under an agreement of sale whereby he or she agrees to buy the property (as opposed to simply having the right but not the obligation to buy the property under an option agreement) upon the occurrence of specifically negotiated conditions. Agreements of sale generally articulate and define the conditions upon which the prospective purchaser must buy the property, while an option agreement might simply give the prospective purchaser the right to buy at a specific price within a specific time.

Under American bankruptcy law and other laws governing insolvency of landowners, an agreement of sale might give the prospective purchaser/developer more protection than an option agreement, depending upon the circumstances and the state law in which the property is located. Hence, the developer must weigh the trade-off of having greater protection under an agreement of sale against the possible loss of discretion and/or flexibility of an option agreement.

The greatest protection with regard to control of the land, albeit with the least flexibility in the event approvals or financing are not available, is achieved when the developer purchases the property outright and then proceeds to obtain approvals and financing. Purchasing property prior to obtaining development approvals is also highly risky but can lead to greater profit relative to the land costs. Such an approach, however, is rarely recommended, even for local developers who *believe* that they can predict the development and financing market with some confidence. For a foreign investor, land speculation of this kind would probably be unacceptable since such confidence in predicting the local approval processes and financing nuances of a foreign market would be exceedingly rare. Finally, the method of acquisition of the property can have federal disclosure and reporting consequences for a foreign person, as discussed in detail later in this article.

THE DEVELOPMENT PROCESS

Government Approvals

As mentioned earlier, one of the most substantial factors in developing real estate in the United States is the process of obtaining the requisite approvals to permit the development and construction.

In the United States, federal law applies relatively little to real estate development, being primarily limited to environmental regulation and certain reporting and disclosure requirements.

Similarly, the various states usually delegate the regulation of land use and development to local municipalities with exceptions similar to the federal context regarding environmental regulation and reporting and disclosure requirements.

Nonetheless, compliance with local municipal requirements can be time-consuming and expensive. Moreover, obtaining final municipal approvals for politically or socially unpopular projects can sometimes be virtually impossible.

Local Governmental Structure

American states are usually divided into counties that can have their own body of regulation for real estate ownership and development. Within counties are incorporated or unincorporated municipalities that may be designated as towns, townships, boroughs, cities, villages, or other local classifications, each with its own codes, ordinances, and collected regulations.

Counties and municipalities will have their own legislative bodies (variously called city councils, county or township commissioners, supervisors, aldermen, selectmen, or other such designations). These legislative bodies will enact zoning, land development, subdivision, and other ordinances or codes regulating real estate development; moreover, these ordinances or codes will frequently reserve discretionary approvals to the same legislative bodies or delegated agencies.

As a control over the generally elected legislative bodies, American state law typically also provides for county and local planning commissions or planning boards whose functions are usually advisory, as well as zoning boards of adjustment empowered to grant variances, special exceptions, or other dispensation to specific property owners to whom the general code or ordinance requirements would unfairly apply. The body of law in every state governing these bodies and their functions is complex and extensive. Moreover, since the growth and development of an area is governed by regulation particular to that area, the process can be an intensely political one.

Sequence and Timing of the Process

Although there are some notable exceptions (the city of Houston, Texas, being one with the highest profile), most of the land area in the United States is subject to these local regulations. Depending upon the political context and the complexity of the planned development, the time involved in locating and obtaining control of a site, and achieving all necessary approvals for a development project can easily take a year or more. A well-informed developer might typically proceed as follows.

After completing extensive market research and demographic analysis, a process that in itself might take months or years, a foreign investor/developer might determine that a 500-unit apartment complex in a suburban municipality surrounding Philadelphia is a desirable project. In the course of canvassing various suburban communites for appropriate sites, the developer will also study the political climate in each suburban municipality with regard to its hospitality and receptivity to development. Once a site is selected, the developer, if he or she has not done so already, will make contact with a well-versed and sophisticated real estate lawyer as well as a professional land planner and/or architect. In order to negotiate an option or agreement of sale to control the selected site, the developer must have a relatively sophisticated analysis of the development potential of the site—hence, the need for a land planner or architect. The option or agreement of sale is then negotiated and signed prior to entering into any public discussions with regard to the property so as to avoid or reduce the possibility of inviting competition.

Once the property is controlled, the developer, together with an attorney and land planner, will commence dialogues with the township and county planning and zoning officials as well as with local community or neighborhood groups or associations. The precise sequence of these discussions and the decision as to which members of the development team should make the contact will depend upon the specific and unique local situation as well as the characteristics of the individuals on the developer's team. Sometimes the developer's local real estate lawyer will have strong relationships with the local officials and/or community leaders; other times the developer's local partner or consultant or the land planner will be the best choice. Whether the community's temperature is taken before or after the local officials are contacted will also vary depending upon the situation.

Once the development team has engendered enough likelihood of a positive political response, formal applications for land development and/or subdivision approval will be submitted. In order to implement this process (or during the course of the preliminary political negotiation), various other professionals and/or consultants may be brought in. These might include traffic analysts, environmental consultants, landscape architects, various engineering disciplines, and so on.

A series of hearings will ensue before the local planning board, the county planning commission, the local governing body, and possibly the local zoning hearing board if variances are required, as well as other more technical bodies. Examples of the technical procedures would include landscaping or shade tree commissions, environmental agencies, streets and highways departments, historical preservation commissions, and signage review boards.

These proceedings can easily take eight to twelve months for a major project and can sometimes take two or three years for the most complex projects.

FINANCING ALTERNATIVES

Each of the five phases of real estate development might have different financing needs that can be financed separately or as a package, depending upon the participants in the overall development scheme and their resources and objectives.

Site Selection and Acquisition Phase

This initial phase will involve a number of predevelopment items of cost. Feasibility studies, professional consultants, legal fees, travel and related expenses, and overhead and personal living expenses (i.e., income needs during the initial exploration period) are but a few. A deposit or option fee, necessary once the agreement of sale or option is entered into, could be substantial depending upon the scope of the project. Generally, a developer should have the funds on its own account (whether by capital or credit) to support this phase. Institutional financing for this preliminary "risk capital" is virtually nonexistent in the American market, and it would be very difficult to bring in an arm's-length "money partner" at this stage since insufficient tangible results have yet been developed to attract such investment at a reasonable price.

Development Approval Phase

At this point, expenses will start to mount up quickly, possibly into the hundreds of thousands of dollars. Engineering and architectual design drawings and specifications will be required and a variety of consultants may be necessary to pursue and conclude the political negotiation process effectively and to make effective presentations at governmental hearings. As with the first phase, the funds to finance these activities are almost always provided from the developer's equity, although an investing partner might be found in return for a significant return (related to the significant risk at this stage). Major developers will often be capable of financing these expenditures by borrowing under established lines of credit or revolving credit agreements secured by general corporate credit.

Construction Phase

Not until the construction and operational phase begins will institutional financing become available. These funds are generally obtained from commercial banks, savings and loans, pension funds, or insurance companies in the form of a construction or project loan. These loans are usually short term, related to the construction and marketing phase, with interest rates that float in relation to the prime rate or other agreed-upon indexes. Generally, the construction lender will want assurance of a permanent "take-out" loan commitment, which can take the form of a commitment from a permanent lender, or a sufficient number of pre-sales contracts if the project is not to be retained.

At a minimum, the loans will typically be secured by a first mortgage lien on the project as well as personal or corporate guarantees.

In the late 1970s and the 1980s, when tax benefits were extremely valuable, an alternative or complement to institutional financing was syndicated investor equity. As tax benefits have dissipated and as the American market adjusts to the changed economics of real estate investment, investor equity will again be available in return for economic benefits.

In the United States, an entire industry arose in the 1980s specializing in syndicating limited partnership investment interests to individual or institutional investors. As the tax benefits dissipate, economic benefits must increase in order to lure this investment market.

The terms necessary to obtain any of these financing sources flow from the general principles of risk and reward. During the predevelopment, construction, and operational start-up phases, significant risks are present and corresponding rewards must be offered to the lender or investor. Cost budgets may be exceeded, strikes may delay completion, leasing or sales may proceed more slowly than planned, and expected rents or prices may not be achieved. The lender or investor properly seeks a greater reward through future participation in cash flow and appreciation for assuming a part of this risk. The partner who comes in early and shares risk expects to receive a greater return per dollar invested than a purchaser who steps forward after the property is in operation with a proven cash flow.

The method by which the site for the project is acquired can also affect the project financing requirements. If land acquisition is required, then that cost can become a part of the total project cost and financing. Alternatively, the site owner may wish to contribute ownership, at a predetermined value, to the partnership that owns the entire project in return for an interest in the partnership.

Foreign Developers' Disclosure/Reporting Obligations

When acquiring businesses or real estate in the United States, foreign developers must be aware that some form of disclosure or reporting to a federal or state agency may be associated with decisions such as where to invest, how much to invest, and the type of entity used in a particular transaction. In a generic sense, a "foreign" owner/investor is traditionally defined as a person who is neither a citizen of the United States nor a resident of the United States for tax purposes. In addition, the term *foreign persons* generally includes natural persons as well as foreign corporations and entities (i.e., corporations or other entities formed outside the United States and its territories), the stock of which is owned directly or indirectly by non-U.S. citizens or residents. Each of the disclosure/reporting obligations discussed below has its own set of definitions of such terms as *foreign person, affiliate, related party,* and *ownership interest,* and the foreign developer should not assume that one definition or exemption will necessarily apply in the context of a different agency's or state's requirement. Moreover, since these and other laws governing foreign developers can change frequently, the reader is urged to consult counsel at the earliest stages of contemplating real estate development or construction in the United States.

As further discussed below, the major federal disclosure or reporting requirements that may be triggered by foreign investment in U.S. real estate include the International Investment Survey Act of 1976 (IISA), the Agricultural Foreign Investment Disclosure Act of 1978 (AFIDA), and the Foreign Investment in Real Property Tax Act of 1980 (FIRPTA). Pursuant to IISA and AFIDA, either the U.S. business entity or the foreign owner of U.S. real estate is required to file various periodic reports with respect to certain specified levels or types of foreign real estate ownership. Moreover, with respect to a sale or disposition of U.S. real estate by a foreign person, FIRPTA may impose certain withholding and reporting requirements on the part of the buyer of the real estate. In addition to IISA, AFIDA, and FIRPTA, depending on the type of entity, the method of payment of the purchase price, and the size of a given transaction, various other federal laws (including securities, banking, and tax) may also be affected, any of which may require some form of informational filing with a particular federal agency. Finally, in addition to the various federal disclosure and reporting obligations that may be imposed on a foreign developer, particular state law requirements may become a factor depending upon the type of entity and/or transaction chosen to acquire U.S. real estate. These filings might include state corporate and/or securities filings, as well as informational filings akin to those required by IISA or AFIDA.

International Investment Survey Act of 1976[1] (IISA)

IISA was passed by Congress in 1976 for the purpose of providing a mechanism to collect information on international investment and foreign trade in the United States. Pursuant to the regulations, the Department of Commerce and the Bureau of Economic Analysis (the BEA) require that reports be filed for each U.S. business enterprise in which a "foreign person"[2] owns, controls, or acquires, directly or indirectly (i.e., individually, as an affiliate, or by merger) 10 percent or more of the voting securities of an incorporated United States business enterprise or an equivalent interest in an unincorporated U.S. business enterprise. The definition of a U.S. business enterprise includes the ownership of real estate.

The report required by IISA must be filed within 45 days of an acquisition and must contain detailed information with respect to (1) the structure of the U.S. enterprise and its current debts, assets, and income; (2) a schedule of the ownership interests in the U.S. enterprise (including a list of the ultimate beneficial owners that are not more than 50 percent owned by another entity or person and their country of residence); (3) the identity of the transferor and transferee (including its legal name, address, citizenship, and principal place of business); and (4) the legal interest transferred (i.e., leasehold, fee, etc.).

Exemptions or exclusions are available from filing for a variety of reasons including the following: (1) the real estate acquired is residential real estate held exclusively for personal use and not for profit-making purposes, (2) if the total cost of the acquisition is $1 million or less and does not involve the purchase of 200 acres or more of U.S. land, or (3) the acquired U.S. business enterprise, as consolidated, has total assets at the time of the acquisition or immediately after, of $1 million or less and it does not own 200 acres or more of U.S. land. Pursuant to the regulations, an exemption also exists for limited partners of a partnership who do not have voting rights in the partnership.

Along with the initial report mentioned above, the regulations require the filing of both quarterly and annual reports, which serve to update the filed information. If, however, the U.S. enterprise does not meet certain minimum total assets, sales, gross operating revenues, or net income after taxes, then it is exempt from filing the quarterly and/or annual reports at such time. In addition, the regulations require the U.S. enterprise to file a survey with the BEA once every five years at specifically designated times, the last of which was due on May 31, 1988.

Agricultural Foreign Investment Disclosure Act of 1978 (AFIDA)[3]

AFIDA and the regulations thereunder require that any "foreign person" that acquires, disposes of, or holds an interest in U.S. agricultural land is required to file a report (Form ASCS 153) regarding such transactions and holdings within 90 days of the transaction. At a minimum, the report requires disclosure of the following information: (1) the legal name, citizenship, and address of the foreign person; (2) if a foreign corporation and its beneficial owners, up and through three tiers of ownership; (3) the type of interest acquired; (4) the acreage and legal description of the agricultural land; (5) the purchase price or consideration paid; (6) the intended purpose of the land; and (7) the date of transfer and the interest acquired by the foreign person. Pursuant to the regulations, agricultural land is defined to include ranchlands, forestry, and timberlands.

Under AFIDA, the following actions are considered to be reportable activities: (1) conversion by a foreign person of agricultural land to nonagricultural land and vice versa, and (2) a change in the status of a foreign person to a U.S. person (and vice versa) who otherwise holds a reportable interest in agricultural lands. Exemptions are available, however, if (1) the tract is less than 10 acres in size, and (2) the annual gross receipts from the sale of the farm, ranch, forestry, or timber products produced thereon do not exceed $1,000.

Under AFIDA, a "foreign person" is defined as (1) a non-U.S. citizen, (2) a nonpermanent U.S. resident, (3) a foreign government, (4) a corporation or other entity created under foreign laws or having its principal place of business outside the United States, or (5) a U.S. corporation or entity in which a significant interest (10 percent or more) or substantial control is directly or indirectly held by a person mentioned in (1)–(4) above.

The Secretary of Agriculture is also granted the power to request that any nongovernmental reporting entity identify any person holding any equity interest in the holder of the underlying real estate. Thus, the Secretary may require that a foreign entity disclose its ultimate "foreign person" ownership interests.

Foreign Investment in Real Property Tax Act of 1980[4] (FIRPTA)

When enacted by Congress in 1980, the stated goal of FIRPTA was to tax the gains of foreign owners upon the dispositions of real property interests in the United States at much the same level as nonforeign owners of real property. The original version of the bill contained a comprehensive system of reporting and disclosure obligations designed to achieve this goal. Although this system was eventually replaced by the withholding mechanism discussed below, under §6039C of the Internal Revenue Code, as amended (the "Code"), the Internal Revenue Service (the IRS) still has the ability to require the reporting of foreign ownership of U.S. real property through annual informational returns that might require the disclosure of the ultimate beneficial owners of such property interests.

Under FIRPTA, any sale or disposition by a "foreign person" of (1) an interest in real property located in the United States, or (2) an interest in a U.S. real property holding corporation is subject to U.S. capital gains tax. The buyer of U.S. real property from a foreign seller is required to withhold and remit to the IRS 10 percent of the amount realized in the disposition.

The amount withheld by the buyer and remitted to the IRS is treated as a payment credited toward the final tax liability of the foreign seller. After the disposition, when the foreign seller files its U.S. tax return and calculates its actual tax liability, any excess withholding is required to be refunded to the foreign seller.

Other Tax Forms

The foreign developer may also be required to file a variety of other tax forms in order to claim either an exemption from taxation or to meet certain disclosure obligations under the Code. While a listing of every tax form required to be filed by the foreign developer is outside the scope of this chapter, §6038A provides an example of one such reporting requirement. Pursuant to §6038A, every domestic corporation and every foreign corporation engaged in a trade or business within the United States is required to file an informational return with the IRS, if such corporation is 25 percent foreign-owned. A corporation is "25 percent foreign-owned" if at least 25 percent of (1) the total voting power of all classes of stock of such corporation is entitled to vote, or (2) the total value of all classes of stock of such corporation is owned at any time by one foreign person. In addition, since January 1, 1991, the disposition of U.S. real estate may require the filing of a Form 1099 with the IRS. Although corporate transferors are exempt from this filing requirement (as are governmental units and certain "volume transferors") and, therefore, need not file a Form 1099 for such a disposition, all federal, state, and local rules and regulations should be carefully reviewed for other filings or disclosure requirements that may be applicable. The foreign developer should also keep in mind that various filings may require periodic updating with respect to material changes to the information set forth therein, while others may be triggered by further acquisitions or changes in ownership holdings.

Federal Securities Laws

Depending upon the structure of and/or the ownership interests acquired in a particular transaction, certain filings with the Securities and Exchange Commission (the SEC) may be required. Pursuant to §13(d) of the Securities and Exchange Act of 1934, as amended (the "Exchange Act"), acquisitions of beneficial interests in U.S. corporations in excess of 5 percent of any class of equity securities must be reported to the SEC, to the issuer of the securities, and to any exchange on which such class of securities is traded. A report must be filed with the SEC within 10 days after the acquisition if the U.S. corporation has registered the purchased class of equity securities under §12 of the Exchange Act. The report must set forth a great deal of information including (1) the background, identity, residence, citizenship, and nature of the beneficial owners; (2) the sources and amounts of funds or other consideration used to make the purchases; (3) the purpose of the purchases; (4) the number of shares of such security that are beneficially owned; and (5) information as to contracts or arrangements with any person with respect to any security of the issuer.

Pursuant to §14(d) of the Exchange Act, any person or group making a *tender offer* that would result in the ownership, directly or indirectly, of more than 5 percent of any class of equity security registered pursuant to §12 of the Exchange Act is required to file a Schedule 14D (which contains essentially the same information as a §13[d] filing) concurrently with making the offer. Moreover, pursuant to §14(f), disclosure that rises to the level of a proxy statement is required if, in connection with the acquisition, (1) persons are to be designated or elected as directors of the issuer without a meeting of the shareholders, and (2) the persons so elected or designated will constitute a majority of the directors of the issuer.

The use of a particular structure, such as a limited partnership, could also invoke the Securities Act of 1933, as amended (the "1933 Act"). For example, limited partnership interests are generally classified as "securities" for purposes of the 1933 Act, thereby requiring either that such interests fall within an exemption or that they be registered before being offered or sold. In addition, the foreign developer should also be aware that each state has its own system of securities regulations (blue-sky laws) that need to be reviewed and complied with in order to offer such interests for sale within the particular state.

Miscellaneous Federal Disclosure Requirements

Various federal laws also have an impact upon foreign bank accounts and money transfers into and out of the United States; these may require some sort of disclosure to or filing with various federal agencies. Depending upon factors such as the type of transfer or the amount of such transfer, the Currency and Foreign Transactions Reporting Act of 1970, the Interest and Dividend Compliance Act of 1983, the Right to Financial Privacy Act of 1978, the Money Laundering Control Act of 1986, or the Money Laundering Prosecution Improvements Act of 1988 may apply in the context of a real estate transaction. For example, under the Currency and Foreign Transactions Reporting Act of 1970, the physical transportation of currency or other monetary instruments in an amount exceeding $10,000 into or out of the United States requires the filing of a form with a particular officer in charge of the port of entry or discharge. Exemptions are available, however, for transfers of funds through bank check, bank draft, or wire transfer. Therefore, if foreign bank accounts and/or money transfers into the United States are contemplated by the foreign developer as a means for payment of the purchase price, particular exemptions or exclusions should be researched under the above-referenced laws.

Two other federal laws that could apply to a foreign developer's acquisition of U.S. real estate are the Foreign Agents

Registration Act of 1938 (FARA)[5] and the Hart-Scott-Rodino Antitrust Improvement Act of 1976 (the "HSR Act").[6]

FARA, which requires certain disclosures regarding the identity and type of activities engaged in by persons acting for foreign principals in the United States, probably would have limited applicability to most traditional real estate transactions. A "foreign principal" is defined as any foreign government, political party, or entity organized outside of the United States or having its principal place of business outside the United States. FARA requires the filing of a registration statement by the agent of the foreign principal who engages within the United States in political activities, public relations, or political consultations for or on behalf of the foreign principal. FARA exempts from its filing requirements any person who is engaged in only private or nonpolitical activities in furtherance of "a bona-fide trade or commerce" of a foreign principal. Furthermore, "trade or commerce" is defined to include the exchange, transfer, purchase, or sale of property of any kind. Assuming the U.S. agent of the foreign developer is merely engaged in nonpolitical or private activities, the agent's activities in the United States should not require disclosure under FARA.

A foreign developer should also be aware of the potential application of the HSR Act, which applies to acquisitions of voting securities, acquisitions of assets, certain formations of joint ventures, and mergers. HSR requires (except in the case of a tender offer) that both parties to the transaction file a detailed application with the Federal Trade Commission (the FTC) and with the Antitrust Division of the Department of Justice (the DOJ). Once the filing has been made, a 30-day waiting period for FTC and DOJ review begins to run. Based upon particular concerns, the FTC or the DOJ may terminate the waiting period, request that additional information be filed by either of the parties, or even extend the waiting period.

In order for a particular transaction to fall within the purview of HSR, it must satisfy a three-part test:

1. One of the parties to the transaction must be engaged in commerce or in any activity affecting commerce;
2. (a) Any voting securities or assets of a person engaged in manufacturing[7] that has annual net sales or total assets of

$10 million or more are being acquired by a person that has total assets or annual net sales of $100 million or more, *or*

(b) Any voting securities or assets of a person not engaged in manufacturing with total assets of $10 million or more are being acquired by any person with total assets or annual net sales of $10 million or more, or

(c) any voting securities or assets of a person with annual net sales or total assets of $100 million or more are being acquired by any person with total assets or annual net sales of $10 million or more; and

3. As a result of the acquisition, merger or joint venture, the acquiring party would hold

(a) 15 percent or more of the voting securities or assets of the acquired person, or

(b) An aggregate total amount of the voting securities and assets of the acquired person in excess of $15 million.

HSR and the regulations thereunder provide a variety of exemptions from its filing requirement, the one most applicable to a real estate acquisition being §18(A) (c) (1). This section provides an exemption from filing for the acquisition of goods or realty transferred in the ordinary course of business. According to the regulations, an acquisition of the voting securities of an entity whose assets consist of (or will consist solely of) real property and assets incidental to the ownership of real property (e.g., cash, prepaid taxes, insurance, and rent receivables) shall be deemed an acquisition of realty. Moreover, except for these entities, no acquisition shall be considered to be "in the ordinary course of business" if, as a result of the acquisition, the acquiring person will hold all or substantially all of the assets of the acquired entity or an operating division thereof. Therefore, to qualify for the exemption, the acquired entity need either consist solely of real property and incidental assets or not result in the acquiring person's holding all or substantially all of the assets of the acquired entity.

Another exemption is provided for acquisitions by "foreign persons" if (1) the assets acquired are located outside the United States, (2) the acquisition is of voting securities of a foreign issuer and will not confer on the acquiring person certain specified levels of control, (3) the acquisition is of less than $15 million of assets located in the United States, or (4) the acquired person is also a foreign person with certain specified minimum aggregate annual sales and total assets in the United States.

> "Foreign person" is defined under this act as a person the ultimate parent entity of which (i) is not incorporated in the United States, organized under the laws of the United States and does not have its principal office in the United States, or (ii) if a natural person, neither is a citizen of the United States nor resides in the United States.

The formation of a joint venture is also subject to HSR reporting requirements if certain specified threshold limits are exceeded. These limits apply to annual net sales, total assets of the parties to the joint venture, and the entity being formed. In addition, certain exemptions under the regulations may apply to particular circumstances and/or transactions of this sort.

State Obligations

Depending upon the type of entity chosen by the foreign developer and depending upon the actual state in which the project is commenced, the foreign developer should realize that state and local disclosure and reporting obligations may also be triggered by particular types of transactions, and that these requirements may vary dramatically from state to state.

With the passage of IISA and AFIDA, many states followed suit and have enacted similar disclosure requirements with respect to foreign investors in real estate. Many of these states focus on agricultural real estate and require disclosure in this respect, but some states actually restrict the foreign developer/owner in the areas of (1) the amount of total acreage allowable, (2) the holding period for such real estate, and (3) the type of real estate. Therefore, particular transactions need to be carefully scrutinized in relation to a particular state's regulations in order to ensure proper compliance. Moreover, each state's definition of "foreign party" and/or "foreign person" may vary. Thus, careful attention should also be paid to exemptions or exclusions that may be available.

Once the reporting and disclosure requirements for a particular state have been satisfied, various corporate and securities issues arising under state law also need to be addressed. Foreign corporations (i.e., corporations not incorporated under a particular state's laws, including corporations incorporated outside the United States) typically are required to file a form that will enable the corporation to qualify to do business within a particular state. The failure to file this form will result in the inability of that corporation to bring a lawsuit within that particular state. The form is normally filed in the Secretary of State's office of that state, and will designate a registered agent to receive service of process.

If the developer decides to form a new entity in the United States to acquire real estate, the form of the entity and its state of origin will also require certain filings upon the entity's formation. For example, a limited partnership that is formed within a given state is typically required to file a certificate of limited partnership prior to commencing its intended business. As previously discussed, the sale of ownership interests in a particular entity may also require state securities disclosure under a particular state's blue-sky laws. Corporate-type filings (articles of incorporation and an annual report) would also be required if a new corporation is formed in the United States. Thus, if the formation of a U.S. entity is being considered, state corporate and securities filings and issues should also be placed on the foreign developer's checklist of legal issues to be reviewed.

Recent Developments

Under the umbrella of the Omnibus Trade and Competitiveness Act of 1988 (the OTCA), two separate provisions (the proposed Foreign Ownership Disclosure Act of 1989 (the Bryant-Harkin Bill) and the Exon-Florio regulations under §721 amending Title VII of the Defense Reduction Act of 1950 (the Exon-Florio Amendment) potentially apply to a foreign developer's investment in U.S. real estate.

The Bryant-Harkin Bill, which was *not* included in the final version of the OTCA, required foreign persons who acquired "significant" or "controlling" interests in U.S. properties or business enterprises to file a report with the Department of Commerce within 30 days of such acquisition. A "significant" interest is defined as a foreign equity or ownership interest exceeding 5 percent of the total interest in a U.S. business or U.S. real property that comprises assets in excess of $5 million or, in the case of a business, one that has recent annual United States gross sales in excess of

$10 million. A "controlling" interest is defined as foreign equity or ownership interests exceeding 25 percent of the total interest in a U.S. business or U.S. real property that comprises assets in excess of $20 million or, in the case of a business, one that has recent annual United States gross sales in excess of $20 million. The report to be filed requires standard information, such as the name and address of the investor, the size of its interest and the consideration paid for the investment for a "significant interest," but requires extensive financial information as well as transliterated foreign disclosure documents for a "controlling interest."

Upon its introduction, the Bryant-Harkin Bill was strongly opposed by the Bush Administration, the Senate Commerce Committee, and the Undersecretary of Commerce for Economic Affairs. One of the major criticisms of the Bryant-Harkin Bill was that the definition of "foreign person" contained in §2(H) (5) (D) was overbroad in its terms and would subject to its reporting requirements every U.S. company or individual that owns or participates in a U.S. business or investment in which a foreign person owns a controlling interest.[8] Thus, for now, the Bryant-Harkin Bill has been tabled, but it provides an example of a trend toward imposing additional reporting and disclosure obligations on foreign investors in U.S. businesses and real estate.

Under the Exon-Florio Amendment, the President would be given the authority to suspend or prohibit a merger, acquisition, or takeover that could result in foreign control of a person engaged in interstate commerce in the United States. The President is authorized to act upon a finding that the resulting foreign control might impair national security, assuming that other provisions of federal law do not give the President adequate authority to protect the national security. Real property acquisitions are exempt from §721 of the Defense Production Act of 1950, but where the real property is part of an existing business or joint venture being acquired, the overall acquisition could fall within the scope of the Exon-Florio Amendment. A concerned foreign developer might consider utilizing a procedure set forth in the proposed regulations, however, whereby a voluntary notice may be submitted by the parties to the proposed acquisition. Once the voluntary notice has been filed, the internal time periods under which the President *must* decide whether or not to take action would begin to run.[9] While most typical real estate transactions should not run afoul of the Exon-Florio Amendment, foreign developers should be aware of at least the potential problem when deciding whether to acquire U.S. businesses.

THE CONSTRUCTION PHASE

Selecting the Architect and the Contractor

When a particular expertise is required (for example, knowledge of the special requirements necessary to design or construct a laboratory building), a specialty design firm and a specialty construction firm must be considered. When a large project is planned, design firms offering a comprehensive menu of services (planning, engineering, programming, landscaping, interior design, and project management) and construction firms with comprehensive resources (construction management capabilities as well as general construction abilities) must be considered. The adaptability offered by smaller design firms and construction firms should never be overlooked, however, on any project, nor should the ability of the local firm to be sensitive to the approval process of the community.

The contractor selection process for private work can be conducted in a far more sensible manner than can governmental construction. In the public context, the lowest responsive bid sometimes results in the contract award, without regard to the fact that the second-, third-, or fourth-lowest bidder may be far more competent and responsible and may have more integrity. For private work, an owner should review carefully the history, track record, and references of the prospective firms being considered. Then their principals and key personnel should be interviewed, with an eye to judging their talent, capability, creativity, understanding of the project, level of commitment, accountability, history of litigation, and cost record on similar projects. A narrowing-down process will begin between the owner's selection committee and the candidate firm—much of it based on objectivity, some of it based on visceral chemistry.

While architects (particularly established architects) prefer a selection method based on reputation and referrals, the owner is often best served by healthy competition. Assuming that an owner can clearly define the services required (apples should be compared to apples), the owner should consider allowing the prospective design professionals to submit design submissions and fee proposals.

Before the owner selects the architect and the contractor, a decision must be reached as to which method of construction delivery is best suited for the project, and how many of the services and responsibilities the architect and the contractor can offer. For example, does the owner desire the architect to design only? Does the owner want the architect to supervise construction? To inspect? How often? Does the owner want the contractor to inspect? How often? Does the owner want the contractor to render construction management services? The owner must then expose these thoughts and decisions to the prospective firms, along with the owner's expectations in regard to their independence, authority, and responsibility. Normally, these candidates help the owner to develop requirements and crystallize thinking.[10]

The Appropriate Scope of Services

The owner generally will want to engage an architect to perform the basic sequential functions historically labeled *schematic design* (organizing the shape), *design development* (defining, enclosing, and equipping the space), *construction documents* (detailing the plans and drawings for the contractor), *bidding and negotiation* (assisting the owner in assembling the construction team), and *construction administration* (monitoring the quality and progress of the work).

If the owner desires to use the construction-management approach (as opposed to the traditional, conventional, and sequential approach), the construction manager can have great input in helping to develop a general cost estimate during the design phase; in planning and scheduling the project time frame; in developing a control model; in preparing a detailed estimate; in monitoring design development; in costing alternatives; and, when the drawings are substantially complete, in tendering a guaranteed maximum price. The more complete the drawings, the less the contingency in the guaranteed maximum price.

It makes sense to bring the architect and the construction manager (or cost consultant in certain situations) on board early.

They can help the owner tailor the project to the owner's needs in the most feasible and economic way, if brought in during the initial planning phase. They can analyze needs, study the constraints of the site, suggest alternative approaches, and help define the overall scope of the project. They can help the owner's planners develop a space and facilities program that will define the owner's height, light, area, quality of material, and maintenance requirements, as well as develop a budget and cost benefit analysis.

Every owner needs site- and scope-planning services, programming services, and architectural-design services. Owners require site, structural, mechanical, electrical, and energy engineering, as well as interior design, cost-estimating, and equipment-planning services. Some comprehensive firms perform all of these services, and there is much to be said for dealing with just one entity to coordinate (and be responsible for) all of these services. On the other hand, detractors of the comprehensive service firm argue that the various segments of the comprehensive group have less incentive toward professional excellence than do independent groups. They argue also that the system of checks and balances afforded the owner by the use of independent groups can also be lost through the use of just one entity.

The contracts with the architect and the contractor or construction manager will set forth responsibilities, obligations, and time frames agreed upon for the rendering of these services and for payment of the agreed fee. The architect's agreement will also list the additional services that the architect is prepared to make available for an additional fee. These documents must be prepared by competent real estate or construction counsel. For example, the American Institute of Architects (AIA) standard industry forms do not include equipment-planning, programming, or interior design services; measured drawings of existing buildings; or code surveys under the basic fee. They would be treated as *additional* services, unless the standard forms are modified. Nor does the most widely used AIA form provide as a basic service coordination of separate prime contractors, services made necessary by the contractor's default, record drawings, change order drawings, start-up of equipment, or any services after the final certificate of payment.

All of the services the owner will require should be identified and the need for these services should be discussed with the design (or construction-management) candidates at the interview stages.

The best cost-saving approach for an owner is to include within the basic fee as many of these services identified (and quantified) as positive needs.

The Appropriate Fee

The percentage fee is not, in your authors' opinion, in the best interest of the owner. Architects and contractors should be paid a fair fee for the work and services they render. Cost does not necessarily mean more work. The choice of a more expensive marble facade instead of the less expensive granite facing, or the impact of inflation on construction material should not present the designer and the contractor with a windfall. There is little incentive to economize under a percentage fee arrangement. If, in a particular situation, a percentage fee must be used, it should be limited by "not to exceed" language in the owner's agreement. The certainty of a fixed fee is suggested as an incentive to get it right the first time and presents the owner with a realistic bottom line basis for comparison among bidding contractors and competing architects. Fees sometimes are calculated on a percentage basis and then, before the agreement is signed, converted to a fixed-fee amount.

Fees can range from a very low percentage on an uncomplicated warehouse building to a much higher percentage on a complicated laboratory structure. Each type of project has a generally accepted fee percentage range that, when blended together with the marketplace law of supply and demand, plus a little need and a little greed, leads to the proposed price. Sometimes architects and contractors will take a little more psychic income and a little less currency of the realm in order to obtain a commission or contract on a high-profile project. Sometimes they are sorry that they did. From the owner's viewpoint, too low a fee may be as detrimental to the project as too high a fee, because the quality of the service rendered for a too-low fee may suffer and negatively affect the project. Generally, fees on alteration work are higher than on new construction.

Architects may seek to insert multiplier provisions into their agreements. Multipliers are appropriate and fair where the services required of the design professional cannot be clearly defined. They are commonly used as a means for paying for additional services as well as a mark-up on consultants' billings. The most common multiplier for additional services is 2.5 to 3 times salaries, plus benefits (termed *direct personal expense*). This amount—expected to cover all of the architect's overhead, miscellaneous costs, profit, and risk—is considered fair in that the architect is paid for each hour of service provided, and the client is paying for each hour of service received. If the multiplier is applied to salaries alone (without benefits), it will be higher.

Protecting the Owner in the Construction and Architect's Service Agreements

When a contractor encounters difficulty during construction or has underbid or underestimated the project, the owner can expect a claim for additional compensation based, in general, on a claim of differing site conditions, changes to the work, construction changes (such as errors, omissions, or ambiguities in the specifications), delay, disruption (such as not making the site or owner-supplied material available, or slowness in approving drawings), or forced acceleration as a result of a refusal to grant appropriate extension.

Good planning and project scheduling, careful record-keeping, aggressive contract administration, and proper project management can help minimize contractor claims, but nothing can help an owner more than an owner-oriented construction document. For example, the owner should seek to require the contractor

1. To include in its bid a contingency deemed sufficient to cover unanticipated site conditions;
2. To disclaim any owner representations pertaining to the site or any reliance thereon;
3. To remain liable for any loss or damage that arises from the work (and not be limited by the terms of a warranty);
4. To maintain job progress and proceed with extra work that may be disputed, regardless of a subsequent resolution of the compensation issue; and
5. To waive certain types of claims for delay damage, accepting an extension of time to complete as the sole remedy.

The owner is well advised to take a hard line in contract negotiations as a defensive measure (although all contracts require trade-offs, of course). The use of experienced real estate or construction counsel here can help the owner receive the project on budget, on time, and without a multitude of contractor claims.

So, too, the owner must require more from the architect than a design and a downstream certification that the project was built by the contractor in accordance with the plans and specifications. For example, the owner should require the architect:

1. To design a project free of defects, to meet industry standards, to be in compliance with applicable codes and restrictions, and to warrant design adequacy (a warranty owners seldom receive);
2. To be the interpreter of the design generated, the judge of the quality of the construction work performed, and the initial arbitrator of job disputes;
3. To be the owner's representative and protect the owner through construction—to make sure that the owner obtains a defect-free building; and
4. To design to a fixed limit of construction cost—or redesign without cost.

The architect's services agreement must, of course, also be tailored to fit the delivery system contemplated and the needs of the project. The cardinal principle for the owner to remember is that it is the *owner's* project, and the owner must be satisfied with the agreement even if it means using an architect who is less prestigious but more accommodating.

THE CONSTRUCTION ENVIRONMENT IN THE UNITED STATES

What's Different About Construction?

Construction, as an industry, is primarily concerned with the improvement of real property; therefore, unlike manufacturing, most of the work must be done at the site of the property to be improved. This means that the labor, materials, equipment, and management team must be more mobile. It also means that, in many respects, each project is like a separate business because the labor, materials, and equipment must be (1) processed, (2) mobilized at the job site,

(3) managed during the job, and (4) demobilized when the job is completed. All this must be done in a relatively short time.

The carrying out of these four steps in any construction project is known in the trade as a "job." Usually, a job consists of one contract, but it may be a segment of one contract or a combination of several. The distinguishing feature is that a job is a logical and appropriate unit for management and, from the contractor's viewpoint, lends itself to use as a profit center.

This pattern is fairly consistent anywhere in the world. In the United States, as in all other countries, there are conditions peculiar to a locality that affect the way job performance is carried out.

Types of Jobs and Contractors

One of the peculiarities in performing construction work in the United States is the fact that the contracts and the contractors who perform them tend to be somewhat more specialized than they are in many other countries. Another peculiarity is the fact that, in addition to the national political jurisdiction, there are 50 state and innumerable local political subdivisions that, collectively, exercise a great deal of control over not only what jobs are done and where they are done, but also how they are done. This diversity of political control modifies not only the effect of local building codes on the physical work but also the relationships between management and labor, and the social and environmental impact of the job itself on the community.

This diversity, in turn, has been at least one factor in accounting for the degree of specialization found within the U.S. construction industry. It has tended to contribute, in some degree, to the success American companies have enjoyed in meeting the variety of conditions they encounter in doing work outside the United States.

The largest and most versatile general contractors are the so-called turnkey or design-and-build contractors, who specialize in very large projects in which the contractor performs all functions from the initial feasibility study through final completion. Typical of the jobs these firms do are power plants, oil refineries, hydroelectric facilities, and similar projects requiring a great deal of managerial and engineering skill.

Next in size and diversity, among the general contractors, are the heavy engineering construction firms, which specialize in earth moving, dams, airports, and very large building projects (such as public buildings, office buildings, large apartment complexes, factories, and hotels). Sometimes these firms perform design-and-build contracts, but more often they do work for public agencies and large corporations that do their own designing and engineering, either in-house or through an architect-engineer.

The engineering and large-building group of general contractors are followed in size by the smaller general contractors, who build office buildings, shopping centers, multifamily housing, single-family home subdivisions, and health care facilities. These are followed in size and versatility by the general contractors, who specialize in home improvements, swimming pools, and repair, maintenance, and rehabilitation jobs. In these last two groups are found the many very small one- and two-member firms.

Cutting across the entire spectrum are the specialty contractors, such as the electrical, plumbing, heating, air conditioning, steel, painting, and masonry contractors, and dozens of others. These are generally referred to as the subcontract trades, although in any given factual situation, any of the classes of contractors referred to above might take contracts as general contractors, subcontractors, or as joint venture partners with other contractors.

Construction management contracts, under which a general contractor, under the supervision of an engineer/architect, will manage and coordinate the work of the various specialty contractors (trade contractors, as they are called in this type of contract) have gained significant popularity among business owners and contractors in the last 15 years. Management contracts vary widely in the relationships among the owner, the architect/engineer, the manager, and the trade contractors.

Another approach having matured during the last 15 years in the United States is the fast-track job, where actual construction work starts before all of the planning is complete. For any newcomer to the construction industry in the United States, however, this type of job needs to be approached with extreme caution. Properly conceived and managed, fast-track work can save considerable time from conception to completion. Ineptly handled, such projects can be a disaster.

TABLE 28–1
Economics of the Construction Industry

General specialty	Major types of jobs	Scope of work	Contract		Major elements of risk
			Price	
Design and build (commonly referred to as turnkey contractors)	Electric power plants Hydroelectric facilities Petroleum refineries Chemical plants Rapid transit systems Irrigation systems	Engineering Financial services Management Procurement Construction	Cost-plus		Time and cost overruns
Heavy construction specialists	Roads Bridges Dams Airports Large buildings	Construction and subcontract management	Unit-price or lump-sum		Unforeseen conditions, cost estimating and omissions, job management failures
General building contractors	Housing Schools Hospitals	Construction and subcontract management	Lump-sum		Cost estimating and omissions, job management failures, unforeseen conditions
Subcontractors	All specialty work in all types of general contracts	Concrete Electrical Mechanical, including heating and air conditioning Steel erection Piping Carpentry Dry wall/plastering Flooring	Lump-sum		Cost estimating and omissions, job management failures, unforeseen conditions

Source: W. E. Coombs and W. J. Palmer, *Handbook of Construction Accounting and Financial Management*, 3rd ed. (New York: McGraw Hill, 1983).

Table 28–1 presents a convenient summary of the broad classifications within the construction industry.

The Traditional and Sequential Approaches

Lump-sum contracts (either competitively bid or negotiated), construction management agreements (either competitively bid or negotiated), cost-plus contracts (with or without a guaranteed maximum price), design-build agreements, and turnkey contracts are all acceptable contracting methods in America's construction marketplace. Each approach has its advantages, each has its disadvantages, and each has its best application.

The lump-sum and cost-plus-fixed-fee methods of construction delivery have represented the traditional methods of construction delivery. Under each of these approaches, an owner decides to build, then budgets, analyzes capital costs as opposed to operating costs (Should machinery be put in to make steam or should the owner lease steam?), and engages an architect to prepare line drawings (the plans) and write prose descriptions (the specifications) to meet the construction needs. The architect prepares a menu of options (Should we have 50 labs or 40 labs? Should we have gold or glass doorknobs? Should we have a state-of-the-art mechanical system or just a good one? Should we spend more for construction to attain lower life-cycle costs?), and the trade-offs begin. The owner selects from the menu and then solicits bids from a contractor or contractors (who solicit prices from subcontractors) to perform the work that the plans and specs (the contract documents) require. The owner enters into a fixed-price contract (or perhaps a cost-plus contract with a fixed fee) with a general contractor and has the building built under the watchful eye of his (or her) agent, the architect.

These traditional, conventional, and sequential construction approaches have been utilized for a couple of hundred years for these reasons: First, there are clear lines of responsibility. The architect, the contractor, and the owner each have a distinct role—there is no duplication of services. Second, the owner presumably gets the lowest contract price through competitive bids. Third, in the event of a dispute between the parties, an abundant body of law is available to govern the resolution. As opposed to the law pertaining to many of the more contemporary approaches to construction delivery, the courts have made their interpretations in this arena. The owner theoretically stays in complete control of the cost of the project. Payments to the contractor are made only for completed work based on a computation of a percentage of completion. Not only does the owner stay in control of the money, but an additional control is afforded by the lump sum itself. It provides the maximum possible protection against surprises, because the risk is shifted to the contractor.

The advantage of the cost-plus contract form (as opposed to the lump-sum form) is that the work can commence before it is possible to establish the true cost of construction. It is best used on large projects (such as power plants or oil refineries) where the entire cost of constructing the complete structure cannot be reasonably estimated. It is also used advantageously where unknown or unanticipated conditions can materially affect construction costs (such as in laboratory or hospital construction) or where the owner may want to change the scope of certain portions of the project. Here, the owner agrees to reimburse the contractor for construction costs as incurred (labor, material, subcontractor cost, taxes, fringes, and other disbursements such as insurance) and to pay the contractor a set fee for services. The theory of the fixed fee (as opposed to a percentage fee) is that the contractor will have no incentive to run up the costs. Under these cost-plus-fixed-fee arrangements, the owner replaces the control-over-price of the lump-sum approach with contractual controls (such as the right to audit progress billings before paying them) and a requirement that there be continuous receipt of contractor's latest cost forecasts, or a guaranteed maximum price (very often so high that it has little effect), or a revolving fund that gives the owner checkpoints on construction cost.

Another control device has made its way westward from England: the target contract. Under this system, the contractor's fee is fixed in relation to the estimate of cost and the estimate of time. By completing the contract below the estimated cost or in less than the estimated time, the contractor earns an additional fee based on the savings in money, time, or both, but if the contractor overruns the cost estimate or the time, the fee is reduced according to an agreed formula.

The unit-price contract should be placed within the category of the traditional methods of construction delivery. Its chief advantage is that it can be used where the cost of performing a single unit of work can be estimated, but the number of required units is not known.

On the other hand, the disadvantages to the owner of these traditional approaches are several. First, the owner must wait until the contractor's bids are in before knowing the cost exposure. Sometimes the bids come in so high that the scope or quality of the project must be reduced to fit within the budget. Second, the owner does not really have the best labor and material cost analyses at the drawing-and-design phase, for there is design professional input, but not contractor input. Third, construction does not start until the drawings are complete. Fourth, a bidding general contractor often bids to the lowest quality called for and tries to up the price later on extras, changes, scope claims, delay claims, and if everything else fails, by crying "fairness" (an equitable adjustment). Other disadvantages are that the general contractor puts a mark-up on all of the subs' work and, in many cases, holds retainages for an exorbitant amount of time. Because most subcontractors know this, they bid higher to cover the cost of their money. Last, the subcontractor usually bids to the general contractor in a fashion whereby each and every contingency is covered; often prices go through the roof.

The Contemporary Approaches

In the 1960s and 1970s, a combination of global politics, economic upheavals, energy crises, material and labor shortages, and other factors resulted in radically varying inflation rates. Sometimes lump-sum bids exceeded the budget by as much as 50 percent. Then, along came construction management.

Construction management, in its broadest sense, means having a contractor with knowledge of construction costs employed at the onset of the project to come to grips with reality early on. The contractor can focus upon the architect's design assumptions, decide how much space is really necessary for the desired uses, resolve the most cost-efficient way to arrange the space or shape or system, and decide if gold faucets are really necessary.

Ask ten contractors, lawyers, or architects to define construction management and you will be given ten different explanations. In fact, only two categories of construction management contracts are meaningful: (1) pure (professional) construction management, wherein the construction manager takes no entrepreneurial risk and is not liable for cost, timeliness, or quality of work, but brings technological knowledge to the design, scheduling, construction, and coordination process as the owner's manager; and (2) contractual construction management, wherein the manager offers expertise during the planning and design stages, works with the architect in making up bid packages, awards trade contracts (with the owner's approval) to trade contractors (the guarantees are between the owner and the trade contractor), possibly performs some work as contractor (usually general conditions work), and coordinates and inspects the work without assuming the responsibilities of the architect. In contractual construction management, the manager (if required by the owner) at a given point in time will establish a guaranteed maximum price. If the owner accepts this price, the owner will assign the trade contracts to the construction manager (to allow for control of the work) together with a financial incentive to recompense the construction manager for assuming the risk.

The advantages of construction management to the owner are that the pure (professional) construction manager, while acting as the coordinating agent of the owner throughout design and delivery (and usually through inspection and certification), owes 100 percent allegiance to the owner alone. The manager is receiving a fair fee for services and is not working for a mark-up or profiting from any entrepreneurial risk. Moreover, construction management allows phased construction: It enables early procurement of long lead-time items as well as the early start of work. Work is divided into bid packages (site preparation, excavation, foundations, construction) performed by multiple primes. Late packages are tailored and honed. In addition, a good construction manager, with knowledge of labor cost and productivity, can be even more experienced than the architect in scheduling, coordinating, and supervising construction.

The major advantages of the construction management approach to the contractor are (1) many jobs are too large for entrepreneurial risk, (2) assembling bids can be quite costly, (3) construction management does not exhaust a contractor's bonding capacity to the same degree, and (4) as a benefit to both the contractor and the owner, trade contractors get paid only if, as, and when they finish (knowing this, the trade contractors can bid lower).

The major disadvantages of construction management to the owner are (1) never really knowing if the guaranteed maximum price of the construction manager (who has worked with the architect from the beginning of the project) is the lowest price that would have been received in a competitively bid project; (2) the owner loses the differential if material prices of items ordered on early lead time drop (for example, steel prices have fluctuated considerably in recent times); (3) it is impossible to put a fix on the capacities of the foundation until you know with certainty the weight of the equipment, and so on, on the top floors; and (4) multiple primes bring multiple problems. The owner may be well advised to have only one guarantor to look to for quality, for cost, and for timeliness and not be subject to everyone in the arena pointing to everyone else.

In the contractor/ construction manager situation (as opposed to the professional construction manager situation), there may be further negatives and inherent conflicts. For example, while the manager is developing design with the architect, the manager can have its own bid and tailor the cloth to fit its own coat. Second, during the construction phase, the construction manager has the responsibility of approving changes in contract documents that the manager helped the architect prepare. There is indeed potential for abuse.

The design-build approach is, in fact, a hybrid of construction management. Here the owner enters into one contract with one entity, who designs and constructs for a single stated price. The owner must describe the desired project with great specificity. Major disadvantages of the design-build approach are that it is difficult to compare proposals, and that by adopting this method of construction delivery, an owner loses the right to first pick the designer and then pick the contractor.

The turnkey approach, a buzzword of the 1970s and a taboo word of the 1980s (because of its negative tax implications), is really the design-build approach plus one extra added ingredient—the designer-contractor supplies the interim financing. Sometimes the turnkey approach encompasses the designer contractor supplying the furniture, fixtures, and equipment as well.

No matter which approach is selected, the standard industry construction-management forms must be modified or, better yet, rewritten to protect the owner's interest. The Associated General Contractor standard forms and the American Institute of Architects standard forms leave much to be desired, if one is championing the owner's cause.

Recommended Approaches for Owners

Three approaches to construction delivery can be used most effectively and encompass the best of the methods developed above. These modifications must be tailored to meet the project's needs.

The first is a *modified pure construction management approach*. Here the owner engages an architect to design to a fixed limit of construction cost (or else redesign) and makes the architect the owner's representative to administer the trade contracts, inspect the work, reject bad work, insure against defects, and certify quality. The owner then engages a construction manager to manage the construction and to coordinate the efforts of the architect, the interior designer, and the trade contractors. The construction manager, as the owner's job manager, brings to the project expertise, essential knowledge of labor and material cost, and awareness of systems capabilities. The manager schedules, coordinates contract documents, and fast-tracks. The manager performs work as a contractor only in the rarest of situations. Like the trade contractor, the manager is answerable to the owner, who keeps control. The manager does not guarantee price, time of delivery, or quality, as the trade contractors do.

The second approach is the *modified contractor construction management approach*. Here the construction manager works with the architect for a fee plus reimbursable costs. The manager than coordinates the fast-track work of multiple primes (in effect, pure construction management). Then, to eliminate the negatives and problems of multiple primes and to obtain the peace of mind of having but one entity to look to for timeliness of performance, quality of workmanship, and a guaranteed maximum price, the construction manager is required to tender a guaranteed maximum

914 Real Estate and Construction

price (which the owner can accept or reject). If the owner accepts the guaranteed maximum price, the fee goes up to compensate the manager for the risk. The trade contracts are assigned to the manager (now contractor) by the owner for enforcement purposes.

Perhaps the *two-phased agreement* combines the best of all worlds. Here the construction manager works with the architect during the design phase for a set fee and helps schedule, engineer, and monitor the design. When the design is complete enough, the construction manager gives the owner a guaranteed maximum price, which the owner accepts or rejects. If the owner accepts, then the construction manager becomes the contractor under a construction contract that has been tailored in a fashion most favorable to the owner—with all costs of work clearly defined with all of its terms complete (except the guaranteed maximum price). This construction contract is attached as an exhibit to the construction management agreement. By not accepting the contractor's price, the owner is free to go out for bids or to negotiate with a new contractor. The major advantage is the clear delineation of responsibility. The disadvantage, however, is that the owner really cannot fast-track (except by the use of a precontract construction document with appropriate assignments, a discussion of which is beyond the scope of this chapter).

Whatever approach is used—traditional or contemporary—the contracts with the architect, the construction manager, or the contractor must be prepared in such a way that authority, accountability, and responsibilities of each are set forth clearly. Who designs? Who inspects? Who approves? Who insures? Everyone on the project must know to whom to turn for a decision.

CONCLUSION

Having considered many of the factors involved in the development and construction of real estate projects in the United States, a foreign company or individual might properly conclude that the excellent rewards to be achieved by a successful project must be well earned by diligent and skillful effort. The development environment in the United States today is a difficult but by no means an inhospitable one. American opportunities stand in stark contrast to those in many other world markets where, notwithstanding diligence and talent on the part of the developer, an unstable government or an unpredictable legal system, currency, or supply of labor and materials can deprive the developer of otherwise justified rewards.

On the other hand, local governments and communities might appear to the uninitiated, uninformed, or uncounseled foreign developer to be as unpredictable as foreign markets appear to Americans. An essential consideration for any developer anticipating entry into an unfamiliar market is how best to obtain the requisite information and familiarity with local laws, customs, and other intangibles. Depending upon the particular assets that the foreign developer brings to the table, this expertise can be obtained in a large variety of ways. The foreign developer might seek a joint venture with a local American developer, builder, financier, or other person who has a particular value to add. Alternatively, most professional contributions (architects, attorneys, builders, planners, developers, etc.) can be retained for a fee, without ceding equity in exchange.

Frequently, when a foreign developer retains local professional assistance, a concern arises as to whether the local professional might have more loyalty to the specific community within which the professional resides and/or practices than to the client. This concern sometimes dictates that the foreign developer retain professional assistance at a regional or state level rather than at the local, perhaps parochial, level. In any event, a foreign developer with a good informational network and with astute, experienced recruiting skills might choose a different course than a developer with less administrative skills but with good access to an American partner.

In summary, the principal lesson from all of the several chapters of this section, and this chapter particularly, is that thorough investigation of the local "rules of the game" is essential before embarking upon a real estate development project.

NOTES

1. Pub. L. 94-472, 90 Stat. 2059, 22 U.S.C §§3101–3108, as amended by Section 306 of Pub. L. 98-573, 15 C.R.F. §806.7 (1988). The 1984

amendment renamed IISA the "International Investment and Trade in Services Act."

2. Pursuant to 22 U.S.C. §3102(3) and 15 C.F.R. §806.7(c) and (e), a "foreign person" includes any individual, branch, partnership, associated group, association, estate, trust, corporation, organization, or government that is a non-U.S. resident or that is subject to the jurisdiction of a country other than the United States.

3. 92 Stat. 1266, 7 U.S.C. §§3501–3508, 7 C.F.R. §§781.1–781.6 (1990).

4. 26 U.S.C. §§861(a) (5), 897, 1445(a), 6039C, 6652(f) (1988).

5. 22 U.S.C §611-21 (1988).

6. Pub. L. 94-435, 15 U.S.C. §18A (1988), 16 C.F.R. §§801.1–803.90 (1990).

7. Pursuant to 15 U.S.C. §18A(a) (2) (A), for a person engaged in manufacturing, total assets *or* annual net sales of $10 million or more will satisfy the test.

8. Representative Bryant's office indicated that he plans to reintroduce the bill at some point, but that a target date was unknown at this point. Senator Harkin's office indicated that he plans to review the Bill and decide whether or not to modify it.

9. As of the writing of this chapter, the proposed regulations under which the Exon-Florio Amendment were published are still in effect. According to the Treasury Department's Office of International Investment, the promulgation of the final rules appears to depend on the reauthorization of the Defense Production Act, which is currently being debated in Congress.

10. For an in-depth discussion of selecting the architect and the contractor, see *The Businessman's Guide to Construction,* ed. Robert F. Cushman and William J. Palmer (Homewood, Ill.: Dow Jones-Irwin, 1980): chap. 2, "Selecting the Architect," by Alan B. Stover, Esquire; and chap. 6, "Selecting the Builder," by John H. Ball.

INDEX